Loris Malaguzzi and the Schools of Reggio Emilia

Loris Malaguzzi was one of the most important figures in twentieth-century early childhood education, achieving world-wide recognition for his educational ideas and his role in the creation of municipal schools for young children in the Italian city of Reggio Emilia, the most successful example ever of progressive, democratic and public education.

Despite Malaguzzi's reputation, very little of what he wrote or said about early childhood education has been available in English. This book helps fill the gap, presenting for the first time in English, writings and speeches spanning 1945 to 1993, selected by a group of his colleagues from an archive established in Reggio Emilia. They range from short poems, letters and newspaper articles to extended pieces about Malaguzzi's early life, the origins of the municipal schools and his ideas about children, pedagogy and schools. This material is organised into five chronological chapters, starting at the end of World War Two and ending just before his death, with introductions to each chapter providing background, including the historical context, the main events in Malaguzzi's life and the rationale for the selection of documents.

The book provides a unique insight into the background, thinking and work of Malaguzzi, revealing, in his own words, how his thinking developed, how he moved between theory and practice, how he border-crossed many disciplines and subjects, and how he combined many roles ranging from pedagogue and administrator to researcher and campaigner. Academics, students and practitioners alike will find this landmark publication provides rich insights into his life and work.

Paola Cagliari, *pedagogista*, is Director of the *Scuole e Nidi d'Infanzia – Istituzione del Comune di Reggio Emilia* [Preschools and Infant-Toddler Centres – *Istituzione* of the Municipality of Reggio Emilia], Italy.

Marina Castagnetti, preschool teacher, is archive curator at the Documentation and Educational Research Centre of the *Scuole e Nidi d'Infanzia – Istituzione del Comune di Reggio Emilia*, Italy.

Claudia Giudici, psychologist, is President of the *Scuole e Nidi d'Infanzia – Istituzione del Comune di Reggio Emilia,* and a member of the Board of Directors of Reggio Children, Reggio Emilia, Italy.

Carlina Rinaldi, *pedagogista*, is President of Reggio Children and of the Reggio Children–Loris Malaguzzi Centre Foundation, Reggio Emilia, Italy.

Vea Vecchi, *atelierista*, is responsible for the area of Exhibitions, Publishing and Ateliers in Reggio Children, Reggio Emilia, Italy.

Peter Moss is Emeritus Professor of Early Childhood Provision at the UCL Institute of Education, University College London, UK.

Series Title: *Contesting Early Childhood*

Series Editors: Gunilla Dahlberg and Peter Moss

This groundbreaking series questions the current dominant discourses surrounding early childhood, and offers instead alternative narratives of an area that is now made up of a multitude of perspectives and debates.

The series examines the possibilities and risks arising from the accelerated development of early childhood services and policies, and illustrates how it has become increasingly steeped in regulation and control. Insightfully, this collection of books shows how early childhood services can in fact contribute to ethical and democratic practices. The authors explore new ideas taken from alternative working practices in both the western and developing world, and from other academic disciplines such as developmental psychology. Current theories and best practice are placed in relation to the major processes of political, social, economic, cultural and technological change occurring in the world today.

Loris Malaguzzi and the Schools of Reggio Emilia

A selection of his writings and speeches, 1945–1993

Edited by Paola Cagliari, Marina Castagnetti, Claudia Giudici, Carlina Rinaldi, Vea Vecchi and Peter Moss

Translations by Jane McCall

 Routledge
Taylor & Francis Group

LONDON AND NEW YORK

First published 2016
by Routledge
2 Park Square, Milton Park, Abingdon, Oxon OX14 4RN

and by Routledge
711 Third Avenue, New York, NY 10017

Routledge is an imprint of the Taylor & Francis Group, an informa business

British Library Cataloguing in Publication Data
A catalogue record for this book is available from the British Library

Library of Congress Cataloging in Publication Data
Names: Malaguzzi, Loris, 1920–1994. | Cagliari, Paola, editor of
    compilation.
Title: Loris Malaguzzi and the schools of Reggio Emilia : a selection of
    his writings and speeches, 1945–1993 / edited by Paola Cagliari [and
    five others]. Other titles: Selections
Description: New York : Routledge, 2016. | Translated from Italian.
Identifiers: LCCN 2015032844| ISBN 9781138019812 (hardback) |
    ISBN 9781138019829 (pbk.) | ISBN 9781315778631 (e-book)
Subjects: LCSH: Reggio Emilia Approach (Early childhood education)
Classification: LCC LB1029.R35 M35 2016 | DDC 372.21—dc23
LC record available at http://lccn.loc.gov/2015032844

ISBN: 978-1-138-01981-2 (hbk)
ISBN: 978-1-138-01982-9 (pbk)
ISBN: 978-1-315-77863-1 (ebk)

Typeset in Bembo
by Swales & Willis Ltd, Exeter, Devon, UK

Printed and bound by CPI Group (UK) Ltd, Croydon, CR0 4YY

Contents

Acknowledgements

This book has been made possible by the generous contributions of many people. As the English-language editor of this book, and co-editor for the series *Contesting Early Childhood*, I would like to offer my special thanks to colleagues in Reggio Emilia including Paola Cagliari, Marina Castagnetti, Claudia Giudici, Francesca Marastoni, Jane McCall, Annamaria Mucchi, Carlina Rinaldi and Vea Vecchi. Without their hard work, sustained commitment and deep knowledge, nothing could have been achieved.

My thanks also to the family of Loris Malaguzzi, whom I met in Reggio Emilia to share the project of this book.

The book would have been impossible without support from the Leverhulme Trust, whose Emeritus Fellowship provided me with funding for archiving, translation and visits to Reggio Emilia; and without the contribution of the Reggio Children – Loris Malaguzzi Centre Foundation.

Finally, I would like to thank Alison Foyle, the editor at Routledge for this book and for the series *Contesting Early Childhood*. Alison has been unfailingly supportive, always offering constructive assistance and backing for this project.

Peter Moss

Credits

Series editor's foreword

Gunilla Dahlberg

In the book *Loris Malaguzzi and the Schools of Reggio Emilia* we are getting a fascinating insight into the story of the twentieth century's most unique experience in education. A story that recently has been described by the Swedish poet and writer, Göran Greider, as one of the *beautiful* stories that has grown out of the bloody twentieth century.

It tells how the women in the small village of Villa Cella, after the fascists had been driven away, and out of the desolation that the war caused, managed to create a school, with the support of Loris Malaguzzi. What today is called 'the Reggio Emilia philosophy and experience in education' was then born.

In his writings Loris Malaguzzi refers to what happened in Villa Cella as one of the events in his life when he felt most alive. 'Beautiful' and 'alive' – a form of aesthetics and ethics in its widest sense, related to meaningfulness, empowerment and openness to change, and fundamental to Malaguzzi's struggle both to renew education and to make a more just and better society for all children.

Malaguzzi had a vision of building new public schools based on democracy and equality. Schools that were value-based and relevant, that could protect children against what in the book he calls 'a prophetic pedagogy', an education built on predetermined knowledge delivered bit by bit, humiliating for both teachers and children, denying their ingenuity and potential. He wanted to protect children, too, from authoritarian teaching methods where children do not have much to say.

Or as Renzo Bonazzi, Reggio Emilia's mayor from 1962 to 1976 and an ardent supporter of the city's educational project, said in an interview in the late eighties:

> Mussolini and the fascists made us understand that obedient human beings are dangerous human beings. When we decided to build a new society after the war we understood that we needed to have schools in which children dared to think for themselves, and where children got the conditions for becoming active and critical citizens.
>
> (Personal communication to author)

How was it that Malaguzzi, together with children, teachers, parents and the city of Reggio Emilia, managed to construct such schools? Schools that intrigue, affect and draw to them so many teachers, politicians, scientists, architects, neuroscientists and artists from all over the world? And how come the Reggio Emilia experience is still 'alive' and has not been ossified, which is so common for similar experiments in different fields?

Many of us have asked ourselves if the anti-fascist struggle might explain Malaguzzi's strong emancipatory idea of childhood. An idea that understands the child *as an explorer and a researcher of the world*. A rich child with rich parents, a child who deserves both rich teachers with a great trust in the potentialities of children and parents, and a school that can meet children's exploring and researching attitude.

The book gives a complex web of answers for what lay behind Malaguzzi's remarkable struggle and endeavour. After following his journey throughout the book I would like to use the metaphor of 'walking on two legs' as a description of him. He was both a remarkable thinker and a unique head of schools. Always standing in both a critical and a loving relation towards expressions of the present. A tireless thinker, who could travel in between the tales of Greek and Roman culture, different scientific paradigms, architecture, philosophy, theatre and art. And at the same time, capable of building up an intelligent early childhood educational organisation.

Being a politically engaged person and an intellectual in its deepest sense, Malaguzzi seems to have been able to stand up, as an independent and free-spirited thinker, to both the political and the academic establishment. This, surely, gave him a space to explore and experiment with new paradigms and new pedagogical practices. He used this space not only to formulate his visions and thoughts in text, but also to put them into movement in a pedagogical practice in a whole city. And he actually managed to build up a unique connection between practice and research.

A unique connection between practice and research

In this book, Peter Moss, with inspiration from the French philosopher Michel Foucault, tellingly describes Malaguzzi and the teachers in Reggio Emilia as *specific intellectuals*. Intellectuals who work out from their own conditions of life or where their work situates them. This is, as Michel Foucault says, a positioning that undoubtedly gives the specific intellectual a much more immediate awareness of political struggles, as well as a different connection between theory and practice.

When the connection between theory and practice is on the agenda in education, the strategy has mainly been that researchers are supposed to inform teachers about their research results, and the teachers are then supposed to implement and practice these results in their own schools. Hence, teachers become consumers of research. This is a kind of relation between practice and research that can be described as research *about* practice.

Malaguzzi chose another interpretation and strategy of research. He saw the need to build up knowledge by engaging with concrete didactical problems appearing in the everyday work with the children. Accordingly, he integrated research into the very organisation and pedagogical work of Reggio's schools.

With the support of pedagogical documentation, the teachers have built into the everyday life of the schools a continuous, rigorous and systematic research process, through closely following and experimenting with what is happening here and now. In this process, the research questions are born out of children's and teachers' relations and explorations of many different themes, such as shadows, rainbows, mathematics and literacy. This is a kind of relation between practice and research that can be described as research *from within* one's own organisation and situatedness.

In this way, besides being a thinker, Malaguzzi was also a 'research creator'. Together with the children and the teachers, he continuously and very systematically followed processes and their consequences for children's meaning-making and learning, something which he always evaluated in relation to the struggle for community building and a more just and sustainable society. It is an astonishing endeavour, given how hard and time-consuming it is to make even minor changes in an organisation.

An intelligent organisation

Following Malaguzzi's tireless struggle to create and enrich such a research process, combined with community building, one understands that it has required a new form of organisation, with new conditions and tools for experimentation and creative cooperative work.

To create change, Malaguzzi from the start constructed an intelligent organisation by building into the schools different supportive structures, previously unknown in education, for example the roles of 'pedagogista' and 'atelierista'. Both of these have different professional backgrounds than the teachers; and both work in close cooperation with schools, engaging closely *in* and *with* what is going on in them. With their different professional identities, and being located both inside and outside the schools, they provide the possibility to support and challenge what is going on in the everyday life of the schools. Also, to support and challenge new research findings, as their function has been to follow and be in relation with the latest university-based academic research.

An ecological ontology and epistemology

Examples are given in the book of how Malaguzzi and the teachers, as specific intellectuals, have integrated professional development into their own organisation as a supportive structure. From an early stage, this integrated, professional development took a stand against the dualisms so prevalent in Western thought. Malaguzzi's poem 'No way. The hundred is there' is an important statement of an education characterised by connections and relations instead of dualisms, such as nature and culture, mind and body, subject and object, theory and practice. This poem also points to the importance of building a transdisciplinary way of working in schools.

A transdisciplinarity also characterises Malaguzzi's own intellectual journey. The reader encounters in the book a serpentine web of the most fascinating scientific and philosophical perspectives. Early on he brought in a holistic and systemic way of thinking, which later opened up for complexity theory and 'a new alliance' between nature and culture. Already in the 1980s he challenged the early childhood field with theories and concepts that had only just recently emerged, such as self-organising systems, dissipative structures, recursiveness, transversality and fractals.

Such theories and concepts can be seen as precursors to the ecological ontology and epistemology that we encounter in contemporary Reggio Emilia. Encountering their use today, we can see that these theories and concepts play a vital role in the municipal schools, functioning as tools and methods for the pedagogical work – like a *tool box* for experimentation, and a *launch pad* for making possible the emergence of new practices.

Behind all this struggle, it becomes obvious through his writings that Malaguzzi had a great trust in what he and his colleagues were doing. A trust built on engagement, intensity and affect, resulting in a power to participate and act. Today this participation and action has its visible expression in the Loris Malaguzzi International Centre, which opened in Reggio Emilia in 2006 as a meeting place dedicated to all those in the world who want to explore the intersection between professional development and research.

A new opening

This ground-breaking book gives the reader a deep and vital understanding of Malaguzzi's thinking and work, which until now has mostly been known through the talks he gave to and through the meetings he had with so many people from around the world.

This encounter with the Reggio Emilia experience, where *new horizons of existence* have taken place and still take place, leaves us with feelings of wonder and enchantment about learning and the world. At the same time it leaves us with a new serenity and responsibility, as it sets ethics and aesthetics in motion. Or in Malaguzzi's own words: '*I have saved my world as I always tried to change it.*'

Introduction

Peter Moss (English-language editor)

The schools are his books

Loris Malaguzzi was one of the most important figures in twentieth-century education. Devoting much of his life to early childhood education and to the municipal schools for young children in the Northern Italian city of Reggio Emilia, he has gained an international reputation in this sector. Yet, symptomatic of the narrow interests that prevail today, Malaguzzi is little known by those who work in other sectors of education, whether with older children, young people or adults; and despite Malaguzzi's clear understanding that his work in Reggio Emilia was relevant well beyond the confines of early childhood, to the renewal of all public education and schooling. Moreover, though he wrote a lot, and could doubtless have pursued a distinguished academic career, his name is not well known among academic educationalists. What he wrote was not for academic journals, and in many ways the clearest testimony to his educational importance lies not in the written word but in the educational project he did so much to create and evolve: a public network of schools, the municipal *nidi* and *scuole dell'infanzia* of Reggio Emilia, the former for children under 3 years, the latter for 3- to 6-year-olds. As others have observed, truly 'the schools are his books'.

Loris Malaguzzi's life, from 1920 to 1994, spanned most of what has been termed 'the short twentieth century'.[1] He was born soon after the end of one world war, and grew up and entered adulthood under fascism and during a second world war. Following the heady days of liberation, he lived the remainder of his life first during the rapid economic growth and social change of the post-war 'golden years', then during the early stages of the rise of neoliberalism to global hegemony. He died after the fall of the Berlin Wall and the collapse of the Soviet regime.

Born in the town of Correggio, situated in the Po Valley in the province of Reggio Emilia, Malaguzzi moved with his family to the city of Reggio Emilia when a young child, and lived there for most of the rest of his life. He also worked in and for the city for many years, an employee of the *comune* [local authority] of Reggio Emilia who devoted himself to a variety of municipal children's services, not just the schools for young children for which he became famous, but also in a pioneering centre for children with psychological problems and in summer camps. Before that, his early working years were spent as a teacher in state primary and middle schools, including a formative stint in a small and isolated mountain village, vividly recounted in the second document in this collection [2.ND], as well as in adult education working with young men whose education had been disrupted by war. With friends, he commandeered the abandoned villa of a fascist boss, to set up a 'people's school', an after-school centre for children experiencing difficulties in middle school. Little wonder then that he had such a wide appreciation of education across the board, and such a broad commitment to its renewal.

This book offers a unique perspective on Malaguzzi the educator: told in his own words. The words are to be found in documents selected from an archive created at Reggio Emilia's *Centro Documentazione e Ricerca Educativa, Scuole e Nidi d'infanzia – Istituzione del Comune di Reggio Emilia* [Documentation and Educational Research Centre] (of which more below). They begin with a newspaper article about literature and culture written in 1945, shortly after the end of the war in Europe when Malaguzzi was 25; and end in late 1993, with some sketched thoughts about a new development for Reggio Emilia's education project, the birth of Reggio Children, 'a place looking to the future' that was founded shortly after his death in January 1994.

Anyone hoping for a sequence of academic papers setting out the seamless evolution of pedagogical thought will be disappointed. But those who want insight into the life and work of an educator actively engaged in public education, intent on building a distinctive pedagogical project in a well-run municipal school system, and for whom theory and practice were totally inseparable, will not be. There are, for sure, articles and speeches containing more sustained expositions of Malaguzzi's evolving thinking, mostly not from academic journals or conferences. These, however, are interspersed with a miscellany of shorter documents, often fragments: letters, announcements of and programmes for seminars and other events held for local people, scraps of autobiography, poems and much more. Reading these you can feel his excitement and frustration, hope and irritation, passion and perseverance as they record the unrelenting and focused effort of this exceptional educator working to build a new public education in a renewed school, striving to bring others along with him but also ready to contend with the many obstacles strewn in the way of this ambitious project.

So what is to be found here are not only insights into the evolution of a great pedagogical thinker, but also into the everyday work of a great educational builder. We see Malaguzzi working with others – politicians, parents, educators, fellow citizens – to make his ideas and ideals happen, not just in one school but in a growing network of schools, a municipal education system that was formally established in 1963 and that today includes thirty-three schools managed by the *comune*, with a further fourteen schools managed as co-operatives under agreements with the *comune* (most of these latter schools are *nidi-scuole*, where a *nido* for children under 3 years and a *scuola* for 3- to 6-year-olds are provided as one educational service in the same building). This is radical public education enacted on an unprecedented scale and sustained over an unparalleled period of time. In this selection of documents by Malaguzzi, we can find some answers to key questions about this remarkable pedagogical experience and ample proof that the schools are indeed his books.

Reading Malaguzzi

Each reader will find something different in these documents, creating their own interpretations of Malaguzzi's words. Malaguzzi would have appreciated that this was inevitable, since he well understood that perspective and subjectivity were not only unavoidable but also to be valued. What follows here, therefore, are some reflections on my own reading of Malaguzzi, what has particularly struck and resonated with me, what meanings I have taken from this rich and varied material.

Like everyone, Malaguzzi was a product of a particular time and place. As already noted, he grew up under a dictatorship, entered adulthood in the midst of a terrible war, then experienced the heady days but also the great turmoil that followed Liberation and the restoration of peace and freedom. Three formative experiences, three 'places where I learned to speak and to live' [2.ND] – teaching in the small, remote and impoverished village of Sologno, the Liberation of Reggio Emilia, and participating in the community effort to build a school in the village of Villa Cella – date from just a few years, during and immediately after the war.

All three of these experiences also took place in a small area of Italy, in and around the city of Reggio Emilia, located in Northern Italy about 70 kilometres to the west of Bologna. Like most Italians, Malaguzzi was deeply rooted in his *territorio* [local area],[2] in particular his beloved Reggio Emilia to which he devoted most of his life. He was a *Reggiano*, and proud of it. Yet this intense local identification and loyalty did not make him parochial. He may have been rooted in a particular culture, but the values and political orientation of that culture were shared with many other *comuni* [local authorities]; and he was in constant and vigorous relationship with the wider world, in the rest of Italy and countries beyond.

This temporal and spatial context must have had a powerful effect on Malaguzzi and his approach to education. It is apparent in his recollection in later life that the immediate post-war years 'were times when everything seemed possible' [98.92]. It is apparent in his strong commitment to democracy as a fundamental value and practice in Reggio Emilia's schools; also in his insistence that the schools should be open to and engaged with not only children's families but also their local communities and all citizens, and that the city itself should recognise, welcome and accommodate children as young citizens (though he thought it remained resistant to such inclusion, being more orientated to the needs and lives of adults, see for example 39.70). It is apparent, too, in his deep respect for children and parents, and his steadfast appreciation of their rich potential, of what everyone is capable of given the right conditions. While his voracious reading and unceasing intellectual curiosity, his love of border crossing into new disciplines and paradigms, his encounters with so many people and experiences from outside Reggio Emilia and Italy, all of which took him and his fellow educators into so many new places, must surely have owed something to growing up under the stifling censorship and other restrictions of a fascist regime.

This context, too, shaped his politics. His ideas and work, Enzo Catarsi comments, 'were influenced by his participation in the struggles of democratic and progressive movements and by various examples of cooperative education' (2004, p.8). He was a man of the left, both in his general attitude to the world and more specifically as a member for many years of the post-war *Partito Comunista Italiano* or PCI [Italian Communist Party]: 'I knew nothing about politics, of the October Revolution, of Marx, Lenin, Gramsci, Togliatti. But I was sure I was taking the side of the weakest, of the people who carried most hope' [2.ND]. In that time and place there was nothing exceptional about this commitment: the PCI had a mass membership in the years after the war, especially in the Emilia-Romagna region where Reggio Emilia is situated. The PCI was also the ruling party in many *comuni*, including Reggio Emilia, and whatever its faults, it provided efficient, honest and progressive local government in stark contrast to that found in many other parts of Italy and, indeed, to the national government in Rome.

It was in such PCI-led administrations that the 'municipal school revolution' of the 1960s emerged in many Northern towns and cities, including Reggio Emilia, producing an exceptional educational experience for young children. Indeed the revolution extended beyond early education, with a shared view of individual and collective rights producing other innovative services, including health care. We can find here the birth of the Italian welfare state.

Several documents in this collection feature Malaguzzi addressing meetings of the PCI or its organisations [e.g. 12.56, 17.59, 59.75]. They not only show the evolution of his thinking and his political engagement, but demonstrate his readiness to criticise and challenge the Party, including its approach to democracy – he was not someone to toe the party line unquestioningly. We can also read him, on several occasions, contesting the views and policies of the dominant party in post-war Italy, the *Democrazia Cristiana* or DC [Christian Democrat Party] and their allies in the Catholic Church [e.g. 12.56, 42.71, 59.75, 61.75]. He was opposed to Church schools, which dominated early childhood education for years, in principle as well as for the way that many were actually run, and favoured a secular education system, arguing in the 1970s for a national system of preschools funded by the State but run locally, by *comuni*. This critical attitude towards Catholic education did not, however, become disdain; several documents emphasise that his political opposition was conducted with respect and a willingness to dialogue and indeed to find some measure of compromise [e.g. 61.75].

But Malaguzzi comes across as highly political in a wider sense of the word, beyond the narrowly party political. He was deeply aware that education was political, because it called for making choices between conflicting alternatives, including values, understandings and ways of working; and not only making choices, but being prepared to go out and argue the case for them. Put another way, he was always wanting to ask critical questions before suggesting solutions, rather than (as is so often the case today) wanting to be told 'what works' without first delving into and arguing about the meaning, purposes and values of education. Malaguzzi, in my reading, is a vivid example of the contention that education is, first and foremost, a political practice. And that overtly political stance was the product of post-war Italy, a context where people argued about real alternatives, believed another world was possible – and assumed education had an important part to play in bringing that world about.

Malaguzzi himself entirely understood the significance of context; it was an important part of what might be termed his paradigmatic positioning – the way he saw, interpreted and related to the world. Other important parts of that position, which he foregrounds increasingly as the years pass, are connectivity and complexity. 'Interconnecting, the great verb of the present and the future' [92.89], as he put it: and in his mind everything did connect, whether the many different facets that made the wholeness of the child; or the interplay of culture, science, economics and politics; or the growing range of disciplines that he was drawn to study, culminating in his fascination with cybernetics and neuroscience, and his insistence on the need for inter- or trans-disciplinarity [88.87, 94.90].

Seeing the connectedness of everything, together with a profound awareness of context and an understanding of the singularity of each person, led inevitably to an appreciation of complexity – and a corresponding abhorrence of the dominant contemporary discourse, with its love of classification and linearity, predictability and certainty, separation and reductionism. This discourse he viewed as outdated and in crisis, contested by new scientific perspectives and understandings: for 'unpredictable today is a category of science' [92.89], while:

> against the old distinction-separateness of sciences (in particular the 'exact' sciences, both technological and human) [the challenge is to] re-establish their inseparability, their communication and integration, in a trans-disciplinary framework which ought increasingly to animate both research and teaching, to defeat the classification of single disciplines.
>
> [88.87]

Such outmoded thinking applied to education led him to excoriate what he termed 'prophetic pedagogy', which:

knows everything beforehand, knows everything that will happen, knows everything, does not have one uncertainty, is absolutely imperturbable. It contemplates everything and prophesies everything, sees everything, sees everything to the point that it is capable of giving you recipes for little bits of actions, minute by minute, hour by hour, objective by objective, five minutes by five minutes. This is something so coarse, so cowardly, so humiliating of teachers' ingenuity, a complete humiliation for children's ingenuity and potential.

[98.92]

Rather than a longing for predictability and regularity, Malaguzzi valued uncertainty, desired wonder and amazement, loved to marvel at the totally unexpected.

Malaguzzi was an educator par excellence and not just an educator, but an educator who assumed leadership for the educational project in Reggio Emilia. What comes across to me in reading these documents is a distinct and important idea of what this leadership role requires, that is if performed as part of a public and democratic education. The political element has already been mentioned, the need to engage with alternatives and to make and contend for certain choices. The importance of participation and respect for all those with an interest in education – in effect, everyone in the city – has also been referred to, to which should be added his belief in the values of cooperation and solidarity. To these qualities, I would like to add what seem to me, from my reading of the documents in this book, to be two more defining features of his role as educational leader.

First, the intellectual educational leader. He was an intellectual who loved the company of other intellectuals (see, for example, his vivid account in the third document in this book of being 'In the post-war city' [3.91]). He was a man of many interests, great curiosity and incessant border crossing, never losing his delight at encountering new ideas, new perspectives and new friends. A man who wrote poetry, loved theatre and drama, and was very well and very widely read. A man who kept abreast of the latest developments and debates in politics, economics, culture and science. A man who wanted a modern education that understood and responded to contemporary conditions and needs and was open to contemporary thinking and knowledge – whilst never losing sight of its responsibility for the future. And a man with a strong critical faculty, applied not only to the outdated thinking and institutions that he found so typical of Italy, and to the organisations of which he was a member, but also to leading figures in psychology and pedagogy, many of whom he also admired greatly and took inspiration from (see, for example, his increasingly critical appraisal of aspects of Piaget's work [25.65, 31.67, 77.ND, 85.85, 88.86, 94.90]).

But these are just some of the ingredients of being an intellectual, the raw materials that enable this role. What sort of intellectual was he? The French philosopher Michel Foucault distinguishes between two types of intellectual. The 'universal intellectual', he argued, for a long period:

> spoke and was acknowledged the right of speaking in the capacity of master of truth and justice. He was heard, or purported to make himself heard, as the spokesman of the universal. To be an intellectual meant something like being the consciousness/conscience of us all.
>
> (Foucault, 1984, p.67)

But since the end of the Second World War, Foucault discerned the emergence of a new sort, the 'specific intellectual':

> A new mode of the 'connection between theory and practice' has been established. Intellectuals have become used to working, not in the modality of the 'universal', the 'exemplary', the 'just-and-true-for-all', but within specific sectors, at the precise points where their own conditions of life or work situate them (housing, the hospital, the asylum, the laboratory, the university, family, and sexual relations). This has undoubtedly given them a much more immediate and concrete awareness of struggles.
>
> (*ibid.*, p.68)

This description of the specific intellectual seems to me to fit Malaguzzi very well, situated as he was in the specific sector of education, aware of and engaged with its struggles, striving to establish new ways of connecting theory and practice. Moreover, he understood the teacher in this light too: in 1975 we find him telling a meeting of the PCI that '[t]he role of the teacher that the need for school renewal calls for is a new type of intellectual, a producer of knowledge connected with the demands of society that are expressed through various types of organisation' [59.75].

Second, the democratic educational leader. Today's new public management calls for hierarchical structures that separate senior officials from those engaged in the everyday work of services, the former controlling the latter at a distance through a web of procedures, targets and measurements. Malaguzzi, by contrast, offers an alternative of democratic and participatory management inscribed with an ethos of cooperation and dialogue and practised in close relationship with the 'frontline'. He is a pedagogical leader constantly engaged with and contributing to the everyday lives of educators and children, working ceaselessly to involve children, educators and parents with his ideas and to learn with them. He did not just plan new schools and ensure their sound administration; he was constantly in them once open, taking the pedagogical pulse, engaging with all and sundry, talking and listening. When he spoke about education and schools it was from first-hand and current experience.

As such, his working life is complex and multi-faceted. So, one moment he is the administrator, the head of the emerging early childhood service in

Reggio Emilia, writing to the Mayor, other city politicians or officials or to schools: about problems with the construction of the new Diana school, or arguing for the school to have an *atelier* [arts workshop]; or warning against the *comune* assuming responsibility for a sub-standard Church-run school; or proposing measures to school staff to implement the *Comune*'s new *Regolamento* [Rulebook]; or chiding some schools for failing to ensure representation at meetings. The next moment he is the educator, organising series of lectures or other events for parents and teachers, in which he also often participates as a teacher. Then he is the pedagogical director, setting out his ideas about summer camps or schools and their underlying pedagogy, to a variety of audiences, locally, regionally or nationally, a role that is inescapably connected with that of pedagogical researcher; research is central to his idea of the identity of the school and the work of the teacher. Another time he is the student, learning from the work on maths of Piaget and other Swiss psychologists, reading prodigiously and widely, wanting to keep abreast of the latest thinking in many fields. He is a broadcaster, sharing this latest thinking and new ways of working with others; while on other occasions, he is a campaigner, arguing the case for more and better services for children and families or for the defence of what has been achieved in the face of threatened cuts – all this within the wider frame of a passionate commitment to the idea of public education. Last but not least, he is a democrat and community activist, building open and participant relationships between the new municipal schools, the families whose children attend them and local communities.

A man, therefore, of great energy and relentless activity, restless and never satisfied; reading the documents often left me breathless, wondering how he found time to do so much. He combined the capacity to think, discuss and do, continuously putting ideas to work and feeding the products of that work back into his thinking, this inter-active process fuelled by relationships, by his daily engagement with fellow educators, parents, administrators, politicians – and children. It is the range and richness of these roles and relationships and their synergy that is reflected in the diversity of documents presented here.

Above all, leading an educational service meant not just knowing about the system, the nuts and bolts of organisation, procedures and resources, important though he recognised that to be. It meant thinking, dialoguing and arguing about education itself. His role as educational leader was not to implement national policy, not to tell others what to do, not to lead a pliant following wherever he chose – it was to create and evolve an educational project in his city, but always in relation with others and in a spirit of participation and cooperation. Following this process of constant co-construction through these documents is a fascinating exercise, spotting the first reference to some feature that has subsequently come to identify Reggio Emilia's educational project, noting why, where and when it emerges, how it is initially conceptualised and discussed, and then how it evolves over time.

Selecting the documents

The very diversity of the documents included in this book, their variety of formats and contents, gives us a unique insight into the man and his work, the times in which he was living and working, the many people and organisations with whom he was in relationship, the subjects that engaged him, and his emerging thinking about children, families, schools and education. They show that Malaguzzi not only spoke a lot, he also wrote extensively. Where have these documents come from and how have they been selected?

They have been selected from an archive created at the *Centro Document-azione e Ricerca Educativa, Scuole e Nidi d'infanzia – Istituzione del Comune di Reggio Emilia*, housed in the city's Loris Malaguzzi International Centre. The formation of this archive owes much to the work of Marina Castagnetti, who has been at the *Centro* since 2000, before which she was a teacher at the Diana school in Reggio Emilia. She found documents in many places, including in municipal schools, each having its own archive, and in the collections of some teachers and *pedagogistas*. She went to the municipal Panizzi Library looking through old newspapers, seeking articles by Malaguzzi and discovering he had had regular columns in the local paper. The *Centro* itself already had 177 audio cassettes of Malaguzzi speaking at a wide range of meetings, as well as a large number of documents that had been published (in Italian) in one place or another. It contained, too, video cassettes, especially from 1987 onwards when the *Centro* was established and began asking for video material when Malaguzzi spoke abroad. Less high tech, Marina also found, buried in old files, other material including notes from meetings. The end result was the creation of an archive of 441 documents, plus a large number of audio and video cassettes.

Building up such a large and diverse archive owes much to the fact that Malaguzzi archived all his papers. This is true, also, of other educators in Reggio Emilia. Moreover, Malaguzzi and other educators took notes about everything. We can see here two important habits deeply ingrained in the culture of Reggio Emilia's educational project. To document so as to be able to reflect, dialogue and make meaning; and to conserve, so as to be able to go back and to re-cognise (a word and concept discussed below).

The archive from which the documents in this book have been selected is not complete; it remains open for the addition of further items. Nor is it comprehensive, not containing all of Malaguzzi's known writings, interviews and speeches. It does not include, so neither does this book, writings, interviews or speeches publicly available in English (see the references section at the end of the book for a list of some English-language publications by or about Malaguzzi); a decision was made not to include these documents, most of which are from the last years of his life and can be read elsewhere. Nor have we included any of the editorials or other articles he regularly contributed to the Italian early childhood magazines *Zerosei* and *Bambini* between 1976 and 1993. Last but not least, the archive contains none of the notebooks that Malaguzzi regularly kept, which contained for instance summaries of his reading, ideas that had come to him and many notes he took at meetings. These are held in a family archive.

Even with these exceptions, the many hundreds of documents in the archive are testament to how much Malaguzzi wrote and spoke about education – and far exceed the space available in this book. A selection has had to be made. This book, therefore, draws on 103 documents from the 400 plus in the *Centro* archive. Moreover, few of the documents are presented whole, a selection being made within these documents with [. . .] indicating where material has been cut. The selection process was undertaken by a Working Group of educators from Reggio Emilia: Paola Cagliari, Claudia Giudici, Carlina Rinaldi and Vea Vecchi and Marina Castagnetti. Together with myself, this group has also formed the editorial team that has produced the book, in collaboration with Annamaria Mucchi of the Reggio Children publishing team. All members of the Reggio Emilia Working Group have worked in and with the municipal schools for a long time and, particularly important, all knew Loris Malaguzzi well. Once selected, the documents were translated into English by Jane McCall, who has lived and worked for many years in Reggio Emilia; she combines expertise as a translator with great knowledge of the subject matter, an invaluable asset in such an undertaking.

The language of Malaguzzi

Translating Malaguzzi's words has not always been easy. He was quite capable of being precise and clear-cut. But on paper and at first glance his words can sometimes seem difficult to understand, on occasion almost impenetrable – even in his native Italian. There are a number of reasons for this. The contemporary context and the references made to people and events may not always be understood by readers today, especially those not from Italy. I have tried to help by supplying an historical and biographical introduction to each of the five periods covered in this book, together with a timeline for Malaguzzi, Reggio Emilia and Italy. I have also added an 'editor's note' by way of introduction to some documents and supplied short footnotes to provide basic information about certain people, places and events that crop up in the texts.

In the case of texts based on oral presentations, the transcriptions may not always be complete or wholly accurate. Moreover, what is inevitably lost in this project, which reduces presentations spoken in Italian to English words on paper, is Malaguzzi's voice, his way of talking, and his body language. Those who knew him well emphasise that he was most at home when speaking, and he was clearly a very gifted communicator, full of passion and 'theatrical, like a magician', as one of the Working Group put it. Another recalled that 'Loris's way of speaking had the style of the narrator. He drew people in, he was very fascinating to listen to, but it took time to fully understand him.' He also held people's attention because he was always in tune with the times, with what people were feeling, so people felt he was talking to them, about matters that concerned them. So while his listeners might not immediately have understood everything he said, he kept them hooked, he pulled them towards what he was looking for, what he was seeking to express, he carried them along, he made them want to go further.

When Malaguzzi spoke, another recalled, he gave teachers a sense of importance, raising the work to an intellectual level that made them feel how valuable it was. He opened listeners up to new horizons and perspectives, to a larger future, to a wider view, to a new world. The operative word, repeated frequently by members of the Working Group, is 'opening': to new ideas, new perspectives, new research, new possibilities. At the same time, he was a good listener, 'he would let teachers present [their work], not interrupt – then comment'. Sadly, we can never recapture these qualities of Malaguzzi, qualities that made him so loved and respected and trusted. What inspired and excited in person may not always transfer equally well onto the page.

Malaguzzi's voice was, of course, an Italian one. He grew up before English had become the dominant global language it is today; he never learnt it. This did not mean that he never travelled beyond Italy, never spoke with people from abroad or never read foreign authors. Quite the contrary. He spoke and read French; and, as the texts that follow show, he was an avid border crosser in every sense of the word, travelling to many other countries, meeting with many European and American educators, and reading a wide range of books in translation.

One aim of this book is to make a body of Malaguzzi's work, written or spoken in his native tongue, accessible to English-speakers who have little or no Italian. But to do this, to translate his words from Italian to English, requires giving some thought to the act of translation. Languages do not translate perfectly; there is no complete equivalence between one language and another. Concepts, terms and other vocabulary may not always correspond, and meaning in such cases can get lost in translation. Presented with a text translated into your own language, it becomes easy to forget this possibility, an especial risk for English-speakers who are so accustomed to everything being served up to them in their native tongue. The danger here is of the Other being made into the Same in moments of false recognition and mistaken equivalence, the alterity of the Other being lost and, hence, the provocation to think that arises when confronted by difference.

So ease of reading may be at odds with comprehension, obviating the struggle to work on the meaning of something different. Translation, too, may lose some of the political significance in the original language. A good example is the competing terms used in Italian, especially in the earlier years of the Reggio Emilia education project, for services for children from 3 to 6 years. These were originally known in Italy as *scuola materna*, with a clear connotation of welfare-orientated services that substituted for mothers and whose staff were primarily to display motherly qualities; the term fitted comfortably with the ideology of Church-run schools, predominant in Italy until the 1960s. But *comuni* such as Reggio Emilia wanted to develop a different concept for these services, as places that were neither home-like nor motherly, but were instead clearly understood to be for children and places of education, a role expressed through the term *scuola dell'infanzia*. To translate both terms into English as 'nursery school', 'kindergarten' or 'preschool' is to lose the competing politics underlying the two different terms and, hence, their part in a wider political confrontation.

Most of Malaguzzi's Italian words, from the documents selected for this book, have been translated into English. But, as the English-language editor, I have chosen to retain a number of important and recurring terms in their original Italian, either because of the risk of losing meaning in translation or to provide a constant reminder to English-language readers that they are engaging with another language, culture and politics. In such cases, where I have chosen to retain the original Italian, I offer an English approximation the first time the word or term appears, as well as including the Italian original and the English approximation in a glossary (see the Glossary to be found at the end of this Introduction). The words that have not been translated mainly refer to services, roles and organisations, the sort of vocabulary that defines the main structural components of Reggio Emilia's education project and the political context in which it evolved.

Then there are other words that are translated into English, but which have a particular meaning as used by Malaguzzi; taken together, they make an important contribution to understanding his perspectives and the distinct identity of Reggio Emilia's pedagogical project. Rather than 'develop', with its connotations of linearity and predictability, people and projects 'evolve' [*evolvere*], responding unpredictably to contingencies, 'a-rythmic and discontinuous' rather than 'a uniform, regular advance' [21.63]. To 'experiment' [*sperimentare*] is a constant imperative, meaning to explore, to try or test things out. And this in turn requires 'verification', to 'verify' [*verificare*] meaning to test ideas or theories in the flow of everyday work, finding out through examination and experimentation if they hold up or not. This can be seen as part of an attitude of 'research' [*ricerca*], an enquiring mind that never takes anything for granted, that treats theories as points of reference but is constantly putting them to the test, verifying them, seeing if they are useful and, if so, in what way. All these qualities are complemented by a readiness for 'confrontation' [*confronto*], a willingness and capacity to question the interpretations and perspectives of others, and to offer your own for similar challenge in frank but respectful exchange – without degenerating into hostility and antagonism.

A number of words are used by Malaguzzi to express his view that everything is inter-connected and inter-dependent, a view that also attracts him to cybernetics, with its attention to systems, and to the writings of Gregory Bateson. There is, for example, a cluster of associated words – 'organic' [*organico*], 'holistic' [*olistico*], 'integral' [*integrale*] – used to affirm that the child cannot (or, at least, should not) be divided into pieces in pedagogical or other work. Other words also refer to various forms of connectedness or interaction, including 'node' [*nodo*], a point in a network at which lines or pathways intersect or branch out; 'contamination' [*contaminazione*] or 'contagion' [*contagio*], to suggest being influenced or touched by someone or something else – but used in a positive sense; and 'articulate(d)' [*articolare*], where pieces connect up in a complexity. 'Ecological' and 'matrix' [*matrice*] refer to the cultural, social and/or political environment in which something develops and emphasise the importance of 'context', a word that itself appears many times.

Two other words are very central to understanding Malaguzzi and the municipal schools. To 're-cognise' [*ri-conoscere*] is fundamental to every process, 're-cognition' being about returning to a previous experience, often with others, to reflect, re-think and re-know its meaning; for example when a small group rejoins the larger group and tells what they have been doing, creating in the process new shared knowledge, whilst themselves 're-knowing' the original experience through sharing it with others. Re-cognition also supports the importance of conserving, since conserved documentation can be subject to re-visiting, re-thinking and re-knowing, providing a rich resource for reflection. Finally, to 'qualify' [*qualificare*] is not about adding a reservation or caveat, but rather refers to giving greater or different value to something, so enhancing its position.

In addition to retaining some words in their original Italian, I have adopted some other conventions in editing this book in English. Resisting the temptation to modernise and sanitise, I have retained Malaguzzi's original language, even where he uses terminology that would not be widely used or acceptable today, for example 'education of the psychically abnormal, those with irregular conduct, and the socially maladjusted' [10.54]. I have retained the original layout of letters and other formatted documents, as well as retaining capital letters and the use of bold or italic fonts and underlinings where they occur in the original documents. I have used square brackets to indicate where I have made additions to the original text or where I have provided an English translation of an Italian term or give the reference number for one of the selected texts. Lastly, I have used the term 'municipal schools' to refer to all services for children from birth to 6 years provided by the *Comune* of Reggio Emilia (or other Italian *comuni*); a more literal translation would be 'communal schools', but this, I think, reads strangely in English and may lead to misunderstandings.

These are issues and conventions that need to be acknowledged and born in mind. But they should not detract from the pleasure of reading Malaguzzi, from the excitement of not knowing what will come next, and from the privilege of entering the life and mind of this amazing educator. Fizzing with incredible energy and boundless enthusiasm, he takes us all on a roller coaster ride, full of surprises and variety. This is education as it should be; not a pallid account of technical practice abetting predetermined outcomes, but a vivid and original story of democracy, experimentation and potentiality.

The organisation of the book

The rest of the book is organised into six parts. The first five, Chapters 1 to 5, present the selected documents in five chronological periods: up to 1963; 1964–69; 1970–79; 1980–89; 1990–93. In doing so, we have largely followed the time spans adopted in *One City, Many Children: Reggio Emilia, A History Of The Present*, the exhibition and catalogue produced by the Reggio Emilia education system to tell the city's story of its education project (Various Authors, 2012). We have, however, chosen to move three later documents to the beginning, because they provide accounts, by Malaguzzi himself, of his early life, giving the reader some important biographical and historical background.

Each of these five chapters has an introduction in three sections. The first sets out the historical context for the period covered, both in Reggio Emilia and Italy, and outlines significant events in Malaguzzi's working life. The second section, written by the Working Group, discusses the selection of the documents that follow, and the themes that they represent. Finally, there is a timeline to enable the reader to quickly check what was going on year by year, for Malaguzzi, Reggio Emilia and Italy.

Each document that follows the introduction for each part is numbered. The first two digits give the document's place in the sequence of selected documents, running from 1 to 100 (in three cases, two or more separate documents have been amalgamated into one document for this publication, hence reducing the original 103 selected documents to 100). The second part of the numbering indicates the year the document was written, with 'ND' indicating there is no precise date known. So, for example, document 59.75 is document number 59, dating from 1975.

The final part of the book, written by the Reggio Emilia Working Group, offers a brief reflection on the educational, political and social legacy Loris Malaguzzi has left us.

Bowing out

Working on this book has been a double pleasure. First, the pleasure of getting to know, albeit second hand, both a great educator and a fascinating person, a man of many interests, many parts and many languages (in the sense he uses languages in his poem about 'the hundred languages of children' [75.ND]). Second, the pleasure of including this book in the series *Contesting Early Childhood*, which I co-edit with Gunilla Dahlberg.

This is the last book in the series to appear under our editorship; we are handing on the task to a younger generation, Liselott Marriett Olsson (from Sweden) and Michel Vandenboreck (from Belgium). Reggio Emilia has figured strongly in the series up to now, both in books by educators from Reggio Emilia (Rinaldi, 2006; Vecchi, 2010), and in books whose authors have drawn inspiration from Reggio Emilia. For Reggio Emilia exemplifies the purpose and spirit of the series: to question 'the current dominant discourses in early childhood, and [to offer] alternative narratives of an area that is now made up of a multitude of perspectives and debates'.

Reggio Emilia is, of course, not the only example of questioning and of alternative narratives, the series contains many more. But it remains unique in its capacity to generate and connect new thinking and new practice, and to enact its alternative narrative in a system of schools that are both extensive and have demonstrated a capacity to sustain a dynamic, experimental and democratic public education. As such it is a reproof and a challenge to a baleful and impoverished current dominant discourse in early childhood education, what I have termed 'the story of quality and high returns' (Moss, 2014), with its instrumental rationale and calculative relationships, its blinkered perspectives and fixation with technical practice, a discourse inscribed with neoliberal values and beliefs, and contributing to an ever-greater governing of children and adults in a society of control.

Reggio Emilia insists another world is possible, rejecting the dominant discourse's dictatorship of no alternative by affirming there are alternatives, and that the political and ethical must precede the technical. More than affirming, but also doing. For one of the great achievements of Reggio Emilia has been to create and sustain a collective educational project, involving the participation and commitment of many, many people – educators, parents, politicians and, of course, children. Loris Malaguzzi's death in 1994 was a great sadness and an enormous loss, but the project survived and continued to evolve. The project proved greater than the man.

This is not to belittle his part in the project. Far from it. If Reggio Emilia survived the death of Malaguzzi, it is in part because he helped to build strong and sure foundations, both cultural and structural, including a body of committed and creative educators; and because he worked at so many levels, from pedagogical theory to the organisation of a network of schools. But Malaguzzi speaks, of course, for more than Reggio Emilia; he is intensely local, a *Reggiano* through and through, but he is also a man of and in the world, a man whose voice deserves to be, and should be, heard wherever there is an interest in education – not just early childhood education, but any education. He is, quite simply, a global figure. With his boundless curiosity, his endless invention and his constant belief in human potentiality, Malaguzzi puts to shame the grey and repetitious maunderings of today's dominant story-tellers with their fixations about returns on investment, predetermined outcomes and applying correct technologies. I can think of no better note on which to bow out and bid farewell to this series.

Notes

1 Originally proposed by Iván Berend (Hungarian Academy of Sciences) but defined by Eric Hobsbawm, the British Marxist historian, 'the short twentieth century' refers to the period between the years 1914 and 1991, from the beginning of the First World War to the fall of the Soviet Union.

2 *Territorio* carries a deep meaning in Italian about local identity and roots, encompassing local traditions, land, foods and wines, the local ways and history, often too the local dialect – all of which vary so much from *territorio* to *territorio*.

Glossary of Italian terms used in the text

Aggiornamento	Regular sessions for professional development and updating each other
Asilo	Earlier term for a centre or school for 3- to 6-year-olds
Asilo nido/asili nido	Centre/s for children under 3 years
Assessorato Scuola e Servizi Sociali	Department/Office of schools and social services
Assessore	Member of the executive of the Giunta, usually with responsibility for a particular department
Atelier/atelierista	Arts workshop/educator with arts education working in atelier
Casa di vacanza	See 'colonia'
Centro Documentazione e Ricerca Educativa	Documentation and Educational Research Centre
Centro Italiano Femminile (CIF)	Italian Women's Centre, connected to *Azione Cattolica* [Catholic Action]
Centro Medico Psico-Pedagogico Comunale	Municipal Psycho-Pedagogical Medical Centre
Colonia/colonie (later, casa di vacanze)	Summer camp/camps for children
Comitato/Comitati di Scuola e Città	School and City Committee/s
Comune/comuni	Local authority or municipality/plural
Consiglio/Consigli di Gestione	School management council/s
Consiglio/Consigli di quartiere	Neighbourhood council/s
Democrazia Cristiana (DC)	Christian Democrat Party
Équipe Pedagogico-Didattica	Pedagogical coordination and support team including pedagogistas
Gestione sociale	Participatory system of governance including representatives of parents, staff and the local community
Giunta Comunale	City council

Gruppo Nazionale Nidi	National Nido Group
Istituzione	An autonomous municipal body for running public services
Nidi convenzionati	Centres for children under 3 years run by a cooperative under agreement with comune
Opera Nazionale Maternità e Infanzia (ONMI)	National organisation, founded by fascist regime, to provide assistance to young children and their mothers
Partito Comunista Italiano (PCI)	Italian Communist Party
Partito Repubblicano Italiano (PRI)	Italian Republican Party
Pedagogista	Worker with psychology or pedagogy degree who supports a small group of *nidi* and/or *scuole dell'infanzia*
Prefettura	Office of the Prefect, the national government representative at local level in the Italian Provinces
Scuola comunale dell'infanzia	School provided by a *comune*, a 'municipal school'
Scuola/e dell'infanzia	School/s for 3- to 6-year-olds
Scuola materna/scuole materne	School/s for 3- to 6-year-olds; term widely used until 1991, most frequently in the state and private sectors
Territorio	Local area, with its culture, customs and traditions
Unione Donne Italiane (UDI)	Italian Women's Union, anti-fascist association with roots in the Resistance movement

Chapter 1

Early years

To 1963

Figure 1.1 Loris Malaguzzi at the *Centro Medico Psico-Pedagogico Comunale* in Reggio
Emilia, 1950s

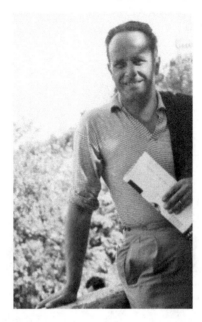

Figure 1.2 Loris Malaguzzi, late 1940s

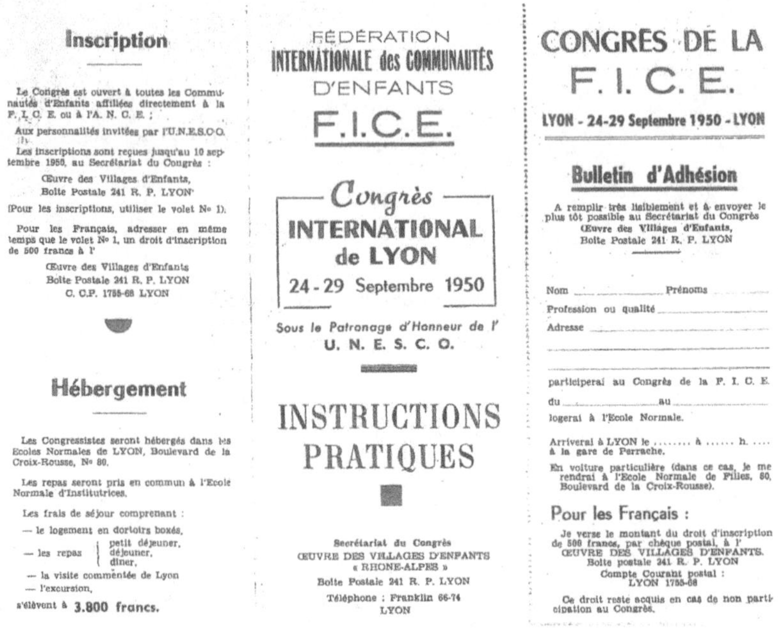

Inscription

Le Congrès est ouvert à toutes les Communautés d'Enfants affiliées directement à la F. I. C. E. ou à l'A. N. C. E. ;

Aux personnalités invitées par l'U.N.E.S.C.O.

Les inscriptions sont reçues jusqu'au 10 septembre 1950, au Secrétariat du Congrès :

Œuvre des Villages d'Enfants,
Boite Postale 241 R. P. LYON

(Pour les inscriptions, utiliser le volet N° 1).

Pour les Français, adresser en même temps que le volet N° 1, un droit d'inscription de 500 francs à l'

Œuvre des Villages d'Enfants
Boite Postale 241 R. P. LYON
C. C.P. 1755-68 LYON

Hébergement

Les Congressistes seront hébergés dans les Ecoles Normales de LYON, Boulevard de la Croix-Rousse, N° 80.

Les repas seront pris en commun à l'Ecole Normale d'Institutrices.

Les frais de séjour comprenant :

— le logement en dortoirs boxés,
— les repas { petit déjeuner, déjeuner, diner,
— la visite commentée de Lyon
— l'excursion,

s'élèvent à **3.800 francs.**

FÉDÉRATION
INTERNATIONALE des COMMUNAUTÉS
D'ENFANTS
F.I.C.E.

Congrès
INTERNATIONAL
de LYON
24 - 29 Septembre 1950

Sous le Patronage d'Honneur de l'
U. N. E. S. C. O.

INSTRUCTIONS
PRATIQUES

Secrétariat du Congrès
ŒUVRE DES VILLAGES D'ENFANTS
« RHONE-ALPES »
Boîte Postale 241 R. P. LYON
Téléphone : Franklin 66-74
LYON

CONGRÉS DE LA
F. I. C. E.
LYON - 24-29 Septembre 1950 - LYON

Bulletin d'Adhésion

A remplir très lisiblement et à envoyer le plus tôt possible au Secrétariat du Congrès
Œuvre des Villages d'Enfants,
Boite Postale 241 R. P. LYON

Nom .... Prénoms ....
Profession ou qualité ....
Adresse ....

participerai au Congrès de la F. I. C. E.
du .... au ....
logerai à l'Ecole Normale.

Arriverai à LYON le .... à ...... h. ....
à la gare de Perrache.

En voiture particulière (dans ce cas, je me rendrai à l'Ecole Normale de Filles, 80, Boulevard de la Croix-Rousse).

Pour les Français :

Je verse le montant du droit d'inscription de 500 francs, par chèque postal, à l'
ŒUVRE DES VILLAGES D'ENFANTS.
Boite postale 241 R. P. LYON
Compte Courant postal :
LYON 1755-68

Ce droit reste acquis en cas de non participation au Congrès.

Figure 1.3 Poster for the FICE International Congress, Lyon (France), in which Loris Malaguzzi participated, 1950

Introduction (Peter Moss)

The historical context

Reggio Emilia, the city Malaguzzi was associated with for most of his adult life, is 70 kilometres to the west of Bologna and situated towards the southern edge of the Po Valley, near the foothills of the Apennine Mountains. Formerly part of the Duchy of Estense, its citizens voted overwhelmingly to join the new Italian state in 1860, when the city's population was some 47,000. In the same year, a charity opened the city's first *asilo d'infanzia* [school for 3- to 6-year-olds], offering free attendance and intended mainly for children living in poor conditions. In 1899, the socialists gained control of the *comune*, and remained in power for most of the time until the *comune* was suppressed in 1926 and replaced by a *Podestà*, an official appointed by the national government. From 1922 to 1943 that government was led by Benito Mussolini, whose fascist regime bequeathed the world the term *totalitarismo* – totalitarian.[1]

Before its eventual suppression by Mussolini's totalitarian regime, Reggio Emilia's socialist administration took a strong lead in developing education, broadly defined. Primary schooling was extended, *colonie* [summer camps] and music schools were established and, in 1913, a municipal *asilo d'infanzia* was opened in the village of Villa Gaida, serving a community with many employed mothers, but combining care with a strong commitment to progressive and secular education, working with the pedagogical ideas of Friedrich Fröbel and Ferrante Aporti. The *asilo* was eventually closed down in 1938 by the *Podestà*, who dismissed it in the following words: 'The municipal *Asilo* of Villa Gaida was opened by a Socialist administration in 1912 as an alternative to the parish [Church] *Asilo* in existence since 1910. In a fascist regime this is not thinkable.' Under fascist rule, therefore, Reggio Emilia was reduced to funding private *asilo* schools, including fourteen Catholic and three charitable institutions.

Italy entered the Second World War in 1940 and surrendered to the Allies in 1943, triggering a German occupation of Northern Italy. A resistance movement organised and grew, fighting and violence spread; Reggio Emilia, like other cities in occupied Italy, was bombed, the Malaguzzi family house reduced to ruins. These were very hard times, both for those actively involved in the resistance (with 35,000 killed in occupied Italy and many others injured or deported) and the rest of the population struggling to survive amid severe shortages, the inhuman behaviour of a repressive regime and the destruction and violence of war. Like much of Northern Italy, Reggio Emilia was only liberated near the very end of the war in Europe, in April 1945.

The immediate post-war years were also hard, with a population confronting the legacy of dictatorship and war. But despite the many difficulties, these were also years of cultural and political renewal, in Reggio Emilia but elsewhere too across Italy. The values of the anti-fascist resistance persisted: solidarity, social justice, peace, democracy. There was a great flourishing of civic society, with a wide variety of political and cultural groups forming, new meeting places emerging and many activities being revived after years of restrictions and censorship, including Malaguzzi's beloved theatre.

Out of the resistance, strong women's organisations emerged. The *Unione Donne Italiane* or UDI [Italian Women's Union] was founded in 1944, an anti-fascist group with its roots in the Resistance movement, committed to women's emancipation and employment and to the rights of women and children; while the *Centro Italiano Femminile* or CIF [Italian Women's Centre], associated with the Catholic Action movement, was founded in 1945 and sought to promote women's participation in society. Many future female administrators in Reggio Emilia and beyond, who were to play an important role in promoting public schools for young children, were members of the UDI.

Party politically, the national government in Rome was led for many years after the war by the *Democrazia Cristiana* or DC [Christian Democrat Party], a Roman Catholic and centrist party that played a dominant role in the politics of Italy for fifty years from its inception in 1944 until its demise in 1994. The second party in size for much of this period was the *Partito Comunista Italiano* or PCI [Italian Communist Party], which gained 23 per cent of the vote in the 1953 election (compared to 40 per cent for the DC) and continued to increase its share of the national vote until peaking at 34 per cent in 1976, close to the DC's 39 per cent. Under its first post-war leader, Palmiro Togliatti, the PCI adopted a strategy of reform not revolution, building social and political alliances (with, for example, the DC and the middle classes) and 'transforming the Communists from a small vanguard group into a mass party in civil society' (Ginsborg, 1990, p.46).

Whilst lagging behind the DC nationally, the PCI was dominant in some areas of Italy and especially in Emilia-Romagna – the region in which Reggio Emilia is situated. Paul Ginsborg, the historian of post-war Italy, writes that 'the Communists reigned supreme [in Emilia-Romagna] from the end of the war onwards . . . [affording] the PCI a quite extraordinary degree of support when compared with the rest of the country' (*ibid.*, p.200); by 1947, the PCI had a membership of nearly half a million people in the region, almost a fifth of the adult population. Space precludes exploring the reasons for this dominance. However two aspects merit attention here. First, it was not based on heavy industry and its proletarian workforce; Emilia-Romagna, after the war, was an area of small businesses, artisans and farm workers. The PCI made alliances with and drew support from all of these sectors, adopting an inclusive strategy. Second, the Party strove to win control of local authorities and demonstrate its capacity to govern well; Bologna, the region's largest city, became the show-piece of Communist local government, and the city's 'efficiency and honesty contrasted favourably with the chaos and corruption in many other areas of Italy' (*ibid.*, p.203). Such local efficiency and honesty was in marked contrast, too, to the inertia and failure to bring about change that marked central government under DC leadership and its unreformed bureaucracy.

The post-war years, and especially from the late 1950s, was a period of economic and material development, culminating in Italy's so-called 'economic miracle'. In the twenty years from 1950 to 1970, per capita income grew more rapidly than in any other European country. And with economic growth and fast rising household incomes came consumerism, urged on by an unprecedented expansion of advertising. Television ownership rose from just 12 per cent of families in 1958 to 49 per cent in 1965, fridge ownership from 13 to 55 per cent, while the number of cars soared from 342,000 in 1950 to 4.67 million in 1964 (*ibid.*, p.239).

With economic and material growth came three demographic and social changes. There was massive migration, from countryside to town and from South to North; between 1955 and 1971, more than nine million Italians moved from one region to another. This in turn contributed to a decline in the strong linguistic hold of local dialect, as people from different parts of Italy increasingly mixed and under the centralising influences of TV and school, with the children of migrant families often turning up at new schools initially understanding little that was said to them. Finally, migration, urbanisation, economic growth and consumerism produced a growing atomisation of civil society with an accompanying isolation of families. The nuclear family was becoming more important than ever, but also increasingly solitary; and while 'this privatization in smaller family units' may have had some good points, it also meant that 'each nuclear family unit tended to be more closed in upon itself, and less open to community life or to forms of inter-family solidarity' (*ibid.*, p.243).

It is against this historical backdrop that we can view the evolution of post-war early childhood education in Reggio Emilia. After the war, Reggio Emilia regained its democratic local government, with successive Socialist-Communist administrations. As the texts reproduced below illustrate, the revived *Comune* became active in many areas, providing a range of services for children and young people, such as *colonie* and a centre for children with mental health problems, services combining medical, psychological and pedagogical functions. It also took seriously its cultural role, supporting theatre, cinema and music, and widening popular participation by attracting new audiences, for example by a policy of low-price tickets.

But until the late 1950s, the *Comune* was slow to give strong support to the needs of women and young children. Early initiatives were taken by private organisations. For example, in the immediate post-war years the UDI opened eight self-managed *asili* for 3- to 6-year-olds within the city boundaries; one of these, the *asilo del Popolo* [school of the people] that opened in 1947 in the nearby village of Villa Cella, would come to play an important part in Malaguzzi's life. The UDI and (with a minor role) the CIF also initiated other projects for women and children in and around the city in the 1950s, including temporary *asili* set up during harvest time, after-school centres and summer camps.

The *Comune* faced external constraints in developing its own services. Despite the restoration of local democracy, central government continued to exert strong control over local affairs, through the powers exercised by the *Prefetto* [Prefect],[2] limiting spending on early childhood services by classifying them as 'optional', and strongly urging that these services be mainly Church run. By 1962, the seven remaining *asili* run in Reggio Emilia by the UDI were far outnumbered by the twenty-two Catholic *scuole materne*.[3] Local initiatives were also constrained by the *Opera Nazionale Maternità e Infanzia* or ONMI [Organisation for Maternity and Childhood], a national organisation inherited from the fascist regime that continued to be the main agency of the State for the health and welfare of young children and mothers, and which opposed the provision of municipal nurseries.

But as Italy's 'economic miracle' gathered momentum and under sustained pressure from the UDI and other organisations demanding the establishment of municipal schools for young children, the *Comune* began to seek ways to establish these services – despite the obstacles placed in its way by the government in Rome. The breakthrough came in 1962. The council that year debated women's employment and the provision of public services. Christian Democrats argued for a strategy of part-time employment for mothers, while the UDI and left-wing politicians called for early childhood services. Under the newly elected Mayor Renzo Bonazzi, who was an ardent supporter of Reggio Emilia's educational project during the fifteen years he held office, the *Comune* decided on the latter course and the first municipal school for 3- to 6-year-olds was agreed: Robinson Crusoe opened on 5 November 1963, housed in a prefabricated building to get around the obstructive regulations of the Prefect.

Reggio Emilia's project of early childhood education had begun. It was an important moment: the local community assuming responsibility for the education of its young children, and also challenging the dominant position of the Catholic Church in this field. In a much later interview, Malaguzzi emphasised that the establishment of Robinson Crusoe school marked 'a rightful and necessary break in the monopoly the Catholic Church had hitherto exercised over children's early education . . . [citizens and families] wanted schools of a new kind: of better quality, free from charitable tendencies, not merely custodial, and not discriminatory in any way' (Malaguzzi, 2012, pp.31–2).

Malaguzzi's life

It was during these years – by turn repressive and liberating, terrifying and exciting, destructive and renewing – that Loris Malaguzzi lived his early life. He describes these times in three documents written between the late 1970s and early 1990s [1.78, 2.ND, 3.91]. Because of the light they throw on his life up to the 1950s, they are the first documents presented in this chapter, even though belonging chronologically to later chapters.

Malaguzzi was born on 23 February 1920 in Correggio, a small town in the Po valley, close to the cities of Reggio Emilia and Modena, and that is today in the Province of Reggio Emilia and the region of Emilia-Romagna. He moved with his family to the city of Reggio Emilia in 1923, growing up under Mussolini's fascist dictatorship. Malaguzzi trained to be a *maestro* [elementary school teacher] at the *Istituto Magistrale* 'Matilde di Canossa' in Reggio Emilia, qualifying and starting work at the age of 18 in 1938, then in 1939 began a three-year course in pedagogy at the University of Urbino in the region of Marche.

Between 1938 and 1950, with the exception of a period towards the end of the war, he worked as a school teacher, including a stint in the elementary school of Sologno, a small village in the Apennine Mountains, which for part of the time he combined with his studies in Urbino. There were later periods teaching in two middle schools in the province of Reggio Emilia. His teaching was interrupted in 1942, when he was drafted by the Republic of Salò[4] to work in a barracks in Bologna, before fleeing to end the war working on the railways. During this time, he experienced the bombing of Reggio Emilia and was in the midst of many other forms of violence that marked the closing stages of the war in this part of Italy.

In 1950, he left teaching in the state sector. He says of this that, though:

> the work with the children had been rewarding . . . the state-run school continued to pursue its own course, sticking to its stupid and intolerable indifference toward children, its opportunistic and obsequious attitude towards authority, and its self-serving cleverness, pushing pre-packaged knowledge.
>
> (*ibid.*, p.29)

Much of his subsequent life was devoted to providing an alternative to this stultifying model of education and the school.

He did not, though, leave the field of education, but developed further his relationship with other sectors, a relationship that had already begun shortly after the war's end. In 1946, he had been one of the founders of the *Convitto della Rinascita* [Rebirth colleges], established by the *Associazione Nazionale Partigiani d'Italia* [National Association of Italian Partisans] and the Ministry of Employment to enable former partisan fighters and prisoners between 16 and 24 to learn a trade, and operated with a strong emphasis on cooperative working and self-government. There were ten of these schools, including the *Scuola Convitto della Rinascita 'Luciano Fornaciari'* in Villa di Rivaltella, close to the city of Reggio Emilia. In 1949, Malaguzzi became director of this adult education school, which was eventually closed in 1954 after what he described as a 'fierce battle' with the Ministry. This experience with the *Convitto* was formative, taking place in a post-Liberation climate in which – as he recounted to Marco Fincardi – 'everything was possible' and one was 'inside a sort of great adventure'.

In the immediate post-war period he also became involved in, and inspired by, another innovative educational project outside the state sector: the new schools for young children being set up by local communities in and around Reggio Emilia, starting with the school in Villa Cella that opened in 1947. Malaguzzi was drawn to this venture when news reached him that 'the people had gotten [sic] together to put up a school for young children' (*ibid.*, p.27). This led, he recalls, to a double-shift work life: 'I started two parallel lives, one in the morning at this centre [the Psycho-Pedagogical Medical Centre] and the other in the afternoon and evening in the small parent-run schools' (*ibid.*, p.29). Here was the beginning of his lifetime commitment to early childhood education. Towards the end of his life, Malaguzzi wrote of Villa Cella being one of three places where he 'learned to speak and to live' [2.ND], the others being the school in Sologno and the Liberation of Reggio Emilia.

Malaguzzi not only taught but studied. Apart from reading prodigiously, in 1951 he participated in a course in clinical and educational psychology organised in Rome by the *Consiglio Nazionale delle Ricerche* [National Research Council]. This was the first education in psychology in Italy after the end of a fascist regime that had cut the country off from the discipline, and indeed all social sciences, including publications and other developments from elsewhere in the world. The course had a profound effect on Malaguzzi. Psychology and the need for a closer relationship between psychology and pedagogy came to play a large part in his thinking, and the qualifications he gained from the course led him to a new stage of his career: one of the founders and the psychologist of the *Centro Medico Psico-Pedagogico Comunale* or CMPP [Municipal Psycho-Pedagogical Medical Centre], established by the *Comune* of Reggio Emilia for school children with difficulties at school, one of the first mental health centres of its kind in Italy. The Centre began its work in 1951, and Malaguzzi played a leading role until 1970, some years after he had also assumed responsibility for Reggio Emilia's first municipal schools for young children.

Malaguzzi found time for other work with children. From its founding in 1948 until 1952, he was an active member of the Italian Commission of FICE (*Fédération internationale des communautés d'enfants*), an international organisation established under the auspices of UNESCO to promote the rights of the child and international exchange, with a particular focus on disadvantaged children. In this capacity, he travelled 'around institutions in our country and Europe for children who were orphaned, lost, or victims of war' [2.ND]; the archive contains a programme for a six day FICE conference on the theme of education, held in Lyon in September 1950, and which Malaguzzi attended (see Figure 1.3). (Ernesto Codignola, President of the Italian Federation of FICE invited all eighteen Italian *comuni* who were members of FICE to this conference; only Malaguzzi and two others, plus Codignola himself, attended.) From the contribution he made to a conference of the *Associazione Pionieri d'Italia* [Pioneers Association of Italy] in 1956, he was clearly involved with this left-wing youth movement [12.56], while between 1953 and 1956, he directed plays at a theatre festival for children held in Reggio Emilia, giving expression to his passion for the stage.

Later in the period covered by this section, Malaguzzi turned his attentions to yet another children's service: the municipal *colonie*, which he renamed *case di vacanza* as part of his renewal project. He led some of these camps, both for Reggio Emilia and the nearby town of Correggio, as well as collaborating with and visiting camps run by the cooperative movement. He drew up new guidelines for the Reggio Emilia *colonie*, in which he called for a basic re-orientation in the way these services were conceptualised, turning away from seeing them as charitable institutions focused on health and towards envisaging them as rights for children focused on education in its broadest sense [23.64]. He also extended their offer, traditionally limited to 6 to 12-year-olds, to 3- to 6-year-olds. These summer camps became important sites for peda-gogical experimentation and, like the *Centro Medico Psico-Pedagogico Comunale*, were precursors for his later pedagogical work in the municipal schools of Reggio Emilia.

By 1963, when this chapter ends, Malaguzzi's career was already rich and varied, with experience of working in early childhood, primary and adult education, as well as in psychological services for school children and summer camps. But this was only one part of a rich and varied life. He was a man of many interests, with a deep hinterland. He was an intellectual, mixing with other intellectuals, not least through his membership of the left-leaning *Circolo Zibordi* from 1946, part of a group actively engaged in Reggio Emilia's cultural and political life (including Renzo Bonazzi, who would become the Mayor of Reggio Emilia during the years of growth for the city's municipal schools). In a post-war Italy freed from years of censorship, Malaguzzi was a voracious reader, an appetite that he retained throughout his life; he was also a sportsman, a poet, an avid follower of theatre and other arts, and a journalist.

From 1947 to 1951 he was editor of the Reggio Emilia pages of the daily Bologna newspaper *Il Progresso d'Italia* [The Progress of Italy], a left-wing publication founded in 1946, while also writing extensively on theatre, cul-ture, education and politics. He wrote, too, for *L'Unità*, founded by Antonio Gramsci in 1924 as the official newspaper of the Italian Communist Party and banned by the fascist regime. His journalism went back even earlier. The first published piece of his in the Reggio Emilia archive is a theatre review dated 28 June 1942 written for *Il solco fascista*, the official newspaper of the *Partito Nazionale Fascista* [National Fascist Party] of Reggio Emilia, at a time when opposition newspapers were banned. Fifteen years later, in happier times, we still find him writing about the theatre, with a piece in *Ridotto* titled '11 eve-nings in a row', reviewing eleven plays performed over a five week period by amateur dramatic groups in different cities including Milan, Parma, Rome, Bari and Venice.

He did more than write about theatre. In 1960 he is directing an evening of Bertold Brecht organised by the *Teatro Club*, which he had helped found two years earlier [18.60]. While the next year, he is to be found introducing a varied, international programme for the eleventh Maria Melato Festival, with a tangible pride in 'our Reggio' and its record – 'a rare phenomenon' – not only for theatre productions but also for opening up theatre to a new, wider audience [20.61].

Malaguzzi was also active in politics during these years. He joined the PCI in 1945, and was a long-term supporter of the cooperative movement, which has deep roots and an extensive presence in Emilia-Romagna. As Paul Ginsborg observes, '[n]o region had a stronger tradition of cooperation than Emilia-Romagna . . . [and] after the war, cooperation flourished as never before (1990, p.202).

Last but not least, he was a family man, marrying Nilde Bonacini in 1944, with whom he had one son, Antonio, born in 1946.

The selection of documents (Reggio Emilia Working Group)

> I have never believed, nor do I believe now, that a story belongs to only one person. Stories are always plural and their origins are infinite.
> (Loris Malaguzzi, 1991, 'In the post-war city' [3.91])

A selection of texts, part of a collection of documents which are all interesting, cannot escape reference to the present, at least we have not been capable of avoiding it (or unconsciously we did not want to). The texts we have chosen tend to acknowledge the genesis of the many ideas Malaguzzi would evolve in subsequent years; to find his creative and critical personality in the projects he tackled and always renewed; and to underline the infinite distortions and critical issues that education and public schooling unfortunately continue to have to deal with, like an eternal, never-resolved motif. The chronological ordering of our selected readings has allowed us – and we think will allow the reader – to enter into and participate in this period of history and its evolution, enabling a better positioning and understanding of the statements, interests and concerns found in these writings.

The first autobiographical contributions in this chapter are exceptions to this chronological criterion, being written later in Malaguzzi's life, but have been chosen and placed here to offer the reader some basic facts for framing the historical and cultural context of subsequent texts in this first chapter. The homage to Gigetto Reverberi is of particular interest [3.91] and allows an understanding of Reggio Emilia's cultural 'humus' in the immediate post-war years. Reading the text, we are offered rich descriptions of the dynamics of encounters with others that accompanied the new cultural ferment in a country emerging from the darkness, and from the civil, moral and intellectual obscurantism of fascist dictatorship. Here the reader will find traces, the start of red threads that will lead to conceptual and organisational choices made in later years, when Loris Malaguzzi was asked to give a pedagogical form to the city's political project, first with municipal *scuole dell'infanzia* and then with the municipal *nidi*.

Gathering together in the city's public spaces (squares, streets, cafés, under colonnades), and the value given to amateur theatre – defined as a 'laboratory of games, ideas and inventions, of precursory facts which produced culture very simply and without school diplomas or academic qualifications' – are elements of a journey that would also leave a deep mark on his pedagogy. We find, too, a concept of democracy and the right to culture of and for all, which would also shape Malaguzzi's pedagogical thinking about the early years. In fact we can connect these ideas and experiences with the school conceived of as a place of participation, debate and research for children, teachers and parents, all able to dialogue, and in a position of equality with academic research.

There is a pleasant surprise in the discovery that from a young age Loris Malaguzzi, who certainly always liked to write, also loved to try his hand at poetry: some of his first compositions, from 1946 [5.46, 6.46] show vitality and optimism. His love of poetry is apparent again in his commentary on Edgar Lee Masters' Spoon River Anthology [7.50], now widely available after the cultural autarchy fascism had forced on the country. But although he is aware of and admires how the words of this American poet are capable of bringing human detail to a universal level, he reflects critically on how much Masters' thinking looks back to the past rather than towards the future. For his entire life, this looking to the future would be characteristic of Malaguzzi.

From his reading of Edgar Lee Masters' work there also emerges another fundamental topic, which would mark his thinking and actions: the social dimension in problems and their solutions; Malaguzzi states that 'tools exist for conducting a shared and common struggle against pain, poverty and death'.

Writing earlier on culture in *La Verità*, the newspaper of the Reggio Communist Federation [4.45], we find the germ of an idea that was to become another red thread: '[t]rue, we cannot create an artist at will, but it is equally true that the conditions for an artist to be born and to develop can be created from now on'. The conditions needed for educating human beings is already, therefore, a recurring subject in this period of very varied writing. For example, we find it when he emphasises the role of environment in the recovery of young maladjusted residents in the *Colonia* Marro [11.54], or in his later piece on 'The Pupil, the Class and the Teacher' [21.63]. We can also add the letter written to parents of children staying at a summer camp [22.63], where he had undertaken radical innovation of the educational project, and in which he underlines the need for their collaboration to construct a proposal for the wellbeing of their children – a strategy for translating into action a unified idea of the child and of her or his experience.

In order to support the need for creating conditions that would enable ideals to give shape to reality, Loris Malaguzzi often participated in political debates. Testifying to this is his intervention in 1959 at the Federal Committee of the regional Communist Party, the first time Malaguzzi took part [17.59]. His words are respectful, but also critical of various aspects of the main speech. He forcefully declares that every political act is a cultural act, so criticising the preceding political analysis for omitting the cultural problems of the times, giving instead too much importance to administrative problems. He invites those present to keep abreast of the times and the evolution of social and cultural battles, to busy themselves with the problems of schooling, the presence of 'Teddy Boys' and new scientific discoveries. He reports the risk for the organised co-operative movements of keeping the technical and the political distinct. And he points to democracy, founded on precise and concrete information, as a strategy for defence against an excessive business logic. He could already see all the dangers, and in fact the course of Italian politics has unfortunately very often strayed far from its initial projects, projects of ideals and projects of ethics.

Democracy is an explanatory concept we find, and will continue to find, on several occasions in Loris Malaguzzi's writings. We find traces of it in the idea of building a 'new public' for the theatre, which in those days in Italy was frequented by the few, an elite. He supports this ideal with a policy of low prices and public transport (conditions again), which enabled Reggio Emilia to achieve results in contrast to other small and medium Italian cities [20.61].

In the city's main theatre, which had come under public management by the *Comune* in 1957, we can also find a solidarity between technical and administrative areas that will be key for constructing the experience of the *scuole dell'infanzia*: Malaguzzi would say in 1963 that 'cultural development is not merely an intellectual fact but *a complex activity with a social and emotional structure*', like education [21.63].

His concept of democracy is also expressed in his commitment to amateur theatre, and later his commitment to dialogue with parents and his optimistic idea of human beings, whom he declares are not pre-determined by their hereditary character or personality [12.57]. This democracy is based on an idea of leaving behind stereotypes and prior judgements or *prejudices* to make space for a commitment to personal knowledge of each being, and to the possibility of being the protagonist of one's own destiny. An interesting definition of education is very closely related to this idea: 'educating means perfecting our knowledge, our conduct, and our feelings' [12.57]. Here it can be assumed that the 'we' he refers to, read in context, are adults in their relations with children: children removed from anonymity, to be known through dialogue, in their contexts and settings, by adults perfecting themselves through these relations. In the 1959 meeting of the Federal Committee of the regional PCI, Malaguzzi proposed another definition of democracy that would be relevant in his work: 'to be able to speak and discuss with awareness, based on precise, concrete information' [17.59].

The *Centro Medico Psico-Pedagogico* opened in Reggio Emilia in 1951 and Malaguzzi was one of the founders. In 1963 he worked on the re-organisation of seaside and mountain *Colonie*. His ongoing work experience in these services influenced his educational thinking, and led him to condemn the backward thinking on which these children's institutions had been based until this time.

His highly productive interweaving of theory and concrete action, begun in these services, was to be a feature of the whole of his life; as was his curiosity and insatiable hunger for the latest studies and theories, and his capacity for immediately merging them into the reality of everyday work, at the level either of analysis or of working hypotheses. For example the modern concept of health inspiring the work of the *Centro Medico Psico-Pedagogico* included the whole individual, and was not narrowly interpreted as an absence of illness. Malaguzzi assigned to education not only the task of teaching but 'its true role of preventative medicine for the individual and society' [8.51].

Adopting the same radical approach, he freed the *Colonia*'s very identity of concepts which, until this time, had anchored and distinguished it: of charity, of patronage, of being a place primarily of medical care in which pedagogy was marginal and insufficient. The new society called for a renewal of intent, both of ideas and education. The *Colonia* had to be a place that attended to a complete state of psycho-physical wellbeing and balance for the child, for the 'flowering' of a good individual and social personality, and where the under-lying pedagogy was a pedagogy of group. This pedagogy and this education had to be relevant to the characteristics of the children of the time, living in a society whose particulars are equally well depicted by Malaguzzi. There are frequent reminders of the extensive organization needed to implement such a project.

We find the concept of health discussed again in an essay of 1953 [9.53]. Here Malaguzzi, in line with the culture of the time, discusses children's draw-ings as tools for psychological knowledge, for psycho-diagnosis and therapy; but with still experimental parallels developed between verbal language and the language of drawing, which identifies similar deep structures and which would open up a new pathway of research, very probably contributing to the eventual *invention* of what would be the *atelier* in the *scuola dell'infanzia*. One possible proof of this can be found in the fact that certain tests referred to here would be used much later in the schools with groups of children: though with an attitude of *lightness* and in an educational – not diagnostic – context, and with a curiosity for trying to understand to what extent the everyday presence of the *atelier* in the schools might have modified some of the results of a draw-ing test, like for example the drawing of 'a lady walking with an umbrella in the rain' (H. M. Fay, 1924).

At one point Loris Malaguzzi makes a claim that may seem risqué for our current cultural times and which perhaps requires an interpretation: 'the *health-ier* the child is the better he will draw'. His attitude, which to our minds is recognisable in all of his pedagogical thinking, and which ran counter to the dominant and very widespread culture, was to choose the idea of the healthy child in opposition to the idea of the child who was always conveyed as weak and needy. 'All children are intelligent, all of them' he often declared.

One further red thread offered in these writings is the resolution of prejudiced and ideological opposites, in a vision of 're-composition' and a framework of complementarity. This would later gain further reinforcement and support from systems theory and complexity theory. Opposition between concepts such as liberty and authority (1957), normality and abnormality (1958), technical and political (1959), a pedagogy of interest and a pedagogy of effort (1963) – these are all overcome in the name of a commitment to re-composition, which accompanied Loris Malaguzzi during his entire life's work.

We are struck by the great importance he gave at this time to the job of parenting [13.57, 14.58, 16.58]: but in contrast to what happens nowadays, the culture of parenting was seen to be a real common good and necessary for a better, democratic society of greater solidarity. An importance that to us seems to be connected, as we have already said, with the idea of democratic culture, not the exclusive domain of experts, and with a recognition of the role of conditions and environment in educational processes. The language he uses with families is interesting: clear and understandable, without losing the competency of an expert, always very lucid, without creating drama but also without mystifying and consoling, even when dealing with problems that often beset parents, such as bedwetting, nervous tics, or more simply thumb-sucking and nail-biting.

The lack of a true educational function in contemporary schools is underlined, and an excessively abstract, self-centred, idealistic and patronising education with a vision of the child passively 'absorbing' is condemned. The metaphor of the child coming into the world armed like the goddess Minerva and beginning her battle is clear. A child, though, who needs adult friends who will stay by her side and dialogue with her.

In his 1958 leaflet on 'Experiences of a School for Parents' [16.58], Malaguzzi proposes participants reflect on concrete cases in order to enable their commitment to personal research and comprehension; this too, we believe, was one of his distinguishing traits, which in a similar way would run through the work of forming teachers in later years. The parents at this 'school' had eighteen lessons, one every fortnight. At the end of this was a very interesting internal inquiry by the co-ordinating group, reporting on statistics about attendance, age, sex and social status of participants and in which, despite the success of the lessons, there is a lucid analysis, a critical and self-critical reflection on the entire operation. For example, the initial error of an overly tête-à-tête relation with families is admitted, and the extent to which increased public debate instead exploded into more enriching, lively discussion. The report recounts the development of this debate, allowing readers (parents, teachers, politicians) to learn not only from the experts, but also from the experience of parents, within that idea of democracy we have discussed earlier.

Timeline up to 1963

Key: *Malaguzzi*
Reggio Emilia
Italy

1860	***Asilo d'infanzia* Manodori opened for children under 6 years; Reggio Emilia votes overwhelmingly to join new Italian state.**
1861	Italian unification (except for Rome and Venetia); first Italian Parliament and Victor Emmanuel II proclaimed King of Italy.
1895	Municipalities permitted to open schools for infants.
1899	**Socialist municipal government.**
1913	**First municipal *Asilo* in village of Villa Gaida: free, secular education for 3–6 year olds.**
1919	Beginning of fascist movement.
1920	*Born in Correggio, 23 February.*
1923	*Moves to Reggio Emilia.*
	Fascist dictatorship begins.
1925	ONMI founded to provide services for young children and mothers.
1926	Municipalities disbanded and responsibilities passed to regime official.
1938	*Completes Magistrali school in Reggio Emilia and qualifies as an elementary school teacher.*
	Fascist government closes *Asilo* in Gaida.
	Racial Laws mainly directed at Jews and natives in colonies.
1938–46	*Teaches in primary and secondary schools in Reggiolo, Sologno, Reggio Emilia and Guastalla, except when called up.*
1940	Italy enters World War II on side of Germany.
	Begins course in pedagogy at University of Urbino.
1942	*Called up by regime in August, for war work.*
1943	**Resistance and fighting.**
	Italy surrenders to Allies; Germany occupies areas not liberated; period of resistance and civil war in occupied areas; 'Committee for National Liberation' created to unite antifascist parties and coordinate Resistance; works in close collaboration with 'Women's groups for defence and assistance to freedom fighters', founded in November in Milan, spreading throughout Italy to mobilise women.
1944	*Marries Nilde Bonacini.*
	Bombed by allies: 265 die.
	Italian Women's Union (UDI) founded, an anti-fascist organisation with roots in resistance, working for social justice and emancipation.

1945	*Joins the* Partito Comunista Italiano.
	Liberated (24 April); Socialist and Communist municipal government; opening of eight self-managed *asili* **for 3- to 6-year-olds between 1945 and 1947, including** *Asilo Villa Cella.*
	Italy liberated (25 April); end of World War II; Italian Women's Centre (CIF) founded, connected to Catholic Action and promoting societal participation of women.
1946	*Graduates from university; son, Antonio, born; joins* Circolo Zibordi; *leaves teaching in state schools; one of the founders of and teachers at the Convitto Scuola Rinascita in Reggio Emilia.*
	Italian Republic established and new Constitution approved.
1947	*Editor of the Reggio Emilia pages of the daily Bologna newspaper* The Progress of Italy.
1948	*Member of* Fédération internationale des communautés d'enfants.
1950	President awards Gold Medal to Reggio Emilia for its contribution to the struggle for liberation.
1951	*Ends newspaper editorship; attends course in clinical and educational psychology at* Consiglio Nazionale delle Ricerche; *one of the founders of the municipal* Centro Medico Psico-Pedagogico Comunale *in Reggio Emilia where he worked as a psychologist for twenty years.*
	Movement of Cooperative Education established.
1952	**Convitto Scuola Rinascita closes.**
1953	*Works with* Teatro per Ragazzi *(a children's theatre) until 1956.*
Early 50s	**Women's organisations organise services for working women and children, including temporary** *asili* **[schools] for agricultural workers, after-school centres and summer camps.**
	New wave of migration, internally and to other European Countries.
1958	*Founding member of the* Teatro Club.
Late 50s	Start of period of rapid economic, social and cultural change.
Early 60s	**Increasing demands for municipal schools for young children.**
1960	**Demonstrations against government supported by neo-fascist party, five shot dead by police and many injured.**
1962	**Reggio Emilia has thirty-three schools for 3- to 6-year-olds: twenty-two Catholic, seven UDI, four charitable; Renzo Bonazzi elected mayor and governs with communist-socialist Cabinet; Municipality agrees to build 5 schools.**
1963	*Consultant to Reggio Emilia's new municipal schools for 3- to 6-year-olds.*
	Municipality opens its first school for 3-6 year olds, Robinson Crusoe.

Three retrospective biographical documents

1.78 Short *curriculum vitae*, 1978

Editor's note: It is usual for *curriculum vitae* in Italy to be written in the third person.

Loris Malaguzzi autobiographical curriculum vitae

Loris Malaguzzi was born in Reggio Emilia in 1920. He worked as a primary school teacher, took his degree in pedagogy and worked as a professor in the middle school. In 1946 he was one of the creators and promoters of *Convitti Scuola Rinascita* [Rebirth colleges] founded with ANPI [*Associazione Nazionale Partigiani d'Italia*; National Association of Italian Partisans] and the Ministry for Employment to help partisans, war veterans and orphans study and obtain a profession; the *Convitti* continued to function until 1952 with exhilarating and pioneering experiences in democratic education. From 1948 to 1952, Malaguzzi was an active member for Italy of UNESCO's *Fédération internationale des communautés d'enfants*, or FICE, together with Ernesto Codignola, Margherita Zoebeli, Don Rivolta and Bice Libretti Baldeschi. In 1951 he attended the first course in clinical and educational psychology organised in Italy, at the *Consiglio Nazionale delle Ricerche* [CNR, National Research Council] taught by Banissoni. He preferred active practice to repeated offers by Banissoni who wished him to continue at CNR, and returned to Reggio Emilia to set up one of the first Italian *Centro Medico Psico-Pedagogico* [Psycho-Pedagogical Medical Centre]. In 1965 with Mazzetti and above all later with Bruno Ciari in Emilia-Romagna he was one of the theorisers and initiators of *scuole dell'infanzia* that were public and directly managed by *comuni*. He saw the importance of processes of renewal in children's education as well as forms of social management, participation and responsibility. Since that time his work has increasingly been absorbed in this field of experience, which allows him to bring together pedagogical research and educational practice, exactly in accordance with his most natural inclinations.

Anticipating themes which are still of enormous significance today, he promoted a national symposium on the relations between pedagogy and psychiatry in 1964. In 1966 with Borghi, La Porta, Volpicelli, Mazzetti, Jovine, Visalberghi and Ada Gobetti he organised and contributed to an Italian–Czechoslovakian Pedagogy Conference in Reggio Emilia, the first ever cultural and political exchange of pedagogical concepts with the area of Socialism. In 1970 he organised a four-day Study Conference in Reggio Emilia on issues of early years education, which drew a thousand Italian teachers as protagonists. This debate re-defined the nature and directions of a large movement for emancipation and renewal in schools for young children.

Since 1970 he has continued with more organic and original work in the *scuole comunali dell'infanzia* of Reggio Emilia and Modena simultaneously.

Today this work constitutes one of the most advanced points of research into methodology and educational practice in the sector, and is a concrete point of reference for those dedicated to the field. The importance of this experience is communicated in books, several publications in leading Italian and overseas journals, television documentaries and interviews, and conferences, lectures and debates in which Professor Malaguzzi is an untiring protagonist with teachers, parents, experts, politicians, early years academics, university centres, and specialist psychology centres in Italy.

✳ ✳ ✳

2.ND Article published in *Ricerche Storiche*, no.84, May 1998

Editor's note: This autobiographical fragment was discovered by Laura Artioli and Carlina Rinaldi in 1997, as part of a search of the private papers of Loris Malaguzzi in the home of his son, Antonio. The search was undertaken at the request of the *Comune* of Reggio Emilia, Reggio Children and the Association of Friends of Reggio Children by *Istoreco*, a society for the history of the Resistance and contemporary society in the province of Reggio Emilia. This organisation publishes a regular journal, *Ricerche Storiche*, and undertakes a range of other cultural activities, including organising visits by secondary school students and teachers to Nazi death and concentration camps and to sites of the Italian Resistance in the local mountains, and contributing to the European Resistance Archive, an on-line archive of interviews with witnesses and protagonists of the European anti-fascist Resistance.[5]

The article below, edited by Laura Artioli, was subsequently published in *Ricerche Storiche* in 1998. She believes that the original text was probably composed between 1989 and 1991, stimulated by exchanges between Malaguzzi and Lella Gandini during the preparation of the book *The Hundred Languages of Children: The Reggio Emilia Approach to Early Childhood Education*, subsequently published in the United States in 1993 (Edwards et al., 2012). In the end nothing of this autobiographical work appeared in the book, although in an interview included in the book Malaguzzi does refer to the importance of the war in making his choice to devote his life to education, 'as a way to start anew and live and work for the future' (Malaguzzi, 2012, p.35). Consequently, as Laura Artioli puts it in her introduction to the Italian article, the pages that follow 'are the only ones in which Malaguzzi wrote about himself, his childhood, his years at *Magistrali* school and university, his first steps as a teacher, of marriage, of the war, of the things that counted . . . [and] for now constitute the only draft of an autobiographical background history'.

That I should take the path of teaching

1.

That I should take the path of teaching and become a primary school '*maestro*' [teacher] was all written in my father's mind. The same went for my brother.

The choice did not follow from any real or presumed vocation, it simply pointed to the quickest career for earning a wage and with that perhaps to keep myself at university.[6] It was a choice with little philosophy in it but one that owed much to my father's modest salary – he was a station master with the Reggiane Railways – and my mother's infinite thrift.

And anyway, like all those of my age I was a passenger willing to embark on any ship.

The first thing I learned at the *Magistrali* [a secondary school for training primary teachers, attended by students aged 14–18 years], from malicious rumours put about by older children in their last year, was that our strict and very famous headmistress wore black knickers to honour the *Duce* [Mussolini] and Fascism. They swore it was true and that was that.

I cannot remember anything I learned. Even when I began my career and urgently needed to.

They were beautiful years, super light, when you could stay afloat with just a few strokes, some wits, a few things learned by heart, some help from more able friends, and a little *savoir faire*. Instead I perfectly remember the faces and figures of companions. And of the teachers: compassionate ones, hard ones, friendly ones.

Among the latter were Don Spadoni and Don Pignedoli (who went on to become a cardinal), the first with his fearless words, and the second elegant and infinitely kind. And with them was Lina Cecchini, with her Aristotle, Kant and Pestalozzi; the sweetest, most motherly of all possible teachers. I kept up relations with all three for a long time.

What is certain is that, despite Gentilian[7] idealism, Catholic spiritualism and the covert black of Fascism, my *Magistrali* studies inspired and reinforced nothing. They [the students] had no vocation either. This was confirmed when, having obtained their diplomas, my friends began working as office clerks, bank clerks and shopkeepers, and only myself and very few others became teachers.

The first wage was there to commend my father's foresight. I was earmarked for the primary school in Reggiolo.[8] My father took me there and he did everything. He introduced me to the senior teacher and the caretaker, and he found me food and lodgings at the *Cavallino Bianco* [White Horse]. Shades of Hollywood!

Meeting the class one children removed every anxiety. We played for days and days aimlessly, freewheeling, and our words saved a beginning that never came. Neither they nor I knew anything. I realised this was the irresponsible seduction that opened the doors of the profession for me. We invented all sorts, and the children were very good at managing to get some reading, writing and counting to come of it.

When we said our goodbyes at the end of the year the drums of war were already beating and I was taking my first university exams [at the University of Urbino]. From that time on school, university and war ran parallel to each other. For me aged 19 years, the three were not yet realities. They were three situations that, with my lack of maturity and consciousness, did not seem dramatic, the way my family was recounting them, or impossible to get through or to combine.

In this naïve state of mind I went off to serve as teacher in Sologno di Villaminozzo[9] at the foot of [Mount] Cusna. It was a small hamlet I didn't know existed. I did know that to reach it I had to walk for kilometres on foot. I will not go into my initial dismay. I will just say it was an extraordinary experience.

2.

Up there, at an altitude of 800 metres, for the next two years I learned a thousand things: the art of walking on foot, of finding my way among trees and rocks, of understanding the false paths and real ones, of wading rivers, discovering the generosity of chestnuts, the friendliness of silences, people's incredible ability for managing, about laces for catching hares, and the infinite depths of poverty in this border land from which the inhabitants continued to flee.

To be attached by a deep friendship with fifteen boys in wooden clogs, clad in enormous handed-down jackets, their thick accent with the French '*u*', curious and quick with self-assured eyes, in thrall to school and sheep, homework and cowshed, charcoal burning and fields.

Getting the school to function in a recently abandoned cowshed, lighting and relighting the stove with green wood each morning, battling with the boys' lateness each day, often helping them to dry still-wet stockings, and supplying them with exercise book after exercise book from the *patronato scolastico*.[10]

To feel loving gratitude for Fortunato's mule, which travelled to Castelnuovomonti[11] each day to supply rice, wine and salami to 146 inhabitants, 147 with me.

To wait longingly for the anomalies of Sunday's gaiety, gentle at first, then noisy and rowdy, which mixed Mass and tavern and finished in the middle of the night with children and women coming to fetch brothers, fathers and husbands.

To stay up for long talks in stone houses with women and men, full of melancholy for children transplanted to Genoa and Milan, and they sitting here watching over their roots.

To grow in harmony with Don Carmine who was also young, brand new like me, in his first job [as parish priest] and resigned to not having a career: without baptisms and marriages, only Mass and extreme unction, frightened of the tavern (where I lived) and ready to use me for children's celebrations, which always got out of hand.

And last of all to play cards, an obligation for *Signor Maestro*, at trump and *busche* [traditional Italian card game]: where the most unfathomable, terrible and comic thing was to see how a novice like myself and the astute wisdom of old mountain folk succeeded in finding secret signals.

Time stretched out a long way and allowed me to read as much as I wished. I devoured Dostoevsky and Tolstoy, Conrad and Rilke, Maupassant, Montaigne, Moravia, Pirandello's theatre and several teaching manuals too. I was not interested in great lessons and great theories. I understood nothing of the aesthetics of Croce and Rousseau, up there they were only ridiculous.

I had to work with practice with my brain divided into five parts in a mixed class, taking children from class one (impossible to call them *bambini*, they were too mature and worldly wise), two, three, four and five. It was a range that tortured a [teacher] just starting out on his profession. And made nonsense of years of *Magistrali* school.

I read newspapers if Fortunato found time to buy them. The war was far off, I dismissed it, I was a long way from the city. I managed to take six university exams. A meaningless ritual with acceptably uneven marks expressed in sixtieths.

I went down to Reggio Emilia twice a month. A quick visit to my family, to my girlfriend, to the library to choose more books.

Over the two years there were two inspections by *Direttore Didattico* Scalabrini who was [based] in [the town of] Carpineti: a glass in the tavern, kind words, all was well.

War existed. I made a hasty visit to Reggio Emilia. A city without words. There were no people. Only persons moving silently. They were searching for provisions. Empty houses. At lunch my father confessed finding food was already difficult. Meat and butter were luxuries. The bread was black [substandard], the shops had very little. When I returned to Sologno I dipped into my savings and bought four lambs, the best ones. I wanted it to be a surprise. It was god-sent meat. The four lambs died on me almost together after licking the red lime holding together the bricks in the houses. It wasn't fair. It would be the only speculation of my life. I didn't confess anything to my family.

My two years in Sologno matured me greatly and shook off the last of my adolescent spots.

Farewells took place in the tavern, a place of sin Don Carmine used to say. But he came too. I received gifts of eight pats of butter, a bottle of herb liqueur, a homemade salami, a small sack of chestnuts. On my part I offered a sweet chestnut cake and a gigantic flask of Tuscan wine. The accordion came too. The children sipped (so to speak) on their fathers' Tuscan wine too.

3.

Adding it up, three years had already gone by as a teacher. If I have recounted them at length, quite intentionally, it is because these were decisive years for me.

I also felt I had grown as a teacher. Certainly I could say I was more thoroughly familiar with a teacher's ways, with the playing up and the surprises of children's ways of reasoning and applying themselves, the fluctuation in the times they spend with things, rather than with representations of things, and of accepting or evading challenges, adopting infinite avoiding tactics; and [I could also say] that I handled better the subjects and activities I was responsible for according to the dictates of the curriculum.

However even the suspicion that children' minds and intelligence had something to do with the difficult processes of learning was still far from my mind. What they learned or did not learn was largely [down to] my strengths or weaknesses, and the children's effort or lack of it.

I had had more than one confirmation that I was good at being with children and that I liked the job. I had learned that even though it was impossible to have the patience of Job it was useless and stupid to lose one's self control. And I had learned it was a good idea to establish a pact of tolerance, of joke and play, of recourse to humour and detachment from my professional role, if I wanted everything to be lighter and more useful: the only way in the end to distance the work of school from a moralising formal superiority, and keep the conversation going with these children, who were distinguished more by cruel ungenerous histories than by their conduct and progress.

The war existed, our bones and consciousness were full of it now. The men were all away at the front. I was called for a military medical. I was let off due to a large peritonitis scar. Teachers were in extremely short supply, they were at the front too. The *Provveditorato* [administrator] offered to assign me to class one in the Via Guasco primary school [in Reggio Emilia], the same school I had attended as a pupil. I remember feeling proud at the invitation. Certainly I was pleased because it slightly alleviated the deep discomfort the military medical had caused me. I knew of friends from *Magistrali* school who were in Albania, Greece and Libya.[12] The school year was coming to an end when the red card arrived forcing me to go to the Via Urbana barracks in Bologna.[13] A barracks of grandfathers. I worked in the warehouse, as quartermaster, [and] as bursar in a school occupied by homeless people after Bologna's first bombing.

The night of 8 January [1944] found me in our house in Via Turri [in Reggio Emilia]. I was with my brother. Fortunately my parents were not in Reggio Emilia. We heard the sound of the siren moments before the American bombers arrived. We escaped towards Via Emilia in the midst of flares and explosions. We made it. We went back to Via Turri at dawn, the house was an indistinct heap of ruins. All we had were the clothes we stood in. We found lodgings in San Pellegrino in a house our relatives had evacuated.

I never went to the front. That is the way the dice rolled. Italy and Fascism were already defeated when I ran away from the barracks.

Life as a fugitive was difficult what with bombings, my terror of the Germans, the blackout, the fleeing to hideaways, sleepless nights in cellars, the ruins, the hunger, the black market and announcements of death.

A pass granted me by the *Wehrmacht* [German Army] helped me as long as I signed up for railway service. It was dangerous work but there was no alternative. I did it going from one station to the next on the Reggio Emilia–Ciano and Reggio Emilia–Veggia lines, which were turning to ruins under the bombings.

On New Year's Eve 1944 I married. I was 24 years old. We put the wedding off until after Vespers [evening prayers], in between pauses in the sirens. It was blackout. We arrived home accompanied by five very close friends. We ate almost in silence. The blackout kept us prisoners. We stayed up all night playing cards and then talking and designing controversial futures for each one of us.

Around us there was already a horrendous history. The city was there with all its destruction, its barbarity, its massacres, its heroisms, its dead, its missing, its survivors. I heard of the deaths of school companions, friends, people I knew.

Everyone was trying to add things up again, to make sense of what had happened in a world that had practised a cult of death for years.

The first months of 1945 were full of premonitions that the war was drawing to an end. It wasn't only Radio London saying so, or what had already happened in the South and Rome. Certain events assumed more and more meaning in our city. Something that until that moment had been just stories was taking on meaning, the presence and strength of partisan struggle. Nazi troops passing through in retreat were real, and the disappearance of Republican guards,[14] and the small bunches of flowers and crosses springing up where Nazi killings had taken place, the heroism of young people who were still without name.

Liberation, the end of the war, came on 25 April [1945]. Partisans entered the city simultaneously with Anglo-American soldiers.

And people were running in the streets, activating the hands, eyes, bodies and thoughts that had been shrivelled for years. Greetings were back again, and tears and hugs and strong voices.

With the spring I stayed out until late at night. I went past hell too: Via dei Servi, Villa Cucchi, the Rifle-range,[15] places of the inhuman.

An unknown era was opening up, a broad horizon where you still could not measure yourself, or measure thoughts and desires. You were in a city that was hoping, and wanted to shout it.

5.[16]

This is the point where some of my life choices were born. I would enrol in the Communist Party. I knew nothing about politics, of the October Revolution, of Marx, Lenin, Gramsci, Togliatti. But I was sure I was taking the side of the weakest, of the people who carried most hope. It was a membership that appealed to the part of me that was a man and a teacher.

Immediately, some days after this, something unexpected and incredible happened. In the chaos of those first days of freedom news arrived that in Villa Cella[17] women and men, farmers and factory workers, doing everything on their own, had decided to build a school for their children. German soldiers fleeing towards the [river] Po had left a tank, some trucks, some horses. It was loot for the people. From their sale money arrived, money to spend immediately. That was how the idea was born.

No-one in the city believed it. I went there by bicycle. Simply everything was true and the women were already there cleaning bricks collected from the war ruins.

Really a school? Certainly, and they took me to see the area and they told me all about it as if the story had already happened, half in dialect and half in Italian as soon as they found out I was a teacher. If that's true come here and teach with us.

The miracle happened. There was a collection, and more money arrived. Every Saturday and every Sunday there was an incredible throng of women, men and children putting up the walls. In eight months the roof was ready. In nine months the school, like a baby, came into the world. In 1947, after official authorisation it started to function.

A self-managed school dedicated to children, designed and created in that place in that way, certainly was not part of the schema and philosophies of the time. It was an exciting anomaly, an invention I liked immensely, and from which many facts of my life would follow.

My childhood? It was tender, idling, curious, thirsty for games and friendships. Full of gaiety in the office worker's house in Piazza Fiume, rich with children, girls and boys and generously tolerant tenants. It was a place that let you play in it from top to bottom, with the courtyard running round it, the vegetable gardens, the attics, the cellars and the front – beyond the metal railings and gate marking the boundary – the enormous piazza. An arena where all sorts happened: from funerals to acrobatics in public, evolutions in cycling, to football matches, to carriages stopping off, to endurance racing, to blind man's buff, and target games with cans.

Then came 1929, which historians remember for the violence of the economic crisis. I remember it for the collapse of the family economy and the irrevocable painful decision to leave the house in Piazza Fiume for one of the small railway workers' houses in Via del Zappello where the rents were much more affordable.

Via del Zappello was in the Santa Croce neighbourhood, across the railway, and ran behind the Officine Reggiane factory, the city's biggest factory, which during the war had 12,000 employees.

A place of workers and blue overalls, summoned imperiously by the factory with the sound of its siren. The workers set out with a small container for their food, and they returned with tired faces and blackened hands. Our house, too, functioned to the rhythms of siren and hammer blows. Clocks lost all meaning. My mother never erred.

It was another world I soon learned to appreciate. I came to know the streets, the lanes and the courtyards, all forbidden stuff [when I lived] in Piazza Fiume. More space, more freedom, more children, more knowing and discovery. The coexistence and interweaving of ages and generations was an adventurous fact: encounters were warmer, at the bowling ground, at the Reggiane workers club, at the train depot. The words of older people, a language with new adult meanings and information, were within everybody's reach. The whole of my adolescence and *Magistrali* studies were set against this theatre.

If what Wittgenstein says is true, that it is important to know places where we speak, I have had three of these places where I learned to speak and to live. [. . .] [I must] hold on to these three places: Sologno, Villa Cella, *La Liberazione* [The Liberation].

With Cella I made a sort of pact of solidarity and another pact with the other six small schools, invented and run by women and the people's movement, in poor outlying neighbourhoods of the city. I would never desert them.

Liberation was in April, in September I was already teaching Latin and Italian to children in the middle school in Guastalla.[18] I accompanied them up to their diploma. Then I made the adventurous and unheard of decision to abandon my career and state schools. It was all too narrow. Outside, after the war, there were infinite spaces and ideas calling to me. I was a journalist with *Progresso d'Italia* and then with *l'Unità*. Then in 1949 I could not say no to the partisans and prison veterans, for whom the *Scuola Convitto Rinascita* had been founded in Reggio Emilia and another eight cities.

And I did not want to say no when they made me a member of the Italian FICE Commission (*Fédération internationale des communautés d'enfants*) that took me travelling around institutions in our country and Europe for children who were orphaned, lost, or victims of war. I said yes to the extraordinary opportunity that took me to the CNR [*Consiglio Nazionale delle Ricerche*] in Rome for six months to attend a course in educational psychology, the first to revive psychology after its ostracism by Fascism.

At the end of the course Professor Banissoni, who ran the Institute [CNR], asked me to be his assistant. I preferred to return to Reggio Emilia and open a *Centro Medico Psico-Pedagogico Comunale* for the prevention, diagnosis and care of children. It was fascinating work, with no let-up until 1970. I left it to accept the invitation of mayor Renzo Bonazzi to become director of the *scuola dell'infanzia* sector, but also because the work had been made impossible by the mystical and destructive attitude of initial converts to early anti-psychiatry.

To a large extent 1970 marked the end of a long professional journey that had never really left the educational field, and my official definitive arrival at the experience of educating children in *scuole comunali dell'infanzia*. In fact I had worked as consultant to the new experience since 1963 (the year the first municipal school was founded), while simultaneously working at the CMPP, and without ever ceasing to help in any way I could with the ventures of the small self-managed schools, which were finally municipalised in 1967. I mean those that survived twenty years of enormous sacrifice.

I cannot say if this point of arrival was the right ending to a chance conspiracy of events, or a conspiracy that in some way happened with a part of me in secret complicity.

You want me to go deeper into this <u>conspiracy</u> for you and declare the genesis of my choice to stay with children and stay with them for a lifetime?

I could get away with it, as others have, by saying if you don't ask me I know, but if you ask me I no longer know. There are choices you feel when they stick to you. But there are choices that insinuate themselves with obstinate lightness, so you think they have grown with you and with events like a mixing of molecules.

It seems to me I understand that every choice is difficult to make with only one hand, and that probably it derives from several hands. From a sort of ensemble of times, facts, persons, echoes, sentiments, interpretations. The play of conspiracy is here.

That the choice had to do with the <u>places</u> of my early life, those of Santa Croce, of Sologno, of Villa Cella, I too suspect myself in part. But I would like to add the <u>places</u> of the war, of the Liberation, of the people, of the events that followed. And above all, with peace, the impetus that longs to make clear again roads dirty with madness.

If you put all these things together they give rise to an X, which is a point that has an oppressive space and that, maybe, you are waiting for. It is the point of the choice.

I don't know if war in all its tragic absurdity, connected with other conspiratorial events before and after, is an experience that can push us into the job of educating as one of the many possible new beginnings for living and working for the future. Especially when war finishes and symbols of life re-appear with a violence equal to that you knew during times of destruction.

I don't very well know. But I think that is the place to look. The place where I lived alliances with children, people, prison veterans, Resistance partisans, in the most intense manner: co-existing with a devastated world, when ideas and sentiments looking to the future seemed immensely stronger than those that stopped in the present. And when it seemed that there no longer existed things that were difficult or incapable of overcoming the barriers of the possible.

An incredibly strong experience, which was shaped by a tight weave of emotions and the more complex discovery of learning and values promising new creativity, and of which we only needed to become aware.

And much as I have often renewed my thoughts I have always remained in that niche.

I have never felt regret for that choice and for what I left or stripped from myself.

❋ ❋ ❋

3.91 Chapter in the book *Omaggio a Gigetto Reverberi a trent'anni dal debutto di Luciano Pavarotti* [Homage to Gigetto Reverberi thirty years after the debut of Luciano Pavarotti], edited by Franco Boiardi, 1991

Editor's note: The book in which this chapter appears was published to coincide with the thirtieth anniversary of the operatic debut of Luciano Pavarotti in *La Boheme*, after winning the Achille Peri Prize, an international singing competition originating and held in Reggio Emilia. By this time Pavarotti was a world famous singer, and returned to perform at the *Teatro Municipale* [Municipal Theatre]. He also contributed a short introduction to the book, which was published by *Associazione I Teatri di Reggio Emilia* to honour the life and work of Gigetto Reverberi, a citizen active in the local cultural scene and who played a leading role in founding the Peri Prize.

Malaguzzi's chapter starts with a quotation from a memoir by the famous Reggio Emilia-born actor Romolo Valli.

In the post-war city

1. 'One evening in the winter of 1946, in Reggio Emilia, a few friends and I were leaving the Teatrino San Rocco in the foggy cold of Via Monzermone. A few minutes earlier we had concluded a "staged reading" of Thornton Wilder's *Piccola Città* ["Our Town"] and once again we had seen how poetic writing, even offered in the humblest and least adorned setting, can inspire pure and absolute emotion in the public. We found good reason for satisfaction and faith in this realisation [. . .], telling ourselves the public in our "small cities" was capable of fresh emotion and enthusiasm denied other audiences in "big cities", perhaps more provided for but certainly less seduced by the enchantment of theatre, a more diffident public, less inclined to give themselves or as Bragaglia[19] has written, to "stay with the play" and "stay in the play". And we wondered, since this was true why the isolation of theatre in our cities should continue. The readings of *Piccola Città*, Irwin Shaw's *Bury the Dead*, recitals of the negro poets, and of Garcia Lorca and Goethe [. . .] were generated by that sincerely felt urgency.'

2. Nine years after that evening Romolo Valli[20] wrote the above memories as a message of good luck and success for young Italian authors and amateur dramatic groups who for five years had been participating in the *Premio Maria Melato* [Maria Melato Prize].[21]

In reality Valli's message, its meaning, and how it was perceived went far beyond the events of theatre. They were a signal, a call to the city. Cultural revival was not only necessary but possible, and the City could make it happen by using its own strengths, its own resources. In reality his event and that of his friends, including lawyer Giannino Degani, had been a *happening*, an act of demonstration and stimulus.

In the meantime Romolo Valli with his friend Afro Saccani, had already chosen his path, which started in that *Piccola Città* reading I had been fortunate enough to witness. He had said his farewells to friends and joined the band of young actors in the *Carrozzone di Fantasio Piccoli*[22] which ventured out into the difficult pioneering world of theatre, a theatre of research capable of 'wider horizons, a new public, greater function and modernity'. That research would continue, always impatient, lucid and rigorous in the *Compagnia dei Giovani* hailed and today remembered as one of the most beautiful, fascinating and innovative casts Italian theatre culture has ever had. Today Romolo Valli, who started out in the small *Teatro di San Rocco*, has returned to his [native] city. [Reggio Emilia's] grand *Teatro Municipale* now carries his name.

3. A fire always needs someone to light it. Credit for a great deal of what would happen in those years after 1946 on the stages of our small city of Reggio Emilia, the small love affairs and great ones with the words of theatre, cinema, music, painting, of cultural and civic debate, must be identified in those first fires sparked in the fog and cold of 1946 by Romolo Valli, who we find in the same year with Renzo Bonazzi and Sergio Borziani inventing the Cineclub in Reggio Emilia which started a second splendid adventure with *Lampi sul Messico* [Thunder Over Mexico].[23]

These things being created in terribly difficult times, in a city attempting to rebuild on its ruins and mourning its deaths in war and in the battles of Resistance, where the shapes and signs of these first spontaneous cultural insurgencies were hidden in small places, in small groups, in scattered places, or more simply in the acts of individuals (I would like to remind readers of Ezio Comparoni's secret literary activity),[24] had the good fortune to immediately cluster and expand, even when there were no pre-established plans, or official announcements and patronage. These acts, intuitions, ideas and protagonism were on different levels. Very often they reflected a humble, popular genesis, and were scattered in different locations, like natural forerunners in a city that wanted to make haste and join the paths of rebirth and culture. They were years when an incredibly strong social energy, with great awareness and utopia, seemed enough to eliminate the limits of time and possibility.

In [the towns of] Cavriago, Fabbrico and Scandiano I remember the people who fashioned inconceivable work and dreams building cinemas and theatres with their own hands; and in Villa Cella and popular quarters of the city the first self-managed children's schools were born. In the city and its province spontaneous gatherings came about that went far beyond a desire to spend time together after the frightening solitudes of war. With these came the first amateur dramatics, the first small theatres, engaging the young and not so young in long rehearsals, and expectant debuts, always with a full house and a completely new public. The *Zibordi*, the *Gallinari*, the *Due Maschere*, Poviglio and Cadelbosco Sopra were all amateur dramatic groups.

These same groups often became organisers of choral music, opera music, and sports clubs, and as we see later, exhibitions of paintings and cultural debate.

Some years later when the Ariosto Theatre re-opened its doors to host the drama season (managed first by the ETI and later by the *Comune*),[25] it already had an open and willing public of a somewhat different kind to traditional theatre-goers.

Memo Benassi, Renzo Ricci, Tino Buazzelli, and *La Compagnia del Carrozzone di Fantasio Piccoli* opened a season that included the best names in theatre, from Carrara to Pavlova, from Emma Gramatica to Salvo Randone, from Elsa Merlini to Calindri, from Diana Torrieri to Vittorio Gassman. In 1949 we saw the return of Romolo Valli in an unforgettable *Miles Gloriosus* by Plautus.

We had the *Teatro dei Gobbi* [company] which was almost a premier, the privilege of seeing Jean-Louis's *Comédie-Français*, and work directed by Louis Jouvet.

In 1949 the city of Reggio Emilia also inaugurated another exceptional event called the *Biennale Nazionale del Bianco e Nero* [an exhibition of drawings and engravings]. At the same time the Cineclub continued its success, as did the opera season and concert season dear to the Reggio Emilia public by long tradition, stimulating the start of a glorious new association: the *Famiglia Artistica Reggiana*,[26] which has played an important role, especially in the fields of music and art.

These were homeless times immediately after the war. There were no places to get together. If you wanted to pass the time with friends, to think and discuss together, you had the streets, the squares and city corners. Sometimes there were homes, or Giannino Degani's studio. Or time borrowed in the *Caffè Cibotti*, the *Caffè Centrale*, the *Caffè Italia*, putting up with people coming and going. Better to brave the fog or the sun under the colonnades of the *Teatro Municipale*, the *Trinità*, or *Piazza del Monte* between statues of Ariosto and Boiardo, if Ezio Comparoni and his friends hadn't already occupied them.

It took the headquarters of *Il Lavoro* newspaper in *Via Cairoli*, and later the *Progresso d'Italia* newspaper opposite the *Banca d'Italia* (with the *Gramsci Circolo* later, and the worthy *Circolo di Cultura* in Via Emilia) to find places to take a break, for meeting, chatting, projects, and political metaphysics. And in them you would find Romolo Valli, Cavicchioni, Gianolio, Masini, Lusenti, Saccani, Rabitti, Morini and Costa.

4. When the socialist *Circolo Zibordi* opened in Via Battaglione Toscano in early 1946, slowly but surely I put down an anchor there. It was a small world but it had ten spirits. You never knew what might be happening, but it was a place like no other, where things really did happen. It was a multi-faceted circle in reality; there were students, workers, office clerks, young developing intellectuals, people waiting, people reading, people getting on with *tresette* and *ramini* [card games], with pool and *stecche* [a pool game]. There was a library that loaned out books and magazines, and a large theatre hall with red velvet stage curtains which transformed into a very happy and noisy dance hall for grand occasions. They were friendly people, [showing] solidarity, always willing to

leave their tables and roll up their sleeves, to wear their Sunday clothes on weekdays and vice versa.

The extraordinary thing, which emerged after a brief apprenticeship, was that anyone who wanted to busy themselves, launch or support the launch of a new idea, or find a familiar stopover passed through the *Zibordi*. The President, secretary and factotum of the *Circolo* was Bruno Prandi, a railway man, but at the centre of this web was a formidable weaver. His name was Gigetto Reverberi, a clerk with the customs house. It was not difficult to pick him out, or become his friend, and I was his friend until death took him from us. He was a man of primordial simplicity, immediate charm, a sort of flame thrower who burned affectionately, and with a voice that knew no low or discreet tones, transported by constant proposals and re-proposals for events and organising projects, which I think he thought up at night. You had to discover the whole of him. He was a sort of totemic object. Everything revolved around him. A Newtonian object, everything gravitated towards him.

The fact is that among the cyclists, volleyball players, special trains leaving for [performances at the] *Arena di Verona*, young and very young painters and theatre players, various musicians, light music singers, sopranos, and tenors, you might meet *maestro* Campogalliano [. . .], Mike Buongiorno, The Cetra Quartet, a young girl called Edmonda Aldini, and Memo Benassi, Maria Melato, Alfonso Gatto, Nando Tartaglia, Giovani Macchia, Anton Giulio Bragaglia, Raffaele De Grada, Mario De Micheli, Ernesto Treccani. And senator Pietro Marani the discreet and protective deity of the *Circolo*.

It was already an era of conferences and public debate. The very first I think. So our company of friends, the homeless ones, would get together and continue to discuss what had already been discussed in the theatre hall. The coming and going was endless. After ETI performances at the Ariosto Theatre there were small picnics with actors and actresses. Later these meetings with actors would be organised by the *Teatro Municipale*.

Already the Zibordi Amateur Dramatic Society was up and running with performances and staged readings, and before the Society there had been an incredible *Compagnia di Operette* which performed an extraordinary score by local citizen and *maestro* Mario Micheletti. There were the first opera concerts and lessons with *maestro* [Ettore] Campogalliano who became attached to our city in a tie of long-standing friendship, and gave it gifts of ideas and lessons in musical culture.

Later the founding of a *Teatro per Ragazzi*[27] [Theatre for Children] was added to the history of the *Zibordi*. It continued for three years, performing a story each year at the *Teatro Municipale* with an orchestra in the pit, and once at Milan's *Castello Sforzesco* where it won first prize in the national competition. I had my part in that adventure together with Corrado Costa and Giancarlo Conte, and I will return to it later. This was the *Circolo Zibordi*, in those poor, penny pinching years. A laboratory of games, ideas and inventions, of precursory facts which produced culture very simply and without school diplomas or academic qualifications. It was a mysterious and anomalous [non-conformist] way of producing culture that was difficult to understand because it was done by simple men, and for this reason difficult to include in officially recorded histories. Among those men was Gigetto Reverberi.

It is not easy to connect the figure of Romolo Valli – who had already won his quota of admiration and gratitude – with that of Gigetto Reverberi. However we have to acknowledge these are the two names to pair together if we wish to understand much of the prehistory and history of the intense flush of love of theatre and music that laid claim on our city.

Deep friendship and mutual admiration were feelings they always shared during two life journeys, between the great actor with the richest, most elegant culture Italy has ever had, and the great-humble provoker and inventor of a hundred theatrical events, whose design for our city was for it to be an unequalled site of creativity and promotional passion.

5. I have taken time over the *Zibordi* world because no tale or story about Gigetto Reverberi and what happened on stage and behind stage at the *Teatro Municipale* between the 1950s and the 1970s could be told without it. Sometimes a genesis is made like Chinese boxes [Russian dolls]. The box that flung out Gigetto Reverberi and the *Zibordi* was Maria Melato's death. It was Gigetto Reverberi who first understood the significance of her death and how much her native city owed her. Only a few weeks later the great actress was commemorated at the Ariosto Theatre in the words of Eligio Possenti (*Corriere della Sera* critic) and in performance of Giacosa's *Come le Foglie* by the *Zibordi* Amateur Dramatic Society.

Others will recount what took place when her body was transported to the *Civico Famedio* [memorial chapel], the honours organised by the *Comune*, how the 'Maria Melato' national festival ensued from that event and ran from 1951 to 1965.

I include myself in the tale only to note that this choice and the way it was realised was one of Gigetto Reverberi's diplomatic masterpieces. The art of negotiation supported by a transparent and impulsive generosity were revealed as one of the gifts in Gigetto's wisdom and foresight. His choice, immediately seconded by the respected senator Marani, was more than just the desire of an individual. In reality his was a political and cultural intuition that built on Romolo Valli's initial story, honouring the memory of this actress in the most enlightened way, intervening during the worst period of the theatre crisis and – importantly – gambling not so much on a traditional public as a new popular public being capable of responding to the offer and taking possession of cultural participation, which until that time had either been something extraneous or denied to them.

6. The *Opera Prima* contest, announced by the *Comune* of Reggio Emilia and the *Società Italiana Autori Drammatici*, was founded in 1957, six years after the first *Premio Maria Melato* [Maria Melato Prize] for amateur dramatic clubs [. . .].

The Festival series provided four elements worth considering: it had enormous success with the public and overcame the 'intellectual' opposition that tried to stop it getting underway; the good, often refined performances by many amateur groups; and a wide and well chosen repertoire that confirmed a solid knowledge of Italian and non-Italian drama, often supported by modern and judicious critical consciousness.

These were all encouraging reasons (in the background was a deep crisis of professional theatre, which was already battling with competition from television) for that first experience to generate another with courageous ambitions and ends: that of launching a national competition for young Italian writers, with full freedom to choose the subject of the drama. The prize was half a million *lire*. A performance by an amateur group chosen by the jury beforehand was guaranteed, and the piece would be included in the 'Melato' series. The project was unique in Europe.

The Festival took on this second commitment, showing itself to be a tool not only for promoting but actively stimulating and searching out new energies and young authors, for bringing them into the limelight to be examined by the public and critics with the declared function of reinforcing and reviving theatre repertoire.

I have to say this choice was debated for a long time. Everyone, whether friends of the organising committee, the jury, or journalists and theatre critics, weighed up the meaning of an initiative that was not too sure of success and was equally well aware of the difficult situation culture and politics were in, especially culture and politics connected with the life of theatre. A life consigned to being a secondary sector, characterised by a historical elitist tradition making theatres mostly the property of people who owned boxes, to privileged minorities of caffè society – as Giovanni Calendoli and Orio Vergani had written: given over to old-fashioned architecture and events, extortionate taxes, frozen repertories repeated *ad infinitum*, and sites partly damaged and disrupted by the tragedy of war. And now, as we have said, they were under siege from television which was eagerly stealing their public and transforming traditions, habits and cultures.

In Italy between 1952 and 1959 performances in theatres dropped by about 50 per cent. Theatre performances were confined to large cities like Rome, Florence, Naples. 'Tours' refused the piazzas of the provinces. Until 1949 the theatre in our city of Reggio Emilia opened only three to four times a year, and only during the winter months.

Yet despite this, an interesting fact was true: while professional theatres produced about 4,000 performances annually, secondary theatre, amateur and dilettante, produced about 35,000 performances much more widely and in outlying places. In effect there was a vast, scattered and submerged world of theatre, denied by official statistics, which was alive and communicating, mostly modest but always genuinely committed. Would this area be willing to embrace the call of the *Opera Prima*? Again, there was a huge area of youth, young unknown writers, rising up with new ideas, new desires, new expectations, who were part of the themes and problems of a society changing and looking for its identity, and anxious to enter it with their own feelings and their own reasons. Was this where we ought to direct our hopes? In Gigetto Reverberi's heart and mind he had no doubt. His task in life was to open up worlds, break down frontiers, and let gifts come forth from them.

We all agreed, as did the *Società Italiana Autori Drammatici*, feeling the gain that would come, and a very noble gain it was, from searching for new names to add to the ranks of playwrights.

7. At the end of these discussions, the mountains of figures, questions and predictions that ended in a 'yes' for *Opera Prima*, each member taking their share of satisfaction, you could only consider the part Gigetto Reverberi had played. How you knew, if there was any doubt about it, was the fact that the project already had an orderly balance sheet and budget, the fact that it had a separate identity from the 'Melato' series but they were immediately re-connected, as if indivisible parts of the same morphological structure, that the names of many people on future panel of judges were already being aired. Where, how and when Gigetto conducted his manoeuvres was not known.

For myself, I presumed to know his ways of behaving, exactly as he had on this occasion. In the final phases, you saw him look smaller, take on a virginal air and act like a fish in the barrel, strangely silent and apparently on the sidelines, but still willing to assent with enormous dangerous genuflecting nods of his large head. All this meant everything was going according to plan. He had already woven his fabric in unknown shadowy corners, just like Penelope in antiquity.

He always orchestrated in that way. When he created the *Zibordi* amateur dramatic society, and the honours for Maria Melato, or began a series of cultural meetings, or the special trains. [. . .] When he promoted the *Premio Avanti* for debuting *Zibordi* opera singers (in 1955) into the *Premio Achille Peri* [Achille Peri Prize],[28] which was run by the *Comune* and the *Teatro Municipale* (in 1969), bringing in *maestro* Campogalliano, who was a formidable figure of a man of learning and music, immediately elected honorary president of the Prize. For himself he reserved the role of organising secretary, then and for all eternity. And lastly, when he sparked the fires that generated the *Teatro per Ragazzi*, once again connected with the *Circolo Zibordi*, and later the *Teatro Club* in spaces in the *Teatro Municipale*.

8. The *Opera Prima* contest, which later became the *Premio del Tricolore*, lasted seven years and took place eight times. There were no other European models for the event. It was an audacious, generous, timely dash of hope that did not disappoint and was capable, in what was almost a desert, of reviving what little theatre culture and vitality was finding its way in the dark. It made a comeback years later with the advent of the *Teatri Stabili* and the *Piccolo Teatro di Milano*, which gained international recognition with Paolo Grassi and Giorgio Strehler[29]

and had contributions from an exceptional generation of artists like Visconti, Gassman, Albertazzi, the *Compagnia dei Giovani*, and contibutions from writers like Diego Fabbri, Italo Calvino and Ugo Betti.

The *Opera Prima* competition was a tool that attracted interest from the press, even managed to gain alliance with television and reward certain competition winners' hard work and texts, and promoted meeting and debate.

I think the authoritativeness of the jury commission played an important role, with Alessandro De Stefano as President and highly cultured members such as Mario Apollonio, Giuseppe Bertolucci, Giorgio Candeloro, Giulio Trevisani, journalists and critics such as Lorenzo Ruggi, Ghigo De Chiara, Icilio Ripamonti, playwrights like Ezio D'Errico and Turi Vasile, actors and directors like Franco Parenti and Sandro Bolchi.

The first *Opera Prima* had ninety-three competitors. Looking back from this distance, the competition lived up to expectations as we have already tried to say. Although it did not unearth masterpieces, it did find well-made, well-inspired texts; it awarded and identified young talents who, when not finding openings in the theatre – which has never valued a national repertory, were often recognised [by getting jobs] on the editorial staff of television, newspapers and publishing, protagonists of excellent careers. Moreover, the competition's value, seriousness and cultural and artistic reputation are further confirmed by scrolling through the names of personalities who accepted invitations to be on the jury. It is not overstating the case to say our city at that time had already assured itself not only cultural activity in several fields (the 'Melato' festivals, the *Opera Prima* Award, the Achille Peri Prize, performances by professional companies), but the credentials of being a city-laboratory which, as the critic Ghigo De Chiari wrote, was a significant and surprising phenomenon in the context of theatre culture in our country.

9. Now it was his turn. I do not know how Corrado Costa[30] would have remembered or recounted here the years of the *Teatro per Ragazzi* between 1953 and 1956. He would have entertained us and transported us to another world, his world, with no lands or boundaries or sanctified memories, he would have transformed the subject into the lightest most paradoxical of subjects. He was always ready – as Ivanna Rossi has said – to gather 'life's honey'. I don't know what way he would have turned the long past game on its head, the tales invented for children, the theatre that seemed at that time more a game than a serious venture.

The texts were his, they were Corrado's, 'The Little Girl Lost in the Carnival', 'The Lead Cat', 'The Snowman', and 'Salvagno the Chicken Thief'. I was director, Giancarlo Conte the choreographer; Mario Novellini the set designer; Angelo Brindani the voice-over; and Ciccio Rocchi the score composer: for fifty children, twenty costume-making mothers, four to six months of rehearsals, performances at the *Teatro Municipale*, with the orchestra in the mystical gulf [orchestra pit]. [We performed at] the theatres of Bologna, Mantova, Riccione and *Castello Sforzesco* in Milan where the company returned in 1954 to win the first national competition.

It all happened by chance in the street, just the way Corrado liked, while discussing whether poetry was something children liked. We put the idea together, we contacted Gigetto Reverberi and the *Zibordi*, we had their blessing and their support. Then we obtained that of the ENAL which at the time counted for a lot. And so this strange ship departed and sailed the seas for over three years.

If humour and poetry are gifts of the gods to change the sense of things, make them more affable and playful, then the tales Corrado put together already had them. A small girl loses ten *lire*, a lead cat is teased, a snowman does not want to die, and Salvagno is a ridiculous chicken thief, all were enough to create surreal, hallucinatory, magically enjoyable plots.

Corrado was always present at the opening. He smuggled himself into the mystical gulf [orchestra pit]. And if the orchestra missed a beat it was due to jests and jokes Corrado made at the most delicate moments, horrifying Gigetto who was always behind the curtains, like an extra bouncer.

I remember how happy he was with these first stories and others published later here and there. Happy that he managed to register with SIAE, the Italian Society of Authors and Editors, which was an ambition he had.

I do not want to say more. Certainly if he were still alive – he hinted to me with fake fright and real laughter a few days before passing away – we would have more opportunities for marvelling and walking the tightrope with his memories, which even he had not explored. Emotions only he was capable of giving us.

[. . .]

10. The task I was given was to talk mainly about the *Opera Prima* and I think I have done that. Though my discussion starts from further back with the post-war *opere prime*, which acted as precursors in some way.

I have never believed, nor do I believe now, that a story belongs to only one person. Stories are always plural and their origins are infinite. What I wish to say is that Gigetto Reverberi was always a significant figure, always at the centre, never on the fringes of these Reggio Emilia stories, and I do not know if they would have happened without him. I think not.

I shared many years, many ideas, with Gigetto Reverberi [. . .] and many of the things he created or championed. I chased the same spirits, and walked along the same stones. I do not really know if we were in love with the *Teatro Municipale* or a greater theatre. About him I have no doubt: it was the latter.

It would be difficult to explain his immeasurable energy that never spared itself, and his instinct and intelligence in choosing, for always choosing what wasn't there because it was the only way of interpreting feelings and expectations, his restlessness to be always doing, and challenging the 'it-can't-be-done's' with a certainty that is very simple and which he made his own, that if you create real facts they will also be real in their consequences. This was where his culture lay (the miracle of an autodidact), his concept of life, and the learning through which he made himself familiar with things, thoughts and persons, even when they seemed to belong to a different and apparently unpursuable universe.

The best and most eminent [exponents] of Italy's music and theatre culture knew his simple and spontaneous charm, which came before the flood of talk and ideas. These immediately revealed his gift for sincerity and the rich competencies he had developed in the field, his organisational rigour that knew no bounds.

[. . .]

This is the story – lying outside any classical canon or Propp's formula[31] – of a man who passed through the history of our city for over twenty years, at a time when each act was an effort of hope and passion. He came from Bibbiano.[32] He was, if you like, born to the art of theatre because his father was the head comedian in a local amateur dramatic society. He used the familiar 'tu' with Paolo Grassi, Giorgio Strehler, Gianandrea Gavazzeni, Luciano Pavarotti, Alberto Zelda, Carlo Maria Badini. He used it with Romolo Valli and the entire city of Reggio Emilia.

Documents 1945–63

1945

4.45 Article in *La Verità* [The Truth],[33] Year I, Number 13, September 1945

New literature, new culture

> *For art to reach the people, and the people art, we must first of all raise the general level of education and culture.*
>
> Lenin

It will be very interesting to see the impact our recent literature will have, in this new atmosphere being established in relation with and as a consequence of the current historical and social transitions. Will we see impetuous and revolutionary metamorphosis or a slow and gradual absorption, like a phenomenon of osmosis? The time is not ripe today for an answer.

[. . .]

In the meantime it is our duty to recognise that an art exists that has lived and prospered in men and things, that has had a function, has been the subject of criticism and acclaim. And it must be recognised that this art has lived estranged from society by a fearsome rift, and that although in the broad view of things this is its greatest fault, it is also its original quality. Today we say the function of this art has been exhausted. However the contributions of these artists cannot be forgotten; their labours, the precious experiences, some more so some less so, are a historical reality and therefore cannot be denied.

Today, faced with new ideals and conceptions that we feel drawing us with all their beauty and justice, we hope for a new expression of our art and our literature, and more than that, new substance. Without this it cannot become part of new ethical and social realities, therefore condemning itself, which would be particularly dangerous for the new spirit of information and education.

[. . .]

Today if we want to find something living we must go back a long way: to Giovanni Verga,[34] an artist who was intimately capable of finding liberating synthesis through artistic observation-sublimation of the popular soul. Whereas D'Annunzio,[35] with his lyrics and prose, the exaltation of form, seems to celebrate the first breakdowns of an Italian bourgeoisie that had always been weakly structured, the Sicilian writer Verga raises a truly revolutionary voice, as if indicating the right road for art. However his call, perhaps because it was not articulated in such highly ornate or elaborate ways [as D'Annunzio], was to no avail. Thus Italian literature stopped at *Malavoglia* and *Mastro Don Gesualdo*.

Writers in the generation from the 1920s to the present day did not see Verga's road, and were drawn to the vacuous current of pseudo-art that merged with a political current as noxious as it was devoid of social layering. Either this or they retreated into interior idylls, more often than not lacking in lyrical emotion – and concealed behind a horribly arcane method, as more or less unconsciously they reflected the rot in an indifferent and egotistical society that was crumbling.

They did not know how to go beyond these limits. For these writers the secret and glorious history of the masses, the worker's soul pulsating in the sweat and daily labour of duty, did not exist. The suffering, the painful experiences that shape our workers and peasants were ignored by these writers enclosed in ivory towers.

For today and the near (or far) future, too heavy a legacy of fossilised ideals weighs on them for them to give us vital, sincere works of art in a context of rebirth. For rebirth we must wait for new artists from the youth and from the people. Because the young masses will be the first to raise their heads and assimilate the reality of our times with a fertile sensibility, just as they did during the struggles of the Resistance insurrections.

The concept of art

However waiting for the birth of an artist does not mean waiting for a miracle from heaven.

True, we cannot create an artist at will, but it is equally true that the conditions for an artist to be born and to develop can be created from now on.

'For art to reach the people, and the people art' – says Lenin – 'we must first of all raise the general level of education and culture.'

Culture needs to enter slowly but surely into the customs of our people. That is why we have to create cultural circles everywhere, in cities and in villages, where all workers can participate, circles that can propose breaking down the walls that today separate culture from the popular masses, with conferences, lessons and debate. That is to say, make these circles into living organisms close to the people, and to the words of the people, with simplicity and dedication, rather than exclusive groups of pseudo-intellectuals.

Culture must become a common estate of all people, not of the select or privileged few.

To provoke this awakening, or better, cultural renewal in the life of the nation we must organise popular universities, create new libraries, make those that already exist into flourishing centres of culture, develop amateur dramatics movements, organise visits to museums and places of art, send travelling exhibitions around the country.

This way the conditions will be created for artistic and social resurrection: it will be enough for the millions of individuals living in ignorance and indifference today to breathe this new air, and to feel the joy of culture, for new ground to be created and bear fruit in the field of literature.

1946

5.46 Poem in *La Verità* [The Truth], Year II, Number 6, February 1946

Mid-September

In mid-September
when pines turn misty
they leave deserted tables
to marmots drunk with sleep
– flocks of sheep
slowly descend the valley
following the footsteps of an invisible god.
The water smooths itself to immerse
the burning sky
now it ruffles
and the grass ruffles
as with a shiver
and there is a cicada missing from the chorus.
There is a faint scent of milk
around

perfumed with juniper berries
And it seems like a slow psalm-singing procession
Mourning the death of things.

❋ ❋ ❋

6.46 Poem in *La Verità* [The Truth], Year II, Number 17, 28 April 1946

My Songs

I know. My voice can only sing
small things already heard.
What does it matter?
I sing! Let me sing!
Here is all the joy of my soul.
   My songs
   will be joys, longing, and child's delirium
Of a man still chasing
   white butterflies on green carpets
and dozing tired
almost oblivious.
They will be dead, mute, nonsensical corners
speaking an inebriated language
only I – perhaps – can understand.
They will be a child's spells in notes of gold:
a little rusty,
vanishing in the fog that oppresses us
with no trace of sound
like rings in marsh water.
Or a man's lament,
shorter than the ocean seagull's cry;
of a man who can no longer struggle
but listens
to the seductive echo
of ancient storms
in shells pure white with froth.

This pale voice that is expressed within
will soon be spent I know.
What does it matter?
Meanwhile I drown myself in limitless labyrinths
of sun.

1950

7.50 Article in *Progresso d'Italia*,[36] daily morning newspaper, 19 March 1950

Editors' note: Edgar Lee Masters (1868–1950) was an American poet, biographer and dramatist, as well as a lawyer by profession. *Spoon River Anthology* was his most famous and acclaimed work, a collection of over 200 free-form poems that narrate the epitaphs of the residents of Spoon River, a fictional small town. First published in 1915, it caused a great sensation for its forthrightness about sex, moral decay and hypocrisy. The first Italian version was published in 1943, in difficult circum-stances. The fascist regime was generally hostile to American literature, and the translated book was slipped past the censor by changing the title to 'Antologia S. River' – 'a collection of thought by Saint River'. The translator, Fernanda Pivano, was eventually imprisoned for this challenge to the system, later commenting: 'The book was super pro-hibited in Italy. It spoke of peace, against war, against capitalism, against the whole weight of convention in general. It was everything the government would not allow us to think [. . .] and they put me in prison and I am very happy to have been there.' The *Spoon River Anthology* became widely known and read in Italy, remaining very popular to this day.

What epigraph for Edgar Lee Masters?

The language of the historic past – explicit language, standing outside all convention, terrible in its tone, dramatic and tragic, veined with torment, regrets and accusations – becomes highly poignant lyricism in the difficult discovery of intrinsic psychological truths.

Cesare Pavese[37] well understands one of Lee Masters' true lyrical and human qualities, perceiving that his way of thinking (his way of life then, and of being a poet) is 'in universals', is expressed 'in universals'.

As Pavese points out, thinking 'in universals' means being part of a society in which pain, spiritual and physical suffering and life's problems have not, as fools believe, been eliminated but where the tools exist for conducting a shared and common struggle against pain, poverty and death. In the [Spoon River] anthology Lee Masters testifies to the fact that in the society he inhabits these tools, these 'universals' are missing – in other words its actions have lost sense and direction.

[. . .]

Lee Masters was more judge than prophet (perhaps his lawyer's toga weighed on him). He could only see 'light' in the past, which is why his ways of thinking 'in universals' ought not to be taken in the most valid, modern and current sense of the philosophical meaning – and maybe Pavese did not take him this way either. For Lee Masters universals were still only an aristocratic way of analysing and thinking (in fact he felt enormous admiration for Greek civilisation). He could not understand humanity's true spurs to growth, how – through purifying dialectic – it reaches inexorably to a future where if there be struggle let it be the struggle of men against things, and not of men against men.

Even today American thinking has not arrived at this truth. Lee Masters, a genuine messenger of poetry that is still living and precious, could certainly not have arrived there in 1914–1915.

1951

8.51 Article in *Collana di Studi Psico-Pedagogici* [The Psycho-Pedagogical Studies Series], Reggio Emilia, June 1951

The Psycho-Pedagogical Medical Centre for Early Childhood Mental Hygiene

The issue of mental hygiene [health] in early childhood is a highly urgent subject for discussion. In Italy certain things have been done in this regard, but in other more fortunate and less war-torn countries the issue has already been concretely transformed into an item on public sector and state authority budgets.

[. . .]

The idea of health must be applied to the physical, affective and mental wholeness of the child: there is no side of a child's complex being that can be hurt or injured without affecting the rest. Dr. Brock Chisholm[38] says, 'Health must be considered as a state of complete physical, mental and social wellbeing and not the mere absence of disease and infirmity.'

If we take this as our definition of health, education is no longer the art of teaching; in its broadest sense it becomes assistance with the psychological growth and maturing of human beings, making possible the growth of a rich, original, socially and individually normal personality. In the same way increasingly significant results in psychosomatic science are revealing the influence of psyche on soma (the correlation between psyche and soma), giving education its true role of preventative medicine for the individual and society.

The connections between mental hygiene [health] and education thus appear to be extremely close. On a practical level the *Centro Medico Psico-Pedagogico* must become an institution complementing family and school, and defending the good of society.

1953

9.53 Illustrated leaflet for the International Exhibition of Children's Drawings, Reggio Emilia, May 1953

Drawing as a tool for knowledge of the child

Are drawings a useful and effective means for studying, and diagnosing, children's intellectual, affective, emotional and volitional qualities?

The answer is decidedly affirmative. Psychology has a vast, rich and exhaustive literature, increasingly solid in scientific terms, and based on rigorously statistical experiment and application that can leave no room for doubt. Thus using drawings as a means of psycho-diagnosis, and as a therapeutic means has become a commonly accepted and universally appreciated technique among followers of psychology. There is no Psycho-Pedagogical Centre (i.e. an institution typically specialising in the clinical study of children) that does not make wide use of them, or testify to their great importance.

[. . .]

The evolution of children's drawings runs parallel to the stages and modes of their language development, of their acquisition of concepts, of their thinking, of their progressive adaptation to and integration with new situations.

The first period of pure idea–motor drawing, or the pure play of movement according to Bühler[39] (the child draws marks, lines, circles, spirals), is accompanied, in terms of language, by the well-known first babbling, of sounds and syllables without meaning, constantly repeated. We are in the preliminary stages of drawing and language. Later the schematic, elliptical and synthetic expression of both marks and the child's first utterances is significant. The child draws a very simple line to indicate a human being or an animal: just as the same child expresses an entire proposition, 'mamma give me something to drink because I'm thirsty', in a single word 'bu'. Then his drawings become richer with particulars and details, with relations and logical connections, and at the same pace his language is enriched with new words, more precise new forms of verbs with connections allowing ordered and finished expression.

Just as one representation in a child's drawings has many different possible meanings (the same representation is used for indicating objects, animals, persons), so his mental concepts have polyvalent meanings (the same word 'draws' different things).

All this demonstrates how children's drawing harmoniously grafts itself onto the integrated evolution of the individual and how it is a concrete expression of the same.

Let us take for example the famous test by Fay, revised by Vintsch, and finally again by Fay, in which a child is invited to express, through the means of a drawing, 'a woman walking, and it is raining'. The trial necessitates an understanding of the theme and an execution of the scene. Depending on his chronological and mental age, the child will give qualitatively different solutions:

from a scribble to a simple *homme-tetard* [head man], to a clear representation of a woman with an umbrella, in movement, with a more or less detailed landscape. The degree of mental development is translated and expressed [in the drawing] by the number and variety of data differentiating sex, the environment, the action and the good logic of the relations.

[. . .]

Editor's note: The section that follows is based on analysis of drawings from 120 children aged 4 to 10 years attending the *Centro Medico Psico-Pedagogico*.

From this we therefore have the rule that drawing reveals mental development, up to a certain age.

1: asexual puppet
2: asexual puppet and rain
3: asexual puppet, rain and umbrella
4: female figure and rain
5: female figure, rain and umbrella
6: female figure in movement, rain and umbrella

	1	2	3	4	5	6
4 yrs	13	7	–	–	–	–
5 yrs	4	9	5	1	1	–
6 yrs	–	4	8	2	6	–
7 yrs	–	1	4	5	8	2
8 yrs	–	–	–	4	6	10
10 yrs	–	–	–	–	2	18

[. . .]

More difficult but no less effective and precious is the study of the child's affective and emotional personality through drawing.

Study is possible both with completely free drawing, and by subjecting the child to drawing tests of a so-called projective character, in that they solicit or prompt more or less hidden elements that form the basis of the child's personality to come to the surface, elements which constitute the child's personal history, type, psychic inheritance, the child's relations with the outside world.

[. . .]

The dimension of the construction of a drawing, whether it is positioned mostly to the left or to the right of the sheet of paper, are other significant aspects; just as the proportional sizes of characters represented are important aspects.

[. . .]

This relation between drawing, intellectual maturity and affect is today precisely restated by psychological studies. Such a proposition shifts, we might say strongly, the traditional problems and methods of teaching art, just as in a broader sense it shifts the entire, integral issue of education. The *healthier* the child is the better he will draw, the better he will create, the better he will be able to express himself and become the active protagonist of his own evolution and of his becoming man and citizen.

But here the concept of health must detach itself from the constraints of old ideas and be applied to the physical, affective and mental unity of the individual. Health must be understood as a state of complete physical, mental and social wellbeing, which does not only consist in the absence of illness and infirmity.

This is the new definition. If the definition of health is understood in this way, then education (education in the holistic sense) is no longer only the art of teaching, but becomes assistance with the psychological growth and maturity of every human being, to allow their personality to expand in as rich and as individually and socially normal a way as possible.

Children's drawing, with its suggestive and precise language, alerts us to this reality and this need. It is up to all of us to capture its essence and work with passion.

Editor's note: The leaflet finishes with the Organising Committee of the International Exhibition and of the Reggio Collection of Children's Drawings thanking 'the Mayor of Reggio Emilia for his kind permission for Doctor Loris Malaguzzi to comment on some aspects and experiences of the *Centro Medico Psico-Pedagogico Comunale*'.

1954

10.54 Article in *Contributions to Social Psychiatry* on the second centenary of the San Lazzaro Psychiatric Institute in Reggio Emilia, October 1954

Two years of Medical-Psycho-Pedagogical Consultorio *activity*

Doctor C. Iannuccelli, Doctor L. Malaguzzi and Doctor M. Montanini

The Medical-Psycho-Pedagogical *Consultorio* [Centre] began its activity in June 1951. It was established by Reggio Emilia's Municipal Administration, and benefits from an agreement between the municipality and the ONMI Federation,[40] which has made premises available at their *Casa della Madre e del Bambino* [House of the Mother and Child].

The *Consultorio* has lived through several experiences, not all easy, especially in the beginning.

These experiences confirm the inevitable difficulties and uncertainties – perhaps typical of a provincial city – connected with creating a modern, scientifically advanced institution, as the Medical-Psycho-Pedagogical *Consultorio* undoubtedly is.

Today the institution is rapidly progressing, gaining respect and trust, and working with increasingly certain and broad perspectives: it has defined its working methods and organisational structure in order to be more clearly distinguishable.

In spite of this there are still lamentable delays in the technical, functional, and inspirational standards of authorities and organisations for the care and education of the psychically abnormal, children with irregular conduct, and the socially maladjusted; those which by their nature undertake activities intrinsically connected with the *Consultorio*. (These [delays] are largely due to lack of funds, or to protocols and laws that have fallen behind the reality and rapid progress in scientific and psycho-pedagogical studies.)

The fundamental themes on which the *Consultorio*'s activity is based are: team work between the paediatric psychiatrist, the psychologist and the social worker; a bio-psychological study of children's individual and social evolution; care aimed at improving the condition of the psychically abnormal; psychotherapy for maladjusted and difficult [children]; environmental therapy, school guidance, screening work in schools, collaboration with parents and educators, and popularising the basic principles of Mental Hygiene.

We have attempted to make an initial analysis of the *Consultorio*'s activity through the statistics and graphs that follow. In the explanatory comments that accompany the data we have included thoughts based on an objective examination of phenomena, and on practical experience developed over time.

This removes the need for any further explanatory notes. However there is only one thing we wish to comment on. Being convinced of the fundamental importance of the family in the process of educating children's intelligence and character, even with abnormal children, we have made a conscious commitment only to admit children for residential treatment in cases of extreme urgency.

Formulating our programme in this way further clarifies the lines on which the *Consultorio* is run; it also explains the low number of cases admitted into institutions. The inadequacies of residential institutions are well-known, especially for difficult and maladjusted children, which means our convictions remain firmly rooted.

Subjects examined

Reggio Emilia: subjects examined 524 (m. 346, f. 178)
Province: subjects examined 126 (m.78, f. 48)
Total subjects examined: 650

An analysis of data regarding those attending the *Consultorio* shows a marked prevalence of males over females: 65 per cent and 35 per cent respectively.

In our experience an explanation of this phenomenon can be found in the following reasons:

a   A higher level of concern for failures, anomalies and intellectual and affective abnormalities in males can be noted in parents and school authorities. No doubt this arises from a mistaken and unjustified conception of social tasks and perspectives, as well as an insufficient understanding of the problems of mental hygiene.

b   Abnormal manifestations are often more evident in boys than in girls, especially regarding conduct.

c   In our judgement there is reason to believe the dynamic of modern life in all its many aspects exposes males, more than females, to experiences which are precocious, disordered and inadequate, and these then translate into an irregular, defective [process of] maturity (a suggestive and interesting topic which merits deeper study).

Obviously although we cannot always draw reliable conclusions from our analysis, owing to the random and non-homogeneous nature of the population examined, we wish to point out that the greatest gap between numbers of girls and boys examined is approximately at the age of six (54 boys, 11 girls). This phenomenon leads us back to reasons we specified above, and the more obvious difficulty of adapting to school life for male children.

The highest number of cases in children of both sexes was recorded at seven to eight years old. [. . .] It is precisely at this age that the school world [begins] classifying achievements and behaviours, makes families aware of them, and sets alarm bells ringing.

[. . .]

The prevalence of the working classes (72 per cent) compared to the well-to-do is a logical consequence of the nature and aims of the *Consultorio* whose services are also completely free. It is consistent [also] with the widely held view that economic instability, with its moral, psycho-physical and educational consequences, is largely responsible for factors determining the lack of harmonious development which makes up the *Consultorio*'s work.

※ ※ ※

11.54 Excerpt from supplement to *Rivista Sperimentale di Freniatria* [Journal of the Study of Mental Illness], Volume LXXVIII, Fascicolo II, 1954

> **Editor's note:** The *Colonia-Scuola* – or special school – Antonio Marro was opened in 1921 as part of the San Lazzaro psychiatric hospital in Reggio Emilia. The *Colonia* was intended for children considered to have 'abnormalities' of character and intelligence, with each child given both a neuro-psychiatric and an educational assessment. The main aim of the school was to enable its students to become employable – though only in manual trades. For more information on the school, see Paolella (2010).

Research on the social behaviour of people discharged from the 'Colonia Scuola Marro' in the decade 1930–1940

Doctor C. Iannuccelli, Doctor L. Malaguzzi and Doctor M. Montanini

The widespread material and moral difficulties individuals encounter today [to achieve] good integration into society are well known. War, social upheaval, ideological conflict, sudden economic loss and rapidly changing fortunes, the never-ending struggle for existence, the rapid increase of technology and great changes in environmental conditions have inevitably led to a lack of harmonious development in social structures, causing a constant strain on systems of adaptation in the individual.

Adapting never takes place without conflicts. On the contrary it consists precisely in resolving them. For this reason intervention by Society is necessary, using all available means – from deeper knowledge of the capacities and possibilities of the individual, to the work of assistance and guidance, and improvement of environmental conditions.

In confronting these problems, in resolving critical situations of poverty, moral neglect, and precarious work, in improving the conditions of people's lives, and thus reducing the conflict and mitigating the strong and often inharmonious influence of instinctive leanings, and finally in creating the conditions for greater knowledge of individual personality and developing the amount and efficacy of assistance which is provided, we can reduce the damaging moral and material consequences that social maladjustment causes the community.

[. . .]

Given the difficulty and time required for a complete investigation of all those admitted to the '*Colonia Scuola*' from the Provinces of Reggio Emilia and Modena since its creation, we have limited our inquiry to those admitted from the municipality of Reggio Emilia, before returning to the subject on a larger scale. Furthermore we have based observations on people who were resident in the Institute during the years 1930–1940.

Whereas this is limited on one hand, it has allowed us to follow social behaviour in our subjects for a period of at least 14 years after discharge, time enough to let us have a complete documentation and evaluation of the vicissitudes in their adult life.

Very briefly we wish to remind [the reader] that the 'Colonia Scuola Marro' was founded in 1921 for the education and instruction of children of abnormal intelligence or character in the Provinces of Reggio Emilia and Modena.

[. . .]

In accordance with the objectives of this inquiry, particular attention was given to the composition and quality of family environments, the kinds of work carried out after discharge from the Institute, work performance, the degree of economic independence achieved, and morality or lack of it in social conduct.

Generally speaking, the family environment is fundamentally important in issues of social reintegration for discharged individuals. In 60 per cent of cases pathological problems were found to revolve around the family (parental mental illness, psychological deficiency, alcoholism, tuberculosis or syphilis). Eighty per cent of family environments were characterised by economic destitution, often accompanied by moral destitution. The breakdown of the family unit was found in twenty-five per cent of cases. Ten per cent of patients discharged were illegitimate.

It is obvious that in the act of leaving the Colonia young people, who need an emotionally and economically secure shelter particularly at this time, are faced with a situation which family instability makes more difficult, their prospects greatly limited by a family environment which is not adequate for continuing their education or suited to orienting them towards employment.

1956

12.56 Speech to the 7th National Council of the *Associazione Pionieri d'Italia* [Pioneers Association of Italy], Milan, December 1956

Editor's note: The *Associazione Pionieri d'Italia* was a youth movement of the PCI, for boys and girls up to 15 years, with the first group established in 1947 in a neighbourhood of Reggio Emilia. In 1950, it began to publish a weekly newspaper for young people, *Il Pioniere* [The Pioneer], whose first editor was Gianni Rodari, a PCI member, who was to become famous for his children's books and was a close friend of Malaguzzi and Reggio Emilia [see 47.73]. The PCI closed the organisation in 1960, partly in response to pressure from the Catholic Church and partly because the Communist Party decided to opt for a commitment to reforming schools, but in so doing abandoned the possibility of its own educational movement for children, leaving the field to the Church.

Speaking at the 1956 National Council, Ada Gobetti (see Chapter 1, n.44) described the API as being 'born in response to deeply felt needs for true democracy: to affirm, against the desolate background of the condition of childhood in our country, the right of children – of all children – to a healthy and joyous education; to give this education new contents, truly democratic, non-confessional, in accord with the ideals that emerged in the struggle against fascism'.

Immediately before Malaguzzi's contribution, presented below, a report was made by Carlo Pagliarini, the API National Secretary, in which he highlighted the 'desolate' living conditions of Italian children, and the failure to address the problems of childhood in the country; the hostile attitude of the Catholic Church, though acknowledging some evidence of changing attitudes, with '[c]ertain manifestations of intolerance and religious war [having] thus faded or disappeared altogether'; and the need for a renewal of schools and the reform of pedagogy based not on class division but on what can 'educate a modern adult, in possession of solid scientific knowledge and a clearly democratic personality'. Pagliarini ends by calling on the meeting to 'begin work on this elaboration of pedagogy' – at which point Malaguzzi took over.

Persevere in elaborating the educational line

We must recognise this study conference appears extraordinarily rich in enthusiasm. There is a great desire in everyone to do, and to do well, and this can be understood from the passionate tone everyone has used in putting forward not only their positive experiences, their uncertainties or unresolved problems, but in the concrete responses, courageous solutions, the criticisms and self-criticism. Should we be going deeper into this debate or going on to a knowledge of Freinet's methods?[41] The question, posed by our friend Dall'Aglio, again testifies to the warmth of attention and the deep interest with which we wish to give order and completeness to our work.

On the other hand we should not be surprised at the many uncertainties that have been expressed. The problem of educating young people is certainly the most difficult of all problems, one which takes the greatest commitment: above all when these educational issues must be concretely translated onto the level of organisation, organisation like that of the Italian Pioneers, which is searching in increasingly better ways for an originality of its own.

Obviously, when venturing into serious research on the founding motives, characteristics and perspectives of an organisation of this kind, the reality of facts in the country in which it exists, the reality of its politics, society and traditions, the pedagogical ferment emerging on theoretical and practical levels cannot be disregarded. If somehow we could simplify the reality of Italian pedagogy and organise it in such a way as to make it more readable and comprehensible, we could see that two channels run through it. The first is one that gathers and pours back the strength of organisation in the Catholic Church, which has an enormous energy, huge resources and centuries of experience. The second channel is made up of democratic and popular organisations, young in years, not so rich in experience, much less rich in resources, but rich in resolve and resolution that perfectly and historically correspond to the needs of emerging social forces. These are increasingly aware of their ways of working and role. However, between these two channels, these two forces – with their very different levels of efficiency – there is a sort of organisational vacuum.

In contrast with what is happening in other countries, *the ideology of third force* – if you will allow me this concise and illustrative term – has not found a way or the means to manifest itself in terms of organisation. However this third force carries out interesting work in the areas of research and pedagogical dissemination, it tirelessly studies modern theories and techniques, and makes original contributions to them, in particular the experience of active pedagogy, and on several occasions it has taken courageous anti-conformist positions on educational issues, and on schooling in general.

It can be recognised that this is all the result of freedom to research, in a sense made freer to the extent that it has never been hindered by organisational or practical needs, which unfortunately often leads to direct and open conflict in our country. Although this particular work in research and dissemination comes from an outcomes-based approach, and thinking we do not always share, in all honesty it must be admitted that we have not seriously and calmly evaluated it until recently.

However going back to the line of discourse which interests us today. What does the phenomenon of this vacuum between Catholic organisation and the organisation of young and very young socialist forces really mean? It necessarily means that because there is no other competing force existing between them, that is capable of conditioning and mediating in some way, the two forms of organisation immediately find themselves in a confrontation. Everyone knows the exasperating extent of this conflict, through the fault of clerical authorities and a portion of the Catholic world, especially in recent years. For too long the fury of this battle – allow me to simplify again – has provoked ideological rigidity on both sides and a paralysis in producing ways to study, to adjust, to renew. Fortunately for some time now the debate has become detached from this violence and taken more considered pathways. To the point where in certain areas of the Catholic world, and we could quote important examples, it is not difficult to encounter voices where dialogues and meeting points are possible on the large and urgent problems of fundamentals and principles in children's education.

The educational situation in Italy is enormously complex (school, free time, the press, cinema, radio, television) and it is not unusual for it to present with dramatic urgency. Certainly one of the most important and widely felt problems is that of modernising schools and the traditional means that are used in educational work, searching out and identifying new tools that correspond with today's children. In this work, in this struggle, the *Pionieri* organisation must do all it can to distinguish itself in a definite way. To this end calm and serious preliminary critical and creative examination of modern psychological and pedagogical discoveries and explanations must be made. Useful and good things can perhaps be found in writing and work in the area of active pedagogy, where as we have seen there is a wealth of experience in our country, at least on the level of theory.

The *Pionieri* organisation, and democratic pedagogy in general, not only have the energy to absorb these modern discoveries and techniques, but to offer more specific contents, new input and important contributions (whereas in the Catholic organisation and pedagogy new ferment often becomes weakened and diminished by fatal conservatism and paternalist leanings).

However in order to do this, we must first eliminate fears and ambiguities. Modernising schools and the principles of pedagogy means modernising legislation, instrumental means, the obvious and not so obvious injustices that continue to slow down the entire scaffolding of welfare and education in our country. We propose this important struggle be conducted side by side with all the forces and exponents of concepts of social and progressive democracy. The place of API is in this frame, on this front. API must set out along these lines, knowing from the start that it must take large steps forward if it seriously wants to progress and transform its essence into something concrete, which expresses the aspirations of children and adults who believe in socialism and the renewal of national society.

On these premises, it follows directly that there is a deep need to clarify the ideals of the institution and translate them into substantial facts and revitalised forms of organisation, until it has the concrete shape of unified ideals in a pedagogy of liberation.

In order to bring about what we acknowledge to be an ambitious programme it is vital to eliminate what small degree of factionalism API may still have; struggle against slavish and anachronistic imitations of the formulas and organisational methods that inspire adult democratic forces; not take up ready-made educational models but respect and adhere to socialist ideology and create models based on our best experiences and traditions and the real needs of contemporary Italian children; clarify our relations with Catholic ideology and religious practice; specify relations with schools and other children's organisations, with welfare organisations and various currents of pedagogical thought.

Then API urgently requires directors and officers who have a better understanding of educational affairs, who are capable of enriching organisational virtues with a more attentive and conscious mastery of educational psychology and methods. However it is obvious that first we need to stabilise and consolidate the tasks, structure and official organisation of API. The constant moving around and replacing of Provincial directors and the directors of outlying areas is fatal for API and leads to the continuous impoverishment of experience and energy; API must not be Penelope's web.[42] First we must look at our connections and relations with other young democratic forces. API can only increase its wealth of experience and influence, and achieve its objectives if it can effectively count on the stability of its workers and adequately available resources.

It can easily be understood that API's programme and politics needs to be framed by the programme and politics of Italy's entire democratic movement. The *Pionieri* movement must be directly and indirectly helped to grow in practical ways unless we wish to sentence it to being useless and trivial. Indirectly by becoming more sensitive to democratic opinion and action on issues of childhood. [Directly] by conducting a broad-scale and unified battle to defend several key issues in the national situation. Today this still means defending and improving state schools, the freedom of teaching, economic improvement for teachers, schools that are possible [to attend] and open for all, more value attached to scientific research, a solution to the problem of ex-GIL and *Patronati Scolastici*[43] assets, the re-structuring and unification of welfare organisation etc.

Only in this broad and dynamic perspective is it possible to situate API's problems correctly and find sources for its definition and improvement.

1957

13.57 Leaflet No.1 in a series *Lessons to Parents* produced by the *Scuola per Genitori* [School for Parents][44] at the *Centro Medico Psico-Pedagogico*, March 1957

The profession of parents

[. . .]

Courageous captains in Kipling's[45] work had to sail their vessels on extraordinarily difficult routes, so tortuous and irregular, he said, they would have broken the back of a snake wishing to follow them. Parents do not have an easier task than Kipling's sea wolves, and the routes they must navigate in order to respond quickly and wisely to the needs of children are no less arduous.

We are among those whose opinion is that *educating*[46] is a more complex, difficult task today than in the past.

[. . .]

A more modest contribution to education is made by the school, which while proving extremely slow in updating programmes, lacking in means and filling children's days less and less, is also at the same time increasingly occupied in dealing with the widespread cultural presence of enormously influential technological media like cinema, radio, television and the press.

Since the turn of the century psychology and pedagogy, driven by a more holistic vision of phenomena, have learned to walk together, made admirable advances in their knowledge of children, and can offer their precious resources of discovery and research. This is what we must turn to and use, this is where we must start.

Above all pedagogy and psychology have helped us to react against an education that is too philosophical, too abstract, too authoritarian, idealistic or patronising, now working with the child-as-myth, now with the 'subversive' 'rebel' child only using adult schema,[47] now with a child to be jealously protected, a small, defenceless, absorptive, passive creature. It is universally recognised today that to understand children, they must be studied as an organic-psychic whole, and in relation to their parents. These relations can only be understood in a dialectical perspective of reciprocal, inseparable relations between living things and their environment.

[. . .]

We have said children are a reality with their own laws. A reality, we must immediately add, that presents with a completely different nature to that of adults, walking along roads in no way comparable with those taken by adults.

[. . .]

Children do not have the adult's capacity for inhibition, children do not know limits, the unreality of imaginary games, they do not know how to free themselves of suggestions they create themselves or receive from the outside world. A chair becomes a train or a pirate ship, a dog seen in the street becomes a giant dog as big as a door in a building, and 'Puss-in-Boots' becomes a character children actually hope to meet or are scared to meet in the street.

Children's ways of seizing on things and phenomena, how they place these within their experience and language is infinitely different from adults. Of the entire and magnificent spectacle of the circus they will perhaps only retain the camel dung. Incapable of creating order and synthesis, they store only the details, which they cannot connect up for a long time except through analogy. 'Coal is like a black stone', 'a mountain is like auntie's hat'. Up to the age of five children are convinced the sun, stones and trees are living things; up to the age of six or seven that moving bodies (smoke, fire) are conscious, that Man makes the wind blow, and drives the sun. Their definitions are instrumental in nature, 'a river is made for sailing boats', 'a ball is made for playing'.

They are egocentric on the level of intellect and affect, and act as if they were the centre of the world. Until the age of four *they do not steal* because when taking a playmate's ball they are merely taking something *that is theirs*.

Their morality has no root in principles. What they judge to be beautiful or ugly, good or bad, right or wrong, are the things their closest, most important *models* judge to be so: mothers, fathers, siblings.

Not possessing a notion of time, children do not possess a present or a future to help them temper or put off the urgency of their wishes. Postponement feels like refusal. If they cry when hungry their mother thinks: 'He's hungry, in a little while I'll satisfy him'. However for the little one this postponement means: 'I'm hungry, they are not giving me anything to eat'. Their reactions are proportionate to this way of thinking.

When they speak, they do not give words the same meanings as adults, and up to the age of school what an adult considers to be conversation is nothing but monologue without too much concern for being understood, much less for appropriating other people's thoughts. This is why many of the 'whys' that are so disquieting and embarrassing for parents are really monologues with no end in themselves, completely undemanding, imitative speech rather than questions they expect to be answered.

These examples can help us understand what has already been said: children's whole life has its own specific dynamics and phenomena, in no way related to that of adults. This more than justifies the appropriateness of speaking about early years psycho-pedagogy.

To know children is to appreciate them, and become more aware of our educational responsibility. However before this it is right to sweep away once and for all the foolish belief that we must wait for a certain age in order to begin children's education – 'they don't understand before that anyway'. Children's character and the personality of the child are constructed from birth, from the first days of life.

[. . .]

Children's evolution is made of progressions, irregularities, conflicts and crises. It is strewn with choices, abandonments, and constant adaptations.

Henri Wallon,[48] one of our most eminent living scholars, writes: 'the Child's realisation of the Adult he will become does not follow a journey without deviations, forks, and roundabout ways. How many occasions will force him to choose between effort and giving up? These arise in the environment, the environment of persons and of things. The mother, relatives, customary and unusual encounters, school, are so many contacts, they are all relations, institutions through which he must become part of society, voluntarily or by force. Language interposes an obstacle or a tool between him and his desires, between him and people, which he may be tempted to circumvent or to dominate. Objects, those closest to him, which have a shape; his bowl, his spoon, his potty, his clothes, electricity, the radio, the most ancient technologies and the most recent, are for him an annoyance, a problem or an aid, they repel him or attract him and shape his activities.'

From the first hours of life children – who unlike Minerva do not enter life armed already – engage in their battles. They are a nervous system developing, a sensibility awakening, an intelligence expanding.

At two months old they smile. This smile is conditioned by a choice and is dedicated to the mother's breast. This first act of intelligence is permeated with affect, emotion guides the choice and stimulates the movement.

In early psychological manifestations emotion, intelligence and movement are in close symbiosis.

However this does not happen, and will not happen later, on the moon. Physical and social environments, mothers, fathers, relationships established, how they are formed and then consolidated, all play a decisive role.

Children *always* face their struggles and conduct them together with adults, but how do these adults help, support, and guide them?

Children's natural tendency to be loved is reinforced because being loved becomes mixed with being nourished and living. Hence the extreme importance of early sensory deprivations. These not only damage the child on a physical level, but on a psychological level, and above all on affective levels.

So as time goes by the responsibilities of parents do not diminish one inch, and their irreplaceable role will always be that of accompanying their children's growth, actively entering into the increasingly intense, wide-ranging and conscious dialogue children compose in the process of differentiation that awaits, another decisively important period.

[. . .]

Parents must understand autonomy cannot be achieved without opposing those who up to now have exercised protection and hegemony.

This crisis is necessary. If it is too weak − Wallon warns − it brings soft compliance and dulled feelings of responsibility, if it is too strong it brings demoralised indifference or a taste for disguised revenge, if it is too easy it brings an arrogance, which completely eliminates its usefulness, submerging other people's existence rather than highlighting it, and can become a possible source of further conflict in which children risk being much more humiliated.

Then children − having finally *revealed themselves* − begin to join *others*, and imitation is the means that satisfies them. They model themselves on people close to them and for whom they feel a powerful attraction. However imitation at this age is as much the desire to replace as loving admiration. Parents must make themselves into *accessible, replicable* models, seriously encourage their children's efforts and their need for identification, at the same time as making the weight of their superiority and guidance felt. At the same time children's socialisation acquires new meaning as they progress unceasingly through their apprenticeship with the external world, wishing to enter into other people's thoughts, collaborate with them, and play *together*. Thus children arrive at the time for school, and another huge leap takes them into a completely original world, new and unknown, with different levels, different habits and demands.

For too long *freedom* and *authority* have been contrasted as two opposite concepts on a philosophical level, two ways of thinking and applying education. Instead *freedom* and *authority* are two needs, two complementary necessities in children. They are led to exercise their freedom within the limits of certain rules and they expect these from adults like a parapet built for their safety. We only need to reflect how children organise games and activities. They make rules and laws for themselves, modify them, update them, and in the end respect them with absolute rigour.

The reader will realise that we have implicitly destroyed another still too widespread fallacy with these arguments, that character and personality are hereditary, 'He was born that way, there's nothing to be done about it' we sometimes hear. Nothing could be more false or illogical. Nothing is acquired in a hereditary way that cannot be corrected, changed or reversed. Character is not received, it is acquired, built day after day, and the overall conduct we express is the dynamic *sum* of infinite additions, and only one of these, merely one, consists of hereditary predispositions. Obviously this formulation gives infinite scope to the possibilities of education, the resources of pedagogy, and the tasks and responsibilities of adults and the social community.

Children's character, their merits, their present and future defects, their intelligence, the way they tackle problems and tend to resolve them, their introduction and concrete integration with the life of the community, the happiness of their living, the wealth of energy and values they are capable of outpouring in the course of their life; all this largely depends on their experience of early childhood, how they lived it, how their parents responded to their needs.

It is a terrible, marvellous and fascinating responsibility.

We say we love children. For our love to be effectively worthy of the task, expressed in activity that is capable of and effects the results we hope for, first we must *know* who we love, be clear and aware in ourselves about the journeys they make to become adults and citizens, and the collaboration they expect from us.

In this sense educating means perfecting our knowledge, our conduct, and our feelings.

1958

14.58 Leaflet No.7 in a series *Lessons to Parents* produced by the *Scuola per Genitori* [School for Parents] at the *Centro Medico Psico-Pedagogico*, January 1958

The child who sucks his thumb or bites his nails

[. . .]

In small children – at the age psychologists call *oral* – sucking accompanies the absorbtion of milk and is not only a source of life but an infinitely pleasurable thing. This pleasure is a gratification with great emotional value.

[. . .]

Other changes come with time and very probably if children are not able to accept them, they will react by trying to recreate the pleasure of early childhood. This mechanism of regression, of returning, of taking refuge in the infant situation and the advantages that derive from it, will be triggered often, each time affective frustration undermines the rhythm of daily life and the child's growth.

[. . .]

Sucking the thumb is neither a bad habit nor an illness; it is almost always a symptom, an external visible manifestation, of a situation of disquiet, unease, and a child's interior maladjustment.

[. . .]

Because children who suck their thumb – like snails retreating into the shell – are children who interrupt contact with the outside [world], with reality, who withdraw into themselves, almost as if falling into a torpor or a completely internalised, secretive soliloquy. They need to be prevented from doing this. One way is by ensuring they are not left alone. Solitude is a dangerous incentive. We must take care they are in the company of other children as much as possible. When two or three children get together we can be certain they will not have idle hands, and the playful society they form will prevent each individual child from isolation and inactivity.

[. . .]

Onychophagia [nail biting], like thumb-sucking, is not an illness; rather it is a symptom of specific anomalies or disturbances in character and behaviour. Onycophagia is sometimes considered to be a symptom revealing nervous illness, moral perversion, or 'deviant' practices.

[. . .]

Certainly nail biting is an alarm bell, which draws our attention to a situation in which a child is ill at ease or suffering.

[. . .]

According to Bovet, after the age of twenty, only 2 individuals in 100 bite their nails. However these figures refer to a survey conducted in Switzerland. From our experience in Italy we calculate the phenomenon – for specific reasons of life and customs – to have a 4–6 per cent higher incidence.

❋ ❋ ❋

15.58 Article in *L'Indicatore*, a bi-monthly journal about literature and other cultural issues, No. 16, EDA, Milan, February/March 1958

A refined bouquiniste[49] in the Italian provinces: the Prandi Bookshop which cultivates precious antiquarian works and original and foreign engravings beside modern books

We do not yet have a history of the Italian *provinces* that understands the essence of their humanity and culture, their ferment, contributions, and battles. Surprising facts and issues would come of it.

What is this *Libreria Prandi* [Prandi Bookshop] for example, eliminating stagnant Italian taste and print collecting in a typical provincial city like Reggio Emilia, renewing a love of art and a market that only seemed to have survived in Paris and London after the romantic and splendid *bouqinistes* along Daumier's[50] Seine? Why does this true struggle in the arts – applauded enthusiastically by critics and artists – come from the provinces?

Such courage and such intelligence must have been born long ago, say from the tradition, and the passionate work of many years in the world of books, culture, and art. [. . .]

In fact the *Libreria Prandi's* noble, generous and liberal character is an old badge that is well known in Reggio Emilia and elsewhere. During the years of dictatorship – insulting for culture and thinking – it continued to be a circle for non-conformism and education, a meeting place for free spirits. Eugenio Curiel, Ernesto Rossi, Riccardo Bauer, confined to Ventotene;[51] and Croce, Einaudi, Bonomi and Tilger elsewhere – to quote only a few names – could write to Nino Prandi and son Dino, certain of finding rare works for consultation, and the most underground texts, together with generous fraternity.

[. . .]

For over thirty years people have entered the shop in Via Cavallotti certain of finding what is most enticing to their taste in culture. Today there is only the slight figure of Nino Prandi, always smaller, his hair always whiter, an agile squirrel among stacks of books and the only one with a key to their order. If there is time we can get Nino Prandi to speak. It does not take much trying, and then, among other things, alongside memories of '*belle*' and '*mauvais époque*', we will discover the scope of his restlessness and dreams, the reasons for his success, and very adolescent dynamism. And we will also have added a lovely book that was certainly missing from our library.[52]

※ ※ ※

16.58 Leaflet No.10 in a series *Lessons to Parents* produced by the *Scuola per Genitori* [School for Parents] at the *Centro Medico Psico-Pedagogico*, July 1958

Experiences of a School for Parents

[. . .]

The costs of organising the Lessons for Parents and Educators course were covered by the *Comune* of Reggio Emilia. The programme included seventeen lessons held twice weekly. However this became eighteen lessons after the need was recognised for two lessons on the subject of 'Children, Cinema, Radio and Television'.

[. . .]

Our initial mistake was complying with requests and accepting a formula of *tête-à-tête* that detracted from public discussion. Instead, unless topics are particularly personal, they should be collected together and debated in public. This system not only contributes to richer debate and sharing experience, it allows a section of the public to cut free from the constraint of an unjustified nervousness and passivity.

Participants only attained the necessary group spirit for the Course to achieve a level of confident efficiency after three or four lessons and discussions. The comments of participants acquired more order and concreteness, respecting and focusing on the subject in question, and connecting and integrating new activities with previous ones in more appropriate ways.

Further gains were noted mid-course, and again it was the way people participated in discussions that was evidence of this, with a higher level of selective and relevant autonomous elaboration. Certain elements of discussion were a clear clue, attesting to some participants acquiring the capacity for using their course experience as a perspective and [to create] working hypotheses.

Others have probably found, as we did, that an element of unease can be sensed in listeners at a certain point, puzzlement that arises from a specific way of addressing these topics, which cannot be separated from what are for them the psycho-pathological nature of processes and explanations, so that mistaken or distorted interpretations, misunderstandings on the borders between 'normality' and 'abnormality' may arise.

The deep-rooted habit of explaining children's attitudes and displays as 'bad habits' or 'vices', or of using reasons that are moralistic, inadequate, outdated and unfamiliar with treating pedagogical problems in the light of dynamic psychology, depth psychology [the unconscious], and paediatric neuro-psychiatry (primary and secondary school teachers) make this phenomenon more frequent.

Therefore we need to take great care: it is a phenomenon that is very difficult to avoid completely, but with skill it can be considerably lessened, and turned into a positive element, which instead helps to upturn old and mistaken positions of interpretation precisely through making use of these *traumatising* conditions.

Aside from pointing out mistakes in children's education [in the family] and explaining means of avoiding and repairing them, we felt a particular need to emphasise the real origins of parental behaviour, their character, their personality, how they reflect the whole of societal life. Though this was done continuously we realised this aspect of the issue needed to be examined and dealt with in a special way for the public to gain as concrete a knowledge as possible of educational processes [in the family].

More expert teachers at the *L'Ecole des Parents* in Paris have warned of this danger and recognised the usefulness of dedicating an entire course of lessons to studying Parent Psychology.

[. . .]

The course aims justified a discussion of the *Consultorio* [*Centro Medico Psico-Pedagogico Comunale*], which gave us opportunities for a discussion of real situations with highly effective examples, and also contributed to making the *Consultorio* better known. In fact we realised teaching is more fruitful when we start with a particular case study rather than general ideas and premises, so that an entire situation can be examined, and a series of practical conclusions deduced immediately and easily, thus stimulating personal efforts of research and understanding.

As we have said our second experience [of running the course] was in Fabbrico, a *comune* of 5,000 inhabitants, thirty kilometres out in Reggio Emilia's 'low lands' [the plains of the Po Valley], and considerably cut off from the city by its geographical location. It has a poor cultural life, is equipped only with primary schools, has a population of peasant and artisan origin, part of which is now employed in industry due to the growing importance of a tractor factory.

The municipal library took care of organisation, and lessons were held in a room in the Town Hall. The course was reduced to seven lessons: Knowing the Needs of the Child; The Left-Handed Child; The Child with [nervous] Tics; The Shy and Frightened Child; The Liar Child; The Irritable and Disobedient Child; Children and Cinema; Methods and Objectives of the *Consultorio*. We took care to focus as much as possible on the most obvious and common problems of family [education].

Enrolment in the course was not a condition. To cover the expenses a Promoting Committee – the Mayor was President – decided on a fee for participating of 50 *lire* per person per lesson.

This small *charge* did not hinder the success of the initiative in any way. There were twenty-four people attended the opening lecture. In the second lesson this number rose to fifty-four. The number of people present became stable at an average of forty-five, and the types of person [participating] also became more stable.

For our part we were concerned with simplifying explanations, increasing concreteness with easy examples, giving the widest possible opportunity for discussion and encouraging this by every means. The composition of the public was as follows: office workers 9 per cent; workers 24 per cent; farmers 15 per cent; housewives 35 per cent; primary school teachers 14 per cent; preschool teachers 3 per cent. The number of women greatly outweighed the number of men: 77 per cent.

Conclusions

From the sum of these experiences we can draw some significant conclusions. We wish to mention the following:

- Courses of Lessons for Parents and Educators of the kind we have set up meet with an extremely favourable reception in this country and correspond to genuinely and widely felt needs, not only in parents but in professional educators.
- Widespread general lack of knowledge of psychology and pedagogy, with roots in children's psychological and historical reality, has frequently been a positive element contributing to the success of the initiative, rather than being an obstacle.

1959

17.59 Speech at a meeting of the Federal Committee of the provincial Communist Party, taken from the minutes, October 1959

Editor's note: Although speaking to a meeting of the PCI, Malaguzzi frequently refers to the co-operative movement. Both were strong in the region and Malaguzzi supported both. Although the PCI initially paid little attention to the co-operative movement, dismissing it as 'reformist', in 1947 it took over the leadership of the League of Co-operatives, at a meeting held in Reggio Emilia. By the early 1960s, 'the cooperatives represented one of the pillars of Communist power in Emilia-Romagna' (Ginsborg, 1990, p.202).

[. . .]

Compagni [Comrades], this is the first time I have participated in a Federal Committee meeting, and my first experience of such a high level in our Federation. Allow me first to say a few words on the issue of methods. To my mind the issue, the subject at the centre of our attention, is a topic of enormous importance and if the report [presented earlier] had been written and distributed to all of us in good time, in all probability our contributions would have been more exhaustive and precise.

[. . .]

My talk will focus on one issue, an issue arising from a point easily made, because it appears that in the group of comrades who worked on the report there is no representative of the Cultural Commission. Now it is evident that certain of the report's defects on this level are largely an inevitable result of this kind of omission, so that the report by Comrade Catelli, a report which to my mind is profound and courageous, and undoubtedly raises a series of issues, perspectives and criticisms, is again excessively given over to administrative problems, and instead leaves aside the cultural issues and other issues, which in my opinion are necessary to complete a general, integral vision of the problem.

An old vice in our local politics and perhaps in regional politics is not recognising, or struggling to understand, that every act of our political life is a sign of culture. As I was saying, it is an old vice in our Federation, because it is one we have commented on several times, and which not only narrows comrades' discussion of certain aspects of the problems being considered, but distorts the objective reality of political phenomena we have before us. It seems right to raise the issue here for a number of reasons, not only because true political examination can only be called this if we are able to address all the problems in a given reality, excluding none. Not only for this reason then, but because one of the distinctive features of the co-operative movement on a practical level, compared to private business, is its social relations, which are instrumental and purposeful. The point I am making about Catelli's report is exactly this: in its political analysis it has not grasped the cultural issues and social issues that are intrinsic to all our political acts, and typical of the co-operative movement.

The needs of political struggle today and always, I would say, suggest to us, and demand of us, that we broaden the area where our perspectives meet. So that each one of our acts, each one of the co-operative movement's acts, must strive to embrace every instance of social renewal, and give them substance through work and objectives that contest and bring advance in the negative, conservative and reactionary aspects of society, whether these are economic, technical, artistic, cultural or social.

[. . .]

I think the reasons for our lack of success can be found in a large and decisive issue that we need to acknowledge – the difficult problem of giving substance to our fundamental political principles and ideals in our everyday practice. To my mind this is the real heart of the problem, it is certainly a real truth, and extremely difficult, to give concrete substance to political activities, based on the ideas and themes that regulate our work today.

[. . .]

It means the capacity of our co-operative members to keep abreast of the evolution of technology, keep up with the tools of knowledge and judgement, participate in all the struggles being carried out around them. The issues of schools, of teddy boys,[53] of scientific discoveries, of educational summer camps [colonie] are not, and cannot be, issues outside the political sensibility of our co-operative movement, or of our co-operative members as individuals, as comrades.

I would like to say it is important at this time that our co-operative member – as well as [knowing about] the play of market prices, and the struggles accompanying his company's life – should also know that Rossellini and Eduardo [De Filippo][54] wrote a courageous letter some days ago to bring the scandal of cinema and theatre in our country to an end. And that while the Soviets are realising their marvellous ventures, scientists in Italy are agitating and striking, disheartened by the shameful conditions in which our governing class holds scientific activity. Then in this sense our co-operative members become truly complete figures, and we no longer commit the error, an error which has been underlined several times during this meeting, of tending to give members a dual definition: members are defined as technicians, members are defined as politicians.

[. . .]

And here we have an explanation of why both the report and comments by comrades do not sufficiently highlight the perspective of the co-operative movement in relation to young people, the turnover of young people, the turnover of positions of responsibility.

[. . .]

When we posed the issue of democracy in the Party we weren't only posing a request to be able to speak. We were not requesting the possibility of intervening, of discussing, of polemic. That is not what we were asking for. Instead, what we were asking for was to be able to speak and discuss with awareness, based on precise, concrete information and on our own critical capacity that becomes deeper because it is based on awareness. That is why today, when we continue to want to defend the concept of democracy and would like this concept to become part of our reports and of relations with comrades, democracy, first and foremost, should have this meaning. It is here that the need arises to extend the area of democracy in our Party, bearing in mind that extending the area of democracy means extending areas of awareness on specific fundamental issues that are particular to the Party.

This is what we mean by democracy. If this concept of democracy can become habitual for us, manage to penetrate into the life of the co-operative movement, then you can be certain a whole quantity of problems, an excessive business mentality, the lack of cultural sensibility, the inability to be coherent with and follow the facts unfolding before our eyes, are all problems which are destined to disappear if the issue of effective democracy enters our co-operative movement.

I would like to go deeper into this issue and touch on one point. The issue of our children's social education is an issue of great importance. I know Co-operative Day was celebrated in the *Colonia* [summer camp] this year. But what did this day of education consist of? Simply a kind of game. Certainly it was capable of moving the children to laughter, of appealing to children's expectations and interests, but that does not make them take one step forward. You took the children in the morning and told them, 'look today is your day, the whole Camp is in your hands, do what you want with it'. Which naturally already contained a large dose of falsehood, because you can never hand the summer camp over to children of ten or eleven years old. That was the first falsehood acted out that morning: 'you will take the pans, you'll heat them on the fire, you'll heat the milk and give it out to the children and you will do all the tasks adult staff usually carry out'.

Now I mean, how did the children accept this? Something fun, something theatrical, like a play – that's all very well – but without understanding the real value there, at least in the intentions of the people trying to organise the day this way. I would like to tell you about a different experience I had in Canazei [in the Dolomite mountains]. I witnessed and had a very significant experience with children in Canazei, and it seems to me that if it were possible to translate it into a situation of social activity like yours (I am speaking about the summer camps) it would undoubtedly contribute to truly maturing the children, and plant a first seed in the journey we need to make.

[. . .]

Is it possible we can never manage to talk of this in a clear and concrete manner, to say bread is bread and wine is wine, and try to get to the bottom of this issue? Otherwise everything is problematic, if we abandon this discussion on fundamental themes and ideals. But we cannot lose ground here in our city, where we have a mandate to work and operate.

1960

18.60 From a programme for a Bertolt Brecht evening organised by the *Teatro Club* at the *Teatro Municipale* and directed by Loris Malaguzzi, Reggio Emilia, June 1960

Editor's note: The *Teatro Club* was established in Reggio Emilia in 1958, with a provisional committee including Loris Malaguzzi. The aims of the Club included 'the diffusion and updating of theatre culture through reading texts of particular importance and current interest, conferences, debates, listening to recordings, meetings with directors, actors, authors and critics, and through every other initiative for stimulating interest in the art of the theatre'. Bertolt Brecht (1898–1956) was a German Marxist poet, playwright and theatre director. He fled the Nazi regime in 1933, living in the USA from 1939 to 1947, when he returned to Europe, eventually moving back to Berlin, where he established the world-famous *Berliner Ensemble* theatre group in 1949.

The evening dedicated to Brecht's work, the programme for which is given below, was directed by Malaguzzi.

TEATRO CLUB
REGGIO EMILIA

FOYER OF THE *TEATRO MUNICIPALE*

TUESDAY 14. WEDNESDAY 15 JUNE 1960 – 21.00 HOURS PRECISE

'I Bertolt Brecht'
EVENING DEDICATED TO B. BRECHT

For the end of the 1959–1960 Cultural Season

An Evening of Bertolt Brecht

Making true an old promise made to itself and to members, the Reggio Emilia *Teatro Club* presents an 'EVENING OF BERTOLT BRECHT' for the conclusion of its second successful year of activity.

Getting closer to the great German playwright, poet and novelist, who theorised a new and original aesthetic of commitment, with a precise artistic and social purpose, is an act and cultural choice of great interest and vivid contemporary relevance. Aware of this, the *Teatro Club* has set about the difficult, extremely demanding venture of offering, in the space of a few hours, a taste – the most representative possible – of the copious and complex artistic creation of B. BRECHT.

The evening's programme has therefore been devised as a selection of several pieces, each one offering an idea, the most typical and representative, of brechtian art.

The evening is divided into two parts. The introduction is in the form of a prologue, leading us to a knowledge of BRECHT the man and artist, and the fundamental principles of his aesthetic.

A reading of one of his most famous didactical dramas follows, 'The Exception and the Rule (*Die Ausnahme und die Regel*)'. This currently appears on the programme of the *Piccolo Teatro* of Milan, and was written shortly before the advent of Hitlerism and Brecht's exile. The rigorous debate of his argument documents an important and decisive period in BRECHT'S[55] ideological and artistic evolution.

The second part of the evening leads us to a knowledge of BRECHT the poet, essay writer and a writer of songs and ballads, which have become highly popular with the music of Kurt Weill, Hans Eisler and Paul Hindemith. There will be a performance of songs with music by K. Weill.

❋ ❋ ❋

19.60 Speech at a meeting of the Federal Committee of the provincial Communist Party, minuted in the form of notes, June 1960

Party activity in preparation for the Electoral Campaign

Salati (speaker preceding Malaguzzi)

Comrades, I believe no one will smile if I state that the administrative [local] elections are of exceptional importance. In fact they take place on a world stage where the part played by Italy goes way beyond the size and dimension of the nation, especially in relation to the political situation in capitalist Europe.

[. . .]

It is sufficient to think of Germany, France, and England itself, where the Labour movement is receiving bad setbacks for its mistakes.

[. . .]

Loris Malaguzzi

Politicise the campaign (peace – region – progress – liberty – socialism) – in agreement with [Nilde] Iotti.[56] Emphasise the local reality, the reality of fundamental themes – the drive, the aspirations, the thirst for progress, for greater comfort.

[. . .]

Lack of schools – professional [technical] schools subordinate – school reform.

Taxes on livestock – monopolies, price of fertilisers – autonomy of the Regions, sports fields – Olympics and general facilities for youth – lack of *asili* [nurseries] – women's emancipation.

The clericalisation of public life. The crisis in art, culture, and sciences and the heavy price the country continues to pay for the government, and the success of capitalist restoration since 1947 with the full agreement between Catholic hierarchies and *big capital*.

1   Italy lagging behind with scientific research.
2   The backwardness of school structures.
3   Obscurantism[57] towards the masses (TV – radio – press).
4   Intolerant and coercive intervention with groups of intellectuals (cinema).
5   The re-launch of Sanfedista,[58] the anathema (the bishops' letter against secularism).
6   The lower quality of life for large numbers of men and youths, influenced by the protection of local interests, by reactionary church-loving, instrumental visions of life, and humiliating compromise.

We must explain how these things empty culture of its inherent work, keep citizens in a degrading condition of lack of culture – tend to neutralise the power of intellect by forcing it into a purely technical role. It is certainly one of the primary causes of disorientation among youth and large parts of the citizenry. The clash between the aspiration for a modern, more advanced life, and Italy's economic and cultural backwardness.

School is separate from life – the protest of young people is directed at individualistic positions of inaction. Youth testifies to the failure of ideas and morals in the governing class. Reconstruction on new, modern, rational, secular foundations.

1961

20.61 Article in a 'Programme of Theatre Activity, Autumn 1961, City of Reggio Emilia, *Teatro Municipale*', Autumn 1961

New Choices for Developing Theatre (by Dr Franco Boiardi, Assessore for Public Instruction)

The *Comune* and cultural organisations of Reggio Emilia – with a commitment not found in many other larger and more important cities – have presented an almost incredible programme of works in recent years, filled the gap in academic institutions, study centres, journals and magazines, and extended their influence to ever more layers of society.

[. . .]

The Maria Melato Festival [see Chapter 1, n.21] with the *Comune*'s support [is] based on the generosity and voluntary work of Italian amateur theatre – which is sometimes almost moving.

Over the years dozens and dozens of plays, the main works of contemporary European theatre, and the highest points of ancient drama have been shown, with the limits that accompany non-professional work, but alive with a sense of love and respect for the dramatic arts and the public.

Meticulous work for organising the public in country areas, and from factories, and a policy of accessible prices, has meant that social classes who traditionally have had no connection with theatre have been drawn in.

The MMF has undeniably made a large contribution to raising the city's cultural tone, through patient and assiduous work. [. . .] Communal management has imposed new criteria: private gain has disappeared, and funds are distributed for good singers, good orchestras, directors etc. [. . .]

These criteria have also been applied to choices of programme. [. . .] This year there are ten plays by major Italian companies, six plays by amateur companies; concerts organised together with the *Famiglia Artistica Reggiana* including [performances by] Milstein, Angelicum, Gulda, Weisemburg etc.; seven operas by Prokofiev, Verdi, and Puccini; the Budapest Ballet and a Modern Jazz Quartet jazz evening. And perhaps a final concert of Schoenberg – something contemporary.

[. . .]

We would be happy – and consider our work more useful for everyone – if other cities joined us so to share programmes and artistic and educational goals. We could do more and better, and for more people. We could offer companies more venues, so encouraging them to try out new, living works, responding to the doubts and spiritual needs of our society. A theatre of problems and not of evasion, a theatre that is an expression of this cultural civilisation and not only past civilisations, a social theatre of debate between spectators and actors, a social theatre of the majority not of an elite, this is the inalienable objective we want to realise through our efforts, which are certainly not small.

Theatre Year Zero? In Reggio Emilia Year One! (by Loris Malaguzzi)

For years there has been talk, discussion, accusations, defence, rhetoric, wailing and sophistry. Theatre is in bed with some limbs already paralysed and others with gangrene. In Rome, where the great surgeons reputedly live, they continue to beat around the bush. Legislation on theatres. Who has seen it? Rather than passing laws millions [of *lire*] are changing hands, so that small and large and secret political cliques, faking sorrow for their *great patient*, can continue the fiction of counting on rosaries of gold.

Amidst the din of real and false 'cries of pain' a book with the title 'Theatre Year Zero', is making modest progress. It was written by Zardi and Bergonzini, a playwright from the younger generation together with a university teacher of statistics. There are figures and documents that would make you shiver. In brief, if we take the number of theatre-goers as the base of our phenomenon and give the number in 1938 an index of 100, we drop down to 91 in 1952, and to 43 in

1959. This is the point we have reached today: the number of citizens excluded from prose theatre in Naples is 97 per cent of the population; 95 per cent in Turin, Bologna and Genoa; 87 per cent in Milan; and 80 per cent in Florence.

The politics of theatre in our *Comune* has created a space in this dramatic context since the *Comune*, with courageous civic sense and an awareness of ideals, became the manager of all things theatre. Our friend Franco Boiardi, *Assessore* for Education, has spoken in another part of this publication, and we cannot see what can be added.

[. . .]

The fact is, we are absolutely convinced that of a hundred Italian cities, our Reggio Emilia constitutes a rare phenomenon, with its intense, lively and varied theatre calendar. Momentous miracles cannot take the credit here.

There are two secrets, plus [the secret everyone knows], Pulcinella's.[59] First our *Comune* has resolutely followed an approach that starts with a full aware-ness that theatre is a high, irreplaceable cultural activity, which should be held in great esteem and treated as a public and social affair of primary importance. Second, for years theatrical life in the city has been organised in a series of initiatives that make it possible to always keep alive an interest in stage events on several different levels. This dynamic has directly and indirectly stimulated the formation of an enthusiastic public, and at the same time the creation of cultural and administrative workers with the ability to give concrete expression to a well-considered politics of theatre.

We do not need to be reminded of the role of the 'M. Melato' annual national amateur dramatic festival for the theatre, or of the *Teatro Club* with its choice of non-conformist and culturally avant-garde shows. We do not need to emphasise the value of their role and perspective in relation to intense theatre programmes.

[. . .]

Without this premise it is not possible to fully understand the meaning of the drama arts festival which is about to start, or the aims it is entrusted with. It immediately appears clear the festival is not only, and cannot be, an academy (in the most positive sense of the word) for the best of Italian [theatre] groups. It does not stand alone; it is part of a general dynamic in a broader politics of theatre in the city (we have already said this).

So choosing groups and texts obviously takes on great importance, just as the issue of finding and organising a public is of decisive importance. The groups are the best of our blossoming national amateur theatre, the works they present are committed works on living current affairs, in a frame of serious and continuous cultural and critical discourse. They help to advance and refine the festival public's knowledge and taste, initiating people to a more continuous interest in theatre, and to being in reality a mostly new and receptive public.

The declared objective, not only of the Maria Melato Festival but for the entire multi-faceted activity that centres on the theatre, is to seek out and form a new public. There is no need to be reminded that this is the problem of all problems.

This brings us to performance prices. [Theatre] prices have been set lower or the same as the price of a ticket for a film at the cinema. Looking for a new public necessarily means considering the price of a theatre performance.

Before the curtain even rises on the first play, these prices mean we can organise season tickets for a large public travelling in from the whole province on special coaches laid on by the organising committee for this season's theatre.

We have before us an interesting and original experiment. Noble and audacious. We already know the social composition of most of this public, which allows us to fill three-quarters of the *Teatro Municipale* with season ticket holders. They are people coming to the emotion of the stage for the first time. People who would never have known the theatre if they had not been offered an opportunity devised this way. They are students, young people, entire families from the *ceto medio* [middling classes] with a longing for theatre, who can only satisfy this longing because the theatre meets them half-way with a very small charge.

The eleventh Maria Melato Festival programme opens with a work by Pirandello, '*Come Prima Meglio di Prima*', in homage to the great author on the twenty-fifth anniversary of his death [. . .].[60]

We will see [Arthur] Miller's 'A View from the Bridge', which was highly successful all over Italy when it was directed by Visconti [. . .]. The courage and maturity of a group of amateurs offers us the opportunity of knowing a work by Miller that otherwise we may never have seen again.

Another privilege amateur theatre offers us is seeing [John] Osborne's 'Look Back in Anger' again, a play which became famous when it travelled round Italy three years ago, causing surprise and controversy everywhere. The play is an expression of the young playwright's position of rebellion and moral anti-conformism.

Another thoughtful choice is one of Marco Praga's loveliest works, 'The Virgins', which will amaze everyone (as it amazed those of us who admired it during the Pesaro festival) with its surprising and wonderful freshness. At the latest Pescara festival, The *Piccolo Teatro* of Turin triumphed with this piece.

We would wait in vain for Garcia Lorca's theatre to be shown by a professional group, tied up in a theatre industry which hardly ever allows cultural choices. Yet our programme includes 'The House of Bernard Alba', one of the great Spanish poet's most difficult and conceptual works.

The festival has another admirable and courageous task. That of *launching* the new young author, Genoese journalist Martini, with 'Angela and the Devil'.

These performances will be accompanied by another two highly original evenings, offered by the FAR [see Chapter 1, n.26] and the *Teatro Club*. These two lively city associations will both put on performances of equal but different

value. The FAR [will present] a concert by teachers and students of the Music
Lycee, and the *Teatro Club 'Come siam bravi quaggiù'*, a cabaret show with an
approach and intentions echoing the post-war experience of *Teatro dei Gobbi*
but presented in a more concrete way. It is a theatre of allusion, of rapid aggression, penetrating parody, satire both subtle and heavy, pressing and whipping
the world of our times. These two shows will enable the public to extend its
artistic emotions. And once again this has not happened by chance, but is part
of a planned framework, [created] in a reality and in a discourse illustrated and
explained at the beginning of this article.

1963

21.63 Speech at a symposium on the 'Relations between Psychiatry, Psychology and Pedagogy', Reggio Emilia, March 1963

**The pupil, the class and the teacher in an educational
dynamic, in the experiences of psycho-pedagogy**

[. . .]

1) This is certainly not the place to attempt a complete answer to the question *what is education?* However, what is certain is that only by removing our
answer from an old, abstract philosophy and starting with the conviction that
education is a fact of society (that school is only one factor in education), and
by moving in the direction of historical investigation, will we be able to understand the meaning and value of education, its definition and mutations.

The French philosopher Durkheim[61] had clear feelings on this issue:

> Every society, considered in a particular phase of its development, has a
> system of education which it imposes on individuals, usually with irresist-
> ible force. It is conceited to believe we can educate children as we want.
> When the way in which educational systems are formed and developed
> is studied historically, it can be seen that they depend on religion, on the
> organisation of politics, the degree to which sciences have evolved, on the
> state of industry etc. If we detach them from all these historical causes they
> become incomprehensible. And then why should an individual expect to
> reconstruct using only the powers of private reflection something which is
> not the work of individual thinking? He does not have before him a *tabula
> rasa* on which he can build up what he likes, but existing realities which
> he can neither create, destroy nor transform as he chooses. He can act
> on them to the degree that he learns to know them, to know what their
> nature is and the conditions they depend on; and he cannot come to know
> these unless he studies them and starts to observe them and interpret them
> like a physicist with matter and the biologist with living things.[62]

By accepting this method, we will inevitably also come to see the composite nature of education, where evolution takes place through the conditioning forces of different elements, sometimes intentional, sometimes deriving from the direct or indirect influence of cultural, economic and social conditions and movements, in the various ages of history.

So today when we speak of 'new education' or 'active education' we wish to refer concretely to a definition given to a certain pedagogy of our times, which is part of a specific complex of values. These values are different to the opposing values of a previous period of pedagogy (values that continue to be discussed and that are open to change and evaluation today), and are inscribed in a historical (or ideological) context that begins approximately at the start of the last [nineteenth] century, at least as far as the affirmation of these values is concerned.

And when we speak of 'new education' and 'active education' we will certainly not forget what sixty years of pedagogical progress has meant, we will bear in mind the different or convergent directions, the current disputes over philosophical, historical, methodological and educational values.

However if we accept the system of fundamental values in *new education*, which for the sake of argument can be summarised as a greater awareness of educational reality based on more rational, systematic and scientific knowledge of children, what is important to underline here is the contribution psychology has made to the evolution and affirmation of this phenomenon, and the contribution general medical science, neuro-psychiatry and sociology have made in more recent times. This point can be borne out with names and facts: from Dewey[63] whose 'laboratory' underlines the need to look at educational solutions in the spirit of research, to the experiences of Gesell, Itard, Seguin, Montessori, Claparède, Wallon, Piaget, Gemelli, and the discoveries made by schools of psychoanalysis, sociology and Gestalt, in particular by Lewin.

2) Certainly the development that interests us most is how modern education, finally freed of last century's philosophical abstractions and understood as a broader issue, can today be seen as a philosophy where the contributions of other sciences, considered outside the field until recently, come together in theoretical and practical ways, in a cultural, scientific and democratic affair. We believe this extension of pedagogy based on a new concept of the sciences is not by chance, and also coincides with the social expansion of education services to involve vast new masses of individuals for the first time in Italy's history.

More recently the close relationship between school and society has been confirmed in growing public awareness of *education as a factor in the development of society itself*. As a result, sociological and statistical studies (which go to the heart of educational debate for the first time in our country) now aim at planning school organisation and orientations in order to respond to productive, cultural and civic needs in the community. It is not exact to say that pedagogy is only science, it continually re-formulates the 'philosophical' values which are present in 'life'. However there can be no doubt that its growing propensity for a scientific spirit, for research and experiment, and the fact that today it no longer only addresses privileged minorities but tends to satisfy the need for culture of ever larger masses, reveals new concepts that are increasingly destined to use the contributions of different sciences and teams of specialists.

3) Turning to psychology and the history of its contribution we must recognise an important fact: psychology was only capable of informing pedagogy after leaving behind the psychology of the laboratories of Helmotz, Weber, Fechner and Wundt[64] (which Claparède[65] called 'a sort of physiological anatomy of the spirit'), and beginning to deal with human beings in their becoming, both the subjects and creators of their evolution, as well as with their functional unity and integrity. The date of psychology's conversion is the date of pedagogy's conversion, the birth of new education. This coincidence is significant, in fact from this moment on the two fields unfold along parallel lines with a growing convergence of interests.

Therefore psycho-pedagogy is not an abstract, a-historical term. It is a reality that has been made in history, advancing and fighting its battles, situating itself as one of the key factors in the renewal of organisation of education, and ways of conceptualising and doing education.

4) Of the various possible reference points in psycho-pedagogy there is one we feel to be compelling and it supports the weave of what we will say today, forcefully underlining *the social structure of experience, of knowledge*.

Certainly by nature and definition schools are places where culture is learned. But schools of this kind, that are not immediately conscious of other values, would be schools of rhetoric, bureaucracy, superficiality, *non-schools*.

What concerns schools, what they ought to be concerned with, are the conditions, the educational ways in which, and only through which, cultural learning takes place and pupils become co-participants in the process. Conditions connected with this fundamental truth [reflect how] cultural development is not merely an intellectual fact but *a complex activity with a social and emotional structure*.

In true knowledge processes the intellectual element never acts with a hypothetical purity and autonomy. It cannot do this. It is promoted and organised in reality by a sort of contaminating dialectic with suggestions and motivations (these become real tools and contents) with their origin in the individual's social and emotional context. We cannot say that this is a truth presiding over the making of culture in our schools always and everywhere. On the contrary, it often happens that we see a tragic and painful decapitation of this truth.

The pedagogical implications are clear then. Above all else education should lead to schools which are concerned with ensuring the most favourable social and emotional situation for children, as an absolutely indispensable condition, because it is integrated with the cultural situation. This way schools not only provide the most appropriate means for cultural learning, they are already creating culture.

5) Education's first and most natural character is collective and social. In the broad fabric of institutionalised systems that order a community, masses of children are organised, who by the fact of entering schools are called pupils. Perhaps there is a difference between the child and the pupil? This issue is not marginal and we shall come back to it later. For the moment we have established something very important: for children entering school this constitutes their first, true and genuine social experience, an experience that situates them, with their evolving personalities, in the midst of a constituted group – or rather a group in the process of being constituted. This phenomenon leads to two kinds of reaction: reactions of a psychological order for the child who, coming to grips with an extremely new experience, must immediately deal with the problem of adapting; and reactions of a sociological order, involving the dynamic of a group settling in. But in the general dynamic we immediately find introduced, and in large measure, the personality of teachers and their actions.

New currents and ways of behaving open up new levels of affect, emotion, intellect and culture between teacher and class, teacher and group, between teacher and pupil, between pupils themselves.

However it is insufficient and distorts our analysis of this phenomenon if we do not take into account the other forces present in this structuring process. These may have their origins in the individual life histories of children themselves, in the variety of their cultural levels and backgrounds, in the way education in school resonates in their family environment, in the ways and values with which all of these are realised, the ways and values with which an organised and historically responsible society accesses and promotes [educational] experience.

So we can immediately draw an important conclusion: examining the fundamental facts of school education leads us to sum up the situation in terms of a psycho-social reality.

Three essential factors interact: the pupil, the class, the teacher. But each one of these draws on dynamics in their own history to constitute a sort of complex chemical process in which a knowledge of the ingredients, how they are expressed, meet and integrate with each other, forms the necessary premise for valid pedagogical action.

[. . .]

7) Our experience as a clinical and consulting [*Medico Psico-Pedagogico*] *Centro* makes us certain that many failures in school, much lack of success, many examples of inadequate learning rhythms, several anomalous behaviours, many examples of a sudden loss of initial enthusiasm on the child's part, the sudden appearance of psycho-somatic disturbances, especially during the first and

second years, are originally caused by encounters with school that have not been well-conducted or facilitated.

For example, the affective needs manifested when children are first at school are of primary importance. Are we sure we give them the necessary time, and provide all the necessary opportunities for the process of settling in to take place in the most congenial way?

A month, the first month in school, dedicated intensely and entirely to deeper knowledge of pupils and their families, lifting them out of an anonymity that unfortunately often lasts for years, might repay itself many times over by favouring the personalisation of education that children rightly request and teachers need.

[. . .]

9) We do not propose here to make a detailed analysis of child psychology at school age. But every pedagogy, however empirical, presumes a passing knowledge of the person to whom it is addressed. This is necessarily true of contemporary pedagogy, which now enjoys an extremely wide-ranging literature in psychology. We will limit ourselves to pointing to the great guiding ideas that condition all serious research in pedagogy today. The first of these is that childhood is an extremely rich and important period of life.

For too long childhood was conceived as a phase of inactivity (and children a sort of larva), from which to be freed progressively in order to arrive at the adult state.

Despite Rousseau's warnings inviting respect for 'the child within the child', we have to wait for the twentieth century before childhood is considered a period of vital dynamism, extraordinarily intense, where the continuous ferment, both physiological and of the psyche, incessantly modifies the characteristics of the child.

Psychology has replaced the concept of a life of slow and simple rhythms becoming progressively more complicated (in old traditions of philosophy and pedagogy) with the affirmation that during every moment of their evolution children live a complete and original life with a unified history. Children cease to appear as simply a reduction of adults, interpreted and known through the adult mentality. We need to know how children are structured. If children are beings that are constantly becoming then we need to follow them step for step.

The *genetic method* will allow us, better than any other, to determine the characteristics of childhood's evolution and give consideration to every moment. The unceasing evolution is not regular, we say it is *a-rhythmic* and *discontinuous*. Radically distinct stages do not exist in children's evolution, neither is there a uniform, regular progress, as if we were simply dealing with quantitative growth.

In growing, children pass through critical periods, nodal points which are signalled to the attention of family and teacher through external manifestations, which are usually a sharp break with previous habitual behaviours.

Wallon [see Chapter 1, n.48] says: 'from stage to stage the child's psycho-genesis, the complexity of its factors and functions, and the contrast of its crises, demonstrates a sort of unity as much in each crisis as between them. It is contrary to nature to treat a child in a fragmented way. At each age they constitute an indivisable and original whole: in the succession of egos they are one, only and always the same human being.'

Among the points of crisis noted by psychology, a crisis appears which affects children at the age of six, when they enter school. During this crisis, working at a deep level, there will be a slow psycho-affective-emotional reorganisation.

10) The extension of the *field of life*, as Zazzo[66] says, leads children to internalise important levels of personalisation and differentiation. Relations and interactions with the community and its forms of discipline (or organisation) increase in quantity and in quality. Children learn to know themselves as a *multifaceted personality*, adapting their conduct when faced with different or particular situations. Rather than being endlessly distracted, they become aware of their capacities, and have a more precise and complete knowledge of themselves. An equivalent evolution takes place in the field of perceptions and knowledge. The different features of objects and situations, until now perceived as a confusion of identities, can finally be progressively identified and classified, so that it is possible to make comparisons and distinctions in a systematic and coherent process. The *thinking of logic and category* emerges, the capacity for subdividing things and the qualities of things into classes, of being precise about their different properties. To use Piaget's expression, they no longer confuse *invariants*[67] with one another.

On an emotional level children begin a journey of affective reversibility, the possibility of becoming their own double and considering themselves as they consider someone outside themselves, making a distinction between their *id* and the *id* of others.

Slowly sentiments begin to replace emotion[68] and are ordered according to logical criteria. On a social level children begin to sense the presence and value of relations with others in an increasingly logical and objective way. It is significant that this phenomenon comes at the same time as another, second phenomenon, whereby analysis-synthesis takes the place of global vision on an intellectual level.

Which might lead us to think that *globalism*, far from only meaning the phenomenon of perceiving images, in reality is the child's way of being more holistic, more total: exactly the way of being that Piaget calls egocentric. So that, together with Laporta,[69] we say just when every detail becomes functional for every other in analysis-synthesis and these coalesce into a unified whole, other children appear as parts of a holistic human framework in the child's now more expanded world, no longer tools but concurrent objects with him in an activity tending towards the common.

These are the particular psychological traits of children attending our primary schools (and obviously the discussion could be richer and more specific).

However it is as well to be reminded that each child's psychological portrait or profile cannot be mechanically deduced from a generalised schema, but [emerges] from an analysis and observation of each individual, built on their original biology, psyche and their personal history.

Certain dissonances might be highlighted, and sometimes these might lead us, after appropriate precautions, to diagnose an abnormality or late development, an anomaly or an affective disorder. However in the majority of cases the dissonances are normal and do not go beyond a range of individual variation that is part of the average. They may simply indicate precociousness, or a relative delay inherent in the child's individual nature.

11) This fact is already evident: the need, according to psycho-pedagogy, to know children as much as we know the things we want to teach them.

Not much time goes by before we are already asking children to obey us, listen to us, acquire habits conforming to the rules of living together in school, as well as to remember and 'to make an effort', *to show their willingness*. We are asking them that is to say, to *try hard*.

When we say this we bring into play one of the most important and debated ideas in pedagogy: *the idea of interest*.

What is interest? *It is the attraction we feel for an object, an act, an idea.*

Research in psychology has established that particular interests are revealed at every age or stage in an individual's evolution, and has outlined some noteworthy generalisations. However, reality is more complex.

Dewey's theory, which insists on the ties connecting each interest and its corresponding need, is well known. He lists four factors: an intellectual element stimulating curiosity, a motor element fuelling action, a subjective element attributing value to the object, and finally an affective element, the desire for the object.

Therefore interest has a global character, which affects all mental processes. It is a far-reaching concept. Interest drives children to seek its object, and in so doing it also guides them in the direction of school activities, obviously to the extent that these are wisely chosen, ordered and distributed.

So we can conclude that a pedagogy capable of energising children's interests, with a proper tempo, creates a tranquil and serene atmosphere in the classroom, conducive to working.

However our attention is immediately drawn to the great ease with which this principle of pedagogy can be distorted. If attractive teaching is conducive to acquisition, then we must be concerned the attraction it exerts is not superficial, that it does not rely on casual procedures, but on the idea under consideration and on the deep interest this stimulates in the child.

Generalising play as a pedagogical procedure is certainly a mistake and its gravity increases with children's age. Psychologically, it can produce quite serious processes of regression.

So it is necessary to distinguish *interesting* teaching from teaching that is merely *attractive*.

However, a pedagogy of interest does not itself escape criticism. In fact it relies on a totally optimistic concept of children's nature, and implies the thesis that education can, and must, look uniquely to children and children's autonomous dynamics.

This type of *naturalistic* thesis is contested by other theses, which give educators their great role. These say that children aspire to becoming adults and their effort is that of an adult. Easy attention is not attention at all, otherwise says Alain,[70] 'even a dog eating sugar is paying attention'.

In reality children want to play but they also want to step outside play, which keeps them in a state of inferiority, and aspire to effort, which they also desire.

The problem lies in graduated trials and efforts. It lies in inspiring children with the idea of their great potential (the marvellous potential of mankind) and supporting this with successes. However it is no less important that these successes should be hard work, difficult and obtained without help.

Certainly interest is an important springboard collecting energy at the deepest level in human beings, the same level as disposition. But are life and its reality really only regulated by interest? It seems essential then that a sentiment of effort should also be developed, an idea of its necessity and awareness of its great human value. This means connecting a *culture of volition* to the transmission of knowledge. It appears clear then that no contradiction exists between these two pedagogical conceptions, which are really more complementary than divergent.

The opposition is not between a pedagogy of interest and a pedagogy of effort, but between a pedagogy of effort supported and enlivened by interest, and a pedagogy either of mere effort or mere attraction. Effort provoked without the natural stimulus of interest and with the assistance of artificial stimulus in the form of penalties, is unhealthy and sterile. Effort generated on the basis of, and following the direction of, extending spontaneous interests that children acquire as they mature, is healthy and normal.

12) All psychology that claims to be rational is founded on dual knowledge of the general child and the particular child. However a psychological description of a school child, even when it brings together these two perspectives, is incomplete if it forgets or neglects the inter-individual influences and reciprocal reactions between children and the environment they live in.

There has already been occasion to signal the importance of school environments as a factor in personal maturation. But recent research in psychology (Wallon for example) highlights the close correlation existing between children's individual development and the nature of the relations they have with the environment. In other words personality and sociality are defined in conjunction, and mutually condition each other.

We can infer then that genuine knowledge of a child is not possible without a psycho-social study leading us to place him immediately side by side with that other living reality, which is the group.

The ensemble of pupils brought together in the same class constitutes a whole for educational ends. Classical psychology (Durkheim in the French school for example) firmly insists that a class is a small society and cannot be conducted as if it were simply an agglomeration of independent subjects. In class children think, feel and act in an original way, quite different from the way they would behave if they were isolated.

A class constitutes a real *collective being*, with its own reflexes and reactions, its own deep and superficial structures, which can be felt empirically when a teacher feels the class presenting evolutions in learning and behaviour, in quantity and quality, modifications, sudden changes of direction or turnarounds, *all together*, and these are almost always unexpected. It is a well known phenomenon.

Some might say, is not a class an artificial group? Is it not made up of children with different characters, from different family backgrounds brought together by an external artificial requirement? Attending school is an obligation children cannot avoid and they must also accept the collective form of organisation despite themselves.

Furthermore, the class or group is exclusively directed by an adult, with attributes of authority and power. Children thus come to find themselves forced to condition or put a brake on their impulses and tendencies, and adapt their behaviour to a new social structure whether they want to or not.

Again children do not spontaneously look for groups except for play activities. These groups may be more or less numerous, stable and organised depending on age (eventually we have the rigidly codified group rules which Louis Pergaud[71] describes in his book 'The War of Buttons', recently made into a film).

So must we conclude there is a marked contrast between a class group and the dynamic of a spontaneous group, because of its artificial character?

In reality this opposition does not exist. Psycho-pedagogy, now analysing the reality of contemporary childhood issues more objectively than in the past, insists on children's need for organisation, the organisation of social meaning, of their sociality. It is an absolutely natural need in the fulfilling of which children find the answer to their fundamental and primitive needs, which they ask us to satisfy so they can grow and mature, be pulled from solitude, from boredom, from 'what shall I do?', and the sense of being abandoned. To the extent that experience has taught us that where this response is missing we find mobs and gangs being formed. The phenomenon has been strikingly apparent in countries destroyed by war. With their schools closed, and teachers lost, youngsters were not resigned to solitude. They organised gangs similar to those that sprang up following the Napoleonic wars, and which inspired Pestalozzi's[72] work.

This is not all. Recently in the news we have heard of a similar phenomenon of confusion, and the creation of gangs in so-called *affluent* countries, where children abandoned by adults and adult society, marginalised and pushed into solitude cannot find their place or role in society effectively, much less the prospect of valid ideals.

Returning to the subject of our interest, we can say the more children participate really and congenially in common life, the more the need for sociality and unity is satisfied. The school group's artificial character disappears as soon as a class ceases to be a constricting environment and becomes a real life environment where children can satisfy their pleasure in growing with others. This process of harmonisation does not take place spontaneously, largely it is the work of teachers whose presence and action prove to be a decisive factor in structuring and giving value to a group.

13) A school group constitutes a human ensemble whose members are tied by close solidarity, and which becomes stronger as the children become older. Children become aware of this solidarity very early on. For example 'telling' on other children is frequent during the initial weeks, and initial months, but rapidly becomes the object of disapproval.

As in all primitive societies affect plays a very large role, it contaminates all rational elements, and is the basis of spontaneous conduct. In the first phase of school life conduct is shaped above all by imitation. The importance of spontaneous imitation in the evolution of children is well known. For example children learn language and acquire a large number of social behaviours by imitating others. By imitating others and 'appropriating' others, children come to intuiting and measuring who they are. The phenomenon of imitation occurs in class constantly. Everyday teaching rightly makes use of it. There can be no doubt of the phenomenon's social essence.

Often imitation takes place at a low level, such as when we find ourselves faced with something that is collectively suggestive, capable of leading a whole class to an unusual or abnormal behaviour. Sometimes laughter is contagious through the whole class, on other occasions it may be an idea or a sentiment, expressed by the teacher or a pupil, that evokes a response from the entire class. This, again, is a phenomenon that if we do not overuse it, can be a potent means of pedagogical action. Another important phenomenon is mental contagion that often shows up in less apparent ways, more tenuous but no less real. All teachers will have certainly found themselves faced with sudden variations in the collective mood. [Sometimes] it seems there are magnificent days, and tragic days, days when children's receptivity is particularly good and days when a thick fog of laziness, apathy, confused and purposeless excitement seems to envelop children, and makes them resistant to any progress.

All these spontaneous behaviours with a collective origin, which make up an important part of the humus in which school activity takes place, need to be known and appreciated for what they offer in terms of usefulness in the complex play of class experience and the educational process.

14) Another important social issue, but situated on the level of conscious thought, is emulation. Really this idea is not as simple and clear as often

thought. In it two different concepts can become confused and it is as well to distinguish them. There is a form of personal emulation, which is a force driving individuals to surpass themselves and their own achievements. This has a more specifically psychological origin, even though it leads to social effects.

The other form of emulation we would like to discuss is of a social nature, and appears in the group context, in fact it does not exist in other forms. It is made up of elements of a different order; seeking public praise, fear of ridicule, seeking reward, and a fear of punishment, disapproval or condemnation by classmates.

So emulation in a group, in a class, tends to manifest itself above all as looking for external signs of superiority. The *value* of emulation seems extremely debatable in these conditions. Certainly it offers the advantage of children in school getting an idea of life outside, where unfortunately competition becomes the general rule. It spurs the child on to efforts for which they might not otherwise have the energy, and acts as a stimulant. At the same time, however, there are many disadvantages.

Emulation in this sense replaces a *sense of duty*, and what was proposed as a simple means becomes an end in itself. A form of *behavioural conditioning* is created, organised on the basis of penalties and prizes. Effort is no longer seen as a necessity and means for achieving personal improvement, but as a means for triumphing over others, and ends up acquiring a discontinuous and opportunist character.

It is easy to identify the importance for children of the group as an agent of dynamism, solicitation and purposefulness on the level of education. However the subjective influences and interactions constantly at work between individual and individual, between child and child, should be considered equally important, as well as those arising from relations between teacher and pupil, and teacher and the pupil group. So that different dynamics with varying intensities are developed in this small society of the class. Sometimes these affect a few individuals, sometimes only a portion of the class, other times almost all or the whole of the class.

Each child thus finds themselves at the centre of a more or less vast social network depending on the degree to which they are capable of creating (or are helped to create) relations with companions, the extent to which they are sought out by others. Inter-subjective relations established in this way define their *personal role* within the group.

This is how an attentive teacher can note the development of ties and relations that go from simple acquaintanceship to friendship, with all the different stages of affinity between. These relations do not necessarily arise only through a preference or an affinity, on the contrary they may be a transformation of rivalry and hostility.

An absence of relations has important significance in itself. An isolated child, ignored or rejected by others, is a case to be addressed seriously. Research and socio-metric inquiry by Moreno[73] for example, offers a rich anthology of knowledge and results.

Based on the reflections we have discussed, as a conclusion it seems opportune and interesting to underline more clearly that, 'classes are a *necessary*

environment for children's complete development and the more solid and extended *levels of socialisation* they promote the higher their educational value'.
[. . .]

16) If we reflect properly, the entire life of a school (like every other aspect of life in a society) takes place within a codified set of structures and rules. Since education is considered a social and ethical imperative undertaken by the State, teachers draw their authority from precise sociological and legal foundations. To this teachers add a second authority, which is tacitly acknowledged by families the moment they entrust their child to the school. Expressed in this way it seems the educational process must be based on the teacher's attitude of authority, and the child's attitude of obedience and subordination, together with a sort of relinquishment of education on the part of the family.

But if this were so, the problem of education would be resolved in a mechanical, hierarchical, disciplinary way. Teachers would *govern* children, the group, the class, the family. We now know that education of this kind makes no sense today, in theory no-one proposes it, no-one wants it. And yet despite everything we can say that something of this profane conception still survives in places where teachers, by *governing*, exclude themselves from the group and the children, cut children off from their families, and cut off their roots from a reality that exists and is important.

If we want educational action to be effective and genuine today, and this is what the State and families want, it must rest on quite different foundations, quite different ties and relations, which can be clearly inferred from modern consciousness, and from what we have discussed here at length.

It is up to teachers to nourish the right ground where they can practice their work and respond to children's need for affection, knowledge and activity.

But what is a teacher for the children? What do teachers represent, how are they seen and considered? How is this judgement evolved and acted on by children? At six or seven years old children's ways of knowing still reflect subjective factors that are highly evocative, permeated with affect, pre-logical, magical, and children are moved to ascribing people and things with powers they do not possess.

The power of the teacher, whatever it is, seems limitless to the child, like an absolute, just as the whole of reality is still seen with eyes that make things greater than their objective size. 'The teacher says so, he wants it like this.' Parents know very well the resolute firmness children use to cut short discussions that appear to be in conflict with, or diminish the prestige and authority of their teacher. These feelings of close dependency require a vigilant, refined sense of responsibility in the teacher, however they are counterbalanced by children's strong trust in the teacher's *justice*.

This is an important fact, which guides children's behaviour and conditions a group's acceptance of the adult figure and their role.

'What differentiates the teacher from the pupils in a group' – says Fau – 'is not only the degree of his knowledge, but the degree of his social adjustment, his personal and social maturity.' What children request before and above all else is that a teacher's personal and social maturity is manifested in an attitude of justice. Children can internalise this aspect of their teacher's personality with rapid and easy intuition, and in order to accept and recognise the teacher as a model, the true head of the group, they require these qualities: that of being just, of doing and judging things with justice.

Before all else the teacher is therefore a factor for unification of the school group. And this is so true that even if a teacher does not possess the qualities necessary for effective educational action their presence will tend to unify the group anyway. But the unification will work against them.

The study of group dynamics, therefore, reveals the prime importance of the teacher's role. A study of the dynamics of individual psychology and of the group poses the fundamental need for a constant readjustment and critical revision of the teacher in the eyes of the class. This attentive, rapid and constantly updated critical revision of the teacher in the eyes of the class and group is a keystone.

Slowly, as children absorb and sediment [experience], and as logic and affect become integrated, the magic submission of children in first and second [grade] elementary classes becomes replaced with an objectivity that creates order in things, increasingly puts them into a spatial and temporal perspective, and provokes new interdependencies and interactions. At nine and ten years old the group already begins to organise on the basis of the teacher's personality (now deprived of magic attributes), interpersonal relations, the children's capacity for judgement and reasoning, and above all based on the appearance of real social sentiment. Teachers no longer rely on children's natural, almost mythical adherence in order to belong to the school group. Now it is based on the need and on the desire of children for collaboration, friendship and *living together*, and the teacher, whether they know it or not, must take into account the children's critical reflection.

A teacher who is not profoundly convinced of these truths or who does not possess a sufficiently supple and finely balanced personality to always respond to the maturing needs of children in a class, runs the risk of being displaced outside it and cutting off the dialogic quality that is the essence and authenticity of an educational relationship. Then they can only work from the outside with acts of dispensation, authoritarianism and bureaucracy, with formal results that only mask the deep wound and distortion that have been caused. Or else, working with the rhythm of a pedagogy which is inert and without history, they will create classes of children who are *neutral*, neither opposed nor tied to them by affection, where pedagogy is reduced to merely reporting the facts, and formative values are necessarily deferred to be dealt with outside school.

For the teacher–pupil relationship to rise to the level of educational happiness it must immediately be made clear that no method is truly fruitful if it does not imply the active and joyous participation of children, does not create a feeling of security, trust and success. Selective schools, that are a mother to the gifted, and stepmother to weaker more needy children, transform teachers into judges but certainly not into educators. Just as schools that do not satisfy children's need for experience, and their need to appropriate *truly scientific and historical* [concepts], giving dignity to their logical and critical capacities, may be places of indoctrination but not of knowledge.

Finally we would like to repeat, and with insistence, that above all schools and teachers who do not realise the social dimension of education fail in their task. Everything that is done is done for the personality of children, who with the force of their nature aspire to increasingly socialised and organised environments in which to meet 'their kind and their equals'.

17) We all know the way things are, the way things stand in our schools today. During our first round table, or first working group, different positions and converging ideas came together to weave an analysis of the educational problems in our country. Do we wonder at this?

Certainly not. Working in groups presupposes a dynamic of differentiation, the comparison of ideas, acceptance and a habit of dialogue on the part of participants, final results that may not always be homogenous and which leave problems open.

In our last talk besides discussing the responsibilities of our public authorities we identified cultural shortcomings on the teaching level as one of the central inadequacies of our schools. Our intention was to express the difficulties we all encounter in adopting genuinely mature emotional behaviours, and the difficulties we encounter – certainly not due to laziness but to the inadequacy of professional and psychological training and lack of socialised and socialising apprenticeships – in adapting to constant research on issues, to examining issues, which above all requires the presence and use of a ferment of ideals.

It cannot be denied that the 1955 programmes for primary school[74] contain at their heart an interesting ferment of ideas. Yet we certainly cannot be satisfied with what has happened in reality. Several factors, some of which we will try and identify, have impeded their progress and realisation. The ferment and the innovative guidelines have fallen on ground (the professional training of teachers) that has not been capable of adequately receiving them and making them bear fruit.

Translating them into reality has been impeded by the absence, even on a theoretical level, of a corresponding identification and development of new methodologies and contents. These alone can contribute to helping teachers imbue practice with the new values.

The philosophies of innovators continue to have a strange and painful destiny in our country (and this is confirmed by the many struggles and words produced fifty or a hundred years ago which still echo among us so long after, unheard and un-heeded). They become absorbed, camouflaged and alienated in concrete practice, at best surviving as isolated and undernourished methodological guidelines in the old system they battled against, giving the impression of becoming established.

[. . .]

Conclusions: We have come to the conclusion of our talk. This is a practical farewell, of work that aspires to putting together a series of indications, attitudes and problems with the intention of calling for more committed reflection, for a greater and more conscious willingness to examine, to criticise and to marvel, in what is essentially an open and scientific attitude to our work and reflections on work.

Together with Claparède [see Chapter 1, n.65], we say 'What is needed is this: the constant presence of a scientific attitude, that is to say the attitude of teachers marvelling when faced with the facts of their everyday professional life, who want to interrogate them, and attempt to obtain an answer by subjecting them to methodical observation and experiment.'

Let us remember [there are no points e, j and k in the following list]:

a   that children are inherently social creatures, and that in the process of knowledge stimulus considerations of a social and emotional nature always intervene.

b   that the nature of children demands that schools [satisfy] their need for socialisation and group integration: this need leads to responses of a sociological and psychological order.

c   that this need is fundamental and its satisfaction is an indispensable premise for further maturation.

d   that children can put in place resistance of a kind that reacts against educational action, through giving up or through aggression and it is the task of the teacher confronted with these reactions to take the only truly pedagogical attitude. This consists not so much in passive acceptance or ethical judgements, but research into and identification of the causes at the root of the phenomenon: 'How is it that in technical institutes we study the resistance of matter, and in *Magistrali* schools [for future teachers] we do not study the resistance children offer or might offer to educational action?' (Makarenko).[75]

f   that it is a teacher's task to work at banishing their god-like nature in front of children, and children should be encouraged in a similarly progressive elimination of affective and intellectual behaviour of a totalising and magical kind.

g   that children's increasing rationality, the progressive sedimentation of their emotional exuberance, which opens the way to the birth of feelings, needs to find rapid, intelligent and passionate support and adjustment on the teacher's part.

h   that the authority of teachers is only fruitful if it is co-operative authority that allows them to enter the group and become an irreplaceable factor in its maturation.

i   that only this attitude can sense in good time when order needs to give way to advice, exhortation to reasoning, when the teacher's action must necessarily begin to support the children's critical reflections.

l   that urging effort without the natural stimulus of interest but helped by the artificial stimulants of penalties and prizes is sterile. Only efforts generated on the basis and following the direction of extending interests that are spontaneous and acquired by children maturing are healthy and normal.

m   that the attitude of teachers who do not adequately take into account the problems their actions constantly provoke through affecting the family environment, and the unstable relations that may result, can lead to a lack of synchronisation [with families] that paralyses their action, with consequences that obviously can be registered in children, in the class, in the family.

n   that for children to be the object of and a stimulus for fruitful observation and fruitful educational processes, they cannot be anonymous, the history of their continuously evolving existence must be known.

o   that the basic attitude of teachers and schools should not be judgement but observation. This frees children of frustrating and coercive pressures.

p   that an excessive pace, especially at the start of school (a phenomenon clearly seen in current school practice and manifesting itself in various forms of disorder and maladjustment that can also be documented at a much later date), and the absence of a vital phase of introduction and adjustment (emotional, affective, intellectual, social, motor, perceptual motor), goes against the nature and the needs of the child.

q   that too great an amount of fantasy and fairy-tale play, continuing with the world of fantasy (without devaluing imagination's distinctive values), can block children in an infantile state, produce regressive phenomena, and a tendency to refuse reality and lose the capacity for observation.

r   that it is mistaken to think that children by their nature aspire to full and total freedom. Aspirations to freedom are enacted only on the basis of progression closely linked to children's personal and social evolution and their evolving need for protection and security. The teacher's task is to be conducive to the acquisition of freedom and autonomy in a secure atmosphere.

s   that stability and continuity of teaching on the part of the teacher are necessary conditions for the continuity and coherence of educational method, and to guarantee the group of pupils a continuity of experience which cannot be interrupted without potentially painful consequences.

※ ※ ※

22.63 Open letter to parents, June 1963

Editors' note: There is an Italian tradition of sending children to seaside or mountain *colonie* [summer camps], especially in the past for children of poorer families whose health and growth were thought to benefit from seaside and mountain air. The tradition began in the nineteenth century and was embraced by fascism, whose buildings can still be seen at the seaside all over Italy. It is still common, in Reggio Emilia and other parts of Italy, for children from around the age of 8 years or so to go away to these camps during the hot summer months, and *comuni* remain much involved in the provision of these services. As well as the benefits of a healthy environment, emphasis is placed on the opportunities these camps give children to socialise. Malaguzzi proposed renaming the *colonia* as the *casa di vacanza* as part of his widespread renewal of these services.

An experiment with the Casa di Vacanza in Igea Marina[76]

Dear Parent,

We are certain you will appreciate this short letter on the eve of your child's departure for the *Casa di Vacanza* [holiday camp] in Igea Marina. Accept it as a way for you to construct an untroubled holiday for your child together with us.

Thank you.

What the Casa di Vacanza offers

Remember the *Casa di Vacanza* does not only offer a holiday that is beneficial to your child's physical development, in an atmosphere of affective care. It offers your child precious new experiences, a great variety and breadth of affective and social exchange, participation and collaboration in an ordered and joyful community life, an education in personal autonomy, new horizons of knowledge, original games and experiments, refining of moral and civic virtues.

The *Casa di Vacanza* should therefore be considered as an occasion of exceptional and original educational richness, involving the child's whole physical, intellectual, affective and moral personality. This awareness and perspective require planning and translation into practice by the institution's Direction [management]. However it also requires specific, careful and clear collaboration on your part.

Feed your child's enthusiasm

Therefore organise your child's departure with loving and intelligent care. Separation from the family is a very important moment and calls for timely preparation.

Help your child to understand the beautiful, joyous, useful holiday awaiting him, and to feel comforted before leaving by the atmosphere of affection that will surround him.

Make children enthusiastic by talking about the new world awaiting them; the sea, the beach, the sails, the shells, the sports equipment, the games in the open air, the toys, the laboratories where they can experiment with a creative spirit, the joy of living with other children, the pride of doing every-thing themselves, the evenings of cinema, of puppet shows, of mime, the card games, the sightseeing, the competitions, the carefree sensation of diving into the water, of making castles and kites.

Check your child's kit

Thoroughly check your child's kit. Check that nothing which has been recommended is missing. Ensure that everything needed is packed in an ordered way in the bag, so that your child can easily find and choose what they need.

Help them to write out addresses on their postcards.

Do not overload them with sweet things, too many toys, too many recommendations.

At the moment of departure show you are confident, do not let him see you worried.

Write to your child often

For children the arrival and handing out of mail (you can easily imagine this) is one of the loveliest and most anticipated moments at the *Casa di Vacanza*, a moment of emotional connection with family, fulfilling their need to be remembered and valued, and inviting them to re-live emotional relations in a new and more mature way.

Write to them often. Write immediately, a few hours after departure. The following day your child will be happy, and their contentment will help us to settle them in this new experience.

Do not tell them news that will make them sad. Instead, ask questions and make comments on their new life, the new relations, the new things they have learnt, their adventures, their activities, their Group mates and the Educator assigned to their Group.

[. . .]

Meetings with parents

Are you thinking of coming to see your child in the *Casa di Vacanza*? Listen carefully. To avoid many inconveniences and in order to satisfy the right and legitimate needs of children and parents, the Direction of the *Casa di Vacanza* has decided to promote MEETINGS WITH PARENTS, one for each stay, on a date to be decided. This will be entirely dedicated to meetings between children and parents.

Editor's note: There is an extra page for parents telling them what their children will need to bring with them.

---

2 pairs of shorts (for boys)
1 pair of shorts (for girls)
3 cotton dresses (for girls)
2 cotton T shirts (for boys)
1 pair of sandals with rubber soles
3 pairs of panties (for boys and girls)
2 pyjamas (for boys and girls)
1 bathing costume (for boys and girls)
2 towels
2 table napkins
1 white cotton hat with all round shade
2 sheets
1 pillowcase
4 handkerchiefs
3 pairs of white socks (for boys and girls)
1 pair of leather shoes
1 pair of rubber soled plimsolls

This material must be placed in an orderly way in the child's personal bag.

> 1 bar of soap
> 1 toothpaste
> 1 toothbrush
> 1 comb
> 2 sachets of talcum
> 1 biro pen
> 6 addressed postcards

This material must be placed in a transparent cellophane bag.

Children's hair should be freshly cut.

Notes

1 Applebaum notes that the term was first invented by a critic of Mussolini, but Mussolini adopted it and offered a good definition in one of his speeches: 'Everything within the state, nothing outside the state, nothing against the state' (2013, p.xxiii).

2 Ginsborg notes that after the war 'the powers of control and veto which the prefects, the agents of central government in the localities, had historically held were not diminished under the Republic. All acts of the municipal authorities had to be communicated to the prefect within eight days, and he then had twenty-eight days in which to annul them if he saw fit' (1990, p.153).

3 The language here is significant. Church and, later, state-run schools for 3- to 6-year-olds adopted the name *scuola materna*, emphasising their 'motherly' qualities and their role of mother substitute. Municipal schools, by contrast, were *scuola dell'infanzia*, emphasising their aim of providing a distinctive environment for the education of young children.

4 The Republic of Salò, or the Italian Social Republic, was a puppet state of Nazi Germany during the later part of the Second World War (from 1943 until 1945), led by Benito Mussolini and his Republican Fascist Party, and based around Salò, a small town on Lake Garda.

5 The Archive's website – http://www.resistance-archive.org/ – includes interviews with Resistance fighters from Reggio Emilia.

6 After qualifying as a primary school teacher, Malaguzzi in 1939 went on to study at the University of Urbino, which he combined with his first teaching job in Sologno.

7 Refers to the philosopher Giovanni Gentile (1875–1944), who described himself as 'the philosopher of Fascism', and ghostwrote *A Doctrine of Fascism* (1932) for Benito Mussolini. He became Minister for Education in 1923, introducing the *Riforma Gentile*, a reform of the secondary school system that had a long-lasting influence upon Italian education.

8 Reggiolo is a small town in the Po valley in the province of Reggio Emilia, about 30 kilometres north-east of the city of Reggio Emilia.

9 Sologno is a small village in the Apennine Mountains, about 40 kilometres south-west of Reggio Emilia and 10 kilometres from the border with Tuscany.

10 A fund established by law to provide support for the education of children from materially poor backgrounds.

11 Castelnuovomonti – or Castelnovo ne' Monti – is a hill town, 44 kilometres south of Reggio Emilia, and considered to be the capital of the Reggio Emilia Appenines. It is 7 kilometres from Sologno.

12 Italian forces were stationed in all three countries during the Second World War.

13 Malaguzzi seems to be referring to some form of draft, requiring non-combatants to work where they were directed by the authorities.

14 The 'Republican guards' were members of the National Republican Guard of the Republic of Salò, the rump fascist state set up in 1943 behind the German lines in the North of Italy. The partisan resistance movement, against the German occupation and fascist regime, began in 1943 and grew rapidly in 1944, with 20–30,000 members by spring 1944 (Ginsborg, 1990).

15 Places used by the fascist regime for detention, interrogation, torture and execution.

16 There is no section 4; the document goes from section 3 to section 5.

17 Villa Cella is a village 8 kilometres west of Reggio Emilia and part of the *Comune* of Reggio Emilia. The school built by the community and run under the auspices of the UDI was the first of a number of self-governing schools for 3- to 6-year-olds opened shortly after the war in and around Reggio Emilia.

18 Guastalla is a town on the River Po 30 kilometres north of the city of Reggio Emilia. The middle school, at that time, was for children aged 11 to 13 years and not compulsory.

19 Anton Giulio Bragaglia (1890–1960) was a pioneer in Italian Futurist photography and Futurist cinema. A versatile and intellectual artist with wide interests, he wrote about film, theatre and dance.

20 Romolo Valli (1925–1980) was a leading Italian actor, born in Reggio Emilia, after whom the *Teatro Municipale* in Reggio Emilia was renamed.

21 A festival with prizes held in Reggio Emilia and named after Maria Melato (1885–1950), an Italian actress born in Reggio Emilia; she is buried next to Romolo Valli in Reggio Emilia.

22 *Carrozzone di Fantasio Piccoli* was a touring theatre company of young actors, including Valli, which was founded in 1947 by Fantasio Piccoli (1917–1981).

23 This film was made in 1933 by the Soviet *avant-garde* filmmaker Sergie Eisenstein (1898–1948), as part of a film project set in Mexico.

24 Ezio Comparoni (1920–1952), whose pseudonym was Silvio D'Arzo, was a writer from Reggio Emilia.

25 ETI (*Ente Teatrale Italiano*) was a public organisation to promote and disseminate drama, music and dance. Founded in 1942, it was abolished in 2010.

26 The *Famiglia Artistica Reggiana* [The Artistic Family of Reggio Emilia] was established in 1946. A foundation supported by the *Comune*, FAR, organises cultural events such as concerts and lectures, and trips to art exhibitions, concerts, plays and places of artistic and cultural interest in Italy and abroad; and promotes young artistic talent.

27 *Teatro per Ragazzi* is a term used to describe theatres and theatre companies dedicated to children, schools and families.

28 Achille Peri (1812–1880) was a composer and conductor born in Reggio Emilia, and also a director of the *Teatro Municipale*.

29 Paolo Grassi (1919–1981) was an Italian theatrical impresario, and Giorgio Strehler (1921–1997) was an Italian opera and theatre director. In 1947 they founded the *Piccolo Teatro di Milano*, the first civic theatre in Italy.

30 Corrado Costa (1929–1991) was a poet and lawyer who lived in Reggio Emilia and was a member of Gruppo 63. Between 1953 and 1956 he organised a theatre festival for children in the *Teatro per Ragazzi*.

31 Vladimir Yakovlevich Propp (1895–1970) was a Soviet scholar who analysed the basic plot components of Russian folk tales to identify their simplest irreducible narrative elements. In his formula, he argued that usually there is an initial situation, after which the tale follows thirty-one functions.

32 Bibbiano is a *comune* in the province of Reggio Emilia, 14 kilometres south-west of the city of Reggio Emilia.

33 *La Verità* was the weekly magazine of the Reggio Communist Federation. Article from the municipal Panizzi Library archive.

34 Giovanni Carmelo Verga (1840–1922) was an Italian realist writer, best known for his depictions of life in Sicily, and especially for the short story (and later play) *Cavalleria*

Rusticana and the novels *I Malavoglia* (*The House by the Medlar Tree*) and *Mastro Don Gesualdo*. He was part of the realist (*verismo*) movement in literature, which emphasised the representation of social and human reality.

35 Gabriele D'Annunzio (1863–1938) was an Italian writer, poet, journalist, playwright and soldier during the First World War. He occupied a prominent place in Italian literature from 1889 to 1910 and after that in political life from 1914 to 1924. Some of his ideas and aesthetics influenced Italian fascism and the style of Benito Mussolini.

36 Established in Bologna in 1946, *Progresso d'Italia* was on the political left and challenged the dominance of more centrist newspapers. Article from the municipal Panizzi Library archive.

37 Cesare Pavese (1908–1950) was an Italian poet, novelist, literary critic and translator. He introduced the *Spoon River Anthology* to Fernanda Pivano, who later translated it into Italian.

38 George Brock Chisholm (1896–1971) was a medical practitioner specialising in psychiatry and the mental health of children, and the first Director-General of the World Health Organization. He argued that children should be raised in 'as intellectually free [an] environment' as possible, independent of the prejudices and biases – political, moral and religious – of their parents.

39 Charlotte Bühler (1893–1974) was a German developmental psychologist. She helped to develop humanist psychology, which emphasises a strong human drive toward self-actualisation, achieved through a developmental process that requires a person's basic needs be met before they can self-actualise.

40 *Opera Nazionale Maternità e Infanzia* (ONMI) was a national organisation founded in 1925 by the fascist regime, to provide assistance for young children and their mothers 'for the physical and moral defence of the race.' It was closed down in 1975. Among the services it provided were maternal and infant health clinics, home visiting and nurseries for children under 3 years. From 1932, ONMI began opening Houses for the Mother and Child, providing a range of services.

41 Célestin Freinet (1896–1966) was a French pedagogue and educational reformer who placed emphasis on active, group-based and cooperative learning, as well as democracy and democratic self-government. In the early 1950s, his work had been recently translated into Italian, and inspired the *Movimento di Cooperazione Educativa* [see Chapter 2, n.2]; Freinet himself attended its first conference in 1952 in Rimini. He was much read in Reggio Emilia during the period when the city was establishing its early childhood education.

42 'Penelope's web' refers to something that is perpetually doing – but never finished. In Greek mythology, Penelope was the wife of Ulysses, who went away to fight in the Trojan war and was feared dead. Importuned by suitors, Penelope stalled for time by working on the funeral canopy of Laertes, her husband's father, pledging to make her choice among the suitors when the robe was finished. But while she worked on the robe in the day, she undid her work at night.

43 GIL [*La Gioventù italiana del littorio*] was an organisation created and controlled by the fascist regime, bringing together all former youth organisations under the motto '*Credere – obbedire – combattere*' (Believe – obey – fight). *Patronati Scolastici* were funds set up in every *comune* to provide assistance to elementary school children through the establishment of school canteens, clothing and footwear grants and distribution of stationery and teaching materials. Malaguzzi here is referring to finding ways to better use these resources.

44 'Schools for Parents' was a concept introduced and promoted by Ada Gobetti (1902–1966), involving a series of lessons for parents on child development and the recognition of disorders in children. Gobetti was a teacher, translator and writer of children's books, as well as having been an active member of the resistance. She edited the journal *Democratic Education* and founded *Giornale dei genitori*, a magazine that provided advice for parents, as well as introducing the work of Benjamin Spock to an Italian audience. She also founded, in 1953, the first *Centro Medico Psico-Pedagogico* in the Rimini area and was a pedagogical consultant from the early 1960s for the first schools for young children opened by the *Comune* of Rimini.

45 Rudyard Kipling (1865–1936) was an English short-story writer, poet and novelist chiefly remembered for his tales and poems of British soldiers in India and his tales for children. Malaguzzi refers to his novel *Captains Courageous* published in 1897.

46 'Educating' is used here, and elsewhere by Malaguzzi, in a broad sense, to encompass the overall formation of the individual and their integration into society. Education so understood takes place in many settings, including both the school and the family, but also in the wider society and through the actions of institutions such as the *comune*.

47 'Schema' is used here and elsewhere to mean 'a mental codification of experience that includes a particular way of perceiving cognitively and responding to a complex situation or set iof stimuli' (http://www.merriam-webster.com/dictionary/schema).

48 Henri Wallon (1879–1962) was a French philosopher, psychologist (in the field of social psychology), neuropsychiatrist, teacher and a Communist politician. He occupied the highest positions in the French university world where he fostered research activity. He presented the development of the child's personality as a succession of stages, some marked by the predominance of affectivity over intelligence and others *vice versa*, a discontinuous and competitive succession between the prevalence of intelligence and affectivity. This dialectical model implied that regression was possible, contrary to Piaget's model.

49 '*Bouquiniste*' refers to the outdoor sellers of old books, journals and so on who line more than three kilometres of the river Seine in Paris with their 900 'green boxes'.

50 Honoré Daumier (1808–1879) was a French printmaker, caricaturist, painter and sculptor, whose many works offer commentary on social and political life in France in the nineteenth century.

51 Many intellectuals and others were confined to the island of Ventotene off the coast of Rome during fascism. This is where the Ventotene Manifesto, which called for a united Europe, was written. The Italians consider this to have been a founding document of the European Union.

52 The original site of the *Libreria Prandi* now houses the Theatre Bookshop. The Prandi Bookshop has moved to the ring road around Reggio Emilia and is still family run.

53 Teddy boys originated in the early 1950s as a British subculture typified by young men wearing clothes that were partly inspired by the styles worn by dandies in the Edwardian period, soon becoming strongly associated with American rock and roll.

54 Roberto Rossellini (1906–1977) was an Italian film director and screenwriter, a leading figure in the Italian neorealist cinema. Eduardo De Filippo (1900–1984) was an Italian actor, playwright, screenwriter, author and poet.

55 'The Exception and the Rule' is a short play that Brecht wrote around 1929/30 as one of several *Lehrstücke* [Teaching plays], which were intended to be taken on tour and performed in schools or in factories to educate the masses about socialist politics.

56 Leonilde Iotti, commonly known as Nilde Iotti (1920–1999), was an Italian politician of the Communist Party born in Reggio Emilia, and the first woman to become president of the Italian Chamber of Deputies for three consecutive legislatures, from 1979 to 1992.

57 The Italian term '*Oscurantismo*' was used in the eighteenth century to describe the antithesis of the Enlightenment. It refers to higher powers opposing the spread of knowledge to the masses and to a blind traditionalism that leads people to oppose all innovation and the spread of new scientific and philosophical thinking.

58 A popular anti-Republican movement defending Catholicism against the ideas of the French Revolution, which mobilised peasants from the Papal States against the Parthenopaean Republic established by Napoleon in 1799 in the former kingdom of Naples.

59 *Pulcinella*, often called Punch or Punchinello in English or *Polichinelle* in French, is a classical character that originated in the *commedia dell'arte* of the seventeenth century and became a stock character in Neapolitan puppetry.

60 Luigi Pirandello (1867–1936) was an Italian dramatist, novelist, poet and short story writer. He was awarded the 1934 Nobel Prize for Literature for his 'bold and brilliant renovation of the drama and the stage'.

61 David Émile Durkheim (1858–1917) was a French sociologist who formally established the academic discipline and, with Karl Marx and Max Weber, is commonly cited as the principal architect of modern social science. Much of his work was concerned with how societies could maintain their integrity and coherence in modernity, when traditional social and religious ties are no longer assumed, and new social institutions have come into being.

62 This quotation from Durkheim comes from an article 'Education, its Nature and Role', published in 1911 in the journal *Éducation et Sociologie*.

63 John Dewey (1859–1952) was an American philosopher, psychologist and educational reformer whose ideas have been influential in education and social reform. A well-known public intellectual, he was also a major voice of progressive education and an advocate of democracy in education.

64 All four were nineteenth century German scientists engaged in the development of experimental psychology.

65 Édouard Claparède (1873–1940) was a Swiss neurologist and child psychologist.

66 René Zazzo (1910–1995) was a French psychologist and pedagogue, whose research was in child psychology where he was one of the first people to study a group of problems relating to dyslexia and disability.

67 'Invariant' is a concept of Jean Piaget, referring to a child's ability to see that some properties are conserved, or invariant, after an object undergoes physical transformation, such as a spherical lump of clay being rolled into a tube.

68 Malaguzzi here may be referring to the distinction drawn by the Swiss psychoanalyst Carl Jung (1975–1961) between 'feelings' and 'emotions'. Emotion is instinctive – and is triggered by situational cues and physiological responses. Sentiment is organised feeling. It is highly socialised, and is developed out of its merely instinctive state by deep thought; it is a combination of our autonomic responses, behaviour as well as cultural or societal meaning. http://www.differencebetween.com/difference-between-emotion-and-vs-sentiment/.

69 Raffaele Laporta (1916–2000) was an educational reformer who became director of the *Scuola-Città Pestalozzi*, the experimental state-run public school founded in Florence in 1945, and a professor of pedagogy in various Italian universities.

70 Émile-Auguste Chartier (1868–1951), commonly known as Alain, was a French philosopher, journalist and pacifist.

71 Louis Pergaud (1882–1915) was a French writer and soldier, whose most notable work was the novel *La Guerre des boutons* (1912) (The War of the Buttons). It has been reprinted more than thirty times, and filmed on five occasions.

72 Johann Heinrich Pestalozzi (1746–1827) was a Swiss pedagogue and educational reformer who founded several educational institutions and wrote many works explaining his revolutionary modern principles of education. One of the institutions he opened was in Stans, a village destroyed in the Napoleonic wars, and which provided for orphaned and war-affected children.

73 Jacob Levy Moreno (1889–1974) was a Romanian-born Austrian-American psychiatrist and psychosociologist, thinker and educator, the founder of psychodrama, and the foremost pioneer of group psychotherapy.

74 This refers to the reform of the Italian elementary school curriculum in 1955.

75 Anton Semenovych Makarenko (1888–1939) was a Russian and Soviet educator and writer who promoted democratic ideas and principles in educational theory and practice.

76 Igea Marina is a seaside town near to Rimini in the region of Emilia-Romagna.

Chapter 2

First steps

1964–69

Figure 2.1 Workshop on mathematics with Loris Malaguzzi, Reggio Emilia, 1966

Figure 2.2 Loris Malaguzzi at the opening of the *Scuola Comunale dell'Infanzia* Anna Frank, Reggio Emilia, 1964

Figure 2.3 From left: Loris Malaguzzi, Germaine Duparc (Director of *La Maison des Petits – Institut des Sciences de l'Education*) and Marta Lusuardi (Head of Organisation for the Directors Offices of the *Nidi* e *Scuole Comunali dell'Infanzia*), Geneva (Switzerland), 1965

Figure 2.4 Loris Malaguzzi, Renzo Bonazzi (mayor of Reggio Emilia from 1962 to 1976), Loretta Giaroni (*Assessore* for Schools and for Social Services of the *Comune* of Reggio Emilia from 1967 to 1975), *Sala degli Specchi* [Hall of Mirrors], *Teatro Municipale*, Reggio Emilia, 1969

Introduction (Peter Moss)

The historical context

The middle to late 1960s saw the establishment of Reggio Emilia's project of early childhood education, with the first municipal school opened in November 1963, the *scuola comunale dell'infanzia* Robinson Crusoe, followed by a second school in 1964, named after Anna Frank, and a third, Primavera, in 1968. Then, following a long struggle with the Prefect,[1] the central government's local representative, two originally self-managed schools were municipalised, including the school at Villa Cella that had so inspired Malaguzzi when local people built it after the end of the Second World War. As a municipal school it was renamed *XXV Aprile* [25 April], the date of Liberation. A period of rapid expansion, in the 1970s, was to follow, but that expansion built on the foundations laid down during this period.

These first municipal schools emerged from a very particular context. This was a period widely known in Italy as the 'fabulous' sixties. It was a time of intense political, cultural and social activity in the city and beyond. The schools themselves were generating experimentation and discussion, but as part of a wider national ferment of debate and initiative on education and public schools, stimulated by organisations such as the *Movimento di Cooperazione Educativa*[2] [MCE, Movement for Cooperative Education] and individuals including Ada Gobetti, Mario Lodi, Gianni Rodari, Bruno Ciari – all good friends of Malaguzzi – and Don Milani.

Schools for young children were only part of the 'fabulous' sixties. Reggio Emilia, but also many other *comuni*, were developing a variety of public services and stimulating cultural activities as part of a wider project of renewal. Bonazzi describes how:

> [l]ocal government functions and policies had to be reconstructed in relation to the requirements and priorities of a country in a phase of rapid and massive industrialisation. The municipal administration [in Reggio] wanted to promote services and initiatives capable of guiding and accompanying economic development, adapting this development to the needs, requirements and aspirations of the life of the community and its single members, not the other way round. To pursue the creation of what was later summarised in a successful slogan as 'a city made to measure for people'.
>
> (Various Authors, 2012, p.88)

These ambitions led to important developments in urban planning, social services and health, in particular 'new' psychiatric services, as well as in culture, where the *Comune* assumed direct management of the theatre, sponsored literary events and concert series, developed municipal libraries and supported innovative institutions including a National Centre for Independent Cinema News and the Antonio Banfi Institute of Studies in Philosophy.

Developments in early childhood education were not limited to Reggio Emilia. This was the period of what Enzo Catarsi has termed the 'municipal school revolution', when many *comuni* in Emilia-Romagna 'pre-empted State-run services by starting up their own services for young children' (Catarsi, 2004, p.8). Reggio Emilia, along with Rimini, Modena, Parma and Bologna, led the way in deciding to start a municipal early childhood education, but close behind were other cities. The 'revolution' was a shared experience, though each city had its own story, its own circumstances.

Eventually, too, the national government was stirred to action. The idea of state-run *scuole materne* had been strongly opposed, not least by the Catholic Church that saw its dominance in this field threatened; even in Reggio Emilia at the end of the 1960s, 80 per cent of schools for 3- to 6-year-olds were Church run. After one national government had been brought down by the issue in 1966, Law no.444 was passed in 1968, which officially recognised the existence of schools for 3- to 6-year-olds and established the state as a provider of these schools (*scuole materne statali*); it also proclaimed the right of Italian children to such education. Moreover, the State could now provide funding for non-state schools, including those established by *comuni*, on condition they took disadvantaged children. Central government, which had favoured church-run *scuole materne* and impeded attempts by the *Comune* to develop its own services, would no longer be an obstacle to the growth of Reggio Emilia's education project.

The law not only provided material support for expanding education for young children, but gave added legitimisation to the very concept. Until Law 444, *scuole materne* had been associated with a welfare role – with helping poor families, with assistance for working parents and with private philanthropy. While the legislation retained this social role, it also affirmed an educational purpose and value and the place of these schools in the State education system. More problematic, the law stated that only women could be employed in these schools for young children, a requirement only removed in 1977.

Whilst this important law was passed by a government led by the *Democrazia Cristiana*, a permanent feature of national politics since the end of the war, these few years in the 1960s did see signs of renewed political and social movements. Reacting to a dysfunctional university system, unable to cope with increasing numbers, a student movement exploded onto the scene in 1967. More than just a protest at bad conditions, it adopted an irreverent anti-authoritarianism, becoming 'an ethical revolt, a notable attempt to turn the tide against the predominant values of the time' (Ginsborg, 1990, p.301).

Though the student movement climaxed in spring 1968, agitation continued through the 1970s. It connected, too, with a new upsurge in industrial unrest that began in 1968, and lasted undiminished into the early 1970s; this in turn gave rise to a new left represented by a 'bewildering number of revolutionary groups' (*ibid.*, p.312) and a 'climate of permanent agitation and conflict' (p.321). Adding to this climate was an array of other social movements, exploring radical alternatives in many fields. All in all, as Paul Ginsborg puts it:

> in these years [1968–73], collective action aiming to transform existing social and economic relations spread into nearly every part of Italian life. Everywhere, but especially in the Centre and North of the country, groups of activists challenged the way in which power was exercised, resources distributed, social classes divided . . . [It was in civil society] that radical alternatives spread most rapidly: 'red' markets, kindergartens, restaurants, social clubs, etc., opened (and often shut) one after another. Their aim was to organise social life along quite different lines, which not only challenged the individualism and segmentation of modern urban society, but also superseded the subcultures of the traditional left.
>
> (*ibid.*, pp.322, 323)

This social ferment and industrial unrest towards the end of the 1960s, with the political pressure it brought to bear, finally forced movement on a long-awaited institutional change. Provisions for regional government had been written into the 1946 Constitution, yet despite being promised as an 'absolute priority', nothing had been implemented, perhaps in part because 'regional devolution meant giving more power to the Communists in the Red Belt of Italy' (*ibid.*, p.271). Now, following elections in May 1968 and faced by growing protest, a new national government (as usual, though, led by the *Democrazia Cristiana*) finally took action, passing a law for the election of regional councils, followed in 1970 by the first elections and a budget law empowering government to transfer functions to regions, as originally set out in the Constitution. In future years, the Emilia-Romagna Region was to form a productive relationship with Reggio Emilia for the furtherance of early childhood education in both the city and the wider region.

The emerging pedagogical project in Reggio Emilia, and Malaguzzi's part in it, indeed the whole 'municipal school revolution' should be seen against this energising and hopeful background.

What is striking about the period covered in this chapter is not only this political, social and cultural background, but also the boldness and self-confidence of cities like Reggio Emilia in taking the lead in developing services geared to contemporary conditions and the improvement of life. This municipal activism was fuelled by a belief in the public sector's ability and duty to run these services, especially the *comune* 'since it was the expression of democracy in the local area' (Various Authors, 2012, p.99). In 1969, Loretta Giaroni, Municipal *Assessore* for Schools and Social Services in Reggio Emilia from 1967 to 1975, emphasised this link to democracy when she noted that 'increasingly the municipality is proposed as a tool for fusing direct democracy with representative democracy. The experience of the protest movement for [municipal] *scuole materne* sees the municipality in this role' (*ibid.*). This strong democratic theme, with the linkage of representative and participatory democracy, can be seen in the creation in 1968 of *Comitati d'Iniziativa* [Initiative Committees] in city neighbourhoods in Reggio Emilia, to press for the opening of municipal early childhood services; their values and experiences were inherited and developed by *Comitati di Scuola e Città* [School and City Committees], established in 1970.

Malaguzzi's life

Malaguzzi in 1964 was already active in children's services in the City, leading the *Centro Medico Psico-Pedagogico Comunale* and reforming the city's summer camps: he had 'extensive experience of working with children and highly innovative ideas on children's potentials and competencies, their ways of learning, and the role of school and education' (*ibid.*, p.83). He was also an important figure in the cultural life of Reggio Emilia. It was not surprising, therefore, that the *Comune* gave him the added responsibility of directing its new schools. He continued this dual role – working with the *Centro* and the municipal schools – until 1970.

For Malaguzzi, early childhood education in the municipal schools was clearly a women's issue, and rightly so. But in Reggio Emilia, and across Italy, there was strong disagreement about the role of women in the family and society. Catholic opinion supported women's family role and confining their paid work to part-time employment. The Left, through the work of groups such as the UDI, argued for women's right to employment, to be full members of society, and for services to support this goal. As noted in the previous chapter, a debate that followed these fault lines took place in Reggio Emilia's council in 1962, prior to the decision to open the first municipal school.

But women were not just the object of debate. Women, women's movements (such as the UDI) and women administrators in local government played an active role in demanding and campaigning for services, services that paid attention not only to their own needs but to those of children as well. From its inception in 1944, central values of the UDI were social justice, employment, peace – and the rights of women and children (*ibid.*, p.67). Women's political commitment, their 'widespread protagonism' for services that would meet their own needs but also children's, created a context 'from which theories of "new" schools sprang, bringing into play the concepts of solidarity between generations, participation in the local community, and autonomous social management' (*ibid.*, p.100).

Like the women campaigning for change, Malaguzzi was clear municipal schools were also there to fulfil an important right for children: a right to early education, education being something that, as has already been noted, he recognised as necessary from birth, since children are (as he later put it) 'born with many resources and extraordinary potential'. From the beginning, therefore, he rejected the idea that promoting early childhood services involved a choice between children or women; they were clearly understood by Malaguzzi and other advocates to be of value to both, offering both the possibility of emancipation.

While very involved in many ways in his home city, Malaguzzi was also deeply engaged nationally, an active participant in the vibrant educational scene of 1960s Italy. He assumed direction of the municipal schools in neighbouring Modena, the first of which was opened in 1964, and continued this role alongside his work in Reggio Emilia until 1974. There was also much exchange with places further afield. Writing later, Malaguzzi, described how he and colleagues from Reggio Emilia 'travelled to gather suggestions from the experience of other Italian cities: Florence, Bologna, Milan, Genoa and Rome' (*ibid.*, p.91). In the late 1960s, Malaguzzi, together with other educators, organised national conferences on early childhood education in various Italian cities.

He was in close contact with leading educationalists of all persuasions, never committing to any one organisation or movement, and basing his relationships on mutual respect and dialogue. One of his closest relationships was with Bruno Ciari (1923–70), a leading figure in the *Movimento di Cooperazione Educativa*, and appointed head of Bologna's educational and extracurricular services in 1966. With his respect for scientific and critical thinking and his belief in the importance of educating the whole child, strong relations with families, collective and democratic working and the physical environment, Ciari was a source of great inspiration to Malaguzzi, a friend he was to describe as 'the most lucid, passionate and acute intelligence in the field of childhood education' (Malaguzzi, 2012, p.22).

But Malaguzzi's interests and contacts were international. As well as Freinet's work in France, Malaguzzi was attracted to psychological and pedagogical developments in Switzerland, participating in the work of the *Centro Educativo Italo-Svizzero* [CEIS, Italo-Swiss Educational Centre] in Rimini. He was later to recall that at this time 'Switzerland was a laboratory of psychological and pedagogical thinking without equal in Europe, with Éduard Claparède, Pierre Bovet, Adolphe Ferrière, the Rousseau Institute, the Geneva School of Piaget and the infinite shadow of Jean Jacques [Rousseau]' (Various Authors, 2012, p.78). This new thinking from Switzerland, but also from other countries, was influential with Malaguzzi and the schools in Reggio Emilia from the start, linking the city into a national and international world of new ideas and ways of working and fostering a spirit of curiosity, experimentation and research. Looking back, in 1993, he recalled how:

> the cultural growth of the schools [in Reggio Emilia] during the 1960s was constructed as permanent research [. . .] [with] much reading (Lev S. Vygotsky, Erik Erikson, Bruno Bettelheim, Adolphe Ferrière, Célestin Freinet, Rudolph Arnheim) and much reflection. [. . .] We organised seminars, open to families, with the most committed representatives of Italian pedagogy. So that in 1965 annual periods of professional development began to take shape such as the Pedagogical November. [. . .] We began an exchange with the Geneva School, which works with active pedagogy and Jean Piaget, we began a dialogue with French pedagogy and colleagues, connected with the thinking and the new techniques of Célestin Freinet.
>
> (*ibid.*, p.91)

After twenty years of isolation under fascism, Italy and Malaguzzi were now well and truly reconnected to the rest of Europe and beyond.

The selection of documents (Reggio Emilia Working Group)

> Either pedagogy – like all the human sciences – is remade, reconstructed and updated based on the new conditions of the times, or it loses its nature, its function, its proper capacity to correspond to the times it lives in, and above all to foresee, anticipate and prepare the days of tomorrow.
>
> (Loris Malaguzzi, 1969, 'The Meaning and
> Intervention of School Management Committees
> in the Scuole dell'Infanzia' [37.69])

The second period we have chosen to organise Malaguzzi's work into begins with the opening of Reggio Emilia's first *scuola comunale dell'infanzia* on 5 November 1963. It was a difficult and embattled opening that shaped many of the choices Malaguzzi would make during the period, and which the reader will find traces of in the selected writings. From that day on Malaguzzi would be associated with the municipal-run schools for young children, a completely new reality in Reggio Emilia and for Italy in general.

In an interview Malaguzzi gave in 1993 he said:

> responsibilities were clear in our minds; many eyes, not all friendly, were watching us. We had to make as few errors as possible; we had to find our cultural identity quickly, make ourselves known, and win trust and respect. [. . .] It was a feverish time, a time of adaptation, of continuous adjustment of ideas, of selection of projects and attempts. Those projects and attempts were supposed to respond to the combined expectations of children and families and to reflect our competences, which were still in the making.
>
> (Malaguzzi, 2012, p.31)

We believe his statement expresses the distinct commitment of the time, a period full of initiatives that Malaguzzi promoted and collaborated on, scattered across the whole region. These ranged over various fields and confronted different subjects: from a seminar on numbers to an exhibition on toys accompanied by a collection of children's drawings, and touching on still other themes in public conferences and professional development meetings. A breadth of interest that was capable of bringing together diverse cultural levels and contexts with an attention, coherence and quality of communication we believe to be quite surprising in the field of education; always striving to make 3- to 6-year-old children and their schools better known to parents and citizens in order to legitimise the investments being asked of the *Comune*. This was an educational and ethical project Malaguzzi felt to be important and necessary for a new society.

The theme of removing children from anonymity is particularly important and had already appeared in Malaguzzi's previous writings and we will find it remains constant over time. It was well defined in the *Casa di Vacanza* [summer camp] project, where he arranges for each child to have a 'biographical record' written up by teachers, which also includes 'a psychological and behavioural profile' [23.64]. At a later date we find him presenting the *scuola materna* experience to the city of Reggio Emilia, giving his assurance that children attending *scuole materne* will not enter elementary school 'anonymous and unknown', but accompanied by materials and documents [33.68].

It should be remembered that Malaguzzi was a marvellous organiser and again, in the *Casa di Vacanza* project, organisation is defined in specific ways that were revolutionary for the times: ratios of adults to children to vary with children's ages, the group considered as a socio–ethical entity, the basic structure of the pedagogy with priority given to 'recovering equilibrium and psychological adjustment [of children]', professional development for educators, planning based on written reference work, and parent involvement. Malaguzzi also proposed using the summer camp buildings, normally deserted in April and May, in a specific programme for children under 6 years, halving the numbers of children attending for this younger age group.

Organisation, which in our introduction to the previous chapter we defined as 'the conditions', is one of the recurring themes in Malaguzzi's pedagogy, and in a speech at a conference in Rimini in 1966, he states 'organisation is always an important pedagogical factor' [31.67]. The venue for the conference was no accident. For it was in Rimini that the *Centro Educativo Italo-Svizzero* was founded and directed by Margherita Zoebeli,[3] becoming a place where the generation of innovating and radical educators, to which Malaguzzi belonged, had access to professional development, meetings and exchange, a crucible where kindred ideas could be debated. The CEIS had close ties with the *Movimento di Cooperazione Educativa*, whose main points of reference were Freinet and an active pedagogy valuing the teacher's role as experiential guide. The intense and close relations between Malaguzzi and Bruno Ciari were generated in this setting.

What strikes us in Loris Malaguzzi's writings is his great commitment to change, to which this very fertile, dynamic period of history was probably conducive. Malaguzzi did not only abstractly theorise, but always firmly fused his ideas (new, revolutionary, borrowed from theories of the time but never in servile, deferential ways) to the construction of new experience and realities. The new experiences looked for (and found) new terminologies: what had previously been defined as a '*Colonia*', mainly conceived in terms of health, prevention and recreation, was changed to a '*Casa di vacanza*': the same process would take place when changing from '*scuola materna*' (school for 3- to 6-year-olds) to '*asilo infantile*', later adopting the term '*scuola dell'infanzia*'.

These were new names for radically different projects and experiences. Another of the many initiatives during this period was the '*Novembre pedagogico*' [Pedagogical November] of 1965, with a programme of five parent conferences and four professional development meetings for teachers [25.65]. We cannot know if professional development in this format was something new for the time; however to us it certainly seems of great import that it was given such visibility and was announced to parents and citizens in a leaflet promoting 'a series of events in November with the aim of giving value to the work and problems of the *scuole materne* and stimulating more thorough knowledge and esteem for them, both in families and in public opinion' [25.65]. Making visible the professional development of teachers (all female since men were excluded by national law until the mid-Seventies) was intended to give value to a profession held in low esteem and associated with a concept of welfare, care and minding young children.

Parents were a necessary presence in the new *scuola dell'infanzia* project, to the extent that Malaguzzi had no qualms about scolding them for their absence from the first *Novembre pedagogico* meeting [26.65]; or recommending they participate at subsequent meetings about the psychology of children aged 3 to 6 years [29.66]. These meetings to enable deeper examination together with experts lead back to the idea of 'discuss[ing] with awareness, based on precise, concrete information', which Malaguzzi used to define democracy in 1959 [17.59]. His reference to the warm rich debate that absent parents had missed in the first meeting testifies to this view.

Legitimisation given by Malaguzzi to the new role of teachers and parents comes together with a new conception of the child and the child's possibilities. He also assigns a non-subordinate role to families, in search of the cultural identity so urgently needed to give impetus to the new politics on childhood, which had been inaugurated with the birth of the *Comune*'s schools.

Malaguzzi was a curious reader and tirelessly read authors of all nationalities with different professional backgrounds. Reviewing his work in this period (published and unpublished), references can be found to Jean Marc Gaspard Itard (physician, pedagogue and educator), Edouard Seguin (physician), Henri Wallon (psychologist, pedagogue and philosopher), Renè Zazzo (psychologist and pedagogue), all French; the Italian Maria Montessori; Jean Piaget and Édouard Claparède (psychologist and pedagogue), who were Swiss; the Americans Arnold Gessel (psychologist and paediatrician) and Jerome Bruner (psychologist); the German Kurt Lewin (psychologist); Anton Semenovyc Makarenko (pedagogue and educator) who was Ukrainian; and many others besides, testifying to Malaguzzi's impassioned and never ending research, sometimes following unfrequented paths.

During this period Malaguzzi appears to be mostly committed to research into defining and legitimising the cultural identity of the municipal *scuola dell'infanzia*. He is extremely interested, too, in the logical structure of thinking and the operational theories of intelligence put forward in studies by Jean Piaget. Referencing a scientific researcher of Jean Piaget's depth, who used innovative and original methods to reveal children and their knowledge processes, is surely a choice intended to give legitimacy to schools for very young children.

An example of Malaguzzi's interest in Piaget comes from 1966. '*L'educazione del bambino dai 3 ai 6 anni*' [The education of the child aged 3–6] was the title given to a series of public lectures held in Rimini in April/May 1966, to accompany a regional exhibition of 'expressive activities', such as drawing and painting. Malaguzzi contributed a lecture on 'The initiation of logical-mathematical thinking, according to Jean Piaget', excerpts from which are included in this chapter [31.67]. Malaguzzi felt obliged to justify choosing a non-Italian researcher as a focus for his talk on numbers in schools for 3- to 6-years-olds, and what emerges is his reaching towards 'the universality, the ecumenism of the culture of our time' – a warning still timely today in a period of conflicting fragmented cultures of identity.

There are several documents in this period on learning mathematics, ranging from professional development to conferences and public lectures. During these years Malaguzzi focuses on the idea that mathematics can be an area of learning for 3- to 6-years-olds, since the 'basic structure of mathematical conceptualisations are identical to the basic structures of thinking' [31.67]. But he immediately places this idea in a broader, more general context, stating that 'logical thinking is constructed and refined as much through the study of science, spoken and written language, drawing, art, music etc. as through the study of mathematics'. This line of thinking anticipated an inter-disciplinary discourse that emerged with complexity theories in the mid-1970s; it suggests a root for his theory of 'the hundred languages', which over time became an emblem of Reggio Emilia pedagogy, a theory in which children (human beings) are recognised as possessing many cultural possibilities, which can too readily be systematically denied and taken away by the culture of school and society.

Malaguzzi's deep interest in Piaget can also be related to his discourse in the previous chapter on psycho-pedagogy as a theoretical frame of reference capable of opening new scenarios for research and action in the childhood services being established at the time. How can psychologists work with pedagogy? The old diatribe between psychology and pedagogy finds Malaguzzi, as always, bringing together apparently opposed elements, choosing, re-interpreting, looking for concrete applications.

He appreciated and took from psychology the methods of observation. These, he believed, were capable of lifting from anonymity children whose identity had been devalued as incomplete and lacking because viewed and evaluated with an adult yardstick; and of discovering and presenting the dynamic processes of their maturation. But always taking a critical attitude to the core concept of developmental stages, supported in this stance by what he saw emerging from the work of teachers.

Malaguzzi aspires to a transition from more experimental science to school experimentation, a process giving pedagogy new life but struggling to make the transition into the reality of school. There can be no doubt of his multifaceted personality, persistently striving to make ideas and desires into reality. The building of beautiful and culturally important schools was certainly one of these desires, and the reason he followed these projects so closely, including their construction. There is a series of documents sent to the Mayor, the *Assessore* and municipal technicians during work on building the *scuola dell'infanzia* Diana, suggesting among other things the creation of an *atelier* environment in the school gardens (and highlighting how important he considered its presence) [36.69], and reminders about keeping to deadlines in carrying out the plans [32.67].

In a document from March 1968 [33.68], Malaguzzi gives an effective synthesis of the research into cultural identity for the new *scuola materna* – that 'many people would like to call *Scuola dell'infanzia* with good cause' – inspired by 'a modern humanism, originating from the essential basis of Piaget's discoveries'. The publication is a sort of manifesto in the simple direct language

Malaguzzi knew he possessed, despite more often being complex, metaphorical and evocative. All the themes developed over the following years in the experience of Reggio Emilia's municipal schools emerge here. It is a sort of list in which Malaguzzi briefly describes conditions for a good school: engagement with families, professional development for personnel, the value of the environment, a richness and variety of stimulus, pedagogical conferences for parents, education exhibitions, observation notes entered in teachers' notebooks, the direct creation of educational materials, study conferences with participants from different cities, connections with the society and culture of the times. Once again he is not afraid of giving clear indications: no to scholasticism, but yes to the importance of observing, stimulating, annotating, re-proposing, examining. He identifies an evolving *university* in the quality of the teachers' everyday work (in his opinion the pedagogical work in Reggio Emilia's schools was a 'true university', that is to say a true and authoritative place of learning), and calls for ties with primary school.

Clearly in this piece he is concerned with reassuring the city, which is not yet used to schools for young children, through his statements on integrating innovation and tradition, and through his cautious and somewhat classificatory attitude towards the capacities of 3- to 6-year-olds. This concern was present in his Rimini talks of 1966 and 1969 [31.67, 38.69], and he raises it here again when he declares the importance of providing differentiated spaces and activities, especially intended to safeguard the youngest children, assigned with mats as spaces and modules for play and work. Although he had great negotiating skills, Malaguzzi was not a man of compromise, but had clear positions he declared with great force. So the care taken not to explicitly oppose traditionally entrenched ideas, instead integrating them into a new system of values and organisation being defined, was probably necessary to keep open channels of dialogue through which the experience could continue and expand.

Another theme proposed by Malaguzzi of great interest today is the organic journey between a *scuola materna* and elementary school: 'the *scuola materna* connects with the school that follows in spirit and in fact . . . [effectively finding] its pedagogical identity in this proper and necessary organic unity, without in any way belittling the features of its profound and authentic originality' [33.68]. Malaguzzi had already imagined this project in 1968, but unfortunately in Italy it has never been completed, in spite of several ministerial circulars written on the subject. 'Organicity' – wholeness – and unity are cross-cutting themes running through the new concept of the child, the idea of involving families, the connections between school and society.

All these issues are raised again in a clearer more extended way in Rimini in 1969, when Malaguzzi examined teachers' cultural and professional background together with an analysis of the real pedagogical situation they worked in [38.69]. The reflection starts from the conviction that children's health and wellbeing are closely tied to those of teachers. His accurate and vigorous analysis makes a defence of the teaching profession, not to preserve the *status quo* with a corporative vision, but to denounce existent situations and propose structural and organisational change: to reduce the child–adult ratio; to abandon the concept of care and offer children and adults new learning objectives; and, above all, to work in groups so as to lead teachers out of isolation.

Malaguzzi was a convinced advocate that the *scuola dell'infanzia*, more than other schools, must look to the future, and that it can be the lever for change and quality in future schools. He also denounces the fact that families often have a minor role in schools; in his opinion it is necessary to reconsider families as authoritative interlocutors and bearers of important experiences and competences, making a precious cultural contribution. Already we have a clear glimpse of the framework and humus of the cultural manifesto Malaguzzi wrote shortly before his death, *Una carta per tre diritti* [A charter of three rights],[4] in which he proposes that the rights of children, teachers and families are indissolubly woven together in schools, and in an education that aspires to call itself such.

The mixing of languages and their concurrent presence, which had already been theorised and distinguished, can be found in a 1969 document [35.69], where the idea that 'without experience thinking is not nourished' [31.67] becomes reality. It is a particularly important piece, first and foremost because perhaps for the first time educational experience with children aged 3 to 6 years is reported in a document where reference theories and educational choices are made clear. What it gives us, Malaguzzi warns, is not *the* itinerary but one of many itineraries for 'orienting the walking together, the growing together'. We can also identify in this piece the re/search for a project thread, feeding the children's motivation and offering them the possibility to be protagonists, not only of single situations and experiences but in the development of the work. The idea that a school is a permanent exhibition of 'precious documentation [that] grows with the story and requires ordered planning inside and outside the classroom' is to our mind the germ of an idea that would be developed over the years to come. The motivation for documentation here is not only the need to legitimise the *scuola dell'infanzia*, making experience with children visible to parents and citizens, but also the offer of 'a constantly available stimulus to children's memory and reflection'.

The theme of organisation is taken up again and we read: 'organisation does not mean systematisation, neither does it means simply adding'. Rather it is a means of comprehensive renewal capable of giving children and adults new conditions, so that the 'occasional, dispersive and spontaneous' are not given too much room. Finally, the piece is a synthesis of evaluation, an impetus to continue methodological experimentation and differentiation in the increasing number of *scuole comunali* in the city in 1969.

On the bond between school and society Malaguzzi asserts forcefully that 'the fate of papers, particularly Education Papers, is to go over the head of reality and present proposals that often do not get beyond paper' [38.69]. The *scuole dell'infanzia*, by contrast, must be rooted in the society and the culture of their time.

Scuole dell'infanzia need alliances, and Malaguzzi was a great weaver of relations. Readers will find evidence of this in the letters of widely differing tenor included in the selection: letters to *Comune* surveyors, to the Mayor, to the Olivetti Company, to intellectuals of various nationalities. All these communications have the purpose of creating precious alliances, that can help give form and legitimacy to this new experience of the *Comune*-managed *scuola dell'infanzia*.

Part of this alliance-building is the project of parent participation, which was essential for giving strength to *scuole dell'infanzia*, generated by the idea of the unity of children's experience and the idea of democracy, both so strongly rooted in Malaguzzi, in the city and in the region of Emilia-Romagna. In Rimini in 1969 Malaguzzi pointed out the risk of schools having a subordinate and marginal conception of families, the result of excluding the real outside world in which children live. This thinking is also the fruit of his relationship with Ada Marchesini Gobetti (see Chapter 1, n.44), founder and director of the *Giornale dei genitori* [Parents' Journal] and an important reference at the time for many parents looking for a new definition of their role in school and society. In 1969, when *Comitati di Scuola e Città* were created in Modena, where Malaguzzi was a pedagogical consultant, their purpose and structure were very different from those of Committees then existing in state schools, whose rhetoric of collaboration and dialogue Malaguzzi denounced as condescending, passive and disguising negative attitudes. He explains that choosing the term *Città* [City] for inclusion in the name of the new management bodies is an invitation to broaden the vision of childhood beyond school, and to keep in mind the unity and complexity of children's identity and experience [27.69].

Already we can see the maturity of a project still living today, proposing the *scuola dell'infanzia* (and later the *nido*) as places producing culture and democracy, and reconciling the different places that figure in children's lives.

Timeline 1964–69

Key: *Malaguzzi*
Reggio Emilia
Italy

1964	**Municipality opens its second school for 3- to 6-year-olds, Anna Frank.** Post-war peak in births: 1.03 million.
1965	**First work in municipal schools with the new concept of an *atelierista*; start of professional development activities.**
1966	**Hearing of appeal (first filed in 1963) by *Comune* of Reggio Emilia to be permitted to municipalise *Asilo del Popolo* in Villa Cella.** Aldo Moro government falls after failing to get approval for legislation to allow state-run *scuole materne*; Bruno Ciari moves to Bologna as director of primary educational and extracurricular services.

1967	**Municipality takes over *Asilo del Popolo* in Villa Cella formerly managed by UDI; later renamed *XXV Aprile*.**
	Publication of 'Letters to a Teacher' by Don Milani and pupils at the *Scuola di Barbiana*.
1968	*Consultant to municipal schools in Modena.*
	Municipality opens third school, Primavera; Initiative Committees created in city neighbourhoods to press for new services.
	Law no.444 approved permitting State and municipal-run *scuole materne;* Law for elections to regional councils starts introduction of regional government.
1969	**Municipality takes over San Maurizio school formerly managed by CLN; later renamed Gulliver.**
	Pedagogical Guidelines (*Orientamenti Pedagogici*) published for state-run schools; Piazza Fontana bomb in Milan, the beginning of the *Anni di Piombo* (Years of Lead), a period of neo-fascist and extreme left-wing terrorism.

Documents 1964–69

1964

23.64 Speech at a study conference *La Casa di Vacanza come Servizio Sociale* [The *Casa di Vacanza* as a Social Service], Reggio Emilia, May 1964

Editor's note: The conference, and Malaguzzi's presentation, are about summer camps, with the traditional name, *colonia*, replaced by a new term, *casa di vacanza*. Other speakers at this conference covered the training of staff, health and hygiene, 3- to 6-year-olds in the modern *casa di vacanza*, motor and play activities, and organisation and administration.

New guidelines for the re-organisation of social services in the 'Casa di Vacanza'

Colonia at the seaside and in the mountains must be freed of the old and traditional concepts of charity and philanthropy, of being places which are largely medical.

This type of *Colonia* is mostly content with [providing] general medical care, and the providentially therapeutic qualities of nature. Ultimately their organisation is based on partly incomplete theory on pedagogical and curative levels, and refuses to recognise a large part of children's issues and vital needs.

Based on subjective sociological evaluation some people theorise the progressive and inevitable decline of the *Colonia* and the end of its social functions, but we reply that this thinking is arbitrary and illogical. A more appropriate evaluation of current sociological data instead leads us to framing *Colonia* issues in terms of necessary renewal, which is the essential condition for an adequate and appropriate capacity for responding to today's emerging social needs – needs which will continue to emerge in the future.

New principles in Organicist Medicine, Mental Hygiene and Psycho-pedagogy, the evolution and transformation of living standards in Italian families and the socio-psychological and moral symptoms these produce, the new needs of today's children – who are certainly in better general physical condition but more exposed to risk while growing up, due to the influence of many factors making traditional education by family and school difficult – and the lack of social services that can help family and school overcome this current imbalanced phase, [these] are all factors that call for a society that is aware of childhood's problems, with urgent and widespread renewal and development of educational structures, methods, techniques and ideals. Naturally these needs also affect the *Colonia*.

New concepts of the *Colonia* must be inspired by modern definitions of health, which is not only an absence of illness, but a state of complete well-being, a balanced psyche in a fully thriving social and individual personality. The *Colonia* must promote and centre the way it organises education on [the basis of] 'historically identified' needs and of collective experience that is constantly re-examined at every responsible level. Above all it must act in the awareness – framed in an objective evaluation of the welfare and education situation in Italy, and despite the limited time [children attend] – that it constitutes an opportunity that is highly conducive to developing original educational experience by virtue of its intrinsic and distinctive features. To the point that certain vital elements could become exemplary models for renewing general pedagogical philosophy and practice in our country.

Based on these considerations we suggest replacing the traditional name '*Colonia*', which is incapable of completely expressing the new values of a socio-pedagogical, techno-organisational reality, with '*Casa di Vacanza*'. This does not mean only continuing the pedagogical action of schools and family, or being in line with it. With careful and considered critical examination, the *Casa di Vacanza* is capable not only of purely supplementary work, but of recovering equilibrium and psychological adjustment.

These designs for *Colonia* education and organisation could be obstructed and deflected on a practical level by a series of problems:

a   the use of *Colonie* where the architectural structure and function have been dictated by old models of community living;

b   educational staff who are inadequately prepared;

c   budgets organised in such a way that the function of *Colonie* with new pedagogical and therapeutic qualities are not fully guaranteed.

Obviously it is essential, therefore, to tackle these three problems in determined and pro-active ways. If they are convinced of the need for renewal *Casa di Vacanza* promoters and administrators must find a solution for problems one and three. As a solution to problem two, given the turnover in educational staff, we suggest setting up special annual courses in education and updating.

In the context of the necessary increase in numbers of *Casa di Vacanza* staff, we also suggest promoting professional development of teams of directors (head directors, psycho-*pedagogistas*, doctors, general secretaries, administrative managers, sector leaders or director's assistants) to establish stable working groups and guarantee continuity over several years' experience.

Another type of problem to be dealt with, which arises from new concepts of pedagogy and therapy, has to do with the criteria for selecting children when this is necessary. Until now these criteria have been almost exclusively dictated by physical and medical parameters and excluded, or undervalued, psychological and pedagogical criteria.

Staying in a *Casa di Vacanza* by the sea or in the mountains also has valuable therapeutic effects for children with personality and behaviour alterations (affective and emotional immaturity; shy, slow, inactive and passive children; children who are over-protected or lack social relations and personal autonomy; children who are slightly mentally underdeveloped, or suffer from hypo-genitalism, endocrine dysfunction, psychosomatic symptoms, reactive personality disorder, abandonment syndrome etc.).

In relation to this problem it would be advisable not just to use referrals and intervention by the *Centro Medico Psico-Pedagogico Comunale*, but look at the possibility of setting up biographical records. These would include psychological and behavioural profiles filled in by teachers each year, along with medical records and objectives. This type of record would accompany children on their seaside and mountain vacations and be completed with notes by *Casa di Vacanza* directors.

A further consideration is the age of children who benefit from *Casa di Vacanza*, which at present is from six to twelve years. If social and medical action by Public Authorities is to be primarily preventative, as it must be, then we cannot understand why this beneficial welfare provision only takes place at six years old. This goes against the need for early diagnosis and identification.

We suggest Public Authorities running *Case di Vacanza* work in such a way that younger children can also enjoy the therapeutic benefits of mountain and seaside breaks. We propose these seasonal institutions also open in April and May for children aged three to six years. Ways of organising this, together with aspects of health and pedagogy, must be the object of deeper study and clarification.

In practical terms renewing the *Casa di Vacanza* needs to deal with three kinds of problem:

1   improving the quality of the daily routine and all the basic facilities (food and board, cleanliness, organisation, general comfort), with the aim of offering hospitality that corresponds to greater needs;
2   re-organising and increasing the number of teams of directors, and staff in various sectors of work;
3   more specific pedagogical guidelines.

The main thread of pedagogy in the *Casa di Vacanza* will focus above all on issues of children's maturation. This term means the whole integral physical, mental, affective, civic and moral development of individual personalities, while bearing in mind some widespread and characteristic traits of children's existential condition today. Bear in mind the disorientation and imbalance young people encounter more frequently in today's society, which can be provoked by a lack or weaker sense of social feeling and interpersonal relations, resulting in solitude and marginalisation. It can be provoked by greater emotional instability, which with other influencing factors (radio, television, cinema, cartoons, news magazines etc.) encourages escapism, passivity, negativity, or adopting heroes or magical stereotypes. It can be provoked by the weakly organised nature of children's cultural knowledge and acquisition, which provokes intellectual and emotional insecurity and creates serious obstacles to the process of maturation. It can be provoked by frustrated needs for physical activity and the acquisition of psychomotor ability, which increase autonomy, control of Self and body schema.

Pedagogical guidelines structuring the *Case di Vacanza* will work towards:

a   creating environments of loving security, with fully efficient health and hygiene;
b   satisfying and increasing social feeling;
c   satisfying the need for activity, movement, play, relaxing nerves;
d   satisfying and increasing the need for knowledge, for doing, for creating;
e   developing a capacity for personal organisation and autonomy;
f   encouraging the practice of courtesy, loyalty, goodness, human solidarity in the widest sense, trust in humankind, reason, science; love of justice, democracy, and peace;
g   satisfying the need for spiritual and religious worship, with maximum tolerance of ideas and faiths.

These structuring pedagogical guidelines must come together and be expressed through:

a   a programme of work with educational situations wisely distributed through the day and the duration of the children's stay;

b   differentiated quantity and quality based on stages of evolution, by age:

6 year-old children
7/9 year-old children
10/12 year-old children

An essential condition for fruitful work in the *Casa di Vacanza* is for educational staff to get to know children fully and rapidly. It would be a great advantage if families filled in specific questionnaires, providing essential data and giving knowledge of the children and their life environments. This act of collaboration is an example of how we can help families to be aware of *Casa di Vacanza* problems in more relevant and conscious ways.

The basis of staff organisation in the Community will be in Groups, which are considered to be a natural, necessary element for the growth of individuality and sociality. The basis of the pedagogy will be Group Pedagogy.

A PSYCHOLOGICAL AND PEDAGOGICAL DEFINITION OF THE GROUP

Groups have been identified as the foundation unit of the *Case di Vacanza* (where they are both an autonomous and an integral, integrating part) confirming the concept of education as the social formation of individuals.

Groups should not be conceptualised merely as an organisational and disciplinary tool but as a situation that is necessary to satisfy the needs of individuals to be educated and mature.

Becoming educated and maturing do not happen alone or spontaneously. They require the protective and liberating presence and participation of adults.

Leaving aside what is perhaps a too indeterminate sociological meaning, Community and Group can be defined primarily as ethical-social entities, which are acquired through ideals, and which inform and steer our evolution through life experience.

On the level of psychology a Group is always considered to be an autonomous but integral situation in an overall vision of the Community; Groups make for a good level of communication and exchange between members, which is a decisive factor for perceiving relations between self and others, others with others, and the system of values being used; and they are a good defence against general organisational pressures.

An educator's task is to facilitate and ensure occasions where each person can create the above dynamics, so guaranteeing the greatest amount of self-evaluation and self-identification.

With reference to the particular way a *Casa di Vacanza* is formed, the Groups are obviously of an institutional kind. We consider the differences between a *Casa di Vacanza* Group and a so-called free Group (in reality these are also conditioned by external factors) to be more an appearance than a reality. We would like to underline that institutional Groups in *Casa di Vacanza* are positively conditioned by their permanence in a time and place, so their experience is more intensely dynamic, and by the psychologically decisive and natural factor of the homogenisation of age, considered not in the strictly chronological sense.

In Groups, and through Groups, children restructure and are nourished through their active participation in the life and company of others (even when this participation is only interior), on the levels of collaboration and tolerance, and the solidarity of shared acquisition of experience, in a framework of shared models and end values.

A Group is a stable community, which is organised and guided by an Educator. It should not be made up of more than 20 children at the same stage of evolution. Owing to particular needs the group of 6-year-olds (usually children with no school experience, or characterised by immaturity) should not be made up of more than ten children.

Educators are an integral part of the Group and their fundamental task is to carry out their role effectively and increase the interior Group dynamic, Group cohesion, and the value of the Group.

They will particularly promote and facilitate children's processes of adaptation. They will monitor and modify the dynamics that form the basis of relations which individuals and the Group adopt towards different activities, other Groups, and the Community.

An indirect factor of primary importance in facilitating adaptation processes is satisfying children's affective needs. Among other things educators should therefore place great value on children maintaining and increasing their affective relations with their extended family through detailed letter-writing. They should also communicate with children's families themselves after agreement with Directors.

During each holiday period, a Parents Party, considered a highly valuable moment in the *Casa di Vacanza* educational structure, should affirm the importance of natural emotional ties and break with the aspects of isolation and closure that were a feature of the old Colonia.

The team of directors in the *Casa di Vacanza* will develop specific work programmes, which document and examine the formative processes of single Groups, the relations between Groups, and Group cohesion in the larger Community unit.

This work of renewing the organisation, conceptualisation and purposes of *Case di Vacanza* can only be done with family endorsement and participation. Families must be taken from a passive position as pure consumers of a service and brought to an active, direct presence and collaboration.

The teams of directors should work carefully and rigorously to develop differentiated educational programmes based on the different states of evolution in Groups. As an indication we propose some general guidelines:

6-year-old children

Strengthen self-knowledge (structuring the self), foster maturation processes through: differentiation and opposition, emotional control, the formation of first social sentiments, mainly through play, co-operative activity, easy experiences of manipulation and drama play.
Autonomy, and the personal organisation of basic functions (dressing, undressing, washing, eating), feelings of property, order, cleanliness, respect for the property of others, respect for the rules of co-habitation.
Refining observation and expressive capacities.
Practising and enhancing motor skills, harmony of movement, command of one's own body.
Responses to early religious problems presenting spontaneously in children.

7/9-year-old children

Giving value to social needs and sentiments and increasing times when the Group is together through: group conversation, play, sport, exercises in artistic expression, education, and harmonisation of feelings of ambition and [self] affirmation.
First guided discussions on issues of organisation, choices in the Group programme, and practical work.
Refining the capacity for observation and research, and for ordering experience.
A considered extension of perspectives on work, on effort, and on success.
Forming a consciousness of the ideal of goodness + through the life of Jesus.

10/12-year-old children

Further and higher awareness in children of the Group and Community, and of personal roles through: Group conversation, more demanding and complex methodologies and goals in play, sport, and expressive and artistic exercise.
Extending feelings of responsibility, behavioural models, help and protection towards younger companions, collaboration with superiors.
Collegial discussion and autonomous development of work and disciplinary plans, within the framework of the overall planning of Community norms.
More intense Group work on the level of researching cultural and scientific ownership of experience.
The purpose of moral and religious behaviour.

1965

24.65 Letter to Berthold Beauverd, June 1965

> **Editor's note:** Malaguzzi is writing to one of the authors of *Avant le Calcul* [Before doing sums], which was published in 1965 as Volume 21 of *Cahiers de pédagogie expérimentale et de psychologie de l'enfant: Nouvelle série*. Beauverd's co-authors included Jean Piaget and other members of his Geneva school. Beauverd played an important role in applying the mathematical ideas of Piaget to the classroom. A seminar for teachers on initiation to number, based on the work of Piaget and Beauverd, was held in 1965 in Reggio Emilia led by Loris Malaguzzi and Dr Carlo Iannuccelli. For more on Malaguzzi's interest in this work on mathematics, see 27.66, 31.67 and 94.90.

8 June 1965
Very illustrious
B. Beauverd
Clochetons 21
Lausanne (Switzerland)

Sympathetically remembering our meeting in Geneva, please accept our sincerest congratulations for your book '*Avant le calcul*', the experiences of which we are trying to transfer into the activity programmes in Reggio Emilia's *Scuole Materne*. We hope to have you as a most welcome guest and collaborator in the Study Conference on learning numbers in the *scuola materna*, which we hope to hold in the Spring of next year.

With best wishes
(prof. Loris Malaguzzi)

❊ ❊ ❊

25.65 Notice from the *Comune* of Reggio Emilia, November 1965

> **Editor's note:** This was the first of what were to become known as 'Pedagogical Novembers', a programme of talks on pedagogical issues, open to families and educators, and featuring presentations from leading figures in Italian education – including Malaguzzi, who organised these events in Reggio Emilia. Reggio Emilia was not alone in holding such public meetings; Bologna, for example, initiated 'Pedagogical Februaries' in 1962.

Pedagogical November Scuola Materna

1 November 1965

The *Direzione delle Scuole Materne* [the *Comune's* office for managing munici-pal schools] in collaboration with the *Centro Medico Psico-Pedagogico Comunale* (CMPPC) is promoting a series of events in November with the aim of giving value to the work and problems of the *scuola materna* and stimulating more thor-ough knowledge and esteem for them, both in families and in public opinion.

For the families

Five conferences will be organised aimed primarily at families, who are increas-ingly being asked for a valid and conscious educational commitment, and a valuable enlightened collaboration with the *scuola materna*.

The conferences will be given by eminent experts on the premises of the CMPPC (via dell'Abbadessa no. 8) based on the following programme:

Wednesday 10 November 20.30
ROBERTO MAZZETTI[5]
Principal of the Higher Institute of Education of Salerno
'*SCUOLA MATERNA*, THE TRADITION AND THE REALITY OF OUR TIME'

Tuesday 16 November 20.30
FRANCO TADINI
Director of the national School Centre for *Scuola Materna*
'THE *SCUOLA MATERNA* AS A SCHOOL OF PARENTS'

Tuesday 23 November 20.30
CARLO IANNUCCELLI
Director of the CMPPC of Reggio Emilia
'THE *SCUOLA MATERNA* AND ITS DISTINCTIVE EDUCA-TIONAL IDENTITY: THE CHILD'S MIND, AFFECTIVITY AND SOCIABILITY'

Friday 26 November 20.30
LORIS MALAGUZZI
Psychologist at the CMPPC
'EDUCATIONAL ERRORS IN THE FAMILY: HOW THESE REFLECT ON THE *SCUOLA MATERNA*'

Tuesday 30 November 20.30
PIER MARIO MASCIANGELO
Freelance Lecturer in Psychiatry
'CURRENT STRUCTURES AND RELATIONAL MODES IN THE FAMILY GROUP'

For teachers in the scuola materna

In order to go more deeply into the cultural, pedagogical and teaching issues in the *scuola materna*, a Study Seminar will be organised by dr. Carlo Iannuccelli and dr. Loris Malaguzzi on 'Initiation of knowledge of numbers and calculation in the *scuola materna*'.

The Seminar is for teachers of the *scuola materna*, and will take place over four working sessions based on the following programme.

Saturday 4 December 15.00 CARLO IANNUCCELLI
'METHODS AND RESULTS OF PIAGET'S RESEARCH ON THE PSYCHOLOGICAL DEVELOPMENT OF THE CHILD'

Saturday 11 December 15.00 LORIS MALAGUZZI
'THE RESEARCH OF PIAGET AND THE GENEVA SCHOOL ON THE FORMATION OF LOGICAL-MATHEMATICAL THINKING IN THE CHILD'

Saturday 18 December 15.00 LORIS MALAGUZZI
'GOING FROM RESEARCH IN PSYCHOLOGY TO RESEARCH IN PEDAGOGY'

Saturday 8 January 15.00 LORIS MALAGUZZI
'EXAMPLES OF CLASSROOM PRACTICE FOR TEACHERS OF NUMBERS'

❋ ❋ ❋

26.65 Letter to parents, 15 November 1965

> **Editor's note:** This letter to parents seems to be a response to poor attendance at the first 'conference' of the Pedagogical November held on 10 November.

To the parents of children enrolled in the scuola materna

Dearest parents

In promoting the series of Conferences for Parents, for which you received the programme some days ago [see preceding document], we have thought above all about you and your children: about your problems, your children's problems and the problems we live through together in that unique and not at all easy experience that is the *scuola materna*.

These are the themes that the series of Conferences proposes to examine, with the intention of helping us all to understand in ever better ways, our vocation as adults and parents: what is a *scuola materna*, what it should mean for you and your children, how you can support this common experience in the best way, what you should and should not do, what are the most advanced results in sociological, psychological and pedagogical research for children to grow without drama and conflict and come to a happy flourishing of their personality.

We must report with a certain disappointment that the opening conference held by Professor Mazzetti of Salerno University (which was highly successful and raised rich and passionate debate) saw the solid presence of teachers and school people – but too weak a presence by parents.

Editor's note: This is a second letter, perhaps drafted by Malaguzzi, to be sent out by the teachers in individual schools to go together with the first letter.

Dear Parents

We are strongly convinced it is our duty not only to propose initiatives, but also not to feel disappointment and to leave nothing untried that could improve and enrich the sensibility of families and public opinion on the most fascinating and responsible issue of our existence, that of education. We call on you to participate in large numbers at the next talks, the first of which will be held on

TUESDAY 16 NOVEMBER AT 21.00

At the Medico Psycho-Pedagogical Centre with speaker Prof. Franco Tadini, Director of the National *Scuola Materna* Didactics Centre, who will speak on

'THE *SCUOLA MATERNA* AS A SCHOOL OF PARENTS'

Certain that you will accept our invitation, we thank you and send you our sincerest greetings.

L'Insegnante Capo Gruppo [Teacher who is the head of group]
La Direzione delle Scuole Materne Comunali

Reggio Emilia, 15 November 1965

1966

27.66 Notes made for study seminars on Numbers, 3 March 1966

Editor's note: These seminars were organised at several different schools in Reggio Emilia over a two month period. Much of the vocabulary here refers to language used by Piaget and the field of mathematics 'operations'. These notes prepared for the seminars are in the form of a series of headings, each of which is developed by Malaguzzi in note form. The first five headings and their content have been fully translated; the sixth heading, on reversibility of thought, is given, but without the accompanying notes.

Study seminar on numbers

REGGIO EMILIA DECEMBER 1965–JANUARY 1966

What mental operations are we interested in?

The mental operations that interest us (because they belong to children of pre-school age) are those that are possible with objects that come to our attention in whatever way they are arranged or distributed.

What are these mental operations?

a   The operation of classification: I can mentally put together objects that have a common quality (a spherical shape, a red colour etc.).

b   The operation of seriation:[6] I can put objects in order according to the degree, the intensity, of their attribute (width, weight, transparency, etc.).

c   The operation of numbering: I can count an assembly of objects.

How are these operations enacted?

All these operations are enacted at the level of concrete thinking. They are logical operations and all arrive at the point of constructing invariables: a class, a series, a numerical quantity, which are realities in themselves whatever the arrangement in time and space of the elements that constitute them or the different compositions they participate in (adding, subtracting).

What are the typical aspects of a class?

A class (white daisies) makes a group of a common quality (being white daisies) and a quantity (the quantity of white daisies). The two essential and interdependent qualities are therefore: comprehension (the quality present in each member of the class) and extension (the assembled number of members in the class).

What are the child's difficulties in understanding class?
The inclusion–property relation fundamental to class
Seriation: another concrete-logical operation
What is a series?
Types of difficulty when making a class

How is the extension of a class determined?

When are two classes equipotent [equinumerous]?

Indicating the building of a class with a number

Are equipotent operations also operations in logic?

What is bijection [one-to-one] correspondence of quality [. . .] (Example: correspondence between a series of dolls and a series of little hats of different graduated sizes)?

From serial correspondence to numerical correspondence

[. . .]

CONCLUSIONS

What is a number?

What a number is arises from what has been said so far:

- a number is at once order and equivalence
- each unit is at once equivalent to all others but also distinct because it occupies a certain order in a series.

However for complete coordination between operations of cardination and seriation children's thinking needs to acquire the character of reversibility.

What is reversibility of thought?

[. . .]

✳ ✳ ✳

28.66 Letter to Dino Perego at Olivetti, 22 March 1966

Editor's note: Olivetti was a major Italian company founded as a typewriter manufacturer by Camillo Olivetti in 1908 in Ivrea; it produced Italy's first computer in 1959 and the first personal computer in 1965. Especially under Camillo's son, Adriano, the company gained a reputation as an enlightened employer, providing a wide range of facilities for its workforce in Ivrea, including a lending library, schools, modern housing surrounded by playing fields and allotments, and mountain-top summer retreats for children; a nursery was opened in 1941, which was advanced for its times, as was its provision of 9 months maternity leave at full pay. The letter below shows Malaguzzi connecting to the company and its social resources.

293/A   Reggio Emilia 22-3-1966

Doctor Dino Perego
Centro Relazioni Sociali 'Olivetti' [The 'Olivetti' Centre for Social Relations]
IVREA
    [. . .]
    We would like to thank you for making the Exhibition of Toys available to us.
    We will no longer be showing the Exhibition in April but in the month
of May, from 22 to 29 to be precise, and as we have already said, showing it
alongside a Collection of Children's Drawings.
    We agree on the costs.
    [. . .]

                                                           Loris Malaguzzi

                              ❉ ❉ ❉

29.66 Notice from the *Comune* of Reggio Emilia, 24 May 1966

Editor's note: The lectures advertised in this notice, probably drafted
by Malaguzzi, coincided with an exhibition of young children's drawings, covering all schools in the province; see the next document for an
excerpt from the programme. Vittoria Manicardi, one of the first *atelieristas* in Reggio Emilia, reports that 'All the *scuole materne* in the province were invited, there were lots and lots of drawings. Together with
the children we took our easels to the municipal Valli Theatre, under
the colonnade. Everybody in Reggio Emilia talked about it for days'
(Various Authors, 2012, p.93).

To all Parents
    We would like to remind Parents that for the occasion of the Exhibition of
Children's Drawings, which is being shown in the foyer of the *Teatro Municipale*
and has been a lively and gratifying success, our *Direzione* [*delle scuole materne*]
has organised two cultural events that will take place on Friday 27 and Saturday
28 May at 21.00 in the hall of the *Società del casino* [in the *Teatro Municipale*]
and which will be held respectively by prof. ENEA BERNARDI from the
University of Florence and prof. LORIS MALAGUZZI. The two speakers
will examine the educational, teaching and artistic issues of children's drawings,
addressing both teachers and parents: the aim of the two conferences is to illustrate the educational values of drawing and to give advice and methodologies
that teachers and parents can use in their educational practice.

In consideration of this we especially recommend <u>that parents participate in the above mentioned events</u>.

Thanking you with feeling

La Direzione delle Scuole Materne

❋ ❋ ❋

30.66 From the programme for an Exhibition of Young Children's Drawings, May 1966

Cover

<u>1ST COLLECTION OF EARLY YEARS WORK AND DRAWINGS</u>
FOR CHILDREN IN *SCUOLA MATERNA* IN THE PROVINCE
OF REGGIO EMILIA
FOYER OF THE MUNICIPAL THEATRE
22–29 MAY 1966

Page 2

Fewer toys
more brushes, more drawing

For your children
fewer toys
more pencils, more crayons, more paintbrushes

Nothing is more conducive than drawing
to children's mental
and affective development

S.T. [Initials refer to a child's name]
10 years old – Tubercular Meningitis
The drawing was carried out by the child during the course of his long stay in hospital.

Too alone, this child. In this drawing he tells us of the fear of dying, the desire to live and the nightmares and anxieties tormenting him.

It is a funeral announced by the ding-dong of a small bell hung from a cross, hoisted onto a death carriage that carries the body of a child as if held in a cocoon. The carriage, drawn by a strange animal, is covered in bloodstains. On the right a pole bears several arrows that have pierced it: one arrow only is hurled in the air and about to pierce it. A pole of torture increasing the drama of the scene.

1967

31.67 Chapter from *L'educazione del bambino dai 3 ai 6 anni* [Educating the 3- to 6-year-old child], published by the municipality of Rimini, 1967

Editor's note: This volume was based on a series of presentations that accompanied a regional exhibition of 'expressive activities of drawing and painting' held at the Sala dell'Arengo in Rimini from 16 April to 2 May 1966; it was published the next year. Other articles are on preschool education in Italy; drawing and painting in the *scuola materna*; *scuola materna* and social-affective maturation; the *scuola infantile* programme; infant psychology; and relations between parents and children. Malaguzzi is described as the 'Director, *Scuole Materne*, Reggio Emilia'.

Initiation to logical-mathematical thought according to Jean Piaget

For a new psychology and pedagogy of the child

1) The presentation in Parliament of a Project for a Law on State *Scuola Materna*[7] has had the great merit of rekindling interest and discussion about the situation of the *scuola materna* in this country on all levels (we are not concerned with other implications here). The time is ripe for critical reflection and discussion of this institution's nature, problems and pedagogical prospects. The discussion has begun, it is already happening, and finally we can see that we have remained silent and given up on the issue for too long, been passive when faced with rich and interesting discoveries in early years psychology, and with the growing mythology of philosophies and methods whose original values have become artificially anachronistic. These values can only gain respect and currency, only be rich in inspirations and lessons if they become part of the flow of time in a constant operation of examination, comparison and experiment.

2) The discourse is at its beginnings. Today for example we propose Piaget's name as a possible point of reference and reflection for people engaging with educational issues in the *scuola materna*. To those who rightly ask us the reason for this choice, we obviously owe an explanation. However before offering our modest contribution to a knowledge of this Geneva psychologist, particularly the areas of his thinking and philosophy that interest us most, let us look together at a series of propositions that attempt to clarify the cultural issues and critiques from which Piaget starts, and which we believe provide clarity and a necessary introduction.

3) The first proposition, which defines a precise ethic of methodology, refers to the universality and ecumenism of culture in our time. Wherever modern thinking takes place and in whatever way, it refers to this dimension. This is our first response to the question of why we have chosen to turn to a philosophy born and developed outside our country and national culture.

4) The second proposition presumes the opportuneness of a critical conscience, both towards our traditional beliefs and the educational situation that really

exists. The passing of time and schools of thought takes place very rapidly today: the distance between Aporti, Montessori and Agazzi[8] is immeasurably shorter than the distance between Montessori, Agazzi and our times. Under the pressure of social-economic evolution, *scuole materne* have emerged with urgency as a social service and as genuinely educational institutions, which are increasingly understood and requested by families. At the same time the contribution and role of psychology to the field of pedagogical disciplines has grown enormously even in Italy, particularly early years psychology, and it would be a serious error not to introduce new discoveries into an updated discourse on the *scuola materna*, which many people would like to call *scuola dell'infanzia* with good cause. From several contributions made by psychological studies, there are two highly interesting and relevant tendencies and forces we would like to extract:

a   The increasingly urgent need felt by researchers, after a fertile period of experimental study of psychological facts considered separately, to start their proper and logical re-assembly into a whole.
b   The tendency to give children's problems of psychology and of life environment a dialectical interpretation, re-affirming the interdependency of factors and rhythms of maturation and the concrete conditions in which these phenomena take place.

This means children's mental structures[9] can be brought forward or put back depending on the conditions and stimuli of their lives, and that the ways (methods, educational practice) in which these processes are initiated and effected are particularly decisive.

Many implications follow from this on a theoretical and practical level, recalling Lewin's[10] intuition when he discusses a close relation between states of knowledge and decisional acts, the connections between cultural life and choices of behaviour.

5) This introduction is for us to better immerse ourselves in the problems of our time, helping us to free ourselves of a tradition complex. Tradition should be highlighted, not negated, through the act of rethinking and reflection in the light of emerging discoveries and problems. Eclecticism? If eclecticism means a situation of growth and examination, of accepting the universal fruitfulness of thinking, there is no need to worry

What is needed (we say this with Claparéde) is the constant presence of a scientific attitude, that is to say our own aptitude for marvelling when faced with the facts of our daily professional life, and a desire to interrogate these facts and obtain answers by subjecting them to methodological observation and experiment.

6) But, some might object, Piaget is a psychologist after all. He recognised himself that until recently he had never posed concerns or problems of a

pedagogical nature in the study and development of his experiments. How can psychology or a psychologist intervene in pedagogical research? This is a very topical question in our country and culture where pedagogical problems are often on too abstract a philosophical level and psychological experiment is viewed with suspicion and scepticism.

We are not going to discuss the issue on a level of principles; old and new diatribes between pedagogy and psychology have always been about the type of relation, interdependency and confluence between the two disciplines.

The facts: the facts convince us that the results and progress of early years psychology have already helped pedagogy considerably. And yet despite the variety of these contributions what has been achieved is far from being completely convincing.

We can see that accommodating different phases of children's development in teaching is more often a programme than a reality, not only for teaching in general but for those methods that take psychological principles as a reference. Much work must still be done to make progress in child psychology, in the conclusions pedagogical methodology must draw from it, and in practical applications of those conclusions.

It seems pedagogy has been revived, Piaget tells us this himself, more by the overall spirit of research in psychology, the methods of observation that cross from pure science into the field of school experiment, than by directly tapping in to discoveries in psychology and using them in its own area.

This process of exchange and interaction between psychology and pedagogy, this filtering of psychology's discoveries into real work and organisation (organisation is always an important factor of pedagogy); this process which means better objectivising the genuine reality and children's genuine personality (not only their general needs but their dynamic processes of maturation) and creating a psychological methodology of work for this reality, an adequate educational methodology – this constitutes a problematic area in Italy. This problem still meets with great resistance, perhaps due to the weight of idealist spiritual tradition, perhaps to the particularly disorganised historical evolution of early childhood services, perhaps to limited cultural and economic resources that demoralise the services, and in particular demoralise teaching staff.

[. . .]

Removing children from anonymity

We must ask our *scuola dell'infanzia* to remove children from anonymity and the unnaturally nebulous nature they have been given, and better distinguish between the ages of three, four and five years (classes i, ii, iii), differentiating modules for organisation, activities, interests, stimuli, and social and cultural exchange.

Already the outline for our *scuola dell'infanzia* stimulates new architectural solutions, new pedagogical spaces indoors and out, new types of furnishing with a general functionality, which can then become complex.

Certainly schools must respect the welfare role that is part of their work, but welfare must be reclaimed as part of education: this is possible through several factors working together, above all through creating a strong educational ambition in school's daily work and furthest aims.

Schools must offer greater cultural ferment, firmly anchored in doing, in producing **experience** and **ways of constructing thinking and personality**.

8) Piaget tells us that without experience thinking is not nourished. Children's logic is the logic of manipulation and personal experience. Intelligence is a system of operations, and operations are internalised only if children have available to them, as well as the passionate and liberating presence of adults, materials that allow them to live their experiences in concrete ways. And the materials, which must be considered as generators and stimulators of experience, must be structured as little as possible; must allow gradually ordered experience; and above all must be part of a cultural ferment conducive to their perfect integration with all other elements of life and education.

Piaget's discoveries make it possible for us to claim that a pedagogy and *didactics* of number have the right to enter our *scuola dell'infanzia*. This is the main aim of today's presentation, because we believe this is the place we can start a description of ideas for innovative pedagogical commitments, which are capable not only of highlighting children's intelligence, but also the values, in all their fullness, that constitute the child. The main rationale for this right is the natural urgency of children's thinking, and the urgency of an education inspired by modern humanism: a humanism with its origins in the essential basis of Piaget's discoveries about the genesis of organisation in logical structures of thinking and about operational theories of intelligence, which mean the first mathematical abstractions and conceptualisations are possible earlier when they are firmly anchored in practical activity.

It is a right that has validity in the authority of Isaacs,[11] when she recommends that it is necessary to 'discover the beginnings of the scientific spirit and the scientific method in the thinking of young children with the aim of ensuring maximum development'; and of Bruner and Burt, who say they are certain that all logic is already potentially present in the experience of young children, to the point of saying, as Mazzucco-Costa emphasises – that we can teach young children anything if we adjust to their cognitive and affective mechanisms. It is a right supported by several research projects, although these are certainly still open to analysis, by Matalon and Inhelder – Piaget's collaborator – by Bang, Nassefor, Gutman and Dienes, and our own Campedelli, Castelnuovo, Petter [1] and Morino Abbele [2]. This right is also supported by concrete experience taking place for some time in *scuole materne* in France and Switzerland in the wake of Piaget's teachings and intuitions. And, finally, [it gains support] from a more organic experience of initiation to numbers that began recently in *scuole materne* in Geneva and Lausanne, based on practical methods translated faithfully from Piaget by Beauverd [3], and organised into a series of trials and exercises of graduated difficulty, and attempting a longitudinal study with evaluation and testing of the different and progressive integrations of logic in children's thinking.

Reading *Initiation au Calcul (enfants de 4 a 7 ans)* [Introduction to Calculation: 4- to 7-year-old children] – Edition Bourrelier, Paris, printed in 1950 and translated into Italian by Nuova Italia in 1956 (but almost unnoticed), which published the talks given by Piaget, Boscher and Chatelet at the Lyon conference of 1949, is enough to understand the extent to which Italian *scuole materne* are enveloped in archaic and false conceptions of the child (leaving aside Montessori schools), defending infantilism at all costs in the face of scientific achievement in psychology and psycho-pedagogy; and to gain some idea of the marvellous and fruitful work that can be done in the field of initiating children to mathematics, thus producing a cultural evolution from the inside that could and must affect – with its coherent and catalysing presence – the entire area of pedagogical and cultural values, and finally find – as Lucio Lombardo Radice[12] hoped – 'the proper position of mathematics in children's culture'.

9) It is not our intention today to give examples of working methods for mathematical initiation that can be used in a gradual and considered way in our *scuole materne* with children of four, and above all five- and six-year-olds. (However on the tables next to us there are some materials inspired by Piaget, which we think are enough to lend documentary concreteness to this talk.) Nor do we intend to put forward here today any critical reflection, for example on Montessori-inspired *scuole materne* where some mathematical **manipulation** undoubtedly takes place, but with processes and purposes that are far removed and in contradiction with our proposals. Today our interest is in outlining general values for a process of renewal, in an initial attempt to compose them into a philosophy.

The paucity, the total or almost total lack of experiment in this country – which is an undeniable fact [. . .] only goes to show the urgency of our work and the actual directions it must take.

For us it is important to conclude by summarising the ultimate meaning of discoveries in scientific psychology. Having identified that the basic structure of mathematical conceptualisations are identical to the basic structures of thinking, we must draw out the consequent implications. Logical thinking is constructed and refined as much through studying science, spoken and written language, drawing, art, and music etc., as through the study of mathematics.

Number is neither intuition nor pure logic, and rests on the long and gradual and increasingly perfected construction of new syntheses of logical operations. That is to say, it is the result of successive acquisitions that begin far away when adults are still children and, as children, are capable of constructing them for themselves day by day through life experience. Using the logic of their age, which is the logic of manipulation, the logic of their fingers, and operating with things, and then with the representations of things, they gradually find relations that exist between things, between things and gestures, between doing and saying, and progressively penetrate into the science of numbers, which in nature is essentially the science of relations.

Lastly I would like to go back to the theme of the value of languages, which is one of the most vital and interesting aspects of early years pedagogy. We know how much the acquisition and evolution of language is of fundamental value for the development of intelligence. Well then, the language of mathematics must be given credit as one of the most powerful and fertile factors in mental and logical-linguistic development. The language of mathematics is conducive to filtering language that is very closely connected with children's personal experience or over imbued with emotional elements. It has its own precious objectivity and rigour of expression, and increases agility of thinking by ordering and enriching structural elements, initiating [thinking] at an early stage to the possession of symbols, and stimulating it to hypothesis and reversibility.

As Mazzucco-Costa rightly likes to remind us, children's early mastery of good language not only affects the level of social communication available to them, above all it is also an important factor in security, self-esteem and self regulation, and therefore an element of irreplaceable value in forming happy, full, creative and critical personalities.

Loris Malaguzzi

---

[1] Through his work *Lo Sviluppo mentale nelle ricerche di Jean Piaget* [Mental development in the research of Piaget], Editirice Universitaria, which we have also used as a source, Guido Petter[13] has finally made the Geneva psychologist's theories known in Italy in an extremely clear overview. For his experimental contributions, Guido Petter is certainly one of the most perceptive Italian scholars in the field of early years psychology.

[2] Morino Abbele was one of the first Italian scholars to theoretically and experimentally look at the problems of the first logical-mathematical processes in thought. [. . .] She conducted her research on children aged 7–8 years, inspired by Piaget and in particular by Dienes. [. . .]

[3] B. Beauverd *Avant le calcul* Delachoux Niestlè (1965). A study seminar on initiation to number, based on Piaget and the didactics of B. Beauverd was held in 1965 on behalf of the *Comune* of Reggio Emilia by the author of this talk together with Dr. Carlo Iannuccelli. Approximately sixty teachers in *Scuola Materna* of the Emilia-Romagna region attended the Seminar.

A series of experimental didactic seminars will take place this year in the *Comune Scuole Materne* of Reggio Emilia.

In the preface to *Avant le calcul*, Piaget writes: 'We must greatly acknowledge [Monsieur] B. Beauverd as having elaborated a systematic experience of initiation to mathematics basing it on the results of psychological analysis in the most comprehensive, capable and original way. The intelligence with which M. Beauverd has been able to identify the essential principles informing logical-mathematical operations and translate these into concrete and extraordinarily varied exercises will be admired . . .'.

An exchange of correspondence both with M. Beauverd and with a group of teachers in Swiss *scuole materne* applying the methods of *Avant le calcul* has created the conditions whereby we can better understand and evaluate the results of these initial ongoing experiences.

Beauverd has written to us: 'These results are more than satisfactory. Above all we are pleased that faced with the diffusion of methods and didactics that put their faith in structured materials, we counterpose a form of teaching that is not at all rigid or limiting, which starts with units and sets perfectly adhering to the suggestions of modern mathematics'.

To be more specific, these experiences show us that the exercises in *Avant le calcul* are highly effective with children of 5–6 years, and can be preceded at an earlier age by a series of exercises inspired by the same original concept. To this end there is much we can use in the French and Swiss literature, and the contribution of constant research and creativity taking place in the *scuole materne* across the border is notable.

Again our results show that the material in *Avant le calcul* can and must be further diversified to extend the ways of stimulating and intervening with children, offering them opportunities for more varied awareness of their powers.

Teachers Clerc Gabrielle and Maire Mariette have written to us: 'Faced with the situation created by the material, children are led to pose themselves questions and problems: which means making children reflect when faced with every situation, avoiding the verbal and mechanical manner that too often has misled us about children's effective capacity for acquiring mathematical concepts'.

❋ ❋ ❋

32.67 Letter to Renzo Bonazzi, Mayor of Reggio Emilia, March 1967

Editor's note: The Diana school, which was named in 1991 by the American magazine *Newsweek* (2 December 1991) as one of 'the ten best schools in the world', took a long time to get from proposal to opening. The original plan was to renovate a cinema on the site, the 'old building' Malaguzzi refers to below. After much debate and delay, it was decided to demolish the cinema and construct a new school building.

Municipality of Reggio nell'Emilia   Reggio nell'Emilia, 3 March 1967
Direzione Scuole Materne
Via dell'Abbadessa 8
Tel. 42875

Dear Renzo,

I would be grateful if you would kindly intervene with Boiardi [*Assessore* for schools] to press for what was agreed to during a recent meeting of the *Giunta* [municipal council] on the already too long and tormented issue of the *Scuola Materna* Diana.

As you will remember it was decided to overcome the last hurdle:

– will the [new] construction work added to the old building leave a satisfactory and adequate surrounding area for children's outdoor activities? – would Boiardi and his office please ascertain this quickly: after which we could finally start work officially on the project.

Twenty days have already gone by:
I think it is opportune to get moving

Thanking you
L'ufficio Scuole Materne Comunali
Loris Malaguzzi

1968

33.68 Article from supplement to newsletter *Il Comune* No.82, 1968

> **Editor's note:** This supplement on schools and education includes, in addition to the article below on *scuole materne*, articles on elementary, middle and secondary schools; physical education; health, culture and recreation for schools; future prospects; and school and democracy.

Scuole Materne Comunali: a pedagogy equal to the children of our time

We believe the intentions and efforts of the *Comune* have not been frustrated for so long on any other initiative as for the *Scuole Materne Comunali*. Having overcome resistance, after ten years of trying, the *Comune* was able to inaugurate its first *scuola materna* on 5 November 1963: the school in via Pastrengo later named Robinson Crusoé [sic].[14] On 9 November 1964 the *Scuola Materna* Anna Frank opened its doors in the Rosta Nuova quarter. On

1 October 1967, after a long dispute which began in 1962, the *Comune* was able to take over running the *Scuola Materna XXV Aprile* in Villa Cella. At the start of this year the *Comune* realised its fourth *scuola materna* called Primavera in the very recently built neighbourhood of the same name. In the current year the *Comune* should start work on its fifth extremely modern *scuola materna* amid the greenery of the Public Gardens in the area occupied by the ex-cinema Diana (the *Comune* Council has unanimously voted on this and is waiting for approval from the GPA):[15] further plans include founding another school in the old Villaggio Foscato quarter and the municipalisation of other schools hitherto managed privately.

There are approximately 400 children attending the *Comune*'s *scuole materne*. There are 18 teachers. The running costs come to 60 million [*lire*, currency used before Italy adopted the euro] annually. Each child costs 600–650 [*lire*] daily. Two buses collect the children. During the summer period about one third of the children enjoy a stay by the sea in the *Casa di Vacanza*, which is the property of the *Comune* in Cesenatico.[16]

Although the *Comune* has at its disposal its own Pedagogical Director, a *comitato di vigilanza* [Vigilance Committee] made up of council-nominated experts monitors life in the institutions,[17] to their great advantage.

The *scuole materne* of the *Comune* have achieved an exemplary level of organisational and pedagogical efficiency: so much so that on more than one occasion they have been the object of illustrated articles and studies by the specialist press and the subject of reflection in national conferences.

Meetings with families, periodical meetings and study days with teachers, pedagogical conferences for families, educational exhibitions, the direct creation of educational material, study conferences on experimental didactics, study conferences with participation by teachers from other cities, all constitute fertile moments of life, updating, and research, which characterise the work in our *scuole materne comunali*.

Creating modern schools for early years presupposes clear and conscious orientations: before all else on the values of the institution, which is considered to be an organised example of public education based on the rights, needs, and psychological and social requirements of the child, living children of our times: and therefore based on a pedagogy whose references are all projected towards today's world and society, but also integrated with the sentiment and intelligence of our tradition.

The whole founding spirit that animates the educational work of children's schools realised by the *Comune* of Reggio Emilia lies in this choice: architectural environments capable as much as possible of housing an active pedagogy; environments of life organised with a richness and variety of stimulants conducive to children's fullest experience and discovery; a community open to cultural exchange with families, and with the world of nature and man; an institution that will not tolerate being thought of as a place of protection, of marginal education, of sub-education, or as a **good and affectionate holi-day** for children waiting for their intelligence to arrive, and elementary school with it.

Culture and instruction – in a sense that has nothing to do with indoctrination or scholasticism [traditional methods] – also have their place in the *scuola dell'infanzia*.

This is an operation of ideals, attempted in the awareness of great difficulties, which at their very least are equal to the optimism that also accompanies such original experiments.

For children of different ages we try to create differentiated educational environments and situations: adapting furnishings, play spaces, the use of materials for development, themes for conversation, and adult intervention. So fairy tales are told and read to children of three years, the adventures of Pinocchio to children of four, and the more structured adventures of Robinson Crusoé [sic] to children of five.

Mats are a space and a module for play and work with small three-year-olds; activity corners with groups that freely compose and re-mix are incentives for small four- and five-year-olds. Painting at an easel with paintbrushes and tempera paints immediately offers children, even three-year-olds, a genuinely expressive joy, which is progressively invited into more and more representative and motivational languages.

Children of three and four years decanting water into bottles and other receptacles are quite happy in their play; and in doing this, as when they manipulate other carefully considered educational materials, they progressively discover laws and relations that will become clearer at five when they decant [liquids] with the conventional measures of a litre, half-a-litre, quarter-of-a-litre etc.

Children play with 'sets' (and this is the most fascinating of our ongoing experiments, introducing the latest mathematical discoveries into the world of children), discovering principles of classification, of correspondence, and of equality and difference step by step, and coming to a knowledge of numbers through this journey.

Teachers observe, stimulate, take notes, re-propose, examine: this is the attitude we try to get them to assume.

Children in the *scuole materne comunali* go to 'school' with their own personal schoolbags: and families, made aware of the journey and the educational choices we wish to make with them in interviews prior to admission and meetings that take place during the year, can appreciate and collaborate, with a totally new spirit that immediately raises the level of work accomplished together on children.

Teachers do not have registers, they have observation notebooks, which they fill with significant events in their work, their experiences, and children's different behaviours, with a spirit of critical reflection and marvelling.

When children take their leave of this three years experience of life and make their entrance into six-year-old school, they do not enter there anonymous and unknown; a personal file with evaluations and judgements goes before them, so that continuity of work coming from elsewhere, begun by others, will be easier for primary school teachers.

In this sense the *scuola materna* connects with schools that follow in spirit and in fact; its pedagogical dimension effectively lies in this just and necessary organic unity without in any way diminishing the hallmarks of its deeply authentic originality.

Loris Malaguzzi
Psychologist of the *Centro Medico*
Psico-Pedagogico of the *Comune* [of Reggio Emilia]

1969

34.69 Letter to the Mayor and *Assessore* for Public Works and the *Assessore* for Schools, 9 January 1969

9 January 1969

To the Mayor
To the *Assessore* for Public Works
To the *Assessore* for Schools

This letter is intended to represent our bitter and pained surprise, and our protest towards the ruthless felling of the trees – all the trees – which ringed the area of the *Scuola Materna* Diana now under completion.

The devastation which has been brought about – and of which we had no forewarning – took place in a few hours yesterday, and the fact – to remain on the level of our own specific interests – will lead to serious problems and serious consequences on an organisational and pedagogical level, paradoxically obliging us to use large beach umbrellas in the heart of the city's green area to protect children from the sun next summer.

What has happened is serious: so serious that we find it difficult to believe the measure was inspired by or decided by *Comune* offices.

Whatever the case, we believe the fact in itself calls for at least some further reflection: and in this further reflection we believe there is room for examining – and urgently – the benefit of an effective relationship between those who have to work – albeit with different competencies – in adjoining or inevitably interdependent parts [of the *Comune*].

Dr. Loris Malaguzzi

✳ ✳ ✳

35.69 From the work plans of the municipal schools Robinson Crusoe and Anna Frank, February 1969

> **Editor's note:** In 1966, two municipal schools, Robinson Crusoe and Anna Frank, started experimental work based on reading two classic books: *Robinson Crusoe* and *Pinocchio*. The work plans were printed by the *Comune* to ensure their widespread availability throughout the system.

Educational experiences with children aged 4 and 5 years, 1969

Why Robinson and Pinocchio?[18]

After three years of work experience in two different schools, we can say with conviction our initial choices were not a mistake.

The results that encourage us today have been endorsed during the course of the experiences themselves, as well as through collegial discussion with teachers and meetings with families. And as they convince us to try them again in other municipal schools we feel it is opportune to offer them to the attention and reflection of colleagues, as one of many possible points of reference that are capable of animating discussion and concrete exchange. We feel this discussion and exchange to be more open and urgent, perhaps because of an increased awareness of the stimulating and innovative pedagogical work taking place in *scuole dell'infanzia*, perhaps because more of this work has been disseminated in recent years, and perhaps because schools are aware of the invitation in the new Guidelines [for state-run *scuole materne*], which aim to encourage experiment and differentiation in methodology 'with the aim of consciously perfecting teaching procedures'.[19]

We hope the intentions that have inspired our choices and experiences in introducing reading and book work into our schools will be understood; to offer children and teachers a working 'itinerary' – one of many possible 'itineraries' that make up the 'work of education'. An itinerary capable of orientating the walking together, and the growing together that are essential elements in an education that is equally reassuring and liberating and which attempts an initial organisation and integration of knowledge on possible and progressive levels. Organisation does not mean systematisation, nor does it mean simply adding, a phenomenon which is often met with due to persistent theories that not only rob children of a portion of their potentials and aspirations, but distort the real process of learning and maturing, leaving too much room for the occasional, dispersive and spontaneous.

The discussion becomes clear if we reflect on the choice of two 'classics' [*Robinson Crusoe* and *Pinocchio*], which are a long-standing and continuous part of the reading of our children and parents. The heroes [of these books] are part of our culture. And we believe the reasons for this to be important.

Some might have doubts about the choice of *Robinson Crusoe*, but they will change their minds when together with us they discover the happy intensity of children reliving Crusoe's stories (with the opportune and necessary devices they can take from our introductory notes to this experience), and how the stories constitute an incomparable fabric of possible dramatisations (which stimulate and support identification and projection, and can be reinterpreted through merging different experiences), and a marvellous source of cognitive and cultural stimuli.

There is a real danger that the various activities illustrated in the work plans might obscure the 'literary' values and ideas in the books. But being aware of this already means we have an effective method of defence at our disposal: as always much will depend on the sensibility and skill of teachers.

We are convinced that one of the values of our experience is a conscious refusal of reading that is passive and passive-making and of abandoning ourselves to its evocations. Children at this age 'read' with their fingers, hands, gestures, actions, with thought that is internalised in movement and in doing, and which strives to find references and connections with adult help.

Helping children to make historical and geographical sense of the events and preparing opportunities for them to encounter and compare contemporary themes and knowledge – as well as enjoying the entire range of emotions, cultural acquisitions and imagination progressively produced by the story through play, manipulation, construction, practical, drawing and painting, and plastic activities – reveals the meaning of our reading, understood as a re-actualising, updating, re-discovering and critical re-approaching of the experience in our own times.

Let it not be said that this is the arbitrary transposition of a method that is correct for older children but not younger ones. If a method is good it is always good and perfectly coherently respected, even when it is proportionate to the effective means of the protagonist. And finally, if method is style, if first and foremost method is attitude, then we believe this style and this attitude rightfully belong in a modern and fecund concept of education.

Our experience remains and we give it to those who want to read it. To return to a discussion nearer home, we believe this experience will be useful for the teachers in our municipal *scuole materne* and children's families. This testimonial is aimed at both, inviting them to a proposal of common work.

Loris Malaguzzi
Reggio nell'Emilia, February 1969

The modest proportions of this work do not excuse us from giving proper thanks: to all the teaching staff in the Robinson Crusoe and Anna Frank schools who conducted this dual experiment with intelligence, dedication and sacrifice: in particular to Sofia Gandolfi and Giovanna Grassi who took the task of summarising the work plans.

We are sorry this first publication does not refer to another two research [projects] already underway in the Primavera and *XXV Aprile* [schools], the first on the theme of Winter, the second on the theme of Poems, Rhymes and Games about Children. In due time these two research [projects] will also be the subject of publication.

Lastly we would like to thank Franco Cigarini, the author of our photographic evidence, we can no longer do without his skills: and Marta Lusuardi, who has co-ordinated all the work of printing.

Robinson Crusoe by Daniel Defoe

Work plan

This work plan is the fruit of experience lived with children in *sezione* [class] 3 (5 year olds) by teachers

> GANDOLFI SOFIA
> OLEARI ESTER
> PONTONI ANTONIETTA
> CASOLI CARMEN
> BRIGHENTI GRAZIELLA
> Of the *Scuola Materna* Robinson Crusoe
> Via Pastrengo
> Reggio nell'Emilia

The experience and the work plans were developed and realised under the guidance of Prof. Loris Malaguzzi.

Choosing the book

No other story seemed so exemplary, both for the singular wealth of themes *Robinson Crusoe* offers to imagination, to reflection and above all to expressive activity and children's busy practicality, and for the vast range of indications and cultural themes the material makes available to teachers and children.

In addition to these more general qualities, we would also like to underline others that contribute to a more exact appreciation of the work:

- the distilled simplicity and linearity of the story;
- the clear-cut and engrossing emergence of Crusoe's character;
- the idea of Robinson as the defence, construction and creativity of human life;
- Robinson's <u>doing</u> as an ideal and concrete retracing of man's <u>doing</u> in millennia of history;

- the ease and congeniality with which children can practically re-live Crusoe's experiences of constructing;
- the rich connections of thinking and action as the key to Robinson's victories and adventures;
- the values Robinson expresses and symbolises as *homo faber*[20] (faith in man's physical, intellectual, moral and above all creative capacities); discovering and trying previously untested aptitudes and capacities; re-working experience of life and culture; critical reflection before and after action; the extension and flourishing of all human resources; the capacity to struggle for victory over nature and reality; the highlighting of social values (Robinson and Friday etc.).

Our work experiences

We and the text

We did not keep to the complete version of the story. We avoided chapters and stories about things we considered unsuited to children's intelligence, interest and emotional level. We simplified and modified the last part of Robinson's story. We did not always fully follow the sequence of events. However summaries in the margins of the work plans clearly show the choices we made.

Storytelling or reading?

The issue of summarising

Topics and motivations

We underline the need to proceed slowly and let ourselves be guided often by children's interests and expectations. We recommend avoiding schematic informative conduct, especially in 'conversation themes' [see below] and other integrated activities. A good knowledge of conversation topics is necessary, and we need to connect them quickly to children's internal motivations, be capable of postponing, shortening and enriching them when this is necessary.

Robinson in the family

Robinson between family and school

During parent meetings the possibility of carrying out and examining shared work on Robinson offered us all a concrete example of how dialogue and exchange between educational experience in school and family can and must take place. The resulting 'method' encouraged further conversation between the two parties and started a journey of identifying other common themes and problems.

Practical and expressive activities

Robinson's adventures have a deep 'hold' on children. This emotional, sentimental and intellectual 'hold' constitutes a valid support for additional conversational themes and for expressive and practical activities. Of these, painting and drawing achieve an unexpected tension and language of representation. Clay work, woodwork and carpentry created much enthusiasm, and some of Robinson's experiences, like cooking meat on a spit, manoeuvring sails, putting up fences and tents, making butter, building trench traps to capture animals etc., which presume a keen sense of organisation, the right tools, and work roles and collaboration between children, became moments of 'choral' participation.

The garden as a natural theatre

The chance to use the garden as a natural theatre to house 'large drama games' was an invaluable and fortunate circumstance. So an old boat given to us by sailors on the River Po, suitably set up and decorated with flags on long poles allowed us to manoeuvre sails, have a perfect pretend shipwreck and other galvanising experiences. In the same way, putting up a hut and surrounding fence made of branches and canvas strips, mostly by the children themselves, triggered enthusiastic adventure.

A permanent exhibition

We have had ample opportunities for seeing how Robinson Crusoe's story stimulates children and teachers to produce a great variety of drawings, paintings, utensils and objects of different sizes. This precious documentation grew with the story and required careful planning inside the classroom and out; to gratify the creators, as a constant stimulus to children's memory and reflection, and as a testament to work done by and with children that families could clearly read and appreciate.

In collaboration with parents

The availability of instruments and materials, and even the realisation of some 'projects' was possible in many cases through parents' help and direct collaboration. This proved to be of great interest and value. Parents showed they were very happy to collaborate, children enjoyed the adult presence, the school was enriched with original experience and moments of authentic community relations.

Editor's note: The publication continues with the work plans from the Robinson and Anna Frank schools; only the former is included.

Work plan: Robinson Crusoe

READING: STORYTELLING	CONVERSATION THEMES	OBJECTS FOR COMMENT	EXPRESSIVE ACTIVITIES	DRAMATISATION AND EXERCISES IN PRACTICAL LIFE
CHAPTER ONE				
Robinson was born in York, England in 1632. Against the wishes of his father, who wants him to be a magistrate, Robinson is attracted to life at sea and runs away from home, boarding a ship on its way to London. The ship is wrecked but Robinson is saved. He boards another ship which is attacked by pirates at sea. Robinson manages to escape and is picked up by the captain of a Portuguese ship going to Brazil.	Map of the world	Globe and world map	Drawing and painting (English and Italian flags; Robinson arguing with his parents; Robinson going to sea)	Putting an old boat in the garden with a mast and sails; drama play
	The island of England	English and Italian flags		
	The sea	Robinson's sailing boat		Basic orientation exercises in the garden
	Life at sea	The compass	Making two flags	
	The compass		Building a sailing boat	
	Other ways of finding the way		Making a rudimentary compass	
CHAPTER TWO				
The Portuguese ship lands in All Saints Bay in Brazil, and Robinson becomes a sugar cane planter. Then he becomes a merchant of elephant tusks and gold dust and finally he is given the job of setting sail for Guinea to find African slave labour to use in plantations.	The various human races	Robinson's journey on the world map	Drawing and painting (Robinson working on a sugar cane plantation)	Write to the Cuban Ambassador to Italy for documentation on the working of sugar cane
	Sugar	Illustrations: sugar cane plantations, the work of man, refineries		Playing shop
		Money (the value and use of money)		Using conventional money

(continued)

(continued)

READING: STORYTELLING	CONVERSATION THEMES	OBJECTS FOR COMMENT	EXPRESSIVE ACTIVITIES	DRAMATISATION AND EXERCISES IN PRACTICAL LIFE
CHAPTER THREE				
Robinson goes to sea again but his ship is stranded on a sandbank. Robinson attempts to reach land in a lifeboat but waves sink the boat. Robinson, the only survivor, manages to save himself and reaches a desert island semi-conscious. The first night he sleeps in a tree. On waking he sees his marooned ship not far from the shore.	Usefulness of swimming Using a lifeboat High tide Low tide		Drawing and painting (Robinson's shipwreck) Drawing and painting (Robinson sleeping in a tree)	Visit to the communal swimming pool Projection of documentary on swimming
CHAPTER FOUR				
Robinson swims to the ship after waiting for low tide. He builds a raft and loads it with everything that might help him to survive: ship's biscuits, dried meat, liquor, woodwork tools, guns, pistols, gunpowder, pieces of sail, rope. He takes everything to the island, then makes more journeys with the raft to get other provisions: compasses, ink, scissors, telescope, wood and even two cats and a dog, and finally three bibles.	The raft	The telescope (magnifying glass) Woodwork tools (hammer, screwdriver, pliers, pincers, saw, plane etc.)	Constructing small rafts and a giant raft Drawing and painting (Robinson transporting provisions and victuals on the raft)	Using a telescope and magnifying glass How rafts float

✳ ✳ ✳

36.69 Letter to the Mayor, the *Assessore* for schools and the Head Engineer of the municipality, March 1969

34/B
Lawyer Renzo Bonazzi
Mayor of the *Comune* of Reggio Emilia

Assessore for City
Schools and Social Services

Head Engineer of
Comune of Reggio Emilia

Work is about to start on the construction of the Municipal *Scuola Materna* in the area of the ex-Diana Cinema and there are some criticisms of the project I think it is opportune you should know about. If these comments are accepted they would require making small adjustments, which I do not think would be impossibly complicated for the competent authorities and funding bodies.

Here are the modifications I suggest:

[. . .]

d) The project does not include an *atelier*-classroom for children working in groups. Considering that *atelier* classrooms represent one of the most original achievements of our experience, much appreciated by children and families, I warmly recommend examining the possibility of installing a small building in the garden (6x4 metres) (perhaps put together with material salvaged from the *Scuola Materna* in Via Pastrengo), which would be capable of housing this type of activity.

Trusting in an urgent and timely examination of the problems illustrated, my warmest greetings.

Prof. Loris Malaguzzi

✳ ✳ ✳

37.69 *'Esperienze nelle scuole dell'infanzia Consigli di scuola–città'* [Experiences in the *Scuola dell'Infanzia* School-City committees], *Documento* [Document] 1, *Municipio di* Modena, October–November 1969

Editor's note: This article, based on a speech in Modena, appeared in the first of what was a proposed series of publications; Malaguzzi also writes a short introduction to the publication. At this time, Malaguzzi was responsible for municipal schools in both Modena and Reggio Emilia.

Participation is an important theme running through Malaguzzi's thinking and work, and led to implementing the concept of *gestione*

(continued)

(continued)

sociale [social management], a system of governance involving repre-sentatives of different sectors of the local community, as an integral part of the municipal early childhood systems in both Reggio Emilia and Modena. The first forms of participation were *Comitati d'Iniziativa* [Initiative Committees], introduced in the 1960s to promote the open-ing of municipal *scuole dell'infanzia*; followed in the 1970s by *Comitati di Scuola e Città*, which were extremely active during that decade. This document is about the origins, rationale and purposes of these *Comitati di Scuola e Città*, which were officially included in the organisation of municipal *nidi* and *scuole dell'infanzia* in Reggio Emilia in July 1970. The Committees played an important role in the management of schools and were composed of a variety of representatives from society recognised with the right of intervention on educational issues: parents; representatives of *Consigli di quartiere* [Neighbourhood Councils]; and citizens 'who believe in the values of the initiative because of a specific cultural interest'.

Introduction

Dr. Loris Malaguzzi, Pedagogical Consultant to *scuole comunali dell'infanzia*, Modena

This publication is the first in a series, inspired by an event we were recently involved in; the constitution of the first *Comitati di Scuola e Città*, which are an original choice for the organisational, social and pedagogical management of children's schools. A turning point when compared with the old work of school Councils, and certainly fertile in values and implications.

This Document presents itself for what it is: a testimonial, a step on a journey, a moment of examination, an organisational tool for ideas, and for all the people who will work with these ideas.

Other documents will come, at short intervals, gathering stimulus and experience from our work with children, with teachers, with families, with administrators, with the City [Modena].

The meaning and intervention of school management committees in the Scuole dell'Infanzia

Talk by Dr. Loris Malaguzzi, Pedagogical Consultant to the *scuole dell'infanzia* of the *Comune* of Modena

Our friend Famigli[21] has already introduced [in the *Documento*] the meaning of this new experience we are about to promote. An experience that, starting from co-operation between parents and teachers (in the old Parents' Councils), should be extended (in the new School Councils being created) into a more advanced form of co-management. We are all convinced of the extreme importance of this initiative, and of the complexity of the task it requires.

My contribution will be to further problematise – examine in more depth – both the values that motivate this choice, and practical and functional aspects.

Perhaps this reflection is necessary on two counts. It can help us avoid the danger of enclosing and impoverishing the initiative in schemes which are purely activist, in contingent and fragile action. However, more than this, it can contribute to giving us the necessary clarity, the awareness, imagination and invention required to identify ways, tools and relations we can work with concretely. Here is a first point: what is the position of pedagogy in relation to this issue?

An answer is only possible if our conception of pedagogy is dynamic, not mummified. Either pedagogy – like all the human sciences – is remade, reconstructed and updated based on the new conditions of the times, or it loses its nature, its function, its proper capacity to correspond to the times it lives in, and above all to foresee, anticipate and prepare the days of tomorrow. (In effect this is the drama and crisis our schools are experiencing.)

In this specific case, a living pedagogy with authentic functions and values, the kind we wish and hope for, seeks to remove the *scuola dell'infanzia* as much as it can from old and new models of welfare, from old and new ways of pretending to educate. There are things no one wants, but that 'hard and obstinate reality', as James[22] says, imposes when environments, timetables, needs, relations and everything else distort the cultural framework of school, so that instead of focusing on children and their rights, <u>the school has to endure adult burdens and contradictions, the delays, disorder and injustice present in adult society.</u>

Releasing the *scuola dell'infanzia* from this ambiguity not only means creating educational institutions children actually need, and endorsing their right to equality in education and study, it is the first stone in the reconstruction of primary schools, which absolutely cannot be deferred, and could innovate education for children of all ages (there are already significant converging ideas on the subject).

The attempts, the hard work, the experiences underway in Modena's *scuole dell'infanzia*, the talks being given today, all go in this direction.

[. . .]

What is children's pedagogy if not the daughter of society, of society's way of being and constructing itself?

The City, how it is configured, its emblematic reality, is an opportune point of reference and polemic, we have said this before. Cities are constructed by adults and proceed based on adults, on a question of age. They are only made for individuals of working age, and are produced in the most material sense. Houses, streets, squares, workshops, cinemas, theatres, automobiles, motorways are built for them.

Those who are truly excluded are the children. Children are completely abnormal in this anthropological model, they put up with its irrationality and its violence, they suffer its constrictions, its prohibitions and repression; the frustration of their most fundamental needs.

They have no choice but to suffer its malfunctions, often in irreversible ways, or naively hope to save themselves by staying very little like Peter Pan who refused to grow up – or get big very quickly, unnaturally taking the giant attitude of Gargantua and Gulliver. They desperately look for salvation in a fairy-tale world that is destined to crumble when the winds of reality blow.

[. . .]

Looking for new relations with parents can only be done based on two premises of decisive value: a school that is consciously open to all hypotheses for freeing and renewing methods and aims; and an organised social context that is equally open not only to recognising but also to stimulating new concepts of citizens' powers, presence and contributions, and ways and times for discussing and resolving common affairs democratically.

Past and present experiences in Parents' Councils have demonstrated these things, but we need to push forward with them with more conviction, more energy, more advanced elaboration. This conference already shows we have the possibility and the maturity.

[. . .]

We know certain important things; that we work in a difficult situation but that in many ways we are privileged.

Privileged because we are part of a conversation with schools, teachers, the *Comune* etc., who are already favourably inclined towards this experience. Because we can count on real organisational structures that already exist; and above all because the *scuola dell'infanzia* is an open, flexible terrain immune to the great virus of bureaucracy, centralisation, sclerosis of organisation, circulars, registers, bulletin boards and grades. And because our parents fortunately are still immune to the opportunism and utilitarianism that very quickly condition them at other levels of school.

Our conversation can take place in this more open fertile terrain beginning with an immediate demystification of certain ideas of dialogue, which were theorised without sparing rhetoric and which only respected form. Fortunately these have disappeared on their own through failure. We are talking of the School–Family Committees and various *Ecoles des Parents*, which above all safeguarded the untouchability, arrogance, and patronising attitudes of old schools and required collaboration in one direction: co-operation with adjusting pupils to passivity and attitudes of passive submission.

These Committees considered schools as a taboo that only knowing, delicate hands can touch, which never belong to parents. So parents who, let us remember, are the recipients, the patrons, and the financers of services have no rights, not even the right to express what they expect, to take an equal part in discussion, argumentation and meetings.

[. . .]

In this framework, full-time schools,[23] which families are strongly pushing for at present, can bring many ambiguities, attempting to find a solution in schools but leaving unaltered the relations and connections education has with the city, with the city's educational and cultural organisation, its civic themes and issues. So they seem to be a choice of the least bad thing, of resigned acceptance, since we cannot construct educational and formative situations outside the traditional connotation of school. So we want to create a children's citadel that is humiliating and artificial in a city forbidden to children. Another act of violence, and a papier-mâché defence against the city's cynicism and oppression.

[. . .]

This is how *Comitati di Scuola e Città* – we will call them this rather than the more restrictive name School Council – could be more incisive on school affairs and on city affairs; cities that must be regained and made-to-measure for adults and for children.

✳ ✳ ✳

38.69 Speech at a *Circondario* Conference on the *scuola* and *nido d'infanzia*, Rimini, November 1969

Editor's note: A *Circondario* is an administrative entity consisting of a grouping of *comuni*. The committee promoting this conference on early childhood education included representatives from seven *comuni* (forming the *Circondario*), three trade union confederations, three left-wing political parties, a Catholic association and the UDI. The Conference followed the passing of a law in 1968 which established the state as a provider of schools for 3- to 6-year-olds, and the issuing in 1969 of the '*Orientamenti dell'attività educativa nella Scuola Materna Statale*' [Guidelines on educational activity in the state *scuola materna*], which are the 'new guidelines' referred to below.

The new guidelines for Scuola dell'infanzia

Prof. Loris Malaguzzi

Director of the *Centro Medico Psico-Pedagogico* and *Scuole dell'infanzia* of the *Comune* of Reggio Emilia

[. . .]

The fate of papers, particularly Education Papers, is to go over the head of reality and present proposals that often do not get beyond paper, or else they age too rapidly compared to things and events, owing to the delays and structural shortcomings of institutions.

Time is pressing and so in order to stimulate the greatest reflection, rather than look at the guidelines again in the light of parliamentary battles and controversy accompanying the birth of State *scuola materna*, we will try to update and organise a series of issues – nothing more – on some very few aspects that, because they affect the guidelines, also directly involve our work today, as workers in early years schooling. A first issue has to do with the guidelines the State has recently given us and relates to the type of school. Someone has written that in reality the State is handing us a school at least one hundred years old (as if the Parliament of 1859 and Minister Casati[24] had approved it).

[. . .]

Now if there is one school experience that is typical, which must look forwards, which demands the active and responsible presence of families, which must respond to the particularities of living environments and customs, which must constantly present the reasons for its actions to the community, which must be as open and flexible as possible, and which must represent a way of educating for democracy through direct, authentic and democratic experiences, then that is the *scuola materna*.

[. . .]

Relations with families go, or they can go, in the direction of rhetorical collaboration, of *scuole materne* that turn into schools for parents and continue to theorise subordinate and marginal concepts of family so that families become passive users instead of being stimulated to participation by ideals and pedagogy. The educational tendencies of a school, which whatever else it is remains an artificial and conventional reality, go in the direction, or they can go, of closing out the world and the external reality, from which children can only be cut off artificially, by an act of violence. The teacher's human and cultural dimensions shrivel, or can shrivel, rapidly and progressively when her field of work, however expert she has become, becomes a solitary process carried out in the often shamefully restricted spaces of the classroom and school walls. This is only part of the critical reflections provoked when we compare the guidelines with real situations.

Another issue we wish to address is in connection with the chapter in the guidelines on the teacher's personality.

[. . .]

This issue involves two kinds of reflection, the first of which is related to teachers' cultural and professional backgrounds, and the second to the real pedagogical situations educators are offered. Both of these aspects are often still distant not only from the reality of our guidelines but from everyday experience.

It is an old story; everyone agrees that the question of initial professional education for *scuola materna* teachers must be dealt with decisively. In reality the situation is becoming irresponsibly worse. The existing *Magistrali* schools [. . .] are no longer the only schools preparing educational staff. In all our cities accelerated courses for *asilo* schoolteachers (the name says it all) are springing up like mushrooms after rain,[25] promoted by mysterious organisations which are clearly and declaredly confessional [religious]. [. . .] In six months, less than it takes for the procreation of a child, diplomas are guaranteed to ill-prepared young girls by people who are even more poorly prepared.

But this is not the problem, or not the only problem, we are concerned with. Our critical reflection would like to touch on the human and professional profile of teachers as defined in the guidelines. The guidelines define the cultural attributes, knowledge of pedagogy, psychology and sociology, the need for continuous updating, the aptitude for establishing positive human relations, the necessary emotional balance, even the gifts of optimism and humour teachers should have. All the qualities that form the basis of a teacher's role, without which relations with children could be damaged, compromised or even become negative. However the non-fictional and non-academic premise necessary for this to happen, for the teacher's basic capabilities not to be worn down and deteriorate, is that the real situation she is given to work in should preserve and defend her endowment, not only that but constantly reinforce it, stimulate it and perfect it. There are several issues at play and we would like to make a plea for two. The first is the context for the teacher's existential reality, which is still firmly anchored in school tradition; working in complete solitude face-to-face with thirty-forty-fifty-sixty children, alone with her problems, alone with the problems children present, and which every child presents.

This is the aspect the guidelines forget and which is of decisive importance. If we want to defend the physical, mental and psychological health of teachers on an equal basis with children's health, then optimal employment of a teacher requires breaking with a situation of pitiful isolation. Working in teams, working as a community, working together, opening up the work of teachers to the stimulus and issues of the outside world are essential points of reference. We must look for alternative ways of conceptualising schools if we want to preserve the figure of the teacher from real devastation of the self. Paradoxically we have to say that solutions to this problem often encounter resistance from teachers themselves, owing to their long and ingrained cultural conditioning. Certainly, another aspect of this problem, which includes administrative, architectural, functional and other aspects, is related to the living conditions teachers and children are expected to exist in.

[. . .]

We are convinced that pedagogy will not co-habit with just anyone. Many, too many, of our schools only pay lip service to pedagogy, and close their doors to even the most humble pedagogy. Despite their intentions, sacrifices and efforts, these schools cause damage and contempt, and are unproductive towards children. This takes place inevitably when teacher–child ratios are distorted and do not respect the thresholds of the possible, never mind the optimal. A woman worn down by work on five to ten looms that she has to oversee simultaneously is a frightening model of dehumanisation, but a teacher face-to-face with thirty, forty or fifty children is no less of a spectacle.

And let us also say this: these are children who spend up to ten or twelve hours a day in the school. The deterioration of teaching staff whose work should last a lifetime, and of children is inevitable: energies and tensions are consumed, children are destroyed. Often both of these happen in irreversible ways. Our effort must be to try and remove young children's schools from old and new models of welfare as much as we can: the ones no one wants but that hard and obstinate reality, as James calls it, imposes when environments, times, relations and all the rest overwhelm any serious psychological, cultural and pedagogical framework. Instead of centring on children and their rights, schools tolerate adult burdens and contradictions, or rather the delays, disorder and injustice present in adult society. Removing the *scuola dell'infanzia* from this ambivalence – in which our public administrators often also become enmeshed, and play the game of a system that allows early years schooling to spread as long as it levels down and doesn't make a difference, doesn't change anything – means creating the educational institutions children need and sanctioning their rightful equality in education and schooling. And it also means releasing a powerful energy for renewing the schools that come after it, offering well-founded plans for pedagogy to take off, for rethinking education's purposes, the contents and methods of schools for older children, pre-adolescents and adolescents, and in this way stimulating a general rediscovery of values that will go much further than the frontiers of schools.

Notes

1 The Prefect refused Reggio Emilia's request to municipalise the self-managed school in Villa Cella, for which there was much popular support. An appeal against this decision submitted in 1963 was only heard in 1966. Central government also impeded local developments through its exercise of budgetary controls, especially over spending classified as 'optional', which included early childhood education.

2 The MCE was set up in 1951, initially under the title of the *Cooperativa della Tipografia a Scuola*, to renew education and introduce the pedagogy of Célestin Freinet.

3 Margherita Zoebeli (1912–96) qualified as a compulsory school teacher at the University of Zurich, and in 1953 founded the first *Centro Psico-Pedagogico* [Psycho-Pedagogical Centre] for the area of Rimini at the CEIS. From the early 1960s she advised the Comune of Rimini on the opening of the first *scuole dell'infanzia comunali*.

4 Available in Italian at: http://www.scuolenidi.re.it/allegati/cartaper3diritti.pdf.

5 Roberto Mazzetti (1908–81) was Professor of Pedagogy and the History of Pedagogy at the University of Salerno, a consultant for *scuole materne* in Bologna (1961–68), and an active reformer of public education.

6 In Piaget's theory of cognitive development, the third stage is called the Concrete Operational Stage. During this stage, which occurs from 7 to 12 years, the child shows increased use of logic or reasoning. One of the important processes that develops is that of 'seriation', which refers to the ability to sort objects or situations according to any characteristic, such as size, colour, shape, or type.

7 In 1966, the Aldo Moro government fell after the failure to get approval for a law to permit the State to provide *scuole materne*. The law, no.444, was finally approved in 1968.

8 Ferrante Aporti (1791–1858), Rosa Agazzi (1866–1951) and her sister Carolina (1870–1945) and Maria Montessori (1870–1952) were all Italian pioneers of early childhood education.

9 Piaget's theory is based on the idea that the developing child builds cognitive structures – in other words, mental 'maps', schemes or networked concepts – for understanding and responding to physical experiences within his or her environment. Each new stage of development is created through the further differentiation, integration and synthesis of new structures out of the old, so that the sequence of cognitive stages is logically necessary.

10 Kurt Zadek Lewin (1890–1947) was a German-American psychologist, known as one of the modern pioneers of social, organisational and applied psychology.

11 Susan Sutherland Isaacs (1885–1948) was an educational psychologist and psychoanalyst, who promoted the nursery school in England.

12 Lucio Lombardo Radice (1916–82) was a mathematician, educator and politician (as a member of the PCI).

13 Guido Petter (1927–2011) was an Italian psychologist and professor of Developmental Psychology at the University of Padua. He published *Lo Sviluppo mentale nelle ricerche di Jean Piaget* (Mental Development in the Research of Jean Piaget) in 1960.

14 The accent is pronounced when speaking of the school although not present in the title of the original English-language book.

15 *Giunta Provinciale Amministrativa*, a State body in every province with the power to approve or veto decisions by *comuni*.

16 A seaside town on the Adriatic Sea, about 30 kilometres south of Ravenna.

17 At the time of this article, the Vigilance Committee of the *Comune* had five members, including the mayor Renzo Bonazzi. Among other tasks, it contributed to decisions about opening new municipal schools.

18 *Robinson Crusoe*, written by the British author Daniel Defoe (1660–1731) and first published in 1719, tells the story of the eponymous castaway on a desert island. Pinocchio, a wooden puppet who wishes to become a real boy, is the main protagonist of *The Adventures of Pinocchio* written by the Italian author Carlo Collodi (1826–90), and first published in 1883.

19 Malaguzzi here refers to Pedagogical Guidelines [*Orientamenti dell'attività educativa nelle Scuole Materne Statali*] issued in 1969 for state-run *scuole materne*, which included a strong emphasis on play, religious education and collaboration with families.

20 *Homo faber* (Latin for 'Man the Creator') is a philosophical concept written about by Hannah Arendt and Max Scheler, which refers to humans as controlling the environment through tools.

21 Liliano Famigli was the *Assessore* for Education in Modena at the time, a politician whose responsibility included early childhood education.

22 Probably Henry James (1843–1916), the American writer.

23 By 'full-time schools', Malaguzzi refers to schools attended from 8 am to 4 pm, Monday to Friday; instead of the predominant model, attended from 8 am to 1 pm, Monday to Saturday.

24 The Casati Law of 1859 was the first law on education of the new Italian State and governed education in Italy until 1923.

25 *Magistrali* schools provided secondary education for students from 14 to 18 years and a qualification for working in *scuole materne* and elementary schools. At this time there were only three such schools provided by the State, leaving the way open for many private providers, the subject of Malaguzzi's criticism including their use of the term '*asilo*' teacher, *asilo* being very outdated and far removed in meaning from the educational emphasis in the term '*scuola dell'infanzia*'.

Chapter 3

Years of growth

1970–79

Figure 3.1 '*Incontri sui problemi dell'educazione infantile*' [Meetings on Issues of Children's Education]: talk by Gianni Rodari (writer and poet), 'Why I have dedicated my latest book to the city of Reggio nell'Emilia', with Loris Malaguzzi, *Sala Verdi* [Verdi Room], Ariosto Theatre, Reggio Emilia, 1974

Figure 3.2 Professional development meeting at the *Casa dello Studente* [Students' Residence Hall], Reggio Emilia, early 1970s

Figure 3.3 '*Documenti, testimonianze, ipotesi sulla difesa e sugli incrementi dei linguaggi di comunicazione del bambino*' [Documents, testimonials and hypotheses on the defence and increase of children's languages of communication], public discussion between school workers, *Comitati di Scuola e Città* and citizens, *Palazzetto dello Sport* [Sports Hall], Reggio Emilia, 1974

Figure 3.4 Public meeting on religious education, Reggio Emilia, 1976

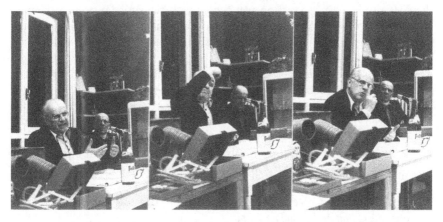

Figure 3.5 Loris Malaguzzi with Goffredo Ghidini (President of the *Consiglio di Gestione* of the *Scuola comunale dell'infanzia* Diana), meeting at the Diana School, Reggio Emilia, late 1970s

Introduction (Peter Moss)

The historical context

The 1970s were years of growth in Reggio Emilia, when the *Comune* expanded its provision of *scuole dell'infanzia*, opening fifteen during the decade, as well as its first *asilo nido* (centre for children under 3 years) in 1971, named after Genoeffa Cervi, the mother of seven brothers executed by fascists in 1943.[1] This was followed by the opening of a further ten *nidi* up to 1979. By the end of the decade, the city provided twenty *scuole* and eleven *nidi*, compared with thirty *scuole materne* offered by other providers, mostly Church organisations (nineteen) and the State.

The *Comune* now provided services for children both under and over 3 years of age, with a strong emphasis on continuity within the framework of a single 0–6 years pedagogical project. Also, significantly, all of these services were made the responsibility of the *Assessore* for schools and social services, unlike national government which, as we shall see, also became involved with services for children under 3 years in the 1970s, but placed this new responsibility with the Ministry of Health. The new municipal *nidi* were, therefore, from the start viewed as educational in purpose, although organised with the needs of employed parents in mind.

An important part of the emerging 0–6 service was the *Regolamento delle scuole comunali dell'infanzia* [Rulebook for municipal schools], officially adopted in 1972. This was 'a synthesis of the nature and characteristics of education in Reggio Emilia' (Various Authors, 2012, p.105); as Carla Rinaldi commented nearly thirty years later, the *Regolamento* 'made clear a concept of school and education as public and participatory, as [a] permanent process, as places in which the culture of children, and human culture are not only transmitted, they are produced'. Its creation was a highly participatory process, involving eight months of work and twenty-four drafts, the final version setting out common principles and guidelines for both *nidi* and *scuole dell'infanzia*, including:

- *Nidi* and *scuole dell'infanzia* as places of education for children, teachers, parents and the local area.
- Educational continuity and pedagogical co-ordination between *nidi* (for children under 3 years) and *scuole dell'infanzia* (for children between 3 and 6 years).
- Pedagogical Co-ordination from *pedagogistas* [workers with a psychology or pedagogy degree who support a small group (maximum 5) of *nidi* and *scuole dell'infanzia*] and psychologists.
- Participation by parents and the local area, organised into periodically elected *Comitati di Scuola e Città*.
- Priority access for children with special rights (the term adopted in Reggio Emilia for children with disabilities).
- The provision of *ateliers* and *atelieristas*.
- Daily presence of two teachers together in each class.
- Permanent collegial work and professional development for all educators (teachers, *atelieristas*, cooks, auxiliaries).
- Male teachers and non-teaching staff.
- Valuing all environments indoor and outdoor as spaces of learning, including kitchens, bathrooms and gardens.

As the *Regolamento* makes clear, Reggio Emilia was not content simply with opening more services. The pedagogical work undertaken within them was of the utmost importance, a priority expressed by the establishment in 1972 of the *Équipe Pedagogico-Didattica* [Pedagogical coordination and support team] – a team of *pedagogistas* and psychologists – following the appointment of the first *pedagogista* in 1970. *Ateliers* also were developed in the municipal schools, along with *atelieristas*, a new breed of educator with an arts background working alongside teachers.

A strong emphasis was placed on participation in the running of services: by children, teachers, parents and the whole local community. In 1968, *Comitati d'Iniziativa* [Initiative Committees] were created in city neighbourhoods to press for the opening of municipal *scuole dell'infanzia* and *nidi*. In 1970 *Comitati di Scuola e Città* were established in *scuole dell'infanzia* and *nidi*, inspired by and drawing upon the legacy and initiatives of earlier citizens' movements. These Committees, which turned into *Consigli di Gestione* [Social Management Councils] in the 1980s, became part of the organisation of all municipal schools, bringing together parents, educators and other citizens in a form of 'social management'. Emphasis, too, was placed on non-hierarchical and collaborative ways of working, which recognised the equal rights and importance of all staff (including, for example, auxiliaries and kitchen workers).

But this pedagogical work was not done in isolation. As well as close involvement in the emerging work of the regional government, there continued to be dialogue and exchange with other cities and towns that were participating in the 'municipal school revolution', places like Modena, Bologna, Pistoia, Florence and Milan, creating a network for mutual learning and solidarity that contributed to the development of services throughout Italy. The *Regolamento* was produced in the first place for Reggio Emilia's municipal schools, but became a 'point of reference for many Italian municipalities' (*ibid.*, p.118). (Though at the same time, some *comuni* were deciding to save money by handing their schools over to the State, which since 1968 had become a direct provider of services.) While towards the end of the 1970s, the first foreign visitors came to visit Reggio Emilia and its schools, from Cuba, Spain, Sweden and Germany, the harbingers of the extensive international connections that Reggio Emilia has subsequently created.

Nationally, this is the decade of the *Compromesso storico* [Historic Compromise], an initiative of the PCI under its new leader, Enrico Berlinguer, to seek an understanding with the main governing parties, the DC and the Socialists, and closer relations between labour and employers, provoked in part by a concern to avoid a repetition in Italy of the 1973 military coup in Chile. This was accompanied by the emergence of Euro-communism, with the French, Spanish and Italian parties moving closer together and reiterating their commitment to a democratic road to socialism and their independence from the Soviet Union. Yet excluded from national government and faced by tactically adept political opponents, these developments delivered few practical gains for the PCI, whose main field of influence remained regional and local government, especially in the 'Red Belt' of regions centred on Emilia-Romagna.

There were, however, other oppositional political forces. Though the student movement had peaked in 1968, it continued to agitate, while unrest among workers continued undiminished until 1973, before waning. A women's movement gained momentum and assumed national proportions, driven by the adverse effects of inflation and economic recession that followed the 1973 oil shock and by the growth of feminist groups from 1970 onwards. These forces contributed to growing demands for new rights in a society undergoing rapid changes, and helped make the 1970s a decade of reform.

Legislation permitted, for the first time, divorce and abortion, and recognised the principle of pay parity for women. Maternity leave was introduced, along with national government support and public funding for the opening of *nidi*. Full-day primary schools developed, a transformation in organisation and pedagogy that led to innovation in schooling. A national health service was established, with the aim of turning the existing disparate and wasteful system into a coordinated whole; and this was accompanied by new legislation on mental health services, intended to replace large hospitals with care in the community.

After first being envisaged in the post-war 1948 Constitution, democratically elected regional governments were finally set up and a range of functions passed to them. This exercise in decentralisation replaced the long-standing system of nationally appointed Prefects with a more local and democratic system of oversight, and introduced a new player into early childhood education (and other educational and welfare areas); one of the first duties of regional governments was to distribute state funding to *comuni* for the creation of *nidi*. (Though, it should be emphasised, regional governments were no solution to the wider malaise of government in Italy; regions did, and still do, vary greatly in performance, as highlighted in *Making Democracy Work*, Robert Putnam's (1993) book about regional government in Italy, which assessed Emilia-Romagna to be one of the top performing regional administrations.)

Reggio Emilia became part of the Emilia-Romagna Region, with its administrative centre in Bologna. Amongst other responsibilities, the Region was tasked with planning and setting criteria for the development of the new state-approved *nidi* in its area, legislating in such matters as buildings, management and monitoring, and providing *comuni* with various forms of support, for example in training educators. Emilia-Romagna took this responsibility seriously, coming forward in 1972 with regional legislation on *nidi*, together with plans for funding and building these new services, having started to discuss and plan even before the national parliament had passed its legislation on *nidi* in 1971. In 1975, a regional conference took place on 'The child as subject and source of rights in the family and society: Creating more *asili nido* and *scuole dell'infanzia* as centres for promoting individual and social education'; followed in 1979 by a conference on 'The educational and social values of the *nido*:

Experiences, reflections, proposals'. Both titles emphasise a clear understanding of the *nido*'s important educational role.

Having taken advantage of a loophole to open its first *nido* before the 1971 law was passed that allowed public funding for this type of service, Reggio Emilia was well placed to play an active part in the development of regional policy:

> In 1970 the Emilia-Romagna region was preparing for the new law by developing proposals for management and initiating discussion on the roles and meanings of the new 0–3 services. Courses for the professional development of future teachers were designed and funded: Loris Malaguzzi was a member of the commission for this work. A different interdisciplinary group made up of architects, urban planners, *pedagogistas*, cooks and health officials worked to define the characteristics of buildings and furnishings for the new nido centres: Carla Rinaldi collaborated with this group.
>
> One year later, when national legislation was introduced, the Emilia-Romagna region was ready to put it into practice. In 1972 regional legislation on the *nido* was introduced together with the corresponding plans for funding and building them.
>
> (Various Authors, 2012, p.114)

But if Emilia-Romagna was to become an example of what good regional government could achieve, this reform was not uniformly successful. Some other regions were inefficient, wasteful and simply reproduced the abuse of power that was widespread in government in post-war Italy. Reform, more generally, was too often marred by poor and patchy implementation. As Paul Ginsborg observes:

> Many of these laws were serious attempts at corrective reform; nearly all of them were poorly executed, and some were not executed at all. By the end of the 1970s, Italy had a welfare state, but it was very much 'all'italiana' [Italian style]. The services . . . often numerous and impressive . . . were frequently poorly administered and always the vehicles of party-political interest.
>
> (1990, pp.394–95)

The local successes of *comuni* like Reggio Emilia and regions like Emilia-Romagna must be set against a national backdrop marred by widespread failure to achieve change.

If the 1970s was a decade of reform, albeit flawed in implementation in many areas of the country, it was also a decade of political violence and terrorism. The so-called *Anni di Piombo* [Years of Lead] witnessed nearly 2,000 murders between 1969 and 1981, involving extreme groups on left and right, and including the 1978 kidnap and murder by the Red Brigade of Aldo Moro, the Secretary of the DC and five times prime minister. Closer to Reggio Emilia, the horrific bombing in 1980 of the Bologna railway station left eighty-five dead and many more injured. Behind this lurked unsettling suspicions that members of State security agencies were connected to right-wing violence, following a 'strategy of tension' that might create conditions for an authoritarian regime:

> Italian public opinion, alerted by some fine investigative journalism, became ever more convinced that a plot was afoot . . . The colonels in Greece had employed [this strategy] successfully in Greece [to justify a coup in 1967], and it now looked as if neo-Fascists and sections of the secret services were trying to repeat the pattern in Italy.
>
> (*ibid.*, p.334)

Malaguzzi's life

Loris Malaguzzi's role with Reggio Emilia's *scuole dell'infanzia* was formalised in 1970, when he officially became Pedagogical Director for these municipal services, leaving his post at the *Centro Medico Psico-Pedagogico Comunale*. Soon after he was given responsibility for the staffing and coordination of a new generation of services, the *nidi*. He played a central role in the development of the *Regolamento*, while he was busy too with the creation of regional policy on early childhood services. As well as pressing forward with introducing the plastic and visual arts as important 'languages' into municipal schools, through establishing *ateliers* and *atelieristas*, he also promoted collaboration with theatre, drama and music, and proposed the appointment of Mariano Dolci as the first puppeteer to be employed by a *comune*.

In 1974, he ended his work relationship with early childhood education in Modena, having previously worked with the *Comune* there, alongside his work in Reggio Emilia. The reason for this break lay in a difference of opinion about future educational strategy, of quality versus quantity. Malaguzzi wanted to concentrate on developing pedagogical work in municipal schools, while the *Comune* of Modena prioritised extending coverage. Whilst pulling out of this relationship, Malaguzzi extended his involvement elsewhere, through his work with the new regional government.

He was present, too, on the national stage, further developing relations with other leading pedagogical figures, such as writer and poet Gianni Rodari, and playing a leading role in conceiving, founding and directing *Zerosei*, a new early years journal for Italy. Carlina Rinaldi recalls how she, Malaguzzi and others 'used to travel around Italy [from the early 1970s], participating in conferences and building relations based on the Reggio Emilia experience . . . [forming] friendships with some cities that still hold fast today' (Rinaldi, 2006, p.159). In 1971, he was involved in organising with Reggio Emilia's schools a conference titled *Esperienze per una nuova scuola dell'infanzia* [Experiences for a

New *Scuola dell'Infanzia*], the first national and secular event of its kind. A few hundred people were expected, but 970 attended, and the three-day conference was followed quickly by a publication that Malaguzzi later described as 'one of the first non-religious publications on the subject of children's education in Italy' (Malaguzzi, 2004, p.12).

At the same time, Malaguzzi continued to read voraciously, avidly following the work of what he termed 'a second wave of scholars', drawn from many disciplines, including psychologists David Schaffer, Jerome Kagan and Howard Gardner, philosopher David Hawkins, cyberneticist and anthropologist Gregory Bateson, physicist and philosopher Heinz von Foerster and biologist and philosopher Francisco Varela. From such varied sources, Malaguzzi later reflected, 'we have received ideas both long lasting and not-so-long lasting – topics for discussion, reasons to find connections, discordances with cultural changes, occasions for debating, and stimuli to confirm and expand on practices and values' (Malaguzzi, 2012, p.39).

What comes across to the outside observer of this decade, apart from the sheer energy, confidence and enthusiasm of the city, its administration and the growing body of educators, is the appearance and practice of values that have come to define Reggio Emilia's educational project. There is a researching approach, applied with great thoroughness to the way the city develops the new *asili nido*. There is a strong emphasis on democracy and participation, both in the management of schools and in the development of policies, apparent too in the drafting and content of the *Regolamento*. There is, too, a clear image of the school, to match the image of the child, the school as a public and participatory institution, a place in close relationship not only with local families but with the whole local community. Closely connected is the insistence that *nidi* were not simply 'child care' centres, places for 'parking' or 'minding' children, welfare services in the narrowest sense, but places of and for education, as much part of a local cultural and pedagogical project as *scuole dell'infanzia*. Last but not least is the combination of intensely local action focused on municipal schools with an ardent engagement with the wider world, a belief by Malaguzzi and more widely in Reggio Emilia that a pedagogical project can be forged that combines strong local roots with a desire to dialogue with a world of ideas, perspectives and experiences.

The selection of documents (Reggio Emilia Working Group)

We can all sense something new is being born, and that past experiences we have lived through are being asked to come to terms with new things, to be lived and expressed in more stimulating ways, with open exchange and broader solidarity.

(Loris Malaguzzi, 1970, 'For a new *Scuola dell'infanzia* fused with families and the City' [39.70])

The 1970s was a period of great ferment and events that disturbed the established order. The war in Vietnam had been dragging on for too many years, unsettling consciences, demonstrating the difficulties in ending a long and useless conflict; feminists occupied piazzas with slogans, wooden clogs and flowery skirts; bomb and terrorist attacks disrupted the everyday life of Italian people; the Red Brigade were authors of several terrorist acts, including the most important, the kidnap and killing of Christian Democrat president Aldo Moro.

There is no trace of these events in the archived writings from which pieces published here have been selected, though we know the extent to which they did cut across life in the schools, often in a direct way, at the instigation of Malaguzzi himself. These writings, rather, mark another particularly seventies phenomenon: transformations designed in the previous decade were becoming new health, social and educational realities, operating at the local level, and officially regulated through laws, rules and guidelines.

The 1970s were years of growing the experience begun with the Robinson school and building the *Comune*'s network of 0–6 educational services. We concluded the period 1963–69 with five *scuole dell'infanzia* but will conclude the 1970s with an extensive network of *scuole dell'infanzia* and *nidi*. This was a political aim, strongly embraced by the *Comune's* administration:

> In 1971, the *Programma per l'istituzione di nuove scuole materne comunali* [Programme for the institution of new comune-run *scuole materne*] was launched. The plan's ambition was certainly a sign of the times: it meant doing a great deal, doing it quickly, to change the world . . . Since Law 444 [Law 444/68, for the provision of state *scuola materna*] was already being declared a failure, partly because it was left unfunded, the *Comune* therefore emerged as the most active agent for policy in this area – [having to act] both as provider and substitute [for the state] – aiming for fifteen new schools by 1971.
>
> (Lorenzi, Borghi and Canovi, 2001)

Here was an organised plan, supported by civic movements, and which proposed strategies for implementation: the recovery of disused buildings, the municipalisation of private schools on request. Malaguzzi watched and accompanied this project with critical rigour. In 1971 he wrote a letter to the *Assessore* for Schools and Social Services, Loretta Giaroni, in which he expresses an exceptionally strong view about the unsuitability of premises at Mancasale, a parish school that had responded to the administration's invitation and asked to be municipalised. It was, he says, a school whose premises are 'incapable of achieving the minimum level of sanitary, psychological or pedagogical decency' [42.71]. The theme of spaces that schools need to realise an educational project was constant in Malaguzzi's thinking and work. His talk – '*La scuola, l'edilizia, l'arredo: vite parallele, vite impossibili?*' [School, buildings, furnishing: parallel lives, impossible lives?] [60.75] – analyses the relation between architecture, furnishings and past educational ideas, still the cause of current problems, and is a statement and denunciation of the inability of sciences, which have always been separate, to re-organise knowledge in unified ways.

At the same time, the school year was dedicated to a deeper investigation of school spaces and environments and how children and adults inhabit them. The research conducted by *atelieristas*, teachers and *pedagogistas*, along with Tullio Zini (an architect who worked with Reggio Emilia's municipal schools for many years, participating in projects and offering advice and consulting) would bring a re-conceptualisation of several spaces (the hall became a 'piazza', the entrance the 'school visiting card', bathrooms became 'interesting places', etc.). Other important changes were the birth of additional spaces in classrooms (the mini *atelier*), new items of furnishing and, in general, new design for interiors. Above all, the diffusion and dissemination of an environmental culture considered as an integral part of education, quite rare in pedagogy.

The problem of quality environments, and more generally of the *scuola dell'infanzia* (and the *nido*), was a critical 1970s theme, but still current today. The meagre resources available for creating childhood policies, a problem in every period and the choice of every Italian government (not only Italian), always bring an apparently sensible way of reasoning: better to have many places with low quality than few places with high quality. Malaguzzi always fought this logic, which seems to insist there is no alternative. We find him promoting a demonstration to petition for '*Scuole dell'Infanzia* for all children' [43.72]. While on another occasion he distributes slogans to be displayed on school walls under the heading that 'This school costs the right price' [74.ND], a message for parents, citizens and teachers, co-participators in the experience through the project of social management.

He also did everything he could for the local administration to build up quality conditions. The *Regolamento*, unanimously approved by the City Council in 1972, is both testament to and synthesis of his commitment. While in a talk he gave at a PCI Federation meeting in 1975 he proposes the objective of a new national law on *scuola dell'infanzia* 'to effectively guarantee every child in this age group [3 to 6 years] the right to attend and the conditions for attending, i.e. attending a *scuola dell'infanzia* run by the *comune*, funded by the State, and planned by the Region' [59.75].

The seventies began with some particularly significant public events, which for the first time included the *scuola dell'infanzia* in their title, both as the principal subject and as the protagonist. These were national conferences, promoted by Reggio Emilia, together with Modena where Malaguzzi was pedagogical consultant until 1974, conferences whose proceedings were published by Editori Riuniti, in an affordable and culturally prestigious series with a wide readership.[2] Of the three-day event held in Reggio Emilia in March 1971, Malaguzzi would later recall in a 1990s interview: 'with notable daring, we organised a national meeting for teachers only. We expected 200 participants, but 900 showed up' (Malaguzzi, 2012, p.33). It was an event that made it possible to publish the first secular work on the subject of early education, *'Esperienze per una nuova scuola dell'infanzia'* [see also 92.89].

In fact the *scuola dell'infanzia* in Italy had been the domain of the Catholic Church up to that time, which was the reason for the *Comune*'s difficulties in opening its first *scuola dell'infanzia*, Robinson Crusoe, in 1963. What is very evident is the difficult and wide-ranging debate with the Catholic world during this decade, of which traces can be seen both in Malaguzzi's response to questions from a Catholic educationalist Luciano Corradini [61.75], and in the document about 'Religious Education and the Education of Children' [65.77]. Difficult dialogues, but always faced up to by Malaguzzi with a clarity of position, which in the following decade would result in the first attempts to build an integrated public system giving legitimacy to all the different providers, as part of governance by the *Comune* of public education policies.

The two conferences at the beginning of the 1970s testify to the large movement for renewal that gathered around schools for young children at the time, and how it was a bottom–up movement that promoted and got change up and running. They were unusual conferences where, alongside *assessori* and *pedagogistas*, approximately twenty talks were given by teachers from Reggio Emilia and Modena, together with testimonials by parents. It was a specific choice: together with research – a strategy for shaping new educational work and tightly interwoven with it, participation and social management were the signature traits of the 1970s. Malaguzzi followed the writing of these presentations personally: a precious exchange of points of view for a shared processing of experience.

The idea of renewal was pursued with determination and tenacity, connecting school with society, removing education 'from its Olympian elitism, from always being over and above, on the outside, from its ignorance and fake neutrality'. This is taken from Malaguzzi's introduction to the conference *'La gestione sociale nelle scuole dell'infanzia'* [Social management in *scuole dell'infanzia*], held in Modena in May 1971, where he also uses the metaphor of a hot air balloon, to warn of the risks involved in distancing pedagogy from reality:

> This game is simple. In simple words, we rise from the ground in a hot-air balloon . . . until the earth is completely flat [and everything looks the same]. [. . .] We use the same discourse for children and things that are not the same. [. . .] This process began before Galileo. We produce a general concept and do not allow it to be contested; if necessary we trivialise and change the terms of the contestation.
>
> [41.71]

Malaguzzi worked on building a new concept of education and of the *scuola dell'infanzia*, intuitively systemic, with its starting point in a new political vision that would be brought to maturity, finding in concrete experience possibilities for self-testing, self-correcting and self-evaluating. A totally new vision of school, developed in the pedagogical, cultural and political experience of previous years, capable of holding together what had previously been thought of as separate: school and family, places of education and society, teachers and parents, teachers and other teachers, pedagogy and politics. In recounting experience already underway, Malaguzzi told the Modena conference that:

> Our children go out from school as much as possible. [. . .] During class meetings and assemblies children's problems, parents' problems, adult problems are confronted and debated. There is no gap between children's affairs and adult affairs, between children's present and future, between the school story and the outside story.

A reuniting of opposites that we have already seen as characteristic of Loris Malaguzzi's thinking in the fifties; and which in Reggio Emilia's *scuole comunali dell'infanzia* found fertile ground during this decade for becoming active experience, capable of building a real movement and concrete facts. A particular and specific feature of Loris Malaguzzi's professional life.

The relationship and connection that education built with the city provided powerful leverage for the change that was sought. To strengthen the connection, each year the *scuole dell'infanzia* worked on creating exhibitions on their premises open to the public. Again in his introduction to the Modena conference, Malaguzzi argues the reasons for inter-dependency between social management and a renewal of school methods and contents. A growing sense of actively belonging to a community experience changed the teacher's identity, allowed her to emerge from anonymity, removed her from her condition of 'deforming solitude' and the authoritarian structure of her role. Collegiality, in a school not separate from social context, is pointed to as a live model of socialisation for children, socialisation not encased in reductive schema or circumscribed by the dynamic of the children–teacher relationship. This is where we find the theme of the three protagonist subjects – parents, teachers, children – in the educational project, a triad bound by ties of interdependency who can only find a way to new conceptualisations of their identities together, in an idea of conciliating rights which during the 1990s would be formulated more precisely in a '*Una carta per tre diritti*' [A charter of three rights].

A letter from 1973, inviting parents to meetings to debate proposals for a new timetable to reconcile the working hours of parents with children's rights, is an example of inter-dependence between social management and school renewal, and of the intention that 'important and urgent topics' are adequately discussed and examined more deeply so as to 'hopefully resolve them rapidly' [50.73]. The proposed discussion deals with a theme that still today continues to be debated: should the *nido* and *scuola dell'infanzia* derive their organisation from constantly changing needs that the world of work imposes on parents, or should they build it starting from educational quality considered necessary to guarantee children the right to an education, and not just to minding? The extensive and heated debate that took place in these meetings led to the extension of opening hours – but only for those with proven need: a conciliatory choice between two points of view that are always considered diametrically opposed, which testifies to how participation, that is to say involving society in educational problems and creating processes of consensus-building, is a fundamental means for shaping a common cultural position.

This is why it is important to be present. In 1973, we find Malaguzzi scolding members of the *Comitati di Scuola e Città* who were absent at the meeting of the *Consulta* because 'the importance of the *Consulta* and the themes being discussed lead us to underline strongly the need for all members of this body to be present' [52.73, which also explains the composition and purpose of the *Consulta*].

New places are needed for consulting and formulating because 'facts are not described, not recorded. They are discussed, investigated, related to each other; precisely the attitude and mental habit we try to offer and live with our children' [41.71]. An attitude of mind, a characteristic of meeting together inside *nidi* and *scuole dell'infanzia*, which today still invites us to think in a different way about participation and our ways of being adult professionals and citizens in children's schools, in a period where social networks have accustomed us to consume news and offer immediate reactions/evaluations. But Malaguzzi does not have an idealised vision of social management, lucidly calling to mind the possible errors: 'expecting to see everything clearly and straight away; being satisfied with the purely formal administrative aspects of issues; sliding into rhetorical patronising attitudes; corrupting the initiative into purely activist or pejoratively pragmatic schemes; impoverishing it in the vacuous exercise of socialisation and simple cooperation' [39.70].

In 1973 Malaguzzi sent to friends and to public figures in culture and academia, the publication 'I Who We Are' by the Diana school. The publication is a compilation of twenty-eight autobiographical stories by children, testifying to the quality of subjective difference representing 'a counter-model to the conformist and repressive models', which would like all children to adhere to the model proposed by the adult. 'I Who We Are', the title considered most appropriate, is a manifesto against 'schools and society, which educate the I and then oblige it to live in suspicion, competition, in rivalry with the other' [49.73]. A value that would be developed during the 1980s in the pedagogy of relations, placing value on the group, large, medium or small.

The educational experience was proceeding well. But this was not cause to halt, because it had yet to free its 'intrinsic vitality, [. . .] it has been more concerned with the present than with looking ahead, to anticipating the days of tomorrow, precisely those that belong to the children of our time' [39.70]. A gaze fixed on the future that we have already seen, and which here meets with an attitude of constant self-criticism, the not-being-satisfied, which was, and still is, the motor of experience in Reggio Emilia's *nidi* and *scuole dell'infanzia*.

In 1976 a document titled '*Bambini handicappati*' [Handicapped Children] was published by the *Comitati di Scuola e Città*. It is a document that synthesises experience realised up to that time 'in a confluence of a political, cultural and practical nature'. It supports the thesis that socially managed *nidi* and *scuole dell'infanzia* can promote an innovative dynamic both on the level of educational work, thanks to their internal organisation and being in a network with health services, and on a socio-cultural level. In fact, in participatory schools a socialisation of problems takes place that lifts families out of their solitude, and the right of access for children with a handicap becomes a theme for debate promoting solidarity: a demonstration that the project of social participation is truly an instrument for change, a place of synthesis and of making new advances concrete.

When Malaguzzi speaks of a 'declared desire for pedagogical research as a permanent method realised together by teachers, auxiliary workers, families, citizens and *Quartiere*' [61.75], this is not a naive or romantic position, but the affirmation of a method striving to re-organise areas of learning for a child who has the right to be considered whole. As we have said this was a period when such mature thinking found concrete implementation. In 1972 the City Council approved the *Regolamento* of the *scuole comunali dell'infanzia*. The document is the result of broad consultation, and reflects the organisational values and conditions needed to maintain and strengthen achievements arising from the many experimentations that had been activated, evaluated and shared. Among other things the *Regolamento* introduced two hours of weekly updating [*aggiornamento*] for all staff, both teaching and auxiliary, and a collaborative role for two teachers in every class: two fundamental conditions. The *Regolamento* defined other important new elements including, after heated discussion, the entry of male teachers and auxiliaries.

Malaguzzi opened the 1972/1973 school year, following the adoption of the *Regolamento*, with two meetings, one for teachers, the other for auxiliary staff.[3] The talks he gave on these occasions were identical in the first part, then more specific to each group in the second. The talk to the teachers refers to the urgency of realising 'new choices in contents, more democratic work creating new relations between school, children, families, committees and neighbourhoods', while proposing 'to develop more fully our cultural levels and our professional capacities' [44.72]. The talk to auxiliary staff proposes a new conception of this role, which means abandoning 'supposed inferiority, the feeling of being incapable or daunted, and [being] aware they represent an educational model and belong to an adult collective whose efforts must come together to create ever improving life experiences for children'. He calls on auxiliaries to be part not only of a working collective, but also of the *Comitati di Scuola e Città* [45.72].

This new conception of professions that previously had little social value is interesting. What had been until then exclusively female roles, and in a period of particularly strong feminist struggles focused on re-appropriating the body, after twenty years of the UDI's focus on women's social role, now found a concrete possibility of freedom and emancipation in schools for very young children. It is no coincidence that these professions, still today generally devalued nationally (and not only nationally), should be highly respected in the city of Reggio Emilia.

The theme of female emancipation in renewed, secular and systemic schools was extended to children, as we find in Malaguzzi's reply to Luciano Corradini, ex-President of the *Comitato di Scuola e Città* of the Diana school, university lecturer, and active in Catholic affairs. In this exchange, published in 1975, Malaguzzi comments that:

> what characterises our way of working is that we refuse the social role models, including those connected with sex, which society distorts and education proposes without critique. These are false and adulterated roles. If we work in *scuola dell'infanzia* in such a way that our children do not find themselves at crossroads, or on separate journeys, with separate activities and behaviours; if we let so-called femininity and so-called masculinity emerge freely and gradually, avoiding obsessively Manichaean attitudes, then I think this is healthy and right.

In the same piece Malaguzzi responds to the accusation that municipal schools engage in ideological education: 'Yes, in the sense of liberating and emancipating children (normal and handicapped), and schools and families' [61.75].

In 1976 Gustavo Selva, news director of RAI [*Radiotelevisione Italiana*, the national public broadcaster] Radio Two, launched a media attack lasting seven days against early childhood politics in the *Comune* of Reggio Emilia, accusing the *scuola dell'infanzia* of being the author of atheist and communist propaganda. The habit of discussion, the concept of schools open to participation, the ties between pedagogy and the real contexts of children's lives, would all be winning strategies for facing this difficult time. The resulting document (not selected here) represented a synthesis of months of debate between parents, teachers, citizens, political groups and the *consigli pastorali*,[4] in dozens and dozens of meetings promoted in and by the *scuole dell'infanzia*. The attack became an opportunity for re-discovering and extending the value of exchange with a wider range of participants, for '[p]luralism, the diverse, the contradictory are in the reality of the world'. Children must not have meaning taken from them; the element of religion is part of reality; however it is necessary to watch out for dogmatism and indoctrination not only in this field, for dogmatism and indoctrination 'can arise within every discipline and every contents'. To conclude, '[a] public and secular *scuola dell'infanzia* that becomes the promoter of these human values, testifying to them through facts and not with words, has already thoroughly accomplished its task of education, in the field of religion too'.

But how to consolidate the new values, how to make them into an active structure, into practice embodied in the actions of teachers, parents, auxiliaries?

Malaguzzi has no fear of formulating concrete action, and makes proposals to the schools. For example, in 1973 he is writing to them about a *quaderno di lavoro* [work notebook], which teachers, auxiliaries, parents and members of the *Comitato di Scuola e Città* and the *Équipe Pedagogica* must participate in writing, and which must seek to be as concrete as possible [48.73]. While the next year, he asks the recently constituted teacher pairs to write work plans together, synthesising what has been done up to that point in time and formulating future lines of work [53.74]. Collegiality, Malaguzzi believed, was a condition breaking with the way school had been conceived until that time; but he also understood that it raised suspicions and objections, including about teacher freedom and 'excessively intense work, ideological pressures, acts of propaganda' [61.75].

New schools were not within easy reach. They required study, intuition, research, trying out, examination: this characterised the decade 1970–79. As with the previous decade, giving visibility to what was being done was also vital and necessary. Forms of communication that had been experimented with in previous years – public conferences, *comune* publications and exhibitions – were augmented by different, more contemporary forms. A vivid example is the celebratory outing for all *scuole dell'infanzia* to San Polo, journeying together in a special, painted train. An event Malaguzzi was careful to promote thoroughly in the newspapers, another form of communication that characterises this decade [46.73].

In 1977 the *nido* becomes a primary subject in Malaguzzi's writings and activities [see, for example, 68.77, 69.78, 71.78]. The *scuole dell'infanzia* had already opened the way, but there was a need to construct a specific pedagogy legitimising the *nido* as a place of education, and not just for minding. Again participation was a priority for shared construction, for hearing doubts and generating questions, capable of orienting the formation of culture and observation. Observation that is necessary to give visibility to very young children and their particularities, to give society an idea of children in their very first years of life, freed of the image of weakness to which they had been relegated until then.

Throughout this period, Malaguzzi maintained an exchange with politics, speaking at meetings where he proposed policies for childhood enacted by the *Comune* of Reggio Emilia as reference points for the PCI's educational policy [55.74, 59.75].

To conclude we can say the 1970s were a decade particularly rich in important issues. They were crucial years for building 'a new conception and reality of educational and social relations', and of:

> schools that untiringly attempt to *bond with reality*, that live on *dialogue's* difficulties and fruitfulness, that finally involve *children's entirety* and not only the part that lives in schools, that never presume and *offer exchange, discussion, and examination*. A school that debates uncertainties, problems, difficulties, and non-successes with parents and citizens, with whom finally it can *grow together*.
>
> [39.70]

An onerous task, which would cause Malaguzzi to say that 'I feel I have left things out everywhere. But this is the talk of the kind of person I am, always distorted by hurrying and running' [61.75].

Timeline 1970–79

Key: *Malaguzzi*
Reggio Emilia
Italy

1970   *Director of Reggio Emilia's municipal scuole dell'infanzia; leaves post at municipal Centro Medico Psico-Pedagogico Comunale.*

Comitati di Scuola e Città established; first pedagogista in post; opening of Theatre Laboratory, a collaboration begins between municipal theatre and schools and Experimental theatre of Puppets and Marionettes.

Twenty regions created including Emilia-Romagna, with responsibility for regulating and funding *asili nido,* nurseries for children under 3 years; new autonomy for municipalities as regions replace *Prefettura* [prefects]; law permits divorce for the first time; formation of Red Brigades.

1971   *Director of Reggio Emilia's municipal asili nido and scuole dell'infanzia.*

Comune opens first nido for children under 3 years, Genoeffa Cervi; first national secular conference on early childhood education, Esperienze per una nuova scuola dell'infanzia [Experiences for a New Scuola dell'Infanzia]; first publication on early childhood education.

Law no.820 introduces full-time primary schools; Law no.1044 recognises *asili nido* as 'social service in the public interest', with national government to provide funding, regional government to regulate and *comuni* to run new services; legislation for paid maternity leave.

1972   **Comune adopts Regolamento delle scuole comunali dell'infanzia [Rulebook for municipal schools]; Équipe Pedagogico-Didattica [Pedagogical coordination and support team]; established 'Encounters with the Fantastic', meetings held with poet and writer Gianni Rodari.**

Emilia-Romagna Region adopts legislation on *nidi*, with plans for funding and building.

1973   **First puppeteer to be employed by a municipality in Italy.**

Oil crisis leads to deep national and international recession; paid maternity leave implemented and national government funds provided for *asili nido*; Decreti Delegati – laws to implement principles of the Constitution in state schools – approved between July 1973 and May 1974.

1974	*Ends his work with the municipal schools in Modena.*
	Referendum supports new law allowing divorce.
1975	Family law includes family rights, equal rights for husbands and wives, new rights for children; national conference in Bologna: 'The child as subject and source of rights in the family and society.'
1976	*Director of new journal* Zerosei *[ZeroSix].*
	First issue of *Zerosei* early years journal; ONMI closes, its responsibilities to regions, services municipalised.
1977	Law no.517 introduces compulsory inclusion into public schooling of children with special rights; Law no.903 establishes principle of pay parity for women.
1978	Law no.194 legalises abortion; Law no.833 establishes *Servizio Sanitario Nazionale* [a National Health Service]; Aldo Moro, President of Christian Democrat party, murdered.
1979	**Comune has twenty *scuole dell'infanzia* (fifteen opened in 1970s) and eleven *nidi*.**
	National conference in Bologna: 'The education and social values of the *nido*: experiences, reflections, proposals'; General election, first fall in PCI share of vote since 1953.

Documents 1970–79

1970

39.70 Speech at the First Citizen's Assembly of *Comitati di Scuola e Città*, *Sala degli Specchi* [Hall of Mirrors], Reggio Emilia, July 1970

Editor's note: *Comitati di Scuola e Città* were first established in Reggio Emilia in July 1970, at the time of the talk transcribed below, but were preceded by *Comitati d'Iniziativa* created in 1968 in city neighbourhoods to press for the opening of municipal schools.

For a new scuola dell'infanzia *fused with families and the City*

I think each one of us senses, and this was true of our preliminary meetings, the meaning of the work being officially launched this evening, which will lead to an official establishment of *Comitati di Scuola e Città*. We can all sense something new is being born, and that past experiences we have lived through are being asked to come to terms with new things, to be lived and expressed in more stimulating ways, with open exchange and broader solidarity. As a consequence we are also well aware of the complexity *Comitati di Scuola e Città* will bring, more with problems of functioning than with their birth.

For a moment let us postpone the attempt at outlining and clarifying the meanings, purposes and contexts of this new body. And let us begin by considering our work. Weighing up our shared experiences as teachers, parents, administrators leads us to a feeling of satisfaction with several aspects. The schools are doing well, they have tried and realised successful innovations that many on the outside envy us, they work and experiment together, two universities have recently asked for degree dissertations on specific activities ongoing in the schools, the children are excellently looked after, they play, they learn, they seem happy, parents are often called for discussions to get to the heart of educational issues, and the exemplary commitment of our teachers has gained them widespread esteem.

Yet we must recognise, now we are at this turning point, although it has not arrived suddenly because we have been reflecting for some time (in the *comitato di vigilanza* [see Chapter 2, n.17], in meetings with parents and teachers), we must recognise our experience has not gone into every single space, has included the bad habits of hesitancy and closure that have not liberated its intrinsic vitality, that it has been more concerned with the present than with looking ahead, to anticipating the days of tomorrow, precisely those that belong to the children of our time.

We feel this projection into the future represents the necessary dimension of a living pedagogy, which has partly been lacking in our schools, and this is what we are attempting to start this evening, together.

The efforts we have made together – to remove the *scuola dell'infanzia* from old and new models of welfare as much as we can, from old and new ways of pretending to educate, the things no one wants but 'hard and obstinate reality', as James euphemistically calls it, imposes too often in practice – allow us to mobilise greater energy.

This means continuing to say no to pseudo-schools. Schools that instead of centring on children and their rights, accept the squandering of their own time and children's. Schools that passively tolerate adult demands and contradictions, the delays, disorder and injustices present in adult society.

Removing the *scuola dell'infanzia* from this ambivalence means creating the educational institutions children need, endorsing their right to equality in education and study. [It means] fighting a sacrosanct battle against selection, discrimination and conditioning, which together shape the nature of our schools and culture. It means laying the first stone for rebuilding elementary schools, something which cannot be deferred, and which could innovate education for young children, older children and adolescents.

This can be done more and better if the *scuola dell'infanzia* (like every other school) fuses its choices and values to a greater participatory presence of families and public opinion, if it achieves greater spaces for children's rights, the rights of new generations in the unceasing play of society's construction.

We believe this directly introduces another important reference for shared reflection: that of examining with the necessary frankness, how children and the entire world of childhood, are involved or defrauded by organised society.

Cities, in the emblematic sense of the word, continue to grow to an exclusively adult measure. They are built for individuals of working age; homes, streets, squares, workshops, cinemas, theatres, cars, motorways are built for them and at the same time they demolish, dirty, pollute and speculate, in a folly of grandeur and self-destruction.

The truth is children are excluded. They are completely abnormal in this anthropological model. They put up with its irrationality and violence, with its constrictions, prohibitions, repressions, and frustration of their fundamental needs.

However the fact is that if cities and houses are not made for children, then neither are they made for mankind.

[. . .]

The violent rupture between private and social life weighs cynically and painfully on those who can defend themselves least (children and at the other end of the spectrum the elderly) and this urgently demands a correction of the system. In this difficult situation schools suffer the same contradictions, whether they know it or not, and they must become promoters of a philosophy and practice, when they have the capacity, by taking on a social role at the same time as they take on their educational role. After all, this is the old and unheeded summons made by the wisest pedagogy, echoing today more dramatically than yesterday.

This is what we are looking for here this evening. Our *scuola dell'infanzia* presents an alternative to old ways of conceptualising and doing education, everywhere and in every way; it is not merely a continuation and supplement to family environments.

Faced with these problems our *scuola dell'infanzia* also has to rapidly change its internal organisation, and above all its methodologies. In the first instance by appealing to the responsibility of teachers and auxiliary staff. What has been lived in segments, in separate different spaces and autonomous actions, must be lived in a seamless common dimension, taking teachers from the deforming solitude old pedagogy gave us (and continues to give us) and situating them in shared constructions, work that calls for exchange, confrontation, updating, that constantly brings into play both personal and private experience; and through this reciprocal dialogical growth and enrichment, brings them to a human and professional awareness of the group.

[. . .]

Therefore *Comitati di Scuola e Città* are being created as a new and original tool for community presence. They presuppose new relations with parents and citizens, and are based on two premises of decisive value: a school that offers itself with full awareness to all hypotheses for the freeing and renewal of its methods and aims; and a social context that likewise offers to not only recognise but also stimulate a new concept of the powers, contributions, ways and times of working democratically.

These two premises exist. Schools have declared their willingness; and parent consensus and enthusiasm have welcomed the creation of the Committees. Together with the busy work some Committees have already carried out spontaneously, and the full agreement of the *Comune* as the managing authority and representative of our city community, these represent a guarantee of success for our intentions.

We must add that we are working in a privileged situation in more than one aspect. Privileged not only because we have the partners already mentioned. But above all because the *scuola dell'infanzia* offers an open, flexible terrain that is still immune to the great virus of bureaucracy, centralisation, sclerosis of the system, circulars, registers, bulletin boards with scores, and because our parents are fortunately still immune to the opportunism and utilitarianism that will quickly condition them in other schools later.

Our conversation can take place on this more open fertile terrain by beginning immediately to demystify certain concepts of dialogue. These were theorised without stinting on rhetoric and were practised only for form's sake, and they have melted away of their own accord through failure and providence. We mean the School–Family Committees and the various *Ecoles des Parents*, which safeguarded the inviolability, arrogance and condescension of the old school, required collaboration in one direction, co-operation with conditioning pupils to passivity and defeatist attitudes. These committees consider school to be a taboo [subject] that only knowing, delicate hands, which never belong to parents, can touch. So that parents, who are – let us note well – the recipients, patrons and financiers of services, have no rights whatsoever, not even the right to express what they expect or to have a non-subordinate role in dialogue, explanation and meetings.

[. . .]

Extending the *scuola dell'infanzia* managed by the *comuni* is a necessary preliminary measure. In fact the State has given us a *scuola dell'infanzia* [managed by the State] at least a hundred years old, as if the Parliament of 1859 and Minister Casati had authorised it.

[. . .]

The pedagogical alternative we propose resides in more than merely meeting, but in the genuine integration of parents, teachers, children, citizens and neighbourhoods, in a renewed and richer vision of society.

This is not all. We feel that even when this happens other geographical and social limits in schools and neighbourhoods can negate other potentials and other yearnings for freedom.

In this framework, full-time schools [not the 8 am to 12 noon half-day of traditional Italian primary schools], a forceful demand being made at this time, can bring many contradictions. It attempts to find an internal solution in schools, leaving unaltered the relations and connections education has with the city, with the city's educational and cultural structures, and with its civic issues and problems.

[. . .]

One last consideration before going into detail. How the *Comitati di Scuola e Città* are composed is a choice of great importance. It is important to recognise the full freedom and independence of Committees in all proposed schemes for organisation. It is our opinion that we could create Committees that go beyond choosing members exclusively among parents using the school. There are parents who have used the school and continue to be interested in new experience; there are representatives of *Consigli di quartiere* who participate in and are the means to extensive and varied relations; there are citizens who believe in the initiative's values because of their own specific cultural interests. These could all enter and become part of Committees. Choices of this kind can already be found in the most progressive examples of our project.

[. . .]

We all make mistakes, but we can acknowledge that these are possible and be on the look out for them. Perhaps we will discover other mistakes in the middle of our journey, and shake them off as best we can.

Some obvious errors might be: expecting to see everything clearly and straight away; being satisfied with the purely formal administrative aspects of issues; sliding into rhetorical patronising attitudes; corrupting our initiative into purely activist or pejoratively pragmatic schemes; impoverishing it in the vacuous exercise of socialisation and simple cooperation, when instead the defining and determining principles of co-management, its ultimate and essential values, are exchange and reciprocal enrichment of our awareness of problems.

While reflecting on these possible dangers, let us conclude by also reflecting on the experiences proposed: a space and quality of intervention where we can build a new conception and reality of educational and social relations, schools that untiringly attempt *to bond with reality*, that live on *dialogue's* difficulties and fruitfulness, that finally involve *children's entirety* and not only the part that lives in schools, that never presume and *offer exchange, discussion and examination*. A school that debates uncertainties, problems, difficulties, and non-successes with parents and citizens, with whom finally it can *grow together*.

Section of Schools and Social Services
Direzione Scuole Materne Comunali
Municipality of Reggio Emilia

1971

40.71 Letter to parents of children enrolled in the *Scuole Comunali dell'Infanzia* of Reggio Emilia and Modena, January 1971

Comuni *of Reggio Emilia and Modena Study Seminar: experiences of organisation and study in the* scuole comunali dell'infanzia

A Study Seminar on experiences of organisation and pedagogy realised in *scuole dell'infanzia comunali* will be held in the *Sala degli Specchi* in Reggio Emilia's Municipal Theatre on 18, 19 and 20 March 1971, organised by the *Assessore* Offices for School and Cultural Services in the *Comuni* of Reggio Emilia and Modena.

The Seminar work will be introduced by around twenty talks produced through group work between teachers in Reggio Emilia and Modena, and a series of addresses by administrators and social management Committee representatives. The work will be enriched with film documentaries, and an exhibition of school activities and materials.

The Seminar does not yet have a precise and complete programme: the promoting organisations are attending to this.

As soon as the programme is finalised, it will be our pleasure to send you formal invitations together with detailed information.

Cordially
January 1971

For the ORGANISING COMMITTEE
Prof. Loris Malaguzzi
Pedagogical Consultant to the *scuole dell'infanzia*
of Reggio Emilia and Modena

Liliano Famigli
Assessore for Cultural Services of
the *Comune* of Modena

Loretta Giaroni
Assessore for Schools and Social Services of
the *Comune* of Reggio Emilia

❋ ❋ ❋

41.71 Speech to the conference '*La gestione sociale nella scuola dell'infanzia*' [Social management in *scuole dell'infanzia*], Modena, May 1971

New socialisation for children and teachers through the experience of social management in scuola dell'infanzia

PROF. LORIS MALAGUZZI: Pedagogical consultant to the *scuole comunali dell'infanzia* of Modena and Reggio Emilia

1. This is a conference for reflecting on and studying issues of public and social management in schools for children aged 3 to 6 years. Specifying the age 3 to 6 apparently reduces the field but in fact includes all the issues that confront schools in general, with their misguided ways of interpreting and doing education. This conference follows closely on the recent conference in Reggio Emilia on work realised or underway in Reggio Emilia and Modena, and attempts a new pedagogical definition of what *scuole dell'infanzia* are. Today these conferences can compare notes and [see how] they have tended to re-examine and discover the theme of research as part of a much broader and complex discourse, and to consider it in the light of facts and values that have always been falsely and deliberately omitted.

This occasion confirms the privilege and power our *scuole comunali dell'infanzia* have of being able to face these important issues not only on the level of ideas but in direct experiment, and the responsibilities they bring of commitment and work. The responsibility of facing the struggle for renewal and transformation without giving in to the temptations of immature protest; of defending ourselves from all forms of devaluation; of maintaining the high levels of educational and cultural ferment that mobilise the development and growth of schools' powers and their new social and pedagogical uses.

A project like this is based on a new and necessary concept of education, removed from its temples, divisions and selections, from its fragmentation and false culture. Education is reformulated and re-invented to include all times and all spaces, where the process of learning and educating that goes from an individual's birth until death is the work of each and every one of us, and over-comes the fixed roles, separations and classifications of educational institutions and individual destinies, which are the most obvious aspect of the distorted nature and failure of school and education.

The concept of permanent education can represent all this, as long as it is not one of the many slogans that pedagogy's inexhaustible and evasive imagination has coined; as long as it is given concrete meaning and is treated as a hypothesis that requires the immediate definition of concrete political, social and educational strategies.

If we want to be coherent with permanent education, and try to realise its aims by identifying education and school with society, to make society into a continuous series of interventions for the education and liberation of human beings, then a decisive large-scale reversal of today's social relations and structures is required, together with research into a new philosophy of human life and culture. Our theme is the clear and irreversible theme of work and struggle striving towards the simultaneous construction of a society and schools which are different to those we have now.

Through these connections we can put an end to the oppositions between a concept and presence of pedagogy and a concept and presence of socio-politics (convenient now for conservatives, now for apocalyptic revolutionaries). We can make a start on re-defining these in more unified ways, through the simultaneous processes of increasing awareness and achieving our objectives.

Several nodes must be tackled, though all depend on a single matrix, and they cannot be tackled without greater consensus, inside and outside the separate entity that school constitutes, making it a protagonist, together with teachers, families, social groups and social institutions.

The issues of social management at the centre of our debate do not merely wish to regain a balance or make formal adjustments to school organisation and functions. We want to initiate a movement and grow it, join together the themes of school, education and society, examine and discover their correlations and contradictions. We want to reveal the instrumental and subordinate role of educational philosophy, but also the meaning of struggles taking place in society and their connections with issues of cultural and professional education for children and young people.

A task of this kind with ambitions like these cannot be separated from large-scale involvement, a mobilisation and the solidarity of the largest number of people possible. Families first of all, then progressive political and cultural organisations, and above all trade unions (of all leanings and types) [perhaps] finally capable of absorbing and uniting in their struggles and work the issues of conditions of life in the workplace, of how the workforce is educated and used, and of education in general.

Reflecting on the experience of Modena and Reggio Emilia, I think it must be acknowledged how important this has been. The participation of citizens, workers' parties and democratic institutions in situations of large-scale mobilisation and struggle, with the presence of the majority of our school workers, has made it possible to expand services rapidly at the same time defending and researching their cultural and political identity.

I think there is agreement that if this experience of social management in the *scuola dell'infanzia* is to be credible and decisive it must continue to grow inside and outside schools, with more involvement of other sectors of society, such as the workplace, workers' organisations and citizens' organisations. It must be offered as the starting point of a process that requires organisation. Above all the model of active responsible participation must be extended to every level of political and administrative de-centralisation, as part of the wider experience occurring in *comune* administrations, in cities, in the regions.

So the capacity of teachers, *Comitati di Scuola e Città* and *Consigli di quartiere* to extend their range of intervention is important. They must go beyond the admittedly important issues of school, of children and families in school, to influence the condition of schools, of families, and of children in their neighbourhoods, in their city and society. This is our great and stimulating objective, where we will try to concentrate our efforts at the start of the new school year with the management bodies that have been created. Some *Comitati* have already spontaneously and intuitively begun to work: we must be more homogeneous, broader, and clearer in the objectives of our action.

2. Which of the many themes can we choose in this attempt of active early years pedagogy to get to the heart of the matter?

Let us take the theme of socialisation. This is a topic, or rather a 'value', that traditional official pedagogy loves to assign to *scuola dell'infanzia* and children's primary needs, and it regularly ends up as one of many 'imaginary representations of self and relations with others' that, Althusser[5] tells us, constitute the misleading game of educational theory today.

This game is simple. In simple words we rise from the ground in a hot-air balloon (official educationalists do not generally have the metal of astronauts) until the earth is completely flat and mountains, valleys and deserts cannot be picked out. Nor can furnace chimneys, mining towers, Onassis' yachts or children in Biafra and Vietnam,[6] the children of workers, farm labourers and emigrants. Then we use the same discourse for children and things that are not the same, and the aforementioned 'imaginary representations' abound.

Speaking 'scientifically' this process began before Galileo. We produce a general concept and do not allow it to be contested; if necessary we trivialise and change the terms of the contestation. So that socialisation and a sense of community are 'no longer something derived from concrete life in a given society, but from the intimacy of our being, a person's inner willingness and dedication.' If a child does not socialise well? 'Certainly – they say – this is because the child suffered a lack of affection, or problems of emotional attachment, as a small infant'.[7]

In the first of these two cases socialisation is presented as an abstract, a-historical fact of personalised, immanent psychologism.[8] In the second case the potentially negative aspects are explained by a lack or a condition left in limbo without exploring the social reasons, and therefore they become inexplicable. This is a convenient and congenial support for conservative psychology.

Again, and the New Guidelines[9] opt for this hypothesis, we say children's lack of socialisation can be blamed on teachers who are not adequately equipped with 'a tendency to optimism, humour and light-heartedness', which are science fiction qualities for those with a passing knowledge of the inhuman conditions most teachers work in, of their inhuman relations with children and vice-versa.

Again, '. . . social development can be taken to mean both growing aware- ness of the fact that in the course of activities we must take others into account and avoid hurting them (untidiness, noise, exclusive use of objects and toys), and also the growing capacity for establishing collaborative relations with others (collective games, activities requiring co-ordination of individual children's contributions, choir singing, recitals etc.)'. Here the premises of socialisation are confined to reductive, primitive, evasive schema and limited to a dynamic that never goes beyond the child or teacher figure (inevitably always female). They are premises that start and end unnaturally on an ethical-moral basis connected with concepts of tidiness and necessity.

3. What socialisation can children learn from teachers for whom an attitude of participation and socialisation is forbidden during inadequate professional development? ('They taught us submission at school', one teacher confesses, 'subordination, to be afraid of several things, afraid of the Principal, afraid of talking, with no awareness of school and its tasks'.)[10] Or from teachers living in isolation, saddened by their working conditions and their frustrated aware- ness? From poor, depressing, overcrowded school environments with nothing for hands to do, from experience (always taught, never learned) inspired by conventional criteria rather than inner needs? What socialisation can they learn from pedagogy that avoids reality, that leaves children's history and conditions outside the door and then creates competition between them? From schools where parents are kept at a distance, held to ransom by awe and fear?

What kind of socialisation can children develop in places where childish behaviour, authoritarianism and vacuity of experience soon kill any growing sense of Self children are constructing, kill their desire to communicate, their joy in living and working together? What socialisation can take place between three and six years of age in environments where the rules only allow female staff?

4. The ways, rhythms and purposes of social development, which we usu- ally consider to be conducive to children's formation, their psychological de-centring and their living together, are not fixed and unchangeable things with dynamics and aims that can be repeated universally anywhere and anyhow. For some time anthropologists have been showing us the results of educational processes inside different cultures.

There are theoretical explanations and practical supports today that [can help] to frame the subject of socialisation and social education. Not by escaping in hot air balloons, but by investigating the world, the relations between indi- viduals, the social uses of school and science, the roles and values we accredit to different ages (childhood, adolescence, youth, maturity, old age).

What we wish to say is if individualism, competition, selectivity, authoritar- ianism, stratification into social classes are all things adults experience and suffer

(Bernstein[11] reminds us it is impossible not to replicate external power relations in school, school organisation, school's production of 'education' and how it defines the concept of educable), then we must reflect seriously when socialising with children (in the sense of giving them a personal and social ethic) on ways to let them escape and be free of a destiny (they are destined to become adults too) that we feel we cannot accept or justify.

It is absurd, for example, to think children's socialisation can take place in separate schools (all the negative connotations of schools today can be included in this 'separate'), if anything it will be a separate socialisation, producing the dynamic that constructs the unacceptable models discussed above.

We have to shift the entire order of school starting with a deep and critical analysis, preparing it for new and radically different experiences of life and socialisation. This is what we have resolved and attempt to do.

For children to acquire the real values of socialisation they must first and foremost be complete, inhabit their body and mind, as well as their history, [and] internalise through real acts and not through preached lessons all the solidarity and freedom the world has for them.

The children of labourers and workers, of migrants from the mountains and the south, children we ask to bear burdens and frustrations that crush adults, children showing the signs of a deprived culture, of adversity, illness and other kinds of damage; children who increasingly come to school hurt and disorientated, often with contorted disintegrating personalities, victims of damage our system inflicts on people's lives, on people's relations with their own children. All these children are asking for the problems they represent to be identified by pedagogy and teachers.

We must not misunderstand. It is not because they want to remain as they are, or because they are requesting privilege or gratification or special education or consoling stories, but so that their problems can cast light on education's overall meaning, bring it down from an Olympian elitism, from always being over and above, always on the outside, from ignorance and faked neutrality. They want to give educators a new sense of their task and power, and lead them to finally taking a position – in a word to living their profession critically, politically. If children's problems and contradictions, which are almost always a reflection of adult malaise and an unjust world, come to school and into teachers' experience, and can be seen in this way, with this potential, [. . .] this immediately focuses our attention on the attitude of teachers. It asks them to abandon anonymity and a mistaken pseudo-cultural self-importance, to stand up for their profession, for schools, for pedagogy willing to defend children and free them, for action connecting interior problems and effects coherently with their external causes.

If teachers accept this awareness and do not limit themselves to an attitude of enlightened intellectualising, then they cannot help but look for remedies in children's lives and the life of the community (and in their own lives). While taking care in their work and behaviour to activate and develop a genuine capacity in the children to observe, discuss, reflect, criticise, to realise what is right in their environment and what is not, and how this might compromise their present and future happiness (extending work progressively, taking into account children's social and intellectual potentials).

Teachers will begin to offer children living models of socialisation not talk, and this can only be done with others, ridiculing their old individualistic attitudes, creating group awareness with colleagues and other adults who spend time with the children, living and thinking together in ways that involve the contents of culture and education deeply. They will see that even when they contribute to and support their school with active socialisation in the work-place (the word 'community' is still distant) their work is pretence and minimal if they do not look for broader connections and exchange outside the school, with parents and people and their problems.

Teachers' attempts to examine their work gain credibility and assurance from the presence of these other participants. The roles formerly reserved for teachers and teachers alone emerge in new original ways in educational and social praxis with multiple possibilities. They replace the solitude and submission, the <u>slow and fatalistic</u> conception of culture, which is destined always to avoid the test of critical reflection on discoveries in thinking, on developments in science, on relations, on changes to human relations in civil society.

We are asking a great effort of teachers, a courageous act of honesty towards themselves, to voluntarily give up things they believed in good faith, so they can participate in building schools together with children, young people, parents and citizens. Schools that are living centres of open and democratic culture, enriched and informed by social encounters that let them go beyond their ambiguous and false autonomy and the centuries-old detachment, and which let them abandon the prejudice of ideological imprinting and authoritarian indoctrination.

Research and experience with methodologies and contents in our schools takes place in a wide-ranging complex reality of human commitment and ferment. We have devoted ourselves for years to the difficult construction of this reality together, trying to take children's social development further than melancholy mannerist[12] models, the disciplinary adaptation pedagogy's frozen imagination still offers in official documents.

Children 'feel' this new condition of life. They take in the first models for <u>living together</u> from how adults, teachers, assistants, parents, neighbourhood men and women work 'together'; they sense how their issues and those of their families and environment become issues for adult attention and care; they feel a stimulating solidarity alive around them. When children understand the wider fabric of this new pedagogy of relations, which sparks off communication and relations between the world of adults and children, between school and outside, between education and the world of work, they perceive more genuinely holistic spaces. (This perception is made stronger when children realise that many daily topics and interests, which are a stimulus to communication and socialisation, are generated not just in personal family experience and school events, but also in experience, events and encounters outside school, where they are active spectators and protagonists, and which are then brought into school by parents, companions, and other adult figures whom they discover to be friend-figures, 'additional teacher' figures.)

Children feel a very important sensation from these things and from teachers' behaviours: that children count in the present, and they count in the future, that what is to come for them is something of great interest and concern for the adults.

5. Our children go out from school as much as possible. They go on foot, on buses, trains and minibuses, with adults from school (without distinction), with parents, with people in the neighbourhood. They go to explore, and to make their own themes that they continue to develop in school. They go to discover what is in the city, and what isn't, to reflect or perhaps gain an idea with adult help of what should be there, what is denied to children even when it exists (problems arise with play areas, managed green areas, urban planning solutions, polluted areas, swimming pools, gyms, libraries, health policies, audio-visual centres, theatre and cinema programmes, and so on). They go to discover where and how their fathers and mothers work (an especially exciting and beautiful experience), something that their eyes and minds are missing and which official pedagogy and publishing compete to hide and distort, [includ-ing] the most varied occupations (building sites, factories, airports, artisans, offices, markets, railway stations, farms). They go to forge relations with cultural and sporting organisations, visit zoos and museums, run in the fields or by rivers, make friends with elderly people in homes, or with children in other schools in the mountains or the lowlands. They invite children in secondary schools, or ask children at music school to visit with their instruments. They go and do puppet shows for slightly older children in primary school, they invite the farmer, the worker, the postman, the municipal policeman, the carpenter, the knitters to recount their stories, and their problems, and they gain some under-standing of what these people's work, and working conditions, mean.

There is a wonderful and extraordinary germinating and flowering of ideas, knowledge and feelings in this rich, varied material[13] that is capable of turning old school contents on its head and giving new direction to journeys of self-affirmation, self-expression, and children's social creativity, which has always been theorised as born exclusively from aesthetic and play activity.

During class meetings and assemblies children's problems, parents' problems, adult problems are confronted and debated. There is no gap between children's affairs and adult affairs, between children's present and future, between the school story and the outside story. The private personal talks initially requested by parents (understandably and legitimately) are progressively integrated into a more complex, wide-ranging discussion that generates a collective awareness.

Children's behaviour is discussed and analysed together with its causes. Disturbances, irregularities, the slowness of some children in class, are not merely described but investigated by joining elements of biology and psychology with social elements and viewing each child as a living part of a system of relations, not a neutral entity. The issue of children from southern Italy, whose presence has grown in our schools, is discussed not in terms of general knowledge or solidarity, but as the starting point for historical and social thinking that frame the issue of the south as a traditional source of exploitation.

The impact on children when fathers go on strike or are made redundant is immediately noticeable. What can we do? Should teachers compensate and distract children or make the issue a subject of conversation, as far as their experience allows? Obviously they should take the second course, and at the same time the issue will be addressed during *Comitati di Scuola e Città* meetings.

There is a decision to admit a handicapped child. This is a broad and important subject, an opportunity for a general discussion on the destiny of these children in a discriminatory and condemnatory society.

When high numbers of children are excluded [from school for lack of places] there is a need to return to fighting for the creation of more school places. People discuss, they understand, they mobilise.

Children aged three reading? In discussion with teachers, with specialists, we investigate to what extent this is something legitimate and to what extent we might be dangerously accustomed to the lure of self-interested and purely precocious performance.

In short, facts are not described or recorded but discussed, investigated and related to each other; precisely the attitude and mental habit we try to offer and live with our children.

Children's growing sensation of actively belonging to a community experience is simultaneous with that of adults (parents, teachers, citizens) in the *Comitati di Scuola e Città*, and soon becomes a sensation of vitality and confidence, and each person young or old feels part of a stimulating circle and conjunction of recognition and exchange. This is what decides the non-authoritarian role of teachers and adults (not ministerial papers and not even sincere declarations of individual willingness), and offers children precious references for the positive construction of their personal identities, and together of a social identity.

Obviously we are not proposing a school in *Wonderland* as Bettelheim[14] would say, but a school brimming with problems and tensions; because our schools do not take their inspirations and contents from within but from the social dialectic of where they are situated, constantly discussing with children the life conditions being offered to them.

6. Summarising briefly, our pedagogical-political hypothesis, from which we expect new definitions of social education and accompanying moral values, is being developed on two connected levels simultaneously. [First] we are working so that children can find a new sense of self and others in their experience, drawing on intuitive and cognitive attitudes, as well as on feeling, breathing

and inhabiting ample, active, concrete spaces that defend and liberate; and recovering the value of a continuity between the world of children and the world of adults, and values that start the children on a first assimilation of sentiments of justice (sentiments early years pedagogy, and not only it, has never included in its numerous forms).

[Second] simultaneously our pedagogy works so that parents, teachers, people, evaluating together and analysing educational issues, can understand how the history and future of children, and the history and future of schools, are closely linked with events and struggles on several fronts of society; and that their task is to be committed, day by day, to a better understanding of causes and forces threatening to keep this unjust world the way it is. To work for a new world, reflected in schools, reflected in children, who while living the present more fully, have the privilege of choosing and creating their future destiny.

Perhaps in this perspective the connections and inter-dependencies between social management, issues of renewing school contents and methods, the roles of teachers, and children's social education will appear clearer and more intelligible. Which we believe will help us to find our way better around these issues, and focus our actions in more effective ways.

❋ ❋ ❋

42.71 Letter to politicians in Reggio Emilia about the *Comune* taking over a parish school, August 1971

Editor's note: The *Comune* had already taken over the management of a number of schools originally opened and managed by UDI. Now it was being asked to assume responsibility for another school, this time attached to a Catholic parish. Despite Malaguzzi's reservations, the school – Mancasale – was municipalised by the *Comune* in 1971, to be followed by another parish school taken over in 1972 and renamed after Bruno Ciari.

MUNICIPIO DI REGGIO nell'EMILIA   10 August 1971
DIREZIONE SCUOLE MATERNE
VIA DELL'ABBADESSA, 8
42100 Reggio nell'Emilia

To the Mayor
To the *Assessore* for Schools and
Social Services – Sig.ra Loretta Giaroni
To the *Assessore* for Employees
Sig. Honourable Otello Montanari

Any possible solution considered for even the partial improvement of the spaces and functioning of Villa Mancasale's parish *scuola materna*, which the *Comune* intends to manage directly from next year, is incapable of achieving a minimum level of sanitary, psychological and pedagogical decency. It is not difficult to imagine the squalor of the time children and teachers will be required to spend in it, relying on the unfortunate and simple naivety of families. We are certain this operation will cause a sharp and sudden reduction in the level of *Comune* work in *scuole dell'infanzia*, which has been built up through hard work.

What makes us intervene on the question, as far as we are competent to do so, is the fear of other similar situations arising for various reasons of limitations and needs.

In our opinion it is dangerous to take over the management [of a school] which will merely be a parking place and [family] substitute in a nineteenth century way, on a seriously different level from other schools run by the *Comune*, especially if it is primarily for children of poor and working-class people, as is the case in Mancasale.

If the *Comune* is going to automatically establish the principle of absorbing existing teaching staff, again in Mancasale, the whole issue is even more serious, raising legitimate doubts about their training and experience of which we know nothing, and the implications of unequal employment which would be created with other staff.

Always at your disposal

Dr. Loris Malaguzzi

1972

43.72 Call by the *Comitati di Scuola e Città* for people to demonstrate for '*scuola dell'infanzia* for all children', June 1972

Editor's note: Malaguzzi drafted this 'invitation' to demonstrate for more municipal schools, an example of his campaigning work. It may not be a co-incidence that the *Regolamento* was unanimously adopted soon after this demonstration; perhaps Malaguzzi saw the demonstration as part of a strategy for keeping early childhood education high on the public agenda, creating conditions for the adoption of the *Regolamento*.

Scuole dell'infanzia for all children

As needs grow, and awareness in families and citizens grows of *scuola dell'infanzia* as an initial form of organisation in the social life of children, and a situation that fights disparities and inequalities between children, the laws and means the government makes available are increasingly shown to be limited and outdated.

Forty per cent of children resident in the *Comune* of Reggio Emilia cannot attend the *Scuola dell'Infanzia*.

Municipal schools this year have received 866 requests for places but only 363 will be satisfied.

Owing to these conditions, which are dramatic in our city and Province but even more tragic elsewhere,

THE *COMITATI DI SCUOLA E CITTÀ* OF THE *SCUOLE COMUNALI DELL'INFANZIA* and the *CONSIGLI DI QUARTIERE*

invite you to demonstrate

→ **WEDNESDAY 28 JUNE 1972 21.00** ←
AT THE MUNICIPAL THEATRE

TO DISCUSS AND IDENTIFY ACTIONS FOR MOBILISING PUBLIC OPINION ON AN IMMEDIATE INCREASE IN *SCUOLE DELL'INFANZIA* AND THE SATISFACTION OF FAMILY AND CITY REQUESTS.

❋ ❋ ❋

44.72 Summary of a talk given by Malaguzzi at a meeting of teaching staff from municipal schools, Reggio Emilia, August 1972

Editor's note: From an early stage, Malaguzzi established the practice, continued to this day, of convening all municipal school staff (teachers and others) at the start of the school year, and presenting directions – an 'opening report' – for the year, including plans for educational work and professional development and anticipated political and other developments. This document summarises the main points raised during his 1972 meeting with teachers; the next document covers the meeting, a week later, with non-teaching staff.

This new school year will be marked by organisational restructuring along the lines proposed in the new *Regolamento delle scuole dell'infanzia*.

This restructuring together with other changes in organisation raise a series of new educational and social issues. If they signify an important turning point in our experience this suggests the urgency of reflecting on our past experience and making new choices in contents, more democratic work creating new relations between school, children, families, committees and neighbourhoods.

For all these reasons this will be a difficult year, greatly testing all our capacities.

The new *Regolamento*, which is the result of a collaborative development, has established some highly important things:

- equality of role for teachers and assistants;
- teachers working in pairs;
- the introduction of male teachers;
- the same working week (36 hours) for all workers, teaching and auxiliary;
- a larger *Équipe psico-pedagogica* with three or four members;
- confirmed and continuous contracts for all temporary staff.

This work will be implemented during the school year. By September 1 we might be able to achieve equality for teaching and auxiliary staff, and pay national insurance for cooks. The other measures will by implemented through the means of public competitions. Perhaps by January or February next year most of this restructuring will be complete.

Although several of the things we have planned will have to wait to become real, the meaning and spirit of the new *Regolamento* must enter into and become part of our work.

We think we can respond to this necessity by increasing collective professional development for workers, awareness of the educational and political values of *scuole dell'infanzia* and schools in general through the creation of more exchange, more discussions on work themes, and giving greater value to relations with *Comitati di Scuola e Città*, *Consigli di quartiere* and decentralised bodies, and finally by making our work with families more continuous and organic.

We further believe it is necessary to develop our cultural achievements and professional capacities more fully. We must be capable of promoting a whole politics of professional development and self development by constructing weekly or fortnightly meetings for study, discussion and examination. The new *Regolamento* is conducive to this because it includes two working hours [per week] dedicated to development activities. Besides teachers these development meetings must involve auxiliary staff, the *Comitati* and citizens.

In order to create an immediate and organic programme of meetings with parents, we put forward this proposed plan: four meetings should be held by September with parents of children just admitted to schools based on a programme grouping the schools as follows:

- Gaida and Cella in Villa Cella
- Villetta Ospizio and San Maurizio in San Maurizio
- Passo Buole, Rosta, Foscato and Sesso in Rosta Nuova
- Diana, Pastrengo, Peep Primavera and Mancasale in Pastrengo

These meetings, we will make the dates known as soon as possible, ought to represent an opportunity for knowledge and discussion on the ways educational experience is moving in the *Comune*'s schools and they will be introduced by talks by members of the *Équipe psico-pedagogica*, and members of *Comitati di Scuola e Città*.

By the month of October class meetings should be held in all schools.

By the month of November all schools should hold parent and neighbour-hood meetings.

In the month of December we will see if we can have meetings in each school with children (and families) who have gone on to the first year of primary school this year.

Immediate problems of a practical nature

a   assigning classes to teachers

b   checking the presence of children and possible substitutions

c   distribution of personal labels (objects and figures for three-year-old children, names and surname initials for four and five-year-old children)

d   more freedom with children's clothes

e   more freedom with the afternoon rest for four and five-year-old children

f   re-organising lunchtimes (knives available for all children, more participation by children in the work of laying and clearing tables, distribution of food by the children, etc.)

g   breaking up collective routines as much as we can (bathrooms, going out, etc.)

h   holding family interviews

i   'facts and reflections' notebooks compiled by teachers as a tool for self-examining experience

j   creation of a dressing-up corner and puppet play in all schools

k   making giant puppets, baggy polystyrene sacks, using air chambers [from tyres] of cars and lorries, large rubber tubes etc. for three-year-old children

l   use of [Richard] Scarry's books 'First words for three-year-old children', the book of jobs for four-year-olds, and Gianni Rodari stories for five-year-olds. Use of the collected poems and nursery rhymes edited by our school's office.

The start of school

To give support to new children from September 1–5, encourage the active participation of all teaching staff and auxiliary staff, relieved of their regular tasks [such as cleaning and cooking].

Use of buses

Not using buses for transport [to and from school] will make it possible to use them more frequently for outings with children. An outings programme should be defined as quickly as possible.

The problem of work placements

The General Assembly [of *Comitati di Scuola e Città*] has decided to reduce the number of placements from *Magistrali* [teacher education] schools to 1 placement in schools with three classes, and 2 placements in schools with more than three classes.

For the moment placements from the *Istituto Professionale Femminile* [Girls Technical School] have been suspended.

ABSENCES[15]

> Absent with justification: Oleari, Casoli, Fieni, Marani, Notari, Lazzaretto.
> Absent without justification: Tabacchin.

❋ ❋ ❋

45.72 Summary of a talk at a meeting of auxiliary staff from municipal schools, Reggio Emilia, August 1972

We must make a great commitment to changing and improving the tasks and roles of auxiliary staff.

Auxiliary staff must have higher levels of participation in educational matters and be able to organise times, alongside their specific tasks, when they can be part of educational activities, discussions and decisions taken by their school.

It is important that staff abandon attitudes of supposed inferiority, the feeling of being incapable or daunted, and be aware they represent an educational model and belong to an adult collective whose efforts must come together to create ever improving life experiences for children. One of the conditions that can make this happen is for staff to actively participate in *Comitati di Scuola e Città* and all the internal and external events affecting their school.

We believe the adult collective should reflect on how they can help each other reciprocally and organise a plan to connect the work of teachers and auxiliary staff, and create situations of co-presence together in the same classrooms.

The first five days of school must be a time for trying out this type of experience. Auxiliary staff (including the cook) must abandon their places of work and busy themselves with teachers in dealing with issues of new children acclimatising to school, taking part in the first collegial discussions of this initial experience.

It is opportune to bear in mind that children's 'conquest' of the environment is best facilitated by all school spaces, including outdoors, being open, passable and accessible to the children.

Again, it is important for workers to agree on general and specific attitudes towards parents who it should not be forgotten are intensely influenced by their children's experience.

Equal working hours for teaching and auxiliary staff is further proof of the new value of cooperation entrusted to adult workers by the Municipal Administration.

We already have enlightening examples (the experience comes from one of our schools) of how new community practices can be created and experienced. Positive efforts have been made in this school to eliminate role differences and hierarchies, so that teachers and auxiliaries take turns with different school activities. By collective decision overtime pay is divided up into equal parts at the end of each term.

Participants [at the meeting] went on to discuss a series of problems of internal organisation connected with schools re-opening, the changeover to a 36 hour working week, keeping records of staff meals and their payment, eliminating bad habits such as staff entering the kitchen indiscriminately and unreasonable work requests.

[. . .]

1973

46.73 An outing by the municipal schools to San Polo, Reggio Emilia, June 1973

Editor's note: Two documents are presented below. A letter from the *Comune*, drafted by Malaguzzi, invites children, educators and families from the municipal schools on an outing to San Polo, a small town about 16 kilometres from Reggio Emilia, taking a local railway line – the *Consorzio Ferrovie Reggiane*, the same line that Malaguzzi worked on for a period during the war (see p.23). This festive event marked the end of the school year. Second, a report by the *Comune*, on this event. Another report of the day – headlined *With a Painted Train they Invaded San Polo: More than 1,500 children, parents and teachers take part in a pleasant and exciting initiative on the banks of the [River] Enza – An unforgettable day for all participants* – appeared in *L'Unità*, the newspaper of the PCI.

MUNICIPIO DI REGGIO NELL'EMILIA
SCHOOLS AND SOCIAL SERVICES SECTION
OFFICES OF *SCUOLE COMUNALI DELL'INFANZIA*

15/6/1973

To families of children attending
To *Comitati di Scuola e Città*
To *Scuole Comunali dell'Infanzia*

A train is departing on Wednesday 20, a different train full of colour, a TRAIN FOR BEING TOGETHER, with children from all the *scuole dell'infanzia*, with staff, Committees and parents.

Our destination is SAN POLO where a grand adventure will begin. Children divided in groups by age will <u>walk</u> to the Lido along three different paths, in the midst of greenery far away from traffic and noise.

There are great surprises waiting for them on their journey, friends with music will accompany them along the way, there will be a tractor to overcome the problem of dawdlers, and refreshments for everyone along the way.

At the end of our 'walk' the Lido in San Polo is entirely ours that day. After lunch we can play, this time old and young together, paint and dress up, there will be a band (as if we needed one) to make our meeting even more festive.

It's a special day, a colourful day, it's a chance to rediscover how important it is and how lovely to spend time together.

MUNICIPIO DI REGGIO EMILIA
DIREZIONE SCUOLE MATERNE
VIA DELL'ABBADESSA, 8

25 June 1973

With a painted train; children and adults together

Children, teachers, parents and *Comitati di Scuola e Città* of *Scuole Comunali dell'Infanzia* spent the last day before the summer holidays on 'A Train and a Walk for Being Together'.

It was a festive mass departure with a special train, a coach and cars that brought about one thousand five hundred people to a hospitable San Polo. A great demonstration of the powers of organisation that were mobilised, and weeks of hard work and imagination by teachers, parents and Committees.

Most of the caravan arrived in San Polo d'Enza on a train painted with suns and rainbows (something which had never been seen before, masterminded and created by *atelierista* teachers, exhilarating the children and astonishing the adults, especially those who work with the *Consorzio Ferrovie Reggiane*). Three itineraries had been prepared in San Polo based on children's ages, one along the river, one through the countryside, and one along the hills, all joining up in that marvellous basin of green and shade, of recreational and sporting facilities, which is the Lido.

The journey on a fairy-tale train throwing ribbons of coloured paper from its windows as it travelled along, the songs, the music of guitars, accordions, violins, even banjos was only the first part of an imaginative programme lasting the whole day. The walks (three to six kilometres long) were full of surreal surprises; giant fish came out of barns to meet children, there were sudden flights of doves, unexpected American Indian camps and dances, clowns asking to join the walks, and treasure hunts.

In the space of a few hours a large dining area was set up at the Lido to dispel thirst and hunger. Mayor Palù of San Polo sent us gifts of two thousand *panini* sandwiches and a band that played for the whole afternoon, amazing children and enlivening the dance and play of children and adults. The band took turns with the more discreet gypsy-like music of the Fabbrico Four, a beat group of four energetic grandfathers whose combined ages come to 280–300 years old.

For hours and hours the Lido's wide dance floors and meadows were the stage for inspired games, enormous rings-of-roses, and never-ending snakes of adults and children.

At 17.00 hours the long, still-partying caravan departed for an astonished San Polo, groups of musicians at head and tail.

[. . .]

❊ ❊ ❊

47.73 Letter to Gianni Rodari, August 1973

Editor's note: Gianni Rodari (1920–80) was an Italian writer and journalist, most famous for his children's books, for which he received the biennial Hans Christian Andersen Award for Writing in 1970. He participated in the *Movimento di Cooperazione Educativa* [Educational Cooperative Movement] (see Chapter 2, n.2) and was a frequent visitor to Reggio Emilia, actively participating in discussions about pedagogical ideas and practice. In the year before this letter, a series of 'Encounters with the Fantastic' were held between Rodari and educators in Reggio Emilia, discussions about languages, imagination, education and creativity that inspired Rodari's book '*La grammatica della fantasia*' [The Grammar of Fantasy]. For further information on the '*Io chi siamo*' project, referred to in the letter, see 49.73.

MUNICIPIO DI REGGIO nell'EMILIA   28 August 1973
DIREZIONE SCUOLE MATERNE
VIA DELL'ABBADESSA, 8
42100 Reggio nell'Emilia

For GIANNI RODARI
Viale di Villa Pamphili, 103
<u>ROMA</u>

Dear Rodari,

We are sending you a copy of '*Io chi siamo*' ['I who we are', mixing 'I am' and 'we are'], a book put together by the Diana children [children at the *Scuola Comunale dell'Infanzia* Diana].

I believe you will have as much fun as we did.

Warmest wishes,
Loris Malaguzzi

❊ ❊ ❊

48.73 Letter to all *Comitati di Scuola e Città* and school workers about work notebooks, October 1973

MUNICIPIO DI REGGIO nell'EMILIA
SCHOOLS AND SOCIAL SERVICES SECTION
OFFICE FOR *SCUOLE COMUNALI DELL'INFANZIA* AND *NIDI*
VIA DELL'ABBADESSA, 8
TEL. 42875

2 October 1973

To all Presidents of *Comitati di Scuola e Città*
of the *Scuole Comunali dell'Infanzia*

To all School Workers in the
scuole comunali dell'infanzia

Writing up all parts of the *QUADERNO DI LAVORO* [Work Notebook] constitutes a moment of great importance, of reflection, and of cultural and professional enrichment for all school personnel working in contact with children. This is why it must be accurate and make an effort to convey experiences, or the syntheses of experiences, that are part of the life of school relations and activities.

This writing is not an academic or formal exercise, what counts is what you say and not how it is said.

There must be an effort to make the writing something in which everyone participates: teachers, auxiliaries, parents, members of *Comitati di Scuola e Città*, members of the *Équipe Pedagogico-Didattica*.

So that the notebook then becomes constructed as a shared experience, and can be turned to, again collectively, for further reflection, in specific professional development meetings or in parents' meetings.

Each school can consider how to organise this experience and how to distribute the various contributions.

We urgently recommend the essence and substance of this work, which is of significant individual and collective value.

(Doctor Loris Malaguzzi)
for the *ÉQUIPE PEDAGOGICO-DIDATTICA*

✳ ✳ ✳

49.73 Introduction in '"*Io chi siamo*". *Autoritratti di bambini di 5 anni*' ['I who we are': Self-portraits by five-year-old children], *Scuola comunale dell'infanzia* Diana, Reggio Emilia, June 1973. Also published in *Il giornale del genitore* [The Parent's Journal], no.11/12, November–December 1973, Year XV

Who are you? What are you like?

To feel happy in a game like this, talking about and drawing yourself (directly etching with a stylus) i.e., being introspective in the two complementary languages of speaking and drawing, is no small thing.

It is **a state of grace** and **wellbeing** current pedagogy generally fails to recognise; **a state of grace** of being able to use the most natural of bilingualisms; **a state of wellbeing** of being able to recount what we are (and not what we ought to be according to the prevailing pedagogy of respectability) just as we like, and without pretence.

Without doubt behind these children there is a long and happy habit of expressing themselves, of looking at themselves, of looking at others, of thinking, of recounting, using all possible languages, in words, images, gestures, with mime and above all the joy and surprise of being and growing up with peers and adults who are friends.

Over a period of three years (the experience of these children now on the eve of their passage into primary school has lasted this long) young children who could hardly separate the **me** from the rest of the world, have learned to separate, construct and describe themselves.

This long, delicate and never-finished process is never acted out in solitude (solitude, including the solitude of home and school, looms threateningly over childhood today) and fundamentally it requires respect and trust on the teacher's part, and freedom on the part of children to try things out and test themselves, alone and with others.

On a practical level, acquiring the **concept of I** (for Erikson 'the point on which we feel firm', for Allport[16] 'the warm region of our being', for Sève 'the meeting point of biological with social relations') requires an intense, varied and calm weaving of personal and group experience. It can be helped by assisting children to have an interest in and command of all parts of their body; strengthening all their languages of communication (words, drawing, mime); refining their analysis and critical distinction in thinking and connecting things; playing equally with the real and the imaginary; becoming researchers and discoverers of a reality that is there and a reality that might be there; feeling the objective and the relative simultaneously; confronting their own point of view with the point of view of others; and perceiving carefully all around them the coherence between what is said (or preached) and what is done.

Understanding the meaning of these indications and translating them into educational and methodological work and content is the responsibility of those working with children in the *scuola dell'infanzia*.

Reading *I who we are*, these twenty-eight identity cards and twenty-eight autobiographical stories using verbal and drawn signs that have been essentialised[17] with amazing ability, is highly amusing and highly interesting.

We cannot attempt to analyse the evident and hidden meanings, or the realistic and symbolic meanings children have used to put together this singular anthology and gallery of personalities and characters. Teachers, parents and interested or casual readers will each try in their own way.

However it is right to make some comments.

The first of these has to do with the dimensions – the quantity, quality, complexity and heterogeneity – of physical features, the dynamics, the relations and the issues animating the world of children. This world we still love to reduce to the 'values' of simple, innocent, virgin and separate (in order not to have to face issues seriously).

The second comment is a note on something extremely important: that each child has constructed themselves in a different way, each child possesses different ways of using thoughts, words and hands, that they have recounted freely what is in their heads, that as Freinet says they can really be 'authors of the printed page'. In short they can constitute a counter-model to the conformist and repressive models of certain doctrinaire pedagogies that are still alive.

The third and last comment refers to the children's attitude. You can clearly feel that although the children accept separation in order to identify and express themselves, they are very suspicious of the operation that was asked of them; you can feel how they wish to be reunited quickly with their other companions. Their **I**, alone, in quarantine, exiled, is a violence, it isn't only a stupid abstraction it is a cruel one.

The **I who we are** invented by children in their own language is a real distillation, of enlightened and cautionary wisdom.

It is an appeal to the people who pretend to be deaf in schools and society, in which the **I** is educated and then obliged to live in suspicion, competition, in rivalry with the other.

❋ ❋ ❋

50.73 Letter of invitation to parents of children enrolled in the *Scuole Comunali dell'Infanzia* of Reggio Emilia, 1973 (no more precise date)

REGGIO EMILIA *MUNICIPIO*
SCUOLA COMUNALE DELL'INFANZIA [NAME]

To all parents of children attending.

The *scuole comunali dell'infanzia* have always refused [to accept] subordinate forms – [being viewed as family] substitution and welfare [sevices] – and defended with resolute firmness their prerogative of educating children.

We believe we should continue to pursue this direction uncompromis- ingly and consistently. Despite our intentions, the danger of *Scuola dell'Infanzia* becoming child minding agencies and places to park children, places where the times, uses and purposes of families, schools and children are conditioned by work organisation, production and profit, is a fact and a looming threat.

The *scuole comunali dell'infanzia* function from 7.45 to 16.00. Children there- fore live inside schools eight hours or more, which is a long time and already often exceeds children's physical and intellectual stamina and the amount of socialisation they request.

Some parents are requesting school hours to be extended until 18.15 pm with the justification of real work commitments and needs. These problems and the weight of all their contradictions are genuine, and we cannot get away from them.

Other parents say they are willing to negotiate on Saturday mornings,[18] where the majority of schools have seen a considerable drop in numbers of children attending.

Might it be possible and opportune to rapidly restructure our working week and school times, and extend our hours of children's care from 16.00 to 18.15 for example, but only for children who do not have the reassurance of return- ing to their family [at the earlier time]?

Might it be opportune and possible to only open some of our schools on Saturday mornings, for children and families who really need them?

And how can we use the extra time our school workers save for the benefit of children and schools?

In order to discuss and explore these important and urgent topics ade- quately, and hopefully resolve them rapidly, all parents of children are invited to participate in a public discussion held on _____ in School at 20.30 precisely.

The importance of these issues makes it unnecessary to recommend family attendance and punctuality.

COMITATI DI SCUOLA E CITTÀ

❋ ❋ ❋

51.73 Letter of invitation from *Scuola dell'Infanzia* Michelangelo to parents, school workers and neighbourhood residents about a meeting on the relationship between these groups, October 1973

MUNICIPIO DI REGGIO NELL'EMILIA
SCUOLA COMUNALE DELL'INFANZIA 'LARGO
MICHELANGELO'
Largo Michelangelo Buonarroti – tel.40779

4/10/1973
To all parents
To all School Workers
To the Neighbourhood Counsellors

- What educational problems do families and children have?
- What responses, tools, and contents do *Scuole dell'Infanzia* use to face these problems?
- How can we get contributions to work together and find times for organic collaboration between school, families and general society?
- How can school workers, parents and citizens realise a new way of educating and a new way of experiencing school?

These themes will be presented and debated during the course of an

ASSEMBLY

held in this school on 16 October 1973 at 20.30. Teachers, parents, citizens and neighbourhood councillors are invited.

During the meeting we will be publicising the election of *Comitati di Scuola e Città* members for the school year 1973–74.

We do not need to stress the importance of the themes. Everyone's presence and respectful punctuality is recommended.

Prof. LORIS MALAGUZZI, Coordinator of the *Équipe Pedagogico-Didattica* of the *Scuole Comunali dell'Infanzia*, will introduce the evening.

❊ ❊ ❊

52.73 Letter to municipal schools about attendance at meetings of the *Consulta*, October 1973

Editor's note: The *Consulta degli Asili Nido e delle Scuole Comunali dell'Infanzia* was introduced in 1972 by the *Regolamento*, to bring together *Comitati di Scuola e Città* and *Consigli di quartiere* – schools and neighbourhoods – and other groups. Its overall aim was to contribute to the formulation of the *Comune*'s early childhood policies including: the programme for new schools; plans for professional development of the school workers; and publicising the roles and aims of the schools. Membership of the *Consulta* included representatives from the *Comune*, trades unions, women's movements, *Comitati di Scuola e Città*, *Consigli di quartiere* and the *Équipe Pedagogico-Didattica*, with meetings at least every three months.

MUNICIPIO DI REGGIO NELL'EMILIA
SCHOOLS AND SOCIAL SERVICES DEPARTMENT
Office of the *Scuole Comunali dell'Infanzia*

To Presidents of *Comitati di Scuola e Città*
To School workers

At the last session of the *Consulta* of the *Scuole Comunali dell'Infanzia e Nidi* representatives from the *Comitati di Scuola e Città* of the VILLETTA, MASSENZATICO, and MANCASALE schools were missing.

The importance of the *Consulta* and the themes being discussed lead us to underline strongly the need for all members of this body to be present.

All *Comitati di Scuola e Città* are requested to guarantee the punctual presence of one of their representatives in *Consulta* meetings.

Best regards

For the *Équipe Pedagogica*
L. Malaguzzi

Reggio Emilia 31 October, 1973

1974

53.74 Letter to teachers about work plans, 12 February 1974

Editor's note: The emphasis on 'each pair of teachers' reflects the principle, incorporated in the 1972 *Regolamento*, that there should always be two teachers for each class or group of children in the municipal schools, who should work closely together.

<u>*MUNICIPIO DI*</u> REGGIO NELL'EMILIA
SCHOOLS AND SOCIAL SERVICES DEPARTMENT
OFFICES OF *THE SCUOLE COMUNALI DELL'INFANZIA E NIDI*
Via dell'Abbadessa, 8 – tel. 42875

12 February 1974

To teachers: _____

Scuola dell'Infanzia: _____

Each pair of teachers is requested to briefly summarise the essence of the ideas, objectives and activities they have completed up to this point, and put together brief working plans, again their essence, which will constitute a concrete reference point in the educational process from March to the end of the school year.

To be more specific on the value of this exercise might we suggest that the request be carried out with a strong sense of commitment on the part of teachers, if possible after discussion and exchanges of viewpoint with school colleagues and also with the *Comitato di Scuola e Città*.

These work plans should be written with three copies (one to remain with teachers, one with the school, and the third obviously sent to these offices) and must be presented by 15 March 1974 – no delay permitted.

These plans, which each teacher pair should write completely freely and fully autonomously (on sheets of foolscap paper), will constitute precious and concrete material for study and reflection, and contribute to supplying a first collection of indications for a wider and more rigorous examination of the contents and methods animating the work of *Scuole Comunali dell'Infanzia*. This will take place in ways to be discussed and agreed at a later date.

Best regards

for the *ÉQUIPE PEDAGOGICO-DIDATTICA*
(Dott. Loris Malaguzzi)

※ ※ ※

54.74 Letter from the Mayor of Reggio Emilia announcing a meeting to be held with various organisations and extract from a speech given by Malaguzzi at the meeting, April 1974

MUNICIPIO DI REGGIO NELL'EMILIA
ASSESSORATO SCUOLA E SERVIZI SOCIALI
19/4/1974

Concluding the series of meetings on issues of early years education, the announced meeting with political, [trade] union and social forces will be held:

MONDAY 29 APRIL P.V. [*prossimo venturo*, i.e. near future]
AT 21.00 AT THE SPORTS HALL

'THE CURRENT SITUATION AND PROSPECTS FOR
EXTENDING *SCUOLA DELL'INFANZIA*'

The following themes will be the focus of the meeting:

The right to public, qualified, free and socially managed *scuola dell'infanzia* for all children aged three to six years.

(Out of a total of 2,727,000 children in this age group in Italy 1,154,000 are excluded from *scuola dell'infanzia*. Out of a total of 4,864 children in this age group in our *Comune* of Reggio Emilia 1,382 are excluded.)

The aims of the movement:

- A new law for extending public early years schools throughout Italy, which are free of charge and open to all children aged three to six years.
- Unblocking the 24 billion [*lire*] set aside for state *scuola materna* buildings.
- Compliance with the Trade Union-Government agreement of May 1973 on increased funding for state *scuola materna*.
- The proposal by Reggio Emilia trade union organisations to use the 1 per cent increase [won in collective bargaining, see p. 211] for extending *asilo-nido* and *scuola comunale dell'infanzia* services, and for transport.
- Greater investment by the *Comune* for more *scuole comunali dell'infanzia* and *nidi*.
- The proposal that the city's public organisations (*Cassa di Risparmio*, ECA, IACP, *Opere pie*)[19] set aside funds to extend *scuole comunali dell'infanzia* and *nidi*.

The movement's operational tools

The roles of *Consigli di Quartiere, Comitati di Scuola e Città*, political and union forces.

Considering the importance of this initiative which coincides with hundreds of families in the *Comune* presenting applications to the City Administration for their children to attend *scuole comunali del'infanzia* and *nidi* next school year,

YOU ARE INVITED TO PARTICIPATE

The meeting will be introduced by the *Assessore* for Schools and Social Services Signora Loretta Giaroni, in the presence of the City Mayor Avv. [lawyer] Renzo Bonazzi. Guido Fanti, president of the Emilia-Romagna Region *Giunta,* will conclude.

THE MAYOR

[FROM THE TALK GIVEN AT 29 APRIL MEETING BY] MALAGUZZI
   [. . .]
For ten years we have been opening our doors to families and parents.

If we have given value to the family, it has been done through this direct, lived, participatory experience we have all created together. Let none of us think an experience like the one we have been capable of creating here can be attributed to one enlightened person, or to a small group of people. This experience began to walk with the legs of a few people, and little by little, grain by grain, it has gathered participation and consensus along the way. Today I say this fact sets us apart, with the kind of vital experience being carried out in our schools, which is certainly an experience of great participation.

And it is necessary today, when we feel we can agree to an exchange of points of view[20] (and it would be a good thing if the exchange were to take place about things and not words, if the exchange were to take place between people and not little sheets of photocopied paper); however it is necessary in my view, to finally compare the facts using documents and evidence, and not emotional states, although I completely understand that these emerge even when we do not intend them to.

If we do not do this, then we cannot understand what this experience we have created means for our city, we cannot understand that, perhaps for the first time in our country, we have given teachers an element of dignity, lifted their material condition from humiliation, given them a legal status that corresponds to the importance of the tasks they are given to carry out. At the same time we have tried to read carefully what we can take from outcomes and lessons in other previous experiences. And then – together with teachers, with parents, with families, and above all with the administrators who have effectively made real things possible – we have tried to create an experiment that is real and historically specific. Because hypotheses can only be freed, and only become science, when there is a correspondence on the practical level between the moment of hypothesis and the moment of trying out: the direct experience.

All this has brought about an important cultural reality. Not only in our city. And at this moment, when we are about to enter into an exchange of points of view, I do not want anyone to think that we will give up anything we have achieved, as part of this exchange. We are not prepared to give up any one of our achievements. And we will not be prepared to give any of them up when the *Decreti Delegati*[21] arrive in our city with their small advances, or perhaps not so small, but small compared to the advances we have achieved in our 'experience', which is the result of democratising the structures inside our schools. Do you think our *comune* schools will be willing to go backwards, and accept what is poor and narrow-minded, what is limited and elusive, but all contained in these *Decreti Delegati*? NO! Since obviously at that time we will be there playing, then we will play with all our means, and all our strengths.

This is not because we wish to negate in any way the awareness of what private Catholic schools have represented for our country. But there is something we want to be more precise about, historically precise and culturally precise, and I would feel I was deceiving myself if I did not do this. When the Catholic sector points out that they are covering for an absent State [in providing early childhood education] we say this is part of the truth. But the other part of the truth is that Catholics have defended at all costs, defended early years education as a monopoly of Catholic education, a monopoly of religious education, and today it looks like this defence at all costs is emerging very dangerously. At least in some sectors.

It is enough to refer briefly to the line certain important papal speeches have taken, enough to remember the statements by Gonella,[22] enough to remember statements by Segni,[23] enough for us to remember several important documents, which fortunately are not hidden in archives no one can use, but can be brought out at times when we want to retrieve the complete account of events that makes it possible for us to distribute our actions and our attitudes in better ways.

[. . .]

✳ ✳ ✳

55.74 Intervention on an agenda item *L'impegno dei comunisti per le elezioni degli organi di governo della scuola nel quadro delle lotte per la riforma*

[The commitment of the communists for elections of school governing bodies in a framework of struggles for reform], at a meeting of the Federal Committee and Commission of the provincial Communist Party, taken from the minutes, October 1974

> **Editor's note:** Malaguzzi is one of fifteen participants whose contributions to this item are minuted. He is addressing new state laws intended to delegate management of schools, including *scuole materne*, to all adult protagonists, including teachers and parents. These 'decrees for delegation' – *Decreti Delegati* – included the establishment of bodies consisting of all teachers (*collegio dei docenti*) and of elected representatives of all staff groups and parents (*consiglio di circolo*).

[. . .]

What I would like to say is that several of the issues *Compagno* [Comrade] Nanni has discussed as if they were conclusive, decided or adequately defined actually offer broad margins and room for manoeuvre.

I think the debate could be more open than he has intimated or attempted to demonstrate. Especially in the situation we have here in Reggio Emilia and Emilia-Romagna, which is firmly rooted in the political and historical context of anti-fascist struggle and its values which continue to offer anchors for our political history: the value of the secular and secularism; the deep level of awareness we have achieved on values of liberty and tolerance etc. In short, I believe the political situation in Reggio Emilia and Emilia-Romagna objectively offers us a capacity and the opportunities for broader discussion than we have had so far.

When we begin to take the measure of this very important theme of school – a theme *Democrazia Cristiana* has kept firmly in its grip since the time of Liberation by using the Catholic Church's capacity and strength for wide-reaching political and cultural action, and actually basing much of its political fortune on the fabric of school – then for reasons I have spoken of (the region's widespread values connected with the kinds of political battle and the nature of their actions since the time of Liberation; the models of government we have been able to establish in the City, Province and Region; the political and cultural nature of initiatives that have marked our political action over the years), I believe all this means we can approach the large theme of the *Decreti Delegati* with a greater degree of confidence than has been the case today.

Even though it is a difficult test, and although the *Decreti Delegati* are mined terrain (the traps have all been lucidly and clearly discussed here today), I still believe there are opportunities for movement, initiative and creativity, in our City and Province, which we can bring into play and which offer the possibility of achieving significant results.

[. . .]

Moreover although we are attempting to bring unity to our discussion of the *Decreti Delegati* by discussing the institution of school as a whole, I think it would be as well to separate the specific features of one type of school from another, without losing sight of continuity and organic wholeness in school as an institution. I think the *Democrazia Cristiana* attitude in our City and Italy will be to differentiate when they consider what kind of battle to carry out in compulsory primary schools, what kind in middle schools, secondary schools and university.

[. . .]

I think the DC and clergy forces will prefer to use tactics inside their own schools and cultural institutions in the City, and will try to limit the discussion, and the breadth and variety of debate, so as to drastically reduce the terms of this large subject of debate to a discussion that is corporate and sectional. I think our problem will be bringing things out into public for confrontation, as much as we can, with the voices of DC leaders, and political voices inside the DC, and the church. And then take the initiative with a series of events, without worrying about selecting the public and the speakers, but aiming for an overall impact on citizens in their neighbourhoods, and on parents and teachers.

I think we really need to reflect on the subject of parents and recover the theme. Parents are a political voice, and I think they have been subordinated for weak political and theoretical reasons.

I believe a Marxist party cannot accept a rigid simplified approach to individuals and human beings, breaking them up into small reductive pieces. [. . .] What is a parent? I think being a parent is one of several attributes of an individual who cannot tolerate internal schism. So all the battle and polemic about the person of the parent cannot be isolated from simultaneous examination of whether surrounding society, culture and the political world, all experience this person of the citizen, the parent and the worker, as one person or not. We must try and remove parents from this fragmentation, this contextualisation, this situating different parts of the person-parent depending on the context, depending on what assignments they are involved in. It is a dangerous operation, because if we accept the idea then we go back to the theoretical and practical possibility of individuals, this person who is necessarily cut up and divided, presenting in different guises depending on where they are [. . .]. We need to recover, and trade unions need to recover, a more unified idea of who workers are, that includes all the aspects of a worker's competencies, and how these can be expressed in different ways.

[. . .]

So I do not want to say, 'Ok then we'll go along with the *Decreti Delegati*, we accept the figure of parents as the *Decreti Delegati* depicts them, and we will give parents the roles the *Decreti Delegati* wants'. Instead the problem is how to create a wide range of global political co-presences around individuals, of political stimuli, and political investments, so that we can ask them for the univocal action and univocal behaviour that signifies absolutely unbreakable wholeness.

Whether parents will represent themselves, or represent political forces, or trade union forces, cannot be decided by voting in favour of this or that role for them. [. . .] The problem is how parents, citizens, factory workers or office workers represent and experience the issues contained in the *Decreti Delegati*. This means we, the [Communist] Party, the trade unions, the resources and the cultural institutions, need to stand beside and stand close to these situations of struggle and discussion. Above all we have to be capable of representing ideas and models, of representing progress in educational and cultural issues, of making a leap forward with all the issues that have to do with our schools.

※ ※ ※

56.74 Note of meeting of *Comitati di Scuola e Città* at which Malaguzzi was present, October 1974

MUNICIPIO DI REGGIO NELL'EMILIA
SCHOOLS AND SOCIAL SERVICES SECTION

MEETING 17 OCTOBER 1974 OF *COMITATI DI SCUOLA E CITTÀ* OF REGGIO EMILIA *SCUOLE COMUNALI DELL'INFANZIA*

Approximately 100 people were present.

After an introduction by *Assessore* Sig.ra Loretta Giaroni the following people commented: Ferrari Tiziano (*Scuola* Robinson), Ottavio Badodi (*Scuola* Passo Buole), Ermes Caraffi (*Scuola* di Sesso), Luciano Guidotti (*Scuola* Primavera), Ganassi (*Scuola* Diana), Bonacini (*Scuola* di Massenzatico), Dott. Loris Malaguzzi.

The following <u>operational decisions</u> were taken:

- Approval of the proposals by *Scuola Robinson* and *Scuola Foscato-Roncina* Committees for the *Consulta Comunale* to promote a meeting for early November of all municipal school committees in the province to discuss local funding issues and the repercussions of the credit block [imposed by government] on social services for early years; on that occasion evaluate the possibility of a provincial demonstration.

[. . .]

- Make a proposal to the *Consigli di quartiere* to start a permanent debate on educational issues connected with the various levels of education. To be specific, School Comittees could organise this open pedagogical examination, involving all citizens in analysis and exchange on how schooling is done in the *asilo nido*, in *scuola materna*, in primary school and middle school. In terms of organisation this would mean inviting the various levels of schools (public and private) present in the *territorio* [local area, see Chapter 3, n.24] and *quartiere* [neighbourhood][24] to present publicly at the beginning of the school year their hypotheses and plans for work (a general outline obviously), the methodology and teaching methods they plan to use. This would translate into an important instance of participation and collective management of educational life, and a stimulus for the work of school Committees allowing citizens and citizens' organisations to have a greater command of the pedagogical criteria necessary for being able to critically interpret different school models, and understand their similarities and differences, distinguishing schools with an authoritarian, isolating, dogmatic, privatising nature from schools with a democratic, open, anti-dogmatic, socialising profile.

The renewal of management Committees in municipal Schools will be prepared from this perspective.

- Another socio-pedagogical intervention connected with the *territorio* could be the organisation of permanent *Quartiere* seminars, with varied programmes, open to participation by *scuola dell'infanzia* and elementary school workers; or open to workers in all educational, health, and welfare services, and any workers in the *Quartiere* who have to do with children.
- We could also evaluate the hypothesis of a joint experiment (between *scuola materna* and elementary school) on some educational projects. The perspective would be that the two different levels of school could begin shared practice, in concrete terms by planning, conducting, and examining certain methodological journeys together (for example between 5-year-old children in *scuola dell'infanzia* and the first cycle of primary school).

✳ ✳ ✳

57.74 Letter of invitation to teachers and auxiliaries to attend courses about logic-mathematics, October 1974

MUNICIPIO DI REGGIO NELL'EMILIA
SEZIONE SCUOLE E SERVIZI SOCIALI
OFFICES OF *SCUOLE COMUNALI DELL'INFANZIA* AND *NIDI*
Via dell'Abbadessa, 8   22 October 1974

<u>COURSE ON INITIATION TO LOGICAL MATHEMATCS</u>
11–12–13 November 1974
18–19–20 November 1974

In the framework of the cultural updating [*aggiornamento*][25] planned for 1974–75, a Course on Intitiation to Logical Mathematics will be held for staff working in our services on 11,12,13 November, to be repeated on 18,19,20 November from 8.30 to 12.30: allowing each pair of teachers working with 4- to 5-year-olds, an auxiliary worker and the *atelierista* to participate in turn.

After a general introduction, the course will focus on <u>games of relation</u> (worksheets and an illustrative leaflet for their use are being printed), and <u>games with Dienes' logic blocks</u>.[26]

These two topics are relevant for immediate use and experimentation with five-year-old children, but we consider it would also be useful for teachers of four-year-olds to be present.[27]

During the course there will be a discussion of experimental results from play with worksheets and logic blocks; these results will be gathered by the *Équipe Pedagogico-Didattica* working with groups of children in different schools.

for the *ÉQUIPE PEDAGOGICO-DIDATTICA*
(Prof. Loris Malaguzzi)

1975

58.75 June 1975

Editor's note: It is not clear what type of document this is, but it may have been a newspaper article – it is signed 'lm', Malaguzzi's usual signature for a newspaper article – or else a report sent to the schools.

The affectionate participation of citizens in the June festivities,[28] data and considerations on the renewal of the committees

While our sister schools from elementary upwards have already closed their shutters, or are getting to grips with final exams, the *scuole comunali dell'infanzia* (closure scheduled for mid-July) are organising two large events, as they do every year: our June festivities and new admissions of children for the coming year.

947 children are requesting admission (the number grows each year) and the number of available places is about 600: although this will probably be

700 if *Comitati di Scuola e Città* and the *Giunta Comunale* both agree to slightly increase the number of places in each class. The Committees are already working on this, and at the same time teachers and parents are busy organising festivities that are an affectionate (annual) appointment with solidarity between schools, families and people in the neighbourhood, young and old.

When we finish there will have been no less than 10–15,000 people-protagonists in the [June] festivities, visiting schools and exhibitions of educational work, participating in initiatives and playing a thousand games invented everywhere. In the Via Balzac *nido*, and the Belvedere and Anna Frank schools, these events confirm the deep ties between those schools and the local citizenry. These ties are one of the most original, distinctive features of our experience in the *scuole dell'infanzia*; this is where the essential hallmarks and the cultural and political examination of our work are created and then return. Those who have a sacrosanct and separate vision of school, or who prefer school not to have ties with so many people, turn up their noses. But all those who approach our schools with souls empty of prejudice can understand and appreciate them. These include Lucio Guasti and Luciano Corradini (who has dedicated an entire chapter to the Reggio Emilia experience in his latest book, recently published by Massimo), who are both Catholic university teachers. Just as in a few days, the Università Cattolica of Milan will make our schools the subject of study and discussion in a day's study of social management in *scuola materna*.

The issue of social management offers an opportunity for some brief comments on the final data from the recently concluded renewal [election] of the *Comitati di Scuola e Città*. Renewal took place in 21 meetings (19 in *scuola dell'infanzia* and 2 in *asilo nido*) and more than 3,000 people participated, which is the same number as voted. [. . .] This operation replaced 40–65 per cent of former committee members, and elected a total of 923 members, and we must underline the exceptional number of men elected in the parent and citizens section (497 men, 324 women). This dispels the old, not entirely disinterested literature that gives women an almost exclusive interest and protagonism in educational tasks and social management organisations.

Some interesting reflections [. . .] come from reading the occupation and the social-political-cultural background of new committee members. There are 214 [factory] workers, 57 small artisans, 9 nurses, 242 office workers, 13 technicians, 59 teachers, 30 small business people, 11 representatives, 7 farmers, 9 independent professionals, 61 housewives, 55 students, 3 members of religious orders. Representation of social-political-cultural elements are divided and composed as follows: CIF[29] (4), UDI (9), PCI (23), PSI (15), DC (19), *Comunione e Liberazione*[30] (2), Catholics for Socialism (1), Parish Councils (22), Parish Priests (3), School Councils (17), Factory Councils[31] (19), Neighbourhood Councils (16).

Besides being a general testimonial to the strong hold educational institutions have on society in our *Comune*, an analysis and synthesis of this data support some detailed reflections:

1   People's openness and presence in the social management of educational institutions appears to be correlated to: (a) the issue's credibility, (b) feeling convinced they count, (c) and that all this is beneficial and useful for comparing points of view, and for changing and improving things.

2   This disproves [the view] that to safeguard social management we do not need regulations, but to compartmentalise and divide responsibilities that are technical-administrative from responsibilities that are pedagogical-educational; that participation should be in <u>tiny doses</u> (drastically reduced attendance) or falsely <u>euphoric</u> (in the sense of a state of permanent assembly-ism);[32] or finally that it should be done only by women representatives, despite what might be suggested by schools entrusted exclusively to women by sexist tradition and design.

3   Other things are proved wrong: that participation in management is a middle-class prerogative; that working-class families and workers tend to delegate to others; that we cannot have participation with such diverse representatives, at least in their credentials that include Factory Councils, School Councils, Parish Councils, Neighbourhood Councils, women's organisations and political parties across the range of our constitutional political parties.

4   These results, of a clearly political nature, contradict *a priori* theorising on politics and social commitment, which rejects collegial, community, pluralistic experience on educational matters.

These are just a few notes in the margins of an experience that is characteristic of work in *nidi* and *scuole dell'infanzia* run by our municipal administration. As we can see it is an extremely delicate experience, and in certain aspects it is an anticipation of <u>political and cultural developments</u> that could be produced on a larger scale in the near future.[33] It is an experience that must overcome many objective and subjective tests and difficulties, and which relies on continuity and on growing consensus and esteem, on democratic coherence, on a free exploration of pedagogy and education (because it is public and open to examination), on open dialogue about all themes (without exception) pertinent to children's education (including religious education's roles and values); finally it relies on the support that will come – we hope this is true – from the desire to live these same issues on a more general level in civil society.

＊＊＊

59.75 Speech to the PCI Federation of Reggio Emilia, 1975 (no more precise date)

Communist commitment in the struggle to making scuole per l'infanzia more generally available

[. . .]

It should be noted that *scuola materna* experience in Reggio Emilia and the Emilia-Romagna Region is a first crucial application of a process of struggle in education that a large portion of democratic anti-fascist culture began at the end of the war by following Gramsci's[34] insights.

It is significant that this experience has become a reality at the height of the crisis in 'traditional' education, a crisis that consists first in the progressively arid nature of the underlying culture that used to inform educational values; and second the persistence of method, content and structures that work to maintain class division and exclude young children from the opportunity of attending school.

[. . .]

The experience of the *scuola materna comunale* has influenced civil and cultural consciousness in large parts and many levels of the community, and has had a strong impact on our social reality and political relations. It has contributed to an increased demand for schools, and involved parts of the population with different motives and ideals in the running and practice of education.

[. . .]

To summarise, the central points expressed by the DC are:

- they refuse the possibility of mass or democratic monitoring of educational methods and content, reporting allegedly chaotic assembly-ism [see Chapter 3, n.32];
- they criticise the chosen pedagogical approach, arguing that it fails to recognise religious values, which ought to preside over education and be its logical objective. This is tantamount to criticising the secular nature of public education and arguing, yet again, that Catholicism is integral to education;
- they see an irreconcilable antagonism in social management between families and other social forces, giving absolute priority to families;
- they see an opposition between the *Équipe Pedagogico-Didattica* and teachers in individual schools, which is part of a reductive, highly negative vision of teacher autonomy.

[. . .]

By contrast, the Communists have confirmed their civic and political reasons for working towards implementing a concept of social services that puts the needs of children's liberation and expression at its centre; not children as an abstraction, but children in concrete terms with their contradictory relations with their environment.

The logical consequence of this premise is that democratic management is a prerequisite and a desire of *scuole dell'infanzia*. They have started to break away from the separation between school and society, and allow families to 'step inside' schools, to intervene and engage with all the issues connected with managing education. Previously these families were either effectively excluded, or involved with subordinate roles.

It should not be forgotten there is a deep 'crisis of identity' in teachers at all school levels; more specifically there is a situation of under-employment, exploitation and devaluation of preschool teachers. The *scuole comunali dell'infanzia* have opened up new economic and social conditions for their workers, and created the conditions for re-evaluating and valuing their contributions, in constant exchange with other members of the [social] management.

We must stress another fundamental aspect defining the political significance of this experience, which is the new power municipal administration has taken on itself by choosing to act in the field of education. This power has been achieved through hard struggle with central state authorities.

[. . .]

The range of social, ideological and political social forces involved in this educational experience has intensified its pluralism, and this is a thread that runs through all the processes we have established for working in politics, art, culture and the sciences. Specifically this means schools are open to experiment, and open to comparing frameworks and values, in ways that always strive to achieve greater levels of rigour and seriousness.

[. . .]

During the initial phases of our experience the *Équipe* carried out a 'directive' role which was necessary for developing methods and contents, for responding effectively to 'pedagogical barbarisation' and disseminating the legacy of the work we were building up. However now it is essential to re-position this role, in the context of giving teachers in individual schools more responsibility including areas of experimentation.

The struggle conducted for innovation has gathered large portions of the community to it, and important new values have become concrete practice for our workers at many levels. This means the conditions have been created for the *Équipe* to spend more time on a higher level, working on proposals, on connecting and unifying, on stimulating workers' fundamental responsibilities, on examining more deeply, and on scientifically co-ordinating the data emerging from our various experiences. All this should enhance the new kind of teacher and her capacity for working in collegial forms and ways.

[. . .]

The teacher's freedom, an achievement with a precise and justified place in the history of mass teacher struggle against a central ministerial and Gentilian [see Chapter 1, n.7] formula for organising teaching, is not an excuse for restoring the teacher's role as sole manager of educational situations, but must be given active meaning. The need for renewal requires the kind of teacher who is a new type of intellectual, a producer of knowledge connected with organised social demands.[35] What allows us to resolve all ambiguity in certain concepts of the teacher is this possibility we must offer them of having a reference point in organised requests by society for new educational methods and contents, and our capacity for making this part of the life of our management committees.

The demand to limit teachers' relations with the outside world exclusively to families (whose presence has been considered vital by communists for some time) therefore becomes unacceptable. If school and family are to have a new function connected with the <u>whole</u> of society then the entire <u>complexity</u> of social, political and electoral needs must be brought into play.

We strongly confirm our choice of valuing parents' contributions to school life in concrete ways, in relation to our understanding of what school is (the testimonial and confirmation of this is in the large-scale active family participation in *scuole comunali dell'infanzia* life, and our choice is certainly not a concession to suggestions other people have made).

[. . .]

Far from proposing to exclude the role of families, our choice aims above all to stimulate the institution of family to open up to society, and this would appear to be the only possible basis for a real re-instatement and re-evaluation of its role in education, faced with the undeniable crisis of parent–children relations.

In our collective experience parents become aware of social, as opposed to private, dimensions in the problems and contradictions they experience daily, and the need for commitment and struggle in facing and resolving these.

Our school management bodies contain all the possibilities required for the work of fusing different elements of society. Their composition officially establishes an important parent presence and introduces new protagonists: teachers, *Consigli di quartiere*, social and political bodies.

[. . .]

It would be a mistake to burden the budget of the *Comune* more than is necessary while expanding [early years] services. [. . .] Workers union organisations have expressed themselves in a mature political way on this issue by making social services part of their platform of demands; [. . .] in many companies in the province unions have asked for <u>an extra 1 per cent in salary [costs to pay]</u> <u>for social services</u>, a concrete sign of growing awareness, the sign of a need that has become conscience, organisation and struggle.

[. . .]

Factory Councils and union leaders have also participated in preparatory meetings for the renewal of *Comitati di Scuola e Città* in *scuole materne* in the *Comune* of Reggio Emilia, and demonstrated their willingness to exchange viewpoints with the *Comune* on all subjects (teaching structures, methods, contents).

[. . .]

The need exists and the possibility exists of taking this struggle to state level and we must decide on objectives that are consistent with this. This does not mean local authorities should no longer use their own funds for the *scuola materna* sector (on the contrary this commitment must continue, and also tackle the delay and lack of commitment of several *comuni*), but it means the *comune* can no longer be considered as a sole funder of the service.

The objective we must fight for is none other than achieving a national law on *scuola dell'infanzia* that effectively guarantees every child in this age group the right to attend and the conditions for attending, i.e. a *scuola dell'infanzia* run by *comuni*, funded by the State, and planned by the Region, which is the proposal the PCI presented for legislation some weeks ago.

[. . .]

Although we must aim for the progressive expansion of *scuole materne*, develop our movement and define the choices of local authorities, this should be conducive to also increasing levels of quality achieved in every area. We must extend an efficient service and a new way of doing school, but avoid practices that produce different levels of quality between schools.

At this point in our experience we must realise the need for going beyond a situation where no organic tool exists for co-ordinating the organisation of exchange, of directions, or of unified syntheses of experience in pedagogy and management. At best this has been work entrusted to the efforts and commitment of Reggio Emilia's *Équipe Pedagogico-Didattica*, but already we are too few in number to respond to increasing needs in the *Comune* of Reggio Emilia.

It is now obvious *comuni* can no longer defer the decision to provide themselves with a specific tool but must introduce an *Équipe Pedagogico-Didattica* into the staff of their local health and social services with the task of intervening in the whole system of early years educational institutions. We insist on pedagogical qualifications for this *Équipe* rather than health, because there is a tendency for some *comuni* and districts to give people with a specialisation in health (and not in education) the work of managing and co-ordinating educational experience in the *asilo nido* and *scuola materna*, which to our minds is a mistake.

Establishing this kind of *Équipe* as part of local health and social services would allow greater development, and richer experimentation and research on the level of pedagogy, as well as responding to a specific need in the *comune*.

[. . .]

With regard to opening hours in the *scuola materna*, our feeling is hours should be based on the principle that schools are offered as a social services for families as well as being tools for children's education. The time children spend in school must therefore be assessed in relation to real family situations. Generally it is true that long and undifferentiated school hours conflict with children's need for other situations and experiences (in the family, in the neighbourhood etc.). However it is also true that the reality of a working family is determined by the working hours of mothers and fathers and the practical impossibility of guaranteeing real family relations outside school hours.

In the light of these considerations we feel obliged to say schools must adapt to factory hours, progressively opening up to workers' children with improved responses to family needs, while maintaining as far as possible the opportunity for parents to collect children at different times.

Certainly one of the most complex issues presenting itself in the struggle to expand state-financed, *comune*-run *scuola dell'infanzia* is the relation we should establish with private sector *scuola materna*. The size and capacity for influence of this school sector obliges the democratic workers movement to form a political initiative capable of commenting on how education is organised and structured.

We must recover the possibility of knowing collectively what reality happens in private *scuole materne*. The citizenry must know the real impact of costs, of teaching methods, and of contents on the family, and how funds flowing into private schools are used.

The Christian Democrats and the Church are asking for a clear recognition of the role of private institutions in the name of pluralism, and a commitment to financial support by *comuni* and the state. We wish to confirm the foundations on which we have acted all these years, fighting for the development of public schools for young children and a stronger commitment by the State in this direction so that all young children be guaranteed the right to attend public institutions.

It is a strange concept of pluralism that leads the State to give up its responsibilities in the field of education. Only the development of public schooling can confirm and guarantee a pluralism of ideas and respect for all faiths and all beliefs.

All the same we cannot help seeing that faced with the State's proven incapacity for extending public schools and the consequences of its culpable lack of interest in the needs of individual families together with the space it allows the private sector for disorganised uncontrolled initiatives, at least this latter sector has had a social function in partly responding to increasingly urgent needs.

All this generates the need to develop initiatives that are capable of establishing dialogue with Christian Democrat and Church positions on the subject of private schools, particularly those requesting financial support. This support cannot be claimed merely on the basis of uncritical recognition of the functions the private sector caries out. This would make the *comune* a mere provider of funds and ignore a basic premise that has guided the action of Reggio Emilia's *Comune* in the field of education, that of unifying organisation and structure with a qualitative definition of education and professional development.

Based on this evaluation, at the same time as defining what commitment the *comune* should make, we consider the private sector's willingness to discuss important points on how private *scuole materne* are organised to be a prerequisite for exchange and dialogue. These points include: management (the insignificant presence of families apart from other considerations); recruitment, professional development, and pay for teaching and non-teaching staff; admission criteria for children; the teacher–student ratio; the public nature of balance sheets; and the fitness of buildings.

To conclude. We confirm our wish to address the issue of private schools with the aim of starting a process leading them to increased quality and transformation. This action fundamentally rests on the maturity of teachers, parents and the community; it means social and political forces must have the desire and the capacity to organise the demand for *scuola materna*, and raise this onto a level of struggle for universal public *scuole dell'infanzia* funded by the state and run by the *comune*.

※ ※ ※

60.75 Essay for the book '*Arredo Scuola '75 – per la scuola che cambia*' [School Furnishing '75 – for Changing Schools], 1975

> **Editor's note:** The essay was also included in a volume, not for sale, edited by ANIC S.p.A. and published by Luigi Massoni editore (Cermenate, Como, 1975); the book was described as a contribution 'to the solution of the principal problems of the country'. It contained eleven chapters, including chapters from the Netherlands, France, Soviet Union, Sweden and the United Kingdom. The first chapter, which is a sort of introduction, is by Loris Malaguzzi.

School, buildings, furnishing: parallel lives, impossible lives?

Loris Malaguzzi, Pedagogical Consultant, Reggio Emilia Comune

[. . .]
The life of school furniture, like that of every other being, is a life of relations: its biological partner is the school, and every place where education is carried out.
   [. . .]
In trying, for coherence sake, to describe the role, the proportions and above all the cultural significance objects of furniture have [. . .], this reflection we are proposing will try and bring together reflections, facts, and references (to do with economy, ideology, science, policy and practice) and re-organise them critically and historically in connection with our schools, and their problems and purposes.
   A fundamental reflection that might help us to begin is to focus on an investigation and reconstruction of mankind's ways of developing over the generations and what trans-generational gestures have helped humans in this destiny.
   And certainly some important considerations would come of it: human beings' long apprenticeship in enriching and adding to the 'cultural' equipment they start with; the fact that their apprenticeship takes place in contexts of social experience; humanity's intentional invention of specific places (and tools) for education alongside the start of relations with other social

institutions; the constant flow of these phenomena, which makes school and its connections with society an inevitably transitory and constantly adjusting reality.

In a proper research into historical events we find that schools have never been their own arbiters or generated significant choices autonomously; they have endured and carried out functions that were given or suggested to them by other centres of power, which means that for long periods of time the flow and dynamic we mentioned above, between school and society, could be said to have taken place in a zone of oscillation that was very contained and determined from the outside.

However it is also useful to remember that for long periods of time school and education were nothing if not – how to say – situated in opposition to society's ways of living, and above all ways of working and producing, and this **separation** was even exalted and celebrated.

The birth of factories – after Galileo's discoveries – opened up a new era: in effect this called for a more rapid and concrete balance and coherence in relations between places of instruction, places of work and social organisation.

The birth of industrial society also meant other things: the consolidation and expansion of schools; the beginning of public intervention in the field of instruction after centuries of Church monopoly; a transition to capital investment; a greater north–south divide always with serious consequences; the extinction of our glorious artisan workshops and a consequent re-organisation of the family; the understanding that professions and culture could have practical uses in the field of industry. These are new, exciting and risky things.

The severe, authoritarian *and curial*[36] stamp of school architecture is the same as we find in the planning and management of new urban developments and which made a focal point of churches, government buildings, law courts, barracks, post office buildings, train stations etc. Together with the alarm and condemnation expressed about the expansion of schools, which were perceived to overturn old values and the old order ('an excessive and extravagant funeral pyre at the expense of true teaching', M. Macchi in *Il Politecnico*, Milano 1860), these [changes] testify that this was an era of great upheaval.

Schools were steeped in decrees, restrictions, authority, surveillance, *nomine regie*.[37] For an almost entirely illiterate population they were full of fear and poverty with ill-prepared depressed teachers – **'we are just people rented out'** (G. Sacchi in *Patria e Famiglia*, 1861)[38] – and teaching entrusted to words descending solely from a high and distant teacher's dais, calculations at the blackboard, and bamboo and willow canes which were poor pre-industrial tools, but effective reminders of discipline and subordination.

Furniture, if there was any at all, was this: a teacher's desk, a dais, five or ten-place desks, a blackboard and a cupboard. These universal objects were found everywhere from preschools to universities and ensured an absolute continuity of function, and above all a complicity with buildings of an equally similar and repetitive kind: a homogeneous and undifferentiated vision of the needs of different age groups, of psychological levels, and ways of learning.

Everything was simplified and reduced, means were few and there was little science, little desire. The problems outside school were difficult and absorbing. Necessary but nonetheless painful changes of leadership were taking place, there was conflict between church and state, conservatives and progressives. The economy was making the enormously difficult conversion from land to factory; unemployment and hunger were creating and organising their own political movements.

There was simply no need for too much analysis of the relationship between school buildings, how their spaces and uses were distributed, and teaching and educational objectives, especially when what was essential had already been discovered – **that is to say, a pedagogy of order and authority was the most convenient and the least expensive**. It cost less because buildings only had to replicate the basic module of a classroom as a container, a straight corridor to make monitoring possible, and very high windows from which only the sky could be seen. It cost less because furnishings were tools of a low standard to which no virtues were attributed, but which limited movement, immobilised the attention and acted as a surface to rest things on. Finally this pedagogy cost less for three very simple reasons: without exception it was offered as the general model for all places and all ages (but oh how many users were excluded!); it could be made to exist in any place in any way – old barracks, old monasteries, old farms – the most **imaginative** places – all with low rents; and above all it cost less because it avoided the thought that times can change and educational ideas can change.

At the same time nascent industry – objectively the birth was difficult partly due to a lack of raw material – asked very little of school either in commissioning potential business or as a qualifier of labour. For the moment artisan workshops remained the best, most economical source to turn to.

[. . .]

When we say a school of reading and writing we mean a school of literacy and nineteenth-century learning, pre-scientific, bureaucratic, hierarchical, centralised, [. . .] an educational project that makes children and young people the holders of incommunicable knowledge and disciplines, represses their spirit of criticism and research, shapes them for passive conformism, authority, discipline, sexual repression, competitiveness, and diffidence towards active responsible social relations; it is a project that is incapable of leaving traces of a culture connected with tradition and memory, or of using research and experimentation as tools for knowledge and discovery, for the promotion of education, culture and society.

Editor's note: There follows a long discussion of how funds have been used over the years, the scandal of wasted money and the many resultant difficulties.

[. . .]

After these revelations it is difficult to define the role of building, architecture, furniture and classroom equipment in educational dynamics and organisation – if possible an education that is equal to the times, or progresses at the same speed.

Even in places like France, where construction work has gone hand in hand with school expansion in a more coherent way, where 74,000 pre- and primary school classes, 3,500 middle schools, and 6 million square metres of secondary high school have been built; where everyone from the Minister, to the *pedagogistas*, to the architects seems to agree on publicly announcing the new education and decrying the errors and backwardness of the old way of education; the amazing fact is that these new buildings seem to have been built with faithful and obsequious respect for an image of the past.

True, here and there in the world there are examples of architecture where everything is coherent and splendid experiences are underway, using spaces and ways of learning for projects of construction and education open to the prospect of change (*pedagogistas*, architects, ergonomists, and designers are observing them together). But these ventures are not generally extensive and will not become extensive until school is free of its historical and political subordination.

Architecture, just like schools, is also first a political object, then a cultural object. There can be no doubt about the close and binding interaction between school architecture, the functions and meanings of its furniture and equipment, and its educational contents, method and objectives. There can be no doubt about this. Nor can there be any doubt that this situation, which is so self-evident and elementary in its logic, has been recognised hardly anywhere on earth and represents a rare state of grace.

School architecture could be said to be twice subordinate, first as architecture and then as school architecture. In our country it pays the additional price of belonging to a concept of school which is not a producer or even a co-producer of culture, but the consumer, part of the Napoleonic codes, of bureaucratic rhythms and with a backlog of needs that prohibit us from rising higher or making a leap forward. We might add it belongs to a pedagogical theory that finds politics, science, technology, commerce and industry as repugnant as other human sciences and activities and as a consequence also research, experimentation, doubt and planning; all the **changing** that constitutes the genuine rhythm of our lives and structure of our time.

And it must be recognised that with few exceptions [. . .], even here in Reggio Emilia, the teaching class, which ought to show the greatest interest in these issues, still seems resigned, willing to act as a humble silent executor.

To find an open and official sign of condemnation and protest we must go back to the investigative Commission of 1963: '**until now we can say that school buildings have never been evaluated in relation to the function they should carry out**'. This is a terribly serious statement.

From what has been said it will immediately appear obvious that the fate of buildings is the fate of schools. If schools do not decide to leave their mausoleums, find strategies for renewal, investigate their own malfunction and waste, acquire and plan the necessary means for a framework of purposeful general objectives for progress, then rather than their birthright of *artes reales*, buildings (seen as a need) and architecture (seen as conferring quality on the need) will become, to put it nicely, *artes sermonicales*: the **pure art of preaching**.

[. . .]

Education's real capacity for starting its own transformation cannot depend on education alone. The amount of time lost, old and new mistakes and problems, above all school's relationship to civil society and work, are facts that young people, families, political forces, trade unions and businesses now understand, and the knowledge has been extended and deepened on the 'inside' through public debate and initial experiences of participation in **collegial bodies**.

The demand for instruction is no longer the old demand for literacy. It is a demand for different knowledge that permits critical capacity and intervention in increasingly wider areas. This is a capacity that must be immediately initiated in active experience of participation in knowledge processes. It is a demand to count more, to experience wellbeing, security and all the civil rights. These things have been induced by social transformation, and emerged in the collective experience of discovering that mass schooling is incapable, unjust and anachronistic: all things that have been greatly increased by general political progress, and especially by our younger generations.

It no longer makes sense to propose the '**shoemakers by nature**' and '**philosophers by nature and education**' so dear to Plato and Gentilian practice [see Chapter 1, n.7] [. . .]. In other words, in the concluding words of the 1974 OECD Report on *Les politiques en faveur de l'innovation, de la recherché et du développement dans l'enseignement*, '**The most basic question is to know how – through school reform – we can achieve a just balance between the rights of the individual and the rights of society as a whole, and how all this can be reconciled into a democratic process creating change and reform**'.

Faure says, '**what we need to do is counter the contradiction which is generally present in the political systems of developed countries: of being pre-technological in teaching and elitist with regard to social recruitment**'.

Tecce says: '**we need to make a decision about the type of society [we want]: this society exploits the achievements of science but does not want to stop cultivating the seeds of ignorance**'.

In all this long history, school furnishings and education, the roles and meanings they have, and those they could have are protagonists that have been forgotten; discreet and vigilant, they always listen with interest.

The case we have argued for buildings and architecture is also true for furniture: without schools and education that desire change, without a society capable of not merely appreciating but actively accompanying processes of transformation, furniture will also continue to be the necessary but servile object it has always commonly been: left out of pedagogical books and studies, undervalued, and misunderstood even by those who use it daily.

[. . .]

Italian furniture factories, some of them illustrious not only through age, continue to weave a fabric conditioned by the market, which does not desire or tolerate a great deal of variation, and so they freeze (and waste) a potential for technique and inventiveness that, if it were freed, would have the energising role of technical, didactical and cultural provocation, developing new ideas on techniques, theories and praxis for places and methods of study and learning.

Much school furniture still bears all the signs of antiquity, especially out in the country: the signs of an attitude that emphasised the pure act of pedagogy that needed nothing else, of nineteenth-century deprivations and all their compensatory forms, and of the atomised pre-scientific culture of our own times.

Some furnishings are trans-generational and remain safe and unchanged though serving generation after generation. Some furnishings go too fast, and their form and use become so evolved they break down centuries-old gestures and seem inconvenient and incomprehensible; either they end up as 'monuments' or they are thrown under the stairs. The arrival and distribution of school furniture often follows a Magellan-like[39] route of bureaucracy and technical specifications. Furniture of an old-fashioned design goes into new schools and furniture of a modern design goes into old ones. Sometimes furniture goes straight to a municipal warehouse because schools have no room for it.

Opinions, including those coming from other countries, all say the same. Furniture is behind the times because that is what we ask for and what is convenient: users say little and stimulate little; administrations love habit; pedagogy continues to be absent; architecture proposes little or not at all, and when it does it has to deal with public administrations and legal constrictions. Students, not having a school they can love, cannot understand the point of furniture. In the long run the deciding factor is cost, which has the advantage over function and aesthetic. It is obvious that a business sector with so few variables means the slow evolution of technology, lazy research and little invention.

Think how things might be if we were able to move things forward in more synchronised, participatory and collaborative ways, with progress in pedagogical research moving together with progress in scientific, economic, artistic and technological research; with the shared examination of results, and the laying of plans in shared ways for investment and development; with complementary work between places of education with their themes and objectives, and the places of production and work with their needs.

Then we would see the great period of furnishings. Finally furniture could express something that has been impossible up to now and which has been its vocation for millennia. It would be fully realised as something living, capable of rich protagonism and a life of its own. It would replace the impoverished image of passive non-essential objects with wonderfully vital images of objects that not only make education possible, but actually produce it.

The fact is, the general and elementary principle of integrating pedagogy, architecture and furnishings - the problem of co-ordinating them; the dynamics and relations they give rise to; determining needs; ways of monitoring, channelling and responding to activities; the possibility of an incentive for flexible and diversified furniture ranges for different interests, activities and uses for different users; coherency with pupils' rhythms and ways of working; activating their capacity for socialising and enjoyment: in a word, the **great subversive potential** the integrated action these three aspects could have in modernizing and introducing new educational contents and methodologies - [this principle] not only constitutes something we are unaccustomed to, but a cultural reflection we are unfamiliar with, and which reveals how abstract and backward our educational processes and practice are.

In reality *pedagogistas*, architects, designers and ergonomists and the disciplines they represent know each other little or not at all, even though they have lived together unknowingly for centuries like ghosts in an English castle. Neither do they know sociologists, doctors, anthropologists, economists, scientists or politicians: each travels with his or her own horse.

If putting all this knowledge together in a unified way means the reorganisation of contributions, of specialisms, interests, research, experimentation, projects and cultures, then this is one of the keys we can offer at the end of this reflection for trying – and not symbolically – to construct a new school with the creative signs of its many co-constructors, those **sottement ingènieuse** people Rousseau's *Émile*[40] derided, because they were busy loving and creating the new.

✳ ✳ ✳

61.75 Article for a magazine *Esperienza*, no.2, published by the *Assessorato Scuola e Servizi Sociali, Comune di Reggio Emilia*, February 1975

Editor's note: This issue of *Esperienza* [Experience] was titled '*Idee, fatti delle scuole comunali dell'infanzia e dei nidi*' [Experience, Ideas and facts in the *scuole dell'infanzia* and *nidi* of the *comune*]. The article takes the form of Malaguzzi answering a number of questions from Luciano Corradini. Corradini was born in 1935 in Reggio Emilia, and was very involved in the world of education, becoming a Professor of General Education first at the University of Milan, in 1980, then at the Rome Tre University. He was also a strong supporter of the Catholic Church, described below by Malaguzzi as 'one of the most open and impassioned voices in the Catholic world and of schooling'. Unfortunately, Corradini's original questions no longer exist, though they are implied in Malaguzzi's responses. In this version, what was originally the endnote to Malaguzzi's article has been moved to the beginning, since it provides the reader with some useful context and background information.

Endnote to the article

Our friend Luciano Corradini, who is one of the most open and impassioned voices of the Catholic world and Catholic schooling, has left our city to take up work in university and the UCIIM [*Unione Cattolica Italiana Insegnanti Medi*, Italian Catholic Union of middle school teachers]. He knows our *scuole dell'infanzia* very well having had direct experience as a parent and as President of a *Comitato di Scuola e Città*[41] (he wrote a detailed and very lucid and affectionate account of this in '*Scuola Materna*'). A year ago he asked us to comment in a completely frank way, the way that has always distinguished our public and private relations, on questions and misgivings certain parts of the Catholic world have on Emilia-Romagna's municipal *scuole dell'infanzia*. It was a legitimate request, which in turn allows him to comment on these issues publicly.

What were these problems? The sense of cultural and political belonging; the influence of ideology; the dangerous mix of social management, teaching practices, and teacher's freedom; sex education and religious education.

The letter published here [see below] is a response to his request, though obviously we only speak for ourselves. As far as we know no use has yet been made of it.

Then why publish it? Because we are certain it is not unethical to do so, and that despite the time that has elapsed and the polemical language it is still relevant. It offers material for knowledge of a debate it is better to have in the open, encouraging the attention and contributions of others. And because it will make our friend Luciano Corradini happy as well as us.

On our experiences

Answers to questions proposed by a friend

Reggio E., March 1974

Dear Luciano

in a country like ours, where pedagogical research and experimentation are banned, where psychologists, sociologists, pedagogists and publishers are forced to rely on imported materials with all the large and inevitable misunderstandings about methods used and results,

where in reality training teachers is almost unacceptable because Italian schools know precious little of what to do with well-prepared teachers, where generally speaking the risk for educational issues is not of being the constant subject of exchange and reasoned reflection, but the subject of malevolence that openly and quite simply leans towards defending the cultural establishment and power,

where when talk turns to *scuola materna* and early years education it risks becoming ill-tempered, making discussion that already is not easy more difficult, about schools that are often sad, mediocre and humiliated, in a state of affairs that cannot be saved even by the generous and heroic offer of voluntary work and commitment,

certainly the *scuole materne* of Emilia-Romagna – the *scuole dell'infanzia* managed by *comuni* – effectively constitute an experience that consciously attempts real research and experimentation, and which has decided to debate and examine the choices made, or that could be made, with workers, families and the people. In short it has turned its hand to building other *scuole dell'infanzia* that are concerned with the educational and learning requirements of children who are far removed from images and roles much current pedagogy and sociology credits them with. Certainly, we were saying, schools in Emilia-Romagna, objectively speaking, have become an experience that is a reference point and so it is legitimate to ask questions in addition to the questions the schools already ask themselves. Let no one think that everything is flowers and roses, that everything has already been invented and realised.

The truth is that Emilia-Romagna's experience, especially for those who live it, is one of ferment and sacrifice: it is a difficult and stressful experience to be faced with a disinterested, distracted, utilitarian, rhetorical and overbearing reality – in school and out.

It is not right to think that experience in the Emilia-Romagna region is uniform. It varies from city to city according to the environment, the traditions and possibilities, for example the city administration or the political and cultural choices, the impact of concrete reality. However some things go beyond these differences and are common: all of them are enlivened by great civil ferment.

Then we come to Reggio Emilia, the city you and I know best. Here our educational experience had a long, determined, gradual, but lucid ten year journey before 1972. This is the year the features and objectives of its institutions were defined in a unified and structured way in a vast people's constituent assembly that lasted eight months and required twenty-four drafts of the 'constitution' (really a *Regolamento* required by *comune* laws). The City Council voted it in unanimously but really the debate took place beforehand.[42]

What are the essential features of our educational experience?

A declared desire for pedagogical research as a permanent method realised together by teachers, auxiliary workers, families, citizens and *Quartiere* (the entire coming school year 1974–1975 will be dedicated to discussing and examining choices made and implemented, one by one). This transcends the reductive and triangular concept discussed in a recent CEI[43] document (the first of its kind to examine *scuola materna* issues analytically), which still reduces relations to 'children, school and family'. It also introduced certain things that the *Decreti Delegati* [see Chapter 3, n.21] will (perhaps) start to implement next year, much earlier.

An insulting, anti-pedagogical 'ban' on male teachers was discarded and the results are extremely encouraging. The teacher's role was re-habilitated with proper wages and a 36 hour working week: with formal recognition that 2 of the 36 hours be set aside for group meetings, school meetings, study, *aggiornamento*, examination, etc. The auxiliary's role was freed so that she can study, meet and discuss on equal terms with teachers, with exactly the same working hours and commitments as her [teacher] 'colleagues', for the first time in Italy.

Every residual notion of hierarchy was done away with. There are no '*dirigenti*' [managers], there are no 'educational directors': there are six co-ordinators [*pedagogistas*] (one for every ten classes), whose intervention, of necessity, is interwoven with the interventions of the seven hundred and more members of *Comitati di Scuola e Città* and other non-centralised administrative, cultural and political bodies in the local area. This defends them from any unconsciously mistaken or inappropriate temptation.

For every 30 children 2 teachers work <u>together</u>, in a permanent break with the impossible and inhuman relations teachers have when they are left alone to experience problems, and the individualistic solitary schema that result. For children who do not have a sufficient guarantee of family care [in the afternoon], a longer day is available until 18.30.

Each school has its own *atelier* with a teacher who specialises in not specialising. The role played by the *atelier* in our educational experience is long in the telling. Suffice to say that through its nature, activities and connections we hope to form a sort of <u>guarantee</u> that our educational experience will remain fresh and imaginative, help the experience not to be trapped in routine and habit, or become over schematic.

The Management Committees – which were born and resisted when no one or very few believed in them – and whose issues you have experienced first hand, are there to testify both to the potential and reality of democratic, human and cultural contributions that schools can make, and to the difficulties they have in resisting and contributing specific and original[44] substance.

What of the 'objections'?

This is not an ideological school, nor party [political] school, or anything of that kind, much less a naturalistic school,[45] a term as unknown in our vocabulary and thinking as it is common in Catholic experience and the pedagogical theories of 'spontaneists' and 'utopists'.[46]

Adults have a permanent historical role in education, and so there is no pedagogy of *laissez faire* or letting things pass, or of cancelling the principles of reality for principles of pleasure; no pedagogy that starts and finishes with rhetoric on children; that does not have to struggle in order to get the means, the spaces and the tools it needs, that does not facilitate children's joy in recognising themselves in the things they do, of being the authors and constructors of their own knowledge as far as possible, observers of the ways society responds to their needs, and of their own and other children's families; that does not have to struggle to get away from anachronistic, unjust forms and contents.

To conclude, by jealously defending children from preconceived and biased models, and giving them back their right to choose who they are from the start, our hypothesis for schools above all defends and liberates the children's role as protagonists, and this must inevitably tend to the side of struggle and renewal.

Naturalistic sex education? What does that mean?

Does it mean sexual education with the utmost naturalness? If so then yes, as long as the subject does not become so specific it moves outside the unified conception of education.

I have to say with extreme frankness that generally those who raise problems and concerns of the kind you report for some time have had a phantom model of sexual education, making it a thing unto itself, and inventing a sexual morality that is as abstract as it is fragile and formulaic. Once again what characterises our way of working is that we refuse the social role models, including those connected with sex, which society distorts and education proposes without critique. These are false and adulterated roles. If we work in *scuole dell'infanzia* in such a way that our children do not find themselves at crossroads, or on separate journeys, with separate activities and behaviours; if we let so-called femininity and so-called masculinity emerge freely and gradually, avoiding obsessively Manichaean attitudes, then I think this is healthy and right.

The other objections are: teacher discrimination, excessively intense work, ideological pressure, acts of propaganda.

It would be easy to respond with the example of the young teachers in Brescia who lost their jobs because they took part in city mourning for the third anniversary of the Piazza della Loggia massacre.[47] They had been officially registered as shop assistants [not teachers] and had been worn down like thousands of other young people all over Italy (including Reggio Emilia obviously).

We have built our experience with the teachers the Italian State offers: not from the seven State *Magistrali* schools,[48] but from the 160 private religious *Magistrali* schools and initiatives the AIMC has run in recent years.[49] These are proliferating everywhere, advertising rapid courses, with no little income for private *Magistrali* schools (let us say 100,000 *lire* for each candidate). And candidates are put through these schools quickly, with organised pre-defined techniques.

Dear Luciano, do you know that if what a high-up ministry inspector told me is true, there is a private *Magistrali* schools in Alcamo [a city in Sicily] that only opens for exams in June and takes 30–40 million *lire* a year?

Well our work begins with these young people. Either we do it with them and experience it with them, appreciating the satisfactions and the social and ethical gains of the commitment we are trying to create together – purposeful, altruistic and social – or the game finishes here.

In reality the game goes on. It is not an easy game, its progress is not linear, tensions flare up, ideas become clearer, attitudes form, questions require answers and constant comparisons, enthusiasms must be measured. A school made in this way, so intentionally grafted onto the affairs of the local area and people, is a school with a high degree of sensitivity that registers, and feels the effect, of every external situation whether private or public. In fact this sensitivity is a delicate issue, but it is the salt and the cornerstone of our experience, and the more it drops the formality and cold mechanisms of pedagogical theory and pure ideology the more human it becomes.

In our experience, which is certainly not immune to limits and criticism, there is room for everything. The broader and more differentiated the politics, the more encouraging this is for our work.

Ideological education?

Yes, in the sense of liberating and emancipating children (normal and handi-capped), and schools and families: in a design like this dialogue finds the space it needs. Perhaps here in Italy though, where 'quiet, don't move' is the fron-tispiece to school and education, there may be people who would prefer us to downplay publicising [our work]?

We have helped, we believe, hundreds and hundreds of teachers; we have tried to persuade several public and private administrators to believe in schools and school renewal. We don't say to them, now you sit there and we will tell you the story. We say, come and see for yourselves, get into the thick of it, into real things. Just this year that is drawing to an end, we have had 179 group visits to our schools. Nothing is organised, people write or phone and ask; we agree together, we are at their disposal, we discuss things openly before, dur-ing, and after. The groups are of many different kinds: 50 per cent are made up of teachers, managers, administrators and architects who are Catholic or thereabouts. The meetings, discussions and exchanges always take place with a high level of cultural interest, which is what we need to reinforce now, at a time when pluralist ideas of education seem to be starting on all sides.

Social management, autonomous practice, freedom of the educator?

From next year Law 477[50] will propose these ideas throughout Italy, which have been a living part of our experience for ten years.

If we take the three ideas as being distinct, separate, living in different worlds that are poles apart, the way it looks from how your question–objection is formulated, then our history would be over: it is a simplified and vain vision. If Law 477 goes in this direction it will cease to have cultural credibility even before it comes to the point of [encountering] real things and facts.

Though people fear this test and see the objective difficulties and risks it pre-sents, schools and education will never understand the meaning of their hard work and their hopes for renewal unless they engage with the unified value of these three situations [social management, autonomous practice, freedom of the educator], in a dimension and dialectic that refuses to put up with or avoid obstacles or lack of engagement: no-one would sacrifice or lose anything, but there would be enhancement of both a specific and a general nature.

This is the – difficult – experience we have been trying for years. We have never theorised fatal or inevitable opposites, instead sometimes – in more fortu-nate situations, and thanks to the reciprocal play of discovery and enrichment – we have achieved encouraging and important results.

That leaves religious education.

Do we want religious education in a society accepted as pluralist, or not? What does pluralist mean? Would we like our vegetable patch hedged in or open? Do we want monologue or dialogue? Do we want religious education in schools with social participation and management, or without them?

Do we want religious education as envisaged in the *Concordato*?[51] Do we want old catechisms or new ones? Why? For whom? How?

Not even the *Orientamenti*,[52] which are certainly advanced and liberal on the subject, seem sufficiently clear to us. For years now, all of us, with our different backgrounds and thinking, have been part of this great crisis of the Christian and Catholic worlds. And again, all of us have become convinced that several ways of thinking and behaving, several political problems that exist in our national society, are directly and indirectly linked with the affairs that take up much of the Church's attention and much of our culture.

In the meantime we need help and clarity from Catholics: a spirit of tolerance, a love of debate, the desire to analyse problems, a refusal for overbearing 'evangelisation'. These are not easy things, but we need to intensify and renew our shared efforts if we want to have them.

Until now we have dealt with these issues directly with families in public meetings (often priests attend these meetings). What comes of this is what we are trying to create. What comes of the meetings is:

- children are not bottles to be filled, they are active interlocutors;
- religious experience is made up of life experience, not of formulas we can impose and reproduce;
- like everything in education, families cannot delegate religious experience to just anyone;
- religious experience has to be integrated into culture, into expectations and the hopes and issues of our times. As you say yourself it must be a 'joy of being, of living, a human possibility' and not as others say, 'the feeling we are precarious, the fate of death, of arriving in the world and beginning not so much to live as to die'.

We respond to religious education in our *scuole dell'infanzia* and give substance to it on the basis of these results, in agreement with our workers, who must constantly compare their 'private' and 'public' consciences.

Are these responses satisfactory for everyone?

When families entrust themselves to a non-private and unbiased place, and this is what they do, then they do not constitute a problem.

Every religious feast is an occasion for our concrete commitment to highlighting the values of existence, of education, of helping and liberating humanity, which are part of the basic messages of Christ's teaching. This is something we feel belongs to us as a choice, as common ground. Some people turn up their noses if we help children to survive in Vietnam[53] or if we go and take our warmth to elderly people in the hospice, or to poor and humiliated citizens.

Is it mistaken? We think not.

This is where the problem lies. And if things are still not entirely satisfactory, then I would like to say the fault is not all ours, just as the credit is not all ours when things are achieved.

I feel I have left things out everywhere. But this is the talk of the kind of person I am, always distorted by hurrying and running.

My greetings to you, your wife, your children, your work.

Loris Malaguzzi

❋ ❋ ❋

62.75 Appendix for the Report of a study commission on '*La Scuola dell'-Infanzia in Emilia-Romagna* – *esperienze ipotesi realizzazioni*' [Experiences, hypotheses, realisations], edited by the *Assessorato* for Territorial Planning, Transport, Building, Emilia-Romagna Region, Bologna, March 1975

> **Editor's note:** The study commission, which focused on *scuole dell'infanzia*, was supported by twenty-five experts from education and architecture. Chapters in the commission's report included: the local area; outdoor space; indoor space; and furnishings, all within the context of an introductory section on the psycho-pedagogical orientation of these schools.

Appendix II: the premises of Reggio Emilia – contributions for designing and using a new scuola dell'infanzia

This part was written by prof. Loris Malaguzzi as a synthesis of orientations in Reggio Emilia

Hypotheses for schools: here the *scuola dell'infanzia* is no longer seen as a separate institution but as a specific, institutional situation of socialisation and of educational, cultural and political processes of responsibility for children, which cannot avoid offering to participate in building an educating society in which its contents and purposes can be debated and integrated dialectically.

The type of architecture cannot get away from seeking coherent formulations and responses: a school where 3- to 6-year-old children can find and construct rhythms of life is a fabric of actions, relations, confluences and contents, tested in the physical-psychological-social-political-cultural spaces inside and outside school.

Children are certainly the primary reference point but idealised anachronistic forms of child-centredness must be avoided consciously: children are part of historically determined and open relations, and the environments they inhabit must reflect this.

This means many things: above all it means education is realised through processes where adult protagonisms and children's protagonisms fuse together in historical-cultural contexts, which must always be critically interpreted, examined and experienced (along the lines we stated initially), and we under-line this is the necessary condition and generator of the contents on which our educational practice is founded.

A school of this kind must closely weave choices of form and function with the *territorio*, which should be as accessible and participatory in educational activity and initiatives as the spaces inside the school: this is one guarantee that pedagogical content and meaning do not become part, as tradition would have it, of alienated teaching based on fossilised things, words and practice done in closed spaces.

Only the mass protagonism of those [currently] subjected to the protago-nism of the few, in school, in work and in life, will make our idea of educa-tion credible and realisable (this will not be easy work or short). This idea is not an opportunist strategy, it is a definite choice, and corresponds to a model of school that is non-ideological and unbiased (this is why they are schools of *liberation*), where dialogue, debate and discussion of ideas and culture make the schools what they are, defend them and reinforce them, and simultaneously make them willing to always stretch further.

Schools are *ensembles of presences and interventions*: of children, teachers (female and male), auxiliaries, parents, citizens, and citizens' cultural, political and trade union organisations. Therefore school spaces must not only include but actually support the presence of this complexity of different groups, and stimulate them into conscious participation in children's issues, into the general issues of childhood, of school and of education.

This raises implications about the types of buildings we need to develop: how to realise this idea of children, workers, parents, visitors and citizens all co-existing, participating, using and running the school, and where the very process of designing this shared life makes all these parties socialise to as great a degree as possible?

These comments already implicitly define several important values, which require the contribution of ideas and responses from technicians and planners. Schools (and the areas in which they are located) should identify opportu-nities for relations with the *territorio* as a source of inspiration, didactics and contents. Piazzas, streets, buildings, people's houses, cultural, recreational and sports institutions, monuments, shops, offices, rivers and woods, factories and places where men and women work all form a vast reading book that can orientate educational activities; and they are all there to be explored and done, where children, teachers, parents and citizens can rediscover a new dimension, the genesis and history of their relations and behaviour, the reasons for their condition and the duality of culture. Then we will no longer have schools that are separate buildings with a modest yard as their outer boundary.

Some traits defining [schools]:

- they should be uninterrupted and transparent tunnels [sinuous, continuous structures];
- they should be places that can accommodate children for several hours a day but also starting points for exploratory outings, and at the same time cultural and scientific receptacles full of discoveries, evidence and problems, gathered in children's research and projects and that constitute the principal road-map for starting out on deeper explorations, greater knowledge and further projects inspired by the outside world;
- places that can accommodate the organisation and work connected with participation and management;
- places that emphasise and sustain participation and management through their propensity and capacity for communicating and telling families and people what they are doing, what they plan and think, through the work of children, teachers, *Comitati di Scuola e Città* and meetings (using entrance halls, walls, larger spaces and areas with freedom of movement as privileged places for encounters between parents, children and workers etc. and as surfaces for permanent exhibitions);
- places capable of finally creating equality between spaces, functions and values, abandoning discrimination, communicating powerful educational images to children and inviting adults, whatever their work, to have a sense of going beyond fixed individual educational roles (rehabilitating kitchens, laundries, ironing and store rooms, that are usually out of sight or hidden);
- places with easily read interiors that can be perceived as an interconnected unified structure people can move through easily, above all places children can make their own and memorise, becoming familiar with the whole and the parts;
- places offering a perception and use of inside and outside as a unified whole, where outside means both gardens and the *territorio*;
- places offering children and school workers (teaching and non) ample opportunities for seeing, meeting, speaking and acting with each other, in daily activities and situations, in planned inter-class situations and activities, and in unplanned play and activity that arises spontaneously through chance encounter, and in meetings children and workers desire and seek;
- places that refuse concessions to home-like or childish spaces, but express thoughtful functional architecture (inside and out) essentially going towards the model of a large *atelier* (more emphasis on doing than on words), understood as an area that is partly organised and partly organisable, where play and work, learning and teaching, personal hygiene, eating and sleeping, being together (in ways we have discussed) can co-exist as equal in value, reciprocally forming a unified fabric of experience;

- *places that satisfy a series of children's fundamental rights-needs*, which are often underestimated and ignored in practice: *the right to reassuring and positive relations with peers and adults*, which asserts the necessity of children enjoying a quality and intensity of exchange and experience adequate to their demands; demands that are bio-psychological, historically defined and connected with schools' purpose of social and cultural promotion. (Therefore: coherence between spatial organisation and function, good ratios of children and workers, definition of professional qualities and content, educational equipment, socialised work etc.);

- *the right to enough room to move*, underlining that 'enough' does not only mean the quantity of space essential for moving around in, playing, learning, socialising, often in immature unskilled ways; it also means the quantity and quality of space and action for children we want to be makers and active constructors of experience;

- *the right to be messy*, which finally frees children to experience, makes them less inhibited and gives them a taste for doing, recognises their right to mistakes and the perfecting power of doing and ranging, especially during activities;

- *the right to noise and to silence, the right to be with others, the right to be alone, to be with a few others*, which are the just response to needs, choices and alternating physiological and psychological behaviours, choices that are completely justified;

- and finally *the right to eat* and *the right to sleep*, which are two fundamentally important rights with psychological, affective, emotional and intellectual implications, the more so because children spend a long and stressful part of their lives in an institution (8–10–12 hours); therefore we request building plans to include kitchens, dedicated dining areas for children and adults, classroom store cupboards that make it easier to put beds away and get them out, and any other elements which might be considered useful for experiencing these two times as pleasurable, secure and gratifying, with as much active and autonomous organisation by children as possible;

- to be specific, we imagine classrooms (with their own bathrooms) which can be separated into spaces for different uses and purposes, in which the large group of children (no more than 25 or 30) and teachers working together in pairs (both sexes) can homogeneously develop their own rhythm of experience together, constructing pertinent educational processes with the necessary continuity; classrooms that are simple to exit and that facilitate outings to do things in different but integrated dimensions (planned or unplanned, these always weave with the lives of others); classrooms that guarantee our idea of highly social and responsible education, the distinctive feature of a just, credible and alternative project for schools.

✳ ✳ ✳

63.75 Speech at a regional Conference '*Il bambino soggetto e fonte di diritto nella famiglia e nella società. Generalizzare l'asilo nido e la scuola dell'infanzia come centri di formazione e promozione individuale e sociale*' **[The child as a subject and source of rights in the family and society. Extending the** *asilo nido* **and** *scuola dell'infanzia* **as centres for the promotion of individual and social education], Bologna, April 1975**

Editor's note: This conference, organised by the Emilia-Romagna Region, coincided with the abolition of ONMI, the national organisation founded in 1925 by the fascist regime, and the transfer of its responsibilities, assets and staff to the Regions and the municipalisation of ONMI's *asili nido*. There were 1,000 participants including educators, public administrators, academics, political and union representatives. The conference was intended to support the extension of early childhood services by drawing on existing local experiences; and to this end the conference was carefully prepared, with three commissions working for several weeks on legislation, buildings and educational content, the last of which was led by Loris Malaguzzi. But in addition to this analysis, the conference also assumed a political purpose, with a renewed democratic commitment from *comuni* to respond to the growing demand for services coming from citizens.

Malaguzzi made three interventions at this conference, two of which are included below. The first is his report to the conference as convenor of the commission on 'contents, programmes and objectives of the *asilo nido* and of the *scuola dell'infanzia*'. The second is some concluding proposals on the *asilo nido*.

Report from the commission on 'contents, programmes and objectives of the asilo nido and of the scuola dell'infanzia'

[. . .]

The idealistic and neo–idealistic perspectives that still have an important role in misleading and hiding things in this country, try to make contents a separate issue that is for an elite competency, divorced from the events that really produce contents and decide their fate. A moral stamp puts its mark on things and acts as a rigorous sentry that keeps politics from entering inside schools. In these mythic schools the role of their young users is to believe in them, and the role of parents is to delegate their powers and rights to them, and only hold rights that are fake and subordinate.

Instead the issue of contents comprehensively re-affirms the issue that schools are concrete institutions, in which processes of professional and cultural 'formation' take place and where the outside world's ethical, cultural and economic conceptions are reflected, in particular the implications of these conceptions for how we organise knowledge.

This means certain essential things:

- <u>contents</u> always reflect an interest,
- contents <u>always connect</u> with the historic present and with cultural confrontations and struggles that are taking place,
- <u>for this reason contents are not</u> and cannot be autonomous choices separate from pedagogy.

This perspective helps us to read and interpret a contents *project*. That is to say, a comprehensive school and education project with the ambition of responding to needs and requests in contemporary children who embody the general situation of society with its signs of deep and highly dangerous instability in its economic foundations and its basic ideals and ideology; or rather a series of responses that are not at all definitive. This project takes responsibility for the conviction that issues of education and schools are just one node in the crisis of contemporary society where there is a decisive and head-on clash between different concepts of children, of human beings and their relations, historical traditions, ideals, political directions, and economic and societal choices.

The design, which will go on to be tested by facts and progressively opened up to exchange and enrichment, can only be born, initiated and informed by political and cultural forces that are interested in school and society's change and transformation. Forces capable of breathing life into the important, urgent work of intellectual and social reform and where – avoiding wishful thinking and irrational attitudes – schools can <u>immediately and concretely</u> commit actively to participating in researching and asserting new values.

This simultaneous <u>political and cultural</u> action rejects delay and accepts being tested by things because that is how processes grow, how awareness and conscience grow, and it can easily be seen in many parts of Emilia-Romagna's experience of governing through elected institutions. Certainly this emerging and particular trait has defined intervention by *comuni* in Emilia-Romagna on issues of school and education, particularly in services for early years.

[. . .]

Constructing educational contents and above all practising them can only take place when there is permanent reflection and critique on the real roles and values that contents have in forming individuals and the society that will welcome them in this contemporary world.

[. . .]

However, to avoid misunderstandings when we speak of contents we must define our fundamental choices. If we want contents to be a part of real contexts, part of unfolding historical events, interpreting these and acting as their protagonist, then they cannot be absolute and final and coercive. They must consist of a series of more complex and coherent hypotheses that are constantly updated and strengthened through interpreting the needs of children, families and society (inseparably woven together), and creating the largest possible movement, the greatest participation, shared responsibility, and determination. These essential issues are the support that makes contents possible, examining and guaranteeing them in a constant democratic regeneration.

[. . .]

Our idea of education clearly means specific institutional times for socialisation, for taking cultural and political responsibility for children. It means the clearly expressed and coherent aspiration of participating in the construction of an educating society where we can dialectically confront and integrate our points of view.

This means offering an unambiguous design for interested schools, but also means offering schools divested of ideological and political bias because they are *interested* in their own construction through dialogue, exchange, debate, and through research into ethics and ideals that express their antagonistic and liberating concept of culture. A content of this kind gives experience credibility and consensus and should be repeated outside schools, in every organised form of civil co-existence.

This is a decisive issue for highlighting the importance of entrusting management to decentralised state structures in a frame of fully valued autonomy, to go beyond what Bertolini calls 'the old vertical logic (inevitably top-down), that is feeding the progressive incoherence of our school institutions, and corresponds to the bureaucratic, largely authoritarian model of our system'.

It is a necessary condition, not only for forming a direct non-bureaucratic experience of school governance that is capable of organising school choices and processes in the local area, but also for practically asserting ideas of participation and democracy and the construction of contents in a social frame.

It is a necessary condition for definitively going beyond school-centred models of education that self-exile or exile society's other sources of education.

And finally it is a necessary condition for intensifying the cultural hegemony of public schools, which makes the right-duty of parents (article 30 of the Constitution) to instruct and educate their children into a great mass movement, eliminating fragmentation, reduction and exploitation of educational management (which cannot be limited today), while giving it concrete powers. It also makes contents and objectives in schools more concrete, and open to the plurality of exchange between political, cultural and religious faiths; it marks the end of illiberal and dogmatic temptations, and respects the freedom to choose, to be a part and a protagonist democratically. This is a right that younger generations ask, with legitimate reason, and a right which must be a pillar of education wherever it is: in the family, in school, and in society.

[. . .]

Participation and social management open up a process of reform and liberation that is more likely to resist assimilation. On these conditions:

a   that we understand the role of the working class and worker organisations in the struggle to transform schools. Because as things stand they represent the forces that are most interested in change, and because they have a real capacity to contribute to the advent of a new culture;

b   that internal and external protagonists of school processes – teachers, auxiliary workers, parents, social and political representatives, citizens – want to participate as equals, and have the conditions that make this possible without privileges of any kind. This is what makes it possible to construct an experience of socialisation, of cooperative filtering, of educating to a participation in which each person feels they can manage their own changes and bring their individual consciousness together with the group's, which is the vital leap in quality;

c   that participating as equals means expressing equal attitudes of willingness and service, personal and group, without loss or paling of individual identities. This attitude is achieved through the value of autonomy and the freedom of new meanings, first for teachers who are requested to leave behind anonymity and play a decisive part which has never been asked of them before; then families, whose fundamentally educational nature is enhanced by becoming integrated into a differentiated social context and who recover their natural historical dimension on a higher level, with a sense of self and of the reciprocal, the shared, of solidarity: and obviously, a richer and more open capacity for education;

d   that the process starts in the awareness that the more consensus and contributions it has, the more it can offer in terms of achievement. Progressive achievements capable of pushing forward with the themes of research, realisation and debate, uniting specific cultural situations with situations of organisation and practicality inside and outside school. So for example the battle to free children from constricting languages and behaviours, which must be understood by teachers and the people, goes side by side with the battle to proliferate school services, improve the standard of spaces and environments we offer children, and the hours, rhythms, relations and tools we give to school workers for their professional competency and development; and again with the intuition that an idea of genuine participatory experience (largely feasible only during evening hours) requires a complete upturning of traditional frameworks of reference with these protagonists as the authors of this new venture. This is the delicacy and complexity of the issue;

e   that the dual operation of participation and management should be trusted to a few vital rules of organisation and methodology, based on free investigation and periodical re-examination, in order to avoid waste and guarantee their democratic and political production and purpose, in the spirit of a general orientation, capable of stimulating the greatest number to participate with the most responsibility; promoting projects and formulating objectives with practical ways of achieving them; promoting the ability to avoid hierarchical action but covering all areas of educational experience; connecting them with general issues; creating stable and wide-reaching connections with cultural and school institutions in the local area, with the *consiglio di quartiere*, the *consiglio di zona*, the *comune*, the region, the state.

In this case again, although experiences in Emilia-Romagna have all started from a common chosen direction, they have not all worked with one single model.

Concluding proposals on the asilo nido

We do not need to underline how children, considered as the subject and source of rights, together with families, have been at the centre of this conference. The idea of children's historicisation [how children are the product of historical development] and interpretations of their needs in growth, health, education and happiness in and outside institutions have been referred to constantly in our talks and discussion. It is a vast theme with broad public responsibilities, and it has had several contributions both during the conference and in the final proposals put together in the working commission.

The proposals are the following:

Asilo Nido *identity and role*

The social and cultural identity of the *Asilo Nido* is constructed in a web of interactions and relations with other institutions in the local area entitled in whatever way to defend the health or increase the education and culture of children and adults, or offer tools for the promotion and security of families.

[. . .]

Work organisation

A fundamental condition for carrying out the tasks and aims of the *asilo nido* is good and efficient solutions for creating relations between architectural features, the distribution of spaces and functions, opening times, work organisation, worker commitment and professionalism and the number of children attending.

The environment. Refined to contain and activate services for very small children for several hours a day, and considering their full range of multiple functional and psychological qualities, environments are defined as an integral part of the overall project of educational experience and play a decisive role for the co-existence, coherency and intensity of response to <u>the request of children to be and to do, and the request of workers to be and to do</u>. This explains the high level of awareness around this issue that we saw both in the conference's preparatory work and in the later work, and the interest and expectations related to contributions from the Buildings, Materials and Furnishings Study Commission.

Children and workers request the best conditions for creating the close and reciprocally communicative relationships that are a prerequisite for producing effective experience – both from the point of view of affect-emotion and the point of view of autonomy, cognition and socialisation – and encouraging participation and social management.

It was widely recognised that an optimal condition for children is to have stable reference persons with whom they can initiate processes of intimacy and refining knowledge, for their security, for greater familiarity with spaces, and for ways of acting and establishing relations with peers and with things.

Implementing all this – this is the precise request we make to the Region and managing authorities where it is their responsibility – plays a decisive role in establishing positive professional ferment and constructing a more solid cultural identity for workers. Specific requests have been forwarded to the Region and managing bodies, in the areas for which they are responsible.

Observation and research

The high number of *Asilo Nido* in our Region is a privileged terrain for observation, study, and research on themes and methodologies that are culturally and scientifically important. Of necessity, before now these were tested in restricted environments or even laboratories.

The need for deeper study of infant behaviour when forming relations with the mother, the family and institutions, in social and cultural contexts where many aspects have changed and are new, is something felt by theorists, researchers, workers in the field and politicians.

In reality observations, investigations and findings are already taking place and interesting references have been made to these in talks and during discussion. We need to offer research more resources, more tools and more opportunities, together with greater organisation, co-ordination and scientific rigour. The intervention of universities, research institutes, regions and *comuni* plays an important and decisive role.

But the area is also open to a different, wide-reaching and fertile application: the exercise of direct <u>observation</u>, which is a cultural and practical conceptualisation for *asilo nido* educators. This form of observation, and it has been said during this conference, becomes a tool that can accumulate and examine experience, and which can refine, develop, and re-qualify our professional conduct. This promotion of <u>attitudes and materials</u> can give the necessary concrete nature to a planned and organised policy of deeper investigations and exchanges that this conference has rightly underlined.

❋ ❋ ❋

64.75 Rough draft for speeches at the time of elections for new members for *Comitati di Scuola e Città*, Reggio Emilia, 1975 (no more precise date)

Editor's note: This was probably drafted at the start of the new school year, when elections were due for *Comitati di Scuola e Città*.

Rough draft for talks on the occasion of renewal [of Comitati]

1. The meanings of elections for renewing Comitati di Scuola e Città

- commitment, coherence, a fact of democracy that has accompanied and sustained our experience for years
- a sign of continuity and vitality
- an act of trust in participation, in collective action, in the democratic management of services
- they highlight cultural values (exchanges of viewpoint, the refusal to delegate etc.) and educational values (socialisation, co-responsibility)

2. Additional meanings

- no to the disintegration of the republican state and its institutions
- no to violence as a political system[54]
- yes to change through participation and democracy

3. The situation of social services in our Comune

- see (statistical data)
- against the influence of the economic situation and dangerous irresponsible theories such as (a) the theme of unproductive services; (b) the dismantling of public institutions and services and handing them over to voluntary or private management; re-assert the community's duty to guarantee satisfactory care for children, which is adequate for their needs and rights through social services; to help with the organisation of family tasks and times; and to make a significant investment of public resources in collective services.

4. The behaviour of the Comune

Adjust monthly fees – vary fees by income – projects for renovation of schools in 1978/79 being examined by the mayor and workers – the opening of 2 *nidi* (Via Puccini and Via B. Croce), and a *scuola dell'infanzia* (Via Samoggia).

5. The institutions [schools]

Integration of institutions with the *territorio* for a system of social cohesion and cultural promotion.

6. The principles and meanings of participation and management, which are essential terms of the educational project

7. Social management's areas of intervention

(Organising the management Committee, organising the working environment, cultural and educational choices, promotional initiatives, economic and political action, monitoring by the assemblies etc.)

1977

65.77 Synthesis of the main points arising at a cultural *aggiornamento* for workers at *scuole dell'infanzia*, Reggio Emilia, Spring 1977

> **Editor's note:** This is a brief summary of a much longer document 'Religious Education and the Education of Children', created at the end of a four month process of examining religious and spiritual education in which priests and parents, as well as educators, participated.

23/11/76–29/3/77

Central importance was given to school's cultural function. It was said that if the essential task of school is to help children interpret human reality, intervene in it and satisfy their right to truth, then we cannot forget that the religious element is undeniably an integral, significant part of this reality.

It follows from this that schools have a duty to provide children with a key for understanding religious facts and issues, being careful their thirst for knowledge is satisfied promptly and correctly, like their questions, their comparisons and their reflections; without ever having recourse on the school's part to removing the genuine personal meanings children are searching for; but helping them to go beyond an assumption of privilege, and go beyond easy false classifications, to get to know and appreciate different attitudes and the benefits that come when there is exchange between them.

Faced with the plurality of [people's] choices, schools must adopt an attitude of equal interest, highlighting the common and more specific values in each choice, and perhaps seeking to examine them in terms of their consistency with the actions of individuals and collectives.

✳ ✳ ✳

66.77 Introduction to the announcement of a photography exhibition to be held in Reggio Emilia, April 1977

> **Editor's note:** Malaguzzi writes an introduction to a photography exhibition – titled 'Children's Experience and Research: In discovery of self and the world' – held in June 1977 to mark the thirtieth anniversary of the *Azienda Cooperativa Macellazione*, a cooperative butchering company. Photographs were invited from all parents of children attending municipal, state or private *nidi* and *scuole dell'infanzia* in Reggio Emilia and the surrounding province, as well as from all workers in these services and anyone working in 'culture and photography'.

Children's experience and research: in discovery of the self and the world

All of us are willing to appreciate children's great thirst for knowing the world. In fact we are all willing to teach it to them: using manuals, books, teaching aids, exercise sheets, audiovisuals, and machines that do everything.

However far fewer of us understand that children wish to discover **the world** for themselves, as far as possible: with their own senses, their own curiosity, their own intelligence, their own hands, their own body, their own store of affect and vitality. They want to research for themselves, try, make mistakes, try again, marvel, understand, imitate now so as not to imitate later. They want to discover the causes and relations between things and facts. They want to play to test themselves and learn how to succeed in situations; make believe to create worlds and things that would be impossible otherwise. They want to speak, write and play music to learn how to communicate with themselves and others.

They imagine in order to invent, they explore in order to examine, they design and plan in order to construct, they socialise in order to ask for help and move on.

Each step forward, each curiosity satisfied, each test overcome, each problem brought closer to the truth, each discovery, is a source of great wellbeing, great satisfaction and great confidence for children. Children know how to know, children can know.

And through knowledge of the world, children come to a knowledge of the self (the shortest way and not the longest, though it might appear so). And the more children know the world, the more they know themselves and can face the world with confidence and trust.

The theme entrusted to the sensibility of those wishing to participate in this exhibition wishes to highlight the meanings and values in our introduction. The task we propose is to use the analysis, the documentation, the story of photographs to catch **images of children in the act of experience and research** and which are generally images of intense work, rare happiness and marvellous processes of growth and enrichment (often these are silent, discreet, un-showy images, but sometimes overflowing with vitality and noise).

❋ ❋ ❋

67.77 Opening report for the 1977–78 school year, Reggio Emilia, August 1977 (transcript from the original cassette recordings)

> **Editor's note:** This wide-ranging presentation is Malaguzzi's 'opening report' at the beginning of the 1977–78 school year, made in the midst of a period of great turmoil in Italy.

[. . .] We feel the need for women's organisations to be more active on these issues (though this is open to opinion). Not so they become issues that are only connected with women's interests but because women's organisations exist and they are a political force and we would like to hear them on these issues.

It is obvious the democratic movement in general has lost several presences that it was capable of carrying along with it on these issues until a few years ago.

We don't believe there are times for discussing the *consultorio* and *scuola dell'infanzia* and social services, and then other times when you have to keep quiet. To our minds this idea corresponds to an absolutely elementary logic. We can't accept there is a time when women's work is considered important and other times when women have to step aside.

And perhaps what we need is a deeper analysis, [. . .] and this issue interests us. Why? Because we feel there is a deep re-arrangement taking place between social services, women, women in the family, parents in the family, children in [school] institutions and in the family; and we feel these crises and the economic difficulties the country is going through force us to review the fundamental issues of social services with great courage, without ever losing sight of their essential connotation.

[. . .]

Some things are already beginning to happen and we cannot stand by indifferent because Italian families use the services to help them in their daily lives, and to help them get by in economic and financial terms. We have to realise that facing the issue of social services on a political level will probably involve looking at a series of problematic areas that have never been resolved: the reform of general welfare in our country, the reform of health services, the reform of local finance. I think the subject of services is an arm and a tool for accelerating several processes in Italy.

We need to carefully analyse the document presented by the Region.

What is our point of view? Ours is the point of view of a group of workers inside these services. We have the feeling that if the institutions and above all the people who work in them had been consulted in time on these problems, this document might not look different but it would contain all the knowledge and interpretations of thousands and thousands of workers and young people who are present and living inside the institutions.

Here there has been no consulting at the preliminary level, nor does it seem there will be any re-examination, or discussion at the grass roots level any time soon, so [the discussion] on these issues, which in our opinion is extremely important, leaves out several facts and phenomena that ought immediately – immediately – to be brought back in.

We need to examine the costs of our schools, certainly. We have done that and several measures have already been taken. The document presented by the unions and the city administration is a confirmation of those measures. The problem now is to examine what the existence or non-existence of social services means for this country, what their role is, what the role of the workers in the services is, what is the role of services in the community, for the collective commuity, and above all what services mean in terms of the enormous political difficulties the country is facing.

There is a series of projects for reforming the *scuola materna* or *scuola dell'infanzia* and it would be as well to run through them and try to grasp (in a very hasty way) the terms and positions of different political parties on the problem of children's education, the problems of the *scuola dell'infanzia*.

How do the republicans [*Partito Repubblicano Italiano*, Italian Republican Party] conceptualise these issues, these facts? They think *scuola dell'infanzia* is a *scuola preparatoria* [preparatory school], a term which is not used completely by chance, because it has its own precise meaning. A school of preparation is a school that precedes and therefore has the task of preparing for. They believe attending school should be made compulsory from age five.

It is not unlikely that things will go in that direction, and so we need to critically review a series of conceptions and assertions we have made over recent years. So what are the risks? The risk is that we resolve the problem of five-year-olds but abandon the problems coming before (four, three, two and one-year-olds) and declare that we are satisfied with a service that is widespread but only one year's experience for children (the year before entering primary school). This concept completely contradicts certain beliefs we have: that children's education begins at birth, that there are differences between children at birth; that overcoming these differences is part of a long and difficult process we have to cultivate in the country's preschool institutions; that we have to give schools the conditions for creating equal educational and formative opportunities for all children. So clearly there are some problems in this Republican proposal, which we put forward based on a brief reading of the project.

Editor's note: Malaguzzi then considers the proposals of the DC and the PSI. He criticises the former especially for their plans on staffing, including the distinction drawn between teaching and support staff and the hierarchical nature of the roles envisaged. His criticism of the latter includes their proposals for larger schools, with six to ten classes.

Then there is the PCI project. The PCI project is the last one. I don't think it has even been presented yet (especially not in the *Camere*).[55] And yet here it is, a project exists, and it has been the subject of reflection and attention on our part and on the part of others.

This proposal does not talk so much about public schools, state schools, and local authority schools but about public schooling, [. . .] This word *public* means going in the direction, or thinking about going in the direction, of not automatically identifying schools either with state authority or local authorities but with a public management in which the state, the regions, and above all, local authorities or *comuni* are all present. We feel this to be the best formula as it allows the highest degree of organisation, of decentralised organisation, with the state, the regions and local authorities all active participants in different aspects.

In this PCI proposal there is a discussion of handicapped children's right not to be put in marginalised-marginalising classrooms and of eliminating special, differentiated classes. The proposal for the Law says literally, 'teachers for support activity', meaning it envisages support activity, guaranteed through the *Comune*'s local Health and Welfare Services. This means that the presence in schools of handicapped children is defined in a certain way, and ways of intervening are viewed and considered in a certain way with the provision of particular measures and tools for support when necessary.[56]

The proposal also includes the elimination of rigid class groups and an orientation towards flexible work groups (this is not a theme we feel indifferent to). You know we have been discussing this important theme for years I would say. It is a complex, very serious, problem.

However our view is that this idea [in the PCI proposal] is merely a response to *avant-garde* concepts and is really contradictory, because if we read the PCI proposals for reforming elementary school we realise that, although their proposals for *scuola dell'infanzia* include the progressive elimination of classrooms and the formation of flexible work groups, when children get to six and go to elementary school they enrol in classes again for the first two years. So they lose their chance of flexibility, and lose their previous experience (if they have had it) by returning to only one teacher; not the multiple teaching roles we would have if a project for flexible work groups were accepted. So this is an issue we need to treat very seriously, which can only be coherent and authentic if it is based on a concept of long-term continuity, and includes the concept of living together in education permanently carried out in flexible working groups.

However it is also absolutely unthinkable for small children (one-, two-, three-, four-, five- and six-years-old) to be moved about indiscriminately between several adult figures (who would probably be switched around for several negative reasons our system suffers). These children would not be capable of finding their identity, or a capacity for projection, or a sufficiently stable identity. Flexibility is an issue that can only be resolved when children have been able to construct sufficient internal personal stability; obviously after this time they are open to experiences of a multiple nature, and a more open nature.

Under the PCI proposals all staff would be state employed. All staff, including yourselves, would go to the state. The timetable would be thirty-five hours a week, with thirty-two hours of teaching and three hours for study, meetings and social management. The standard for schools is set at ninety children, with five teachers. Schools would open seven to ten hours a day. All state schools would transfer management to the local *comune*, which would also own the property and contents. Local authorities then, the *comuni*, would be the direct managers of an educational experience at the same time as owning it. This changeover of ownership is not merely a transfer, it is an acknowledgement of local authority's capacity, and legitimacy to intervene in decentralised matters.

Certainly, based on our experience I would say this project [the PCI proposal] is the most acceptable, or at least more connected with the type of experience we have realised to now.

We have some misgivings about some of the things we have tried to discuss. We have misgivings about five people with ninety children, which would not guarantee the equal functioning of different classrooms and different times of the day. If the school works for eleven hours we cannot see how two teachers can be together even for a short time in the day. They would greet each other on the doorstep, one going, the other coming.

There are some problems of this nature. There is no indication of the number of children per class. So we have to refer to reform for elementary school taken to Parliament by the PCI. In their proposal we find: the number of children is twenty-five; each pupil assigned to one class; the first two classes have only one teacher; classes that follow (be very careful) immediately involve multiple figures and break with the figure of the single teacher.[57] These include not only teachers of letters (Italian, language, etc.) and teachers of science subjects (maths, etc.), but also teachers of expressive activities (an issue we are interested in), music and singing teachers, and teachers of physical education. The proposal therefore envisages the co-presence of various professional qualities, which are capable – we hope – of forming a cohesive unit, which is not easy [. . .]

The last issue is handicapped children. We have to try and reflect during the course of these days together on the issue of handicapped children. We have a dispute that has not been concluded with the city administration and the unions.

For those of you who know the history and events tied up with the theory (political–cultural theory) and the practice, a very interesting book by Jervis has just come out.[58] In our city Jervis has made a very strong impression, which can still be felt today. He is a man with an extraordinary culture and his influence has gone beyond this province and affected a series of cultural aspects and issues that are international. What is important to understand [. . .] is his attempt to tell the story which started in Gorizia before it came here, and involved primary schools and the universities. There are some very interesting sources in the book, which can help us understand [. . .] a central problematic node of psychiatry which is: do we want to totally negate psychiatry or critically use psychiatry? This is still the central issue today. Towards psychiatry should we have an attitude of totally denying it, or should we have an attitude of using it critically?

Jervis acknowledges several large issues are still unresolved, that have to do with the subjectivity of health service workers, and the subjectivity of affected children and families; and he finally goes beyond the generalisations [and situations] where political problems come first and always first, ending up with declarations of an ideological nature without ever really getting inside the complexity of these extremely difficult and painful and suffering situations (like all the difficult situations of our existence).

[. . .]

What are our thoughts? I will try and sum up the essence of the discussions we have had during our experiences, so they are absolutely provisional attempts, but attempts where I think we manage to identify issues of definition, and therefore also issues of implementation and practice.

Handicapped children (in our opinion) are children who for different causes (the genesis of these causes is never separate from the moment of social and political–cultural definition) display a difficulty in development, in learning, and in socialisation. This means we are moving towards the distinctions that are more complex than those generally made in certain places. Not in all places.

What does this mean? It means that handicapped children present difficulties of different kinds, and therefore on different levels, and of different nature, and the matrix of these is very connected with social issues, but not exclusively. However it is part of a very complex and difficult process. They have difficulties, determined by fact, that have to do with physical mobility, which means the child's body, the child's physical state; or with their development (i.e. the gradients and rhythms of development of a biological character); or with learning (i.e. processes of knowledge acquisition and socialisation). What we want to underline is that this particular aspect is not disconnected from others, it is connected with all the others although it can signify, in quite a physical way, the difficulties that might affect a child already objectively and subjectively in difficulty, in issues of their relations with others, who may have other rhythms of development and other physical capacities, other capacities for learning and other capacities for socialisation. This kind of problem does not melt away, we cannot simplify it, it cannot be reduced and broken down in terms that are completely incongruous. Problems have to be faced with all their complexity and all their objective difficulties.

So, what responsibility does each one of us have? The need for a deep understanding of the singular situation in which this handicapped child lives. When children are challenged by the same illness, the same handicap, or suffer the same difficulty on a clinical level, no one has the permission to think they can be treated in the same way. The life story of each child – of their late development, or their difficulty – is a story defined, presented and constructed in unique processes which each child experiences as part of their own life experience (in the home, in the family, in the condominium garden, in their specific situation). This means we must go towards a constant analysis of issues connected with knowing the nature of this child's difficulties.

We need to arrive (this is another central issue) at developing intervention that is unified and does not merely affect the part or piece of the child most denoting a difficulty (as if a child could be taken apart and divided up in some way). It must be unified provision. And one of the primary, most privileged opportunities for this kind of unified provision is in schools, which are organised situations in children's lives, and where (if the action is well conducted) we can achieve the most advanced results – at least theoretically.

If we assert the need to re-constitute the child as a whole, even when they are in difficulty or suffering in some way or in some part; and if we confirm our idea of unified intervention involving the whole of the child, then it is no longer thinkable to intervene with the work of diversely qualified professionals (here is the technician, here is the doctor, here is the pedagogue, here is the orthopaedist, here is the speech therapist and so on) in non-integrated ways. We absolutely cannot design unified intervention if we do not work in unified ways with the various disciplines and with the practice of those disciplines. This means there is no situation of identifying a handicapped child that can be exclusive or only pertinent to one of the disciplines working with the child. We question what was recently stated in a health and social services document, which discusses exclusive situations with exclusive responsibilities for certain parts (the time of diagnosis belongs to these technicians, the time of intervention belongs to those other technicians), conceptually reconstructing the nodes Jervis and the new psychiatry has been trying to fight in recent years.

Where does all this lead us?

It leads us to theorise that there is no moment in our work with handicapped children, or with children in general, where fragmented intervention is tolerable.

We must know children together, putting together all our disciplines and the people who practice them; arrive at a project of shared intervention sharing the design of these interventions; we must activate the school situation as a dynamic situation, a particular situation for children's affairs; we must look for all the necessary equipment in schools, which means having all the tools as part of the dimension of school, the dimension of education. This is the great transition we must promote; the transition from therapy outside schools and therefore in differentiated marginalised conditions, to therapy activated in the richness of school normality, in the richness of the normality of socialising with other children.

[. . .]

You know that we have to decide together how to manage *tempo lungo*.[59] We have agreed with unions and city administration that by the end of September we will have an answer to all our questions; and also long before that, propose how schools will organise *tempo lungo*.

This means, in my opinion, every school should begin reflecting on how it intends to organise *tempo lungo* in the coming year. Ways of organising are not neutral for parents who wish or choose to have their children participate in *tempo lungo*. I think there is a meeting on the issue on the 7th [of September] with the *Comitati di Scuola e Città*. Which means by the 7th you must already have come to a fully considered decision, school by school, on how to organise. You know there are two [possibilities]: *tempo lungo* for the *tempo continuato* and *tempo lungo* for the *tempo spezzato*.[60]

We believe schools will evaluate the quality of choosing one or the other in a serious and committed way and be capable of understanding it is still the child at the centre of the demand, while bearing in mind we cannot deny ourselves or forget ourselves: we are a presence too. But we have to try and reconcile these two apparently contradictory requirements in the most decent way.

[. . .]

I'd like to comment on what these three or four days mean. During them we will be working together to try and understand a series of important issues. They are important because they represent themes we find in our work project, but above all they will be important if we can all make them into constant reference points (this is the effort each one of us must make). So we will proceed with addressing these different themes in a serious, committed way, exploring them more deeply, but we will also try to constantly connect them together even when apparently they seem separate. We will re-connect them with each other, but above all we will re-connect them (within the limits of our capability) with more general political affairs, which is the context where our themes, our issues are situated.

This discussion includes an attempt to construct material for reflection on affairs of a political, cultural and pedagogical nature, of a general nature and a local nature. We want above all to try and understand what preschool institutions (the *nidi*, the *scuole materne*, the *scuole dell'infanzia*) mean, but also what families, children, men, women and society as a whole mean; what the schools have solved and not, and the issues on which we urgently need to take a position.

It is an attempt to develop a deeper understanding of the general situation we and our educational experience are situated in, with our specific nature that is the result of a history no one has invented and which in part was contingent upon historical, cultural and political situations of a certain kind. And research together for a new and different position in the frame of general politics, which influences larger problems of a political nature, touching deeply on issues of the education of the individual, and in particular the education of children.

We have also tried a deeper investigation of themes that have to do with the education of children's thinking. That is to say on the whole of children's education today, in a very particular situation, that categorically requires us to analyse, with more commitment and more seriousness, what the effective needs of children are today and what kinds of response we have given children, what kinds of response children expect of us, and what responsible reflections we can have on such delicate important problems.

We have identified another important theme for investigation and reflection that has to do with three very connected constants: the child, the family and society. Because we all feel – in ways that are confused to a greater or lesser degree – the situation is certainly not conducive to having many clear ideas in one's head. In any case we feel today that several problematic areas affecting society as a whole strongly influence all aspects of culture that affect children, society and the family; how they relate to each other and the ways they refer to each other.

Another theme we will be trying to understand is the meaning of the educator's role today, in a situation where concrete experience requires further reflection. What is our task inside the institutions [*scuole* and *nidi*] regarding children, regarding parents, regarding expectations, regarding a series of problematic areas that our contribution could help to unravel? We do not consider ourselves as an appendage that is cut off from politics, or cut off from the economy, cut off from small or large events that are often defined rather euphemistically as 'outside' our schools. We know the moment has come for us to resume a more pertinent evaluation of issues that have to do with the role of this profession; the physical reality, the psychological reality, and the cultural reality of this role, with the level of culture and politics educators can have today.

Another aspect is to try and understand more, to dig deeper than we have done, on problems to do with the organisation of work at a very delicate time, above all for this aspect (perhaps we will return to this during the course). Addressing issues of work organisation means trying to harmonise it with all the other issues we are going to address together, trying to thoroughly talk through the organisational requirements of our work, so that it is work we believe in (no small issue), work where we manage to find our identity, and where children also manage to find their own identity. So that we become an experience where families feel their needs, requests and demands are respected. Certainly this means going with a fine tooth comb through a series of delicate, extremely delicate issues. And we will come back to this theme of delicacy and these aspects during our days together.

[. . .]

Editor's note: Malaguzzi moves on to discuss the Italian welfare state, which he criticises for guaranteeing access for all in theory but failing to remove 'shameful causes and differences', for being perfect in theory but inefficient in practice. A series of important facts are transforming society and family, and the ways families actually exist are distant both from the old patriarchal family model and the simplified nuclear family 'beloved of sociologists'. He notes that enormous amounts of money are transferred from one place to another: both directly and indirectly by means of services, such as schools, health and social services. The different types of family income, both direct and indirect, have transformed and upturned relations between man and woman, husband and wife, family and children, family and relatives. Untaxed, 'black' work and enormous quantities of overtime all have repercussions on the life of the family. He asks what all this has brought about. A great increase in private consumption, extreme mobility and a fast changing reality in terms of needs, habits and tastes.

In our country the lesson connected with building a welfare state, as far as this has been possible, is that it has required (and still requires) a greater deployment of energy, which means a greater deployment of waste. So it is easy for critics (especially in other countries when they refer to Italy) to speak of a country where the welfare model is probably the most perfected on a theoretical level, the most wasteful on a concrete level, the most expensive as a matter of fact, and also the least efficient of all countries.

[. . .]

[In society] there has been an accentuation of external aspects, which is not a minor matter, and we need to evaluate this for the good things about it and the bad, however it is something new. Certainly this extroversion brings a range of aspects and issues that affect all individuals profoundly, and inevitably also affect children, with their children's dimension and measure.

There has been an accentuation of emulating and competition. People attempting to work with problems that are part of education, and who work with our experience of education, in a way that is alternative to emulation, individualism and singleness, cannot feel indifferent to a problem of this kind.

There has been an accentuation of philosophies that attempt to push individuals to live above all in the present, to progressively demolish any philosophy that takes a long-term political and historical perspective in any way. The appearance of the young philosophers, the French philosophers, and the success they have enjoyed recently is a response to this. There is a total negation of long-term philosophies, a total negation of long-term politics, a total negation of the advance of projects, and a desire for sudden and absurd renewal that turns the world upside down. We are in an extremely complex, and extremely difficult situation, in which I think our way of working must be continuously examined.

The significant aspects of *nidi* and *scuole dell'infanzia* are situated in this reality. Each one of us feels we are faced with a turning point and we have felt it in several examples of objective conditions: the disputes we have had, the issues with unions, issues with the [city] administration, issues in our place of work, the relations between us, the relations between us and our work, children and families. We have been feeling all these things for some time now, and we feel them as something inside, something for which we can no longer find the autonomous, reasonably satisfactory response, and commitment, of some years ago.

The sensation is very very widespread, less in our city than other cities (and we will speak of this too), but even in a region like ours we see the phenomenon of young workers in the region's preschool services abandoning, dropping out, fleeing towards other employment, and other kinds of commitment; the level is still hardly noticeable (but it is there).

This is something new and we are only just feeling the first signs. The fact that a region like ours – where the issue of educating young children was taken up as a commitment of a political and moral nature, of an ethical nature and with great commitment – is beginning to see these signs of disaggregation and flight from the services means we lack the capacity, or the possibility, of identifying enough with our work conceptually and educationally. So our attention for these aspects and phenomena must be very high.

[. . .]

Editor's note: Malaguzzi now discusses the recent history of *nidi* in Italy. He refers to Law 1044, passed in 1971, in which after a decade of campaigning, especially by women's organisations and political parties, the State accepted responsibility for services for children under 3 years. He reminds his audience that the Law led to a five year plan to open 3,800 *nidi*, but that a year after the end of the plan, only 221 *nidi* are up and running, 431 under construction and 289 with contracts out for tender; and that a number of regions, mostly in the South of Italy, despite having money, have built no *nidi* (e.g. Abruzzo, Molise, Puglia, Calabria, Sicily, Campania, Sardinia). By contrast, the region of Emilia-Romagna already has 174 *nidi*. This points, he thinks, to social, political and cultural differences between regions, and is a 'grotesque demonstration of inability' to respond to commitments and to new laws. He adds that the *nido* comes after other problems have been solved, it cannot go before and that without resolving basic problems at the foundations of society, it is meaningless to speak of 'education', of the 'child'.

At this point, in our opinion, there is an equally important assertion, which is this. At this time, when we are being asked to critically re-evaluate our whole educational experience (rightly so I believe) no-one (not even us, especially not us) is authorised to separate topics from one another, to address the theme of school services as a separate theme, as a sector; as if it were possible to deal with the important theme of social services in our country by separating it from all other aspects of an economic, civil and administrative order. This is a test of our ability to always hold the discourse firmly on this connected level and never let anyone in through a sectoral pathway, or through a separate corridor.

The other comment it is fair for us to make is that the history of these last years has taught us something (certainly we started with more privileged background situations than other countries). I think we have to acknowledge it has been the cities and the *comuni* who have understood and sensed their cultural and political role in relation to the services, in relation to the *nidi* and *scuole materne*, in relation to the education of children, and in relation to family demand. This capacity of the *comuni* and the cities, to constantly test themselves, accepting their responsibilities – certainly not only financial – but their great political and cultural responsibilities, has made it possible for the *comuni* to progress to a consciousness of cultural and educational issues, even those of a pedagogical nature, and this has made it possible to raise the sensibility of public opinion on problems of education, the problems of schools, and problems of children's education. What I mean is, this direct practice in the field, more than anything else, gives us the possibility and the capacity for promoting, for consolidating, for enriching the quality and the breadth of our work.

❊ ❊ ❊

68.77 Invitation to parents, workers and citizens to attend a public meeting on children and the *asilo nido*, December 1977

[Cover Page]

20.30 Wednesday 14 December, 1977

SALA DEL TRICOLORE
(Municipal Town Hall)

Let's Discuss Children and the *Nido***

THE INVITATION IS TO PARENTS, TO WORKERS, TO CITIZENS

[Inside Page]

- Children at the *Nido*: their problems, parents' problems, *nido* workers' problems
- Education in the family and education in institutions

- The false problem of children's spontaneity
- Prejudices about children
- Gratification and frustration in children
- When and how children communicate and express themselves without words
- How adults change children and how children change adults
- Children's socialisation
- When does intelligence begin in children, how is it expressed, and how can it grow?

Speakers

Renzo Vianello
(Lecturer in Psychology, Padua University)

Francesco Tonucci
(Researcher, CNR *Consiglio Nazionale delle Ricerche* in Rome)

Loris Malaguzzi
(Psycho-pedagogista, Director of 'ZEROSEI' journal)

1978

69.78 Article from the magazine *L'ente locale e i servizi sociali e sanitari* [Local authority and health and social services], Year IV, No.1–2, ESI, January–February 1978

> **Editor's note:** Malaguzzi wrote this article at a time of widespread criticism of children under 3 years attending *nidi*, criticism that he later wrote was driven by 'the rediscovered writings of John Bowlby and Rene Spitz . . . [and] the resistance of the Catholic world, which feared risks and pathologies in a breakdown of the family' (Malaguzzi, 2012, p.39).

The need to overcome separation between the contents and organisation of services

Loris Malaguzzi

There has been no exchange of experience or deep exploration in our country on *scuola per l'infanzia* issues and this has a negative impact on the difficulties inherent in our work given the delicacy and importance of our reference point, which is the dimension of children and families.

These are also times of great difficulty on cultural and pedagogical levels. There can be no doubt a series of conservative moves is being attempted through Europe and these are particularly pronounced in relation to the *asilo nido* and the *scuola materna*.

The time has come to face up to reflection, in the form of discussions and probably disagreements, on a series of issues, themes and 'reminders', in democratic worker circles.

The issue of the *asilo nido* that families, mothers and women feel they need is probably the most sensitive issue in Italy today; political forces seem to have taken sides on the problem but the capacity for really engaging with the subject, for a continuous heightened level of involvement, is missing. Those of us who work in these institutions have felt a sudden fall in ferment, attention and interest, and often we find ourselves alone in dealing with the problems we face, which are by no means simple.

This is a problem that also affects our managing authorities, the regions and *comuni*, especially smaller ones, who are being asked to make serious choices without valid guidelines even of a cultural kind. Even in Nordic countries, where pedagogical literature has produced images of exemplary and emblematic situations, changes in the political context began some time ago to unleash a ferocious campaign against institutions for young children.

This issue concerns us, because the idea of exchanging points of view on theoretical and philosophical levels, is something that defines both the right and the left. We need to propose themes and issues that can be discussed with the contradictions and paradox [of different viewpoints] and where final results correspond in some way whether you start from the right or the left. This means we have to address a series of issues and experiences that will rapidly create interest here in our country. We have many examples; it is enough just to travel to some regions to find an obstinate resistance to the *asilo nido* with families and mothers struggling to find the courage to take their children to a *nido*.

So we must be on the offensive and carry out a large campaign, and not wait to be forced onto the defensive, which is why we need to be culturally equipped and request contributions from the centres that produce cultural elaboration,[61] we need to define the issue in terms of research and investigation on a university level, and identify specific situations that offer intense discussion here in our country too.

In places where *nidi* exist we need to be capable of presenting experiences taking place inside them, because there is a serious lack of reference materials. And we also suffer the handicap of a psycho-pedagogical culture that stubbornly continues to concentrate on the adult figure, particularly mothers, and therefore creates an obstacle to serious investigation of the attitudes we need to produce in our institutions – on relations, relationships, psychology and pedagogy, and we have to do this if we want them to stand up to vigorous comparisons, not the simplistic kind or that lead to easy simplifications.

We cannot always reduce reflection on the *asilo nido* to merely administrative issues, as often happens. Inside the institutions we must create a capacity for constant exchange on all issues, including economic and political, especially when these suggest or attempt reducing or lowering the quality of our experience, which instead should be defended through open exchange that could be wider.

There is the problem of costs, and I think we can insist it is not possible to continue along the lines we have followed until now. This poses the problem of redefining spending and the contents that have a significantly social nature, not just for direct users. We have to reject the logic that constantly separates how learning is organised from how services are organised.

This is a political battle and it has to be articulated in specific ways, but we must be aware of the risks of separating interventions.

If we had been more capable of mobilising around conceptual coherency between preschool institutions, perhaps today we would not have built *scuole materne* and *asili nido* in separate structures, which reproduces the same logic of having the mental health *consultorio* [clinic] in one place and the paediatrician's *consultorio* in another.

It is no longer possible to think of the *asilo nido* as a building that takes children and keeps them there from morning to evening. We know that the amount of time children spend in an institution is highly significant for our work and the responsibility and co-responsibility we take.

This means being capable of expressing the contradictions we experience in our work, and asking for contributions, not only from society but from political forces and union movements, in order to resolve them.

One more problem this raises is opening hours, and this implies several issues; the institution's relations with families, and with the times, rhythms and conditions of employment and production in our country. This is a theme requiring very troubling but necessary reflections of a pedagogical nature, but they cannot be excluded from our overall reflections.

※ ※ ※

70.78 Press release about a professional development session for *nido* workers, February 1978

MUNICIPIO DI REGGIO NELL'EMILIA

SCHOOLS AND SOCIAL SERVICES DIVISION
SCUOLE COMUNALI DELL'INFANZIA AND ASILI NIDO
Via dell'Abbadessa 8

17 February 1978

To the City Press
To local radio and television services

AGGIORNAMENTO MEETINGS
FOR *NIDO* WORKERS

Starting at 8.30 this morning (Saturday 18 February) an ***aggiornamento*** meeting will be held in the Students' Residence Hall in Via dell'Abbadessa, for workers in municipal *asili nido*.

The themes of the meeting will be:

'SOME CRITICISM OF CONCEPTS OF CHILDREN'S EGO-CENTRISM'
'PSYCHOLOGICAL AND CULTURAL PROBLEMS OF FEMALE WORKERS IN THE *ASILO NIDO*'
'ASPECTS OF PERCEPTION IN VERY SMALL CHILDREN'
'HOW MOTHERS TALK TO CHILDREN'

these will be conducted respectively by

Dott.ssa CARLA RINALDI
Dott.ssa PINA TROMELLINI
Dott.ssa MARIA PIA DESTEFANI
Dott. LORIS MALAGUZZI

❋ ❋ ❋

71.78 Programme for a two day seminar for *nido* workers, July 1978

[Cover Page]

Comune di Reggio Emilia
Assessore for Schools and Social Services

SALA DEGLI SPECCHI
Teatro Municipale
10–11 July 1978

OBSERVATIONS IN THE *NIDO*
STUDY SEMINAR
8.30–12.30 / 15–18

[Inside Page]

THE IMPORTANCE OF OBSERVATION IN THE EDUCATIONAL WORK OF THE *NIDO*
Introductory notes by LORIS MALAGUZZI

Talks and discussions on:

1.

The birth and adventure of children's names, in the family and the *nido*: interpreting their meanings.
Children and mirrors (collected situations).
Speakers: ANGELA DODI, TIZIANA GUIDETTI for the Via Guasco, Pradarena, and Picasso *nidi* collectives.

2.

Experiences of perception and cognition in children 16–36 months, through games of recognition, logical pairing and tactile recognition.
Speakers: MARZIA MARANI, ANGELA PREGREFFI for the Allende and Sole *nidi* collectives.

3.

Observations on multiple aspects of reading, comprehension and visual image memory in the *asilo nido*.
Speakers: ELUCCIA FORGHIERI, LORENZA RABITTI for the Arcobaleno and Genoeffa Cervi *nidi* collectives.

4.

Variations in children's behaviour related to variations in adult behaviour.
Speakers: ALFA STROZZI, CAROLINA CANTARELLI for the Alice and Pierino Rivieri *nidi* collectives.

Communications

by ANGELA PINOTTI and IVANA ROSSI, 'Autonomy in *lattante* infants [3 to 9 months in September]' and 'Improving *lattante* children's spaces'.
by PATRIZIA PANCIROLI and MARIA PIA DESTEFANI, 'Children with their own images in photography and their own creations'.

Observation through video recording

The methodology of observation. Communication in children aged 0–3 years (documents video-recorded at the CRESAS in Paris).[62]

Comments by <u>LAURA BONICA</u>

Verbal and non-verbal communication in structured situations – eating and playing – and possible errors in adult behaviour (documents video-recorded in the *Nidi* Pezzana, Meloni, Albertario in Carpi).[63]

Comments by <u>NADIA BULGARELLI</u>

1979

72.79 Programme for a seminar for workers in municipal schools, July 1979

[Cover Page]

Comune di Reggio Emilia
Assessore for Schools and Social Services

SALA DEGLI SPECCHI
Teatro Municipale
7–12–13 July 1979

OBSERVATIONS
STUDY SEMINAR ON THE EXPERIENCE OF CHILDREN IN
MUNICIPAL *NIDI* AND *SCUOLE DELL'INFANZIA*
8.30–12.30

[Inside Page]

PROGRAMME

- The methodology and ends of observation: Dott. Loris Malaguzzi

NIDI

- The interactions of *lattanti* [3 to 9 months in September] (CANTARELLI CAROLINA, PANCIROLI PATRIZIA)
- On [children's] first mark-making (RIFREDDI TIZIANA, SONCINI CARLA)
- Interference or intervention or interaction and possible modes of adult behaviour in the *Nido* (ALFA STROZZI, PAOLA FONTANESI)
- Behaviour and verbal interactions in 2–3 year-old children while eating lunch (MARCO FIBROSI, CELMENTINA GHIZZONI, ANTO-NELLA COCCHI)

- Different behaviours of families and children at the *Nido* entrance (GUIDETTI TIZIANA, LUCIA GATTI, GIULIANA CAMPANI)
- Perceptions of shapes and colours in children aged 20–36 months (RITA MONTECCHI)

SCUOLE DELL'INFANZIA

- Children's operations with colour (MARA DAVOLI)
- The images of school in children's families, in a particular reality (TINA BERTANI)
- Experiences with water (MARA BARBIERI)
- Ideas from the *camera oscura* (MIRELLA RUOZZI) with projected slides
- Opportunity in classroom work (VEA VECCHI) with projected slides
- Notes on reading and writing (PAOLA CASALI, LAILA MARANI) with projected slides

❅ ❅ ❅

73.79 Excerpt from an interview in *l'Unità*, 8 December 1979

Editor's note: *l'Unità* is an Italian left-wing newspaper, founded by Antonio Gramsci in 1924, one year after Mussolini came to power; it was the official newspaper of the PCI and more recently supported the Democratic Party. It closed temporarily in 2014, following financial problems.

In centres for early childhood in the Comune of Reggio Emilia [introductory headline]

A large experience of democratic commitment [main headline]

An interview with Loris Malaguzzi, pedagogical coordinator of the Comune's preschool services – Approximately 5,000 people involved in renewal of Comitati di Scuola e Città.

[. . .]

What is the significance of renewing Comitati di Scuola e Città in preschool institutions?

[. . .]

What are the values accompanying the theme of participation in these first institutions [schools] for children?

Participation (and this is the value of collegial bodies) remains the same as always, a sort of challenge to society (as well as immediate, real, progressive change) when a political governing class does not want it, does not include it and does not replicate it either on a level of social organisation or on the level of custom and culture.

The meaning of this political event [committee renewal] lies in this contradiction, and gives us an indication of what kind of difficulty participation and social management (two complementary terms) encounter.

There is a sense that the theme of participation will be one of politics' important themes in coming years. Families who bring their children to the *nido* and *scuola* have several wishes and requests they put forward. They want reassurance that the services are good ones. They want to understand more; as if they are asking for help with problems increasingly difficult to manage in the home.

The same requests come from teachers but the other way round. They want to understand more about what happens, why it happens (to them and to children), what happens in the family and outside it. There is a discovery of a mutual incompleteness, as if the profession of teacher and the profession of family need to take a new look at themselves and re-construct, not through a formal and token continuity with one another, but through more intensive meetings, exchanges of viewpoint and commitment. On the *nido* and *scuola dell'infanzia* level this is the new fact we need to deal with and interpret.

We have very little time, less and less time, and schools and families have to rely on the quality of the meetings for this new idea to work.

No date given

74.ND Slogan distributed to the municipal schools, no date

Editor's note: Although not signed, this slogan was drafted by Malaguzzi, in campaigning mode.

THIS SCHOOL COSTS THE RIGHT PRICE

IN A COUNTRY WHERE OFTEN RESOURCES ARE
THROWN AWAY
AND WASTE IS PROMOTED OR TOLERATED

NO   TO SAVING AT THE EXPENSE OF CHILDREN
NO   TO BETRAYING THE RIGHTS AND NEEDS OF CHILDREN
AND FAMILIES
NO   TO EXPLOITING SCHOOL WORKERS
NO   TO REDUCING QUALITY OR ACCEPTING SURVIVAL WITH
LOW QUALITY *SCUOLE DELL'INFANZIA*

❋ ❋ ❋

75.ND Poem written by Loris Malaguzzi, no date

Editor's note: This is a shorter and earlier version of the poem 'No way. The hundred is there' that was to become famous. The poem is written in capitals in the original text.

CHILDREN HAVE A HUNDRED LANGUAGES: THEY ROB
THEM OF NINETY NINE
SCHOOL AND CULTURE
WORK TO SEPARATE
BODIES-MINDS
MAKING THEM THINK WITHOUT THEIR BODY
AND ACT WITHOUT THEIR HEAD
MAKING CONFLICT BETWEEN
PLAY AND WORK
REALITY AND FANTASY
SCIENCE AND IMAGINATION
INSIDE AND OUTSIDE

★

THE SELF PORTRAIT GAME
I LOOK FOR MYSELF TO FIND MYSELF
AND TO HOLD MY HAND

★

THE PAINTING GAME
I TALK
I TELL THE STORY
THAT I INVENT
FOR ME, FOR YOU,
FOR US, FOR ALL OF YOU

★

THE WOODWORK GAME
HEADS THINK
THEN
HANDS SPEAK
ONE CREATIVE THOUGHT GENERATES ANOTHER

★

THE MUSIC GAME
SOUNDS TOO

CAN BE GENERATED
BY THE IMAGINATIVE
USE OF REASON

★

THE SCULPTURE GAME
REINVENTING THINGS
TO INVENT SOMETHING OTHER

★

THE PRINTING GAME
FOR TELLING
WHO I LIKE
THE THINGS I LIKE

★

THE DRESSING UP GAME
I AM
I WAS
I NO LONGER AM
I NO LONGER AM
I WAS
I AM

★

THE PUPPET GAME
PUPPETS
FOR THINGS
I WOULD SAY
THAT I WOULD NOT SAY
THAT I WOULD DO
THAT I WOULD NOT DO
FOR MAKING POSSIBLE
WHAT IS NOT
AND IMPOSSIBILE
WHAT IS

❋ ❋ ❋

76.ND New responsibilities for *Comitati di Gestione*, no date

Editor's note: There is no date on this document, but it was written by Malaguzzi after 1977, possibly in 1978. Nor is it clear for whom or why the document was produced.

The proposal of entrusting *Comitati di Gestione* [Management Committees] in *Asili Nido* and *Scuole Comunali dell'Infanzia* with the direct management of catering is intended to achieve a series of objectives and results.

a   Adding this important responsibility to the *Comitati*'s range of tasks high-lights the functions of participation, intervention and autonomy. It is a task the *Comitati*, with their experience and their real willingness and capacities, guarantee they are capable of carrying out.
b   Bringing families closer to the experience in schools is conducive to better and increased control of the quality of dietary ingredients and how they are prepared, above all the weekly menu will be richer in meat.
c   It brings a significant saving in the cost of procuring foodstuffs as we have managed to obtain quotas of meat, oil and butter from AIMA[64] (other *comuni* have already obtained these).
d   Thanks to the expected savings, families' monthly contributions will be as low as possible (savings from the project are expected to allow *Comitati di Gestione* to cover the cost or most of the cost of buying educational materi-als and materials for school use).

Detailed analysis where this is possible seems to indicate savings of 30 per cent, especially with the AIMA agreement. This is a saving of approximately 57 million *lire* per year, based on overall expenses of 190 million in 1977 for purchasing foodstuffs.
   [. . .]

※ ※ ※

77.ND Draft of a lecture, no date

> **Editor's note:** This document has no place or date attached to it. However, the fact Malaguzzi refers to a book by Howard Gruber, not published in English until 1974, suggests the document dates from the second half of the 1970s. It is possible that Malaguzzi was preparing this lecture for a professional development meeting with teachers from the municipal schools. The original was completely unpunctuated.

The education of logic and thought

[. . .] [W]e will try to give our version of certain issues, but it is only one of the possible versions we could give and the word 'end' has not yet been written.
   [. . .]
[We] need to try and understand what lies underneath the surface of differ-ent civilisations, the ways in which different civilisations express their philoso-phies and different cultures, and their different cultural and political situations, understand whether the issue of school and therefore the issue of education and

of children's formation, and the issue of educating thought, evolve in totally similar ways. [That is] if we accept as true that more than one philosophy exists in the world, and that there are several ideologies, with several philosophical, ideological, cultural and political organisations, and that each of these cultural organisations in reality has sub-organisations acting in them, given that no organisation is monolithic enough to rigidly forbid the possibility of different currents existing side by side (this is not a problem that is dead, it is still alive today). When we discuss and deal with them on a general level we become aware of an essential prerequisite in order for thinking to have its own progress, its own development, and its own evolution in as free a way as possible: it must be made possible for thinking to explore freely. I do not think we can get away from a matrix of this kind.

An extraordinarily interesting study has recently been made by Gruber.[65] It is a very exciting historical examination of delays in the rhythm of the development of thinking. The topic fits because we have Piaget's entire philosophy and frame here [today]. Certainly Piaget is a necessary point of reference but one on which we need to make a series of critiques, and we will attempt to do that, for example by trying to understand the thinking of Bruner[66] who comes to us from an American civilisation, an American culture in a certain mould with a certain historical origin, and certain qualities related to the fabric of its society and its relations with production, property and the concept of liberty. What about European thinking though; or the thinking of Luria, Vygotsky, Leontiev,[67] who I think have translated issues currently existing in the Soviet Union in the most significant ways for us. So we have different fields that are totally removed from each other and where we necessarily have to go and dig down. Here inevitably we will find fundamental differences on a cultural level and therefore on the level of organising schools and above all organising thought.

I would like to return to the issue of Piaget's stages of evolution which, as Sergio has said, start with the sensory-motor stage, go on to the representational or pre-operational period, the operational period, and the formal period. First of all we have a sequence of this kind in individual evolution, and if we accept this we have to understand why we accept it. It seems from various investigations that certain aspects of Piaget's hypotheses can be credited with being universal, so where do the fundamental differences lie? They lie in the rates of development of these stages and therefore the ways the stages develop. Do we sometimes find accelerations? Are accelerations something that is possible? Can external action stimulate an individual and accelerate their processes of growth? If these things are possible then how can the action of education be carried out? Is it right to accelerate certain cognitive structures that belong to the child and to the individual? Is this also consistent with concepts of health? Is acceleration something which is objectively beneficial to children from the point of view of health? Because this might be the risk; it may be that acceleration is something adults are especially interested in. You understand this? It might be adults above all, and it is easy to find examples: how many mothers, and how many fathers do we see with a weakness for immediately vaunting how precocious their child is, both in physical development. . . .

Editor's note: The remainder of this sentence is missing.

This is where the baby foods, the vitamins, and the homogenised baby foods connect up. This is where the market forces and giant companies make their grand entry and become established. So as we can see, it is a good thing to talk about [children's developmental] processes but clearly we should never forget their close relation with other processes we have been taught to see as un-related and separate. The fact is they are intimately connected. So now we have to make an effort to recover the whole rather than accepting separation and divisions. Again there is much discussion needed on this.

There are some very important issues. For example if we briefly look at the United States, [. . .] American psychology and pedagogy took a great leap forwards in 1958 after the Soviet Union launched a Sputnik[68] into space. It was an earthquake! The Soviet Union launched a Sputnik into space and America, which considered itself to be a highly technologically developed nation (with reason I think) was surprised, appalled, humiliated by this great space exploit, and they immediately tried to remedy the situation by summoning all their possible resources and trying to put them together. They wanted to look at what American education and pedagogy had been doing on the level of education, on the level of professional development, and on the level of educating younger generations. Obviously they had been doing things pretty badly if they hadn't made possible the technical prowess achieved elsewhere.

So there was a great revolutionising of American pedagogy at that time. All the American educationalists were summoned, and the psychologists were all brought together, all the sociologists were summoned, and the scientists were summoned, and the mathematicians were summoned. It was one of the greatest meetings ever held of the best American minds and the concrete point all of them had to investigate and research into was how to critically revise the pedagogical methods that had been in use until that time. Identify the mistakes that were being made, understand the reasons for them, and try to understand and intuit the innovations that were necessary for educating individuals. I should say 'privileged individuals' in inverted commas, above all; those individuals called upon to tackle and resolve problems at the highest level, the great problems of technology, the great problems of leaders in American culture.

Good then, well what came of this? Bruner came of it and it might be interesting to connect Bruner immediately with the great figure of Dewey because this is where Bruner comes from. American pedagogy and American philosophy – at least the best of America – identified with Dewey's thinking for many years. I remember – but perhaps you won't – that after 1950, in around 1956 and 1957, Italian journals were all discussing Dewey in some way, either in dialectical or highly polemical terms. The Marxist journals were all full of debate on the thinking of this great and extraordinary figure, and perhaps we need to rediscover him again today.

So then what does Bruner maintain? He maintains it is necessary to fight '*nozionismo*'.[69] First of all, let me say this to my mind is a sacrosanct issue and we are agreed with him on this. That is to say, we need to fight the idea of simple information as a summary of facts, data and events; and, for example, try to go beyond the traditional stages of maths and maths learning. We need to start with a perception of a number through its graphical form, how we draw it (and not only graphical), and slowly going on to what the meanings of numbers are, to the topological meanings, and then on to initial numerical operations, and then classification and serialisation work, and so on. And, as Bruner says, try to draw out the ideas and original structures that exist in every specific [discipline].

This opens up a large problem, which has not yet been resolved. It is a fine thing to say education must be a whole, that it should be capable of weaving individual disciplines closely together and moving towards their meeting in a wholeness. However, if it is true each single discipline has its own spirit and its own specificity, the risk is that the quality of these individual disciplines then becomes lower. For me personally the great problem today is not how to re-formulate situations from the past in opposite terms, but how to move towards a form of renewal that attempts to interweave the single disciplines and make them interact in a way that has never been done before in learning; at the same time as allowing each discipline to have its own specific itineraries and journeys of progress so that it returns to us with what it has found. We are proposing something in very uncertain terms, which does not envisage abandoning specific disciplines but at the same time does not want to exalt them; something that would like to have the disciplines penetrating each other and reciprocally enriching each other. And then with this constant fusing and contamination, and from the dialogue between one specific area and another, culture would have a more holistic and unified image of itself. To my mind this is the great issue, and it is an issue that is not without political, economic and social repercussions. Certainly it would have these!

For a comparison let us take Bruner's position, which is typically American, as an example. I am retuning to this because I went off at a tangent earlier. Well, things aren't always straight and linear.

What Bruner says is, that's enough of teaching facts, we have to go in the direction of teaching structures, from where we get structuralism. What do we mean by the word structure? We mean an entity that is composed of different elements that are capable of co-existing with each other, capable of being together, and which are characteristic of a certain discipline. This is not a simple concept; however we feel that a language [like maths], and the learning of a language, has its own intrinsic and specific way of moving and acting. Maths moves around in an area that is contaminated by other languages in several ways, but it definitely has certain typical aspects of its own. We are capable of understanding that different forms of expression, expression through drawing, through painting, through art and so on are not completely unrelated, but we also understand they are specific, and that each has its own cultural matrix and its own cultural connotations.

So where does Bruner's defect lie? After he has discovered all these things he continues to believe that structures are inside the individual disciplines, as if they were frozen inside them. And even though he says we must abandon *nozionismo* and reach the structures, what he means by structure is a sort of distinctive hallmark inside each single discipline, as if it were the discipline itself that generates the structure – which is not true. And what Bruner does in this way is to keep things separate, because a wider definition [. . .], a definition that brought in sociological, political and evolutionary issues, on the levels of culture and politics, would be too risky and too dangerous. So if we follow Bruner's thinking we go directly to the sophisticated outline of separate individual matrices. And on a social level this means that people who have money, have money and those who do not, do not. You understand this? What I mean is that power on an economic level is not up for exploration or analysis, it has to be accepted as it is, because each human situation has its own self-generated matrix, which has produced itself and the situation.

Now you understand it cannot be true that the structure of a discipline is generated by the discipline itself, in an uncontaminated way, because instead it is generated by a multiplicity of influences. Human culture is certainly all like this. When all science as Newton had conceived of it exploded in a physical and clamorous way when it was confronted with Einstein's new hypotheses, then everything collapsed. It wasn't just the structuralism of matter, and of science, or of a discipline, it was the entire conception [of the world] that completely collapsed.

Then again we have Piaget, who gives us these elements, or stages, or evolutionary steps, in the individual and in the child. Again he avoids examining the external social and cultural influences and whether we accept the stages or not, and Piaget admits this himself, we cannot single out forces in the individual, in the child's school life or family life, as contributing to rates of development. [. . .] We have to always bring all the factors that could stimulate, or inversely stimulate (stimulation doesn't go just in one direction, it goes in more than one) into Piaget's structures and their rates of evolution. And clearly we must also take into account the history of an individual's evolution, but how?

If we can imagine we are in a sort of laboratory; let us suppose a child still has pre-operative thinking and is a child acting with very low, very infantile logic, not to fault the child of course, absolutely not. This is the child's condition, and we on our part would like to accelerate the child's learning processes and get on to the stage that follows. On a pedagogical level we try and do our best: we let the child have the necessary opportunities; we stimulate the child with words and images, and through the opportunities we offer, and we try to get the child to achieve the second stage as quickly as possible. This is what we do consciously or not and whether we see it clearly or not. I think it is clear that in our schools and in our work we have a tendency to act in compliance with this type of expectation and with this type of end. The problem is that as we proceed based on education and pedagogy's refined techniques, there are two worlds, one inside the child and the other inside us, and these two worlds are not apparently part of our relationship; and yet they have a deep bearing on us and on the child, on the relation between us and the child, and on the relationship between the child and their family.

Gruber is the first [. . .] to explore the issue of time, and the question of how long it takes to achieve a positive evolution. In an exemplary and terrifying documentation he analyses certain historical facts. For example he takes Galileo's entire story: he discovers all the notes Galileo made, and Galileo's letters, the notes he made in the margins of books he was reading, and in the little notebooks he kept as a sort of intimate diary. Above all he takes Darwin and diligently tracks him from the age of twenty. He tries to comb through all his notes and letters and he realises that Galileo, but more especially Darwin (for whom he has a personal weakness and affection) both consciously delayed the public announcement of their discoveries, he discovers they were held back by a series of fears and threats, by the models they would clash with. [. . .] And these same things are constantly repeated in children's education. If Darwin kept the innovative nucleus of his reflections and discoveries closed off inside himself for fifteen years, then probably we can find something similar in our schools and in the education of young children.

So, in reality a child's evolution can evolve slowly, or not evolve, or evolve with difficulty, or rather than being a long straight line it can be a contorted line that goes back on itself, with sudden stops and sudden responses. Because, let us be careful, there can easily be repressive forces at play that block the evolution of a child's potential, and it is as well for us constantly to take into account the underground incidents, the influences, tensions, coercive fears, stresses and anxieties that a child might feel inside. Where perhaps our teaching and the family's teaching with the models we offer them, or models children receive from outside, press on them dogmatically or para-dogmatically and do not allow the courage that is vitally necessary for children to soar in many directions and try out many models and behaviours, whose results the child must not be afraid of. If children are afraid of the outcome of an experience they are about to have, it is all over.

Faced with the way in which an adult proposes things, a child might feel inhibited; so these ways are crucial to freeing children up. The history a child has inside them is not just a story of the present; it is the story of the past, and it is the story of the future. Where ideological pressure exists in children's education and intimidates children with its authority, with its exclusivity and the one way, then clearly education is not being done, certainly liberal education is not being done. This is education that is not inclusive, and where we are not freeing children, not respecting the rhythms nature could and would allow if they could move very freely without brakes and without stops.

So on this issue of stages, this issue of progressing from one stage to another, actions which are external to an individual count for a lot in accelerating or delaying situations or causing them to regress and this is all important. And as always educators must perceive the whole world, and not just a part of the world. I do not consider tolerance to be a primary concern in an individual's attitudes, because tolerance is based on a very hypocritical form of authoritativeness. Instead the important issue is to appreciate diversity, to appreciate the concept of democracy that there is in diversity, and do our utmost to be conducive to the concurrent existence of different things and exchange between them in our *modus vivendi*.

[. . .]

Perhaps rather than trying to understand one aspect of our problems and work, and then another, and then another, we could turn to German Gestalt[70] thinking and try to broaden the field of vision together so as to gain an understanding of the entirety of the relations in that field. This means that for us (at least for me it means) that pedagogy is not totally cultural, and that politics plays the role it has to play, so that our discourse inevitably is also always a political discourse whether we know it or not. It is about working with cultural choices, but it clearly also means working with political choices. And so we must understand what things we can use as a positive reference and the things that should cause us to feel perplexed for a moment.

I would like to conclude with a reminder that we must be on our guard concerning Marxist currents from the Soviet Union. Even though Vygotsky, Luria and Leont'ev take the concept of evolution in individuals as constantly and closely interwoven with historical, civil and political evolutions, with the advance of customs and culture (and all the connotations culture and politics have); and even though they have recovered the value of the environment in forming individuals, and the value of educators and education, they then conclude by saying that children's education is necessarily inter-psychic, and that it only becomes intra-psychic later. This is an issue that makes me very suspicious and I will try and explain why. I am always highly suspicious when a theory spells out two different situations in the individual. We cannot cut an individual into pieces, not in any way or for any reason; and we cannot say that up to a certain point education must proceed based on certain values, and that then from a certain age on it must proceed on a different level and in a different dimension.

What do we mean when we say inter-psychic education? We mean education which is realised through a plurality of *inter* relations, relations among many, where a child is one of several. On the one hand, we have education that is of an individualistic kind, with the myth of individuality, and creating a myth is something completely different from respecting the individual. On the other hand, we have education that glorifies socialisation and education as sociality. Certainly education is inter-psychic. But theorising this kind of education as 'primary' education, as children's and individuals' initial 'emotive' part, and saying that intra-psychic education only comes later, so that children only become the agents of their own achievements and experiences at a later point, that children only achieve this capacity at a later time, and so they evidently did not have it at birth – all this is highly suspicious to me. First of all no one can guarantee that this intra-psychic capacity is born at a certain age (it might never be born at any age). This is to injure the capacity of the individual for autonomous and creative self-organisation, which we should not only connect with the start of [formal] education, we should connect it with education from the beginning of an individual's life.

I believe an acceptable cultural matrix can only be found in a dialectical relation between inter-psychic and intra-psychic education and not in trying to conciliate the two. In an education where we are capable of self-producing, self-organising and self-making as participants in our own destiny and in our own education, in a context that is permanently dialectical; and [in an education that] avoids all risk of mythically exalting the individual on the one hand and an exaggerated collectivism on the other during the situations where education is produced.

The problem is this. If we start with concepts of this kind, how can we make them all reflect and resonate in concrete terms in children's education, and therefore in our work, and therefore in the relations we have with children; starting with the small children who attend the *nido*?

Notes

1 Genoeffa Cervi died the following year, it was said of a broken heart when her home was burned a second time.

2 '*Esperienze per una nuova scuola dell'infanzia*' [Experiences for a new *scuola dell'infanzia*] and '*La gestione sociale nella scuola dell'infanzia*' [Social management in the *scuola dell'infanzia*], both published in 1971 by Editori Riuniti, Rome.

3 *Consigli pastorali* [pastoral councils] are the bodies through which Catholics help parish priests in every parish to foster pastoral activity.

4 Auxiliary, or non-teaching, staff include kitchen and cleaning staff, and are all part of the school *collettivo di lavoro* [work group].

5 Louis Pierre Althusser (1918–90) was a French Marxist philosopher.

6 Aristotle Socrates Onassis (1906–75) was a wealthy Greek ship owner. Biafra and Vietnam refer to wars that claimed many victims, including children: the Biafran war (1967–70) ended the attempt of Biafra to secede from Nigeria; while the war in Vietnam (1955–75) was fought between North Vietnam, supported by China and other communist allies, and the government of South Vietnam, supported by the United States and other anti-communist countries.

7 These two quotations are from a talk by Aurelio Valeriani – '*L'educazione emotiva, affettiva, morale e sociale*' [The emotional, affective and moral education of the child] – given at the eighteenth National Congress organised at the *Centro Didattico nazionale della Scuola Materna* [National educational centre for the *scuola materna*] Salerno, in 1969.

8 'Psychologism' accords to psychology a central role in explaining other, non-psychological types of fact or law.

9 The 'New Guidelines' refers to the '*Orientamenti dell'attività educativa nella Scuola Materna Statale*' [Guidelines on educational activity in the state *scuola materna*], published by the national government in 1969.

10 From *Bambini mani in alto* [Children hands up], testimonies of a group of *scuole materne* teachers published in 1971 by Collettivo C.R., Milano.

11 Basil Bernstein (1924–2000) was a British sociologist known for his work in the sociology of education.

12 Mannerism was a period of European art that emerged from the later years of the Italian High Renaissance around 1520 until about 1580, and was notable for its intellectual sophistication as well as its artificial (as opposed to naturalistic) qualities.

13 In a footnote, Malaguzzi adds: 'It is interesting to remember and take note of the betrayal consciously practised by Italian schools towards certain choices in the Elementary School Programme, which reminds teachers to "start from the child's concrete world", "make the environment and its multiple aspects a reference point for every other activity of observation, research, reflection and expression", "to communicate the joy and a taste for learning and doing for oneself to the child, so that they conserve this habit after their school work, for the rest of their lives"'.

14 Bruno Bettelheim (1903–90) was an Austrian-born American child psychologist and writer. He gained an international reputation for his work on Freud, psychoanalysis and emotionally disturbed children.

15 Having struggled for teachers to be entitled to time to attend such meetings, Malaguzzi is clearly concerned to ensure there is a high level of attendance, and that any absences are for good reasons.

16 Erik Homburger Erikson (1902–94) was a German-born American developmental psychologist and psychoanalyst known for his theory on the psychosocial development of human beings. Gordon Willard Allport (1897–1967) was an American psychologist, one of the first to focus on the study of the personality, and is often referred to as one of the founding figures of personality psychology.

17 'Essentialised', as used here, refers to the attributes that make up identity and is closely linked to the notion of definition.

18 Initially all *nidi* and *scuole dell'infanzia* were open on Saturday mornings. Later they were reorganised so that some remained open on Saturdays; then all were closed.

19 The *Cassa di Risparmio* is a local savings bank; ECA (*Ente Comunale Assistenza*) is a body set up in 1937 to hold the funds of various religious charities suppressed by the Fascist administration; IACP (*Istituto Autonomo Case Popolari*) is the local administration of a public housing scheme; and *Opere pie* refers to charitable organisations.

20 The exchange Malaguzzi refers to seems to be with other actors in early childhood education, including the State and the Catholic Church.

21 The '*Decreti Delegati*' (or *Provvedimenti delegati sulla scuola*) were a collection of six laws approved between July 1973 and May 1974, constituting the first attempt to apply the principles of the Constitution to state schools in an effective, ordered and coherent manner. These laws included the establishment of school governing bodies, school districts and new institutions to inspect and evaluate schools.

22 Guido Gonella (1905–82) was a Catholic thinker, journalist and politician, becoming Secretary of the DC party. He founded *Il Popolo*, the official DC newspaper.

23 Antonio Segni (1892–1971) was one of the founders of the DC party, becoming Prime Minister and President of the Republic.

24 The word *quartiere* is used for 'neighbourhood'; the *Comitati di Scuola e Città* seem here to envisage the *Consigli di quartiere* as a possible bridge between schools and their local communities. Soon after, the word *territorio* is used for 'local area', which carries a deep meaning in Italian about local identity and roots, encompassing local traditions, land, foods and wines, ways, perhaps the dialect, the local social system and local history – all of which vary so much from *territorio* to *territorio*. Used in relation to education, it can be valuable as a way of activating local support and resources, and generating pride in building a local project rather than using a standardised educational model.

25 The term 'updating' – *aggiornamento* – is often used in Reggio Emilia in the context of professional development.

26 Zoltán Pál Dienes (1916–2014) was a Hungarian-born mathematician who dedicated his professional career to improving mathematics education all over the world. He was a world-famous theorist and introduced revolutionary ideas of learning complex mathematical concepts in fun ways such as games and dance.

27 Teachers and children remain together during children's three years at *scuole dell'infanzia*. So teachers of 4-year-olds would continue to teach these children in the next school year, when 5 years old.

28 'Festivities' refer to the parties organised by each school for children and parents at the end of the school year.

29 *Centro Italiano Femminile* is a women's group associated with the Catholic Church.

30 *Comunione e Liberazione* is a lay movement within the Catholic Church, founded in 1954.

31 Factory Councils spread rapidly through Italy in the early 1970s. Members were elected in secret ballots by the whole workforce, and all could attend their meetings. Their roles included developing trade union activity in each workplace, taking initiatives to resolve workers' problems and contributing to the development of trade union strategy. They began to decline in importance in the mid-1970s, with the established trade unions exercising increasing control (Ginsborg, 1990).

32 'Assembly-ism' refers to the assembly of equals as the basis for debate, discussion, organisation and political decision, in contrast for example to the election of representatives to whom responsibility for decisions is delegated.

33 Malaguzzi might be referring here to the Reggio Emilia experience prefiguring the 'historic compromise' proposed by the PCI leader, Enrico Berlingeur, which envisaged an alliance with other parties, including the DC.

34 Antonio Gramsci (1891–1937) was an Italian Marxist theoretician and politician, a founding member and leader of the PCI. He was put in prison by the Fascist regime, where he died.

35 Malaguzzi here returns to a constant theme: the need for teachers to be included in organisations that enable wide participation and deliberation about social demands, for example *Comitati di Scuola e Città*.

36 'Curial' refers to the administrative apparatus of the Catholic Church.

37 *Nomine regie* means, literally, royal appointments, but is used here to mean unelected power.

38 Malaguzzi refers here to an article by Giuseppe Sacchi in the first issue of a new journal *Home and Family: Journal of Popular Education*.

39 Ferdinand Magellan (1480–1521) was a Portuguese sailor who led the first expedition to circumnavigate the world, leaving Lisbon in 1521.

40 *Emile, or On Education* or *Émile, or Treatise on Education* is a treatise on the nature of education and on the nature of man written by Jean-Jacques Rousseau (1712–78), and published in 1762.

41 Luciano Corradini was President of the *Comitato di Scuola e Città* of the Diana school in 1970–71 and later wrote: 'how much good [it did me] to dedicate large numbers of days and evenings to socially managing his [son's] school together with parents and teachers, an exceptional director [Loris Malaguzzi], and a local citizen who represented society' (Various Authors, 2012, p.129).

42 Malaguzzi here refers to the *Regolamento* – or Rulebook – for the municipal schools adopted by the *Comune* in 1972 after months of discussion in the city. For more on this, see the introduction to this chapter and document 44.72.

43 *Conferenza Episcopale Italiana* [Italian Bishops' Conference] was established in 1952 and is the official assembly of Catholic bishops in Italy. One of its tasks is to oversee relations between the Catholic Church and public authorities.

44 The 'Management Committees' referred to are the *Comitati di Scuola e Città* that the *Regolamento* established in every municipal school, consisting of elected representatives drawn from teachers, parents and local citizens.

45 The 'naturalistic school', ignoring God and spiritual explanations, is posed in contrast to the religious school.

46 Malaguzzi refers here to different groups who believed radical consciousness would emerge from the oppressed masses without any intervention or mediation.

47 The *Piazza della Loggia* bombing took place on the morning of 28 May 1974, in Brescia, Lombardy, during an anti-fascist protest. The terrorist attack killed eight people and wounded over 100.

48 *Magistrali* were colleges for training teachers for *scuole materne* and elementary schools, entered at the age of 14 and providing a four-year, upper secondary qualification. This training was replaced by a university-based graduate education in 1998.

49 *Associazione Italiana Maestri Cattolici* [Italian Association of Catholic Teachers], founded in 1945, includes teachers, administrators and inspectors in early childhood and primary education.

50 Law 477/1973 was one of a number of laws that constituted what was termed the *Decreti Delegati*, which delegated management of schools, including *scuole materne*, to all adult protagonists. For more on these laws, see 55.74.

51 The *Concordato* was part of the 1929 Lateran Pacts made between the Catholic Church and the Italian State, which gave the Church considerable influence over public education.

52 The *Orientamenti dell'attività educativa nella Scuola Materna Statale* were guidelines on educational activity in state-run *scuole materne*, published by the national government in 1969.

53 The Vietnam War, which lasted from 1956 to 1975, brought enormous destruction and suffering to Vietnam, and neighbouring Laos and Cambodia. The schools in Reggio Emilia provided aid to children in Vietnam including contributing to an initiative by the Region to offer Vietnamese children a *scuola dell'infanzia*.

54 Malaguzzi was drafting these notes in the midst of the *Anni di Piombo* [Years of Lead], a period of widespread social conflict and terrorism.

55 The *Camere* are the two houses of the Italian Parliament, the Chamber of Deputies and the Senate of the Republic.

56 This discussion of education for children with disabilities takes place in the context of a subsequent law (517/77), passed in 1977, which established the principle that all such children from 6 to 14 years should be included in ordinary schools, that class teachers should prepare educational plans, and that these plans should be supported by specialised teachers providing 'didactic support'. These children – described in Reggio Emilia as 'children with special rights' – had been attending municipal *scuole dell'infanzia* in the city since the 1960s.'

57 Malaguzzi here contrasts the PCI proposal under which children would get a new teacher each year as they passed up the school, with the practice in the municipal schools in Reggio Emilia where teachers stay with their class as it moves up in the school.

58 Malaguzzi is referring to Giovanni Jervis (1933–2009), director of psychiatric services in Reggio Emilia in the 1970s. During this time he wrote *A Manual of Critical Psychiatry*. Part of the movement to close large institutions for psychiatrically ill people and move all psychiatric services into the community, given official sanction in the 'Basaglia' Law of 1978, Jervis later became critical of how these closures had been implemented.

59 *Tempo lungo* (long or extended time) refers to organising extended opening hours in some municipal schools, up to 6 pm, for children with employed parents.

60 These are two options for organising teachers' time. *Tempo continuato* is a continuous working day for educators, for example 9 am to 3 pm; while *tempo spezzato* is a split shift model, for example 9 am to 12 noon, then 2 to 5 pm. After much debate, the *tempo continuato* was adopted.

61 Malaguzzi often uses this term, referring to places where culture is available to the public and where culture is pieced together, created, constructed. In Reggio Emilia, these places are understood to include the *scuole dell'infanzia* and *nidi* since children construct culture in these institutions. In this article Malaguzzi means libraries, places of debate, theatres, political circles and other associations; he would probably include such organisations as the UDI and *Comitati di Scuola e Città*.

62 CRESAS is the *Centre de recherche de l'éducation spécialisée et de l'adaptation scolaire*, which was established in 1969 in Paris as part of INRP, the *Institut national de recherche pédagogique*.

63 Carpi is a town situated between Modena and Reggio Emilia.

64 AIMA, *Azienda interventi mercato agricolo*, was a government agency set up by the Ministry of Agriculture and Forestry in 1966.

65 Howard Ernest Gruber (1922–2005) was an American psychologist and a pioneer of the psychological study of creativity, his work leading to several important discoveries about the creative process and the developmental psychology of creativity. A main interest was the history of science, and particularly the work of Charles Darwin, and in 1974 he published *Darwin on Man: A Psychological Study of Scientific Creativity*. Named by the magazine *American Scientist* as one of the most important scientific books of the twentieth century, the book was both a case study of the nature of creativity and a contribution to the history of science, demonstrating the slow, integrative processes of creative thought, and that such thinking is the solving of many problems rather than a 'eureka' moment.

66 Jerome Seymour Bruner (1915–) is an American psychologist who has made significant contributions to human cognitive psychology and cognitive learning theory in educational psychology, as well as to history and to the general philosophy of education. He became a frequent visitor to Reggio Emilia from the 1980s onwards and was made an honorary citizen of the city in 1996.

67 Alexander Romanovich Luria (1902–77), Lev Semyonovich Vygotsky (1896–1934) and Alexei Nikolaevich Leontiev (1903–79) were Soviet developmental psychologists. Luria and Vygotsky helped develop a theory of human cultural and bio-social development commonly referred to as cultural-historical psychology.

68 Sputnik, launched by the Soviet Union in 1957, was the first artificial satellite to orbit the earth; it came as a shock to the United States, demonstrating the Soviet Union's scientific capacity.

69 By '*nozionismo*', Malaguzzi refers to acquiring knowledge of facts related to a discipline without having any organic or systematic understanding; it has overtones of superficiality and sterility.

70 Gestalt psychology is a theory of mind, originating in late nineteenth-century Germany, whose central principle is that the mind forms a global whole with self-organising tendencies, considering objects in their entirety before, or in parallel with, perception of their individual parts; suggesting the whole is other than the sum of its parts.

Chapter 4

Opening to the world
1980–89

Figure 4.1 Loris Malaguzzi, Nilde Iotti (*Presidente della Camera dei Deputati* [President of the Chamber of Deputies] from 1979 to 1992), Ugo Benassi (Mayor of Reggio Emilia from 1976 to 1987) at the opening of the exhibition '*L'occhio se salta il muro*' [If the Eye Leaps over the Wall], Reggio Emilia, 1981

Figure 4.2 Loris Malaguzzi, 1980s

Figure 4.3 International Study Group visiting the *Scuola Comunale dell'Infanzia* Diana, Reggio Emilia, 1980s

Figure 4.4 Meeting with Howard Gardner on the 'Theory of Multiple Intelligences', for teachers in *nidi* and *scuole dell'infanzia* of the *Comune* of Reggio Emilia. From left: Howard Gardner (psychologist, Professor at the University of Harvard) with interpreter Enrica Bondavalli, Ettore Borghi (*Assessore* for Schools and Deputy Mayor of the *Comune* of Reggio Emilia from 1982 to 1987), Loris Malaguzzi, Reggio Emilia, 1985

Figure 4.5 Loris Malaguzzi, *Scuola Comunale dell'Infanzia* Diana, Reggio Emilia, 1988

Introduction (Peter Moss)

Historical context

While the 1970s was the decade when the first overseas visitors came to Reggio Emilia's municipal schools, the 1980s was the decade when Reggio Emilia went out into the world to share its experiences and, in the course of doing so, began building a large international following. While increasing numbers of people journeyed to Reggio Emilia, their visits becoming more formalised during the decade with the organisation of week-long Study Groups, Reggio Emilia reached out to many more through its travelling exhibition, first called '*L'occhio se salta il muro*' [If the Eye Leaps over the Wall], later renamed 'The Hundred Languages of Children'. Drawing on some of the most significant project work from the schools, this was, in Malaguzzi's words, 'an exhibition of the possible' (cited in Vecchi, 2010, p.27). Shown first in spring 1981 in Reggio Emilia itself, in autumn of the same year it travelled to Sweden, attracting tens of thousands of visitors to Stockholm's *Moderna Museet* [Museum of Modern Art] and establishing a close relationship between Reggio Emilia and many educators in Sweden that has lasted to the present day.

Sweden was only the first stop. The exhibition began travelling throughout Western Europe, while in 1987 a second updated version began a North American tour. Indeed, the exhibition was to be continuously updated and translated into different languages, with work from other schools being added. By 1995, shortly after Malaguzzi's death, the exhibition had been to forty-four venues in eleven countries. In a matter of a few years, *The Hundred Languages of Children* had brought Reggio Emilia's pedagogical work to the attention of a vast new audience and, together with the Study Groups, helped create an international network of people engaged with the city and its schools for young children.

The exhibition was symptomatic of an important value: the need to make the educational work in Reggio Emilia visible and transparent, to share democratically with everyone what was going on in the *Comune*'s schools. We have already seen this value applied locally in earlier years through exhibitions and other events held in the city, the creation of public moments for the educational project, opening it up to the wider community, seeking to make the public more competent alongside the growing competence of the schools. And now the new exhibitions extended this work to the wider world, to become on a global scale (as Vea Vecchi puts it) 'a place of communication, professional growth and visibility for the public beyond our highest expectations' (Various Authors, 2012, p.151).

During the 1980s, further important developments occurred within the city, some motivated by growing financial difficulties, due in part to central government cutting funds to *comuni* and reducing local autonomy, which included a ban on new public sector jobs.

In Reggio Emilia there was strong pressure on the municipality to rethink organisation and reduce costs in municipal *nidi* and *scuole dell'infanzia*. In the School Management Councils (*Consigli di Gestione*) there was constant debate on the idea of quality, not negotiable, and high levels of participation by teachers and families played an important role in defending municipal education. It was felt in more than one area that social needs had diversified and become more complex. New ways of doing things were searched out among the difficulties, meetings were held between various cities to compare notes and build practicable and effective strategies.

(ibid., p.143)

One of the new ways of doing things introduced an important organisational development. In 1986, the first agreements were made between the *Comune* and cooperatives for the latter to provide *nidi*, which would follow the pedagogical principles and ways of working of the existing *nidi* directly run by the *Comune*. Two 'cooperative *nidi*' opened that year, the first in Italy, setting a precedent for future growth in local services (though two schools run directly by the *Comune* were also opened, in 1987 and 1988).

Openings were made to the Catholic Church and its schools for young children. Relations between *Comune* and Church had not always been easy. The Church had resisted secular education for young children, objecting to the provision of these services by the State and showing its suspicion of *comuni* when, in a 1976 radio broadcast, municipal schools particularly in Reggio Emilia were accused of practising a 'sinful and corrupting' materialist pedagogy and contrasted unfavourably with the 'superior' morality of autonomous religious schools. Matters came to a head again in 1986, following a new Concordat between the Italian State and the Vatican[1] and the subsequent agreement between the Italian education ministry and the Italian Episcopal Conference (the official assembly of the bishops in Italy). This agreement required schools to provide religious instruction, with two hours a week proposed for *scuole dell'infanzia*, though families could opt out if they did not want this for their children. Once again, Reggio Emilia responded by opening an extended dialogue, involving families, teachers and Church authorities. The result was an agreement to provide some funding for Catholic schools, to support staff development.

Reggio Emilia was not alone in maintaining a local educational project. Despite the financial benefits to be gained by handing over schools to the State, progressive *comuni* retained their commitment to young children and continued with the development of innovative work in their own schools. Solidarity and dialogue between these experiences was supported by the *Gruppo Nazionale Nidi* [National Nido Group], founded in 1980 at a meeting in Reggio Emilia with the aim of promoting debate on issues related to the provision of services for children under 3 years. During the 1980s, the *Gruppo* organised meetings across Italy to exchange and discuss experience.

However, the distribution of *nidi* was very uneven across the country. Despite funding being allocated after 1971 to all regions, by 1980 60 per cent of these services were to be found in just three of the twenty Italian regions, all in the North and including Emilia-Romagna. This region had one *nido* for every 338 children compared to just one *nido* for every 6,248 children in the South of Italy. The 1971 law had predicted the opening of 3,800 municipal *nidi* in five years – yet after ten years there were still only 1,510. Once again, national initiatives had failed to deliver for all children in the country and in parts of Italy public funding seemed to have vanished into thin air.

If the *Gruppo Nazionale Nidi* provided one new national forum to discuss early childhood education, another was provided by a new journal. Following the sudden closure of *Zerosei* in 1984, a meeting in Reggio Emilia led to the founding of a successor – *Bambini*, a publication that continues to this day. So despite a background of economic difficulties, the *Gruppo* and *Bambini* provided welcome opportunities to generate collective energy and offered examples of the value of solidarity and dialogue.

Nationally, after the stagnation of the preceding decade and a sluggish start to the new one, there was an economic recovery as the decade progressed; growth was strong from 1984 onwards, bringing a new period of material prosperity. Despite the terrible bombing of Bologna rail station in 1980, terrorism declined and the four years of coalition government under Socialist leader Bettino Craxi (1983–87) brought political stability; the 1980s, indeed, were dominated by an alliance between the PSI and the DC, with no inkling that both parties would implode and disappear in the next decade. After nearly twenty years of acute crisis, 'Italy seemed at last to have been pacified and on capitalist terms' (Ginsborg, 1990, p.407). This political stability did not, however, provide a basis for national reform. Rather, as in the decade before 1968, 'the economy was booming, the material bases for reform clearly existed, but the centre-left politicians let the opportunity slip by' (*ibid.*, p.419). Matters were not helped by the decline of the PCI during the decade, meaning no credible alternative existed to the seemingly perpetual rule by DC-dominated governments.

But some things were changing. A referendum in 1981 that gave support for the 1978 abortion law confirmed a shift in social attitudes, even if the country was still far from achieving gender equality. Issues of ethnic equality also arose as Italy by the early 1980s was no longer a net exporter of labour, but was becoming a country of immigration, though without any social policies in place for receiving new citizens. Ginsborg highlights another important social trend of the 1980s: a continuing decline of collective values and, spurred by increasing material prosperity, 'a new age of familism: families have become ever more concerned with their own wellbeing and less with the collective problems of society as a whole' (*ibid.*, p.413). Yet, he concedes, the picture of 1980s Italy is not quite so clear, since rising familialism was matched by 'significant evidence of new associationism in Italian society: voluntary work, recreation clubs, cooperatives have all flourished as never before' (*ibid.*). An estimated one in five Italians were involved in such activities, and using the concept of 'social capital', Robert Putnam was to show how levels of such civic engagement were related to effective government – with Emilia-Romagna having the highest levels both of regional government performance and of associational life (Putnam, 1993).

Malaguzzi's life

Loris Malaguzzi was actively involved in all aspects of the evolution of early childhood education in Reggio Emilia. His continuing role of sharing new thinking from a wide range of disciplines is captured here in this recollection by *atelierista* Vea Vecchi, who remembers how in the 1980s:

> together with the daily task of making teachers and atelieristas grow and develop together, Malaguzzi also organized many ongoing education initiatives. Some of these, for example firing clay, were specifically for atelieristas and we were always requested to take part in other initiatives, for example in mathematics and science. We listened to lectures on the latest discoveries in the field of neurobiology, which then we discussed among ourselves trying to understand the possible effects on our work. In the world of Italian education I think we were among the first to discuss Edgar Morin's theories of complexity, the theories of Ilia Prigogine on entropy and time flow, Francisco Varela's theories on learning, Gregory Bateson's on mind and ecology, Mandelbrot's on fractals and other experiences. The working environment was a place of strong cultural growth.
>
> (Vecchi, 2010, p.124)

He was also deeply engaged in Reggio Emilia's opening to the world, playing a pivotal role in the creation of the exhibitions:

> Each [of the selected] school[s] prepared more than one proposal which evolved and matured through revision and discussion with Loris Malaguzzi. It is not easy to convey the atmosphere of excitement and interest in which we worked. [. . .] We all felt Loris Malaguzzi to be a distinguished pedagogical and cultural reference. We were conscious of the depth of his constantly updated reading, his capacity for processing and his curiosity for the new. [. . .] They were lively meetings. Malaguzzi was very severe in his evaluations, but he was equally generous and attentive in recognising the competencies of others: he loved and knew how to compare and appraise ideas and thoughts without any preconceived hierarchy. I think all of us, Malaguzzi included, came out of these meetings with a good feeling of intellectual and human growth.
>
> (Various Authors, 2012, pp.150–51)

But Malaguzzi's role in Reggio Emilia did change in the 1980s in an important respect. In 1985, at the age of 65, Loris Malaguzzi formally retired from his position as Director of Reggio Emilia's municipal schools. But he did not retire from his involvement in early childhood education: locally, regionally, nationally and now also internationally, his work continued. He kept a small office, next to the *Assessore*, and frequently visited the schools. From its inception in 1980 until his death, he was President of the *Gruppo Nazionale Nidi*; he was a founder and director of *Bambini*, to which he frequently contributed; and he acted as consultant to the regional government. At the same time, he continued to support the work of Reggio Emilia's municipal schools in many other ways, meeting with visiting study groups and accompanying the Reggio Emilia exhibition on a number of its overseas tours.

The selection of documents (Reggio Emilia Working Group)

> Is it possible, is it legitimate to cheer (yes, in sport jargon) for certain theories on the brain rather than others? I know much is still unsettled. But in the meantime we must take into account that studies are advancing very clearly [. . .] Scientific, technological and ecological research with the new disciplines has generated (and will generate) the emergence of a natural epistemological frame that involves contemporary knowledge with the entire span of cognitive, biological, evolutionary sciences. Advancing new cultural paradigms, new modalities for thinking of the world, new conceptualising about the relations between the human sciences and the natural sciences, and about the limits, the scope, the creative possibilities of human connections.
>
> (Loris Malaguzzi, 1988,[2] not included in selected documents)

Looking for the themes that stand out in the 1980s, some remain vivid in the memory of those who experienced those years in Reggio Emilia's *nidi* and *scuole dell'infanzia*. One is undoubtedly the exhibition 'L'occhio se salta il muro', inaugurated in 1981 at the Museum of Modern Art in Stockholm, where it was a great success, so much so that it was hosted there again some years later in an updated version with a new title: 'The Hundred Languages of Children'. Stockholm was the start of a long journey around the world for the exhibition, ambassador for the construction of an international network, which is vast today. The exhibition revolutionised the lens for thinking of children and a possible new educational methodology.

In the schools of Reggio Emilia the exhibition marked a point on a journey, an occasion for *ordering and communicating* the new ways of working educationally from the previous decade, and allowing our experience to advance with further research and discoveries. The most important and decisive, which revolutionised ways of working for teachers, *atelieristas* and *pedagogistas*, and generated interest on an international level, was the attention given to observation and documentation of children's processes, a *transition in design* from which it is impossible to turn back towards the didactics of the past.

Another characteristic element of the period was the fascination, almost elation that Malaguzzi felt towards the developments science was making through inter-disciplinary forms: theories of complexity, the neurosciences, ecological models of human development, studies of the genome and DNA. These constituted a theoretical frame, which brought to crisis the certain and absolute scientific paradigms that education had depended on. Scientific theories and evidence were now confirming choices previously made in Reggio Emilia on the basis of ethics and values.

Yet another element that to our mind distinguished these years was the attempt to constantly evolve participation, by parents and citizens. In previous decades there had been much talk of social management, and much had been done to construct it in new ways, assigning it a role of great significance in school life. It is our impression that in the 1980s we find in Malaguzzi's words a stronger emphasis on competencies that need to be acquired to have strong and vital social management.

In sum, therefore, three elements seem to us to identify this decade: international dissemination and exchange of Reggio Emilia's philosophy of education, characterised by educational advance derived from the observation and documentation of children's processes; a new framework of cultural and scientific references strengthening already implemented choices and intuitions in organisation and giving new impetus to the theme of educational design[3]; and a strong call for competent social participation.

The 1980s begin with a document signed by workers in the *Comune's nidi* and *scuole dell'infanzia* at the regular meeting that started each new school year, expressing solidarity with Andrei Sakharov, winner of the Nobel Peace Prize, and subjected to repressive measures in his country, the Soviet Union [79.80]. This is an important document because it testifies to how education, at least in Reggio Emilia, is not neutral; it clearly takes sides in the important events of its times, and, above all, cannot accept any form of totalitarianism and fundamentalism, because education feeds on freedom and critical thinking in a dialectic exchange between different points of view. This is an invitation to daily critical thinking that also has to do with educational methodology, confirming the value of *collective professional development and updating* both as a vital time for the choice and timing of subjects for discussion, and for a lively communication of shared syntheses that have been achieved. The same attitude is apparent in Malaguzzi's analyses of what is taking place socially and politically, in meetings with *Consigli di Gestione* [School Management Councils]; an example is his discussion of the proposed reform of primary school in 1982, which generated debate and led Reggio Emilia pedagogy to argue why it was against lowering the age of compulsory schooling [80.82].

As before, it is the image of the child that orientates choices. It is not precocity that should be sought, rather wellbeing, wholeness and overall maturation. In a talk given at the 1984 Conference '*Il bambino e la scienza*' [The child and science], Malaguzzi moves from the idea of growth in the economic field to the idea of growth in the field of pedagogy, inviting us not to be concerned with the rate of growth, but with the nature, quality and structure of growth [84.84]. The dilemma Malaguzzi says, is crucial: 'Is childhood a world we leave never to return, or is it a world we leave when we get bigger, and can go back to freely?' Here he forcefully says 'no' to accelerating children's growth through intensifying their production in selective and taxonomic ways, maintaining instead the need for slower and broader processes, capable of activating everything the child possesses.

In this text he highlights once again the extent to which children and adults are both and at the same time part of interwoven life processes, even when they appear distant. A 'normalisation' of childhood can, therefore, only take place by 'liberating it from artificial isolation'. With the term 'normalisation' Malaguzzi indicates the necessary cultural process for leading childhood out of opposed stereotypes (childhood as a time of magic vs. violated childhood), which prevent us from welcoming its biological and cultural identity as an organic part of the existential journey of the individual and society. Only the normalisation of childhood can lead to an adequate politics that recognises its rights and potentials.

Malaguzzi confronts relations with science, regretting that its dissemination and application in daily life is insufficient to produce effective changes. He denounces how it is difficult to speak of science education for young children, and at the same time highlights how in effect children practise scientific research because they possess the necessary requisites of the researcher: curiosity, wonder, concentration, the pleasure of understanding, the ability to find relations between things, acceptance of different points of view. Malaguzzi proposes the thesis of a new relation between children and science based on statements by renowned physicists and quoting a sentence of Piaget's: 'the ideal I am trying to realise personally is to remain a child until death' [84.84]. His participation in the debate about two cultures (humanities and sciences) is evident in these pages, which forcefully return to certain issues that Malaguzzi discussed on more than one occasion with various academics and where we clearly perceive how his is a holistic, inter-disciplinary and intra-disciplinary approach, which becomes structured as the theory of the 'hundred languages'.

Malaguzzi embarked on a truly profound and fruitful dialogue with David Hawkins, philosopher and scientist [see Chapter 4, n.14]. They were both convinced that children take the same attitude towards the world as scientists: asking questions, asking questions of themselves, advancing and trying out hypotheses, developing and revisiting theories. Their journeys and languages of research will not tolerate the confines of disciplines, but are constructed through the action and experience of daily life and the participation of others, children and adults.

There is an unbroken thread in Malaguzzi's writing that situates education and pedagogy not in an abstract context, but strongly connected with social and political reality. His concrete proposals for education always start from an analysis of the current situation. So in his talk to *Consigli di Gestione*, already referred to, he deals with the role of women – a theme returned to on several occasions over the years – and how they have to put up with a double work-load, a situation related to an archaic mentality in society, which is partly trans-mitted to children and schools [80.82]. Malaguzzi argues that this is one reason why welfare-type services (e.g. 'childcare'), only regarded as useful to the eco-nomic relationship between work and family, are generally accepted without adequate critical evaluation; while on the contrary *nidi* and *scuole dell'infanzia* that have a broad educational purpose, like those in Reggio Emilia, are not considered to be productive for the market and can therefore be subjected without thought to inadequate funding and negative political decisions – for faced with economic recession early childhood and school services, now as in the past, are among those subjected to the largest budgetary cuts.

Malaguzzi also argues that the diminished importance of identity in family roles and of the family in society, still true today many years later, is causing a crisis in the confidence of many people, making it necessary to research new identities and different roles. He refers to the necessity of giving 'individu-als a sufficiently deep level of self-listening, a feeling of self and sense of self' without which 'everything else is destined to slide'. If families experience the present in a painful way it is difficult for them to make projections into the future; in the same way, if children have interesting experiences, it will be easier for them to be able to construct their own identity, but if memory is painful, awareness of the present will be weakened and elaboration of a future will become more difficult.

It is probably because of the phenomenon of 'weakened family identity in society' described above that Malaguzzi points to the need to connect the desire families have for getting together with an increase in competent participation, because only then will democracy be able to develop. A competency consisting of culture and of great human and political sensibility is necessary, 'competent participation that is in constant flux', competency acquired by absorbing families and workers into the process, and also by explicitly inviting teachers to include social management in their professional development, because only this inclusion can lead to more complete quality in education.

Competency in families and workers is born of exchange and dialogue, as we read in a document from 1982 on adult/child relations, an exchange between parents on the *Consiglio di Gestione* of Diana school and Malaguzzi, which became a publication distributed to all parents. These reflections were disseminated through class meetings, because 'we are always trying to build a network reaching many ears'. These exchanges were related to concrete situ-ations, where the aim was to unite children's rights with those of adults, and to deal with the issue of mutual understanding between home and school. Malaguzzi faces reality in pragmatic terms. Children's experiences will neces-sarily be *kaleidoscopic*, meeting with many points of view and diverse situations. Multiplicity of experience is positive: what is important is that all experiences, even those distant from each other, are re-connected when parents and children are together again, because this will support children in articulating their own philosophy [81.82].

Malaguzzi creates continuous connections between an educational philosophy he considers just, for the good growth of children, and the choices that derive from it, implemented in Reggio Emilia schools, and says: 'the problem of problems lies in being capable of having different experiences but maintaining a close connection between one experience and another'. This sentence expresses one of the most radical convictions of Malaguzzi's thinking. In a society that was increasingly characterised by the fragmentation of educational opportunities and stimuli offered to children (courses in the gym, swimming, music, dance etc.), and where children could find themselves changing activity and educational style more than once during the same day (school teacher, family, trainers, musicians etc.), Malaguzzi proposed schools might be the place in which to produce synthesis and exchange, helping children to find a deeper unity, capable of going beyond all this running from one place to another, and from one adult to another. School could be and had to be the place for learning to re-process and to build the meanings of action and of being in the world.

This was above all for children. But it was no less important to offer parents and teachers the possibility of greater unity for their own actions, looking for coherence even in discontinuity and in differences. Here is where the theme of continuity emerges, a theme we will find recurring in several writings of this period, a continuity seen by parents in the 1982 discussion at Diana to be desirable and necessary in the relationship between school and family. But Malaguzzi proposes replacing this concept with one of dialogic capacity, the capacity for self-interrogating, for asking oneself questions, and for reciprocally exchanging information. In an open letter to families in 1983 he proposes the need for agreement between school and family on the themes of children's growth, in order to 'promote a more concerted shared co-responsibility in choosing contents and educational methodologies' [83.83].

Malaguzzi dedicated much of his thinking and much of his time to the *Consigli di Gestione*, addressing them in different ways. It is difficult to compare the role of these Management Councils in Reggio Emilia's schools with the role commonly assigned to such bodies in more traditional institutions. As we saw in the previous decade, Malaguzzi several times took a position in the debate surrounding the *Decreti Delegati*, the national government's proposals for school governing bodies, whose implementation was never fully realised, and which betrayed many of the hopes and possibilities that had been entrusted to them. In reality their implementation in schools prevented any form of real participation: rather than re-activating debate, an amendment in 1977 reduced the *Decreti* even further to a mere formality of a bureaucratic-administrative nature confined to the role of checking. For Malaguzzi all this was truly and profoundly wrong, since he considered participation (and social management) to be an essential quality of learning and of being a school.

The importance given to the *Consigli di Gestione* in Reggio Emilia's educational project is clear: 'Essentially, the educational hypothesis in our *scuola dell'infanzia* is a hypothesis of participatory education', as part of a solidarity of practice and ideals. In this thinking, Malaguzzi was also stimulated by encountering the theories of Urie Bronfenbrenner [see Chapter 4, n.18], in which he was particularly interested, but which also generated some criticisms, expressed publicly in a debate with Bronfenbrenner during the Ancona conference of 1986. Organisation as always accompanied theory, and for *Consigli di Gestione* Malaguzzi proposed a structure made up of work groups, each dedicated to a theme: the environment, external relations, issues of educational methodology, and analysis and examination of what was done in school. He proposed a time schedule for each group, because time too is a content of participatory processes [93.ND].

So in this decade's documents, Loris Malaguzzi's strategic educational, cultural and political vision, in which family and citizen co-management/participation is one of the most defining conditions of the pedagogical project, can perhaps be understood with greater clarity. At the same time, however, he was committed to an educational approach that did not betray the child whose image had always been stated. Malaguzzi confronted this commitment with a critical spirit, as always moving across different domains – science, art, architecture, the economy, union politics, with different forms, written and oral, in different places, with different interlocutors, but always seeking to involve many people.

In 1985, to restore centrality to the culture of *nidi* and *scuole dell'infanzia*, and to oppose proposed legislation to lower the age of compulsory schooling, Reggio Emilia responded by organising a national Conference, in which the municipal schools presented their most recent and interesting educational experiences. For those present at the time it was an important event, whose title reflected the contents: '*Esperienze e problemi: Modelli e congetture teorico-pratiche nell'educazione dei bambini*' [Experiences and problems: theoretical-practical models and conjectures in the education of children] [85.85]. The Conference was preceded by specific work over a whole school year in the *nidi* and *scuole dell'infanzia*, where material had been distributed and investigations conducted on widely diverse subjects, from the more traditional – such as drawing and mark-making and mathematics – to the new, such as computers, all addressed in an interesting and often innovative way. A vast panorama of teaching experience was presented at the Conference; many teachers, *pedagogistas* and *atelieristas* explained their own work. The most formative part was the deep exchange that took place between colleagues, and above all with Malaguzzi himself, who closely followed the process of the projects from inception to presentation.

Malaguzzi ended the conference with criticism of the 1969 Ministerial Pedagogical Guidelines for use in state-run *scuole materne*. Once again his words communicate an image of intelligent children, capable of expressing themselves in a range of different languages, creative in all their approaches, even with new tools such as the computer, which at the time was much debated and regarded with suspicion by many educators. While discussing information technology, he reflected on another older subject, drawing and mark-making [*grafica*, see Chapter 5, n.14], which Malaguzzi defines as 'part of [our] biological programming', and which is fine-tuned and diversified through life's experiences. Among drawing's multiple possibilities Malaguzzi underlines 'pleasure' as a form of energy contained in the act of drawing and identifies its different forms, referring to the reading of a drawing as an act of responsibility and competence.

One of the projects presented, '*Approcci per il futuro. L'intelligenza dei bambini, l'intelligenza del computer*' [Approaches for the future: Children's intelligence, computer intelligence] was conducted in a truly experimental way. In addressing the topic Malaguzzi immediately distanced himself from either prejudice or infatuation with new digital tools, hypothesising instead friendly relations between children and computer science, with children as designers and not only users, their intelligence encountering and confronted with another intelligence, that of the computer.

In consultation with the *Istituto di Cibernetica dell'Università di Milano* [Cybernetics Institute at Milan University], he chose the LOGO computer programming language created by Seymour Papert at MIT as the most appropriate for the approach he hypothesised, for the clarity of its logical structures and its simplicity of language.Only the graphics part was selected, using a mechanical tortoise, 'a little 3D technological animal' facilitating identification between children and the tortoise which, controlled by children and simultaneously visualised on a screen, moved around a large area leaving a trace of its journey with a small pen.

The children, talking and acting, attributed the computer with powers but also with limits. 'The computer thinks, if it is big it thinks more; it isn't intelligent, they have made it intelligent'. A deep investigation continued in the following years, on a road charted by the first experience. In 1988 Malaguzzi promoted and conducted updating meetings on the theme with teachers, in which he proposed analysis of conversations between 4-year-old children, from which a variety of images of computers sprang, some more joyful (a tool which has light-hearted powers such as dancing or entertaining), others more serious (such as writing, counting, having encyclopaedic powers, 'If there's something I don't know, the computer will know'). All, however, providing competencies that are useful and become manifest in a game that reproduces an organised society inhabited by characters like school teachers and policemen, but where there is exchange and relationships with characters the children love such as UFO Robot Grendizer and others. The children soon understood that to establish relations with the computer they needed to find a different common language: 'The computer obeys us, but if I don't write things the way it wants, what happens is it doesn't give you the answer'. An analysis that Malaguzzi used to critique the rigid stages of Piaget's theory on the development of children's thinking.

The intention of these formative meetings was to give teachers an articulated and complex conceptual framework that would welcome new theories, in which to situate their own work with projects and methodological development; it was not to offer them methodological models and techniques. A few years later Seymour Papert visited Reggio Emilia and showed great interest in the experiences realised in the *scuole* and *nidi*, especially in the field of computing. These were the years, too, in which Malaguzzi initiated intense exchange with the post-Piaget Geneva School, in particular with Donata Fabbri and Alberto Munari, who sought exchange with Malaguzzi and the Reggio Emilia experience on various occasions.

Malaguzzi also encountered the work of Edgar Morin and found himself in great sympathy with his thinking: to think without ever closing a concept, to re-establish connections between what appears disconnected, to strive to understand the multi-dimensional nature of events, like the interweaving between human sciences and natural sciences. Continuity and discontinuity are seen as elements not in opposition, with contemporary epistemology leaning towards a knowledge based on theories of complementarities. There were other fruitful encounters. The discovery of nerve growth factor by Rita Levi Montalcini confirmed the vision of the brain as an organic and dynamic structure of neurons and synapses, with abundant cooperation and synergies: a great challenge and an opportunity for education. 'A brain that is not caged in by genes escapes the old deterministic absolutes. Its structure and its functioning are those of a species that nature has privileged with resources disposed to change through experience, education and the adventure of living' [88.87].

We remember very well the updating meetings Malaguzzi had with school staff, during which problems posed by philosophers of science were analysed, exploring how they connected in concrete ways with our work with children. Children, Malaguzzi reminded us, not only know how to learn, they know how to learn to learn, a further invitation to teachers to privilege knowledge through action that transforms. Methodology (didactics) was advancing constantly in thinking and in educational strategies: that is how these years appear in the memories of teachers who were present at the time in Reggio Emilia's *nidi* and *scuole*.

In 1980 Malaguzzi convened a series of dialogues/meetings with teachers to analyse the theme of '*programmazione*' or 'planning'. Imported from the field of industry and the English-speaking world, Malaguzzi thought it had been abandoned too hastily by pedagogy: 'a necessary undertaking to contradict theorising the non-professionalism of educators. [. . .] What we are proposing is open-eyed planning, but these are conclusions we will have to come to during the course of these days' (the text referred to is not included in this selection). This is a broad cultural framework within which Malaguzzi affirms the importance of distancing from macro-pedagogy and getting closer to micro-pedagogy, to know children better, and to adopt an 'artisanal' conception of education: for pedagogy does not allow a complete and absolute control of situations, it is not an exact discipline. But in 1982, with the *Consigli di Gestione*, he puts forward the risks of '*programmazione*', to be countered with educational design, which 'we consider to be permanent, and therefore constantly open . . . We have always refused to make a programme, because the risk of a caged-in programme is that in some way it generates caged-in experience'. Returning to an earlier theme, he proposes the need for 'founding the entire educational experience on an interlocutory and participatory base, in all its parts: professional, project, technical, relational' [80.82].

Malaguzzi, always a great reader, seemed to multiply his reading and discoveries when he retired in 1985. He took notes, interpreted and re-formulated what he read, met the *Équipe Pedagogica* to share his deeper investigations and reflections. In the writings we have selected, the philosophies of Gregory Bateson and Edgar Morin are among the most frequently quoted, indicative of revolutionary thinking and of ways of accessing knowledge in which interconnection is defined as ' the great verb of the present and the future' [92.89]. Malaguzzi laments the fact that neurosciences are not part of teachers' professional development, when it is relations between biology and knowledge that constitute the future cornerstone of every inquiry into the nature of being.

Recalling the American biologist Barry Commoner, Malaguzzi declares that 'ecology will certainly be the alphabet of the future. We are part of an ecosystem . . . our earthly journey is a journey made together with the environment, with nature, with the cosmos . . . [This is] where the great web of our lives exists' [90.88]. He speaks of the child as a designer, desirous of realising projects. And in the same talk to a workshop on *progettazione* in the *scuola dell'infanzia*, he declares the educator's profession to be one of uncertainty, and says that we must restore uncertainty 'as something we can live with and use in practical ways [. . .] Uncertainty can be turned into something positive when we start to test it and see it as a state of ferment, a motor of knowledge'. Connected with this idea, the 'research-action probes' proposed by Malaguzzi are 'a situation channelling conjecture towards the gathering of children's behaviours, procedures, interpretations and activities, around a circumscribed, defined experience . . . with a limited, appropriate number of children'; and requiring teachers to exercise 'far-sighted and meticulous tuning of observational methodology.' A probe, he continues, is an 'observation of observation and above all knowledge of knowledge, which remains one of the most fertile, sought after phenomena in the field of individual knowledge processes and relations between individuals.' The experience of probes was, for *pedagogistas*, teachers and *atelieristas*, one of those situations that profoundly modifies ways of being with children, letting their points of view emerge and making them visible. It was like crossing a ford in a river from which it is impossible to turn back [89.88].

In the writings and talks of the late 1980s, reflections about states of being are very present, such as disequilibrium (considered a source of energy) and equilibrium, continuity and discontinuity. All elements in which conflict and uncertainty are considered permanent states and acceptance of risk a condition of normality. As a consequence stumbling becomes an important tool in methodology because it interrupts a path of normality and allows sparks to be ignited and because, by creating crisis in what exists, it helps a process of restructuring and renewal. Disconcerting situations are necessary to children to lower the threshold of routine.

At the *Marzo–Aprile Pedagogico*, an initiative in 1989 repeated for several years with fruitful re-launches and critical analysis, Malaguzzi goes back over the most important choices made over the course of time and evaluates them in the light of new research. Choices such as teachers working together, systemic use of space, outings, social management and highlighting the introduction of the figure of the *atelierista* as 'a sort of desired turbulence stirred up in the schools' [92.89]. Already in 1988, he had underlined how 'all the connections we were aware of, all the connections we were capable of, have been realised in some way as part of our organisation' [90.88], adding, 'we have never accepted divisions, separations or hierarchies in children's formation'.

In a conference organised by the CGIL trade union in 1986 he publicly expressed his distress and intolerance for a trade union politics which, by not being capable of including the large themes of public schooling as part of a historical evolution, cannot be an active and credible participant, denouncing in this way union and political silences and absences [86.86].

In the 1970s, Reggio Emilia had built up a network of twelve municipal *nidi*, and after 1977, as recorded in the previous chapter, they became a primary subject for Malaguzzi's writing. In 1980 he was a founder of the *Gruppo Nazionale Nidi*, of which he was President until 1994; the intention was to co-ordinate exchange and give impetus to experiences being developed in different parts of Italy. Some of the pieces included here are taken from talks given by Loris Malaguzzi in opening or concluding conferences promoted by the *Gruppo* during this decade (La Spezia, 1981; Pistoia, 1982; Orvieto, 1983; Venice, 1984; Ancona and Turin, 1986; Riccione, 1988). These conferences drew (and today continue to draw) large numbers of *nido* workers, looking for deeper cultural, social, political and pedagogical analyses to strengthen their daily educational work and to help prevent *nidi* becoming a mainly welfare service.

During the Turin conference of 1986 Malaguzzi emphasised that 'an idea of the child is always an idea of a social and cultural nature'. He refers to ecological development as Bronfenbrenner proposed it, an interconnection between children and environment. He stresses the choice of a constructivist and interactional education 'because it overcomes a tension . . . between empiricism and rationalism, between resources that are innate in character and resources that are acquired or of an acquirable character'. Malaguzzi argues that quality is the *nido*'s best defence; and he proposes the *nido* as 'a micro-system . . . in which there is the greatest possible internal communication, the greatest dialogical exchange between children and children and children and adults'. In this way it assumes a large role in society, 'the only place today . . . which receives values from the private world for the public, and from the public world for the private' [87.86].

Speaking at the *Marzo–Aprile Pedagogico* in 1989, Malaguzzi was inspired by a passage from *Alice in Wonderland* in which Alice, in a soliloquy that must be understood as an 'extreme provocation', wonders: 'Who am I then? Tell me that first of all. And if I am a person I like being I will come up, otherwise I shall stay down here until someone comes to get me. I would like very much for someone to put their head in here and say something, because I am tired of being alone'.[4] Alice's words, which gave the title to a major conference held in Reggio Emilia in March 1990, take on the value of a cultural and pedagogical manifesto, an appeal once again to recognise childhood as having an identity, and also 'the right of childhood to testify to an identity accepted and shared by children. Children ask to be loved, not only in order to be loved, but in order to love, to be understood in order to understand'.

Browsing through many of Malaguzzi's writings can generate a feeling of disconsolation in the reader because we are still faced with problems that have never been fully resolved, even today, and with concepts like continuity in a 0–6 educational project, which still need to be argued, defined and defended. However, at the same time, at least here in Reggio Emilia, one also feels optimism, because we have managed to carry forward a quality educational experience and make it evolve through choices that have not always been easy. Today as then, with great perseverance, conferences continue to be organised and we strive to keep educators, administrators, politicians and families together, aware that only through broad and competent participation can the current conditions of the educational services be maintained and advanced.

Timeline 1980–89

Key: *Malaguzzi*
Reggio Emilia
Italy

1980	*President of* Gruppo Nazionale Nidi.
	Bologna station bomb kills 85; *Gruppo Nazionale Nidi* founded.
1981	**Exhibition 'If the Eye Leaps over the Wall' opens in Reggio Emilia, then travels to Stockholm.**
	Referendum supports new law allowing abortion.
1984	Concordat between state and RC church, includes
	religious instruction in schools; magazine *Zerosei* closed.
1985	*Retires as Director of municipal schools; continues to collaborate with Reggio Emilia comune on activities linked to the Exhibition, on a project about children and computers at the* scuole dell'infanzia *and on the creation of the Documentation Centre; and continues to collaborate with Emilia-Romagna Region to bring the Exhibition to the United States; Zerosei magazine becomes Bambini, with Malaguzzi as Director.*
	Conference *Esperienze e problemi. Modelli e congetture teorico-pratiche nell'educazione dei bambini* [Experiences and problems. Theoretical-practical models and conjectures in children's education].
	First edition of new magazine *Bambini*.
1986	**Comune makes first agreement with cooperatives, to manage two *nidi*, the first experience of this kind in Italy; agreement between *Comune* and FISM (Catholic inspired) *scuole materne*; Sergio Spaggiari becomes Director of municipal schools.**

1987   **Documentation and Educational Research Centre opens; exhibition
        – renamed 'The Hundred Languages of Children' – continues to
        tour Europe and is first shown in the USA (San Francisco); visits to
        Reggio Emilia schools first organised into 'study groups'.**
        552,000 births: half peak level in 1964.

Documents 1980–89

1980

78.80 A Call for Peace and Freedom by Workers in the municipal *scuole dell'infanzia* and *asili nido*, January 1980

The news that the eminent Soviet scientist and Nobel Peace Prize winner A. Sakharov[5] has been subjected to severely repressive measures by his country's authorities has rightly caused outraged responses around the world.

In this appeal we also wish to express first, our complete solidarity with all the men and women who are suffering censure, marginalisation and criminal conviction for their ideas; and second, our complete condemnation of every method and concept that is totalitarian and fundamentalist in nature and seeks to suffocate freedom of thought, freedom of expression, and freedom of cultural, political and religious dissent.

[. . .]

More than ever we are conscious that children's education in school and the family cannot be kept separate from the most important issues and problems threatening all humanity. We feel anxiety for the future, but hope and trust in <u>human reason</u>. In this appeal we would like to express our deep conviction that the common resolve of men, women and children who aspire to living in a world of peace, liberty and democracy, a world that fully deploys the best and most positive expression of each individual and every people, constitutes an invincible tool for mobilising the conscience and actions of all to look for ways for the salvation and progress of humanity.

Through our everyday experience as educators involved in the municipal *scuole dell'infanzia* and *asili nido*, we have learned the high and essential value represented by human solidarity and collaboration, by respect and value for different opinions, by determining and creating conditions for an ample and free expression of different cultural, political and religious ideals.

Therefore it is our hope that every human being, every people and every country that loves progress and civilisation will wish to lead the affairs of humankind back to the path of dialogue, co-operation, disarmament and peace, each with their own original contribution.

Educators of the municipal *scuole dell'infanzia* and *asili nido*
participating in the *aggiornamento* of Saturday 26/1/1980

❊ ❊ ❊

79.80 Opening report for the 1980–81 school year for all workers, Reggio Emilia, August 1980

Editor's note: This document, prepared for the report that Malaguzzi regularly made to all workers from the municipal schools at the start of the new school year, begins by listing 'Tasks for the Collective' (i.e. all adults working in each school), including social management, *aggiornamenti* [professional development work], cultural initiatives, audiovisual and educational materials, outside areas and equipment, administration and external relationships. It goes on to discuss 'spaces and tools for documentation and communication' and 'meetings with families'.

Indicative data for organisation and planning of the educational environment

[. . .]

*Self-*aggiornamento *of collectives*

(Themes of meetings)

Self-*aggiornamenti* meetings at frequent intervals involve worker collectives in *Nido* and *Scuola dell'Infanzia* in a shared and rigorous re-thinking of the issues that on different levels are part of the experience they are conducting together, to improve conditions in which the experience itself takes place (environmental, psychological and professional) and the educational and cultural results expected from them, particularly to the advantage of children.

In order to be fruitful each of these work meetings needs to select topics in good time, engage with them in the most concrete way, and check that they are just and functional.

The quantity of topics and the need to engage with them in good time through close and productive debate and exchange might suggest ways of organising that differ from the traditional module, in which an agenda is addressed by the whole group together. More flexible and separate methods could sit alongside this, for example sub-groups in the collective group could simultaneously engage with different topics, carefully identified and well distributed, which could then be brought together for a shared synthesis.

This type of hypothesis reinforces the need for each collective group to increase its capacity for critically self-examining experience, which is rightly considered among the most formative and productive capacities.

No one can completely list or define the topics for these meetings. In part they derive from the living experience of each school institution.

[. . .]

We have tried to list some relevant topics [. . .] that can be included in a project for activities in the first quarter:

- The correspondence between indoor and outdoor spaces and the educational project, children's ages, needs and experiences (examining elements in the organisation of children's spaces and activities).
- Examination of the efficacy of educational materials and tools, large objects, corners and children's activities.

[. . .]

1982

80.82 Speech at a meeting with *Consigli di Gestione* [School Management Councils],[6] Reggio Emilia, September 1982

The education of children between family and institutions in a period of cultural change and presentation of projects for reforming the scuola di base [elementary school][7]

The following different suggestions have been put forward by the Ministry for Public Instruction: the first year of elementary school for children aged five, the last year of *scuola dell'infanzia* available for all children, and the last (third) year of *scuola dell'infanzia* compulsory [children aged 5 to 6].

[. . .]

Why are we against bringing forward the age of children [starting elementary school]?

Because we are convinced the problem today is not so much making children precocious [doing things at an earlier age], but constructing situations for their wellbeing, for a full life, for their enrichment and overall maturation, and we must work with parents and families so that they can understand this. This important theme should always be at the centre. Instead what happens today is a curious phenomenon whereby faster children, and precocious children and children with multiple resources for study, application and performance (children in school, doing horse-riding, judo and dance etc.) represent a form of status symbol; a new form of status that families increasingly desire.

[. . .]

We could say that today women are subjected to the double effort of projecting inside the home and outside it. However this external projection outside the home never fully allows them to make their job central because it is only part of a cumulative workload that includes housework and bringing up children.

This is not all. The most delicate issue is that with their children women make the effort required of them owing to the treatment they are subjected to, using the means and possibilities they have available to them. But while they are doing this, we are personally convinced they have a function that is half submerged in ancestral ways of thinking about women and female roles and conditions, while the other half is fully thrown into the situations of our times today. We have proof of this in the fact that the job market has sectors that are open to women and sectors closed to them. The open sectors are those working with services and care, and only these, because the philosophy in our system only allows women to work as long as when they leave the home they carry out services with a close and intimate relation to their role in the family.

[. . .]

The second issue is that when women are the people employed in a service it means that the service may be much weaker.

The third [issue] is that because generally speaking services are not something [regarded as] necessary or productive, but merely useful, fluctuating politics can be applied to them that change from one moment to the next: 'We will open a service; we will close a service; we will have fewer services than the demand for them, always; we will take it out on the services'. In every country around the world faced with recession, services pay the highest price together with schools.

[. . .]

Fragile, more shadowy and less substantial, not as strong, with attitudes that often alternate, highly unsettled and restless: I believe this is the nature of children today, and above all the nature of the family today.

Just as children are partly looking for their identity through contact with us, families are also looking for their identity and cannot find it in the collective community. So I believe a phenomenon exists of weakened family identity in society, which exactly corresponds to the loss of children's identity in family relations. Now you understand, until we can give individuals a sufficiently deep level of self-listening, a feeling of self and sense of self, then everything else is destined to slide, lose shape, become changed, and suffer the consequences of a lack of organisation in children's initial formative experience. An insecure child can only look on things, events and facts with an insecure vision. Children who only live experience a little (and it seems to me today's children are in this situation) are children who cannot make memories or stable memories emerge sufficiently. So even memory is not constructed, and children cannot manage to build a personality for themselves, because personality is made up of the constant re-reading and constant remembering of the past, of comparing it with the present and the future. Above all else children today lack a past, and when the past is missing clearly the present becomes very weak, and the possibility of projecting into the future is almost completely eliminated.

I think families are experiencing the same drama. There are families living in the present with too much suffering and who have very little past behind them to retrieve from, who do not have the capacity, or have very little capacity, for projecting their existence, their future and their destiny into a longer perspective. We must begin discussion on the quality of life.

[. . .]

Today there is a need for participation with a wide range of interests. Above all participation that has an interest in developing competencies during those times when the desire for gathering together, participating and sharing problems is most evident. We have to think in terms of more genuine forms of protagonism, which are stronger and more competent, and more substantially democratic, because democracy is only effected when the model of competencies is as homogeneous as possible, so that discussion, dialogue and exchange are all on the highest level.

[. . .]

We know very well that getting people to come together cannot be summoned up like a miracle, but this means accepting that getting together is a problem, a process and a hope; it is a project that is decided, consolidated, made concrete and materialises in the course of a long, delicate and difficult process.

[. . .]

What we ask is for teachers to embed social management as an element of their profession, of their culture, and therefore of their actions.

[. . .]

> **Editor's note:** At this point, Malaguzzi discusses the necessity of planning work in a unified way and considering the child as a whole, in contrast with the way culture is often broken up, perceived and consumed in pieces and parts.

Some of you have experienced children going to elementary and middle school and understand the distance there is between a project that unifies languages, and a project that separates languages. This is not a simple discussion and I do not want to make it appear so.

The problem of subjects and disciplines and of the parts of a culture exists, certainly it exists. However I think to a large extent a pedagogical process can only really be a project of re-organisation, the progressive and permanent organising of forms of children's thinking and behaviour.

Now it is clear all of this is part of a permanent process of *progettualità*.[8] Which means we do not have a perfect and completed project. Intentionally we are faced with a process of *progettualità* that we consider to be permanent and therefore constantly open. [. . .] Permanent *progettualità* is the primary value in our contents. If someone asks us for a programme we say we don't have one. Notice that this is no coincidence: in twenty years we have never created a programme, even though we have always worked with work plans and with work projects. But we have always refused to make a programme, because the risk of a caged-in programme is that in some way it generates caged-in experience. But this originality [in our work] is formed through a very long process, which is the process of research, the process of curriculum project and planning, the process of controlled execution, of evaluative analysis of the results, and the process of decisions. This process also affects every action we carry out. There is a situation when we think, when we carry out research about the things we know and a project on the things we would like to do. Then we go on to an evaluative analysis of the results, and immediately after that we go ahead with our choice. I don't think these ways of working can be made different.

[. . .]

We must agree on the fact that education cannot be managed, education cannot be done, children cannot be brought up, without us having a specific competency, which is not a bookish competency or an enlightenment competency [i.e. rigidly rational]; it has to be a competency made up of humanity and culture at the same time, and therefore of great human and political sensibility.

How can we acquire this competency?

For us this is a fact and a process, so that on this issue we place ourselves with something that is the equivalent of all our culture, our sensibility, our ideas, and our cultural, human, political and ideals background; and all this culture, which constitutes our existential history, is offered in a process, becomes part of a process, which we agree and wish to accept and which drives us along with it, absorbing educational workers, families and themes, towards a definition of participation. And so participation becomes competent; not in the sense that we create participation so competent it has nothing left to achieve in terms of more or greater competency, but competent participation that is in constant flux: let's say participation that is 'competent and permanent'. By saying permanent we mean the gradual acquisition of new and progressively higher conditions of competency, regarding themes and issues.

[. . .]

All this leads to an important definition, which is that of a pedagogy and didactics of competent participation.

❋ ❋ ❋

81.82 Conversation with members of the *Consigli di Gestione* of the *Scuola Comunale dell'Infanzia* Diana, November 1982

Editor's note: The three parent representatives on the *Consigli di Gestione* of the Diana school who participated in this conversation were Franca Catellani (FC), Valeria Catellani (VC) and Giuliano Rovacchi (GR).

Malaguzzi (LM) is described as both Coordinator of the *Équipe Pedagogico-Didattica* of the *nidi* and *scuole dell'infanzia* of Reggio Emilia and as Director of the *Zerosei* journal published by Fabbri.

Adult–child relations

GR: Dr. Malaguzzi, at the last class meeting some parents raised the need to start examining an important theme more deeply: the relations between adult and child. We examined the problem in a *commissione di lavoro* [work commission] and tried to identify topics in the theme to discuss in the next class meeting with all the parents whose children attend the *scuola comunale dell'infanzia* Diana. We would like to take some new topics to parents at the next meeting, enriched by this conversation with you. [. . .]

VC: Until now we have spoken about children's rights, but at this point I would like to say parents have rights too, couples, and men and women individually, have rights: the right to a space for themselves. So how can we manage to reconcile these two things?

LM: Children must know how to live both in contact with adults and in contact with peers, and I would not say being close to adults is necessarily more important for children than the experience they have with friends and peers.

It is important for children to live experience on different levels, to be faced with different situations, and faced with different difficulties and responses, because the world is a very diversified place, not a world the child should perceive as uniform. It is an extremely diversified world and children's experience of each situation they are immersed in should enrich them, so that they can structure that experience into a sort of child philosophy.

What is important is that when they are temporarily away from each other, or even very far away from each other, the situations in the life of a couple and the situations in the life of a child are situations that can be re-lived by both the child and the parents when they are back together again. What I mean is: it is possible to be far away and still be extremely close when memory unites the child and the parents, even if distance keeps us apart for a while.

In effect we can be very close when we are apart and very far apart when we are close.

GR: Of course, but there must also be some issue of continuity between these various situations otherwise there would be breaks in the child's life and in adult–child relations.

LM: This is a very important theme and a theme that is at the centre of debate among *pedagogistas*. That is to say, what kind of relationship should there be between families and [school] institutions. Some people talk of continuity. I am one of those people who say continuity cannot be, we cannot go chasing after it, because objectively the two experiences are different. What is important is to open up to a capacity for conversation and keep it going constantly, the capacity for inter-rogating oneself, for asking oneself, for exchanging information, for decisions taken together, for making choices together; and for trying to discuss and understand more deeply together the specific qualities of family experience and of experiences that take place in the [school] institution, where children live experience with thirty, sixty, ninety children of a similar age, in a completely different environment from the family environment, and with different rhythms of time.

So the large theme is one of managing to bring about the most pro-ductive conversations possible, connecting the very different nature of these different experiences.

Thus the problem is not merely the relation between family and school, because that would be a simplification: that is to say, families must question themselves internally about how they can develop a coherent attitude towards their own children. There are some children who live a lot of their time in the family and yet really they are distant from the family.

[. . .]

This means making it possible for each one of us to belong to a com-munity, to feel we are tied to a group in some way, also affectively, but capable of not losing the warmth of affection and the value of affection at times when distance separates us from one another.

This is true for adults but it is also true for children. Our school organisation also privileges clear points of reference. The class is a stable point of reference, and from there children can move around in spaces with greater confidence. The continuity of the adult figure with chil-dren is another organisational feature full of important responsibility, and it is also the form of organisation that responds best to children's needs. That is to say, children must have a capacity and possibility of having points of reference, and when they have them then they can detach from them.

VC: But when there is more than one point of reference this can create con-tradictions for children. So how much does this influence the relationship in the family between adult and child, between parents and children?

LM: I think this is one of the situations we absolutely cannot ignore. That is to say, the natural situation is to live in a world where contradictions are a permanent given fact and give us a rough ride. The earth is not made of easy and endlessly flat ground. Our life is often made up of situations that are not smooth, or easy, or undemanding. The problem is how to equip ourselves and equip children for living a life that is not smooth, with an adequate capacity for self-determination and self-control.

So in education we must proceed as if children's situations might be situations of disequilibrium, and education must have the capacity to equip children to get through moments of this kind.

VC: We can't strictly call them contradictions, but we could say they are experiences children must have in order to arrive at acquiring their own critical capacity towards things.

LM: Exactly. So the problem of problems lies in being capable of having <u>different experiences</u> but maintaining a close connection between <u>one experience and another</u>. This means a capacity for dialogue between experience and experience, a critical capacity on the child's part for knowing to adopt a certain behaviour in this situation but, in a different situation, to necessarily adopt another, and in yet another different situation to adopt yet another. That is to say, this flexibility in children's behaviour is something we have when there is equal flexibility in the behaviour of adults.

[. . .]

1983

82.83 Speech to the National Conference of the *Gruppo Nazionale Nidi* [National Nido Group], Orvieto, March 1983

> **Editor's note:** The paragraphs below are taken from a much longer talk. Malaguzzi speaks against the background of prolonged recession and cuts in public expenditure.

New conceptions for the nido and early years institutions in a society in crisis and obliged to change

Like the old sea routes recounted in Kipling's tales [see Chapter 1, n.45], there are times when it seems the long accumulation of problems and difficulties becomes extenuating and brings the power of reasoning to crisis point, and with it the possibility of taking control of things again. We are probably at one of those times. And this coming together [at the conference], all of us coming together in the one place (there is hardly room for us all), certainly has the mark of widespread anxiety, but is also the sign of a desire and a determination to understand the situation's meanings together and, if we can, to find our way out of it.

I do not think there is anything to marvel at (as some might) that such a wide range of issues is included in a conference on the *asilo nido*, which is a young, very young institution; and even when we put its many social and cultural values together, it appears to have relative value compared with the situation of enormous conflict and the problems in politics, economics, traditions and civilisation that are threatening our everyday life and our futures.

The fact is that apart from its specific nature (which we will examine in detail over the next few days in order to understand better), the *asilo nido* here stands for many other things. Each one of us can feel how, beyond the apparent slightness of our subject, there are many crucial issues of society at stake: how the State respects rights and supports needs, how it distributes and protects its resources; the position it takes on families, women, children, educational themes and work organisation; how it intends to tackle the economic crisis and decline of morale; what choices it will make to reduce misspending and public debt; if it has the necessary resolve to put an end to tax evasion and injustice; and how it will distribute the (inevitable) burden of these necessary sacrifices. Will it prove capable of abandoning the old choice of being pitiless with the weak so that children, women, the young, the elderly and the disadvantaged are always the great target to regularly aim at?

In short, is the State capable of coming through this crisis while safeguarding the qualities of life we have achieved in recent years, which constitute a precious legacy and distinguish a civil, democratic and just society capable of responding to the new needs it has created for itself?

All these things come in through the tender walls of the *nido* with all the reality and hope they contain, which includes the whole area of needs and rights in childhood, mothers, women, families and more; to the point of [the *nido*] bordering on the more general philosophy that touches essential issues of economy, politics and culture, which today all lie in the balance, so much so that the matrix and fundamental guidelines [of this philosophy] are threatened with being overturned (we must be aware of this).

So to open discussion on the *asilo nido* is to open a wide range of several complex issues full of implications.

[. . .] Identifying and defining the most relevant references [for our discussion] leads us to organising relevant material for *nido* issues in three directions.

Editor's note: Malaguzzi then discusses (1) political-administration issues; (2) socio-historical issues; and (3) cultural issues.

❋ ❋ ❋

83.83 Letter to parents about *Consigli di Gestione*, September 1983

MUNICIPIO DI REGGIO NELL'EMILIA
ASSESSORATO SCUOLA INFANZIA E ASILI NIDO
Via dell'Abbadessa 8

OPEN LETTER TO PARENTS
ON THE THEME
OF RENEWAL OF *CONSIGLI DI GESTIONE*
September–December 1983

We think it is right and just to inform you that by next December (probably in the first ten days) a renewal of the _Consiglio di Gestione_, which have been in office for two years, will take place in all _Comune_ preschool institutions.

This is an important event first and foremost for all families and school workers, who are asked to organise in order to bring more strength, democracy and competency to all forms of collaboration, research and exchange that promote a more concerted shared co-responsibility in choosing contents and educational methodologies; and guarantee that every single institution will have at its disposal the necessary tools and functional efficiency for responding to its tasks and objectives.

We believe families will easily be able to identify the meanings and values contained in this initiative.

Essentially the aims of the proposal are to:

* strengthen the quality of educational and professional standards in institutions through more rigorous strategies of participation and social support;
* intensify, as systematically as possible, reciprocal knowledge and exchange on educational experience between family environments and that of the institution, to increase reflection and convergence on common themes of children's growth and advancement;
* consolidate children's reassuring image of the rich protective fabric of social relations and cooperative interactions between adults whose interest in them takes different forms, at a time when models of impersonal conformity, the drive to precociousness, and violent and divisive images are insistent;
* offer parents a concrete opportunity for increasing and orientating knowledge and competency in areas that have to do with their specific role;
* allow workers and teachers entrusted with the delicate and always difficult task of raising and educating children to feel a concrete and stimulating social solidarity, and take the opportunities for learning and evaluating that are so vital in raising their professional level and culture;
* and finally, contribute to giving each _nido_ or _scuola dell'infanzia_ its identity of public purpose and public responsibility conferred on it by social mandate.

The reasons why, since their inception, _nidi_ and _scuole dell'infanzia_ have chosen participation and co-management with families and citizens as one of the most defining qualities of their pedagogical project will appear clear.

In the period of time leading up to December the institutions will promote a series of initiatives and meetings that aim to deepen understanding and disseminate themes to do with _Consiglio_ renewal.

We ask families to participate as much as they can, and are certain of their sensibility and sympathy for the great importance of the events connected with renewing the *Consigli*.

FOR THE *COORDINAMENTO PEDAGOGICO DIDATTICO ASILI NIDO E SCUOLE DELL'INFANZIA*
(Prof. Loris Malaguzzi)

1984

84.84 Speech at a conference '*Il bambino e la scienza*' [The child and science], Scandicci (Tuscany), November 1984

Childhood and the child between prejudices, reality and science

[. . .]

3

Breaking down this kind of [official] inaction [towards childhood policy], and the paradoxical public legitimisation of bad governance, in which 'prejudices' become transformed into political and cultural facts, and events play their part, means progressing on theoretical and practical levels with a more just and truthful objectivisation[9] of childhood and the problems connected with family and social environments. It is a question of **normalising** childhood, and it isn't hard to understand how much historical-critical process, of research and knowledge, of culture and politics, will be necessary. Normalise it in the subversive sense of [. . .] cleaning it as much as possible of the highly interfering imagery that blurs and alters its biological and cultural identity, above all through silence and metaphor. So that we can begin to **see it** and to **practise it** as an age, a part that is organically and historically included in a longer existential journey, **which we leave by becoming bigger** and which we can **return** to – certainly with problems, but no more than with other forms of leaving and returning.
    [. . .]
    Normalising childhood does not mean simplifying it or reducing its complexity. It means above all freeing it of all artificial isolation and not its specific transitory evolution – as far as the knowledge we have up to now is concerned (which is still very little and uncertain) – and also [freeing it] of its historical mediation if it is true, as I believe, that **objectivisation** of childhood is always inevitably connected with an **objectivisation** of adulthood. **Children and adults always transit simultaneously through cultures and social spheres, and the relations between them (their being and their becoming) are part of interwoven processes even when they seem distant, or even contradictory.**

In other words I like to think that if adult women and men could be guaranteed a more peaceful and secure existence, ridding them of the enormous anxieties and fears that threaten them today (especially today), with higher levels of knowledge and literacy, of sentiment and reason expressed with full creative freedom, and a higher consciousness of solidarity, then they would be freer to revisit their entire lives (childhood included) with a stronger memory, taking recollections, images, experience, wishes and fantasies to add to their history and consciousness, and having a completely different philosophy of relations, with themselves and with children. This might in turn herald a new culture of humanity and children, conducive to changes in the quality of life that no one can deny are within reach of human volition and action.

It is in the fabric of these propositions, and by setting aside old and new forms of extreme imagery, that we find the most promising ideas for a theoretical and practical project of children and adults together, that cancels everything disallowed by the traditional asymmetry: children who are weak, who just survive, who do not know, and adults who are strong, enlightened and knowing; or turning all this upside down, children who live in a golden and divine age with adults living in a corrupt, apocryphal age. This kind of distancing precludes any real shared protagonism in exchange and relations.

If a children's project exists not just in fairy tale and legend but in the history of mankind, then it taps into the biological, existential and cultural continuity that flows dialectically from children to adults and from adults to children.

[. . .]

6.

I would like to better re-formulate a proposition/problem I made earlier and that is crucial for me: it posits children's 'normalisation' as a necessary event for continuing to talk about and with children, and see them as a unified whole. 'Is childhood a world we leave never to return, or is it a world we leave when we get bigger, and can go back to freely?' I know this question is a difficult, complex and even painful one, because we need to strip it of all the encrusted layers and attributions humanity has always unearthed – symbolic, allegorical, mythical and religious – whenever we have wanted to go back in time, and laboriously retrieve our childhood, and often through childhood our own [adult] dimension. History, art and literature are full of examples of this kind.

Otherwise there would be no explaining something I experienced recently when I asked some well-known friends – poets, literary critics, artists and scientists – to contribute their thoughts on childhood. I met with refusals, walls of difficulty and diffidence, declarations that they were incapable or powerless, had no desire to, felt reluctant: 'Ask me anything but not to talk about children'.

Carlo Bernardini,[10] who later gave me a lovely contribution, wrote: 'I am indebted to the children of the *scuole comunali* in Scandicci [Tuscany] for so many things, but I don't talk about it, because I have the impression I appear ridiculous: <u>where a man gets lost</u> – people say'. Getting closer to childhood, in the material and immaterial sense, is still very difficult.

Reflecting on this fact I recently came across an illuminating proposition. I did not find it in a book of pedagogy but in an essay on economic policy. 'Where does, and where will, the failure of Keynes' *dirigiste* policies and Friedman's liberal politics lie?'[11] They share a preoccupation with the <u>rate</u> of growth. While the real problem lies in the <u>nature</u> and the <u>structure</u> of growth.

There are meanings and connections to be found in the incisiveness of this proposition, which if we transfer them into a pedagogical situation can help us resolve one of the most crucial and impassioned themes in reflections today on children, children's education, and our adult action.

Good. Then let's ask ourselves questions. 'Is what worries us, or what should worry us, the rate of children's growth? Or is it not rather the nature, the quality, the structure, of their growth?' The two theses are opposed, and I agree with the second. I feel a grudge towards the first. Because the second of the two, and I think this can be seen with the naked eye, is the one that allows us to attempt achieving the normalisation of childhood that to now has eluded us.

Instead of aiming for a Taylor-type[12] growth of children through laws of rate [of return] and the selective intensification of tools of production [to be applied to children], normalisation aims at slower, broader processes. These are capable of activating everything children possess in and around their intelligence, including the forgotten parts and those said to be transient or inferior, the *cognitio inferior* [inferior knowledge] as they used to say, which also contribute to profit of a very different nature and structure.

The problem is seriously complex because objectively <u>rate of growth</u> with its rigid rules of profit is <u>a law of capitalist consumerism</u>; and because it has already gone from being a <u>category of economics</u> to becoming a <u>category of customs, culture and values</u>; and because in this version it is already a living thing in the character of many people with low, medium and high levels of culture; and because there are already several signs that certain currents of pedagogical thinking are formulating general theory borrowing copiously from the methodologies of economics.

I would like to emphasise that this <u>standard of rate [of growth]</u>, which is already part of organised work with implications that have serious consequences if they go unguided and uncontrolled, has already visibly insinuated itself into human history, compressing and bringing forward people's ages and experience – paradoxically at a time when life expectancy has become longer.

[. . .]

7.

Science and science education can play a large role in this controversial picture of children if they help rid us of metaphorical and reductive models, of conventional truths about childhood (and adulthood) that resist change in both popular and academic culture, that resist in shared understanding and in current educational practice, and above all resist in the pillars of our consumer society. Paradoxically ours is a society informed by science and technology in other areas, which means that the massive and widespread presence of science and technology in what we could call the 'key' areas of human production (but not diffused, distributed, or made part of our <u>everyday</u> knowledge processes) has not been enough to produce any shift in educational culture and procedures (up to now) or to constitute a reassuring element for our present and future existence.

Here we have one of the crucial points. We all feel we are faced with enormous changes in knowledge (including science) and children also sense this. But what is our adult relation with this increasingly eclectic and pragmatic knowledge, which co-habits with technologies, economies, demographics and ethics that go in different directions? Where and how do we construct our competencies and where do we affirm them? What different directions are we taking with the efforts and challenges we have undertaken for long years, for ends and ideals that still retain their intrinsic purpose despite everything? Perhaps one of our highest objectives is to govern the encounters and collisions between the most vital parts of our old humanist culture and those of technological culture.

Whatever the case, our adult responses will also <u>contain</u> children's and we know little of the ways they are adopting and organising their ideas, thinking and feelings in order to understand the world.

What I mean is the battle and challenge for science and educating to scientific thinking, however exhilarating it is and rightly so, can only start with some difficult observations. Because science itself and the philosophical praxis of science are in a crisis of transition, together with all the branches that stem from them.

One of the risks [we run during this conference] is to reduce children to an epistemic subject (or object), removed from any historical and social context when we place them beside science. This is the reason we are concerned with giving some background and figures.

I think it is right and opportune to focus closely on some issues before we start. The first is to clearly state the age of the children we are discussing. For my part I make reference to children aged 3 to 6. The second is an attempt to give an updated definition of the concept of science, given and considering it has several disparate attributes today. The third, when we have defined it, is to establish if and how it is practicable as part of an educational and didactical project and therefore what its purposes are. That leaves procedures, rhythms, didactics and values: a vital subject that clashes with cultures and competencies that are backward and unused to them and is still waiting for much knowledge-based and experiential material.

While we wait for help in order to better understand points two and three I must say I have great difficulty in talking about science and science education in any version when it is intended for children. I can see others have the same difficulties as me. Bernardini makes a reference to children's 'non-specific scientificness'. Guidoni wonders if the issue is not more one of 'children and knowledge' than 'children and science'. And Bernardini and Guidoni are both scientists who have worked with children. I see Toraldo di Francia,[13] another scientist, has sparked an important topic for reflection that is too often completely skipped over when he asks if all the holistic, egocentric, animistic etc. visions of children are not at odds with science and are really old clutter we ought to throw out.

And I have something unsuspected, completely unpredictable, in my ears. The confession of a scientist like Jean Piaget almost at the end of his long work: 'the ideal I am trying to realise personally is to remain a child until death'. And this, though not an act of weakness, is a surprising act of rhetorical fading away that we need to reflect on.

Each of these references is full of deeply controversial issues and questions. I can only take a position, and they will be barely stated positions, on some of the many possible theses:

- It is not only legitimate but urgent to reflect on the relationship between science and young children, on science and children's pedagogy. The legitimacy comes from the simple fact that children are already immersed in and have experience of life in the physicality, imagery and languages of science and, above all, in the languages of its technological applications. The urgency arises from the awareness of our delays in producing interventions.
- In general parents and school culture cannot see or appreciate these procedures or co-participate in them. If only they were able to appreciate what Hawkins calls 'messing about'![14]
- Children already experience scientific practice and research of their own accord when opportunities and help exist, in the sense that they possess the necessary requisites of curiosity and concentration, the need to understand and pleasure in understanding, the ability to find relations between things and events, to feel wonder when these do not agree with what they were thinking (the wonder, Gargani reminds us, that makes scientists leap from their chairs), to accept points of view that seem better than theirs, and even transit from simple causal relations to the initial formulations of progressively extendable laws.
- There is a real pragmatic resemblance – resemblance not coincidence – between children's qualities and actions and those in [psychologist] Ada Fonzi's definition of science:

> A progressive construction in which each piece of knowledge acquired puts a question mark over the original design and transforms the ends of the work. Non-success is re-absorbed and becomes the source and drive for research into new relations and the formulation of new laws. Testing is science's ultimate truth but since we are not dealing with

teleological truth it is always subjected to counter-proof and examination. Paradoxically the most transient knowledge is precisely the knowledge which is scientific, the only kind that will admit the possibility of self-negating.

This definition contains much of children's procedures. It seems to me that procedure and method are scientific values we can ascribe to children, who are innate carriers of what we could call an <u>epistemological</u> curiosity for researching into meanings, for which their experience of life has a clear and coherent need.

• Based on my experience the possibility of working in small groups provides children with the conditions that are most conducive to doing 'science' by producing co-operative and conflictive exchanges, above all of a cognitive-linguistic nature, and by also being conducive to the assimilation of adult help in circular ways (with adults picking up on the <u>high points</u> of what takes place).

• Children '<u>doing science</u>' constitutes one of the most privileged situations for adults who wish to learn the art of the interlocutor, which substantially means silencing their own thought processes and perceiving the very different processes children choose for learning and understanding.

[. . .]

1985

85.85 Two speeches at the conference *Esperienze e problemi. Modelli e congetture teorico-pratiche nell'educazione dei bambini* **[Experiences and problems: Theoretical-practical models and conjectures in children's education], Reggio Emilia, May–June 1985**

Editor's note: This four day conference was organised by Reggio Emilia for 'friends, Italian and from abroad, with whom we have exchanged reflections for some time on the themes of early years education'; 400 attended, including groups from Sweden, Denmark. Switzerland, Luxembourg, Germany and Spain, as well as participants from all over Italy. The conference presentations were made by educators from Reggio Emilia's schools and drew on projects and other everyday work. Among the issues 'confronted' in the conference were the situation of childhood today; how children represent, express and invent images; what they look for and how they construct their intelligence, including

(continued)

(continued)

when confronting the artificial intelligence of the computer; and a new pedagogy of childhood and a reform of the institutional framework. The conference included a presentation on a project 'The Intelligence of Children and the Intelligence of Computers' undertaken by a number of municipal schools and state elementary schools in Reggio Emilia 'stimulated by the awareness that civilisation is strongly marked by the presence of IT conditions and [these] will condition the growth of children from their earliest years of life'. Malaguzzi made two interventions.

Introduction to the second day of the conference

Editor's note: Malaguzzi begins with an introduction to the history of different scientific and educational attitudes to children's drawings, mentioning the theories of Arnheim, Luscher, Piaget, Stern and Laubenfeld, but also how Rousseau, Pestalozzi, Spencer and Froebel did not see its possibilities. He discusses Montessori's attitude with her interest in copying geometric figures, and Lombardo Radice and the use of drawings to reveal psychological disturbances.

[. . .]

What is the language of drawing for us? It is one of many languages children bring with them, a natural language belonging to all children, which constantly and continuously mixes with all the other languages. This is probably what gives rise to the need to be very cautious when we evaluate and reflect on operations in children's drawing because a language made in this way and defined this way will absolutely not tolerate a unilateral approach. Interpreting drawings (which is above all the adult responsibility) must be done not in order to go and dig up presumed or real images of the child, but in order to learn together where children direct their capacities, what their rhythms are, what their choices and motivations are (whether spoken or unspoken) and above all to learn what our job is. This is done both by listening and by intervening to produce the circularity of situations pedagogy must realise (the most difficult pedagogy and the most productive) if it wants to carry out its responsibilities.

[. . .]

Drawing is one of many languages children have, and a language which is part of their biological programming (like all the other languages) and it is refined and diversified through children's life experience. Like all languages it is highly complex and so we could define it as a multi-factored, dynamic and evolving unified act, and therefore an act which is multivalent, with several meanings, where several different and disparate factors come together, apparently distant but always present together, unfolding in unified processes of progressively increasing unity and with dynamic aspects. Children's journey in drawing (through the drawing, through this evolving language because it constantly accompanies children's evolution) produces different and sometimes discordant attitudes towards the relations between themselves and the world, between themselves and things, between themselves and situations, themselves and feelings and so on.

[. . .]

Please allow me to use the term 'pleasure' in place of other terms. I do not wish to use it psycho-analytically. 'Pleasure' is a typical word, removed from its psycho-analytical meaning, and I mean 'pleasure' as a form of energy. Think of it in this sense, while I attempt to list what these 'pleasures' might be that a child seeks, sometimes finds and sometimes doesn't, sometimes intentionally and sometimes not, because children's lives are very complicated, and children's encounters are never scheduled to happen on this or that particular date.

What 'pleasures' constitute the act of drawing then? Our work today, especially this morning wishes to concentrate our capacity for looking into children aged 3 to 4 years, the age when the first germs of direct and explicit figurative transposition are activated.

The pleasure of play, which we must not lose sight of when we look more closely at children's production and our own production on children, because it is certainly part of the inventory of pleasures that are part of children's lives.

There is a pleasure of storytelling, which is extraordinary in children's first approaches to life, and I consider it a pity that children lose this art during the course of their lives. But beginning on this subject would lead us far away.

There is motor pleasure on children's part, bearing in mind that muscular and nervous activity immediately makes states of pleasure possible. Psychoanalysts also speak of pleasure that is hedonistic and that is sexual in muscular work and motor activity.

Visual pleasure. There cannot be a pleasure that does not also belong to the eyes and the visual.

Rhythmic-temporal pleasure: when a child draws several times and goes in several directions in an unpredictable succession. This is often not what we think it is, because children are content with the pleasure of rhythm, the rhythm the pencil or felt tip pen flows with, how it breaks up the space, and how it becomes an element of space and time.

Spatial pleasure: the pleasure children take in being able to organise and govern spaces. Most certainly this pleasure is born with the child, it is in the child and these things are all present, all present together when the child is born (so do not imagine we have a date for them in the history of a child's evolution). This is one of those issues where discussion would lead us far away.

There is a self-identifying pleasure, which is that of assigning identity to things they are doing, given that not only adults but children seek, through words, the definition, identity and identification of objects, words, things, feelings and so on.

There is the pleasure of repetition that the child pursues through long repetition and is an acquired competency children can only let go at a later point when they start to realise they are acquiring many competencies that they can abandon this one. Repetition is a pleasurable game for children. Just think how many times children love to be told the same tales, the same stories, using the same words and the same situations. This need is part of the child.

There is the pleasure of knowing, and undoubtedly in the act of drawing there is also the pleasure of learning, of knowing and of fixing the event, the happening or the object in terms of knowledge.

Another pleasure is that of relations, of being able to communicate through using this language. There is introverted communication, and extroverted communication. Communication can go in infinite directions and we cannot always understand the exact direction of children's communication. This communication includes all the possible forms of communication, those that go inside and stay inside, those spoken and expressed, and those that are unspoken because they sit intimately in a sort of private cave; children's thoughts, situations, words.

The last pleasure is aesthetic pleasure. Here again we need to retrieve aesthetics from the old theories of a philosophical nature and give it credit because it is clear that a good form (using the language of the theory of form), an organised form, a balanced form is what makes a child say 'I have managed to make a really good drawing', and children know when this is true. I know very well how difficult it is to try and investigate what a statement of this kind by children contains deep down; but there is certainly an aesthetic pleasure in children, which is probably closely woven with symbolic aspects and the pleasure of symbol, which is another pleasure in the same family as aesthetics, and which can conclude this list of pleasures.

If all these factors can be at play in producing drawings, then what kind of product are children giving and offering us at any given moment in time? If all this is a shadow, and all this constitutes material that penetrates, a mixing and alchemising that circulates inside children and leads them to find a finished form of expression, then this is what children are giving and offering us.

I believe there is the play of self-regulation in children, which is partly intentional and partly not. It is difficult to try and follow to what extent this fixed point of the child's drawing really gives us a finished operation. The last operation to have been completed is the one we have to read and it may well happen that one aspect of the several we have discussed emerges more than others. Sometimes we are clearly being offered a drawing through the pleasure of play, other times a drawing might be playful and narrative together, or again a drawing might be rhythmical, and so on. It is like a die with many sides: children throw the dice and often they know which side will come up but often they do not know what side they want or wish for. Children will try anything, they are orientated in ways that are difficult to interpret for adults. When the die comes to a halt there is probably a mixture of all these pleasures, with one pleasure [in particular] emerging.

So, reading children's drawings is something very serious, very committed, very difficult, very responsible. To interpret a drawing we need to have competency, passion and a capacity for getting inside the children's situation and the operation they are carrying out, while bearing in mind that probably every form children offer has a completed aspect but is also in some way transiting, in the sense that it is in transit, that it might be a representation of transit. So that our interpretations should probably be of a context and of a situation, and we cannot approach any of children's operations without also admitting the context of yesterday's operation and perhaps of the operation they will carry out tomorrow.

In every form, every act, every field and every level children propose, there is always a great risk for us. This is the risk of being subjected to forms of suggestion that the culture of humanities has soaked up from the culture of science, so that it quickly moves on to classify and to categorise. The risk we run is of classifying too quickly and putting things in order too soon, without thinking sufficiently, without waiting sufficiently long, of not knowing how to wait, and not knowing how to interpret children's acts.

In this way the subjectivity of today's theme, or the objectivity of today's theme, disappears and becomes confused, but that was my intention: to go back into the important, difficult and complex circuitry of children, of children's thoughts, their acts and their attitudes. In this way I think I have brought a language back into the totality of our languages, which until now has been kept pitifully marginalised and disconnected in a very foolish way.

[. . .]

The intelligent and careful observation of children can offer practice and pedagogy very useful and rich information. In other words we have started on a journey to the source of children's thinking, we know that children's thinking is generated above all when it is dealing with problems, and that it develops when it is researching solutions to problems in the same way as adult thinking; and this is something we have attempted to highlight on several occasions during these days [of the conference], knowing that children's thinking is inextricably composed of cognitive elements and of non-cognitive elements.

***

Editor's note: Malaguzzi then introduces the day's forthcoming presentations.

***

To conclude, it is important for us to underline how, from the research that has been [presented], a rich, strong and complex idea of children's thinking emerges, which is far removed from the usual static, reductive and one-dimensional images that continue to be presented in much of preschool and school publishing with its widely circulating little books on pre-reading and pre-numeracy. It is urgent for us to underline – and this has been said often during the last few days – that children's intelligence should not be humiliated, that children's intelligence asks adult intelligence to be on the same high level as children's expectations and potentials.

The issue of childhood, and educational and institutional issues

I think Italy, in homage to science education, is literally sinking under basins of water measuring the capacity of an object to sink or float. I think this is the stage we are at in research in education when we are addressing children. Or else we classify shells and bounce ping-pong balls and impose an observation for the record.

We are in times where new terms like taxonomy, curriculum etc. are all the rage, and these are names that come from other places (although this is certainly not what is bad about them); but they are flooding our schools with a dry and rigid terminology, compared to the needs of the teaching profession, which are different.

Here [in this conference] we have seen procedures followed by children. To my mind this is something extraordinarily important at a time when there is still debate about authority and non-authority in the difficult relations between adults and children, on whether adults can suppress or actually do suppress children's freedom, and whether children feel hurt or humiliated by the collaborative presence of adults.

These are important themes that continue to thread through the great debates in philosophy and pedagogy. Instead I believe it is possible to be part of an operation that literally turns the problem on its head, and takes us by the hand to lead us – if we want, if we are willing, if we have the capacity, above all if we have the willingness – to realise a pedagogical construction which is this: where we clearly see the progressive definition of situations, which have been gradually thought out and reflected on through explicitly comparing them with friends and companions. Essentially, a presentation in images offers a continuous sequential organisation of children's actions, words, thinking, reflections and criticisms as well as the circularity gathered up by the teacher, again sequentially.

This circularity contains the great secret of transmitting knowledge and of being with children, the great secret of educating children. In reality what are teaching us how to be educators and teachers are the trajectories children take, the signs, the traces, the pathways children show us they have taken (this is true of the children we have seen here today). Our task is to look very carefully and listen very carefully, looking inside ourselves to try and find the difficulties, the rhythms, the possibilities, variables and contradictions, which in part must be kept as they are so that they become the laws the children find, and because no one is asking us to impose laws on children that are absolute, final and rigorously and scientifically exact.

Life is long, experience is long, children's rhythms are rhythms that must be respected, like laws that we absolutely have to respect.

Earlier while looking at some computer slides we spoke about algorithms. I think that if you reflect now and put together the whole story of the coffee or tea [in the presentation we saw], and if you reconstruct the story in images through deconstructing the single acts and single processes, then you will come to a form which is immediately distinguishable and with a very precise identity: where children are experiencing algorithms in completely natural terms, as part of an action, a term, a word and a process, and which until now could only be found in dictionaries or alien scientific languages.

What we have seen, what we are discussing, is an extremely important question because I think it can give us an answer to many of the questions we have posed during the conference and which we will probably continue to pose inside ourselves and in the external world.

I do not much like to make comparisons but I think we have to make them. Let those who have experience of spending time with children, talking with children, and above all understanding the words of children, spoken and unspoken, think about how a problem of this kind (the problem of measuring) could be treated. The market is full of tools and there are precise methodologies: Cuisenaire Rods, Gattegno Rods,[15] Montessori Rods (my apologies to Montessori for naming her here but her rods do not evoke particularly happy thoughts). It is important to understand that in this kind of operation, when we go and ask the market or ask for things or tools invented by pedagogical researchers etc., we become aware of their limitations and rigidity, of their incapacity for communicating and speaking; and of the risks we take when we offer them all boxed up, then taken out and put on the table, and invite children to put the rods in a row or put the different measures in a row.

Our polemic with Piaget also lies here. Because really this [what we have seen today] is the clinical attitude that is necessary, not his. His clinical research was done on children without the children knowing, unprepared children suddenly put there, in front of things: the clinical interview is a misleading thing, painfully and seriously misleading.

The great problem to my mind is the fact that truly clinical interviews with children come about through a history, through a dimension of journeying, through long intervals and through children's capacity for activating in play, where it is no longer possible to rigidly delimit play from work.

Reflection, reasoning, the desire to be protagonist, the desire to play, the desire to participate, the capacity for thinking ahead and anticipating; this is the real clinical discourse we should use to replace the clinical discourse of a Piagetian order.

It seems to me all these things are important, and I felt I ought to underline them for the value of their immediate use, their immediate capacity for connecting up in rapid synthesis an operation of the kind we have seen presented [today], and which like all the others we have seen has cost long investments of strength, energy and patience, and above all of qualitatively refining adult behaviours towards children.

We can find many keys in this work to the large questions, and the small ones, which constantly arise to remind us of the difficulties that are part of work like ours.

1986

86.86 Speech at a national conference of CGIL-FLEL School, Reggio Emilia, January 1986

Editor's note: Malaguzzi is speaking to a national conference of the school section of the *Confederazione Generale Italiana del Lavoro* [CGIL, Italian General Confederation of Labour], a national trade union. CGIL was formed by agreement between Socialists, Communists and Christian Democrats in June 1944. But in 1950, Socialists and Christian Democrats split to form their own organisations, UIL and CISL, since when the CGIL was influenced by the PCI. It remains the largest trade union in Italy.

[. . .]

This is not an issue that only influences the *nido* and *scuola dell'infanzia* but the entire school system, and the cultural conception accompanying the education of very small children, older children and young people of all ages.

The conceptions the CGIL has gathered together up to this point really are conceptions I believe to be extremely negative, and which still weigh heavily on our perspective today.

[. . .]

What I mean to say is that any discourse of union politics or general politics that does not take into account the historical and evolutionary aspects of situations will find it difficult to actively participate in the conversation and to be listened to on the central and most important issues we are confronted with today.

[. . .]

The problem is that state *scuole materne* are schools that suffer from an unexplained absence, from oversights and negligence of a political and trade union origin, which affect the functions of the local authorities and affect the school [section of] the CGIL union directly. It is not possible to produce a working week that includes no time for reflection on what takes place, and this is something that has been claimed as a right in trade union contracts. But [in practice] no-one does those hours. There is complicity with a rule of silence on this issue that is affecting everyone on all sides. On a practical level it would be possible to publicly denounce the Ministry for Public Education for the failure to carry out its public duty, because no-one is checking and no-one is doing the six hours included in the contract. And so they become a feature that either we have the courage to throw out; or if we include them, then they must be used for the purpose of *aggiornamento* and for reflection etc.

On the issue of professional development, if we accept a coherent 0–6 project, then we also need to be coherent on the level of professional development, so development must be as unified and similar as possible for both parts [services for children under and over 3 years].

[. . .]

Then the problem becomes one of understanding what it means to live in a profession that is diminished and abandoned, left there like a relic, an issue it is as well to keep one's distance from.

❋ ❋ ❋

87.86 Speech to a conference 'Quale futuro per l'asilo nido' [What future for the asilo nido], Turin, December 1986

> **Editor's note:** This excerpt is taken from a speech by Malaguzzi to a three day national conference of the *Gruppo Nazionale Nidi*. As well as speeches, a whole day was given over to working groups on topics such as: relations between families, *asilo nido* and experiences of integration in the *nido*; the planning of educational activity in the *asilo nido*; and problems of relations and educational continuity between the *asilo nido* and *scuola materna*. The conference ended with a speech by Senator Elena Marinucci, President of the National Commission for Promoting Equal Rights between men and women, on 'Is the public *nido* as it is configured today the only just and possible solution?'

For a children's ecology at the nido: quality of the environment, of work organisation, of relations with the family, of workers' professional culture

[. . .]

Over the course of recent years the discussion of what constitutes a pedagogy capable of giving identity to the *nido* has made great headway; it has met with different positions on its journey, still meets with them today, and will continue to do so in the future. In my opinion what is needed today is to try and give the *asilo nido* an identity of a philosophical nature, an ideological nature if you like, a pedagogical and cultural nature, where *nidi* are set up as institutions with a profile not so much of welfare, care and substituting the family, or only of these; but as institutions that instead take up the task of participating and co-participating in children's education consciously and with all the necessary sense of responsibility.

[. . .]

[B]ecause quality is the best weapon the *nido* has in order to be confirmed as an institution capable of having the esteem, credit, capacity and sense of responsibility that are due to such a delicate institution.

An idea of the child is always an idea of a social and cultural nature. In the *nido* today, in the form it takes in Piemonte,[16] Emilia-Romagna and other regions, I think this idea is always the same image the collective community has of the child, of childhood, of the family, of school, of education, of women.

This idea of the child – at least the one we are trying to work with in our Emilia experience, in my city – is an idea that is attempting to incorporate a triad of influences,[17] which obviously people may agree with or not. However [our experience] is trying to put them together because no one model today constitutes an adequate reference point, and considering the changes there have been in society, in cultures and in images, changes that follow on one another regarding issues of early years education, we need to look towards a series of references.

[. . .]

So why a constructivist, interactional, Piagetian idea inside young children's education?

First, because it overcomes a tension – and be careful because I am speaking of a tension still in place, which has not ended – between empiricism and rationalism, between resources that are innate in character and resources that are acquired or of an acquirable character; while also underlining how children's development is conditioned both by the competencies of the child-organism, which includes an idea of the biological programming children carry inside them, and by the influence of the environment as recorded by Piaget.

[. . .]

Bronfenbrenner's[18] idea of ecological development is what I would annex on to this first Piaget-inspired part. This takes place between an active or very active organism, the very active child, and its environment, but also through the way this child–environment interaction is conditioned by interconnections – this is what Bronfenbrenner says – and these interconnections are as decisive as specific educational events effected in a given situation are important and decisive. This interconnection is always active, and therefore constantly, continuously in a state of change and fluctuation between different environmental situations: those that are immediate, those that are less immediate, and those that are further away.

It seems to me that the great breadth of Bronfenbrenner's work is that it seeks a new understanding of the nature of children, who are not only immersed in their immediate environment – which may be family, or *nido*, or any other institutions, but are also influenced and conditioned in some way by the media and through parental input and a family culture deriving from environments that are further away, and other environments that are even more distant. It seems to me that this is a sufficiently composite picture, sufficiently broad and sufficiently complete, with the influences constantly at play in those situations where we seek to activate direct and directed processes with children. And the interconnections have to do with children, but they also have to do with all adults who are a reference for children in any way. So I must be very careful about the child's history and the child's present, but I must also simultaneously be very careful about the history of the adults who spend time with this child, or who are called on, professionally or not, to spend time living together with the child.

The concept of environment has expanded, the problems have become more complex and this complexity gives voice and is laden with significance and meaning. But it is probable that the delicacy of children's education can only be carried out with the greatest dignity if it colludes with environment.

The third issue I refer to is the idea of pleasure, which in a way is taken from Freudian philosophy, but can also be seen as a type of sentiment and as a type of pregnant intelligence, and therefore as an energy force, the searching out and final satisfaction pursued by the child; and which is capable of resisting even when asked to overcome difficulties caused by appropriate reminders from the reality principle.

A sense of pleasure or a feeling of pleasure can be an extremely important and defining reference in the relations we as adults should have with children, bearing in mind we are speaking of a sentiment that embraces the whole of the child and that explains their obstinacy, which is an obstinacy we perhaps ought to summon up more than we do. The obstinacy children pursue their ends with, their directions, hopes, desires, research and need to understand, in an extremely complex world that includes people, includes things, includes children's imagining, and in which this sort of drive for the satisfaction of pleasure always persists; and this seems right to me, something that is right if it is part of human nature.

So then, children who love to grow, children who more than protection need situations that are both reassuring and problematic, children who love doing, love exploring and love understanding, children who never put off to a future date the start of their desire for the pleasure of understanding, of penetrating into the meaning of things, events and relations etc. And this desire is not only impressed figuratively but also concretely on how the environment is constructed, on how work is organised inside the *nido*, and on the openness and culture that must concern adults working in the *nido*.

I will say this, and I am going into a more open polemic because it is a theoretical framework that goes beyond both a pedagogy of contingency and a pedagogy of necessity: the concept of total ungovernability on the one hand, which is a pedagogy of the contingent; and of absolute and total governability on the other, which is a pedagogy of necessity. These two concepts to my mind stand outside all philosophy of life or philosophy of education, because in reality they do not correspond to any objective reference point and because both of them, the pedagogy of contingency and the pedagogy of necessity, one ungovernable and one governable, coincide in that they both leave the child in the background. Children on the one hand are perennially left waiting and dominated; and on the other hand, a great busyness is set up by adults with a series of propositions, appointments, dates, times and hours in which children's development and maturation takes place to a predetermined design. However this framework I have tried to define, can help us to define education in family environments and in institutional environments.

[. . .]

What I mean in more concrete terms is that the *nido* is revealed, becomes defined, or as Bronfenbrenner would say is identified, as a micro-system,[19] [. . .] in which there is the greatest possible internal communication, the greatest dialogical exchange between children and children and children and adults; and when I say adults I do not only mean adults working there on a daily basis but adults outside, the ones that constitute the users. We have to put this pivot of children–teachers–families at the centre and have a cultural kind of convergence expressed in terms of organisation, times, the mode of approach, the mode of reflection, collegial discussions and choices etc., with shared participation by families, so the *nido* is hallmarked as an institution that is natural in some way and can immediately be dialogically open, not only on the inside but with the outside.

[. . .]

Because the *nido* is a terrain welcoming children and families, and welcoming material and immaterial problems, this fact alone – whether we want it or not and whether we are aware of it or not – gives the *nido* authority and an important role in society. The fact is the *nido* offers us the only place today, and I don't know about the future, but today it is the only place we can try out and exercise an exchange of points of view, shared participation, open discussions between family users, children and teachers, where all of these can immediately be disentangled. It is the only possibility our Italian culture offers today as an open field, and a concrete field, for reflection and discussion, with a commensurate relation between private and public, and which receives values from the private world for the public, and from the public world for the private.

1987

88.87 Draft text, possibly for a book that was never completed, December 1987

Editor's note: It is not known what book Malaguzzi had in mind when he drafted this text. However, Malaguzzi made it clear that he thought there should be a book about the educational experience in Reggio Emilia, even though in the end he never found time to complete this project. The original text has many notes written in the margin, though not by Malaguzzi. They may be by Laila Marani who, with Laura Artioli, curated a historical exhibition about Reggio Emilia – *Città, gente, bambini* [City, people, children] – in 1988, shortly after this piece was written.

Text for the book

I.

No-one, least of all those whose work it is to educate the younger and youngest generations, can be permitted to avoid reflection on the changes and the questions in culture and life that social behaviours and scientific and technical innovations are suggesting.

There are several references. Those I will comment on here have been selected because they are more directly implicated in problems of a theoretical and practical nature to do with the theme of knowledge and therefore of education. There are two of these and they both relate to the world of reason and of ideas, how ideas are born and constructed, and ideas about mankind and the world.

The first invites reflection on the genesis and formation of knowledge and learning based on the thesis of a strong current of research, which seems to me the most interesting and fertile and which expresses the most recent developments in different sciences (physics, biology, evolutionary, epistemological) starting in the 1940s. Those were important years, emblematically marked by the birth of cybernetic thinking, the first scientific venture of an explicitly interdisciplinary character.[20]

The second [reference] discusses the latest interventions in neurosciences on the nature and functions of the brain and the nervous system and concerning human behaviours. These offer several points of connection with the thesis of the first proposition.

Both topics, although with different procedures and times, clearly break away from the paradigmatic tradition of science, to advance innovative theses and hypotheses that can make knowledge processes and issues, and the uses and ends of rationality, more complex and in some ways more democratic.

The importance of our entire discourse calls for certain additional comments. It is urgent owing to three growing convictions. That today, as never before, science and technology provoke enormous consequences for knowledge processes and human relations. That science and knowledge are cultural, economic and political entities whose strength of impact and acceleration have never been so integrated, and so capable of transforming the world. It now appears increasingly clear and ascertainable that different moments of development in the history of the sciences and their governing principles have had (and have) consequences for how the image of human beings (and children) and their cognitive, ethical and social strategies become reformulated.

2.

Regarding the first reference, the reinterpretation of knowledge processes and ways of knowing, this has arisen through contemporary critiques and studies of positivist and post-positivist scientific theories, which for the whole of the nineteenth century and part of the twentieth, seemed committed to classifying, ordering, dividing and generalising the disciplines; to celebrating laws that were attributed with completeness, absoluteness, eternity, predictability, and the valued quality (the Archimedean points)[21] not only of being capable of guaranteeing research methods and results but also explaining and generalising phenomena. This cultural and scientific system, in the opinion of researcher Mauro Ceruti,[22] can appear as the extreme secularisation of what was previously explained by the reasoning of myth. Experts in the natural and physical disciplines, which claimed objectivity and liked to call themselves exact sciences because they were founded on definitive and certain principles, are the same experts in the front line today claiming unchangeable models no longer exist. Just think of molecular biology and genetic engineering and how they are defining possibilities for revising the 'natural' codes of evolution itself.

It is a fact that biology, evolution theory and physics, like cybernetics and cosmology (scientific cosmology is a recent discipline because the universe in its wholeness has only now become a scientific subject, after being the prerogative of religions for centuries), like psychology, cognition, anthropology, cybernetics and the neurosciences are rediscovering their nature and a need for relations that imposes strategies for re-connecting, for hybridising concepts and elements that until recently were considered unnecessary and even incompatible.

On a level of general science we are going from a normative epistemology intended to disentangle the complexity of phenomena and arrive at laws and simplified certain orders, to an ecological epistemology, which by refusing all temptation to select and enclose the real in stable and omniscient structures accepts multiplicity and complexity, accepts the co-existence and inter-penetration of scientific and cultural events. This is an epistemology that requires us, says Morin[23] – who is working on redefining reason in problematic terms no longer presided over by the traditional epistemological rules – to think without ever fencing concepts in, to break the closed circles, re-establish connections between what is (or seems) disjointed, and strive to understand the multidimensionality of facts, their singularity and their integration. To the point of suggesting we expand the scientific and cognitive meaning of weavings between human sciences and between human sciences and natural sciences, which underpin the design of a virtuous and ecologically productive structural coupling between organism and environment.

On the levels of ethics and values a possibility is being outlined of an approach to our human journey that is no longer carved up and divided up as it was in the old divisive propositions that have defined Western culture since Descartes. This is a reformulation of the image of human beings, no longer opposed to nature or fleeing nature to construct a sort of autonomous kingdom for themselves and their culture, with the complicity of scientism and humanism imprisoned in false and moralising contradictions.

The old division between humanist culture and scientific culture gives way to the territory of solidarity, common observation points, complementarity and useful exchanges of method and experience that help us consider fields of learning not as monads[24] but as influencing entities. At the same time, we must recognise, in relation to our current historical condition, that we have a pressing opportunity, which is, as Gregory Bateson reminds us, to 'bring our system [the human and the natural] back into an appropriate synchrony or harmony between rigour and imagination, between the necessities, both vital, of compatibility and change'.[25]

3.

This already clearly raises questions about many of the foundations and purposes of science, knowledge and ethics, the ways we have looked for, inherited and transmitted them until now. As part of this large picture we will take only a few partial and constituent elements to guide our more immediate capacity for reflection.

We will begin with the old association-equivalence between concepts of evolution and continuity and the accumulation and linearity of psychogenetic processes, which were among the strongest research paradigms of the XIX century and later, and which were also quickly assimilated by currents of psychology and pedagogy. The theses we propose – in a perspective that uses facts and concepts from biology, psychology and sociology in a dynamic of interdependency and filiation – point to more complex and non-univocal journeys in thinking that branch out in forms and rhythms that are not easily identified or categorised, not necessarily linear or always cumulative, with unexpected feedbacks and comebacks, and combinations and creations that weave the unexpected and intentional together; where the ways and the rhythms of onset, development and changes in thinking and knowledge alternate between subjective and objective, in modules and cycles that often are governed but also often are not, and which are subjected to the influence of cultures and behaviours in ways that can be explicit, hidden, or even unconscious. The presence of cognitive and disciplinary socio-genesis is underlined.

Continuity and discontinuity are not in opposition, responding to logics of their own; sometimes they converge, sometimes they do not, however they are certainly complementary.

In the same way the concepts of order and disorder, which were seen as the negative of each other, bend to the point of being in dialogue and even generating each other. In short, faced with the concept of opposites contemporary epistemology counter-poses a concept founded on the dynamics of complementarity, as if opposites are demonstrating they belong to the same conceptual ecology, to a history of reciprocal co-production, to a desire for unified perspectives.

States of non-equilibrium not only have a positive role of beneficial change in forcing breaks and reconstructions upon logical, affective, communicative and relational schema, but – in an analogy with Prigogine's[26] discoveries in other fields – can play a constructive role, opening up dynamic instabilities and complexities that classical research did not include and re-establishing the co-existence of reversible and irreversible structures.

There are those who see how this concept looks anew at the meaning of regulatory equilibrium, which was constantly sought and valued in Piaget's genetic epistemology; how it calls for redefining the genesis of the processes that make up thought and behaviour, and in a broader sense, the conception of adaptation itself. This is no longer seen as a regulator of equilibrium, in the sense of adjusting to and synchronising with the environment, but re-proposed as mastering capacities and creativities on the part of human organisms for maintaining open viability with the environment itself.[27]

In the field of the evolutionary sciences the environment is no longer seen as a cause but as a fluid structure of relations with which the organism communicates, multiplying the intensity, variety and procedures of its adaptive solutions, and the constructive nature of its interactions.

In other words the relations between subject and object could be thought of as moments of a history of reciprocally producing and reconstructing relations. In this sense real and possible lose their position of disconnected fixity and are instead identified as unstable constructions, shifting in their relations, and never excluded from our acts or choices.

This is not all. If knowledge is a relation of information between subject and object and of provisional and constantly shifting formulations, then clearly the problem of epistemology is located at every level, very strongly changing the boundaries and procedures in child psychology that are still in force today defined by stage-based taxonomical norms. So that starting times and finishing times no longer exist, and we have times for a *forma fluens* [fluid form] that uninterruptedly re-organises meanings, which are always interconnected and open-ended. The psycho-genetic development of viability with the environment, knowledge and culture, therefore has very deep roots and branches and is born when life is born. It is a period of immediate and very intense adaptive, cognitive and affective exchanges, which impose themselves as vital and necessary not so much or merely for survival but to comply with the principles of research and adopting meanings that belong to the human species. These do not necessarily correspond in quantity and quality with levels and processes of maturation, because development, in accordance with Bronfenbrenner's hypothesis, is nothing other than the constant modification of ways in which an individual perceives and engages with their personal and historical environment.

And (I realise these have only been rapid notes) I think I will conclude this space I have dedicated to the first reference I announced at the beginning. It has focused on the genesis of formation, knowledge and ideas, and refers to the theory and epistemology of complexity, in which the trans-disciplinary studies of several scientists and philosophers of our times come together.

To summarise, we are faced with three complementary stories.

One of these brings to crisis the certainties and myths of knowledge based on scientific and epistemological tradition.

One accepts the challenge of a new adventure in knowledge that, through its complexities, more deeply explores the directions of a new formation of learning and a new relation between the individual, nature and culture.

One goes against the old distinction-separateness of sciences (in particular the 'exact' sciences, whether technological or human) and re-establishes their inseparability, communication and integration in a trans-disciplinary frame-work, which should increasingly give cause to research and teaching to break down the development and classification of single disciplines and social aspects that correspond to them.

However partial these elements are that I have taken from my personal preferred readings, they cannot be made to total up like clues in scientific results, unless it is to express a more general paradigm that attempts, as Gianluca Bocchi[28] advises, to break down at its very roots what seemed to be the acquired order of our century: a separation between the philosophy of knowledge and the anthropology of knowledge.

The indications for reflecting on education (which has been closed for too long in a separation as simplifying as it is unrealistic) and for a philosophical, ethical and aesthetic transmission of knowledge that looks to the future, are partly obvious, partly need to be identified, partly have to be carefully and responsibly discussed, and in part must be created. If these reach people – and inevitably they will, they will also rightly reach children and their journeys of experience and culture.

The second reference I announced at the beginning has to do with study of the brain and the nervous system based on the latest contributions from the neurosciences.

The topic suggests many directions. For myself my expectations go in the direction of recent research, which – in contrast with current tendencies that are almost exclusively directed towards solving scientific problems and explor-ing inanimate or living material – privileges the study of structures and func-tions of the brain at the same time as consciously getting closer and closer to humanist disciplines. To achieve what Rita Levi Montalcini,[29] Nobel Prize

Winner in Biology, clearly states is a single objective: 'to understand the nature of human beings and improve the quality of life, not merely for part of the human species but for all humanity. Knowledge of the brain is not only the key to understanding the universe, it is the only hope human beings have of understanding themselves.'

The latest achievements in the neurosciences have led to a series of extremely important propositions. In the first place the brain is no longer seen as a structure immobilised by genetic programming and removed from chance and environmental variables. Nor is the brain seen as a structure whose functions are deterministically dependent on specific centres or which is made up of separate, non-communicating neurons.

Through its hundred thousand billions of neurons cerebral mass has spectacular internal resonances that participate in the acts of human beings, whose intelligence (however you define it) is the fruit of synergic cooperation between the parts of the brain. Synapses, which are plastic connectors of neurons and which can be modulated and modified, testify to the interactions and circuits that take place in the brain.

The evolution and involvement of neurons (like those of the synapses) is dependent on environmental events and factors that are only just beginning to be known and distinguished today.

Above all specific centres in the brain intervene with functional support in cases of pathology.

Rita Levi Montalcini's discovery of the growth molecule [nerve growth factor] produced by the body and by environmental influences leads to new hopes: the molecule appears to be a sort of medicine that activates and repairs neurons affected by illness and deterioration. This is a sensational discovery awaiting confirmations and deeper understanding and represents a high point in the scientific choices of neuroscience.

The latest news coming to us from research carried out in the United States of America offers a similar reading, this time for small children. Using highly sophisticated technological equipment it has been confirmed the energy metabolism (the important operational activity) of the brain of a two-year-old child is already the same as that of an adult, and that in four-year-old children the metabolic rate is twice that of an adult, because the greatest proliferation of synapses (whose decisive importance we have discussed) takes place during the first and second period of childhood [up to 3 years and from 3 to 6 years]. This delicate time is accompanied by processes of synapse selection that give rise to the structures of circuits and interactions between brain cells.

According to studies by Max Cowan[30] at St. Louis University this period of synapse proliferation could comprise a privileged time for deciding the quantity, and above all the quality, of neuron connections and their potentially alternative functional pathways.

Using a high number of pathways well or using few pathways in an unsatisfactory way is a fact that depends on the quality and generative capacity impressed by our environmental and educational situations. What this means is that the role of the first periods of our life is confirmed as decisive in many aspects for learning processes.

These results and the results connected with neuroscience research mentioned earlier are situated in the frame of a scientific philosophy that re-establishes extraordinarily interesting perspectives on human nature and evolution. A brain that is not caged in by genes escapes the old deterministic absolutes. Its structure and its functioning are those of a species that nature has privileged with resources disposed to change through experience, education and the adventure of living.

1988

89.88 Draft for a speech on research action probes, Reggio Emilia, April 1988

Editor's note: This document comes from the personal archive of Vea Vecchi, one of the first *atelieristas* in Reggio Emilia. A 'probe' *(sonda)* is an action arranged by teachers in a defined area to go deep down into knowledge of children's knowledge processes and increase the capacity of adults for forecasting, documentation and interpretation. An example is 'Shoe and Meter' (Castagnetti and Vecchi, 1997). The term *sonda* was used for the last time in 2002 in *Tra scrittura e segni* [Between Writing and Signs], on the construction of the written code by children, though there is no particular reason for it falling out of use

- Children possess the capacity for self-constructing.
- Children not only know how to learn, they know how to learn to learn.
- Children privilege knowledge through transformative action.
- Children learn and know by transforming.
- In transforming children anticipate, conjecture, try out and check through images and representations born of co-ordinating meanings, that are progressively born of actions and their co-ordination with memory.
- Children proceed and structure, structure and proceed.
- Procedure and structure are a distinct, complementary pair that give rise to productive circularities.
- Structures are a cognitive plateau,[31] a key-schema which, through abstraction, unifies meanings into a more general all-encompassing meaning.
- Utilising or inventing structures implies a use of procedures. However procedure calls for knowledge of structure (sometimes only traces of structure) that are already available or are gradually acquired in the course of activities and the achieving of an end.

- Once they have been discovered, structures leave behind the functions, pragmatics and procedures that provoked and generated them, and by becoming keys and tools for interpreting other procedures, and other cognitive pathways, they become a-temporal and trans-functional. Waiting for other a-temporalities and trans-functionalities.
- Children are self-organising and co-organising organisms, through the action of the environment. They move between personal and social competencies. Between personal and biological constraints and environmental constraints. They play an active role both in the social field and that of knowledge.

Until twenty years ago psychological inquiry (with tests, questionnaires, interviews etc.) into evolutionary behaviours contemplated a *tabula rasa* child. Subsequent investigations have alternated between a vision that is naively naturalistic (see the behaviourist child) or naively a-temporal and a-historical (simplified into linear stage-based evolution), even when attributing the child with possessing constructive, generative capacities (see the Piaget child). Almost always they have privileged the asymmetrical conditions of child and adult, and have compared the reality and quality of relations in family environments and extra-family environments for reasons more historical, political and cultural than intrinsic.

In this framework, and for these non-stated reasons, we should not be surprised at the weakness and lack of research in the field of the influences and interactions in the world of childhood, between children of similar ages, and between peers.

It is a world filled with prejudices, which are reductive, imitative, distracting and inconclusive. Above all it is full of the un-confessed adult fear of losing the ability to govern. However this world is a terrain, like no other, for the experience children avidly seek, and is predisposed in original ways towards the needs of socialising, communicating, exchange and discussion; towards the needs of dialogue and co-operation, which are fertile for the formation of intelligence, of thinking, of learning styles, of languages, of harmonious behaviours, of one's own identity and the identity of others. Finally it is privileged terrain for adults for observation, for reflection, for a knowledge of strategy and evaluation of the ways children produce and construct their conduct for knowing and evolutionary forms of knowing; for the possibilities [it offers] for adults to self-evaluate and self-adjust their expectations, their hypotheses, their capacity for predicting and reflecting on the acts and choices they realise with children. Therefore it is terrain that, through reciprocal evolutions, reinforces the knowledge of children and adults, produces professional development, and improves the quality of their relations and interactions.

What is a research-action probe?

A research probe is a situation channelling conjecture towards the gathering of children's behaviours, procedures, interpretations and activities, around a circumscribed, defined experience: that strives to know the quality and variety of the influences of children on children.

It is carried out with a limited, appropriate number of children, to ensure the best recording and understanding of facts, and the forms they take. For this reason it requires far-sighted and meticulous tuning of observational methodology.

The probe can assume different forms, courses and times (expected or unexpected) before and during its course. With this flexibility it follows there must be an equal flexibility of situations and of adult conduct. Adjustment strategies escape any form of prescription.

The course of a probe may be entirely undertaken by children autonomously, with an adult attitude of non-interference and only of support. Or it may be opportune, depending on each case, for adults to include themselves with complementary interventions and stated aims, in order for the probe to regain its original strength. Then the probe intentionally becomes a project with intersecting pathways of research and action alternating between children's autonomous activity and the circular, co-operative entry of adults.

All probes transform, in their course, into sequences with different rhythms and intentionality, which may temporarily lose and re-find their direction. However this is meaningful too. Above all, it [probes] invites us to understand that <u>interpretation</u> is important but that <u>comprehension</u> is even more important. (If possible referencing other elements of knowledge we have of the situations and experiences of the protagonist children.)

Sometimes a probe configures in an intertwined way, like craftwork re-using its own material for increasingly purposeful transformations and constructions: like a tree from whose parts other parts can be generated.

On its journey every probe discovers other possible probes that can be engaged with, or can be moved and postponed to another time.

There can be different geneses for the title and objectives of the probe: they can derive from normal situations of observation where events emerge that are considered important to explore and examine more deeply; but they can also derive from the reflections and competencies of adults, where adults feel it is opportune to investigate particular topics.

Since unambiguous and planned methodologies between observation and phenomena do not exist, it is necessary to be aware that every result achieved provides nothing other than indicative data to be evaluated and generalised with caution. We also suspect that any recordings (simultaneous with observations) will be partial; that already recordings are a subjective interpretation in some way; that facts are contaminated by expectations and a pressure to know in the observers; that whatever happens the results are above all connected with that particular contextual situation.

Awareness of all these things reduces the possible risks for adults, and can help them to go from subjective impressionistic evaluations to indications that are more defined, more probable, more transferable and better transferable. It can help them above all to refine their competencies and their styles of educational behaviour.

To conclude: a probe is an opportunity and a tool, organised in order to achieve <u>observation of observation</u> and above all <u>knowledge of knowledge</u>, which remains one of the most fertile, sought after phenomena in the field of individual knowledge processes and relations between individuals.

※ ※ ※

90.88 Talk at a workshop on *progettazione* in the *scuola dell'infanzia*, 1988 (no more precise date)

To tell the truth I do not know exactly what will come out during the course of today's meeting. What I wanted to say immediately is that today's specific theme of discussion can only apparently [. . .] be kept inside a narrow container [. . .]. And so instead today we will try and take to the open sea, try and open the container up and declare ourselves; in a series of reflections, hypotheses, conjectures, sources, and with supporting statements that come from new forms of research, culture, philosophy of science and philosophy of life, and which perhaps can help us understand things that have been changing around us in recent years, mainly in these years of the universe.

I realise the lives of children in the *nido* and *scuola dell'infanzia* today will be immersed in combinations of humanity, science and culture in the year two thousand that will be very different from our lives now.

I think our talk has to begin here, at this point that has hardly begun [to be discussed] at all. It would be interesting to understand the reasons – historical, political, cultural and scientific – that paradoxically have held sway, held power and domination, over a series of phenomena and reflections. Reasons that have not allowed what is instead the simplest, most elementary approach and substantially the most vital: an approach that could give us an idea of ourselves as connected to and tied with the environment, with nature, and with the cosmos.

It would be interesting to go back to the origin of this phenomenon because I think we would find a resistance in ourselves that we are not sufficiently aware of. [In fact] we do find them, I have found them in myself, and I think you will find them too. They are living objective resistances to how we can transform our old-fashioned ideas, and a resistance to other ideas that are alternative and capable of substantially changing our concept of ourselves, of the environment, and of culture. Above all change our concept of knowledge and the ways and processes through which our knowledge – and the knowledge of children, young people, adults and the elderly – evolves during the course of our life.

[. . .]

Every second of our life is wrapped up in issues of nature that border on the environment, and border on the cosmos, and what I mean to say is that although we are contained in these issues every day we still feel them as extraneous, and our culture approves and keeps our detachment at very high levels.

[. . .]

Ecology, as Commoner used to say – he was an old American pioneer[32] – ecology is certain to be the alphabet of the future. We are part of an ecosystem and we must be convinced of this, that our earthly journey is a journey made together with the environment, with nature, with the cosmos; that our organism, our morality, our culture, our knowing, our sentiments, are all connected with the environment, with the universe, with the world, with the cosmos. And this is where, Commoner said, the great web of our lives exists, in this grand dimension, a dimension we find difficult to measure but which is the dimension a web requires; and whatever happens it comprises our life's terrain.

Perhaps this means we are trying to persuade ourselves that the connections (or interconnections if you like) there are in the world are stronger than we think, and that many aspects of our lives, even our most interior life, beat to the same rhythms and meanings as nature. The change of time and weather [that comes] with the seasons is a change we feel is ours, not only because we are part of it, but because we are part of it as protagonists with our sensibility, our expectations, our situations. Just as the alternation of day and night are a part of our rhythms, of our biorhythms, and just as day and night are part of and belong to the world's life cycles.

Perhaps we could think in terms of a coupling, a coupling of structures, and maybe we should spend more time on this. You see, we are speaking about very big things, the coupling of structures between mind and nature. 'Mind and Nature' is an extraordinary book,[33] which I invite you to read because it gives our [human] dimension its place as one part of a structural coupling, between us, our organism, and the organism outside us.

[. . .]

There is a kind of circularity and a very wise circuitry, which has always been and continues to be, and today we feel an impelling need to make it the object of our reflection.

[. . .]

To my mind the relation between biology and knowledge really is the crux and fulcrum of every enquiry into the nature of being: the nature of our being and the nature of being in a wider sense. It is a relationship that identifies and perhaps helps us better understand the potentials available to us, the knowledge processes through which we try to increase our culture, increase our learning, and the passages of our life and our living. Montalcini has already invited us to reflect that knowledge of the brain is not only the key to interpreting the universe but the only real hope humans have for understanding themselves.

[. . .]

Again some words from the old fighter of American ecology [Barry Commoner] who was a *maestro* [teacher], a *maestro* to the whole world who said: look, today we need to get culture moving, above all by making it start anew with another way of thinking. So planetary thinking, in the sense that it is time to understand our thinking can only find its equilibrium, perspective and progress through a conscious connection with the whole planet. [And again] he said: be careful because a second measure is to start thinking prophetically, in the sense of addressing the possibilities contained in important concepts about this adventure that connects our life with the life of the universe.

[. . .]

In substance we are being invited to take a different train from the one we have been on until now, to try and create a unity of contents, of learning, and of disciplines that have always been left outside the so-called science of pedagogy and the science of education.

These connections are important, but the connections we have brought here today do not open up completely new frontiers. Certainly, a large part of the frontier is new. But if we reflect on our experience over the course of these years, it seems to me we can say all the connections we were aware of, all the connections we were capable of, have been realised in some way as part of our organisation. What I mean is: think a bit about the figure of the pair-teacher [teacher working as part of a pair] and our attempts to connect up things that traditionally were not connected; our taking care with the connections between environments [spaces] that contain a connected vision of systemic space, which is what a *nido*, and what a school can be.

Our attempts to go out often [from school] is a way – a rather naïve and insufficiently valued way – but one of several demonstrations of ways in which we have tried to make something that was an intuition into something concrete over the years. The issue of social management, which I believe to be part of the great theme of conferring a socialised, participatory image on parts that are usually divided and separated. And the very idea of the child we have tried to bring forward is a highly inter-related idea; we have never accepted divisions, separations or hierarchies in children's formation.

We have always theorised that the parts of a child are parts that have to be connected, because they are naturally connected with each other, and therefore to divide, separate and take them to pieces would be a sort of violence.

The very activities we have suggested over the years have always been activities connected with each other, in an attempt not to accept discrimination [between different elements of] early childhood learning processes and contents.

[. . .]

It is not a coincidence that [Howard] Gardner's talk, Gardner's definition of intelligence, sounds the way I will tell you.[34] Intelligence is the capacity for solving problems, and I do not think any of the old or even very old pronouncements on intelligence would refuse to start with this kind of argument. Intelligence is the capacity to solve problems and Gardner adds: or 'to fashion products that are valued in one or more cultural setting'.

Be very careful, because the great strength, the great history, the great power of American civilisation passes through this point. It has in it a very specific, detailed idea, particularly today. Intelligence is what is capable of producing products. However, perhaps not everything that is produced by human imagination, human thinking and human reflection is synonymous with *products* – unless we are now to include several things humans have done, and continue to do, which we have attempted to remove from this category and never included in such a narrow, contingent idea as *production and product in one or more cultural settings.*

We only need to reflect here for a moment to understand this is a class-based idea, that it is an idea of an American kind, and of a historical, political and economic kind.

[. . .]

[Gardner] indirectly infers that the seven intelligences [he describes] are all already inscribed in the individual and do not arise at a certain point of the individual's evolution, which means all our work would have the objective of journeying and progress, but each time following one of these seven intelligences.

Seven intelligences, which he says are not only of a bio-genetic character and therefore already part of our inheritance; but he also says, with a lightness that is typical of American culture, that any teacher can identify the seven intelligences perfectly well (if she has not already identified them) in the space of a month, the way they appear in the child and what their strength and capacity are. I think this must necessarily be a process linked to a familiarity with American 'testology', where it is enough to do some tests on an individual and immediately the individual has been defined and measured in some way.

[. . .]

If you read a series of contributions in recent years from the level of experimentation, investigation etc., which seek an explanation of why children are not all the same and why children are not all like [each other], why they are so un-alike, you will see them resorting to the word 'style'. That is to say, allegedly children aged two and three establish a sort of style, a sort of differential communication compared to others. However this does not take into account that life's processes are much longer term, and that however many intelligences we have, the construction process is very long; and that therefore variables are constantly present, and I do not think we should let these variables pre-establish or pre-define distinctions, differences or hierarchies ahead of the time it takes children to do so, objectively and logically.

This does not take away the fact that our children are all different, and that every child is a never-ending discovery on our part. But if we place ourselves in the position of trying to discover even children's emergent character, our profession will always be faced on a daily basis with 'nomadic [impermanent] images' that are less intense, faded and absolutely insignificant. So we feel that although we have an awareness of children's distinguishing traits, there are no tools that persuade us which things to push [educationally] and which things to get rid of.

[. . .]

If we say children are not all the same, are we convinced when we speak that we are speaking to each one of our children, or are we talking to classes of children? Just as when we have our children work, are we really convinced we are producing an operation that is distinctive, or do we realise that perhaps we are working in ways that do not take differences between children into account, and even risk increasing them by not giving children what they feel a greater need for in one situation than in another?

What of children's maturation processes then? I would say maturation takes place based on drives arising from genetic inheritance. If this maturation of the brain-organism forces the child's evolution to stay within certain rhythms and rules, then we might think this maturation is often reached before, or after, the effective maturation of children's capacities. This is the series of large questions we can ask ourselves and that we have always asked ourselves: questions posed with great difficulty because they have to do with governing difficult territory. It is probably a question of recognising our research as the only great freedom we are allowed, as a great possibility and resource, a great opportunity, and then trying to solve problems along our journey.

However there are certain things we can do. We can think that if children are different, and precisely because they are different from one another, then we need to use more appropriate and coherent strategies than ones that do not take these facts into consideration, or that think all children and all human beings are the same, that there are no differences, or that our task is to eliminate the differences – when instead our problem is to differentiate, by listening to the multiplicity of differences.

The problem now is how to put this together on the level of education. No one of us, I think, is aware of or knows what the journeys and itineraries are and in our last meeting I talked of these being part of the maturation of an organism in its entirety and complexity, with a hard core and a soft core. In the hard core our margins of freedom and access are limited; but when we refer to the soft core there are no limits to our possibilities for intervening, except biological limits. That is to say, all children speak, all children walk (leaving aside the phenomena of deviancy and accident) and I want to say that there are certain journeys that really accompany the maturation and directions belonging to all children.

[. . .]

What we can do is develop our imagination as much as we can in connection with opportunities for children to encounter realities, and invite them to choose from a range of possible responses, invite them to choose paths they consider might be the most congenial.

However again there is another risk here. I think you can see it immediately. It may be true children have always had certain paths [to follow], but no-one can say children are not capable, perhaps with a little help, of re-directing towards other paths: I mean to say ours is the 'profession of uncertainty', but life is a profession of uncertainty.

Well, if this elasticity exists above all at the very start of life, at about four, five, six and seven years old; if this flexibility is there and if this possibility of environmental stimulus is genuinely capable of becoming inscribed in the quantity and quality of connections – in synapses on a cerebral level, the most significant parts, which will have a primary role in the different behaviours we will have – if all this is true, then we must make haste and work, and not wait for children to reach a certain stage before we begin. I think this is a realisation that is still only partly felt, and which is still not provided for or sufficiently informed on a level of psychological and cultural awareness.

[. . .]

It is dangerous to think our intelligence autonomously constructs the world; on the other hand it is just as dangerous to think the world constructs us. The problem lies in this unsolvable contradiction, and in finding the intersecting space that permits a capacity for collaboration, a capacity for hooking up, for professional development that translates into participatory working capacities, sometimes in antagonistic ways and sometimes in complementary ways. So what I want to say is that probably knowledge processes must be re-examined as part of a circularity, part of a perpetual circular flow – in which several names and terminologies must be dropped.

[. . .]

I am anxious now for us to confront a problem. A problem that comes into our daily work in a highly concrete way, into our relations with ourselves, with children's culture, and above all with children's learning. It hinges on issues connected with attempting to define programme and strategy in exhaustive terms, to clarify the precise differences that exist between them.

[. . .]

This means we will see (but we certainly will not be able to do it today) how far we can get with defining programme, which means planning ahead not only for final objectives but for the procedures that lead to the objectives. Instead we feel the necessity and urgency – not only professional but human – to face up to problems, events and situations in ways that are free of programmed restriction, and trust in a sort of strategic capacity, in strategies for intervening. This should not be considered so much an ABC, a complete and defined alphabet, but as a possibility which, in order to be realised, requires processes of experience, requires competency, and above all requires an understanding of the ways we are capable of pushing in the direction of conjecture. Certainly this means in the sense of what is a matter of opinion, certainly, but opinion backed up with corroborative documents to the greatest possible degree.

Anyone whose formation has taken place in recent years is familiar with two terms; one is the process of induction, and the other is deduction. I think philosophy and pedagogy always bear in mind inductive and deductive processes. Instead, I wish to add another term which is not generally considered, and which has been re-discovered through modern semiotics: it is abduction.[35] This term is not used with such familiarity as the other two.

Just to give you an indicative example, I will say that induction refers to a thing that will be so, that is so, and will be so. Deduction refers to a thing that must be so, in that it must be so on the basis of elements and platforms of a general nature. Deducing makes something descend from something else, inducing means rising up from something else. Instead abduction remains as a form that leads us to a thing in the sense of its probability, in a probabilistic sense.

[. . .]

Abduction, I would say, is the art of the detective who does not start out from a certain position, but who follows, with a selective flow, the pathways, clues and traces, which might lead him to the discovery of the assassin or guilty party, but who is always willing *a priori* to constantly adapt his strategy and thinking.

Now in my opinion this third form of thinking, abduction, is something that is part of children from the start.

Because children have a freedom at their disposal, which makes those who have it feel they are its prisoner. In what sense do I mean this? In the sense that we adults are unlikely to pursue probability, and instead pursue certainty, we have objectives, we choose. But they [children] do not yet have Archimedean points [see Chapter 4, n.21] that have the strength and leverage of knowledge. We find it more difficult to consider that, as well as constituting a recursive strategy, abduction may also lead to a conclusion and an objective. That precisely because it constantly goes back on itself and contains no certainty but pursues the probable through a series of clues, it is I think an attribute we can credit children with from the start.

[. . .]

What of strategy? On this level of abduction strategy certainly has much greater room for manoeuvre.

[. . .]

Strategy is at once a biological and a cultural necessity, because strategy meets with the willingness to live in symbiosis with uncertainty. [. . .] Therefore I believe uncertainty should be freed of its small degree of negativity and any denials of its virtuous nature; it must be brought back as a constituent element of our lives, of our relations with ourselves, with others and with nature. Bearing in mind we must fill uncertainty with a contents that is positive in some way if we want to be capable of restoring it as something we can live with and use in practical ways as a constituent element of our growth.

Then uncertainty becomes a constant and permanent reality, and can act as an alternative to less uncertain notions; it becomes a force, an energy we can always find inside us, in our capacity to problematise and give responses – sometimes connected with a hope, sometimes connected with a precise purpose and objectives, sometimes with precise and pertinent knowledge.

Uncertainty can be turned into something positive when we start to test it and see it as a state of ferment, a motor of knowledge.

[. . .]

What difference is there between programme and strategy?

Briefly I would say programme is an idea that already contains a certainty of prescription and that predicts situations of enactment. So that procedural schedules are already inscribed in this *ante*-thinking, this premeditated thinking, and through these procedures and a series of coherent contingencies, programme comes to achieve its objectives: it is a capacity for prediction, it assigns human beings with a programming capacity.

We are not playing with this capacity for programming; we will see how we need to redeem it and combine it with strategy. Strategy is also capable of attempting to foresee things, and has the awareness to attempt a pre-vision of a series of objectives; it is aware that its adventures are partly expected, partly not expected, and partly completely unexpected. So strategy requires a capacity for flexibility, a capacity for attention, reflection and for changing attitude, for distancing ourselves from behaviours: a quality of great elasticity that belongs as much to logic (in the truest sense of the word) as to logic coupled with sensation, a perception of reality in the presence of which a dialectical union is born.

Children's learning and our learning, what have they been, what can they have been, what can they be, if not procedure of a strategic nature, if not the constant different ways of putting things together in relation to evolutions in reality? This is intelligence, the capacity to produce strategies, and strategies are what inform learning. This means that at the foundation of children's learning (and our learning too) we can agree that a situation of strategy – the capacity to deal with situations and problems by letting go of our old ways of putting things together and to feel no nostalgia for them – is truly a condition of great and happy intelligence. Through reflection and exploration this capacity can lead us to achievements in faraway territory.

[. . .]

The problem is that in this way we cannot accept the opposition between programme and strategy. Perhaps the problem is to see, for each level of school, how much programme can take on different nuances; where strategy can be present on our [adult] part and re-present in terms of how we do things with children; because the two issues [programme and strategy] are not mutually exclusive. I would say strategy is naughtier; naughty in the sense it goes off on its own account etc., it goes together with children's psychology more, and this is not only my opinion. Perhaps it goes with adult psychology too: if we had fewer brakes and fewer blocks, fewer inhibitions than we have inside us, then perhaps we would like it better too.

For me pursuing this possibility has become a sort of mythical adventure. This capacity for having a greater freedom of strategy at our disposal, for our acts, our behaviours, and for our thoughts.

[. . .]

Programme or strategy: which of the two is richer and more fertile? I have no doubt: strategy is certainly the richer and more fertile of the two. Certainly programme is necessary for constructing and hypothesising an event and the future in some way, but it rests on a theory of certainty that does not belong to us. The problem is how to govern this mixture of programme and strategy with great wisdom, with modifications of character and contents etc. I think every attempt at programme, especially in the first part of children's lives, is an attempt against nature, against that indeterminate and undetermined part of genetic legacy, against the strategic part, the designing part of the organism, of the brain, of children's human condition etc.

[. . .]

Morin [see Chapter 4, n.23] also concludes that certainly the problem is that while programme can be born of strategy, strategy cannot be born of programme. Therefore, the important quality of strategy (to me it seems an art) can also be found where, for the sake of opportunism etc., we give space to programme.

[. . .]

The image of the child is a precarious image, an oscillating image that changes with history. Today's image is an image we have to discuss, can discuss. [. . .] However the fundamental problem is to understand the credit we want to give children. The things we credit children with are partly bound up with choice, partly with assumptions in our choices, partly with cultural informa-tion, and partly because we allow ourselves to be subjected to opportunistic or necessary events in which we produce our approach to aspects of children. What I mean to say, therefore, is that it is extremely difficult – and here we need to open a detailed parenthesis.

[. . .] We must be more aware that the idea of a describer who is external to situations or the external observer is in a period of decline and in a highly controversial phase; so that today it seems inevitable that once we accept the constant circularity between ourselves and the world it is clear none of us is an external observer. We are an inside observer, an internal observer. So all the issues of the capacity, possibility and competency of observation as a source of information have now fallen into crisis; it is a situation we have walked with too much confidence and bravado. As if we were capable of detaching, and producing a distance not only from children but from our own selves; and much of us is inside children . . . so the issue is even more critical.

The child is a child about whom we have to make up our mind, make up our mind on the qualities and competencies with which we want to attribute them.

We must bear in mind the initial part of our talk; that part of the child is always predetermined and part is not predetermined; and I can think of these as two constraints giving a child its characteristic traits, which always find a way of emerging and which are necessary for the child's survival. If we have an idea of constraint that is connected with determinism of a genetic kind, but also accept the same word – constraint – for a part that is mobile and available, the part of freedom in an adult–child environment, then perhaps we will arrive at a more pertinent and precise idea of two autonomous parts: two autonomies that simultaneously need to always keep their identity and always mix, with the possibility of change. So the problem of knowledge and the problem of adaptation is no longer as Piaget saw it, where adaptation was the optimal form of adaptation to an environment – as if there was an infinite scale for the capacity to 'optimise' adaptation.

[. . .]

What we want to underline today – underline with a secular conception (because what we are discussing is a secular conception and I say this in very clear terms: thinking and believing etc. continue to be preferences that are free and recognised, legitimate preferences each one of us chooses). So what I wish to underline is that on issues connected with creation, connected with evolution, with the world, with our events, we must not always refer to a perfection outside us. I am making a secular construction in the sense of recognising the meaning of each person's limitations and the meaning of their power. And perhaps through this dual concept we can express ourselves with greater freedom than we have been able to do before.

[. . .]

The most recent books say that each act in itself is knowledge, and that necessarily each act is not a description but an interpretation.

[. . .]

We need to understand that not all acts (as we were saying the other day) bring great richness to the child. There may be acts that remain acts in the grammatical sense of the word rather than the meaningful semantic sense. We probably need to assimilate strategies that are conducive to children's capacity for intervention and to acts that do not remain as a mere manipulation – [that is as mere] manipulative changes and transformations – but which let children have the time, the possibility and the favourable advantageous situations for attempting to create an abstraction from a material, mechanical or intelligent manipulation . . . without immediately categorising it (interpretation). The sort of abstraction that lets children build up a provisional law, or a provisional schema, which orients and deciphers and makes it possible for them to get by for the moment, and then using that intelligent schema they can make themselves busy.

[. . .]

I want to say that a sense of wonder, almost certainly, is something which is part of human nature and we would be in trouble if it weren't. It is a co-participatory and enticing act of sharing by children, which can be related to something that is happening where they might be the author or the protagonist but not necessarily. Think of the kinship between wonder and strategy, because we are much more likely to have wonder in strategy than in programme, although we cannot exclude it surfacing there too.

Perhaps what interests us is understanding how wonder is a tool that is naturally part of children, but that we can also use it to maintain their capacity for ferment at high levels in all the pauses in explorations and research they unceasingly carry out; that we can also make it a tool and a pillar in the complexity of process, of delicate process nudged along by children's expectation of wonder, or recover it as an element [in process] as wonder that is born in children.

I do not know how many games of wonder you have transcribed in your *diario di continuità* [continuity diaries] with children. Wonder is different from marvelling.[36] Wonder is subtler, lighter, and we pursue it because it is worth the effort: you can pursue marvelling too but it meets with lots of doubts and questions; you never know if it is spectacle, or a theatrical kind of marvelling. But wonder has a sense of the sun, of fullness, of *eros*[37] and festivity children feel, when certain attitudes produce the wonder, or when they realise they can see a discrepancy, a gap or a vertigo and that beyond them wonder lies.

[. . .]

Sometimes, more than a rich array of equipment, our gestures are enough to confirm or not confirm children's sense of wonder. Our gestures and our expressions are enough to heighten children's sense of wonder, or diminish it. I wanted to say that these are all very subtle dialogues, but subtle dialogues are the ones that bring a greater capacity for meaning.

❋ ❋ ❋

91.88 Article in *ALFABETIERE '88'* [Alphabet '88'], a booklet produced by *Scuola comunale dell'infanzia* Diana, December 1988

For a listening we must re-discover

We must acknowledge that, despite our merits, as adults we talk about children a lot, talk with them little, and listen to them even less.

These three propositions (which we certainly do not like) are not absolutely true. However it cannot be denied they refer to much of family experience and very much more to school experience.

Which confirms a trait – quite a definite trait – of our adult culture and our childhood culture. All this does not happen (or hardly ever happens) in the first two years of a child's life. Then, there is an extremely beneficial and responsive interaction between adult and child, who call to each other, nudge each other, wait for each other, continue each other, in a splendid and productive circuitry of communication.

Why this shared play, this extremely fertile sort of ping pong, right and vital, should then fade and become debilitated is a disconcerting fact.

And yet we understand very well that in so doing we are breaking the rules, robbing children (and ourselves) of play that is of vital importance. We are interrupting an invaluable flow of comprehension, adaptation, discovery and invention, of reciprocal respect and mutual advantage.

So then?

The problem lies first of all in un-packing our three propositions, and in accepting a scale of values. The first proposition can be left in the waiting room. The second is important. But the third – the listening proposition – is decisive: both for constructing the sense and pleasure of communicating, and for language competency, something that is true not only for the children but also (a fact we may marvel at) for adults.

The thesis is this, if we cannot learn to listen to children, it will be very difficult to learn the art of being with them and conversing with them (in the physical, formal, ethical and symbolic senses of the word). Not only that: we will find it difficult, perhaps impossible, to understand how and why they are speaking; what they are doing, asking, conjecturing, theorising and desiring, what their privileged messages are, what procedures they are exploring and choosing to gain affection and knowledge.

And what of the children?

The parallel language (uncommunicative because each child is supposedly speaking for themselves) that Piaget and other child psychology experts have fixed as a necessary phase in children's linguistic, social and cognitive evolution, can in reality be presumed to be a loss or closure of dialogue in the adult environment, when communication loses the strength to connect and ends up running away in parallel rivulets. It is not lost on us what this means for pedagogy, tempted today more than ever to reward a one-way flow and the prescriptive might of the adult word. A theme that has been central since the very outset of our educational experience and in the efforts of our teachers in the *scuole comunali dell'infanzia*.

There is one last issue I find urgent. What does not-listening, not being disposed to listening, seeing, observing and interpreting children's actions and their questioning and constructive logic, mean for adults? We would say a loss of wonder, marvelling, reflection and the gaiety that children's facts and words are capable of spreading when we find the desire and time (oh yes, time too!) to enter into their play and daily work. These are feelings we cannot do without, because they are what push our daily thinking, *progettazione* and imagination forward, as well as reflection on our relations with children, and with our offspring.

These short and laborious notes are not here by chance. They come as the prelude to a fortunate opportunity: that for listening to and interpreting talk that children have with themselves and with others, taken from contexts of varied experiences in school.

It is similar to raising the blinds or [the lifting of] a bank of fog.

Sometimes the language appears clear and limpid, sometimes hidden and masked, sometimes it needs to be deciphered like Etruscan tablets, with meanings that must be searched for in seemingly impossible combinations and relations, or a magical, surreal logic; sometimes again by sewing together fragments of sounds, visions, memories, of words spoken by adults or in the media.

Or it can also be none of this, all much simpler: discourse declaring affections and friendships, or intervening with absolute nonchalance in the grave existential problems of adults (giving us the measure often of how much better children are at listening than we are), or apparently taken from scientific arguments and completely unsuspected social issues.

In short our invitation is to listen to what we sometimes do not have the time or the patience to listen to, and which is none other than that extraordinary laboratory (the child) living by our sides.

It is no coincidence that this unusual offer, the privilege of this understanding, of highly enjoyable interest and no little surprise comes during the days of Christmas.

The days of Christmas – freed of clamour – are days when listening can give us particular sensations and values of rediscovery and of reflecting more intimately on the ways children think and believe they are growing up.

1989

92.89 Speech by Loris Malaguzzi, Reggio Emilia, April 1989 (transcript from the original audio recording by the *Centro Documentazione e Ricerca Educativa*)

> **Editor's note:** This speech is described as being given at the *Marzo–Aprile Pedagogico*, which may have been a period of events on educational topics open to all educators, parents and other citizens.

Our children: beautiful heads rather than heads full[38]

My thanks to Eletta[39] and all the friends who over the course and turning of time have contributed to this very long spiral [the history of Reggio Emilia's municipal schools]. It is a spiral that has grown over time and changed over time, a very long journey in history that has gone through moments that were not always in a straight line but has always had on its side a capacity for coherently keeping to the trajectory, to the sightline.

It is a long story, and the generations are changing, and I do not know how much these memories can be shared. Young teachers entering now probably do not live the same things, with memories of the kind we carry within us. In many ways these are extraordinary memories, and we certainly should be recounting them in much more documented ways, more written ways I mean, writing the phases of these memories, their moments, their origins. I think the original hallmark is a hallmark we still have, and I think it has been shared over the years, with a memory that has never lost its capacity for selecting out the things that are worthwhile from things that are not.

Our story was born some days after Liberation. It is a long ago era, but an era we still feel inside us. It is a story that was born of an intuition in people less disposed in some ways towards what I would call the current culture. It was born based on an intuition, on concreteness, on a hope and a utopia, which meant they started without anyone else suggesting things to them, they started building their school in Villa Cella. It was not their school – in a certain sense yes it *was*, but more than that it was the school they wanted for their children: a kind of redress, a redemption, a strong creation, strong with the hope an initiative of this kind could contain within it. And working on Saturdays and on Sundays – they were labourers, and land workers, they were factory workers, and the women were labourers too; so in the space of a few months, working Saturdays and Sundays, they built the school. It was a school born absolutely just like that, the way a mushroom can grow by surprise, without anyone suggesting anything to them and without any guidelines from anywhere.

And I still remember the conversation: on the one hand their very thick dialect and on the other how incredible that the conversation should take place between me and some of these women cleaning bricks. There. To my mind this is probably the font that contains the great generative strength that is capable of leading to different shores in children's education. It was felt so keenly by these people, participating so much, and was something the official culture was only just beginning to glimpse. To my mind those bricks, taken from bombed out houses, cleaned one by one, made into a building, give exactly the sense of the journey we have made. One bit at a time.

These were times of a great flowering, and even schools could be set up without being ordered: they were all on the city outskirts, especially in the poorest parts. When I say poor I am referring to a very great poverty, really very deep, on a very great scale. So the schools of Sesso, Massenzatico, Foscato, Masone and Santa Croce were born. They were created through direct self-management and their great problem was one of survival. Hopes were many, but hope only just managed to weave in with questions of an economic and financial nature. The problem was to ensure the survival of the schools and the survival of hope: above all the survival of the children.

I know diets today are under discussion. At that time there were no special diets, diet was cyclical and we progressed according to the season. We always ate eggs, which were offered to us by farmers, and chestnuts when there were chestnuts. The menu was the sign and the cross of a great generosity. Recounting these episodes, which today would seem absolutely incredible, there is a point where I would like to halt the memories, because I know that when memories return they re-invent themselves in some way, and I really do not want to re-invent anything.

So then, the story of schools for [young] children in our country is a story interwoven with many events, and many vicissitudes I will not discuss too much.

However historically and politically it is a very strong affair. You all know that the issue of whether to create *scuole materne* or not moved forward slowly [. . .]. The struggle lasted eight years, and really it began two years before that, so from 1958 to 1968 there was a Parliamentary battle that was essentially on the right of the State to have its own *scuole materne*.[40]

In 1966 Moro's government fell over this issue, which means *scuola materna*, schools for little ones, little schools, school for the wee ones was a very significant crossroad, very difficult to deal with. Perhaps we should not marvel more than necessary at these crossroads in history. At that time it was a historical crossroad. Past experience had led to an absolute monopoly of [Catholic] parishes in early years education with situations we can hardly criticise. We have to give due consideration to the work the parishes did, just as it is important to acknowledge the great amount of voluntary work in schools in the humblest parts of the city. This [voluntary work] seems to be disappearing today, when we consider the way things are going, how things are moving forward, how they are progressing. However this [kind of work] remains a great opportunity for culture, not only for existential and human adventure.

The country was being rebuilt and many meanings became grafted onto the issue of schools for young children during the reconstruction, and were also grafted onto changes in the organisation of the family that began to emerge at this time and were unstoppable in the 1960s and 1970s, and from 1970 to 1975 – I think this was the great time of movement, though the later changes are probably still ongoing and so it is difficult to determine its trajectory. However, more than anything else the issue was connected with changes in the meaning of education, and this problem was social in nature and administrative in nature: it was a problem that was political and cultural in nature. It was a huge issue. Consider that when we [the municipal schools] were born, officially in 1963, all the other schools that had been invented, that had sprung from the people's invention, had fallen behind, or fallen in action. Some managed to resist until 1967.[41] The *Comune* finally managed to municipalise them in 1967, and bring an end to this great odyssey of extremely difficult survival that was the hallmark of the birth of these somewhat irregular and alien creatures.

In 1963 we [the municipal schools] were born. I will not tell you how but obviously we were born after fortunately overcoming long, strong and obstinate opposition, since the *Comune* could not be allowed to directly manage educational affairs. This is an important issue I have always fought for personally and most determinedly. It was a great opportunity for the historical left. The historical left has always been very backward on the issue of understanding education, and above all on understanding childhood. So this was an absolutely radical turning point in the long tradition of struggle and politics. To me it seemed essential, and of vital importance, that together with the issues of administration [by the *Comune*], there should also be a presence [by the left] in the facts of education, in the fact of being part of understanding and managing, of a capacity to grow awareness on the very delicate and very important issues of children's early education.

The Robinson school [first municipal school opened] was born, and I would just like to say the name was not plucked from the air. It is a name that is well-meant, giving centrality to the adventures of a man, to the adventures of the birth of an institution, for the first time taking place with a sufficient guarantee of survival behind it.[42] [. . .] However I want to tell you that curriculum design began immediately with teachers – and this to my mind is one of the most important things – curriculum design that today perhaps would make us smile, legitimately I think. But at that time it was something completely new, especially in the education of young children and in schools for young children, something completely new that one could design [an education], that one could attempt to leave behind daily improvisation, the improvisation of minute-by-minute, and attempt to re-construct something more monitored, more monitor-able, something longer, with more intersections, more combinations that could be re-combined. Above all it let teachers – the very first teachers – go from nothing to something. Because the secular experience of schooling and of a [school] service was absolutely virgin territory. So I remember from the start that interwoven with the birth there was this first conscious germ of rigorous application, as far as it was possible, of what I would call an educational design.

The school was born in 1963 when the battle in Parliament [over public provision of schools for young children] was at its most tense, and the battle continued for five years. However I do not want to remember the Robinson, which has its anniversary this year: we send our best wishes and congratulations. I wanted to remember the way the city of Reggio Emilia was continuously intersected by the planning of research and cultural events. In 1963, at the same time the Robinson school was born, we organised a conference in Reggio Emilia that was incredible because it was on a theme that is still underway; research and debate on this theme are still ongoing. The conference was on the relation between psychiatry – it was called psychiatry then – between psychology and pedagogy, and it is still a current theme. The conference anticipated by years the appearance of reflection on these themes. Themes that are still asking to be interwoven, and where the lack of this weaving, for people attending to work like ours, is something we feel and suffer.

In 1966 we held an international conference, the first international Italo-Czechoslovakian conference. It was a highly successful conference and all the most illustrious names in Italian pedagogy were present, from De Bartolomeis to Visalberghi, Borghi. This was an event that marked the city of Reggio Emilia as already having a vocation for culture, for research on a cultural level.

In 1968 something extraordinary happened. For the first time, secular *comuni* from all over Italy came together in Bologna to reflect on issues of *educazione dei bambini* [early years education]. I remember it was an incredible occasion. To think that the secular sector was capable of rallying together on a theme that had never gone beyond theoretical statements, to [reach] a place where themes put down roots in very concrete reflection.

In 1970 the first *asilo nido* was born in Reggio Emilia, one year in advance of [national law] 1044. Again this was something extraordinary, illustrating a capacity for translating into action things that might [previously] have remained on a level of ideas and thinking.

In 1971 we held a conference on social management [in early childhood services], two words worn threadbare today. However to speak of social management and family participation – real concrete participation, not participation preached or written in frontispieces – was again something very big and new in terms of experience at that time. It underscored – I would say it *re*-scored – the parental mark of the first schools [for young children], which I discussed with you earlier.

For the first time in 1971 we had the courage to organise a National Conference in our city; the first national study conference. The theme was very ambitious: 'Experiences for a new *Scuola dell'Infanzia*'. It was the first time secular Italy had managed to organise a meeting of such importance and such vitality. Remember what transport and communication were like at this time. We thought 200 or 250 people at the most would come, and we would have been over the moon. We found ourselves at midday with 750 people from all round Italy, and some even from abroad. I remember we had to change the *Sala degli Specchi* venue in a great rush. Overnight we moved the exhibition that was on in the *Teatro Municipale*, and held the conference in the theatre.

Again it was an exceptional experience. The first time an attempt had been made to put together experiences from here and there – there were not many – that were capable of making a public statement directly related to the values of the newborn experience [municipal *scuola dell'infanzia*]. A book was produced. It is impossible to find the book now, it can only be found in libraries. However I believe it represented the first organic attempt in our country to give a voice, sufficiently concrete, sufficiently organic, to the issues of early years education.

In 1974 we even had a conference on Graphics [drawing and mark-making, see Chapter 5, n.14] and again it was an extraordinary conference. I am remembering it now because it was a little lost in there with my memories. It was an extraordinary conference because we not only invited psychologists and *pedagogistas* to discuss drawings (graphics), for the first time we also invited semioticians,[43] and nobody knew what these were. And we also invited biologists, and no one knew what these were either or what they could do for us with this kind of theme. In some ways we anticipated many of the issues that are still open-ended in the field, and we will come back to those later. The question of biology on a level of professional development has yet to come: it has not registered yet, and it is still only half an issue.

In 1975 there was a large conference in Bologna.[44] There was a strong attack in 1975 by Catholic forces on the radio, but we won't talk about that [actually in 1976; see pp.166, 277]. Again it became an episode in our history, an episode that can be explained very rationally, and I think they had reason to produce this kind of attack, concentrating especially on our city [of Reggio Emilia], which was seen as a sort of epicentre for an increasing phenomenon related above all to [educational] activity by *comuni*.

In 1963 [in the *scuole dell'infanzia*] we had two classes [of children]. At the end of the 1960s we had twelve. Between 1970 and 1975 we progressed to fifty-four classes. Think how extraordinary this trajectory was. This really was the [. . .] easiest season in many ways, and the most thrilling, because there truly was a capacity for word to become fact, for word to become bricks. And here we must remember our mayors, all of whom continued in a direction anchored to the values of this initiative, the kind of initiative we are trying to remember.

Then came another extremely important episode. In our opinion it was incredible that men could not be employed in the *scuola materna*. Not only was it sensible to feel this way, I would say it was an awareness, a feeling that a profession like this could not be denied to male teachers.

It was prohibited, **the employment of male teachers was forbidden** [by national law]. We broke the wall of resistance, we broke it [in 1972 in the *Comune's Regolamento*], and twenty days later a circular from the Malfatti Ministry [of Education] was on the desks of every Italian administrator based on our initiative, reminding them it was absolutely forbidden for any State administration or State representatives [e.g. state-run *scuole materne*] to open the doors to male teachers. This problem has still not been resolved, the problem of teaching for ever given over to women. The issue of teaching only being a job for women is not just about freedom of choice, it is an extremely complex issue that represents a serious obstacle for every man who comes forward wishing to teach in our schools.

This again is a very complex, delicate theme. So I would like to say that men did pass over the threshold with us. I remember the first men employed in the *asilo nido* and *scuola dell'infanzia*. It was a great event for us, and I think we were aware of it, but it was a great event for children too, and for families. It is something that, thinking back today – and we have fewer men today than we had then – was a sensational discovery, which pedagogical literature has not been capable of adequately remembering nor been sufficiently capable of highlighting as a necessity and opportunity for children who from a psychological and anthropological [human] point of view are very obviously asking for relations with both sexes, which are not partial and halved or forbidden.

Well I could go on with this history, but I think it is time to stop, except to remember certain things that are still alive inside us, alive in the sense we are still researching them, still realising them.

The problem of Social Management, despite crises in the collegial bodies, is something that has been maintained. And though it now takes different forms and has new difficulties it is still a cornerstone of our experience, which must not lose such a vital, fertile contact.

The problem of teachers' co-presence [having two teachers in each group]. If I were to tell you the adventures we had in order to obtain a measure like this! Fully aware that still today we cannot do education, and cannot even aspire to doing education if this principle is not included in a project or package. [This principle] is more organic, more extended, more systematic, and includes forms of organisation that are capable of letting pedagogical ideas and practice take their course.

The entrance of the *atelier*. The other day a [female] friend from another country said to me, 'We were amazed when you spoke of *ateliers* as a sort of desired turbulence stirred up in the schools.' And effectively speaking, the *atelier* was one of several measures capable of sweeping away tradition, sweeping away traditional organisation. We did not really know very well ourselves [what would happen], but we did know it was important to provoke a break, provoke some less convenient directions capable of breaking with the professional and cultural routine that we were interested in removing.

The problem of including **aggiornamento** [professional development] in our work contracts. If you think what this has meant in battles, not just here [in Reggio Emilia] but especially in other places. [. . .] This *aggiornamento* included in our working week, this [form of] social management, is something of extraordinary value.

In the same way our sensibility towards handicapped children was of extraordinary value. In 1970 we had twenty-five [of these] children in the *scuole dell'infanzia*. I mean the sensibility towards bringing in difference, fully aware of what we were doing, and of what would be produced in the way of the educational dynamic.

However I believe this spiral of continuity that has existed relies above all on a level of theory, on a project of research, and this was elaborated during the journey, but in some ways it was already [there], sufficiently clear and aware inside us.

I do not wish to insist on these issues. The problem I would like to discuss this evening is another. It is to see instead how to further complete and push forward with our theorising and research, while taking into account all the mutability, all the changes, that have happened or are happening. Constantly keeping before us above all the fact that the children we have today are the children of the year 2000. To my mind this is something of a cultural and political nature that ought to tie us to a sensibility and extreme awareness.

We are working in difficult times, so mutable, so constantly changing for children, pushed beyond our capacity for prediction because the future today is difficult for us to govern. The problem of today's children is a great problem, requiring a great capacity for selection, for producing choices, for producing choices that break with the recent and distant past, and that hold within them at least the conditions of a possibility, of a possible trajectory, of seeing the future by keeping at hand everything the present gives us today. In the present there are many things, many complex things, many intersecting things, many good things, many things that are not good, many bad things. There are many chances, many possibilities, many positives and many risks. Our period is one of extremely rich elements, mixed with the possibilities of an extremely complex destiny.

So, I think we could start with this invocation by Alice [in Wonderland]. An invocation it seems to me that could very well be included not only symbolically, but as a reminder we cannot be indifferent to. At a certain point Alice, this extraordinary girl with a philosophy that is not only adult, but who loves with a youthful philosophy of extreme richness and extreme provocation, wonders in a soliloquy:

> Who am I then? Tell me that first. And if I am a person I like being I will come up, otherwise I shall stay down here until someone comes to get me. I would like very much for someone to put their head in here and say something, because I am tired of being alone.[45]

Images of great significance echo here. Still today children are asking who they are, if you will tell me who I am. And if I like this 'I', then I shall come up and stay with you. But if you will not pick me up, and if you cannot help me find my identity, well then I shall stay here, but I am tired of being alone.

It is an important document, a document I think has relevance not only for today, it will be relevant tomorrow too, because the question of children's education, the question of relations, the question of children's identity, all constitute a very difficult anthology. The great issue is for us absolutely not to impede childhood from giving testimony about itself. These are not simple assertions because clearly there is a contradiction here. What needs to be done is to give them the capacity; but how do you give the capacity if you do not concede the rights? The right of [children to be] able to testify about themselves, to be the protagonists themselves, identified in an identity they like too.[46]

Starting here we could attempt to reconnect the grand designs, the grand theories and the grand problems with the problems associated with our everyday experience with children. This is something Italian pedagogy lacks, because it is closed up in its books, in its textbooks, closed up in cellars and in attics in a constant and obsessive re-reading of old texts about old problems, and above all, it is in an utterly cramped, unliveable space.

What attempts can we make? I do not know. All I can do is make a series of public statements, from which you can draw a series of invitations and suggestions, to be examined and re-examined on the level of action. That is to say on the level of choosing and selecting actions that we are obliged to carry out in our work.

It seems to me the first issue is the crisis, or the end – yes, I think the end – of science as a teleological reference point, the inflexible source, all-knowing, all-foreseeing. You can try and work out for yourselves the kind of pedagogy we use if pedagogy is presented as science. Good, well you ought at least to have raised some doubts. Several implications can follow on from it and I think each one of you can already draw them out.

Never again can any area of learning predict every eventuality. Today the unpredictable is a category of science. This statement is related to the previous one, but gives even greater strength to possible interpretations each one of us can make. What is necessary on our part – the time has come – is to analyse the significance and above all to understand the significance that the development of science, the development of technology, of information, of economy, of consumption, all have for reformulating our image of children and humanity, and of cognitive, ethical and social strategies.

Effectively, whether we know it or not, whether they tell us or not, whether it is guaranteed or not, whether it is imagined or not, we have to work with an image of the child, a fundamental image of the child, which comes from far away. Later we will see how this image of the child comes from far away on a level of biology. It is important to know in this moment that the formulation of the image of the child, and of human beings – every time I say child I am saying human being, even though I never actually say it, the formulation of the image of the child and human beings we are faced with, of their cognitive, ethical and social strategies [. . .] [is] extremely connected and tied to a series of facts and large phenomena that govern us, and that we have to deal with every day. Here again, how can we pick out a thread capable of leading us to reflection of a practical nature about the choices we make of a procedural and tactical and strategic character in education? This is a problem.

Reflect on the fact – again this is absolutely necessary – that biology, evolutionary theory, theories on the evolution of humanity, the species, on the evolution of the cosmos, are completely peripheral to our formative culture, and not only for teachers, but for young people, the younger generations. For the first time physics, chemistry, cosmology, study of the mind, the neurosciences and cybernetics are discovering their [own] nature – this is what we are not capable of taking in. They are rediscovering their true nature. This means physics, chemistry and biology etc., have been hibernating through the rigid [period of the] laws of science and have paid a high price, but now they are producing something of great value: the necessary re-combination of disciplines. Not only does each discipline understand it cannot get by [alone], it also understands the meaning of solidarity and transculturality.

On the level of pedagogy, the indications are very clear. This solidarity, this interaction, this inter-relation between disciplinary forms, between forms of knowledge, should tempt us to look anew into our experience.

Think of the great challenge being played out in our times with philosophy and around philosophy, where for the first time the human sciences and the natural sciences are weaving together. This is a passage humanity has never experienced before. A great passage, heavy, weighed down with responsibility, especially if we consider how close the year 2000 is, and that our children will become a more advanced generation.

This is a grand theme, which cannot merely be a declamation, a regional or political slogan. It is an important idea that we have to try and bring together each day in terminals capable of producing a new kind of research, a new kind of learning, a new kind of sensibility, a new kind of sentiment, of imagination, of logic and rationality.

Above all, as Bateson a great pedagogue suggests, [. . .] the necessity [of considering] ties between our whole system and the system of nature in a way that makes them capable of synchronising rigour and imagination on one hand, and compatibility and capacity for change on the other.

This means we must bring a number of aspects back into consideration: aspects that are inside us as information but not inside us as thinking, sensibility, perception and levels of awareness. All of you know that for these aspects to come full circle in a reformulation of thought, culture and knowledge, of ways of accessing knowledge and acquiring culture, certainly represents a very difficult problem: however it is one we have to pose.

So our thinking must be less disjointed than thinking we have been capable of up to now, and we still continue in this way today. There is not enough time today to discuss with you how division, opposition and dualism are categories that were much used by the old kind of science, and because of the strength and pressure of the old kind of science. . . .

Editor's note: This sentence is unfinished.

Do not think in purely scientific terms, these are terms of an economic order, a political order, terms of an ideological order. This is a very large issue.

In ourselves, and also in the children, we must try and produce the maximum cognitive flexibility, must feel we are always willing to pack up our suitcases [and move on]. There are values that are strong, but other values advance faster than the immobility of these values. We all know them. However I think the great problem is to go in the direction of the capacity to cross borders, and to stock up on supplies of things we thought were unending, perhaps until a moment before.

The second issue – for ourselves above all, and then children, young people, younger generations – is to teach an understanding of interpretation, personal orientation and re-orientation, the orientation and re-orientation of theory and practice; rather than adapting to and perfecting oneself in professional and scientific material that has been handed down to be applied and replicated. Here we [face] the whole problem not only of '*formazione*' or professional development, but of '*aggiornamento*' or professional updating – for which we probably need to look for keys.

Think of interconnecting, the great verb of the present and the future. A great verb we must be capable of understanding deep down, and of conjugating as part of our hard work; bearing in mind that we live in a world no longer made of islands, but in a world made of webs. In this image there is the construction of children's thinking and the construction of our own thinking. A construction that cannot be made up of islands that are separate, but which belong to a great archipelago, to a great web, in which interference, interaction, inter-disciplinarity is the constant, even when we cannot see it, even when we think it doesn't exist, or that it isn't there. Interdependence is there.

So then, on the level of pedagogical and theoretical choices I think there is much work to be done.

Bear in mind the other important fact of obsolescence in learning and knowledge. Being with children I think we notice and register a sort of loss. This is not a cyclical loss, it is a loss whose motivations and causes we cannot immediately decipher. Certainly, however, we are dealing with what is for us a large phenomenon; the falling away of culture and professionalism. In the sense that these must both be constantly stocked up and [re]supplied for the new problems that are born of evaluating the present and our attempts to interpret what the future may be.

A great care with values. I believe values are of primary importance, together with selecting and choosing, and a capacity for penetrating the great forest of today's large themes. However I also think [it is important to have] a capacity for observance of human values, ethical values, the values of solidarity, of interdependence, the values of organisation. These are the great values we must work with, and they are also the great values we must somehow make germinate in children.

Again, reflect on the transition from an idea of heteronomy [action influenced by a force outside the individual] in the construction of knowledge to an idea of autonomy. There is a large choice we must make in areas where we become aware that, as part of our efforts, we are working with operations that are perhaps too heteronomously accented, too strong, and not always appropriate for children. We must try instead to give much more trust, much more credit, to children's autonomous capacity for growth: not only physical growth but the manipulation and re-manipulation of the discoveries of the senses, of the perceptions, suggestions, intuitions and pathways that children also have.

And perhaps transmission too.[47] Because no one wants to forbid transmission, no one wants to ban it. However there is transmission of a conservative nature and transmission of an innovative nature. Transmission of an innovative nature not only brings us closer to the large themes we have attempted to illustrate here, it is also the only road that allows us to truly produce a real and genuine closeness to children. Because the children's desire is exactly this, to be innovative, to be part of an innovation they can feel, as if it were a physical sensation, of movement, of dynamism, inside them.

The third question, and I'm cutting very short here, is the problem of whether this theoretical frame can in some way benefit from ideas and strengths that come from the neurosciences. Neurosciences are another absolutely foreign chapter in professional development and it is impossible to understand (obviously it *is* possible to understand) how such an important subject connected with the brain. . . .

Editor's note: This sentence is unfinished.

Not only is it the least known machine (the least known tool, not machine), the least known tool in the entire universe, it is certainly also the means, the medium, the terminal through which we decide if we are capable of understanding more of our life, of our possibilities, our potential, our substance, and of the things we do not know.

However, I must be short. Neurosciences belong together with a hypothesis like ours, in the sense that they give it strength by affirming that certainly the cerebral device [brain] is the design of genes; but that synapses, the neuronal connectors, are tools that, though they are with a child from birth, in reality become selected and reinforced, multiply or decline during the first years of life. This is something extraordinary, which can give a theory of this [our] kind stronger application.

The other question, which to my mind is extraordinary, is that the brain functions in groups: solidarity between hundreds of billions of neurons is a characteristic. Again this solidarity in our brain cannot only remain in our brain: it must also be capable of being realised, and of entering into, passing into, our values. And these values are not necessarily biological in nature. This is a very good value.

The [different] parts of the brain know very well how to assist each other. Now this capacity for rushing to assist where something is not functioning, where something is deteriorating etc. is another [example of] the brain's wisdom. You will say, and I say, it is a wisdom of nature, a great wisdom, which must not remain stored up there. We have to take it and draw it down: manage to introduce it in some way into pathways of a social order, pathways of a political order, and into pathways of a philosophical order.

I will not tell you of the latest discoveries, made at the University of California, and the University of Chicago.

Editor's note: Calls from the audience for more information can be heard on the tape.

Very well then. At two years old the child is already an extraordinary child. The child is a laboratory eating up more sugar than an adult consumes, eating up more glucose, in the sense that a working brain is a great devourer of glucose. Well then, at two years old a child manages to make their brain work, in short the brain manages to make the child work, by means of large consumptions of glucose.

The latest discovery at the University of St. Louis indicates that selection, not only of the neuronal synapses, the bridges that constitute solidarity and the capacity for connection, the capacity for interdependence etc., is constructed in the first years of life. Up to the age of eleven it seems this construction is variable, both in quantity and quality, based above all on the real life experiences of the world and society that a child has.

[. . .]

The first period of life is the most fertile for every kind of learning. This again is an important issue, like a rocket with more than one stage, though stage is a word we should abandon absolutely. In any case the image is that of a rocket with different stages, and the first propulsive force is what gives greater strength to the stages that follow. However we have to be certain, we need to be convinced that this is a very important statement. There are very important reflections to be made here. But I'm not going to make them. [He laughs.] I'm going to skim over them. I just want to pause with you on what I think is the central topic.

There is no need for me to recount the journey up to the present day of the cultural sciences, and the psychological sciences, in terms of their interpretation of the child. Or how the most recent interpretation, given to us (not only) by Piaget and by Garcia in a posthumous book[48] finally senses that everything we have considered before now as sensory-motor intelligence in the first years of life instead belongs to a logic of meanings: which means reconstructing, through a celebration and recognition of the great potentials children act out on the level of meanings.

No act of the child after birth can be perceived as devoid of meaning in any way. This is absolutely not possible. Think of it as you wish, think of the dawn, think of the sun coming up, think of the night disappearing, think of forms being born, think of the glimmers of light being born, think of the wind, of the smells, of the tastes being born in that moment. I don't know if this is the dawn of a child but what is important is feeling convinced these are all meanings that leave some kind of trace: and there is no action, no act, no act in which a child is a protagonist, or of which a child is the recipient, which does not contain a meaning in it above all for the child. It cannot be there is no trace.

The question I especially wanted to underline, as I conclude, is of arriving at an even closer, if possible more analytical reading, of why historical theory has been indebted to and conditioned by the themes discussed this evening. This would be another way of revealing how theoretical authenticity or non-authenticity has often also completely misled us, in good faith.

However what is important today is for us to reaffirm a strong conception of the child. This, to my mind, is what we need to do.

[. . .]

Probably children have a need to produce situations that disconcert, that lower the threshold of the routine they are forced to experience, both in family and school environments. They feel a need to emerge from the indistinct, and they do it through exaggerating, through understatement, through extremely bold imaginations, and through documentations that are completely unthinkable on our [adult] part. To be attentive to this is sufficient for us to become more used to the confusion, the surprise, the extraordinary marvelling children lead us to with testimonies you cannot read in the mainstream literature. However, the children declare them, in support of facts and events that evidently are born inside them. Without us being able to understand how, or why, or how they are capable.

No date given

93.ND Speech to school staff, no date

> **Editor's note:** This may be a presentation made to staff from the municipal schools at some form of *aggiornamento*, either at the opening of the new school year, when all staff were present, or at another meeting when all schools sent representatives. The date may be 1984.

Proposals for an educational hypothesis that is participatory and democratically managed

Scuola dell'infanzia

Public and participatory schools

Essentially, the educational hypothesis in our *scuola dell'infanzia* is a hypothesis of <u>participatory education</u>. In the sense that it recognises and enacts the needs and rights of children, families, teachers and school workers, actively to feel part of a <u>solidarity of practice and ideals</u>.
    [. . .]

> **Editor's note:** Malaguzzi goes on to call for a 'new culture of educational processes', including teachers and families and a 'new diffused social consciousness of education', which emphasises the need for 'interaction between competencies and cultures', underlining the 'incompleteness and complementarity of parts' and highlighting the 'ethical and productive values of dialogue and research'. In a section headed 'the value of experience, the value of democracy', he argues for an educational project that adopts the 'method of democracy and confrontation as a permanent choice, developing processes of individual and social participation and co-responsibility'.

Adapting methodology and educational practice in schools

A school with the ambition of constructing its own experience and being identified with participatory values has to adapt its contents, and its working methodology and practice.

[. . .]

It must be capable of internally living out processes and issues of participation and democracy in its inter-personal relations, in the procedures of its *progettazione* and curriculum design, in the conception and examination of its work plans, and in operations of organisational updating, while always focusing on children, parents, and the *Consiglio di Gestione*.

This simultaneous referencing is very important: essentially it consists in basing each element in the whole of the educational experience – professional, *progettazione*-connected, technical and relational – on a foundation of dialogue and participation.

In the same way, identifying the themes that determine our general planning on an operational level – the objectives, the intermediate and end points of our working plans, the directions of our methodology and practice – must avoid two equally evasive practices as much as possible. The first aspires to being a complete educational project but conceals its incomplete philosophy behind rhetoric as an excuse for vague improvised practice; the second refuses precise choices in the area of professional development in deference to children, whom it is presumed have their own development programme and must avoid contamination from any perspective.

So that one of participation's tools and objectives is this: collegially organising deeper exploration of cognitive methods for knowing and evaluating children's and adults' concrete behaviour - by bringing together information from multiple observations and fields of experience - until procedures [that can be] used operationally can be defined, again collegially; and gather from what is contingent or a detail or separate or private, the reasons, causes and hypotheses that might be behind them, how much they may be part of more general phenomena or similar stories, and the cultural and political aspects that often explain them, and in any case come to a truer and fuller analysis. By making it participatory in this way, we give the work of education the meaning of a genuine practice of solidarity, of inter-subjective proposals and research, of effectively checking our own personal action, and of a project turned to social ends.

[. . .]

Participation and democracy as open processes

Participation and democracy are not facts of nature, which are given and complete. They are specific forms of a life of relations, of personal and collective organisation, that can be upheld with legislation, and that as part of the unfolding of history and culture derive from continuous and open processes.

Participation and democracy are part of, and a result of, processes that can be promoted and organised: this precise interpretation gives us concrete indications and possibilities for work that concerns workers and direct and indirect users of the schools.

Levels of participation and democracy grow with organisational capacity, the suitability of tools, the clarity of the objectives that support our work and their capacity for mobilising, and with coherent behaviours and purposes in those who though they start with positions and possibilities that are not the same, can identify with participation.

Participation grows and safeguards democracy and liberty, liberty and democracy grow and safeguard participation.

A need for change and faith in the possibility of change as the promotion of a higher and more just degree of individual and collective wellbeing are the elements that justify participation and make it move forward.

If the project of democratising schools is separated from a process of changing their functions and purposes it will be very difficult to realise and share.

Participation and democracy have a historical and cultural meaning and only have the strength to mobilise when they take on the task of reform and stimulus to transformation. This is even more so when reform and transformation do not only affect schools but a society that is fundamentally anchored to a model of accumulation as a private project and an organised induction to private consumption, which endorses norms of competition, the marginalisation of individuals, groups and classes, and which objectively creates obstacles to democratic cohesion and interaction between the school community and the civil, social community.

THE ORGANISATIONAL STRUCTURE OF THE EXECUTIVE GROUP
in the *Comitato di Partecipazione e Gestione* [Participation and Management Committee]
BASED ON WORK THEMES

General Coordination	General coordinator Secretary
Organisation of Work	• admission of children, defining costs • relations with teaching and auxiliary staff • hours, shifts, tasks, holidays • relations with families • para-scholastic initiatives (*tempo lungo* [see Chapter 3, n.59]), *settimane verdi* and *azzurre* [green and blue weeks], summer time, trips, itineraries for visits etc. • celebrations, entertainment

Organisation of Environment	• caring for, and adapting indoor and out-door environments • ordinary and extraordinary maintenance • furnishings, equipment, materials for educational and school use, • functional services (kitchen, laundry, transport etc.)
External Relations	• relations with *Comune*, neighbourhood councils, cultural, recreational, sports institutions, local polyclinic, social and health services, educational institutions, collegial bodies
Educational Issues Cultural Issues	• cultural and educational organisation of the school related to objectives • interaction between the school community, and the civil and social community • general planning, planning by sector • curriculum objectives, analysis of the progress of objectives • establishing work groups and consultation groups • promoting larger meetings on educational work • cultural initiatives, cultural and experiential exchange • planning initiatives, participating in cultural initiatives together with neighbourhood committees • Relations with the *Coordinamento pedagogico didattico*

General Guidelines

Meetings of *Comitato di Partecipazione e Gestione:*	once a month
Meetings of executive group:	3 times a month
General assemblies of users:	twice a year[49]

Notes

1 The 1984 Concordat replaced an earlier treaty signed in 1929 by Mussolini and Pope Pius XI. The new treaty ended Catholicism's status as the state religion of Italy and officially guaranteed freedom of religion for non-Catholics.

2 From an editorial in magazine *Bambini*, No.5, May 1988.

3 'Education design' refers to the constant work of verifying how the underlying values of connections, relations and aesthetics are being realised in every aspect of the school as a complex system.

4 The actual words written by Lewis Carroll are 'Who am I then? Tell me that first, and then, if I like being that person, I'll come up: if not, I'll stay down here till I'm somebody else – but, oh dear! . . . I do wish they *would* put their heads down! I am so *very* tired of being all alone here!' The version quoted by Malaguzzi suggests a responsibility for 'someone' (an adult) to 'get me' (a child).

5 Andrei Sakharov (1921–89) was an eminent nuclear physicist in the former Soviet Union and a Nobel Prize Winner. He was an outspoken critic of the Soviet regime, ordered into internal exile in January 1980 after an interview with American television, in which he called for the withdrawal of Soviet troops from Afghanistan.

6 In the early 1980s, *Comitati di Scuola e Città* took the new name of *Consigli di Gestione* [Management Councils].

7 After the title, the text says that 'this synthesis has not been re-read or corrected by the author', implying that the text is a note taken of Malaguzzi's presentation.

8 *Progettualità* refers to the process of building or evolving a project. It is closely related to the noun *progettazione*, used in Reggio Emilia in opposition to *programma* or *programmazione*, which implies predefined curricula, programmes, stages and so on. The concept of *progettazione* thus implies a more global and flexible approach in which initial hypotheses are made about classroom work (as well as about staff development and relationships with parents), but are subject to modifications and changes of direction as the actual work progresses.

9 'Objectivisation' here refers to the need for a more empirical understanding of childhood, based on observable phenomena, in contrast to prejudiced understandings.

10 Carlo Bernadini (1930–) is a physicist and professor at Rome's La Sapienza University.; he acted as consultant to some schools in Tuscany. While he was convinced that maths/physics thinking could only be generated through strictly maths/physics activities, Malaguzzi maintained it could be supported by other languages such as drawing, music, dance and oral languages.

11 John Maynard Keynes (1893–1946) and Milton Friedman (1912–2006) were famous economists who adopted very different positions on the workings of the economy.

12 Frederick Winslow Taylor (1856–1915) was an American mechanical engineer who sought to improve industrial efficiency through systematic observation and study and the application of 'scientific management'.

13 Giuliano Toraldo di Francia (1916–2011) was an Italian physicist and philosopher.

14 David Hawkins (1913–2002) was an American professor whose interests included the philosophy of science, mathematics, economics, childhood science education and ethics. He visited Reggio Emilia on several occasions. A chapter in his 1974 book *The Informed Vision, Essays on Learning and Human Nature* is titled 'Messing about in Science', in which he speaks of three phases of school work in science; one of these he calls 'messing about', in which time 'should be devoted to free and unguided exploratory work'. During this phase, 'children are given materials and equipment – *things* – and are allowed to construct, test, probe, and experiment without superimposed questions or instructions.'

15 Cuisenaire Rods are learning aids for exploring mathematics and learning mathematical concepts, such as the four basic arithmetical operations, working with fractions and finding divisors. In the early 1950s, Caleb Gattegno (1911–88), an Egyptian educationalist best known for his innovative approaches to teaching and learning mathematics, foreign languages and reading, popularised this set of coloured number rods created by the Belgian primary school teacher Georges Cuisenaire (1891–1975).

16 Piemonte is a region in the north-west of Italy, with Turin as its capital city.

17 In accompanying notes, Malaguzzi refers to '[1] the idea of the child [being] influenced by the constructivist idea, interactionist in itself, with; [2] an ecological idea of development and of the child like Bronfenbrenner draws for us in his most recent writings. To which I would personally again add, connected above all with; [3] shared participation in pleasure, which to my mind [. . .] has a psychoanalytic derivation.'

18 Urie Bronfenbrenner (1917–2005) was an American developmental psychologist – but born in the Soviet Union – who is best known for his ecological systems theory of child development. This theory, sometimes known as human ecology theory, identifies five environmental systems within which an individual is embedded and interacts: microsystem, mesosystem, exosystem, macrosystem and chronosystem. His book *The Ecology of Human Development* was first published in English in 1979.

19 The micro-system is one of Bronfenbrenner's five environmental systems within which the individual is embedded. Closest to the individual, it includes family, friends and services like schools.

20 Cybernetics is a transdisciplinary approach to exploring all forms of systems – mechanical, physical, biological, cognitive, social. It foregrounds connectivity, interaction, feedback, emergence and complexity. It first appeared as a discipline in the 1940s. An important figure in the field, who helped extend cybernetics to the social sciences, was Gregory Bateson (1904–80), whose work is often quoted by Malaguzzi.

21 An 'Archimedean point' is a hypothetical vantage point from which an observer can objectively and in totality perceive the subject of inquiry. It represents the ideal of 'removing oneself' from the object of study so that one can see it in relation to all other things, but remain independent of them. The expression comes from Archimedes, who supposedly claimed that he could lift the Earth off its foundation if he were given a place to stand, one solid point, and a long enough lever. Sceptical and anti-realist philosophers criticise the possibility of an Archimedean point, claiming it is a form of scientism.

22 Mauro Ceruti (1953–) is a philosopher who in the 1980s introduced into Italy the issue of epistemology of complexity. Between 1986 and 1993, he worked in France at the *Centre d'Etudes Transdisciplinaires, Sociolgie, Anthropologie, Politique*, directed by Edgar Morin.

23 Edgar Morin (1921–) is a French philosopher and sociologist known for the transdisciplinarity of his work. He has paid particular attention to acknowledging and working with complexity.

24 'Monad' refers to a concept of learning as a sequence of steps.

25 This quotation comes from G. Bateson (1979) *Mind and Nature: A Natural Unit*. New York: E.P. Dutton, p.223.

26 Viscount Ilya Romanovich Prigogine (1917–2003) was a Belgian (though Russian born) physical chemist and Nobel Laureate noted for his work on dissipative structures, complex systems and irreversibility. In his 1996 book, *La Fin des certitudes*, published in English in 1997 as *The End of Certainty: Time, chaos, and the new laws of nature*, Prigogine contends that determinism is no longer a viable scientific belief. 'The more we know about our universe, the more difficult it becomes to believe in determinism.' This is a major departure from the approach of Newton, Einstein and Schrödinger, all of whom expressed their theories in terms of deterministic equations.

27 In Italian Malaguzzi uses '*vie dell'agibilità*' and immediately after gives the English word 'viability'; it is not clear if he offers 'viability' as a translation or whether it is a word he has come across in his reading.

28 Gianluca Bocchi (1954–) worked, at the time this text was written, at the Faculty of Psychology and Education Sciences at the University of Geneva; today he is a Professor at the University of Bergamo. He played an important part in introducing complexity studies into Italy, especially through *The Challenge of Complexity* (1985), a book written with Mauro Ceruti, about the transformation of paradigms and ways of thinking that characterise the science of our day.

29 Rita Levi-Montalcini (1909–2012) was an Italian neurologist who, together with colleague Stanley Cohen, received the 1986 Nobel Prize in Physiology or Medicine for their discovery of nerve growth factor, a small secreted protein that is important for the growth, maintenance, and survival of certain target neurons. In 1987 she published an autobiography, *Elogio dell'imperfezione* [In Praise of Imperfection].

30 Maxwell Cowan (1932–2002) was a neurobiologist best known for discovering that during the development of the brain, considerable numbers of nerve cells die and many pathways are reorganised. He showed that these two phenomena are widespread in the developing nervous system and together play a key role in refining the brain's initial connections.

31 Malaguzzi here may be referring to the work of Gregory Bateson, which also influenced major poststructuralist philosophers especially Gilles Deleuze and Félix Guattari. In *A Thousand Plateaus*, they wrote: 'Gregory Bateson uses the word plateau to designate something very special: a continuous, self-vibrating region of intensities whose development avoids any orientation toward a culmination point or external end.'

32 Barry Commoner (1917–2012) was an American biologist and a leading ecologist who was among the founders of the modern environmental movement.

33 *Mind and Nature: A necessary unity* by Gregory Bateson was first published in 1979 and summarises his thinking on the subject of the patterns that connect living beings to each other and to their environment.

34 Howard Earl Gardner (1943–) is an American developmental psychologist, best known for his theory of multiple intelligences, set out initially in his 1983 book *Frames of Mind: The theory of multiple intelligences*. He has had a long collaboration with Reggio Emilia, including shared research projects.

35 Malaguzzi later refers to abduction being worked on by Charles Sanders Peirce (1839–1914), the American philosopher, logician, mathematician and scientist, sometimes known as 'the father of pragmatism'. Pierce said of abduction that it is 'the process of forming an exploratory hypothesis', 'the first step of scientific reasoning' and 'neither more nor less than guessing'.

36 Malaguzzi draws a distinction between *stupore* (translated as wonder) and *meraviglia* (translated as marvelling). The distinction does not work very well in English, where 'wonder' and 'marvel' have similar meanings.

37 *Eros* is one of four words in Ancient Greek that can be rendered into English as 'love'. The other three are *storge, philia* and *agape. Eros* refers to 'intimate love' or romantic love, though it has also been used in philosophy and psychology in a much wider sense, almost as an equivalent to 'life energy'.

38 The title refers to a book by Edgar Morin, *La Tête bien faite. Repenser la réforme, réformer la pensée* [The well-made mind: Rethinking reform, reforming thinking].

39 Eletta Bertani was the *Assessore* for education in Reggio Emilia from 1985 to 1990 and first President of Reggio Children (1994–2000).

40 Malaguzzi refers to the long struggle for public provision of early childhood education for 3- to 6-year-olds, opposed in particular by the Catholic Church. This led to the fall of the national government led by Aldo Moro in 1966, before legislation was finally agreed in 1968, recognising and supporting provision by the State and by local authorities.

41 Of the eight self-managed schools for 3- to 6-year-olds opened between 1945 and 1947, including Villa Cella, three closed between 1953 and 1962; the remainder were taken over by the *Comune* of Reggio Emilia between 1967 and 1973.

42 A 5-year-old boy attending Robinson school explains the relevance of the name: '[Robinson Crusoe was] an adventurer, he was very, very courageous and went to sea because his passion was going to sea. A passion is something you have desired for a very long time, and then you do it always' (Various Authors, 2012, p.91).

43 Semiology is the science or study of signs, signals and symbols, especially in language and communication.

44 Malaguzzi refers to a conference organised by the regional government: 'The child as subject and source of rights in the family and society. Creating more *asili nido* and *scuole dell'infanzia* as centres of individual and social education promotion'.

45 *Alice's Adventures in Wonderland* (commonly shortened to *Alice in Wonderland*) is an 1865 novel written by the English author Charles Lutwidge Dodgson (1832–98) under

the pseudonym Lewis Carroll. It tells of a girl named Alice falling down a rabbit hole into a fantasy world populated by peculiar, anthropomorphic creatures. For Lewis Carroll's actual words, see n.4 above.

46 The next year, a major international conference was held in Reggio Emilia drawing inspiration from the quotation from *Alice in Wonderland*, titled '"Who am I then? Tell me that first". Knowledges in dialogue to guarantee citizenship to the rights and potentials of children and adults'. More than a thousand people participated from all over the world to discuss the learning, the rights and the potentials of children and of adults [see 95.90].

47 In this paragraph, Malaguzzi demonstrates his reluctance to adopt dualistic, either/or positions. Thus it is not a matter of being for or against transmission, but of the context and manner in which transmission occurs, in particular whether it occurs within a conservative or innovative idea of the child, knowledge and learning. It is consistent, too, with his ideas about the protagonism of teachers.

48 J. Piaget and R. Garcia (1983) *Psychogenese et Histoire des Sciences*. Paris: Flammarion. Published in English in 1989 as *Psychogenesis and the History of Science*.

49 This refers to General Assembly Meetings (*Interconsiglio Cittadino*) made up of representatives sent by *Consigli di Gestione*.

Chapter 5

The final years
1990–93

Figure 5.1 Conference '"*Chi sono dunque io? Ditemi questo prima di tutto*" *(Alice) – Saperi a confronto per garantire cittadinanza ai diritti e alle potenzialità dei bambini e degli adulti*' ["Who am I then? Tell me that first" (Alice) – Knowledges in dialogue to guarantee citizenship to the rights and potentials of children and adults], *Teatro Municipale*, Reggio Emilia, 1990. Speakers are from the left: Luciano Corradini, David Hawkins, Loris Malaguzzi, Paulo Freire, Andrea Canevaro, Mario Lodi

Figure 5.2 Public at the Conference '"*Chi sono dunque io? Ditemi questo prima di tutto*" (Alice) – *Saperi a confronto per garantire cittadinanza ai diritti e alle potenzialità dei bambini e degli adulti'* ["Who am I then? Tell me that first" (Alice) – Knowledges in dialogue to guarantee citizenship to the rights and potentials of children and adults], *Teatro Municipale*, Reggio Emilia, 1990

Figure 5.3 Opening of the Reggio Emilia *Institutet*, Stockholm (Sweden), 1993. In the foreground, from left: Vea Vecchi (*atelierista Scuola Comunale dell'Infanzia* Diana), Harold Gothson (Reggio Emilia *Institutet*), Loris Malaguzzi, Anna Barsotti (Reggio Emilia *Institutet*)

Figure 5.4 International Study Group visiting the *Scuola Comunale dell'Infanzia* Diana, Reggio Emilia, early 1990s

Figure 5.5 Cover of the programme for the Kohl International Teaching Award ceremony, Chicago (USA); on the back, notes written by Loris Malaguzzi, outlining the talk he gave on that occasion, 1993

Introduction (Peter Moss)

Historical context

Sadly, the 1990s proved a short decade for Loris Malaguzzi, with his unexpected death at the beginning of 1994. The decade, however, started on a high note, with Reggio Emilia hosting an international conference – "'Who am I then? Tell me that first'. Knowledges in dialogue to guarantee citizenship to the rights and potentials of children and adults' (a title inspired by Lewis Carroll's *Alice in Wonderland*) – that drew many participants from around the world as well as overseas speakers including David Hawkins and Paulo Freire. The next year, under a headline that read 'The 10 best schools in the world', the American magazine *Newsweek* identified the municipal *Scuola dell'infanzia* Diana, representing all of Reggio Emilia's *nidi* and *scuole dell'infanzia*, as the most advanced in the world for early years education.

This growing international interest and recognition, including increasing requests for support with service and professional development, led to a new project to help organise the relationships between Reggio Emilia and the world beyond. What happened has been described by Eletta Bertani, first President of Reggio Children from 1994 to 2000:

> Our city also had to fully take on the new responsibility towards all those people around the world who wanted to converse with our pedagogical experience, and therefore equip ourselves with suitable means. So that in February 1993, taking up a proposal Loris Malaguzzi had put forward for some time, a group of citizens launched an appeal in the city which gathered many respected supporters, to set up an International Centre to support and give value to the educational experience of Reggio Emilia, and formed themselves into the Reggio Children Support Committee.
> (Various Authors, 2012, p.190)

The new organisation, Reggio Children, was formally inaugurated in March 1994, as a public–private company established by the *Comune* and other interested parties to manage the relationships between the city's schools and the outside world. It has evolved since to assume a range of functions including arranging Study Groups, undertaking consultancy work, organising a variety of research and other collaborations, designing and managing exhibitions and publishing.

Meanwhile in Reggio Emilia itself, new services continued to open during the course of the 1990s. These included three *nidi* run by co-operatives and one *nido* self-managed by parents, all with agreements with the *Comune*; two *scuole dell'infanzia* managed by the *Comune* itself; and an experimental space for afternoon use by children and adults together (*spazio incontro*, space for encounter). Two new premises were opened to rehouse existing municipal *scuole dell'infanzia*, with one being located together with a *nido*. Alongside these developments, three new state-run *scuole dell'infanzia* were opened and two municipal *scuole dell'infanzia* became state-run.

This expansion was needed to meet increasing demand, as the city population rose rapidly – from 137,000 to 150,000 in the 1990s – as a result of a rising birth rate and further migration, now mainly from outside Italy.

This was not the first wave of migration to Reggio Emilia, but it was certainly the most substantial and visible. In the 1960s migration had been mainly from the south of Italy, particularly Calabria and Puglia; during the 1970s people migrated from Egypt and were often employed in steel works; in the 1980s migration was from Ghana, Tunisia and Morocco. In the 1990s the city, characterised by a local economy offering many different work opportunities, became part of the global flow of migration: from eastern Europe to China more than one hundred different nationalities and provenances brought new cultures, but also new fears and new conflicts. Defining a new identity for the city was not an easy course.

(ibid., p.169)

Nationally, the government in 1991 issued new *Orientamenti dell'attività educativa nelle scuole materne statali* [Guidelines for educational activity in state-run *scuole materne*], which (despite the title) among other changes renamed state-run *scuole materne* as *scuole dell'infanzia* – accepting a terminology and identity long advocated by the educators in Reggio Emilia.

The early 1990s saw Italy moving into crisis. The economy slowed again. More terrorist outrages occurred, most shockingly the assassination in Sicily within a few months in 1992 of two magistrates – Giovanni Falcone and Paolo Borsellino – and their protection details, by the Mafia, the criminal organisation they had been charged with investigating. Even more momentous was the collapse of the post-war political order. The PCI split in 1991 into two new parties, the *Partito Democratico della Sinistra* [PDS, the Democratic Left, which adopted a more democratic socialist position] and the *Partito della Rifondazione Comunista* [Communist Re-foundation, which maintained a communist identity]. Then following a judicial enquiry – *Mani Pulite* [Clean Hands] – that uncovered widespread and deep-rooted corruption, both of the main parties in government during the post-war years, the DC and the PSI, dissolved themselves, hopelessly mired in scandal. Bettino Craxi, leader of the PSI, and prime Minister from 1983 to 1987, fled to Tunisia to escape jail; the entire political class were similarly discredited.

In their place emerged new groups and parties, notably the *Lega Nord* [Northern League], a federation of regional parties in Northern Italy, expressing deep resentment of national government in Rome and with (as they saw it) the waste of their resources on an inefficient and corrupt South; and *Forza Italia* [Forward Italy], a party founded in 1993 by billionaire tycoon Silvio Berlusconi. Elections held in 1994 confirmed this political transformation, producing a coalition government headed by *Forza Italia* and supported by the *Lega Nord* and the conservative *Alleanza Nazionale* [National Alliance]. The players may have altered, but the dominance at national level of the centre-right remained.

These changes were felt in Reggio Emilia, too. For the first time, after local elections in 1995, the city was governed by a centre-left coalition, under the *Ulivo* [Olive Tree] banner, spanning a range of parties including the recently formed PDS. In the same elections, the *Rifondazione Comunista* party gained just 5 per cent of the vote, and went into opposition. This marked the end of a political era.

Malaguzzi's life

Now entering his 70s, Loris Malaguzzi remained an active presence in Reggio Emilia and its municipal schools. Vea Vecchi recalls 'the wonderful meetings that were held where Malaguzzi, always an avid reader, brought us his latest findings, always extremely up-to-date and, particularly in the 1990s, related to the areas of neuroscience and scientific philosophy' (Vecchi, 2010, p.48). He was still an important figure nationally, continuing as President of the *Gruppo Nazionale Nidi* and director of *Bambini*. If not a member of the commission that drafted the new national Guidelines for early education, his influence was felt indirectly through the impact of his work on those who were members.

He was working on developing his last major project, which was the creation of a new organisation he named Reggio Children. He was also active abroad and witnessed the increasing international standing of the city's educational project, which he had done so much to bring about. In 1992, he was awarded the LEGO Prize, in recognition of his outstanding contribution on behalf of children and young people. A year later, he received the Kohl International Teaching Awards, in Chicago, on behalf of the municipal schools.

Loris Malaguzzi's death, from a heart attack, was sudden and unexpected, on a cold winter morning in January 1994; a few months after the death of his wife Nilde, to whom he had been married nearly fifty years, and of his brother.

It is a tribute to him that Reggio Emilia's project of early childhood education was able to survive his death, and to continue to flourish; he had laid strong foundations for a continuing project that had developed a life of its own.

The selection of documents (Reggio Emilia Working Group)

I would like to quickly give a sort of strong image, an image of a political, geographical and economic nature [. . .], [of] a world no longer made of islands, intervals, spaces, oceans and mountains, [but] a world made of a network. [. . .] It is important we know that this network form of the world corresponds perfectly, I believe, with the network image of our brain and the functioning of our brain. [. . .] There is a network between the brain and evolution, between neurons, the world and the world of children. [. . .] I think this strong image may be pertinent for schools, for the functioning of schools, for the organisation of schools, for school logistics, for

education, pedagogy, didactics, learning, knowing, that can be in a network form, with the possibility of reciprocal contaminations and of interactions.
(Loris Malaguzzi, 1990, Speech to an international conference 'Who am I then?' [95.90])

It is not possible to find completeness or maturity reached in the journey of Loris Malaguzzi: his sudden death at only 74, while still fully and restlessly engaged in his research and analysis, gives us – just as he theorised in children's development – theories suspended between equilibrium and disequilibrium, between continuity and discontinuity. Furthermore, working on texts that are mostly transcriptions of spoken words results in complex interpretation and comprehension, because when talking without notes – as Malaguzzi usually did – we cannot always be certain the words or verb constructions really mean what they seem at the first reading. However, given that above all Malaguzzi spoke and worked, more than wrote, engaging with this transcribed oral work allows us to better study and investigate his thinking, to better understand his extremely refined philosophical thinking, woven through with diverse dimensions, cultured and profoundly human.

We will not systemise what is not systemised. Instead, though dealing with such a very brief period (1990–93), we will try, without making them banal, to follow the threads Malaguzzi appears to have woven, taken apart and re-woven in his long work of research and dialogue with the contemporary world he was experiencing.

The 1990s opened with an international conference, the preparation of which we met in the 1980s, with a title taken from *Alice in Wonderland*: 'Who am I then? Tell me that first'. More than one thousand people and around fifty speakers from Italy and other countries participated in the event: among them were Father Ernesto Balducci, Paulo Freire, David Hawkins, Mario Lodi, Alberto Munari and Mira Stambak. The conference came just over a year after the fall of the Berlin Wall, and in his opening talk Malaguzzi situates the event as part of the great political changes, also relating it to new discoveries in science: 'These subjects do not hover or circle above education: these are subjects that are part of the themes, the sensibility and the restlessness, which must be inside schools that are confused like our Italian schools' [95.90].

Essentially this introductory talk has three subjects. The first is a denunciation of a society composed of castes and sects and of a culture cut into slices, incapable and unwilling to 'begin the difficult art of inter-disciplinarity or of trans-disciplinarity', which are the keys to understanding the world and inventing 'new keys in a very short space of time for keyholes we do not yet know about'. Scientific theories were finally offering a basis for getting past the Manichean and disjointed positions Malaguzzi had always fought in philosophy, ethics and politics. The image of the world as a network, like the network of the human brain, is an image with great visual and cultural impact, which Malaguzzi seems to have adapted from the ecological perspectives he refers to extensively in these selected texts, an anticipatory and visionary image of a reality – of the Internet and social networks – that shapes our world today.

A second subject is subjectivity, often 'impeded, subjected, not encouraged in the fullness of its gift-giving', and not to be confused with individualism. Malaguzzi proposes subjectivity as part of a culture of liberty, of democracy, of choice; he connects it with a biological and cultural right made of an evolutionary dynamism – the right to enter into life actively, to be credited with resources, competencies, interactive capacities, relational reciprocity, constructive intelligence, conjecture, and negotiation with things, with ideas, and with others. Wise nature, he observes, gives children a prolonged period of apprenticeship, but she also gives adults a prolonged period for evaluating, weighing up and analysing. Society, instead, cuts back on the time available to adults and children. Time is a significant issue: giving children time (and childhood is the right age) for ownership of different points of view, to break down barriers, formulate transgressionary choices, to range freely with the imagination, in essence to construct with full freedom, but also in a dimension of participation, the art of learning to learn.

The third topic Malaguzzi discusses in this contribution is the child, the principal focus and dominant theme of this period. Reading through the texts selected for this chapter they compose a theoretical and value-based declaration and positioning on the idea of the child, which – Malaguzzi says – is a necessary premise for every pedagogical theory and project. A shared scale of values is essential to avoid the risk of daily life dictating its rules, increasing the thirst for immediate achievements. Instead, paradoxically, 'our children lack a public declaration of identity' to save them from the meagre word 'protection', a word that stands out in the UN documents on childhood published during those years; and which, perhaps, still today, too often prevails in common thinking about children. For this absence of a public declaration on childhood, Malaguzzi denounces his day as a period in history not only economically difficult but culturally aggressive. Unfortunately we can only agree with his evaluation even when referring to the present: the current era continues not only to be fragile and uncertain on an economic level, it is also violent on a cultural level, especially regarding childhood.

'Certainly even today if we put all the keys in our pockets together they cannot produce the right image of children', admits Malaguzzi. Scientists studying children have always found strong and unpredictable qualities in them: but immediately, perhaps out of fear, they proceed to box them in, to put them into cages of schema, so activating a sort of defence not only on the scientists' part but on that of families and schools. Leaving room for the unpredictable, the surprising, happenchance, without which our species would be terribly depleted, perhaps no longer exist, is vital for children and for human beings, while pedagogy and schools think they have to put the brakes on their play. Malaguzzi would first call this controlling cultural attitude 'prophetic pedagogy' in a commentary accompanying the showing of *The Hundred Languages of*

Children exhibition in Bologna in 1990; an exhibition that through field work and observations, carried out in schools by adults maintaining an ability to marvel and wonder, offers a testimony to the capacity children have for sweeping away all taxonomies and any idea of stages of development. He discusses the concept of prophetic pedagogy again, two years later, in a speech at a book launch in Reggio Emilia [98.92].

In his introduction to the 1990 international conference in Reggio Emilia, Malaguzzi makes a particularly strong and pregnant statement when he states that all children are rich [95.90]; while in an interview soon after he states that children 'immediately [situate themselves] in a world of communication and exchange' and from birth therefore they become an 'active co-habitant' [94.90]. Poor children then are only those who are not recognised as bearers of a sufficient measure of identity to claim a strong dialogic spirit, rich intelligence and curiosity in others. Such poverty is not inscribed in children as a biological fact, but socially inscribed in the absence of those public declarations of identity referred to earlier. Children are curtailed, are thought of as poor, *tabula rasa*, because this vision is useful to the politics and economies of governments, who 'know exactly where to divert the money, the wealth, and the things that are necessary'.

Elsewhere Malaguzzi declares that identifying or declaring a child to be poor is more convenient because identifying them or affirming their richness requires overturning the current logic. So it is extremely important to credit children with enormous potential but also necessary to be able to count on 'strong political and cultural commitment [. . .], capable of contributing to the overturning of many current paradigms making society an unwelcoming place for children – who are not the subjects and bearers of needs, but the bearers of rights, values and competencies' [94.90]. During a talk at a 1991 Conference, on 'New ideas for early childhood', Malaguzzi also distances himself from the child of psychoanalysis and the child of Piaget, offering a much more complex concept of the competent child than the one that has been frequently used – overused – in the years since his death.

Malaguzzi deals with the image of the child in complex ways. In the first place he tells us a competent child does not mean a self-sufficient child, and introduces the theme of context: going from child to context means accepting a complexification of the issue. Referencing Heidegger, who maintains context holds and breaks a subject (i.e. it can enrich a subject's subjectivity or swallow it up until it has disappeared), Malaguzzi puts forward the idea of an agent-child in 'a context, of which they are in part the author, in part the co-author, and in part someone requesting [help and protection]', and poses this as 'a value which has to be declared this way, it has to be attempted this way' [96.91]. He then proposes that self-regulation is a powerful concept, but one which must be understood to be part of a much more complex and lively dynamic. Children's 'co-existence . . . is obviously an identity connected *with*: it is contextually connected', an image biologically rooted in the species and in pre-natal life, an image of the child as interactive (capable of acting) and constructivist (equipped with limited self-regulatory capacities outside context). So this biological root does not mean genetically programmed determinism or essentialism: in fact the brain has great plasticity and environment plays a strong role.

'What to do?' Malaguzzi asks himself – and asks us. A first answer is not to classify things too quickly, offering 'a range of experience, [and a greater] possibility of producing encounters with the whole range of genetic specificities and potentialities' [94.90]. Again, flank the child with interlocutor-resources, rather than protectors and instructors, so the child can learn the art of choosing and creating, rather than the art of imitating and consuming models.

Themes of context and how identity takes root biologically also posit the issue of nature–culture, nature–nurture opposition. Malaguzzi takes the position that objects have a cultural nature, they are not *objective:* 'objects are something we have to read, the way we read a book' [96.91]. Children pass through, are mediated by, microcosms, which are historically specific and have laws, rules, empathies and revulsions. This reminds us of adult responsibilities – politicians, teachers, managers – each one using the competencies, possibilities and powers available to them.

Malaguzzi critically discusses the vision of the self-constructing child and returns it to an idea of contextuality, where acquisition processes run in constant flows, which also include the adult: a flow of processes that allow adults to listen to children and listen to themselves at the same time, a strategy privileging learning compared to teaching. Not learning as reproduction or comprehension, but 'rather as a complementary process of constructive self-education and co-education, through the uninterrupted interactions and inter-subjectivities of ideas and acts between young and old, and between the children themselves, in all the multiplicity of their geneses and forms' [94.90].

In his speech of thanks at the prize-giving ceremony held at the Kohl Foundation in Chicago in 1993, Malaguzzi again offers us the image of the child as producer of culture, bearer of a capacity for producing further culture and contaminating our culture [99.93]. He reconfirms his earlier words, from 1991, when he invites us to take the child 'from an image of self-constructor with no interaction', towards an image 'of hetero-auto-construction', which is not dependent on stages ('We perhaps do not have time to speak ill of stages today') but welcomes the richness of multiple and contextual interactions [96.91].

These pages – so rich and detailed – can help the reader develop a more precise idea of the image of the child, a fundamental concept for all educational politics and choices but often paradoxically also held at a distance by psychology and pedagogy. Malaguzzi denounces this short-sightedness as the loss of capacity for reading the world in intelligent and contextualised ways that are capable of highlighting 'the sensation of complexity'. He also denounces a culture that oppresses children, not with conspicuous forms of violence, but with public rhetoric opening up trapdoors of precociousness, with the disowning of their rights, with their public invisibility, and with a consequent lack of dedicated politics.

This elaboration is strongly contextualised by the problems of these years. It was a difficult period for Italy's early years services. Economic problems in *comuni*, especially those investing in *nidi* and *scuole dell'infanzia*, led many (even those that were left-leaning) to consider handing these services over to the state as a way out of their predicament. It is what happened in nearby cities such as Piacenza. For Malaguzzi, this was not only an abandonment of services for the citizenry but of a cultural and political process.

At the time Reggio Emilia was experiencing a substantial increase in its population owing to large flows of migration, with rising demand as a result. As always the city chose the less simple road-map to respond to changing demographic and economic conditions and heightened demand. A project, '*Progetto Infanzia*' [Project Childhood], was developed to value the existing services and offer investment, constructing the combined efforts of the municipal, state and Catholic schools, together with educational co-operatives, into an integrated system.

During these years the national government published the new Guidelines for educational activity in state-run *scuole materne* (in 1991), a complex and advanced piece of work Malaguzzi had been watching carefully and appreciatively. The problem he often criticised was the total divergence between the words of the guidelines, the organisational choices of state regulations and trade union choices formulated for teacher contracts. This discrepancy (reflected, for example, in teachers working fewer hours with children and together with other teachers, the absence of professional development time, the lack of pedagogical co-ordination/support) highlighted the absence of political and cultural thinking on childhood on the part of politicians and made the choice of many *comuni* to let their schools become state-run even more painful. In this context readers will appreciate Malaguzzi's perseverance in working on and declaring the image of the competent child and consequently the qualities needed in educational contexts.

In its issue of 2 December 1991 the US magazine *Newsweek* declared the *Scuola dell'Infanzia* Diana, representing the network of *comune*-managed educational services in Reggio Emilia, to be the most advanced school in the world for the education of 3- to 6-year-old children. The article dramatically increased the renown of this educational experience, drawing other newspapers and media to investigate the story. Among documents from this year we find the text of a television interview: in the manner and time television permits, Malaguzzi synthesises with ability and to effect the main themes that shape Reggio Emilia's educational project [97.91].

This recognition, and the greatly increased number of requests for professional development, visits and international collaboration, became the starting point for developing a project, personally followed by Malaguzzi until his death, for the construction of an organisation able to support Reggio Emilia's *nidi* and *scuole dell'infanzia* in 'the defence of children's rights'. Included in these selected writings the reader will find declarations that Malaguzzi proposed for use in communicating this new project – what was to become Reggio Children – to the public [100.93].

This theme of international recognition re-emerges in the launch event for the book *Infanzia e Scuola a Reggio Emilia*. Malaguzzi underlines how this award has created strong ripples abroad and in the media – but not in the national Education Ministry nor among the powers-that-be on the left, who though they are not governing the country could have taken advantage of Reggio Emilia's recognition to put forward proposals for the national educational system. This deafening silence was broken only after Malaguzzi's death with the advent of a centre-left coalition government, when a national Education Minister, Luigi Berlinguer, visited Reggio Emilia's schools for the first time.

During his talk at the launch of the book on childhood and schools in Reggio Emilia [98.92], Malaguzzi offers a reconstruction of the history of the schools, finding their roots in the experience of the *asilo del popolo* [people's school] that opened in Villa Cella immediately the war ended and was strongly desired by women who saw children as the great historical agency through which destinies that they did not want to see repeated could be liberated. Malaguzzi credits these women with great and powerful energy, organised, capable not only of producing theory but going out and entering politics, capable of understanding and closely following the needs of the people and finding the right responses. Women whose organisations lined up on opposite political sides, but who were capable of working together for an objective and going beyond their opposing positions.

In Malaguzzi's effective metaphor the necessity of women entering the workplace covered the sphere of rights with a thin veil: services had been secured and secular schools had been secured as spaces not only of political, historical and cultural production but of the educational production to which children had a right. At this point, however, Malaguzzi introduces a critical perspective, in which he accuses women's movements of not accompanying the journey by going deeper into constructing an identity for the schools, but of turning their attention instead to other issues, for example the struggle for securing autonomous decisions about their bodies.

Malaguzzi also harshly criticises the indifference of politicians to educational issues, not interested in knowing what happens in schools: 'what is lost is the global vision . . . [that enables us] to understand what is happening to the future conditions of citizens' [98.92]. Finally he denounces the absence of debate on the subject of the family, above all on the father figure, identified primarily as a political subject and worker: when in reality 'you cannot think of a worker's conditions or a labourer's conditions as starting and ending in a factory: there is a human, existential, cultural, affective continuity with the family environment, and with the family nucleus' [98.92]. Instead, in Malaguzzi's opinion the family must play its role, must make its own contribution and share in the educational project. Parents, together with children and teachers, make up an inseparable triptych of subjects that form the foundation of making education: to them Malaguzzi dedicated *'Una carta per tre diritti'* [A charter of three rights], which began to take written form in January 1993, after years of constant and continuous thinking and coherent choices in educational action.

It is difficult to find a conclusion for this last chapter, nor do we wish to: the thread of Malaguzzi's life on earth was suddenly broken, and inevitably his words were also interrupted. We will see in the next chapter how his legacy has remained alive and vital, the generator of many more experiences – which had often been conceived and prepared by Malaguzzi himself, such as the birth of Reggio Children in March 1994. However for one last time we will entrust ourselves to his voice, in two messages which are not so much a farewell as good wishes for all those working in education:

> [Our experience in Reggio Emilia] has gained its identity through a crucible of debate, exchanges of points of view, and dialogue; it is a history with the obstinacy to continue to live, the strength to live, because I believe we can say a sort of fever, of internal revolt, is first and foremost good for health; and that it is also one of the infinite variations on happiness.
>
> [95.90]

> Perhaps more than a nostalgia for the past we need nostalgia for the future. Children, the children that are and the children to come, are waiting for us there in the place where nostalgia for the future is capable of arriving, and let us all hope we are there too.
>
> [99.93]

Timeline 1990–94

Key: *Malaguzzi*
Reggio Emilia
Italy

1990	**'Who am I then?' international conference organised in Reggio Emilia.**
1991	**'Newsweek' magazine nominates Diana School, representing the system of municipal schools in Reggio Emilia, as most advanced in world for early childhood education.**
	New *Orientamenti dell'attività educativa nelle scuole materne statali* [Guidelines for educational activity in state-run *scuole materne*], includes changing the name of state *scuole materne* to state *scuole dell'infanzia*; PCI splits into *Partito Democratico della Sinistra* and the *Partito della Rifondazione Comunista*; *Lega Nord* established as a political party.

1992	*Awarded LEGO Prize.*
	Mani pulite [Clean hands] begins, a nationwide judicial investigation into political corruption; Mafia murder magistrates Giovanni Falcone and Paolo Borsellino in Sicily.
1993	*Malaguzzi's wife, Nilde, dies in November.*
	Kohl International Teaching Award (Chicago) to the municipal schools of Reggio Emilia.
1994	*Dies in Reggio Emilia, 30th January.*
	Reggio Children founded.
	DC and PSI parties dissolved after mounting scandals; *Forza Italia*, headed by Silvio Berlusconi, launched.

Documents 1990–93

1990

94.90 Interview with Loris Malaguzzi (no record of who the interviewer was and where the interview appeared)

Editor's note: This document comes from the personal archive of Vea Vecchi.

[. . .]

LM: A declaration [about the image of the child] is not only a necessary act of clarity and correctness, it is the necessary premise for any pedagogical theory, and any pedagogical project. So then. What is the image of the child? What is the child's bio-cultural reality? What are their rights of personal and social autonomy and subjectivity? What are their rights of citizenship?

The primary issue, on my part and on our part, is declaring the historical, biological, psychological and cultural nature of how the child enters life. Children are the fruit of life itself, and from the very beginning as new-born babies they weave dynamic processes of interactive co-existence and growth with life, and from birth they continue with their specific ways of relating. Their interactions with adults, cultures, environment, things, shadows, colours, spaces, times, sounds, smells and tastes, immediately situate them in a <u>world of communication and exchange</u>, from which they take and receive, combining and selecting sensations, emotions, sentiments – traces of what Watzlawick[1] calls 'different realities' – meanings they gradually learn to distinguish, organise and process. The world passes through them as they pass through the world.

It is a widely shared opinion that children at birth are ready to experiment with most if not all the fundamental sensations peculiar to our species. This opinion is very well expressed by Jerome Bruner: childhood is an inheritance of human evolution and its destiny is to develop an exclusively human culture. From the start childhood brings a model making it possible to grow a human being who is a user of sociability, learning, knowledge, communication, language, sentiments, symbols, imagination etc.

The child is already [from birth] an <u>active co-habitant</u> asking to be treated and recognised as such (this is what widely goes unrecognised, not only on a basis of persistent old prejudices, but of theorisation and practice, which have always been hegemonic and up to now have found an indistinct, indefinable, poor, *tabula rasa* image of childhood to be convenient). Choosing the aspect of children as organisms disposed to interaction and active self-construction (creatures among creatures Bateson would say), as possessors of a great dynamism that is evolutionary and expansionist, and of initiative, dialogue and exchange, confirms a new synergic vision between two orders, the <u>biological</u> and the <u>environmental</u>, and puts the old opposition between <u>innate</u> and <u>acquired</u> away in the attic.

In the field of psychology and education this concept re-establishes recursivity between usually separate elements: mind and nature, body and mind, subject and object, dependency and autonomy, integration and differentiation, intra-individual and inter-individual, rationality and affectivity, children and adults, children and children, objectives and procedures, theory and didactics, instruction and education, integrating them in inter-related, complementary processes. It is a concept that marks a starting point (though it will take much more than this) in pre-figuring an ecological child and an ecological perspective, which by considering society as a globally interactive context highlights the concept of interdependency as one of its functions and choices, as one of the functions and choices of the educational field.

The absurd thing is that this explicit public declaration of the identity of the child, which is the proper and necessary premise on which to base our theoretical foundation when starting work, is a quite unusual operation in a world that is usually unclear and dominated by praxis (or at any rate doing) without the need for prior references. At this point allow me to say that <u>hiding</u> children, leaving them in mystery, in the inexplicable, or what **Lacan** calls '**desêtre**' [variously translated as 'dis-being' and 'un-being'] in the unsaid, is to my mind a historical and cultural <u>block</u> that is still scrutinised with too little courage; something that has been extremely painful for many people, from Socrates to Campanella, from Ellen Key[2] to

Maria Montessori. It is where two cultures and all their logical and illogical political effects continue to meet and clash.

To put it crudely, I repeat, unidentified children who are declared poor are more convenient than children who are identified and declared as rich. Poor, indistinct children without qualities stay where you put them, you can describe them as you wish, without gender, or role, or history; they put up with any kind of pedagogical theory or application, and you owe them no future or even laws. You can create institutions without quality for them, give them poorly trained, poorly paid teachers, with poor prestige. Programme-based curricula, which are fashionable today with their emphasis on efficiency and their fiction of signs, arrows, scales and lesson-packs, are a misguided progressive riposte that re-objectifies children and teachers, hiding them in the way we discussed earlier.

With children who are declared rich you have to overthrow all this stuff, give them a mind and not a head, give them laws and ethics, guarantees, investment and rights. You have to set up new institutions, learning and culture for them, with long-term investments that impose long-term social policy and a completely different citizenship. In the background you can imagine the play of the undying powers of control over education and knowledge: the sacred reliance on family, the subaltern roles of women, the conformism imposed on social services, the doling out of blame and responsibility which must always be private and can never be public.

The shocking phenomenon of school drop-out and 'death', and the gap between education and the job market, which are highly visible truths in our country, do not necessarily represent calamity and injustice from certain points of view: they are the major (hidden) manifestation of public sector racism in Italy and the end point of a long schooling, which is not allowed to function or be loved.[3]

In short this 'strange situation', to use the words of Mary Ainsworth[4] (although she used the expression elsewhere), is a dangerous anomaly. It explains why some people say there is more control over [concern about] washing powder than for children in the European Economic Community [precursor of the European Union]. Or it is why, on the authority of Jerome Kagan,[5] Americans (but not only Americans) hold independence and individuality in high esteem and then end up nonchalantly considering children as undifferentiated, dependent creatures.

It is why terribly sad and escapist reactions are common in the psychology of children and teenagers faced with these incredible blackouts [sic] and nonsenses [sic], and which are on a par with Gregor Samsa[6] who had no reason to transform into a beetle in a show of desperate gaiety, except his desire to escape the grip of a petit-bourgeois family and society, which does not tolerate diversity, rigour or fantasies.

These rapid assertions suggest certain things: that it is opportune and our moral duty to credit children, all children, with resources, possibilities and capacities that are much greater and much more universal than believed; that it is necessary to constantly research educational strategy that starts with concepts based on the respect and promotion of these traits defining children's reality; that all this is not an obvious given unless there is strong political and cultural commitment on its side, capable of contributing to the overturning of many current paradigms making society an <u>unwelcoming</u> place for <u>children – who are not the subjects and bearers of needs, but the bearers of rights, values and competencies</u>.

This last definition of the nature and project of the child – each and every child (as well as every human being) – is the reason for our convictions, our hard work, and our attempts to make our organisational and methodological architecture correspond to them, for the professional nature of our relations and for our values – which we are willing to confirm today even more than yesterday.

This first discourse introduces a second morally necessary declaration: on the cultural choices that have supported our recent work, with adjustments, mediations and re-interpretations partly suggested by experience, partly by outside events and educational policy, and partly by wider comparisons that have been facilitated by international contributions and contributions from diverse disciplines in the last decade.

With the premises we have put forward, it is clear our choices have been in the direction of currents of thinking that define children first and foremost as disposed to and active in constructing the self and knowledge through social interactions and interdependencies: that as much as possible we have tried to hold together processes that are biological, political, cultural and – in the spirit of the times – also ecological. The webs of our inspiration connect up with constructivist and socio-constructivist theories; theories that generate a creative conception of development and knowledge. To be more precise, our references go from Piaget's genetic epistemology (but not the pedagogical interpretations that have been made to derive from it) to experimental theories of complexity: from Morin to Varela, Bateson to Von Foerster and Prigogine, from Mugny to Doise and Moscovici. And never ever forgetting Dewey, Wertheimer, Wallon, Claparède, Vygotsky, Bronfenbrenner, Hawkins, Arnheim, Gombrich, Papert, H. Gardner; and for the area of the neurosciences Edelman, Rosenfield, Levi Montalcini, Dulbecco and others we will mention later.

Indicators emerge from these contributions – or can arise if we are competent – that help us without any kind of obligation to try out educational strategies and attempt responses that are more far-sighted and just – the most democratic and progressive – to the problems, demands and troubling questions posed by the society of our times, and above all the ethical and civic repercussions they bring with them. These are strategies that privilege learning compared to teaching. Not learning as reproduction or as understanding through external induction, but rather as a complementary process of constructive self-education and co-education, through the uninterrupted interactions and inter-subjectivities of ideas and acts between young and old, and between the children themselves, in all the multiplicity of their geneses and forms.

This thesis obviously looks with great suspicion on any <u>ideology of gift</u> (children born with gifts that are already predetermined); and on any precocious judgement that tries to evaluate and distinguish children's presumed points of strength and weakness, such as the claims to an early <u>channelling</u> of talents, aptitudes and styles that are allegedly incontrovertibly dictated by genetic inheritance. Such claims forget that plasticity is one of the central nervous system's characteristics and that the brain continues to grow and organise its neurons and synapses during the first years of life, thus declaring its susceptibility to experiences children live.

However I imagine we will return to this critically important subject, if you agree.

Interviewer: *Agreed. Excuse me if I stop you for a moment. The <u>suspicions</u> you have listed are understandable. But today there is much talk of the <u>learning styles</u> and <u>aptitudes</u> that are said to be part of hereditary factors, said to design each child's diversity, and which could justify individualised educational intervention.*

LM: The originality and singularity of each individual are incontrovertible facts. However adopting diversity by <u>prescription</u> and declaring it to be diagnosable and readable from the start should truly frighten us. Individual differences have their own journeys to make in order to be realised. And then how are they realised? In fully coherent and realised ways or ways that are reductive and non-coherent compared with their potential? This complicated issue will not tolerate simple answers, which seem unwilling to confess the limits of our knowledge.

I know there is a lot of talk today of <u>styles</u> and <u>aptitudes</u>. But what are the tools for their identification? Anglo-Saxon 'testology', which is nothing but a ridiculous simplification of knowledge, and a robbing of meaning from individual histories?

I believe these theories on styles are bolstered above all by the just fear that children's differences might not be respected, but also by the collapse of our waiting times [willingness to wait], and again by the great desire to give things a name. Studies of hereditary factors tell us a lot about the transmission of physical traits, but little about traits of temperament, and hardly anything or nothing about cognitive styles and personality. The biology in this field owes much to genetics. When genetics says we are living organisms, it is not saying there is anything that is already absolutely codified in our genetic inheritance. When it says genes are polymorphous [occur in various forms], it wants to underline that for their realisation they have to reckon with the environment. When it adds that learning corresponds to changes in synaptic connections it is declaring the power of the quantity and quality of learning. This is also Howard Gardner's thesis and he is recognised as being above suspicion, competent and of impartial judgement.

What should we do? First, put aside any rush to categorise. Secondly, vary, multiply, intensify, re-invent and re-listen to children's activities, behaviours, words and languages. Support and make use of their interests, their forms of learning, choosing and communicating. In short, widen the net that we and the children use to fish the sea. The more we extend the range of experience, the greater the possibility of producing encounters with the whole range of genetic specificities and potentialities: those ready and eager to germinate, those that are undecided, and those that are sleeping and need a shake.

To continue with our discourse. Looking suspiciously does not mean ignoring children's diversities. It means not avoiding the other question of the hows and whys of the phenomena that accompany development whether still ongoing or already established: the meaning of certain similarities and differences, of certain sudden halts and equally sudden accelerations, and so on. The real problem is that pedagogy – and this is another difference between it and psychology – must, as it were, walk with flat feet. It has to proceed with patience and caution, with doubt and conjecture, must place itself in different points of view, see much and listen much, ask itself if what is taking place is external to it, if the rhythms and qualities of its work are capable of meeting with children's expectations, motivations, their levels of maturation, their requests for affect and socialisation. Before being a court of judgement, pedagogy is the preliminary hearing, the inquiry, the reflection and the unclosed parenthesis.

Moreover – and I apologise for insisting on this subject, which is of vital importance from both an epistemological and educational point of view – I confess there is a characteristic of our species that has always impressed us deeply: the extraordinary length of childhood. In Tolstoy's opinion, it is as if an eternity passes between birth and five years old. I think this gift of nature is significant, an act of wisdom, a splendid advance notice as if nature were saying: this long time respects the long time of maturation and development and the patient times children need in order to learn to learn, negotiate their great and difficult achievements, which they accomplish with this world, and put down roots in life. This far-sightedness cannot be wasted, and neither should it offend; instead it should be remembered in this period of insane Taylorism,[7] waste and acceleration mania [that applies] towards children too.

However this long period of childhood is also an act of generous wisdom towards us adults, as if it recognises the great difficulties and responsibilities of being with children and educating them, and effectively indulges us and helps us with our potential errors.

It is legitimate to hope that ecological awareness, with its immediate expansion of consciousness and radical strength that forces our thinking to review the disconnected ways society–nature relations have been habitually considered, will constitute a very good reason for modifying several paradigms of production (including how society and culture are ordered) and obviously our regulatory ideas[8] of ourselves, our own formative processes and those of children.

Some nuclei for the design of education? That of beginning the battle against the arrogant Cartesian rationality and anthropocentrism that sustain human/environment duality – they are contradicted by events but hold enormous sway over all our acts; that of denouncing everything that stems from [a way of] thinking that cannot see the systemic inter-related quality of phenomena, the reciprocity between different fields of nature, and between living and knowing; and finally that of understanding the connections between the crisis in ideology and the unbearable, illogical vehemence of conceptually absolute universes, which are the precursors of old and new fundamentalisms.

More than so-called exercises in ecology, to my mind education's task and especially with children, is to derive values from the propositions discussed above, which can preside over new contents and ways of promoting them. This is not an easy task certainly but it is a wide-reaching one and it starts [in this way]: by reviewing the concepts that form the basis of organising teachers' work today, so isolated, divided and distant from families and the problems of children themselves; by reinforcing the sense children have of belonging to a wider more varied world than family and school; by appreciating children's exploratory, curious subjectivity and inter-subjectivity, and the different systems of relations and theories they freely construct in putting together competency, information and sensibility; by helping children master their relation with reason and procedure, which can lead to infinitely extended possibilities, to webs, hypotheses and knowledge; by emphasising the value of communication and dialogue through expanding the range of their experience; by intensifying their discovery of environmental resources and condemning any offensive use of these; and by privileging the values of connection over the values of antithesis and hierarchy. This is an ecological and systemic vision that penetrates deeply into our very ways of acquiring knowledge: it stands beside reality and, as Bateson hoped, it contests 'man's habit of changing his environment rather than changing himself'.[9]

| Interviewer: | *Could the force and passion with which you describe childhood not give rise to suspicions of a return to idealism and child-centredness?* |

| LM: | The accusation of child-centredness does not scare us, and nor do accusations of idealism and naturalism, which mean losing a sense of the complexity, the transitions and transactions, and of the inter-dependencies of children's historicity [historical reality] and real contexts. What of Helvetius and Rousseau? No, children are neither perfect nor equal by nature. However their marvellous intuitions help us make wide-reaching choices, which in times of incomplete democracy force us to reflect seriously on current conditions of risk, the negation of childhood's lives, roles, rights and values, which are connected with the same risks in adult life. Do we really need to refer to the increase of social violence, of places of suffering and de-humanisation? |

The problem is to see whether current forms of democracy are compatible first with themselves and then with other new forms of development; whether they are capable of going beyond several of their individualist, competitive, selective priorities on the one hand, and contradictions between growth, prosperity and universal citizen's rights on the other, and [if they are capable] of bringing an end to a system in which principles and values do not translate into codes of public and private solidarity. As editor Carl Rowan wrote with all-American sarcasm in the *Washington Post*, 'the word problem – especially when it refers to individuals – has no legal currency in our country but if we put it together with social it becomes obscene'.

Obviously in a polluted ethic there is no room for several things, and even less for a genuine culture of the child, on whom blessings are lavished and solemnly promised, written up in International Charters – and then constantly retracted, instead of the universal recognition of children's biological, historical and civil rights, which would help them (and adults) not to feel like objects to be raised, but like subjects who need to be perceived as individuals; as persons who <u>know</u> and who <u>can</u>, who are looking for an interlocutor/resource rather than a protector and instructor, the better to learn the art of choosing and creating rather than a conformist art of imitating models and consuming the infinity of derivatives that stem from those models. Perhaps a recent reflection by the governor of New York state [Mario] Cuomo can be linked to this arid sense of life: '<u>There is a recurring theme. That in America something is missing. People can feel it but they can't express it. What is it? This America does not have ideals</u>'.

Without ideals and without co-participation in a shared and shareable scale of values, daily life ends up by dictating its rules. It curtails imagination, and minimises the self, as well as our sense of the other; it corrodes the project of expectation and the unpredictable; it fractures the sense of sustained relations and thought; it turns into egoism; and it increases our thirst for immediate achievement, disrupting the ways capabilities are measured and rapidly consuming what experience gives (or does not) give us. It leaves behind those who do not yet go at a running pace and those who no longer can, and children are among them.

Neil Postman has written – with much ado – on the disappearance of childhood.[10] His theory of a return to a mediaeval kind of childhood in the year 2000, with confused boundaries between childhood (which is one of the greatest, most humanist inventions of the Renaissance) and the age of adulthood, is a warning on which we can reflect even if we do not share his cultural reasoning.

Personally I remember being enormously impressed by the foresight of *Learn to See*, a book I never tire of mentioning by David Hawkins, again a child of America:

> <u>I do not know how to marshal the evidence or state the thesis with the proper qualifications but speaking bluntly I feel we are busy building a society in which children are not wanted. I am not talking about the birth rate but about the estate of childhood. Much of our present zeal for reform in education is consistent with the interpretation that we don't really like children and want to get them over being children as early as possible. I do not suppose that these symptoms are a result of individual choice but rather of the failure to make corrective choice in the face of pressures which tend to squeeze out the child-centred institutions, family or school.</u>

This was written in the 1970s when Italy was reconstructing. America was far away but its models were the precursors of many influences. Today the world has grown smaller but the critical nature of childhood conditions has grown greater, and the conditions of youth as a consequence. The shadows – which were fought with absolute prescience by a giant like John Dewey, taken up by Hawkins, and denounced in different ways by Postman, Rowan and Cuomo – for some time have also been present in Italy and Europe and are already spreading more widely.

The reason I insist so much on these revelations is simple – they are just one aspect of many references we owe to the cultures of American society, with which we certainly have all sorts of debt. Human affairs have many of their most immediate rhythms and questions there today. If this insistent attention for what is happening in the USA seems suspect, and if it distracts us from a time we can feel getting closer, when encounters, clashes and interweaving between cultures, politics, religions, races, languages and traditions will lead to the kind of <u>mutation</u> that has never been seen or imagined before, then this is a criticism that is entirely appropriate.

In this framework of undefined and unpredictable presents and futures education's challenges, rather than disappearing or becoming diminished, expand until they call to mind unforgivable premonitions.

All this pushes us to challenge the contents of several widespread laws and customs and favour the exit of childhood from its great womb of (not only) prejudice and distorted representation, which is widespread in different cultures and similar to Moscovici's <u>consensual universes</u>[11] – always repeated but never proven.

We can be certain that childhood is partly, but not only, a cultural construction. In itself this statement is both incontestable and contestable. What continues to surprise us [. . .] is that instead of looking for children at the beginning of the tunnel we find them at the end, wholly based on the rules, behaviours and convenience of the world as adults live it. This logic concedes nothing to the critical experience of those who lived before [today's] children, and it is incomprehensible why a historical and human order of this kind should be so irreversible.

The real risk is of allowing the currency of a <u>public rhetoric of childhood</u> to circulate, so that moralists and redeemers alike throw themselves into it, leaving trap doors open for all those who do not wish to change anything.

Interviewer: *I know you have always been a great admirer of Jean Piaget. How did this connection, so important for your development, arise? I remember one of your articles in the 1970s hoped that study of the Geneva thinker would draw out new tools for thinking in addition to possible innovations in methodology and didactics in children's education. Now, years later, I feel there are critical reflections.*

LM: Nothing will ever be able to take away the precursory genius of Piaget, whose fascination increases enormously when you enter into his programme of research on genetic epistemology, which strives to identify the relations between biology and knowledge that form the [generative] matrix of cognitive processes. This undertaking had never been attempted before, and its creative reach and roots are still germinating today in the wider furrow of experimental epistemologies and theories of cybernetics and of complexity.

It goes without saying that we too have <u>constructed</u> ourselves partly using the bricks of Piagetian constructivism. This was in the nineteen sixties and seventies. Personally I was very excited about activism in the new schools and the work of Bovet, Claparède, Freinet and Ferrière[12] (whom I had met, very old and very loved, in the fifties at a conference in Lyon of FICE – an international federation co-ordinating the children's communities that arose immediately after the war – and where I participated with Ernesto Codignola and Margherita Zoebeli). Piaget was the man announcing a real revolution of psychology.

My reading, my friend Guido Petter[13] – one of the Geneva school's first Italian ambassadors – and Madame Duparc, who was director of the famous *Ecole des Petits* and whom I had met at conferences, all convinced me to pack my bags and go to Geneva. The true greatness of Piaget still escaped us, but not the greatness of the child he was describing, the fabulous ways he interrogated the child, and the inexhaustible research into processes whereby children organise their intelligence.

Piaget was away from work [when I visited Geneva]. I had a long visit to the famous *Ecole des Petits* and the good fortune to meet Doctor Beauverd who was presenting a book on thinking and mathematical games deduced from Piaget's investigations at the Geneva institute [Institute of Educational Sciences, University of Geneva, where Piaget was the Director between 1938 and 1951]. It was completely new. Beauverd authorised me to translate it. I was naïve. I discussed it with Italian friends and a rival publisher took the idea. That was when I wrote the article, and organised seminars on the genesis of numerical thinking and children's thinking. The subject entered into Reggio Emilia teachers' working plans for years. [See 24.65, 25.65, 31.67.]

Younger researchers (from Mounoud, Le Moigne and Apostel to Munari, Bocchi and Ceruti) have been debating the *maestro's* theses for some years.

What are our reservations and criticisms? Briefly they lie with the Geneva child who is camped outside human history and society, a knower in one-directional, cumulative and linear ways, too caged in by stages of development in an inflexible order, too predictable and immune to affectivity, emotions and fantasies, too wrapped in excessive formalism; and this was also recognised by Garcia, who with Piaget was co-author of the last book, which appeared after the *maestro*'s death [see Chapter 4, n.48].

Interviewer: *You said to go back to the discourse on biology, a subject that gets little or no hearing from educational theoreticians and practitioners. In what way do you speak of it, and how do you connect it with issues in children's education?*

LM: Allow me some memories. Several years ago we organised a conference on perception and the language of mark-making and drawing [*grafica*]¹⁴ in children. There were five of us introducing at the conference: two *pedagogistas*, Francesco De Bartolomeis and I; a psychologist from Padua University; a biologist from Parma University; and a science researcher from Genoa University. There was very lively discussion, with several opinions diverging and very few agreements. We were on the right road but we couldn't synchronise our vocabularies and concepts. We were ill-prepared for weaving the voices of different disciplines together. On the other hand the presence of the biologist and the semiotician gave some people the opportunity to accuse us of materialism and technicality.

That is how things went that time; but we can't rule out things might go the same way again today. The fact is there is an obstinate and anti-historical loyalty to a cultural tradition that keeps knowledges distinct and separate, and accounts for the incapacity even of educational philosophy to leave behind old paradigms and have the clear-sightedness needed to outline the properties of children, teachers and their professional development. This phenomenon is still very marked in Italy and is common on an international level. It is only in the English-speaking world that we see certain changes of direction registered in the social sciences, which have started combining with biology, mathematics, information technology, biochemistry, neurobiology, and in particular with research into the structure and functioning of the brain. We can find documentation of this different cultural perspective in recently translated works by Bruner, Gardner, Kagan and Brazelton and the insistence with which they send out messages for psychology to join biology, and create a new closeness with the theory and practice of pedagogy.

To my mind these couplings are still not enough to come close to the trans-disciplinary cultural model at the basis of the birth of cybernetics in the 1940s and the first cultural alliances (so dear to Prigogine [see Chapter 4, n.26]) that seem today to be an inescapable response to the human and planetary problems afflicting us, and in which pedagogical research is incapable of being included or is left out through weakness and ignorance. However, here again, options are necessary because biological theories do not all speak with one voice. I think agreement is easier if we talk of biological–cultural theories.

Our option is for the dynamic vision of biology that comes to us from several schools of research where the names of renown are Gerald Edelman, Rita Levi Montalcini, Renato Dulbecco (Nobel Prize in medicine and neurosciences), Israel Rosenfield and Jean Pierre Changeux. The most important aspect is the aims of dynamic biology whose investigation of the brain is connected with themes of cognition, behaviour and human destiny. 'The objective' – says Rita Levi Montalcini – 'is to understand the nature of mankind and improve the quality of life, not just for part of the human species but all humanity. Not only is knowledge of the brain the key to understanding the universe, it is the only hope human beings have of understanding themselves.' And, Gerald Edelman continues, '[o]nly if we free ourselves of deterministic mental schemes in interpreting its working can we understand the human brain, its plasticity and its unrepeatability'.[15]

The greatest strength of the dynamic vision of neuroscience is the plasticity of the brain, no longer immobilised by genetic programming or made up of separate and indifferent structures and nerve cells. [Instead] nerve cells are linked by connectors (called synapses and whose organisation is particularly significant), which in turn merge together in aggregates or poly-functional maps to give us the incredible image of a building site where different functions and consequences are assembled, no two ever the same, all according to a common shared plan.

Interviewer: *If we think that the brain has a hundred thousand billion neurons and a network of connections expressed in a number with thirty-six thousand zeros, then this building site has its feet in fable. It is the most complex place in the universe, the most sophisticated system evolution has ever produced.*

LM: Exactly. The critical assertion is that genetic information and dynamics seem not to be enough either to establish connections between billions of neurons (nerve cells), or to determine the synaptic connections and networks of the inter-communicating maps that fuel cognitive and intellectual activity through chemical and electrical signals. These complex webs of relations, it is claimed, are integrated and differentiated under the influence of information and interaction with the outside world.

Renato Dulbecco's thinking takes a similar position, 'the human brain escapes genetic determination more than might be supposed': as does the thinking of Jean Pierre Changeux (renowned neurobiologist and director of the Pasteur Institute in Paris) who describes intelligent thought as a global event including contributions from the body and as 'a melody of ideas, a symphony of mental images generated singly, in aggregates, or all together, by neuronal assemblies that are activated with a common vibration simultaneous with different human behaviours: and when these assemblies – through resonance – provoke other ensembles these become available for creative acts'.[16] Israel Rosenfield strongly insists that creativity is a constitutional trait of the brain's functioning: 'Creative ability, the capacity to create without limits, seems to be the fundamental characteristic of our brain. What is surprising is that the neurosciences are beginning to explain this.'

This narrative clearly urges us, based on the brain's inherent plasticity, to never think of biological and experiential factors as independent forces. Their complementarity, together with their co-constructive variance, opens the door to a clearer awareness of educational processes. But for those interested in the education of young and very young children, the area and the quality of intervention are even more urgent and decisive, in homage to the metaphor, American again, that a child is similar to a rocket with different stages, and that what is decisive is the propulsive force of the first stage.

From the point of view of science, using sophisticated tomography techniques for the first time, we have the words of three researchers who, though working at a distance from one another, concur in their findings. In short, H. Chugani in Los Angeles, P. Hutternlocher in Chicago and M. Cowan in Saint Louis have found: that the metabolism of a two-year-old (their glucose consumption) is the same as that of an adult; that the growth and re-arrangement of brain cell synaptic connections takes place intensively in early childhood; and finally, that the quality of connection pathways varies greatly depending on pathways in life. That is to say an absence or poorness of one can lead to inactivity and weakness in the other. Indisputably the first period of our lives is the most fertile for all learning.

Perhaps this chat has been a little long. It hasn't seemed that way to me because I have reasons of subjective interest and gain; personal convictions, intuitions, fears and hopes. But why do I say only subjective and personal? Or [is it also] group?

I know very well we cannot eliminate the doubt that opting for the theories of dynamic biology described here might be an option that will change, based on biological investigation in the future. Is that a question of science? Or is it a question of ideologies and politics?

What I wanted to emphasise particularly are the concepts of ties, relation, interaction, complementarity and interdependence, which simultaneously emerge both in the forming of the brain's maturational changes and in the forming of individuals and of life events. Not one of these concepts, or the philosophies that are expressed in them, whether we take them alone or together, pre-defines times, modes, rhythms, directions and destinies that are predictable and can be guaranteed in any way.

What is important is choosing an axis of principles and values that is capable of indicating and transferring coherent ways of knowing, thinking and deciding the issues in educating ourselves and children (and not only these).

This concept of tie and of connection, where we can glimpse the fabric of cybernetic thinking, is the basis of the definition of mind [sic] or mental system Gregory Bateson has given us. For Bateson the mind is a mobile aggregate of parts, a process of organisational and interactional sequences between multiple parts. And this connected image also reflects the peculiar essence of the substance of living in the opinion of a very modern thinker like Norbert Elias:[17] so that interdependency is the founding and teleological nucleus of our living.

※ ※ ※

95.90 Speech by Loris Malaguzzi at international conference '"Who am I then? Tell me that first". Knowledges in dialogue to guarantee citizenship to the rights and potentials of children and adults', Reggio Emilia, March 1990 (transcript from the original audio recording by the *Centro Documentazione e Ricerca Educativa*)

Editor's note: This international conference attracted an audience of a thousand, and a wide range of speakers from Italy and abroad.

All of us feel we are here today to speak of things we are not able to analyse if we stand still and things stand still. We feel that the things we speak of are on the move, objects are walking, feelings are changing, words are changing, the world is changing. Not only is this the first generation to have to decide if the world and the universe are to continue to survive or to die. It is perhaps also the first generation [. . .] to discover that if they want to, if they are able, if they have the capacity, then the hard times of the cold war, of clashing, have come to an end.[18] No-one knows yet in what ways young people have experienced the many years we have lived as adults. We do not know. However we do know young people today are faced with planetary transformation, and perhaps the greatest transformations are to come. We are faced with phenomena of extraordinary importance that for the first time make it possible for young people to distance themselves from a measure of reality they were perhaps running from, escaping, not helped by families, or by schools, or by culture, or by the measure of political attitudes. For the first time they can autonomously imagine for themselves what it could mean to have a world free of something, not yet free today or fully capable of taking the ethics of co-responsibility to the level of credibility of something great. These subjects do not hover or circle above education: these subjects are part of the themes, the sensibility and the restlessness, that must be inside schools that are confused like our Italian schools, and perhaps not only our Italian schools, if they are to be capable of listening to the serious things rolling down the road and not remain silent about the restlessness and questions children and students have inside them.

One of the most painful things I have experienced in recent years, in recent months, in recent days, has been the revolt of Italian university students. In most of our cities Italian students have occupied universities. I have experienced the phenomenon with great sorrow, faced with these young people's great immaturity, which is borne out in their words, their discourse, their slogans. I wonder where on earth they have been living before now, where this immaturity on several issues (not all issues) has come from. Certainly they are someone's children, they are children of our schools, children of our universities. Where is their sense of reality, of analysis, of criticism? Where is their sense of having registered events and phenomena?

Universities pursue their own pathways, their own disciplines, their own subjects, their own exams. There is a line, a sort of highway, where you have to travel the way God commands, and where each day students [face] enormous humiliation, perhaps no-one knows [how much], with the inefficiency of the service and simple questions that never get an answer from bureaucracy. Young people come from other cities, from far away, they count their pennies, counting them so they can eat. There is insensitivity. Society in our country today is a society of corporations, sects and castes, each with its own etiquette and salaries. Salaries to be increased or decreased.

Our culture has been cut into slices, the way you slice a watermelon. Every professor divulges their own learning, which, great as it may be, is simply inadequate if they do not take the trouble (university does not consider it) to go beyond their specifics and begin the difficult art of inter-disciplinary or trans-disciplinary work where subjects and knowledge, even distant fields of learning and subjects, begin to dialogue. The world can only be understood through these keys. Each one of us carries a very small key, perhaps the key to our car, or our house. But the keys to the world demand a multiplicity of keys, and therefore a multiplicity of forms of acquired and integrated learning, the capacity to find different answers to different questions and utilise different keys for different uses. Above all we will need to invent new keys in a very short space of time for keyholes we do not yet know about. This is one of the issues we could stop and think about.

I would like to quickly give a sort of strong image, an image of a political, geographical and economic nature. It is an image that takes us into the changing of the world. A world no longer made of islands, intervals, spaces, oceans and mountains [but] a world made of a network.

It is a powerful image. It not only leads us into a shrinking world (not only symbolically), it also describes a world different from the world of the past. Now we begin to see a world not made of coexisting islands, separate parts, distant unique languages, but a world held in a web. Migrations, changes of tradition, changes of language are all in this web. We must think of everything happening today, everything that will happen in the next few years, to understand it is a powerful image to keep. Powerful because we can transfer it to many other fields; the field of imagination, of scientific knowledge, of pedagogy, of culture.

A world of networks is a world that communicates even when it does not wish to, a world which has the same destiny even when it seeks out partial, different destinies; a world where beliefs, old fundamentalisms and new ones, will perhaps come round again, we do not know how or in what way, we do not know how history will resolve its knots. However it is important we know this network form of the world corresponds perfectly, I believe, with the network image of our brain and the functioning of our brain. It is a powerful image, an image of extraordinary correspondence. It contains great significance, the significance of distant and diverse images that are capable of coinciding, in terms not only of form but of life. The parts of the brain are distinct, separate and interconnected. If we read the pages of the great French researcher Changeux [see Chapter 5, n.16], we hear him speak of the brain as an arrangement of instruments capable of producing extraordinary symphonies depending on which areas of the brain are stimulated, stimulus from the outside and other impulses coming from the inside.

If a part of the brain falls ill other parts respond. They assist the weak part and, whatever else happens, work in a symbiosis of great solidarity. There is a network between the brain and evolution, between neurons, the world and the world of children. Again this is an extraordinary thing. The brain is effectively concerned about all of us, but certainly it is also the most delicate and sensitive organ, with a vocation of love for children. For the first two years [of life] synapses, cell connectors, are created based on children's life experience. Many connections fail, other connections emerge depending on the child's quality of life experience and leaving a margin for change. This inter-dependence between an organ like the brain and a person playing out their first experiences of life and taking a part, or a portion, of that organ with them, to me seems extraordinary.

However there is also an interactive network between the brain and intelligence, cognition, sentiment and emotions, which also consolidates unification on this level. Fields of learning, the disciplines, the sciences (social sciences, human, and any other sector of the sciences) today need an interconnectivity that has never been achieved on a cultural level. (Except in the 1940s when cybernetics was born, but this invention touched the sensibility of [only] a few and did not touch the sensibility of many.)

Learning and knowledge belong to a network. Even Gardner [see Chapter 4, n.34] who works on seven intelligences cannot escape the question of whether these intelligences are based on a co-operative capacity and he recognises that a co-operative basis exists. We believe less in seven (seven isn't necessarily a number we always like). We are more in favour of an extremely complex form of intelligence until someone can disprove us. Bearing in mind that as things stand today intelligence is commercialised, sold and taught in schools as a factor of production, depriving mankind and the meaning of intelligence of its sensibility, relations, interactions and inter-connections with all other human spheres. It is not possible to extract powdered intelligence in some chemical laboratory. Intelligence will be discussed over and over for a long time to come. It is something we do not know, however we know many things about it, and very often we pretend not to know them.

I think this strong image may be pertinent for schools, for the functioning of schools, for the organisation of schools, for school logistics, for education, pedagogy, didactics, learning, knowing, that can be in a network form, with the possibility of reciprocal contamination and of interactions, when a school lives in a network, and the network gathers the vital elements into a whole, making it possible for that place to have cultural renewal, which is also psychological and spiritual renewal. These things are not taught in university. They are things you only learn by working in the field.

Editor's note: The next sentence is not complete because of a break in the tape.

Again, this form of network also contains the death of all the theories of disconnectedness we have followed, and continue to follow. Opposing theories, Manichean interpretations. Zero tolerance, zero comprehension, clashes between discipline and discipline, between mind and nature. The death of these Manichean or disconnected positions can produce the co-existence of extraordinarily effective and productive images in human society, not merely on an educational level but also on the level of culture and professional development, a capacity for complementarities we have never known before, never previously been given to our work and thinking. It can open up to a much more human culture, more genuinely humanistic and scientific than ever before. There are probably people who will find themselves unemployed after the death of Manicheanism and disconnection. Many people will be unemployed in Italy. All the people specialised in disconnectedness, in fragmentation, in Manichean opposites will be unemployed. Aggressive when others do not concur with their theoretical supposition (a kind of nastiness that takes place at a high level, at university level, at the level of high learning). Some people will feel unemployed because they have no one to fight with any more. This is something I will not be crying over.

The children. There are some extraordinary things. I don't know whether we need several keys; but certainly even today if we put all the keys in our pockets together they cannot produce the right image of children. Historically speaking, going back over our own terrain, our [Reggio Emilia's] strength in resisting for so many years comes precisely from this fact that every other week, every other fortnight, every month, something unexpected, something that surprised us or made us marvel, something that disappointed us, something that humiliated us, would burst out in a child or in the children. But this was what gave us our sense of an unfinished world, a world unknown, a world we ought to know better. A world that is a living witness to the children.

To be capable of maintaining this gift of marvelling and wonder is a fundamental quality in a person working with children. Otherwise we just leave the task to scientists who are genuinely capable of jumping out of their seat when faced with a new invention. For our part, we have little familiarity with children's forms of thinking, their potentialities, their uncertainties and certainties. [. . .] Until now anyone who has come close to genuine knowledge of children, who has attempted to bring their knowledge as close to children's knowledge as possible, discovering qualities in children so rich, so strong, they had never been foreseen – every time this has happened everyone has drawn back.

The second issue is that, very often, these great discoveries of children's unsuspected qualities are immediately, or almost immediately, enclosed in a sort of box. Almost as if we were scared they might emerge in a way that would make us doubt our own level of learning, our own knowledge, our own capacity for governing the type of relations we have with children. This is a large phenomenon emerging strongly in families today, and equally strongly in all kinds of school for all ages. There is a kind of defence mechanism, growing together with a dam of blocked out facts and events and phenomena. Revealing our defences, our expectations, and things we do not expect. We find it difficult today in an uncertain situation, a situation which is not easy, to include them, bring them in. It is worth reflecting on this issue because recently I have become more convinced of a transition in the family whereby the children are not actually children. Families have children who are part of the family, and continue to be sons and daughters, but they can't manage to be *children* at the same time.

There is a very well-known linguist in our country [Simone Raffaele], and I like to quote him because his is an extreme case, and also an amazing case. He is an academic in psycho-linguistics. He had a little girl, and this little girl had grown up to be six years old. He was a great linguist and an excellent father. The immediately amazing thing is that a father so renowned on a scientific level, so renowned in the area of forms of language, including children's forms, so renowned in the area of possible connections between theory and practice, and so close to his own child, only realised when she was six years old that, for example, children can transgress with words, transgress with word formation.

One day the little girl said, 'Daddy I've invented a word. Would you like to hear it?'
'Of course, what word have you invented?'
'Maistock'.
'I beg your pardon?'
'Maistock'.[19]

It is hard for a father to have to lower himself a little and ask a little girl what a word means.

'What do you mean by that?'
'You must never drink Stock liqueur!'

The linguist father was struck dumb. He began to measure the distance between *Stock* and *mai*. He did his sums and opened his tool box. It doesn't fit. The word doesn't fit. Where has the little girl got *mai* from? Where did she find *mai*, and where did she find *Stock*? On the television perhaps, in the advertisement for this well-known liqueur. But how did she manage to put *mai* with *Stock* and *Stock* with *mai*? He did not know the answer. From that moment he paid more attention to the little girl. The amazing thing is that attention can come at five years old, six years old. In the home of a scientist who knows very well you have to be a scientist father even when a child is very young. Perhaps the fact of being a scientist makes them so confident they can't imagine children will wander from the score they have been given.

I am at the seaside, on the beach. It is a short holiday.

'Papà, how many days are left?'
'What do you mean how many days are left?'
'How many days is it to the end of the days?'
'What do you mean, how many days to the end of the days?'
'How long is it to the end of the time?'
'What time? The time we are spending at the seaside?'
'No, no, no. When will days finish forever, when will the days of days finish, and time will be finished?'

This is where the traumas are. Even a linguist or a scientist is permitted to make a rapid preliminary inquiry into the amount of worry, anxiety and uncertainty they ought to manifest or conceal in some way, here and elsewhere, faced with a '*maistock*' or '*days*' attitude. Children are full, and adults only have ears for the things they want to hear, not for things they have not decided about yet.

We have been working with shadow. I would like to tell you about two or three things that are extraordinary, which only those spending time with children manage to wrest from them, in completely anomalous, irregular ways. We played with shadows, we chose a game of shadows and played for a month, a month and a half, with children of three, four and five years because it seems to us the subject of shadows has absolutely no literary or scientific presence in family or school language. No family discusses shadows. Very few mothers speak about shadows to their children. So the children were absolutely virgin and we thought getting closer to shadows might return something interesting. Extraordinary things returned, interesting things. With work like this you see how many rules we have been subjected to for years, how many norms have been set down, how many stages predicted. You see how many gradients, like staircases, children have to overcome first. The children made a clean sweep of many conventions that are still standing on the level of science, or pseudo-science, of research, of descriptions of research and culture, on the level of pedagogy and education.

You remember how Piaget gets a girl to hide a watch. It is one of the classic examples. Is memory present? Is memory not present? Is perception present? Is perception not present? Memory is not present because the girl loses track of the watch and does not ask if the watch is hidden under the cushion. Well, we have Mariano who is a colleague of ours and goes around the schools, and he has been playing with very young children, two, two and a half years old, and with shadows. The children have enjoyed themselves immensely. The incredible thing is you have to stimulate children to realise they have a shadow by them, otherwise they would not see it. There are old people, and adults, who give very little importance to their shadow. Perhaps they look at them once in their lives and then abandon them. With the three-year-olds we thought we would catch them out, that they wouldn't be able to give us answers at their age.

'Shadows are made of sun'.
'Shadows walk with the sun'.
'What if it rains?' Trick question.
'They go inside us because they don't want to get wet'.

You can make comparisons, make bridges of relations, look for coherence and lack of coherence; however there is a full assortment here already to makes us reflect on children's possibilities. At a certain point the children go from exclamations of this kind, which are ephemeral, sudden and improvised, to more rigorous formulations, as if they wish to lay down a rule. So they try. These are the same children but with a few weeks or a month more experience; free experience, played experience, with adults assisting in a non-interventionist way.

One child says, and he thinks he is making a proposition of universal logic, 'Everything has a shadow except ants'. This is the title of the book we wrote [Sturloni and Vecchi, 2000]. But another child is a little surprised. For a moment he does nothing. Obviously he is thinking how to engage with a proposition that is not correct, something he does not consider correct that the first child has said. He thinks about it, he selects, and he is infinitely mature, infinitely wise, because he could attack in a hundred ways, he could enter into conflict a hundred ways. No, his form is so elegant and gentle, 'Even little stones make a shadow. Big ones make them better.'

If you think about it you can find the fabric of maturity here, a sense of the other, opening out, egoism scrapped, egocentrism cancelled. These hypotheses open up to other things, and other processes of interpretation if you follow the things through.

We took the children into a different situation. We took them to the public gardens in the evening, in the dark. There was some angst and anxiety on the parents' part, children out at night etc., and great joy on the children's part. They chased around, they played, they didn't remember the shadows. First they had time to play, talk among themselves, tell the day's stories. Then the theme of shadows reappeared, and reappeared very genuinely, in a very fertile way. The children had to deal not only with moonlight but with street lamps. It is hard for the children to understand street lamps exist, hard to understand there is another source of light, which is not only the sun on the one hand and moon and stars on the other. Finally somebody discovered the street lamps existed and immediately there was very passionate discussion. Because the lamps were playing very strange tricks. If two street lamps were close by, objects could be doubled up, there might be two shapes joined, and a bigger, darker black one in the centre. The children are faced with the disruption of their previous theories, the entrance of disparate theories, and they feel a sort of fear. They feel they are losing the safe ground acquired and treading instead on ground they do not know. Who will save the situation? There is always a child who saves the situation. A child who after doing his sums becomes a sort of Pythagoras and establishes for the other children in clear terms that: 'In the deep of the night you can see five shadows. Then early in the morning we have two, then during the day one, and in the afternoon one as well, then in the evening three, and when it is midnight five.'

We can laugh at the numbers, but we can't laugh at the capacity children have, through an almost impossible interpretation, of aggregating elements that will constitute the density of a meaning, propositions with the universal nature of a value. Extraordinary.

The final game was to invite the children who know lots about shadows, or who know little but lots more than before, to invent shadow riddles for their mothers and fathers – if they want. We don't know what happened in the families. This adventure is still ongoing, but I think there will have been some lively meetings and sittings:

'Can the shadow of a rubber be as long as a pencil's?'
'What happens when a little shadow goes inside a big one? Does it disappear? Or is it underneath?'

In this game the children turn into small Oedipuses, [. . .] enriching an experience played out with other children in new conditions. In this way they reassure us they possess talents not generally judged to belong to children. These children probably appear inconvenient in some ways, a bit of a nuisance, children that pose problems, pose whys, pose problems and enigmas; children who ask. In my time we used to ask a lot. Today's children are used to asking fewer questions, which means perhaps they have lost a capacity for conversation, for communication in the family that perhaps used to flow more. Adults today have a greater ability to turn aside conversation, to consume it or joke about it until it disappears. A sort of blanking out. We need to think about this more. These are facts that our linguist does not know what to call and calls 'vague facts'. He has written an opportune book about them (not a great book but worth reading) called *Maistock: Language explained by a young girl*. He began when his daughter was six. What happened before is something we cannot understand – why he did not instead have the eyes, hearing and attention for the germination, the beginnings that deserve to be greatly marvelled at.

These things are important because they teach us that children do things we don't expect, and vice-versa we do things they don't expect. This lack of understanding does not concern me if it leads to a capacity for journeying and transit, in the direction of enhanced awareness of what marvelling and wonder we have available to us from things that may happen. When lacking, it is one of the things that make children perceive men, women, adults and teachers as ridiculous. We must not think children are incapable of making judgements, they make exceptionally fine-tuned and precise judgements. Perhaps the children we are describing elude the current models and meanings that appear in the literature. Perhaps they are children who challenge the regularity and imperturbability of scientific learning; the kind that claims to cover every eventuality, every situation, every event, and which will not accept the unpredictable and chance as categories in their own right.

Unpredictability and chance are categories of a scientific nature, which absolutely ought not to be missing, despite being anathema to behaviourists today. Neither should they be missing in children's behaviour or attitudes. We should not reach the point of the recent new *scuola materna* programmes, which speak and write about play. [. . .] What is written is that adults and teachers (no longer educators) should organise things so that nothing improvised or left to chance happens. This means we must rein in the non-rules of play, the freedom of play, the fertility of play, the great capacity of all games for being played from different points of view. Without even giving children a chance to improvise. If this came true the human species would die out, because if the human species does not continue to play with the unforeseen, with chance, with probability and improbability, if it stopped improvising [. . .], then it would be a very poor, much poorer, species. I do not know if we would even continue to exist.

At this point I would like to take the discussion back to what children can be. Again a powerful image: there are rich children and poor children. We [in Reggio Emilia] say all children are rich, there are no poor children. All children whatever their culture, whatever their lives are rich, better equipped, more talented, stronger and more intelligent than we can suppose. On the other hand poor children exist. They are not poor in the class-based way identified up to now, but poor like Alice [in Wonderland]: poor in the sense they do not feel that measure of identity they need to survive. These are the poor children. The rich children are those requesting rich intelligence in others, rich curiosity in others, a very high and advanced capacity for fantasy, imagination, learning and culture in others. It is not possible for us to continue to tolerate in silence, with a universal complicity, that human intelligence and individual intelligence be wasted, consumed, come up against obstacles and go unused. It is not possible for us to constantly cover everything up in a collective unspoken agreement. Nor can we think of children as objects we can deprive, offload, declare poor, declare impoverished. Poor children get what adults want for them. They can be left outside the door, put inside the door, have any kind of schools, any kind of teachers.

Instead rich children must be richly acknowledged. However all children are rich, this is the issue. I know what you might say, but we start from a strong position, strong with reality and hope, and we have a lot of confirmation coming from different areas, coming from discoveries in the neurosciences and biology. For example biology is a subject that has no existence on a pedagogical level, it is absent, no-one knows about it. [Yet] our life is in there. How can we under-nourish it so?

If we start from the concept that all our children are rich children, and all need acknowledgement, all need great respect, much more than we concede today, we are crediting them with the capacity, the talents, the resources that must emerge because children possess these qualities. If we start from a small and needy poor image of the child, as happens in European countries, and happens elsewhere in even more dramatic desperate terms, then immediately a sort of hierarchy arises of a racist kind [. . .]. Travelling around Italy, travelling around Europe, travelling everywhere, you find these differences. Certainly, the differences exist.

[. . .]

If we were to go in this direction we would go towards a strong image and a strong pedagogy. Weak pedagogy for poor children is the pedagogy of nurses. [. . .] We are at a point in history where fake science really is being used in a culture of nursing that above all saves the poor and weak. However the children we generally see are not poor and weak. They are absolutely normal children, absolutely pre-disposed to joy and gaiety, pre-disposed to growing, to singing; and [yet] they are restricted. It is my impression that after all our achievements over the years, after all the events of history, all the scientific discoveries, the *tabula rasa* image of children still predominates. The anonymous child, the silent child, the child forced to be silent, the child who does not speak, the inaudible child, is a child who will go along with anything. Adults, the economy of adults, the economies and policies of governments, know exactly where to divert the money, the wealth [. . .].

The last issue is subjectivity, because to my mind among children's rights subjectivity is one of them. It is absolutely impossible to deal with a theme of this nature if we do not also open up cultural processes of subjectivity at the same time, processes which are completely absent on the level of the literature and of the culture, and which have traditionally been viewed as heretical because individual subjectivities lead to forms of individualism. Again, the problem is one of recovering a new conception of the theme of subjectivity, in new forms that go with our times. By culture of subjectivity we mean an absolutely contemporary culture of liberty, of democracy, of choices. Because without subjectivity there is no possibility of free choice, and this means depriving individuals and depriving children of a condition that instead is essential and vital for giving continuity to individual strength and hope, for attempting to do justice to potentials that until now have been barred precisely and obviously by virtue of a subjectivity impeded, subjectivity subjected, not encouraged in the fullness of its gift-giving.

A culture of subjectivity means, in this field, seriously thinking about children. It is a completely different culture from the culture of individuality. The culture of subjectivity is something very different. It penetrates deep into the child. It penetrates deeply and critically into concepts that appear still to regulate the rituals of behaviour. It means acknowledgement of the biological and cultural rights of the [human] species and its integral development. We connect it, immediately, to a right that is biological and cultural in nature; it means crediting the resources, the strong evolutionary dynamism we recognise as present in all children. Recognition for the right of competency. [. . .] The discovery of children's competencies is one of the greatest, most productive and most generative discoveries ever made, also in terms of subjectivity and rights. Recognising children make an active entry into life, because an active entry is what children make. Crediting children with interactive capacities, with relational reciprocity, with constructing intelligences, constructing hypotheses, constructing elements for testing these hypotheses; and with the things that issue from their hands and their minds, with adjustments certainly, and creations – some transgressing, with negotiating with things, with ideas, with others. We are saying things that truly belong to children. But without credit for these things, the meaning and value of subjectivity will find it difficult to survive for long with their necessary richness, with the right to live in these times, with children's times.

This is a large subject. There is no other creature in the world with such a long childhood as human beings. We have to think that Nature is not stupid, that nature is very wise, and if Nature has given children such a long period of growth, of life, it must mean it recognises children have many things to overcome, many obstacles, they have to learn, have to comprehend, have to compare, have to enrich: they have to learn and a very long apprenticeship and internship is needed.

The other part of nature's wisdom is what she gives to us, in the sense that for we who are adults, we who are parents, we who are teachers, she gives us an infinite childhood, an infinite distance to realise how complex children's growth and evolution is, for us to realise the mistakes we make, what the child is achieving, what they achieve with us and despite us. Nature gives adults and pedagogy a great length of time for evaluating, for weighing up, for analysing, for introspection; a truth and times that of necessity are indispensable for children. Instead, think of the death of time today, the closure, how time has been cut in schools and institutions, times dictated by others, by production, by women's work and the time women have, by men's work and the time men have.

This question of time is a very strong question; it is enough on its own to overturn and revolutionise the lack of respect for time in pedagogy and schools. The right to play, to be idle, the right to work, in short a right that is as broad as possible, that if a child wants to be a Chagall character flying over houses then let him; if a child wants to be Ptolemaic, well let him be Ptolemaic, he can stand in the centre and the others will run around him. This too is experience. If he wants to be Copernican then let him be Copernican and he will see the movements are different.[20] If he wants to withdraw with computer games, let him withdraw with computer games. This is the moment to let children interiorise different points of view, different points of life, different life choices, transpositions of life, transgressions, to break the dams of rationality and range far and wide with the terms of imagination.

If only we were able to credit our children, these children we have, much more than we have up to now. Our children lack a public declaration of identity. We hear talk of laws, but if you read the UN charter [United Nations Convention on the Rights of the Child] you realise the word that appears most is 'protect', we must protect children, as if it really were an inferno and we needed Moliere's fake doctors, capable of helping them and saving them.

Even though this is not an easy time on an economic level, [. . .] these are also times of several assaults on a cultural level. Not least because here on home ground we have theorists of Italian behaviourism and neo-behaviourism, reborn with a rigour, dryness and aridity that perhaps are revenge for the times we had no behaviourism and there were other theories, a sort of vendetta. The keys of Italian behaviourism today are extremely narrow-minded, extremely argumentative, full of completely gratuitous certainties. This operation of intelligence, which can only be made fruitful and only analysed with quantitative analysis.

I believe a National Council for Evaluation is being created. We have *scuole materne* with no identities, elementary schools that after thirty years have had a programme for ten and there is no sign of anything passing, secondary schools that no-one has touched for the last sixty years, and universities which are what they are. Discussing the addition of another inefficient public institution connected with functions that are inevitably ambiguous in content, means and purpose, in a situation of this kind with collapse and ruin being registered everywhere, sounds like avoidance, like blackmail in an unacceptable situation.

[. . .]

I wanted to say that aggressiveness is often shown to theories like those discussed this morning [. . .] and that being more aware in our reading, interpretation and analysis can help us have the right attitudes and behaviours.

We will cut short our history here. But I believe [our experience] has gained its identity through a crucible of debate, exchanges of points of view, and dialogue; it is a history with the obstinacy to continue to live, the strength to live, because I believe we can say a sort of fever, of internal revolt, is first and foremost good for health; and that it is also one of the infinite variations on happiness.

I would like to finish here.

1991

96.91 Speech by Loris Malaguzzi, Reggio Emilia, February 1991 (transcript from the original audio recording by the *Centro Documentazione e Ricerca Educativa*)

Editor's note: This speech may have been given to mark the publication of an edited volume – *Manuale di psicologia educativa. Prima infanzia* (Handbook of educational psychology: early childhood) – edited by Valeria Ugazio. The book, published in 1990, challenged some widespread views about very young children, arguing that they are capable of multiple relationships and are active agents in processes of social construction.

New ideas for early childhood

[. . .] Valeria Ugazio[21] is very interested in family therapy and how it is possible to go from family therapy to new ideas on children. This is an issue and interpretation we share with her. In her book (which is a collection of different contributions) I think she gives ample recognition to interaction as a central value, a unifying value, for those people accompanying children and accompanying children's growth not only on a human, inter-human and inter-personal level, but on the level of taking the professional role of adult and teacher.

We have already insisted on the value of interaction on other occasions and I do not know if we will touch on it today, though it seems we might. It is a central issue on which we can construct a series of values that are pedagogical in nature but also a series of values of a human nature; which is why this issue of interaction must be placed at the centre of all our reflections and, if we are capable, these reflections must be translated into acts and facts that lie in close continuity with the creature that accompanies us: a smaller creature who continues to be the subject and object of our attention. I say the small object of our attention, but I don't know if that corresponds to the way we denote the children we are following. Children are small but not in the sense of being weak, or of being without virtues: these are children with virtues, children with great strength, children with great energy, children with a great thirst and hunger, children with a great desire to grow, to grow in today's times, and grow – I believe – above all in the midst of children.

I do not know if we will have time, but if there is a time today when celebratory words are worth something, then they should be celebrating children with children. This discovery is not yet adequately supported by research; but on a human level it truly represents an important [value/insight],[22] rather than the image of children taken to an institution that substitutes for a mother who is perhaps absent or perhaps working. I think families today must above all be capable of appreciating what they have and expand their judgement to take in these institutions as they really are: the fact that children can live with other children, which to my mind, historically speaking, is one of the greatest resources and perhaps the one most ecologically capable of helping families; the one most substantially capable of helping us to bring up children.

[. . .]

[Valeria Ugazio's] book is titled *Manuale di psicologia educativa. Prima infanzia* and it underlines the area of early infancy [birth to 2 years] as a new subject of research, which is beginning to open up, a subject that was undervalued in the past and until relatively recently. Essentially in the last twenty years research in psychology has discovered the value of first and second childhood [birth to 2 years, and 3 to 5 years] and especially first childhood, from which we can derive an image that is not only of a philosophical nature but also human and cultural; and from this in turn there emerges another type, which is partly continuous and partly discontinuous with the child of early infancy, and this is the child of second infancy.

There are two terms Valeria Ugazio uses and I think it is worth mentioning them. The first term she uses is that of the 'precursor' child: children running ahead of their times, children who know how to keep up with their times, and children who are capable of adjusting to their times. Therefore these are children who are equipped with an amount of energy and who, certainly, ask adults for help, assistance and protection, but above all are constantly looking for ways out both from an excessive subjection to adults and from adults' scant consideration of them. 'Precursor' children construct themselves by constructing things around them: these are children who know how to find ways, forms and languages (non–verbal and verbal) that are capable of including them in the world with an activity, with a personality and with a style that belongs to each child, and makes each child completely unique.

The second term Ugazio uses is the child who belongs to a promiscuous world and this is the 'promiscuous' child. That is to say they are children today, in the society we find ourselves in today and they are children who long for promiscuity, which is to say for change: a change in the style, the possibilities, potentials and resources of having relations with different types of figures: with fathers and with mothers, but above all with boys and girls. It is clear at this point that we are beginning to see some fundamental aspects that are a firm part of a strongly rooted image of the child; of the kind we hope it is possible to welcome and accommodate. This means producing a series of diverging [points of view] that we will not dwell on, but essentially they are divergences with the psychoanalytic child: we are in a different world, we are distant (though we also have to reflect). We are also distant from Piaget's child: a solitary child who somehow self-regulates by himself, as if endowed with recurrent energies capable of self-producing, of actively self-reproducing on their own, of being gradually built up and gathered by the child.

We are distant from Bowlby's famous attachment, which in many respects has represented a sort of obligatory step on research journeys owing to the author's authority; and also because he supported a thesis it is not easy to argue with or dismiss in a few words, on the intimacy and the dyad between mother (actually an adult but mostly the mother) and child – and therefore on the issue of attachment. Clearly we have tried to slightly fray the edges of his theory of attachment in the few propositions we have discussed up to now, because we have said children substantially are looking for a progressive distance and progressive autonomy, and this important issue is something that concerns families – mothers and fathers – but it is also something that concerns teachers: therefore we are trying to accompany children into moving further away. We need to discuss how this distancing takes place and what kind of interior attachments (material and immaterial) accompany this unfolding of children progressively distancing themselves, above all from adult models.

We are very distant from Watson's *tabula rasa* and therefore from all behaviourism, and this includes the new faces of behaviourism [. . .]. We are also distant from information [processing] theories,[23] because we believe information in itself to be something that is extremely lacking, devoid of a much more complex and complicated contextualisation than any form of behaviourism is capable of achieving or manifesting with all its *conjunctive* capacities.

To go from an image of child to an image of context. At this point we need to develop our idea but we do not have the time. However I believe we will refer to it in a conference we will be holding specifically on the issue of context. If we think about it then certainly we know what context means: children who are tied to a context or grafted into a context and who must be identified, perceived and mediated through their contextualisation. But when we say context we immediately understand we are faced with an image we can feel has a complete form, and yet at the same time the image and the form is incomplete. We have to reflect very hard on what this means because it is easy to say 'context' just like that, in a very general way and [think we] understand what it is – *oh very well then, we will surround this child with something different, what shall we use?* If we think about it at a certain point we begin to realise the construction is always limited in some way, always artificial in some way. Although I think we also need to admit that our entire culture is artificial and an artifice in some way. However we will go back to this later.

To go across from child to context means we have to accept a complexification of the issues, accept entering a much more complex tunnel. On the other hand – and we all understand this very well because human experience counts for something – no tree we have ever seen has been removed from its context or made to leave it: so we no longer know which has the greater value, the surrounding context or the image we put in the centre.

There is a proposition we could take for ourselves because it completely covers the problem of attempting to give meaning and substance to this particular image of context. At a certain point Heidegger[24] recognises that a place is only defined [. . .] in relation to its district or region: the vast background that holds it and also acts as a ground. These terms he uses are extraordinarily evocative: 'hold' until it is impossible to extricate the tree from its 'ground'; but on the other hand we have backgrounds that break the tree down by including it until it has been completely swallowed and eaten up. We are attributing the tree with a subjectivity, but the tree can lose this subjectivity to its ground (partially or entirely). Children are the same and we are the same. There are contexts in which, however we place ourselves, we have the feeling we no longer know what kind of judgement is being expressed toward us: if we are being judged for what we are, or for what there is behind us; for what we say, or the story behind us; for the things we say, or the conceptual trees – the ideas etc. – situated outside or inside ourselves. I think this issue needs to be analysed, because the problem with context is understanding whether it can be fenced off with barbed wire, or if it is simply a convention which, by convention, we accept.

What if I leave a context? Can I leave a context? Let's say I can leave the context, but then do I take the context with me, or do I go over into another contextualisation on the level of philosophy, and on the level of . . . etc.? There are several problems generated at this point, which from the point of view of formal logic and philosophical thinking are extraordinary. But we will set these aside for the moment. However I believe an in-depth analysis of the logic of context, and of the logic of contextualisation, would also lead us, if that is what we want, into polemic of a philosophical, social and political nature. It would lead to us understanding certain phenomena that have taken place and continue to take place. Simplifying in the extreme, we could say that what is happening now is essentially a perversity of context. And at this point I will stop.

So let us abandon the self-sufficient child because this is another image we need to distance in some way. Children are not self-sufficient, and we do not credit them with self-sufficiency either on the physical level or, above all, on the level of growth – of the constructions, relations and relationships that will weave children's growth, in contexts where children act simultaneously as agents and recipients. This is the great duality and validation of the value children have: of being the agents of their own construction. This is how it must be declared and this is how we have to attempt it. We can only do what we can, but in my mind it is clear this fact is a value that absolutely cannot be overlooked.

The second fact is that children are self-producers, they self-sufficiently construct ideas and new things and the world. And here we take the meaning of self-sufficiency to be relative self-sufficiency because clearly children's co-existence – owing to how they are born, and owing to why they are born, and owing to when they are born, obviously this identity is an identity connected *with*: it is contextually connected. So clearly we must take all these connections into account: all the direct and indirect layers, all the stimuli, all the reasons that make a child a subject situated in a context of which they are partly the author, partly the co-author, and partly someone requesting – requesting help and protection, but which has to be understood in very relative terms and not what I would call traditional terms. This child does not have, as Piaget said, a capacity for complete self-regulation (and this is taking us into a second phase of ideas that lead to contextualisation). So children's self-regulating capacity is a very strong concept that we must never lose sight of; but at the same time we must also have a sense of its limits and a sense of its fullness, which can only come to children through dynamics that are much more complex and capable.

Children are interactive and constructivist: these, I would say, are the fundamental things. They are interactive because they have an active capacity for doing, for doing *with*, for doing with; and at the same time they are constructivist children in that we credit them with self-regulatory capacities, in a limited way outside context, as I said before. When we see them in a context (and this is how it is, it cannot be otherwise), then obviously the dimensions of the proposed dynamics modify these self-sufficient children, who are somehow capable of turning into giants, and becoming progressively more giant until they acquire their ultimate form of becoming, which is the adult form, the form of an individual etc.

At this point I don't know what to do, because I have tried to simplify this image to the utmost. If this were the kind of image that came to me from biology I would be more convinced that individuals, and children as individuals, are born with laws of continuity for re-making and re-constructing the species, with virtual potentials already part of the image of the child even before it appears physically in the world: in the uterus, in the mother's womb. And this raises important problems and important issues on the theme of when individual life begins, on the issue of motherhood, the issue of birth, and of children's rights, of abortion and so on. You do understand. We all have to put these problems somewhere. But it is clear to me personally, and I think of myself as secular (at least I have always tried to be), that when I embrace this image of the child conceptually, I do not know if I should anchor it very deeply and strongly, because deep deep down what I find is a series of images and generative forms, and there are probably also certain values it is hard for me to get away from. And in some way we cross the boundary into a different place.

There then. So where can we find a biological image that can help us understand to what extent biology proposes destinies? Since I am distant from all possible forms of determinism, clearly the issue for me – and for you – is an issue that deeply touches our intelligence and our sensibility.

Some very recent research allows us to introduce several very amazing and highly significant elements into our research reflections. This research was done with advanced technology and therefore with means we do not have and do not know. Essentially it is connected with the interaction inscribed in the very early life processes between mother and child. I am not re-proposing the Bowlby dyad, I am proposing an aspect [of the interaction] that is extremely significant for me: does interaction have a biological foundation or not?

The focus was on breastfeeding and the problem was the issue of children's phases of sucking and pausing during their breastfeeding. Let me remind you there are two phases, an active phase of sucking, and a phase of rest, of pause, that only the human species has. The first thing that seems extraordinary is this alternation. I am speaking of alternation because it is another of the terms we need to reflect on at length. This alternation has its own *process* of regularity and stability for the whole of one of children's first life journeys. Each four to ten sucks the child stops, has a pause, waits, then returns to the mother, sucks for another six to ten times, and then pauses again. Think carefully and read this alternation as something that can lead us to another place that is much further away, and where we can note the processes, the several processes, we see in our daily family life and school life, where alternation exists absolutely as a pre-requisite of life. If we weren't capable of achieving a capacity for alternation we would be destined to exhaustion, probably to the point of dying.

Alternation then. Let us be careful about what this alternation means. Let us ask ourselves why these phases of activity and pause exist. Are the reasons physiological in nature? No. No because the child does not need to pause to breathe, because children can swallow and breathe simultaneously, they have absolutely no need to take a pause. And yet, and yet, children pause. It is not a question of being out of breath at a certain point. No, there is nothing the child lacks, not even breath. One could think a certain amount of tiredness might be an influence. But there is no tiredness in a child who is feeding. And if we are still uncertain then the research records tell us that if this tiredness hypothesis were valid then the length of the active and passive phases, of the pauses, would probably be irregular. Instead they have their own regularity. This is the extraordinary thing. So the alternation absolutely cannot be attributed to the child's tiredness.

Perhaps it happens to let the mother recover her energy.

Editor's note: The next sentence is lost in the changeover of tapes.

Therefore we must use words that we have used already in other fields. I would say the active phase and the pause phase, the rest phase that is not rest but a pause, which is really a pause that is not a pause, because this pause provokes what I would call various responses, and that is the extraordinary thing. So what happens? What happens if you watch what mothers do (even first-time mothers breastfeeding their child for the first time) is that you realise something rather significant. When the child sucks there is a sort of silence between the two, and as soon as the child stops sucking and enters a passive phase the mother immediately begins to speak, almost as if the pause allows the mother to make an intervention (she chats, makes statements, pushes, encourages, compliments the child etc.). Then there is a point when the child goes back to feeding and there is a sort of silent collusion, a sort of silent complicity, almost as if they need to find some moments in their journey when they are running and some moments when they are not, pausing in a journey capable of producing an alternation, a dynamic.

So it is an amazing elaboration, and precisely because it is produced at the beginning [of life] there is a reliance on something that is in some way biological and physiological in nature. What I want to say is that all these things are extraordinarily important as we discuss interaction today and as we discuss alternation. No one would be able to speak. I would not be able to speak at this moment if we had not been educated to alternation. On a level of language acquisition alternation is a great achievement, which is terribly hard and difficult for children; and yet it is also enjoyable for children.

To have no alternation means to overlap, it means there is chaos, it means talking ten at a time, it means not understanding that language is something that you start off in order for the other to understand, and that above all you have to understand if the other has understood exactly what you meant to say: so there is an extremely complex, and extremely complicated *recursiveness* to it. But it is also extremely gratifying when you discover the taste for dialogue, the taste for words, the taste for the communication coming and going and re-connecting up to re-construct ground, to build places of encounter and of dialogue, of words, of ideas. It is an extraordinary thing. And this behaviour is also of great value on a social level, on the level of socialising.

I do not think we would be able to live without alternation. And without alternation children would not be able to play. There is a type of alternation that is part of the learning process in children, and certainly this is a process of adaptation, of adaptation through interaction. The last thing I will say on this episode [of the breastfeeding], and which to my mind is fundamental, is that there is no explicit intentionality, because the entire operation takes place without intentionality. Intentionality is something those with experience of intentionality have. But a mother aged 18, or 16, or 15 years old, with a child for the first time, does not have intentionality: she has pathways, she has intuition, she probably has something that derives from the culture, from the biological culture, or the culture of biology I mean. So it is an extraordinary thing.

If this is how things are, if this is how it is, then I think it is difficult for those who wish to attack us, or attack a position like ours [with our image of children]. And clearly they would have to attack in a way that would be very dangerous for them rather than us. However if all these [things we have seen] are true, it is also true that we must stake our work, and our professionalism, and our culture, on this card. It seems to me that this is our field of application.

An aspect I would like to return to is artificiality and artifice. As long as we agree on what it is. We all understand very well that the word 'artifice' contains various meanings, however let us all also agree on the fact that substantially all our life is artifice: an artifice with laws, rules and anarchies, with things that blow out and then re-light. But I think we can agree, after understanding together what we mean by artifice, that in some ways life is typically a great artifice.

The value of objects, be very careful, the value of objects. [. . .] Perhaps it was Piaget who discovered the function of objects and I think it was a great discovery in the process and flow of progress at the research level. But objects for Piaget are in some way inert and all the properties and qualities are given over to children, to the child's capacity for coordinating and the coordination of an action they are carrying out on an object, or the coordination of actions between one child and another, and another; or between the child and an object or objects; or situations that are caused in some way by objects.

For the first time we are now discovering that objects are part of a thinking society. [. . .] They belong to a thinking society not only as a production, as if the aspect of production were to die the moment the product is produced: inside each object there is a frighteningly rich human history. This thing I am holding in my hand [a microphone] is not a find from an Etruscan tomb or an Egyptian tomb, it is an object with its own history, which is not a dead history but a living history, and it is living to the point that it conditions me to speak at a certain distance from it and achieve certain effects. For the first time we are inscribing the value of the object in itself, with a series of meanings and significances that are more significant and meaningful [. . .]; and I believe much of the philosophy behind the *designers* of our times is connected with this injection of animistic history into objects, which are no longer something detached from us but prostheses of ourselves. I mean the chairs you are seated on, this book-rest, the environment, our clothes, the pens and biros you are writing with are probably objects that are strengthened when we include them in a conception that gives them value; they can acquire a role of great importance on an educational level, and on the level of the relations we have with objects as adults.

Many people have relations with objects that are almost fetishist: the purchases we make, the selections we make, the things that come into our homes, the things that match with our taste or are far removed from it; things we no longer accept as merely functional (which was a permanent aspect of rationalist architecture and philosophy) but have something they call *soft* [sic] qualities. Objects are something that we have to read the way we read a book, and if we could read objects the way we read history, read events and read culture, then we would probably have a very different kind of relationship with objects, and a different relationship with the great object of Nature, coming together with which signifies a great act of constructive re-connection. And all this might make some people think we are going too far beyond the confines of pedagogy; instead it is pedagogy that has always done without these things. [. . .] Pedagogy and psychology have always gone without these things: but we cannot assign psychology with the task of being inert. Part of the reason is that psychology continues to feed on itself obsessively, like the institution of school feeds on itself, and the way the cultural tools we have today constantly chase their own tails, and are never capable of connecting *with*.

And all the authors you find in these books all lament one thing, all of them: they all sense (as our American friends sense) that you cannot only work on the form of things. That is not possible. It is not possible only to work on images. That is not possible. The problem is how to reconnect the images with the substrata, and the connections and the relations and the interactions, in a contextualisation that expands out in concentric circles, and which would certainly lead us back to a sense of the world's complexity, and to a capacity for reading the world intelligently.

[. . .]

So then if we think objects are prostheses (which means they live with us, co-exist with us), then think what this means for an architect starting from the premise that objects are simply objects that need to satisfy a function; or instead the architect – the *designer*, the man, the men, the women – who chooses an object because of a sort of bond that goes beyond the bare bones of function: and this is an extraordinary thing. Then let us bring all this into our relations with children, let us bring it back to our relations with children and objects. Let us bring it into the topic of the materials we adopt: we adopt them in a careless way, in an absolutely unconscious or degraded way, I don't know which. What I do know is that using materials for their own sake, and buildings for their own sake, smells a great deal of un-inhabitability. By 'inhabitability' I mean the satisfaction, the sense of relish, the sense of gratification, the sense of pleasure you feel in a situation that is contextual, but doesn't only correspond to a physical need for protection, but instead is also something you like. Try and think what all this means.

I am saying all this because in reality children are mediated through objects, through their relations with objects, through the functions objects have and the value objects have for mediating inter-personal communication, self-perception, enjoyment of self when we are in individual solitude; [the value they have] for mediating ideas of production and construction that are part of the real world, and freer more fantastical processes and ideas that are part of playfulness and games etc. So if we think all this is a problem then probably we are dealing with a problem we have underestimated. Therefore we have to agree on this and start making it the object of our reflections.

Substantially children (and this is the artifice) are mediated through microcosms, and these are historical microcosms with a historical date and historically true. They are mediated through microcosms that contain forms and materials, but they also contain principles and laws and rules: they contain empathies and revulsions. It would be difficult to say that all this is not part of an artifice: it is a man-made artifice but it is still an artifice. So children are mediated through microcosms. They might [have been part] of a Spartan microcosm. Think what it means to say a Spartan microcosm, or an Athenian microcosm, or a Babylonian microcosm: and inside these microcosms I think we will find a series of images, and perhaps we will find others in our thoughts and our reflections. What I mean is, the concept of the self-sufficient child – if it still exists, the autarchic child constructing and self-constructing alone, must be distanced and brought back to contextualisation, so that the process of acquisition of ideas can run along in constant flows.

So now we come to the problem of stages. Let us take them and throw them out of the window. Perhaps we do not have time to speak ill of stages today, but there are several aspects here to convince us that breaking flow into stages means submitting to the rules of the municipal police. But we will not be subjected. We [want to] create the kind of encounter that is continuous in a way, and yet also highly discontinuous, and discontinuing of its own accord.

And perhaps this is not only a hymn to freedom and the greater space we could work in. In this image [of the child] there is always simultaneously an image of the adult, because everything I have said to now is only apparently directed towards just children: adults and children are always completely joined in an idea of identification, of complicity, of children with adults (and if possible, adults of our times with children).

So I wish to say the great impact children have on the world is in their approach, which is of an interactive nature, contextual nature, social nature, so that discussing the socio-genesis of mental processes takes on a meaning we can accept more safely. It is an issue that Vygotsky raised in very clear terms and today we can say that Vygotsky's contribution was extremely important and is still important today. It would be difficult to cook up a dish we like without also having recourse to Vygotsky in some way. However I would say there is an excessive attachment to reality in Vygotsky, and a probable loss of a series of elements that refuse to be included and regimented in an excessively realistic form.

If children are agents and recipients, then we believe adults must be agents and recipients too. So look how much protagonism we are beginning to find.

And all this is also thanks to journeys of research that have tools for observation we did not have in the past. If we think of everything that comes with cameras: in terms of micro-analysis, the capacity to go back and forth, of pausing and deconstructing photographs, deconstructing images. I can take a thousand images in a fraction of a minute so we have ways of getting closer, which are much more productive and capable of giving us signs and information. And our interest must therefore be an interest that is much more focused on the processes than on the results, because process becomes the pillar holding things up. Process as the pillar: well we could transfer that onto a political level or onto the level of policy.

But what I want to say is that process allows us to listen to children and simultaneously listen to ourselves. Bear in mind that when you are not listening to the children then essentially you are not listening to yourselves. And then afterwards it becomes difficult to discover the sense and the meaning. So this is the great new thing and certainly it is surrounded by large obstacles (obstacles of a physical, legislative and cultural nature), but this is the important issue and all the new themes that are part of contemporary research stem from here: co-operative learning in children, conflict in children, socio-cognitive conflict. Everything that happens in children is a process of constant negotiation where children lose and re-discover their identities. And on the process of forming the Self we could examine several important issues. Does the Self hang on one coat-hook or on several coat-hooks? Do all these coat-hooks grow simultaneously at a certain contingent age in an individual's life? Does the Self also continue to construct and deconstruct in the course of time and over the course of the years? These are issues where, again, no one can use the language of certainty, but they are surely issues we must not lose among ourselves.

So the image of the child must be turned around completely, but what does this turnaround consist in? [. . .] The problem is how to take the child from an image of self-constructor with no interaction, to an image instead that is hetero-auto-constructive. The issue of asymmetry between adult and child has let us create a great deal of confusion on the nature and processes of knowledge learning, and we are still paying for this today. So clearly, what can school legislation offer but a simplified version of its entire project of content and form, and the nature of its organisation and regulations, and not what an educational process means, what it means to respect the times and rhythms, the pauses and alternations of an educational process.

This process [schools are using] produces constant discriminations, and attempts to contain any possibility of differentiation beyond a certain threshold. But the problem with knowingly and consciously pursuing categorisation, which inevitably leads to stages (because when I say categories I am speaking of stages), is that stages are a sort of finishing post. Some people arrive: but those who don't are not included in the category, they belong to a category I invent – I am inventing it. And then another category comes after it. What I mean is that if we validate the principle of judgement exclusively in terms of quantity this can only produce a classifying, categorising attitude – in all the judgements, subjects and objects that have to do with me.

So the great problem is to go from the vision of a child who has to be created, to the vision of children constructing themselves with others, and who therefore combine – in terms I am not able to express very well (I don't think anyone is able to express very well), in terms that are still confused, but which are terms of alternation, conjoining, interweaving, distancing and mixing, between times of activity and times of pause. That is: times when children self-construct through reflection of a subjective nature and therefore, in that moment, through their own autarchic productivity; but who absolutely cannot loosen their ties of a biological, cultural nature that are the social aspect of their venture. This cognitive venture, like the venture of growth and the venture of constructing oneself, the venture of growing, is a venture that has a social nature not an individual nature. It is a venture of a social character: with everything a proposition of this kind brings with it. Perhaps now we can better understand the meaning of the precursory world of children, which we discussed earlier. Children are forerunners, who are capable of being *forerunners* of themselves, and at the same time they know how to interweave and conjoin, depending on events, depending on chance and the uncertain, and depending on necessity. And all these interweavings and close conjunctions with situations can partly be predicted, but we cannot predict them entirely, and instead they constitute one of children's fundamental features.

[. . .]

And in my opinion all this is something important, which should be taken up by everybody, though perhaps in very different ways, because different actors contribute different topics. My judgement is suspended because these themes are being sold as new but in reality they are not new, or very new. They are part of cultural currents that have not found ways to flow into their cultures in more widespread ways: into academic culture, into 'learned' culture in inverted commas, and less 'learned' culture in inverted commas.

It remains to be understood what other issues can influence and converse with this interactive relationship we could have with children and among ourselves. What is the strength and importance of prejudice? What is a prejudice? What is a social representation? What is a psychological attribution? Are they stumbling blocks, obstacles, mistakes and living fossils that accompany us? Or are they under- or over-evaluations of objects, pieces, words, conversations and images we carry in our minds?

[. . .]

You will never get children to be interested in a tree or a leaf. A child has to understand that a leaf is a living context, a contextualisation of life, in itself. A leaf, a bud is a contextualisation. If it is living this is simply because life is a context, a ramification, a continuous interaction. The tree has its interaction with the earth, with the air, with the sun, with the moon, with the dark, with carbon dioxide, with oxygen. If children can perceive the contextual form, the interwoven ecological form, then they will be able to give life to objects and more meaning to things they feel are alive but don't perceive as a part of living nature. We have seen that when we want to get children closer to leaves we have only managed to do so when the children perceive the leaf to be a living thing, a living organism: an organism that breathes, dies, lives, is young, ages, is an infant, and is then consumed – consumed by the earth I mean – and that comes back to us in some way.

What I mean is: there is the story of the leaf, and then there is our story, you understand? And until you get the children closer . . . there is nothing [. . .].

[. . .]

❋ ❋ ❋

97.91 Text of an interview by Canale 5 TV channel, *Scuola dell'Infanzia* **Diana, Reggio Emilia, December 1991**

> **Editor's note:** This short interview at Diana school, presumably forming part of a news item by an Italian TV channel, followed an article in the American magazine *Newsweek*, titled 'The 10 best schools in the world', in which an international jury identified the municipal *Scuola dell'infanzia* Diana, representing all of Reggio Emilia's municipal *nidi* and *scuole dell'infanzia*, as the most advanced in the world for early years education.

The project in our schools is one that aspires to giving the greatest value possible to the child, which means crediting children with resources, with talents and with potentials that are much richer than we think; and letting children represent themselves with the richness of their intelligence, of their languages, of their openness to things, in a way that above all is conducive to their capacity for self-direction, self-learning and self-organisation.

This absolutely does not mean excluding the role of the adult, who is capable of seeing, listening and understanding: of much listening, of introducing themselves into a state of permanent interaction with children; offering them learning situations of great diversity, in the sense of being able to give them time – and time is an extraordinarily important entity in a situation where everyone is robbing children of time. Instead we are for respecting time as much as possible. Children have their own times, which are subjective and objective, but they are extraordinarily important times, and if you respect them then the children repay you with creations and learning that leave you amazed.

Perhaps the attitude that is necessary is an attitude that remains open to wonder and to marvelling. If you are equipped with this – you as an adult – then children will respond to you with a great openness to wonder and to marvelling. Children are not looking for dull continuity, they are looking, avidly, for what changes, what transforms, and what becomes other than itself.

1992

98.92 Speech at the launch of a book *Infanzia e scuola a Reggio Emilia: Le iniziative del CLN e dell'UDI per la scuola materna* **[Childhood and school in Reggio Emilia: The initiative of the CLN and the UDI for the scuola materna], Reggio Emilia, February 1992**

Editor's note: Malaguzzi is speaking at an event to mark the publication of a book, edited by Lino Rossi and published by the UDI, about the creation of self-managed schools for young children in Reggio Emilia and the role of the women's movement in this process; the book covers the period from 1945 to the end of the 1950s. The book launch took place shortly after the American magazine *Newsweek* named the Diana school as the most advanced in the world for early childhood education, an event that Malaguzzi starts by referring to.

[. . .]

This capacity of an Italian pedagogy to be exported is a great event. So great that it has received many congratulations, phone calls, letters and telegrams from places everywhere, from friends in Italy and friends abroad; so it can be no coincidence we have received nothing, not even a short telegram, from the Minister of Public Instruction [Italian Education Minister], who I think we represent worthily enough and with enough distinction for him to be moved enough to make his presence felt. I want to say we have received no recognition from the shadow Minister of Public Instruction either [opposition Minister for Education], which means these two Ministers (one in the shadow and one in the light) really have more in common than just the strange coincidence [of their roles]. And perhaps these are things we need to understand and reflect on.

How can our story begin? I won't say when it began because it is too many years and too long ago, but perhaps understanding the beginnings means understanding many of the things that happened later. Many things and many facts came together: the ingenuity of the people (their astuteness even) and the hard times, the extraordinarily hard times, managed to make something come of the long underground status of the self-managed schools. At that time being a self-managed school meant sacrifice and caring of a kind it would be difficult to renew and make credible today. Anyway these self-managed '*scuolette*' [little schools] resisted for twenty years on the absurd foundations of sacrifice and precariousness, with their existence never guaranteed, very low pay, the meals only confirmed from day-to-day, and going ahead for certain when food arrived at 10 or 11 am. We only knew if we could pay the teachers their very low wages on around the 26th, 27th, 28th, 29th [of the month]. You never knew what might happen: but in some extraordinary way these schools had this form of precursory social management.

Families owned the management. I remember the parents, and above all I remember these '*scuolette*' that came before us [the municipal schools]. I remember the school born in 1945 on the decision of the women, a women's choice, with no invitation, no encouragement, and no [ministerial] circular. The school was born spontaneously, and this remains an unusual event even in the history of our city; because still today behind this there are clear meanings that we have perhaps lost in a way. You have to think these women decided to sell things, objects left by fleeing Germans, and they decided to do it immediately. And they decided immediately because they had the wisdom, yes, the wisdom to foresee that if they left it a little bit later then very probably the delay would become much longer. They had to decide before someone else or something else arrived. The decision was of a spontaneous character: a decision that had to have immediate effect. And this is where we see the birth of an idea that was so anticipatory, of building a school there in the little square of this small village.

It was a school made of bricks. They worked all day Saturday: the women worked, the men worked, youngsters worked, children worked. They went to the river and collected sand, and they went to collect old stones from houses ruined by bombing. The women wanted a school that was theirs and that belonged to them. They wanted the school because they were convinced (there was much naivety, but much excitement and much passion too), they wanted it because in their minds owning the premises was directly equivalent to owning the school, and owning the school might mean owning their children's lives and their children's destinies. So much so that I remember, at an advanced stage of the project, they discussed whether to build a small apartment for the teacher (two very small rooms) as if they were afraid she might run away from one day to the next, and with this little apartment they could offer a sort of extra guarantee that she wouldn't run away, but instead would make this great statement of theirs, this enormous statement, possible to realise immediately.

I don't think they had many ideas in their minds about female emancipation or all the things, thoughts and ideas that came after and matured later. They were 'catapulted' in the direction of the child. The child was the great historical object, the great cultural object: children, poor children, the children of farm labourers, the children of poor women, children with a great centuries-long poverty behind them. No-one steeped in that destiny could escape it. The chance of a school would let children climb the ladder, perhaps just enough to lead them to some form of delivery, some release from the destiny their parents did not want perpetuated. And to my mind this was the great gesture, the greatness of the women's gesture in Villa Cella, the greatness of these mother-women; and I think this aspect needs to be underlined because later it became an issue for women who were not necessarily mothers, and not necessarily out working.

So probably it was a form of maternal instinct integrated with other aspirations. They managed to build what they built, and that was the start of eight other 'little schools' of ours scattered around the outskirts [of Reggio Emilia] in the poorest neighbourhoods. And what these schools had to do was gradually establish a presence (ahead of everything that happened shortly after), a presence at the time children needed it most.

When we speak of children we cannot speak as if we were discussing today's children. Children then were extraordinarily poor, extraordinarily thin, and extraordinarily undernourished, from years of war. The signs of rickets were obvious for all to see. The children were dialect speakers, they only spoke dialect and couldn't understand a word of Italian. Their mothers' proposal, their hope, was to entrust them to these miraculous people, people who had been miraculously saved: these were the first teachers. It was as if they, by knowing everything, could guarantee the mothers' aspiration that their children would leave their destiny behind and put themselves in a higher place.

I remember these were times when everything seemed possible (perhaps I have said this before), times when it seemed everything was possible. At that time, after the war, after the grief, and after the ruins, there was a very strange phenomenon, impetuous and strong, it made possible a great longing, great fervour and great excitement. It was the ridiculous capacity of being able to think anything, and to think that anything could be physically realised.

I remember at that time, the same time, the factory workers and land workers in Fabbrico put up their cinema, their theatre. The same thing happened in Cavriago, and the same thing happened in Scandiano.[25] It was a time when any idea could be taken and realised with ingenuity and intelligence. It was a time of a flowering of ideas, a flowering of practical capacity and not only speculative capacity. It was all symptomatic of a culture that was appearing for the first time in history, advancing timidly, and advancing with passion, advancing very reticently, and very naively with many illusions. In essence it was the advance of an estranged citizenship, which was asking to knock at the door – it was knocking on the door and opening the door – and to be able to enter the tangle of problems that were part of the country's reconstruction, part of the terrible unemployment, and with hunger on the increase (hunger that had been accumulating for years). This great need was – I think – a need for great solidarity, and the solidarity was infinite, a solidarity unknown today.

I remember Vallini.[26] That was a time when the *mondine* [women rice workers] spent the summers in the Piemonte rice fields. I don't know if you remember the De Santis film?[27] I think the film romanticised Piemonte and the rice fields, the mosquitoes, spending the entire day bent double in the mud, in the water, planting out rice plants. I remember the idea Vallini had, this woman from the country, I think she was from Novellara [a small *comune* near Reggio Emilia], and she had the idea of opening an *asilo nido*. I'm speaking of the 1950s, and she opened an *asilo* for the children of *mondine* women so that they could leave home with greater peace of mind, feeling safer. You could take your pick of these gestures of great significance and great solidarity.

I remember the time was so magic that after I had made sure the women in Cella were completely serious, I remember a month later near my home there was a villa abandoned by a member of the fascist hierarchy and we assumed that as a fascist boss he would be away for at least a year, [perhaps] two or three years, I mean long enough for us to get inside the villa perhaps. And it was all possible, it was possible to get inside: duplicate the keys, open the doors: it was possible. The lack of public order at the time was great, very great. And in there, in the villa, I remember Professor [Sergio] Masini and I we made an enormous banner: 'Scuola del popolo' [The people's school]. Names like that make us smile now, but it was a people's school. And we opened it: for three seasons we opened an after-school centre for middle school children suffering difficulties with Latin, Italian and maths etc. What I am trying to say is this: it was possible, it was possible to do anything.

I think it is also worth remembering the Convitto Scuola Rinascita [Rebirth college] set up in Reggio Emilia in 1946 for war veterans and partisans. This was another extraordinary invention. An invention created in the attempt to compensate the youth and men all over Italy who had absolutely not had time to fully acquire professional skills because they had spent several years fighting: so they were people without a profession, without anything. Italy was there waiting to be reconstructed, and competent profiles needed to be created, capable of getting deep into the reconstruction. It was the only way to find work for them and highly qualified work. The diplomas at the college – I want to remind you of the diplomas because again they were the result of very precise choices – the choice was to create site managers: three years of study and the men became site managers. Site manager meant getting them in as part of the work of building reconstruction in our country. In another course, again there were three years [of study] and the men came out as agrarian technicians. Agriculture was all to do with land at that time. Anyway these adventures tell you how generative those years were, and how capable they were of evolving things which are absolutely impossible in normal times.

And I think when we remember all this we remember it together with the great contribution and great support women gave, organised and otherwise. In all these things we have discussed, and in many more it would be worth discussing, I think the strong drive and impetus belonged historically to the women's movement. Women were strong at that time, they were organised, not only were they capable of producing theory, they were capable of getting out and entering politics, capable of closely following people's needs, and capable of finding the right responses.

Today when I am speaking of women I do not only want to speak of women in the UDI, which was certainly the strongest and most powerful organisation; I would also like to talk about the CIF [Centro Italiano Femminile], which was a Catholic organisation (a weaker organisation). And certainly these were different entities with different inspirations, but what I want to say is that very often we found ourselves working side by side in extraordinary ways, and in times when everything was dealt with confrontationally, in radical ferocious terms. And yet you would find women in the UDI, women in the CIF, and women working with the parishes, all side by side on children's affairs. Perhaps what I wanted to say is that this fills in the picture of a landscape that might otherwise be left a little empty.

Then there was the great second period: the time when organised women began enriching their theory on issues of female emancipation. I think this was a very difficult passage but it was already part of women's consciousness; and although perhaps it couldn't be spread enough everywhere, the germs of consciousness were already present in the women in Reggio Emilia who were leading women's movements and city organisations. I think they already understood perfectly (with intuition that seems easy but wasn't easy then) that enriching the theory, with all the illusions and limits that came to be understood later, made it possible to extend the possibilities of women's journey through history in a difficult society, or in various difficult societies (because there were constant clashes between them). The movement helped us a great deal; the movement and its direction, which in some ways anticipated (by a short time) the great movement that was one of our largest phenomena, and is perhaps still too little reflected on, and which saw people in the south moving north, young farmers abandoning the country and coming into cities, and above all women leaving the family to start facing the problem of work outside the home.

This large movement had great political and cultural depth. It was the first time women had left the family nucleus and left the home to transfer their commitment, intelligences and hard work outside. Certainly it was a need, and an economic need, but the necessity cloaked an area of rights with a very fine veil: rights that women were acquiring very slowly and which went way beyond the world of work. It was not possible to access the world of work without services behind them. This was not possible – but the services were not there. There was a network of parish schools [for young children] (with all their limits but with all their merits too); there were the little self-managed schools living in great poverty, and living the issues of pedagogy and education in great poverty (the problems were enormous). At the same time there was this need, to move forward on the subject of guaranteeing services available to families.

A large phenomenon arose at this point (and we will need to return to this with 1976, when other large events took place nationally). What happened? What happened was that private schools, the schools that were a monopoly of the Church (by tradition at that time) were debated in Parliament for eight years. Almost as if the State did not have the right to run its own state pre-schools (this parliamentary battle was eight years long, like the War of the Roses, or the war to conquer Troy). It was a massive confrontation. Finally in 1968, [Law] 444 was passed and the possibility began to take shape of enriching the old network.

We and our first *scuola comunale* were born in 1963. Repeatedly over the years (because we had begun ten years earlier) the *Comune* had deliberated about directly running *scuola dell'infanzia*, but explicit forces and implicit forces (the Prefecture and others) brought their absolutely and ferociously rigid *verboten* [sic] [veto] to the council meetings.

In the end, where politics (that kind of politics) cannot go, more astute politics arrives, of mandarin directors with enough astuteness and enough wisdom to fool the Prefect and council minorities (but benevolently, lovingly) and manage to get schools [for young children] agreed on through a series of strategies: they had to be on wheels, they had be mobile, and transferrable from one place to another, because the law laid down that state schools could only be created where a network of private parish *scuole materne* did not exist. Therefore they were second class schools, category B schools, subsidiary schools. The great problem was how to start this experience of secular schools, which were beginning to surface in our country for the first time, beginning to acquire the dimension of a service, beginning (if they were also able to do this) to find an identity, which was not only political, not only historical, not only cultural, but educational: the educational identity that children's education necessarily requires.

Perhaps there was a point here, a moment, when contact was lost between the [school] services and the women's movement. I think it began around the beginning of the 1970s. Until the 1970s women had battled constantly for fifteen years and achieved what they achieved, going from family rights, to the great ten year battle with ONMI (*Opera Nazionale Maternità e Infanzia*) from 1960 to 1970, to their capacity for arriving at the proposal and foundation of another institution, the *asilo nido*, which started to open in 1971.

To my mind this is when some sort of separation happened and I think it came at a cost to women, but it also came at a cost to other elements further removed, and not only for women. Because women, driven by reasons that have not been sufficiently explored, went in another direction at that point: I think it is possible to accuse the movement of this. A movement so strong, so large, so victorious, so pregnant, that in fifteen or twenty years it had been able to create transformations and extraordinarily important decisive reforms. My impression is that at the time they did not only re-direct elsewhere, they also lost an opportunity for understanding that it isn't enough to be able to establish a service: you have to give it an identity and a content, you have to give it values, you have to spend your time and your capacities and your intelligences on it, to penetrate and understand and comprehend what is happening in it.

Women's destiny is related to children's destiny. Still today the value of childhood is the value of woman. And the value of woman is the value we are able to give children.

There is a sort of fracture, a switch, when you go from the time of securing the service to the time of trying to continue to follow it through: not only because you know the enormous impact it can have, on the level of women's psychology, women's emotions and needs and requirements, but because securing a service is not simply that: it means securing a new situation and a new dimension too. It guarantees that the other projects you have with women will be strengthened by a level of coherence, a dimension of coherence and quality, by the quality of children's education.

Another thing I think women lost is that men were absent at that time – they were elsewhere – and the issues, the field and the arena [of school services] were all essentially given over to women. The men were racing off in other directions following journeys of their own. What I mean is, this [educational] discourse unfortunately has always clung to and been rooted in women's female capacities (for better or worse). And I feel there was a loss of the capacity for consolidating the institutions they had secured, of feeling a need within them to learn and know about how a service is never neutral, never an autonomous thing, how its story does not come from inside: a service is a sort of constant broadcaster of feelings, knowledge, aptitudes, of *feedback* [sic] and responses that come back to you and then go out again. So on the level of women constructing and of women guaranteeing that the [school] service had the framework of their ideals, that it is an integral part – that, in my opinion, is something that came to be lacking.

[. . .]

On the other hand the situation was difficult because the fact is the men didn't understand what the value of family could be. I remember the endless discussions in places that were set apart, and you could not get them to understand. It was the 1970s when the *Decreti per gli organi collegiali* [laws on family representation in schools, see Chapter 3, n.21] came out, establishing whether or not families would play a role [in school education]. But theory and thinking at the time separated men, and separated male workers, as a subject that might be contaminated in some way by belonging to a family. So there was no family, there were no women, there were no children.

The great subject for the women of Cella had been the children, and now the great subject [of the times] became men: in the sense of a political man, the working man, the working-class man, the man as representative of the working classes. Not only were women and children completely marginalised, they were dangerous. The discussions we had! Trying to get people to understand that we cannot think of a worker's conditions or a labourer's conditions as starting and ending in a factory: there is a human, existential, cultural, affective continuity with the family environment, and with the family nucleus. This was something the men, the militant men, could not understand. And I think this also had an effect on declarations on the part of the women, which were missing [this element].

[. . .]

Certainly services have multiplied now and we can say that ninety per cent of our children are welcomed into *scuole materne*. [In Italy] there are all kinds of schools: there are uninhabitable schools, schools where children never know if they have to go, or if they can, if they will be able to eat, or not able to eat, if they are certain of getting a sandwich, or certain of not getting a sandwich, certain of having a teacher, or certain of not having a teacher. Despite the easy praise and emphasis we can give to the *scuola dell'infanzia*, it still does not have an identity: I believe these are schools that still need to lay claim to their full identity, but are not up to doing so.

So now that these services exist we see enormous gaps of disparity and of dysfunctional times opening up and widening. On one hand women's time is weighed with more problems, anxieties, needs and requirements, but correspondingly certain times are progressively being cut. So you can imagine what happens every time we go back to this topic and take up the theme of women, and of mothers and fathers. What is the meaning of these dysfunctional times, and of the disconnect that has become an organic (and perhaps irreversible) fact between some times getting shorter and shorter and other times getting longer?[28] Time isn't only quantity it is quality too, and it brings all sorts of new problems: difficult problems, subtle problems, anxious problems, problems of organising our families, and of finding a unity between all the different times that are part of our family life.

I think this is a phenomenon that we need to re-focus our attention on. And in the same way we must consider the issue of [school] autonomy to be a lost battle, which the secular community has not been capable of advancing. These things have fed an increase in the centralisation and nationalisation of [school] services, of the whole [school] network,[29] and they raise large questions about the corporative birth of different teachers' organisations. So that we now see twenty to thirty unions that belong to the tertiary [service] sector, belong to the public sector, and belong to teachers, in schools that have essentially become welfare [services]. These schools are full, full up with people, schools that want to be full of people, ships overflowing with people, ships that do not let anything go because everything is ultra-guaranteed; they are schools that have lost their taste for culture, lost all interest in living with children and young people; schools that do not know how to make themselves loved. Sociologists like to cite several causes when they discuss student 'mortality' [drop out], but they always forget to reflect on schools that are not lovable: and if children cannot love their school in any way then they will end up abandoning it and looking for other solutions. This is the drama of our times.

So that we feel swamped by an abominable situation from every point of view: from an ethical and moral point of view; from the point of view of respect for the individual; of violence and the daily spectacle of the mass media, the emerging vulgarity, and the lack of safety and autonomy when all of us want safety and autonomy guaranteed. These are all elements the Minister for Public Instruction does not discuss: great educationalists, from directors to inspectors, avoid discussing them as if a membrane stops things filtering into the bodies – considered impermeable – of women, men and children; and especially of women and men working by the side of children. There is a frighteningly strong culture of alienation on this level, which is frighteningly productive of great suffering, and therefore of great loss: a loss of ferment, a loss of hope, a loss of illusions, a loss of the capacity for playing by the rules in a difficult game, and I believe this is an element that has little part in politics, even when politics makes large investments in educational themes.

But this topic does not come up. No, there is talk of salary factors, of pay packets, of pay rises etc., as if all this corporate claiming has eaten up politics. Some people are beginning to say, and they are the most courageous at a union level, 'Yes if we look back over our history we realise that pay and pay claims, which are sacred and can't be marginalised, have ended up eating up all the other pieces of politics'. But we must not lose these other pieces even when we go and decide a pay claim, quite to the contrary. We lose public opinion in situations where the differences and the indifference are too great (we experience this first hand each day), and politicians are too insensitive to all these things. They have their presence and their protagonism on the level of providing institutions. But the defect in the world of Italian politics, and especially on the left (but not only on the left, on the Catholic side too), is this way of feeling unduly indifferent, which is greater in the secular area than for Catholics.

Feeling indifferent to the ways destinies are constructed, to the fate of children, very young children and young people at university level. Just quoting some figures on the failure of Italian conditions is enough for us to understand. [. . .] What is still missing is what happens inside schools, what happens inside universities, what happens inside the *asilo nido* and inside the *scuola dell'infanzia*. That is to say, what is lost is the global vision that would allow the political world to have all the elements necessary – integrated and relating to each other – to enable it to understand what is happening to the future conditions of citizens to come, and which perhaps also explain the 'Reggio Emilia' phenomenon. I could open up a few chapters on this subject but I prefer not to.

This is where I conclude my talk. It has been a very quick tale. We need to go back and understand the line and direction Italian pedagogy has taken. We must understand that this prize we have been given [by *Newsweek* magazine] recognises that one of our values (and this has been understood more by people outside Italy than by Italians) has been our original identity; and this identity is explicitly opposed to pedagogy of a behaviourist nature, which is pedagogy that has had the good fortune of being very easily applied, and has had great success because it is simple easy teaching, where you pull out the worksheets and glue them to exercise books. When it is practised on this level, the profession becomes so easy there is no understanding of the damage it inevitably produces, for the future and in the present. This kind of pedagogy is part of what I call 'prophetic' pedagogy. When we showed the [Reggio Emilia] exhibition in Bologna we had to give it a title.[30] I remember I resorted to this phrase because I knew very well who it needed to be addressed to. 'Prophetic' pedagogy knows everything beforehand: it knows everything that will happen. It knows everything and it has no uncertainty, it is absolutely imperturbable, it contemplates everything and prophesies everything and sees everything; sees everything to the point that it is capable of giving recipes for the parts of an action, minute by minute, hour by hour, objective by objective, five minutes by five minutes. This is a coarse and cowardly thing, which is humiliating to teachers' ingenuity and a complete and visible humiliation of children's ingenuity and potential.

But what do we see at this level? Are there battles? Are there clashes over these issues? No. None. There are none. [. . .]

The award we have been given is an award that we deserve (without too much emphasis) for what we have been capable of doing, for everything we are continuing to do, will continue to do, but cannot continue to do the same way we used to. Today there is a greater responsibility, a greater duty, things we have to reflect on. And this reflection, which we have started, must go on, must understand what is going to happen now in our [educational] experience. It is extraordinary that our experience has not only received this award, which is a sort of Hollywood Oscar, or look at it whatever way you like – it is what it is.

The fact is that *we* are already in the European Community when Italy still doesn't know if it has the requirements for entering. We are already in it with this experience: our relations and our weavings have already been going on in Europe for twelve years – so we are in. We are already part of reflections on a European and international level. We are already in there, already participating, already active in inter-cultural European bodies on themes that are directly or indirectly the same as those of this evening's meeting. We have a vision of the future which, although it is uncertain like all the futures we can think of or imagine today, it is a future connected to the present through a series of ties, and with its roots in a series of facts. The problem is this: an adventure of this kind, having arrived at this point, must continue to be a good adventure, must be revisited, must be closely followed. And above all it still needs support, despite all the merits of our comunal administration (which absolutely no-one wants to forget) and which has constantly ensured and guaranteed the possibility of our schools' survival for so long: it has always looked on them with very benevolent eyes and great love.

The problem is to see, based on a core [experience] like this, if it is not also possible to reflect on where the city has fallen short and still falls short in relation to a legacy of this kind. If there is a feeling of sufferance in any way it is that this experience has not been able to impact beyond the physical limits of the schools, it has not impacted outside the school walls. Outside, in Italian schools, in Italian pedagogy, and overseas pedagogy it has had a great impact. But it hasn't managed to impact on the city, not in such a way as to be able to think Reggio Emilia not only has the most advanced schools but could be a sort of capital. They called us a capital in the hard years, in 1967, when they called Reggio Emilia the capital of all that rebellion and subversion we were accused of.

But what we have lacked is the capacity to take other situations, to show other situations, other moments, other possibilities, other occasions, which would let the image of this city grow. [So we could then say] this is a city that not only has the most beautiful schools, it has them because it is the most beautiful city on issues of childhood.

1993

99.93 Speech on receiving the Kohl International Teaching Award, on behalf of the municipal schools of Reggio Emilia, Chicago, May 1993

Editor's note: The Kohl International Teaching Awards were given by the Chicago-based Dolores Kohl Education Foundation between 1985 and 1994, to honour elementary and high school teachers as well as media and lifetime contributors to the field of education. In 1993, the Educational Award was given to the municipal early childhood services of Reggio Emilia.

A gulf is always needed, for men, for children, for women. It is an enclosed place, a more silent place, a place where we can think more, and think better. What will we do, all of us, in this gulf?

We will think about what we have done and what we have not done, for us and for the children, we will also try to understand the reasons why an experience of this kind not only lies behind us, but is also still before us. Certainly in our boat we will leave the gulf, perhaps with a stronger awareness of children's rights. The rights conceded by the UN and by UNESCO are no longer sufficient. Children no longer need charity, or offerings, we adults need first and foremost to be convinced that children are not only holders of rights, but that they are holders of their own culture, they are holders of a capacity for developing more culture, and they are capable of building their own culture and contaminating our culture.

I do not know whether you have ever thought that the wind can have shapes, or a shape: where can I find a shape for the wind? Zen philosophy helps us Westerners to understand that the shape of the wind is none other than the bodily shape of the trees, it is in the trees that we have to find the shape, the shapes, of the wind. And we take this tree as our emblem, as a model, as strength, a tree with stronger roots, so that the strength of the tree can also flow into us, into the people, into children.

Perhaps more than a nostalgia for the past we need nostalgia for the future. Children, the children that are and the children to come, are waiting for us there in the place where nostalgia for the future is capable of arriving, and let us all hope we are there too.

✻ ✻ ✻

100.93 Notes made by Loris Malaguzzi about Reggio Children, 1993

Editor's note: These notes were originally written out by Malaguzzi, summarising his thinking about a new organisation to structure Reggio Emilia's relationships with the outside world. They were then divided up and put onto cards for wider distribution; each section of the grid below represents a card. The organisation Reggio Children was founded two months after Malaguzzi died.

REGGIO CHILDREN

Another resource
for the children
the families
the teachers
the city

REGGIO CHILDREN

A re-investment of resources
put together in 30 years of work
and of passionate intelligence
by teachers and parents

REGGIO CHILDREN

A stronger image
for an experience
that has flown
and is flying
in the world

REGGIO CHILDREN

Once again let us get together
to help every child
to be what they think

REGGIO CHILDREN

A school extending
beyond our borders
that reinforces and diffuses
the rights and the hopes
of children

REGGIO CHILDREN

To export a history of the
intelligences and smiles of children
to many parts of the world
is a title of joy
and prestige
for our city
and our people

Notes

1   Paul Watzlawick (1921–2007) was an Austrian-American family therapist, psychologist, communications theorist and philosopher. A theoretician in communication theory and radical constructivism, he made contributions to the fields of family therapy and general psychotherapy.
2   Tommaso Campanella (1568–1639) was an Italian philosopher, theologian, astrologer and poet, best known for a utopian treatise *La città del Sole* (*The City of the Sun*). Ellen Karolina Sofia Key (1849–1926) was a Swedish writer on many subjects in the fields of family life, ethics and education and was an early advocate of a child-centred approach to education and parenting. She is best known for her book on education, *Barnets århundrade* (1900), which was translated in English in 1909 as *The Century of the Child*.

3 Malaguzzi in a footnote refers to statistics showing the growing drop-out rate of children and young people as they passed through the Italian state education system, so that of every 100 children enrolled in middle school, only eight eventually gained university degrees, one of the lowest percentages in Europe.

4 Mary Dinsmore Salter Ainsworth (1913–99) was an American-Canadian developmental psychologist known for her work in early emotional attachment with the 'strange situation' design, as well as her work in the development of attachment theory.

5 Jerome Kagan (1929–) is a leading American developmental psychologist.

6 Gregor Samsa is the central character in *The Metamorphosis*, a novella by Franz Kafka, first published in 1915. The story begins with Samsa, a travelling salesman, waking to find himself transformed (metamorphosed) into a large, monstrous insect-like creature.

7 Taylorism, or scientific management, is a theory of management that analyses and synthesises workflows, to improve economic efficiency, especially labour productivity.

8 Malaguzzi is, perhaps, referring to Kant's use of 'regulative', referring to how reason guides our work in striving for knowledge, helping us to correct errors and arrive at more comprehensive insights.

9 From *Steps to an Ecology of Mind* by Gregory Bateson, first published in 1972.

10 Neil Postman (1931–2003) was an American author, media theorist and cultural critic. In his 1982 book *The Disappearance of Childhood*, he attempts to explain why the dividing line between childhood and adulthood is rapidly eroding in contemporary society, and why the social role of the child may well disappear in modern industrial society.

11 Serge Moscovici (1925–), a Romanian-born French social psychologist, first used the term 'social representation' in 1961 referring to a stock of values, ideas, metaphors, beliefs and practices that are shared among the members of groups and communities. He postulated two universes: the *reified* universe of science, which operates according to scientific rules and procedures and gives rise to scientific knowledge, and the *consensual* universe of social representation, in which the lay public elaborates and circulates forms of knowledge which come to constitute the content of common sense.

12 Adolphe Ferrière (1879–1960) was a Swiss educator and one of the founders of the progressive education movement. He set up an experimental school ('La Forge') in Lausanne, Switzerland, but had to abandon teaching due to his deafness. In 1921, he was a member of the first Executive Committee of the New Education Fellowship, for which he wrote the charter. Other members of this league included Maria Montessori and Celestin Freinet.

13 Guido Petter (1927–2011) was an Italian psychologist who did much to disseminate the work of Jean Piaget in Italy, and undertook extensive research on cognitive development, language, psychology of adolescence, parenting and educational psychology.

14 In Reggio Emilia they talk about the language of *grafica*, which includes very young children's signs (sometimes thought of elsewhere as scribbles) and also actions like drawing on a stone with water, or drawing in sand with a finger, or how a wire sculpture in two dimensions can be a drawing.

15 Gerald Edelman (1929–2014) was an American pioneer in immunology, embryology, molecular biology and neuroscience, and won the Nobel Prize in Physiology or Medicine in 1972.

16 Jean-Pierre Changeux (1936–) is a French neuroscientist known for his research in several fields of biology, from the structure and function of proteins to the early development of the nervous system. These words of his may come from a 1987 article in the newspaper *la Repubblica*.

17 Norbert Elias (1897–1990) was a German sociologist of Jewish descent, who later became a British citizen, and developed a theory of civilising (and decivilising) processes, focused on the relationship between power, behavior, emotion and knowledge.

18 The Cold War, a period of prolonged military and political tension between a Western bloc (USA and Western Europe) and the Soviet Union, is commonly held to have ended

around 1991, with the overthrow of Communist regimes in Central and Eastern Europe and the dissolution of the Soviet Union.

19 'Mai' means 'never' in Italian, while 'Stock' is the name of a well-known liqueur.

20 Marc Chagall (1887–1985) was a Russian-French artist; Claudius Ptolemy (90–c.168), a Greco-Egyptian astronomer, who held that the earth was at the centre of the universe; and Nicolaus Copernicus (1473–1543), a Polish astronomer who formulated a model of the universe that placed the sun rather than the earth at its centre.

21 Valeria Ugazio (1949–) is a psychologist, a family systemic psychotherapist and Professor of Clinical Psychology at the University of Bergamo, with a particular interest in relational psychotherapy.

22 The word after 'great' is missing in the transcript. 'Value' or 'insight' are offered as a possibilities, given the sense of the sentence.

23 The information processing theory approach to the study of cognitive development evolved out of the American experimental tradition in psychology. The theory equates the mind to a computer, which is responsible for analysing information from the environment.

24 Martin Heidegger (1889-1976) was a German philosopher, widely seen as a seminal thinker in the Continental tradition, developing a ground-breaking philosophy that influenced literary, social and political theory, art and aesthetics, architecture, cultural anthropology, design, environmentalism, psychoanalysis and psychotherapy.

25 Fabbrico, Cavriago and Scandiano are small *comuni* in the province of Reggio Emilia.

26 Velia Vallini was a partisan, a leader in the UDI, a member of the PCI and the provincial *Assessore* for health (1951–74).

27 Giuseppe De Santis (1917–97) was an Italian film director, one of the most idealistic neorealist filmmakers of the 1940s and 1950s. Malaguzzi here refers to his film *Bitter Rice* (1950), the story of a young woman working in the rice fields.

28 In his discussion of dysfunctional times and of times getting shorter and longer, Malaguzzi seems to contrast the longer hours demanded by paid work and the shorter hours left for family time. He may also be referring to the long-running issue of the opening hours of early childhood services and primary schools, and the tension between parental demands and needs, often for longer hours, and the hours of attendance deemed best for children. For an early discussion of these issues in Reggio Emilia's municipal schools, see 50.73.

29 Malaguzzi refers here to *comuni* who have handed their own schools over to the State.

30 Malaguzzi first used the term 'prophetic pedagogy' ['*pedagogia profetica*'] for a commentary he wrote for *The Hundred Languages of Children* exhibition when it was shown in Bologna in early 1990, two years before this speech.

Walking on silk threads

Reggio Emilia Working Group

Selecting texts by Loris Malaguzzi and making a synthesis of each decade as presented in this book (a project long hoped for that has come true, thanks above all to the passionate and competent commitment of Peter Moss, whom we warmly thank) has meant greater emotion and awareness, revisiting a history that precedes some of us, which some of us experienced first hand, and which we are still living. Turning our gaze to the past is never simple, it reawakens memories, reinterprets events and provokes comparison with the present.

Certainly what emerges from the words of Loris Malaguzzi is a portrait of an exceptional man, but also the portrait of a city that has been capable of discussing and of facing change in original and often counter-current ways, of battling to evolve into a society it believed to be more intelligent, cultured and fair for all.

What legacy has Loris Malaguzzi left us? To the city and those of us who live in the present, he has left a precious treasure to be defended and nurtured: the awareness that respect for children's culture is closely tied with respect for ourselves and the civilisation being constructed. The awareness that no problem, however complex, can be resolved without innovating our thinking and creating connections with the context in which it is situated. An innovation, however, that does not betray basic values and ethics that have accompanied the constructing of our educational and political thinking.

It has not been an easy journey. Malaguzzi says this several times: and we repeat it, those of us who have continued on the road mapped by Malaguzzi and many others, participating in the educational project with enthusiasm, hard work and creativity. It has always been like 'walking on threads of silk',[1] keeping a fine balance and often at risk of falling, not as poetic as the quote would make it seem. It means having the courage to take decisions even if they go against the flow, when there is a risk of making mistakes, being exposed to potential error because the situation is not clear. It means 'avoiding opportunist and obsequious attitudes towards authority' (Malaguzzi, 2012, p.29), discussing and exchanging points of view constantly with other realities, trying to evolve situations that appear stagnant and irresolvable.

Revisiting almost fifty years through Malaguzzi's writings and speeches, we understand some of the capabilities needed to construct durable innovative projects that require and defend quality: intelligence, creativity, rigour (stringent rigour), courage, patience, perseverance, the capacity to make connections and to argue the case for these projects. A general attitude of great human solidarity – social, cultural and political.

What legacy has Loris Malaguzzi left us? It is a question we cannot avoid, and above all however difficult, we cannot avoid a self-evaluation. There are several moments when we find ourselves thinking, what would Malaguzzi do in this situation? What would he have to say about the choices we are making? Though times are very changed, they still offer up the same problems encountered on more than one occasion down the years, but they seem always new and more difficult when they need to be faced, and hopefully resolved.

Some positive and important evolutions have become reality. In 1994, immediately after Malaguzzi's death, the Reggio Children project became reality and over twenty years it has grown and extended its activities substantially, communicating and valuing the points of view of children beyond the boundaries of school education, and increasingly recognised as an international representative of educational experience in Reggio Emilia's municipal *nidi* and *scuole dell'infanzia*.

The Loris Malaguzzi International Centre was born in a project renovating the ex-Locatelli Parmigiano-Reggiano warehouses, and opened to the public in 2006. It represents a laboriously constructed dream and a courageous choice, its full potential not yet expressed but capable of embracing many ideas. Perhaps this truly is the gulf Malaguzzi spoke of [99.93], where we can put down anchor to reflect and think, and talk together with a *planetary* gaze on the conditions of childhood and, as a consequence, on human existence and about our planet.

The international network of dialogues and contacts has continued to expand and the *Reggio Emilia Approach* is now an acknowledged reality that the various philosophies of pedagogy must consider, despite there still being some resistance in certain cases.

In 2011 another partner in this system was born, the Reggio Children–Loris Malaguzzi Centre Foundation, whose purpose is to improve and develop the life of communities in Reggio Emilia and the world, and for whom key words are research, internationalism, solidarity and educational quality.

Reggio Emilia's municipal network of twelve *nidi* and twenty-one *scuole dell'infanzia* – managed since 2003 by the *Scuole e Nidi d'infanzia – Istituzione del Comune di Reggio Emilia* [Preschools and Infant-Toddler Centres – Istituzione of the Municipality of Reggio Emilia], which is also responsible for relations with affiliated, officially recognized and state *scuole dell'infanzia* – is a living reality and one of quality (a fact absolutely not to be taken for granted). These services continue to realise journeys of research and interesting educational projects in their everyday lives, they face change and new cultural challenges with courage and originality, they continue to work with passion and intelligence to involve families and citizens in competent forms of participation. It would be blameworthy and naïve to think this long and passionate continuity of social and educational experience is simple, or has been simple. Reggio Emilia pedagogy must constantly confront (and clash with) cultural images of the child, of the teacher, and of the school which are very distant from those declared and made real in daily work inside its own educational services.

The reality of Reggio Emilia's municipal *nidi* and *scuole dell'infanzia* has become an increasingly well-known reference point throughout the world. It represents a reality that is *possible*, a concrete hope for those who believe education, children and young people merit all of a society's attention and respect.

Many of us feel this as a responsibility and a political commitment requiring the rigour, the courage and the creativity of continuing to make difficult choices, sometimes, often, in contrast with what might appear to guarantee widespread social consensus. Will we be capable of continuing to walk on threads of silk, without losing our balance, without the thread breaking? We can only partially prepare for the future, readying the conditions whereby the declared philosophy is not betrayed through action and practice. But there are many hurdles and stumbles along the way; the economic crisis, still deep and critical, and current culture make everything more complex.

We often repeat to ourselves that, by virtue of its profession, pedagogy must always have an optimistic attitude. Even through long nights and heated discussions Loris Malaguzzi managed to preserve an optimistic gaze that was lucid and wide-reaching. He had a visionary capacity, both cultural and political, which anticipated the future through concrete action and choice. Quoting Paulo Freire, Malaguzzi loved to say that daring the future is not a risk, it is a necessity of human dignity.

Note

1 These are the words of Loris Malaguzzi, taken from Malaguzzi, 2004.

References

Applebaum, A. (2013) *Iron Curtain: The crushing of Eastern Europe 1944–56*. London: Penguin Books.

Castagnetti, M. and Vecchi, V. (eds) (1997) *Shoe and Meter*. Reggio Emilia: Reggio Children.

Catarsi, E. (2004) 'Loris Malaguzzi and the municipal school revolution', *Children in Europe*, 6, 8–9.

Edwards, C., Gandini, L. and Forman, G. (eds) (2012, 3rd edn) *The Hundred Languages of Children*. Santa Barbara, CA: Praeger.

Foucault, M. (1984) 'Truth and power', in P. Rabinow (ed.) *Foucault Reader*. New York: Pantheon Books.

Ginsborg, P. (1990) *A History of Contemporary Italy: 1943–80*. London: Penguin Books.

Lorenzi, O., Borghi, E. and Canovi, A. (2001) *Una storia presente. L'esperienza delle scuole comunali dell'infanzia a Reggio Emilia*. Reggio Emilia: RSLibri.

Malaguzzi, L. (2012, 3rd edn) 'History, ideas and basic philosophy', in C. Edwards, L. Gandini and G. Forman (eds) *The Hundred Languages of Children*. Santa Barbara, CA: Praeger.

Moss, P. (2014) *Transformative Change and Real Utopias in Early Childhood Education: A story of democracy, experimentation and potentiality*. London: Routledge.

Paolella, F. (2010) 'Un esperimento di profilassi sociale. La colonia-scuola "Antonio Marro" di Reggio Emilia' ('An experiment of social prophylaxis. The special school "Antonio Marro" in Reggio Emilia'), *Rivista Sperimentale di Freniatria*, 134, 3, 23–34.

Putnam, R. (1993) *Making Democracy Work: Civic traditions in modern Italy*. Princeton, NJ: Princeton University Press.

Rinaldi, C. (2006) *In Dialogue with Reggio Emilia: Listening, researching and learning*. London: Routledge.

Sturloni, S. and Vecchi, V. (eds) (1999) *Everything Has a Shadow except Ants*. Reggio Emilia: Reggio Children.

Various Authors (2012) *One City, Many Children: Reggio Emilia, a history of the present*. Reggio Emilia: Reggio Children.

Vecchi, V. (2010) *Art and Creativity in Reggio Emilia: Exploring the role and potentiality of ateliers in early childhood education*. London: Routledge.

Other articles by and interviews with Loris Malaguzzi available in English

Malaguzzi, L. (1993) 'For an education based on relationships', *Young Children*, 11/93, 9–13.

Malaguzzi, L. (2004) 'Walking on threads of silk' (interviewed by C. Barsotti), *Children in Europe*, 6, 10–15.

Malaguzzi, L. (2009) *Conversations with Loris Malaguzzi* (edited by J. Moestrup and K. Eskesen). Odense: Danish Reggio Emilia Network.

Other articles and books about Loris Malaguzzi available in English

Hoyuelos, A. (2004) 'A pedagogy of transgression', *Children in Europe*, 6, 6–7.

Hoyuelos, A. (2013) *The Ethics in Loris Malaguzzi's Philosophy*. Reykjavik: Isalda.

Smidt, S. (2013) *Introducing Malaguzzi: Exploring the life and work of Reggio Emilia's founding father*. London: Routledge.

A selection of other resources about the Reggio Emilia educational experience available in English

Fasano, M. (2002) *Not Just Anyplace*. Reggio Emilia: Reggio Children.

Malaguzzi, L. et al. (1996) *The Hundred Languages of Children, exhibition catalogue*. Reggio Emilia: Reggio Children.

Rinaldi, C., Giudici, C. and Krechevsky, M. (2001) *Making Learning Visible. Children as Individual and Group Learners*. Reggio Emilia: Reggio Children.

Various Authors (2010) *Indications of Preschools and Infant-Toddler Centres – Istituzione of the Municipality of Reggio Emilia*. Reggio Emilia: Reggio Children.

Various Authors (2011) *The Wonder of Learning, exhibition catalogue*. Reggio Emilia: Reggio Children.

For further information

www.scuolenidi.re.it
www.reggiochildren.it
www.reggiochildrenfoundation.org

Index